SOUTH AMERICA

EUROPE

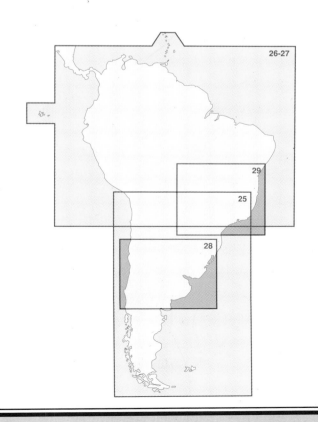

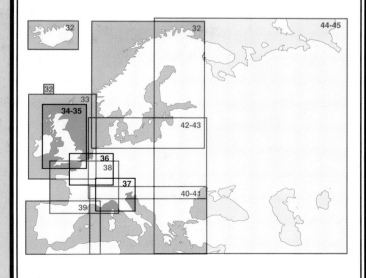

COLLINS

ILLUSTRATED Atlas OF THE WORLD

HarperCollins*Publishers*

Collins Illustrated Atlas of the World

Collins
An Imprint of HarperCollins*Publishers*
77-85 Fulham Palace Road, Hammersmith, London W6 8JB

First published by Bartholomew 1987
First published as Collins Illustrated Atlas of the World 1995

Printed in Great Britain by the Edinburgh Press Limited

ISBN 0 00 448231 X

The publishers acknowledge the assistance of the following in the preparation of material used in this publication: Dr Walter Stephen, Senior Advisor, Curriculum, Dean Education Centre, Edinburgh; Alistair Hendrie, Assistant Headteacher, Portobello High School, Edinburgh; Andrew Grant, Principal Teacher, Geography, Wester Hailes Education Centre, Edinburgh; Stephen Hamilton, Principal Teacher, Geography, Broughton High School, Edinburgh.

The publishers are grateful to the following for providing the photographs used in this atlas (picture number(s) shown in italics)
Travel Photo International: pages xxii-xxiii, savanna, rain forest, prairie, northern forest; page xxii, *7;* page xviii, *2;* page xv, *11;* page xvi, *4, 5, 13, 14;* page xx, *7;* page xxi, *2;* page vi, *3, 4;* page viii, *3, 4. Photographers' Library:* page xxii-xxiii, scrub *Chris Knaggs photograph,* desert *Oliver Martel photograph;* page x, *8 Clive Sawyer photograph;* page xiv, *8 Ian Wright photograph;* page xvii, *9 Tom Hustler photograph;* page xx, *4 Robyn Beeche photograph. Biofotos:* page x, *5 Heather Angel photograph;* page xx, *6 Andrew Henley photograph;* page xxi, *3 Soames Summerhays photograph. The Photo Source:* page xii, *10;* page xviii, *4;* page xiv, *7. Wade Cooper Associates, Edinburgh:* page xvi, *12;* page xvii, *10;* page vi, *1. Pictor International:* page xiv, *6;* page vi, *2. B. and C. Alexander:* page xxii, tundra. *Bruce Coleman Ltd:* page viii, *6 WWF/Eugen Schuhmacher. Mepha:* page xviii, *1 C. Osborne photograph. Michael Scott:* page xxii, woodland and grass. *Yorkshire and Humberside Tourist Board:* page xi, *2. Spectrum Colour Library:* page xiii, *12, 14.*

HH 7987

CONTENTS

THE WORLD

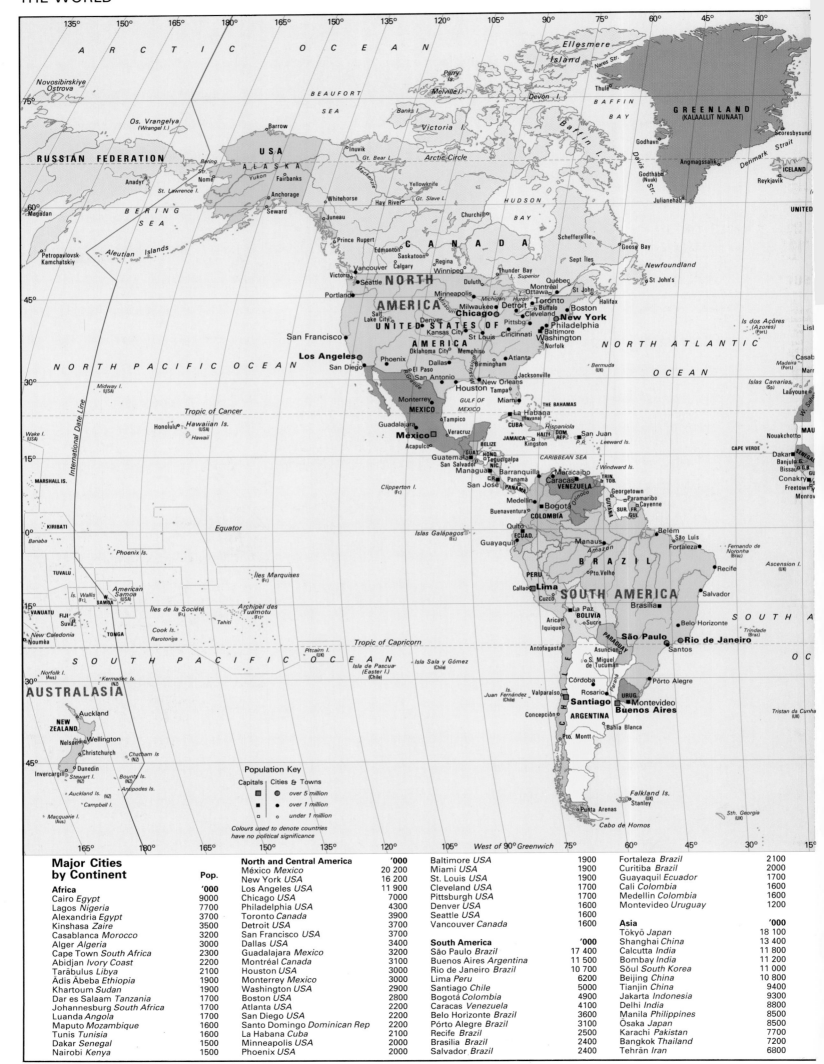

Major Cities by Continent

Africa	Pop. '000	North and Central America	'000		'000	South America	'000		'000	Asia	'000
Cairo *Egypt*	9000	México *Mexico*	20 200	Baltimore *USA*	1900	São Paulo *Brazil*	17 400	Fortaleza *Brazil*	2100	Tōkyō *Japan*	18 100
Lagos *Nigeria*	7700	New York *USA*	16 200	Miami *USA*	1900	Buenos Aires *Argentina*	11 500	Curitiba *Brazil*	2000	Shanghai *China*	13 400
Alexandria *Egypt*	3700	Los Angeles *USA*	11 900	St. Louis *USA*	1900	Rio de Janeiro *Brazil*	10 700	Guayaquil *Ecuador*	1700	Calcutta *India*	11 800
Kinshasa *Zaire*	3500	Chicago *USA*	7000	Cleveland *USA*	1700	Lima *Peru*	6200	Cali *Colombia*	1600	Bombay *India*	11 200
Casablanca *Morocco*	3200	Philadelphia *USA*	4300	Pittsburgh *USA*	1700	Santiago *Chile*	5000	Medellin *Colombia*	1600	Sŏul *South Korea*	11 000
Alger *Algeria*	3000	Toronto *Canada*	3900	Denver *USA*	1600	Bogotá *Colombia*	4900	Montevideo *Uruguay*	1200	Beijing *China*	10 800
Cape Town *South Africa*	2300	Detroit *USA*	3700	Seattle *USA*	1600	Caracas *Venezuela*	4100			Tianjin *China*	9400
Abidjan *Ivory Coast*	2200	San Francisco *USA*	3700	Vancouver *Canada*	1600	Belo Horizonte *Brazil*	3600	**Asia**	'000	Jakarta *Indonesia*	9300
Tarābulus *Libya*	2100	Dallas *USA*	3400			Pórto Alegre *Brazil*	3100			Delhi *India*	8800
Ādis Ābeba *Ethiopia*	1900	Guadalajara *Mexico*	3200	**South America**	'000	Recife *Brazil*	2500			Manila *Philippines*	8500
Khartoum *Sudan*	1900	Montréal *Canada*	3100			Brasilia *Brazil*	2400			Ōsaka *Japan*	8500
Dar es Salaam *Tanzania*	1700	Houston *USA*	3000			Salvador *Brazil*	2400			Karachi *Pakistan*	7700
Johannesburg *South Africa*	1700	Monterrey *Mexico*	3000							Bangkok *Thailand*	7200
Luanda *Angola*	1700	Washington *USA*	2900							Tehrān *Iran*	6800
Maputo *Mozambique*	1600	Boston *USA*	2800								
Tunis *Tunisia*	1600	Atlanta *USA*	2200								
Dakar *Senegal*	1500	San Diego *USA*	2200								
Nairobi *Kenya*	1500	Santo Domingo *Dominican Rep*	2200								
		La Habana *Cuba*	2100								
		Minneapolis *USA*	2000								
		Phoenix *USA*	2000								

Population Key

Capitals | Cities & Towns
- ■ ● over 5 million
- ■ ● over 1 million
- □ ○ under 1 million

Colours used to denote countries have no political significance

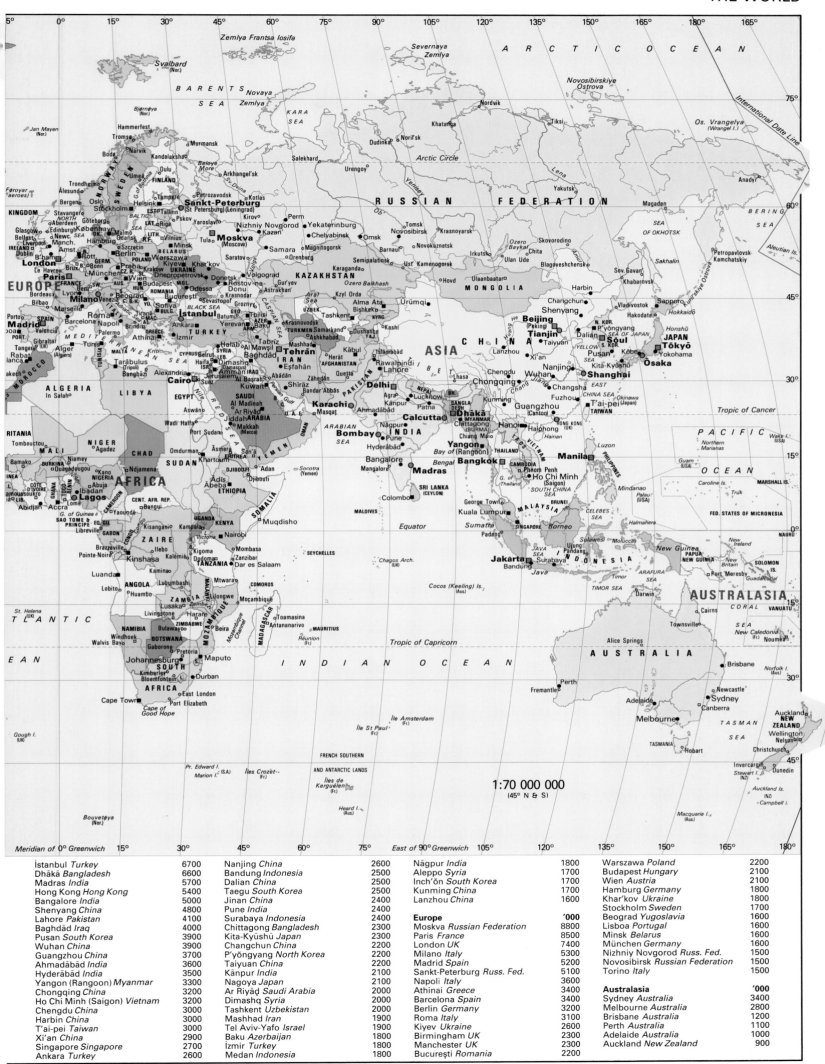

1:70 000 000
(45° N & S)

İstanbul *Turkey*	6700	Nanjing *China*	2600	Någpur *India*	1800	Warszawa *Poland*	2200
Dhåkå *Bangladesh*	6600	Bandung *Indonesia*	2500	Aleppo *Syria*	1700	Budapest *Hungary*	2100
Madras *India*	5700	Dalian *China*	2500	Inch'ŏn *South Korea*	1700	Wien *Austria*	2100
Hong Kong *Hong Kong*	5400	Taegu *South Korea*	2500	Kunming *China*	1700	Hamburg *Germany*	1800
Bangalore *India*	5000	Jinan *China*	2400	Lanzhou *China*	1600	Khar'kov *Ukraine*	1800
Shenyang *China*	4800	Pune *India*	2400			Stockholm *Sweden*	1700
Lahore *Pakistan*	4100	Surabaya *Indonesia*	2400	**Europe**	**'000**	Beograd *Yugoslavia*	1600
Baghdåd *Iraq*	4000	Chittagong *Bangladesh*	2300	Moskva *Russian Federation*	8800	Lisboa *Portugal*	1600
Pusan *South Korea*	3900	Kita-Kyūshū *Japan*	2300	Paris *France*	8500	Minsk *Belarus*	1600
Wuhan *China*	3900	Changchun *China*	2200	London *UK*	7400	München *Germany*	1600
Guangzhou *China*	3700	P'yŏngyang *North Korea*	2200	Milano *Italy*	5300	Nizhniy Novgorod *Russ. Fed.*	1500
Ahmadåbåd *India*	3600	Taiyuan *China*	2200	Madrid *Spain*	5200	Novosibirsk *Russian Federation*	1500
Hyderåbåd *India*	3500	Kånpur *India*	2100	Sankt-Peterburg *Russ. Fed.*	5100	Torino *Italy*	1500
Yangon (Rangoon) *Myanmar*	3300	Nagoya *Japan*	2100	Napoli *Italy*	3600		
Chongqing *China*	3200	Ar Riyåd *Saudi Arabia*	2000	Athinai *Greece*	3400	**Australasia**	**'000**
Ho Chi Minh (Saigon) *Vietnam*	3200	Dimashq *Syria*	2000	Barcelona *Spain*	3400	Sydney *Australia*	3400
Chengdu *China*	3000	Tashkent *Uzbekistan*	2000	Berlin *Germany*	3200	Melbourne *Australia*	2800
Harbin *China*	3000	Mashhad *Iran*	1900	Roma *Italy*	3100	Brisbane *Australia*	1200
T'ai-pei *Taiwan*	3000	Tel Aviv-Yafo *Israel*	1900	Kiyev *Ukraine*	2600	Perth *Australia*	1100
Xi'an *China*	2900	Baku *Azerbaijan*	1800	Birmingham *UK*	2300	Adelaide *Australia*	1000
Singapore *Singapore*	2700	Izmir *Turkey*	1800	Manchester *UK*	2300	Auckland *New Zealand*	900
Ankara *Turkey*	2600	Medan *Indonesia*	1800	Bucureşti *Romania*	2200		

NORTH AMERICA

1:35M

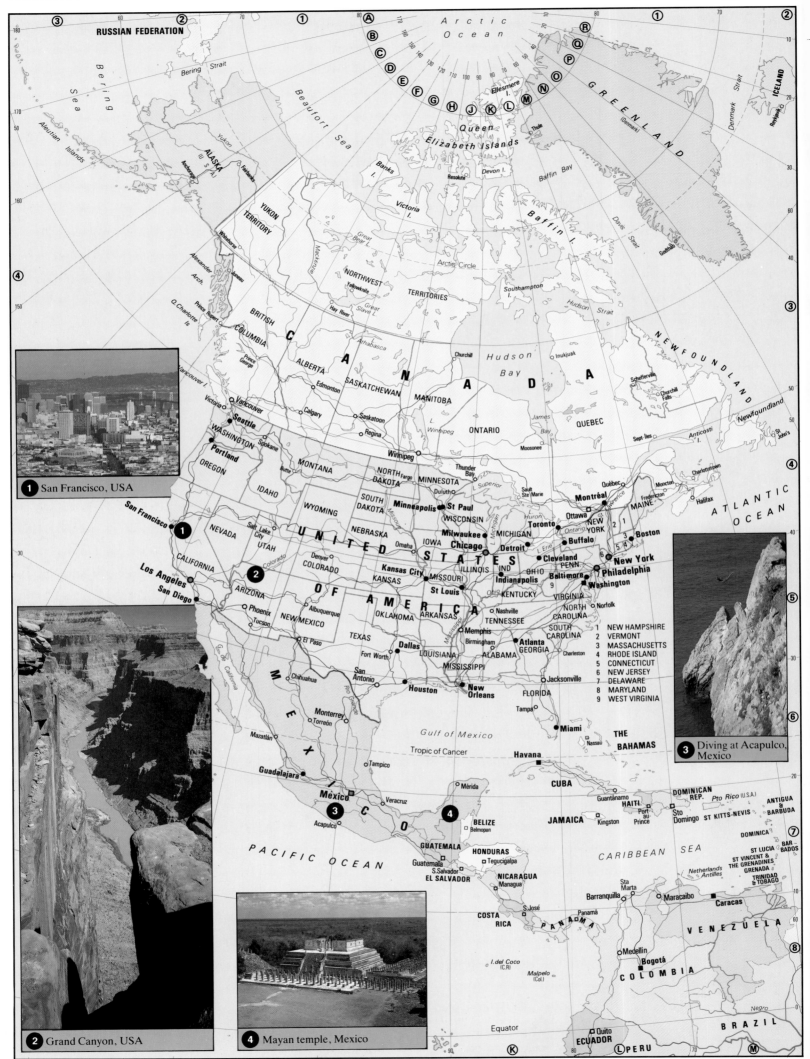

RUSSIAN FEDERATION

Arctic Ocean

GREENLAND (Denmark)

ICELAND

Bering Strait

Bering Sea

Aleutian Islands

Beaufort Sea

Queen Elizabeth Islands

Ellesmere I.

Banks I.

Devon I.

Resolute

Baffin Bay

Denmark Strait

Reykjavik

ALASKA U.S.A.

Anchorage

Fairbanks

Yukon

Victoria I.

Southampton I.

Baffin I.

Davis Strait

Godthåb

Arctic Circle

YUKON TERRITORY

Whitehorse

Juneau

Great Bear L.

Mackenzie

NORTHWEST TERRITORIES

Yellowknife

Hudson Strait

NEWFOUNDLAND

Alexander Arch.

Prince Rupert

Q. Charlotte Is

Hay River

Great Slave L.

Inukjuak

CANADA

BRITISH COLUMBIA

Prince George

Athabasca

Churchill

Hudson Bay

Churchill Falls

Schefferville

Vancouver I.

Victoria

Vancouver

ALBERTA

Edmonton

Calgary

SASKATCHEWAN

Saskatoon

Regina

MANITOBA

L. Winnipeg

ONTARIO

James Bay

Moosonee

QUEBEC

Sept-Îles

Anticosti I.

Newfoundland

St John's

Seattle

Spokane

Winnipeg

Thunder Bay

L Superior

Sault Ste Marie

Québec

Moncton

Fredericton

Charlottetown

Halifax

Portland

OREGON

Butte

MONTANA

IDAHO

NORTH DAKOTA

Fargo

MINNESOTA

Duluth

Minneapolis

St Paul

WISCONSIN

L Michigan

L Huron

Montréal

St Lawrence

Ottawa

MAINE

ATLANTIC OCEAN

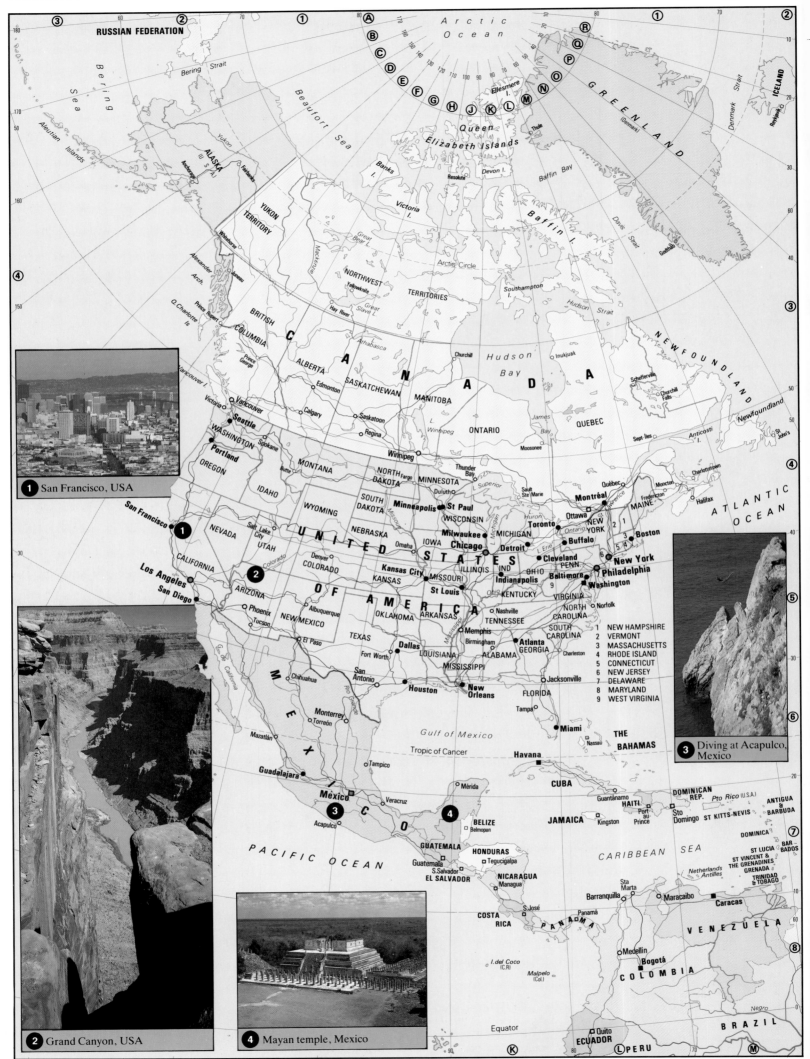
1 San Francisco, USA

San Francisco

NEVADA

Salt Lake City

UTAH

WYOMING

Colorado

SOUTH DAKOTA

NEBRASKA

Missouri

UNITED STATES

Omaha

IOWA

Milwaukee

MICHIGAN

Chicago

Detroit

Cleveland

L Erie

Toronto

Buffalo

NEW YORK

Boston

2 1
3
5 4

New York

Los Angeles

San Diego

CALIFORNIA

Denver

COLORADO

OF

Kansas City

KANSAS

MISSOURI

St Louis

ILLINOIS

IND

OHIO

Ohio

PENN.

6

9

Baltimore

Philadelphia

Washington

1 NEW HAMPSHIRE
2 VERMONT
3 MASSACHUSETTS
4 RHODE ISLAND
5 CONNECTICUT
6 NEW JERSEY
7 DELAWARE
8 MARYLAND
9 WEST VIRGINIA

Phoenix

Tucson

ARIZONA

Albuquerque

NEW MEXICO

AMERICA

OKLAHOMA

ARKANSAS

TENNESSEE

KENTUCKY

Nashville

Memphis

VIRGINIA

NORTH CAROLINA

Norfolk

SOUTH CAROLINA

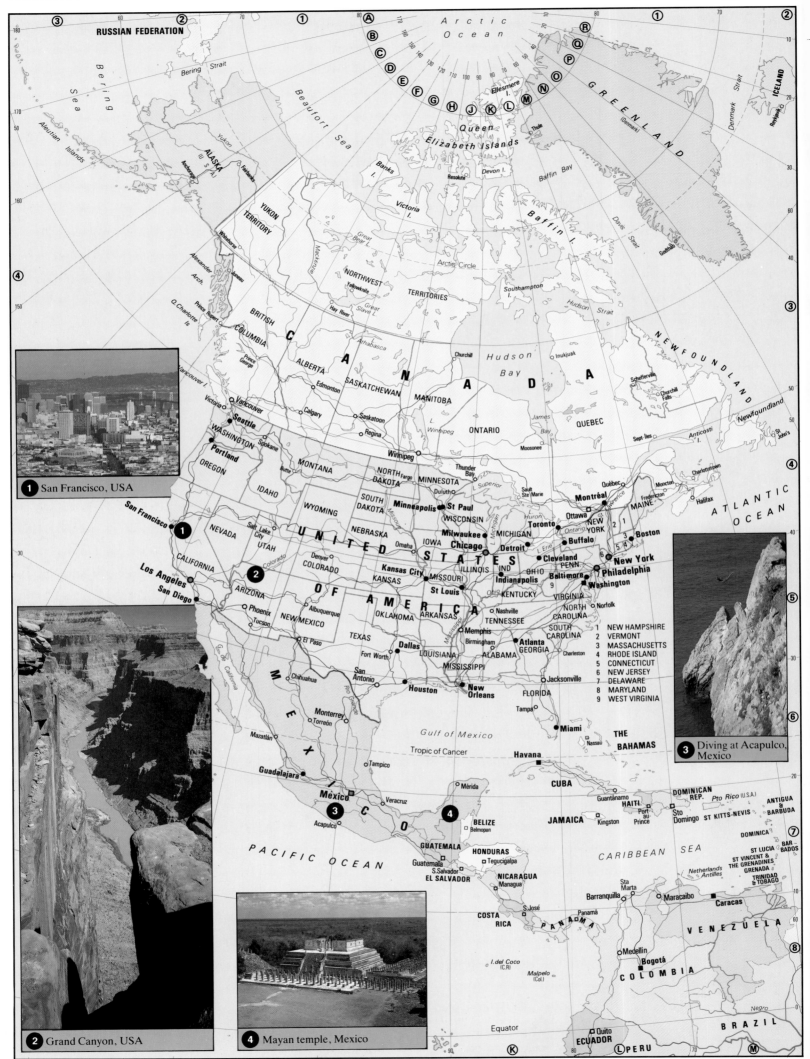
3 Diving at Acapulco, Mexico

G. de California

El Paso

TEXAS

Fort Worth

Dallas

LOUISIANA

MISSISSIPPI

ALABAMA

Birmingham

Atlanta

GEORGIA

Charleston

Rio Grande

San Antonio

Houston

New Orleans

FLORIDA

Jacksonville

Chihuahua

MEXICO

Monterrey

Torreón

Tampa

Miami

Gulf of Mexico

THE BAHAMAS

Nassau

Mazatlán

Tropic of Cancer

Havana

CUBA

Tampico

Guadalajara

Mérida

Veracruz

México

Acapulco

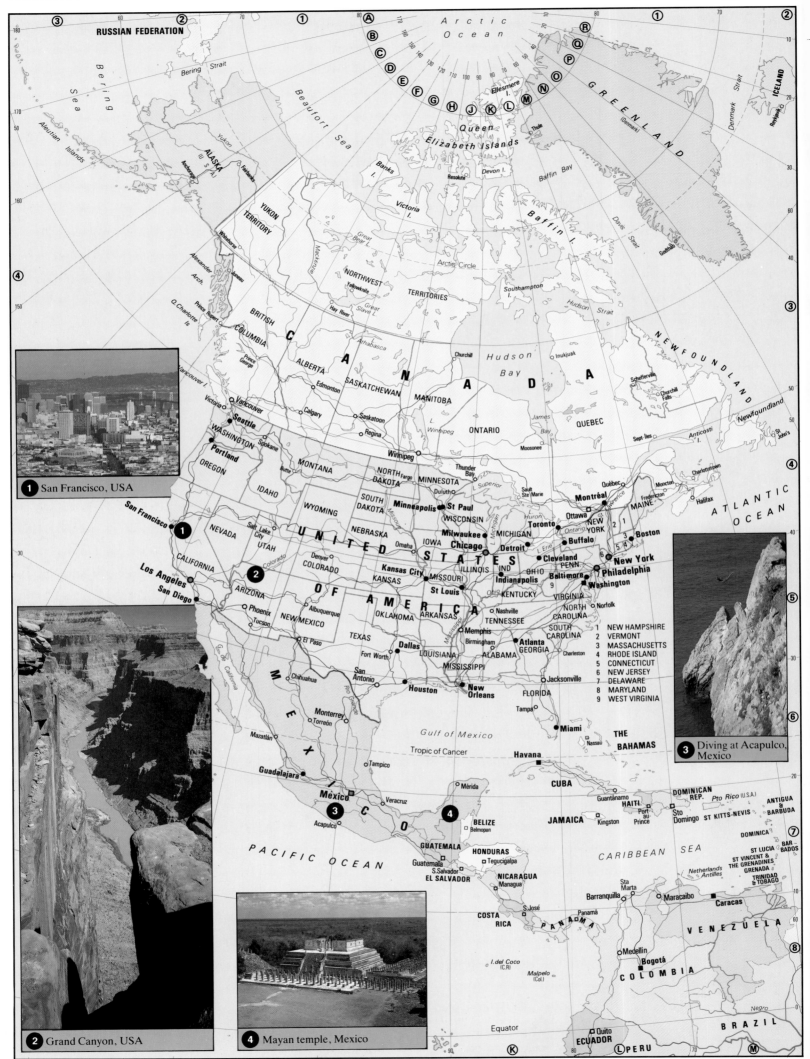
2 Grand Canyon, USA

PACIFIC OCEAN

Guantánamo

HAITI

Port-au-Prince

DOMINICAN REP.

Sto Domingo

Pto Rico (U.S.A.)

JAMAICA

Kingston

ST KITTS-NEVIS

ANTIGUA & BARBUDA

DOMINICA

ST LUCIA

BARBADOS

ST VINCENT & THE GRENADINES

GRENADA

TRINIDAD & TOBAGO

BELIZE

Belmopan

GUATEMALA

Guatemala

S.Salvador

EL SALVADOR

HONDURAS

Tegucigalpa

NICARAGUA

Managua

CARIBBEAN SEA

Netherlands Antilles

Sta Marta

Barranquilla

Maracaibo

Caracas

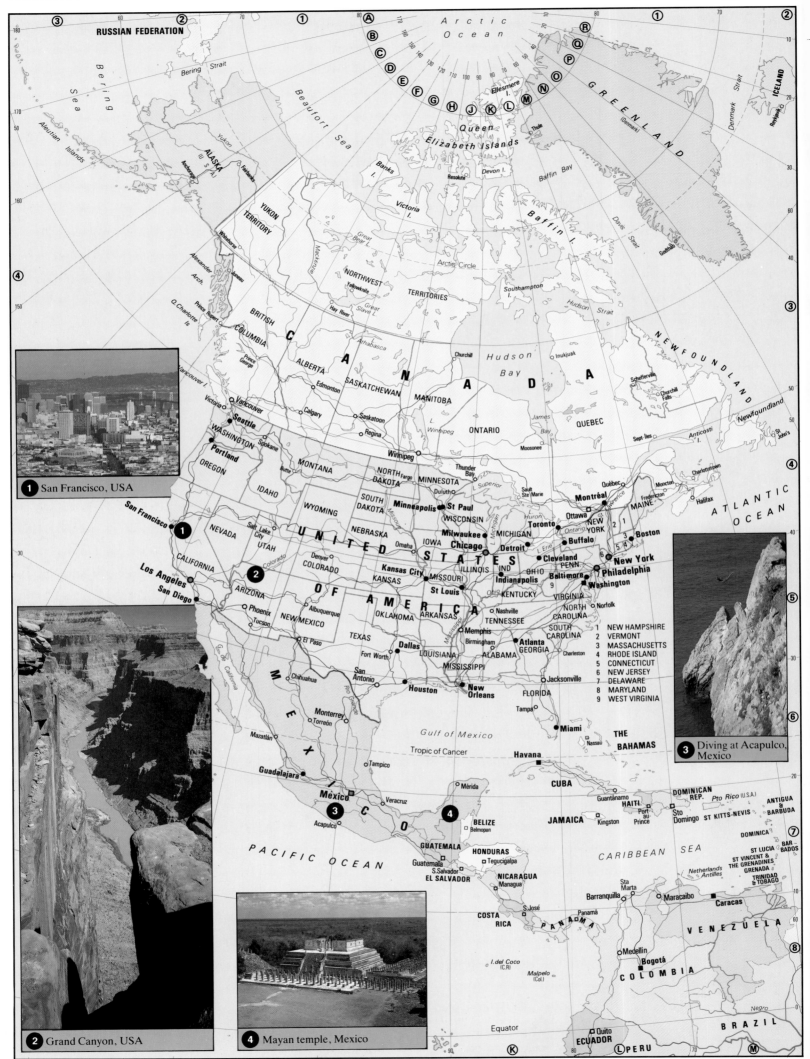
4 Mayan temple, Mexico

COSTA RICA

S. José

PANAMA

Panamá

VENEZUELA

I. del Coco (C.R)

Malpelo (Col.)

Medellín

Bogotá

COLOMBIA

Negro

BRAZIL

Equator

Quito

ECUADOR

PERU

VI

FACTS ABOUT NORTH AMERICA

1 In 1906, the city of San Francisco was almost destroyed by the fires which resulted from an earthquake. The city was hit by another large earthquake in 1989. Beneath the city runs the San Andreas fault, where two of the 'continental plates' which make up the earth's crust slide against one another. When they get jammed together at any point, pressure builds up beneath them, until finally they are forced apart. This causes an earthquake because of the sudden release of so much energy. The longer the plates stay jammed together, the greater the build up of pressure and the greater the strength of the final earthquake: in 1906, land surfaces in San Francisco moved as much as 6metres (20 feet).

2 The huge Grand Canyon in Arizona, USA, was gouged out of the rock by the Colorado River after the land was uplifted. It is as much as 1·6 kilometres (1 mile) deep, a maximum of 29 kilometres (18 miles) from rim to rim and no less than 446 kilometres (277 miles) long! The Grand Canyon is still being carved deeper (though very slowly) by the river.

3 At La Questrada, Acapulco Mexico, divers often swoop 36 m (118 feet) down into the sea. This is the highest dive which people do regularly.

4 The Maya were a people who lived in southern Mexico and Guatemala 1400 years ago. They built great cities with stone temples, public buildings and palaces. The picture shows one of their buildings which can be seen today. It was built without help from any modern machinery.

Cattle	Fruit	Wheat	6 Nickel		
Hogs	Sugar cane	Maize	7 Lead		
Bananas	Timber	Minerals	9 Silver		
Citrus fruit	Tobacco	1 Bauxite	11 Uranium		
Cotton	Coal	3 Copper	12 Zinc		
Fish	Oil	5 Iron	13 Asbestos		

NATURAL VEGETATION/PRODUCTS

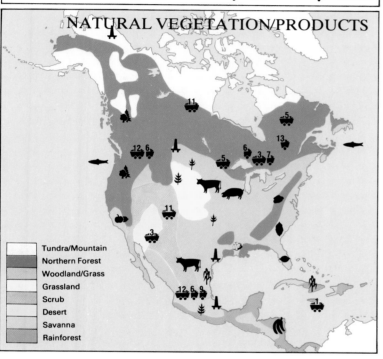

Tundra/Mountain
Northern Forest
Woodland/Grass
Grassland
Scrub
Desert
Savanna
Rainforest

POPULATION

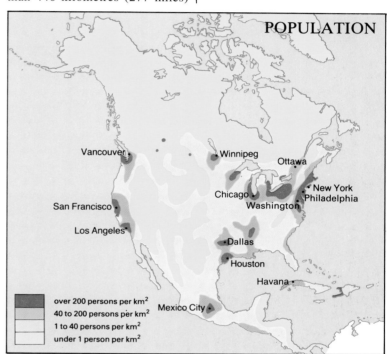

Vancouver, Winnipeg, Ottawa, Chicago, New York, Philadelphia, Washington, San Francisco, Los Angeles, Dallas, Houston, Havana, Mexico City

over 200 persons per km²
40 to 200 persons per km²
1 to 40 persons per km²
under 1 person per km²

CANADA

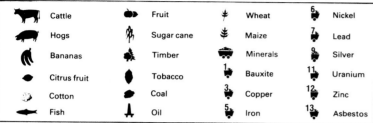

Area: 9 976 147 sq km (3 851 790 sq miles)
Population: 27 300 000
Capital: Ottawa
Languages: English, French
Currency: Canadian Dollar

CUBA

Area: 114 524 sq km (44 218 sq miles)
Population: 10 600 000
Capital: Havana
Language: Spanish
Currency: Cuban Peso

EL SALVADOR

Area: 20 865 sq km (8056 sq miles)
Population: 5 300 000
Capital: San Salvador
Language: Spanish
Currency: Colon

GUATEMALA

Area: 108 888 sq km (42 042 sq miles)
Population: 9 200 000
Capital: Guatemala
Language: Spanish
Currency: Quetzal

JAMAICA

Area: 11 424 sq km (4411 sq miles)
Population: 2 500 000
Capital: Kingston
Language: English
Currency: Jamaican Dollar

MEXICO

Area: 1 967 180 sq km (759 528 sq miles)
Population: 88 600 000
Capital: Mexico City
Language: Spanish
Currency: Mexican Peso

NICARAGUA

Area: 139 000 sq km (53 668 sq miles)
Population: 3 900 000
Capital: Managua
Language: Spanish
Currency: Cordoba

UNITED STATES OF AMERICA

Area: 9 363 130 sq km (3 615 104 sq miles)
Population: 248 700 000
Capital: Washington
Language: English
Currency: U.S. Dollar

SOUTH AMERICA

1:35M

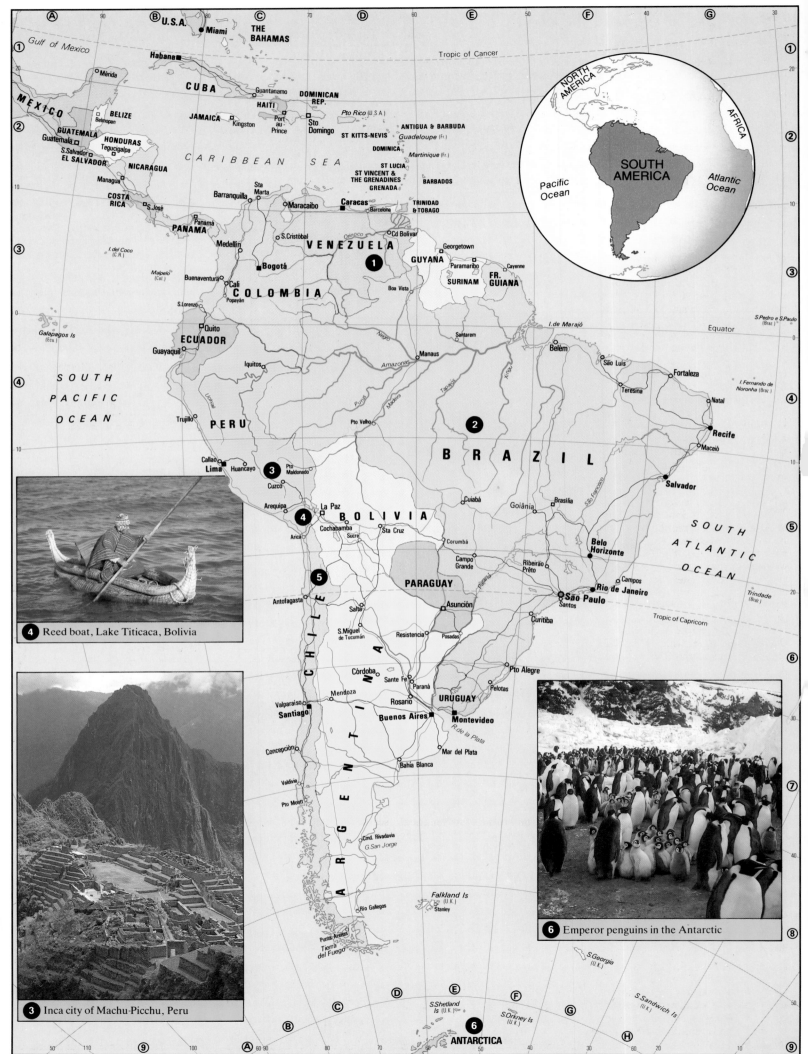

0 250 500 750 1000 km
0 250 500 mls

Gulf of Mexico
Tropic of Cancer

Miami

THE BAHAMAS

Habana
Mérida

CUBA

MEXICO

Guantanamo
DOMINICAN REP.
HAITI
Port au Prince
Sto Domingo
Pto Rico (U.S.A.)

JAMAICA
Kingston

CARIBBEAN SEA

ANTIGUA & BARBUDA
ST KITTS-NEVIS
Guadeloupe (Fr.)
DOMINICA
Martinique (Fr.)
ST LUCIA
ST VINCENT & THE GRENADINES
GRENADA
BARBADOS

TRINIDAD & TOBAGO

BELIZE
Belmopan
GUATEMALA
Guatemala
HONDURAS
Tegucigalpa
S.Salvador
EL SALVADOR
NICARAGUA
Managua
COSTA RICA
S.José
Panamá
PANAMA

I. del Coco (C.R.)

Barranquilla
Sta Marta
Maracaibo
Caracas
Barcelona
Cd Bolivar
Orinoco

VENEZUELA ❶

GUYANA
Georgetown
Paramaribo
SURINAM
FR. GUIANA
Cayenne

S.Cristóbal
Medellín
Bogotá
Buenaventura
Cali
Popayán
COLOMBIA

Boa Vista

Malpelo (Col.)

S.Lorenzo

Galapagos Is (Ecu.)

Quito
ECUADOR
Guayaquil

Equator
S.Pedro e S.Paulo (Braz.)

I. de Marajó

Iquitos

Negro
Amazonas
Santarem
Belém
São Luís
I. Fernando de Noronha (Braz.)

Manaus

Japurá

SOUTH PACIFIC OCEAN

Trujillo

PERU

Purus
Madeira
Tapajós
Xingu

Fortaleza
Teresina

B R A Z I L

Natal
Recife
Maceió

Callao
Lima
Huancayo
Pto Maldonado ❸
Cuzco

Pto Velho

❷

Salvador

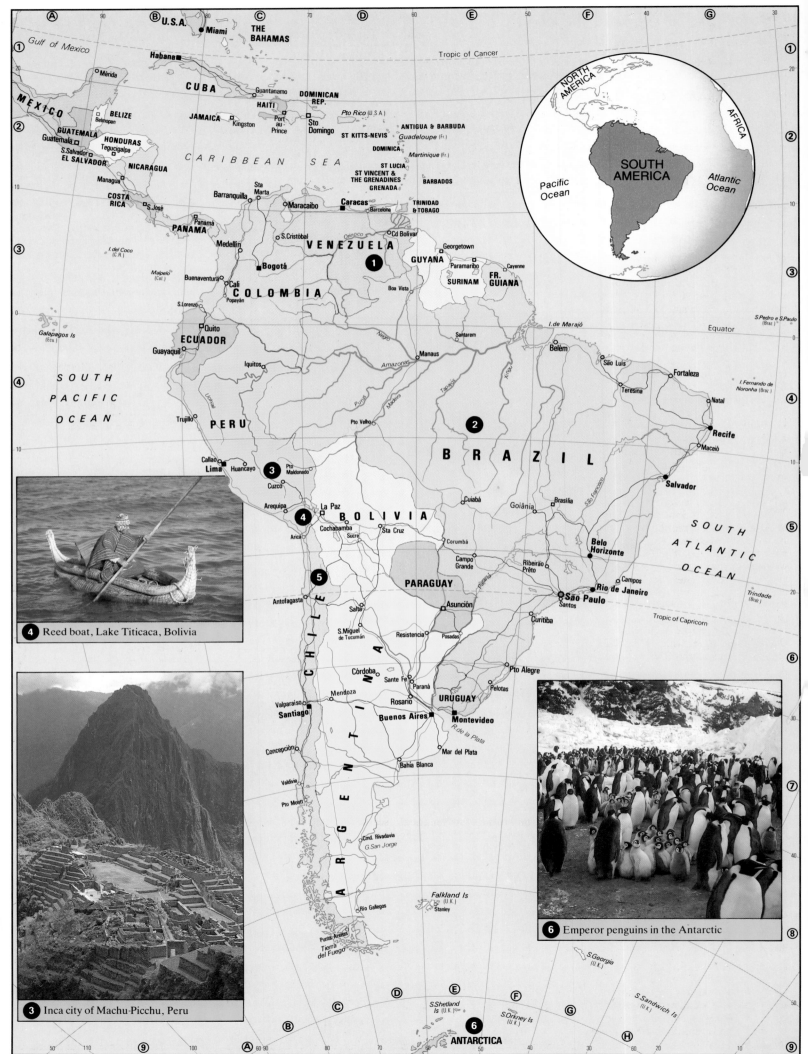

❹ Reed boat, Lake Titicaca, Bolivia

Arequipa
La Paz ❹
BOLIVIA
Cochabamba
Sucre
Sta Cruz
Arica

Cuiabá
Goiânia
Brasília
São Francisco

SOUTH ATLANTIC OCEAN

Corumbá
Campo Grande
Belo Horizonte

Antofagasta ❺

PARAGUAY
Asunción

Ribeirão Prêto
Campos
Rio de Janeiro
São Paulo
Santos
Curitiba

Trindade (Braz.)

Tropic of Capricorn

Salta
S.Miguel de Tucumán
Resistencia
Posadas

Pto Alegre
Pelotas

A R G E N T I N A

Córdoba
Sante Fe
Paraná
Rosario
URUGUAY
Montevideo

Mendoza
Valparaíso
Santiago
Buenos Aires

❸ Inca city of Machu-Picchu, Peru

Concepción
Valdivia
Pto Montt

C H I L E

Mar del Plata
Bahía Blanca
R.de la Plata

Cmd. Rivadavia
G.San Jorge

Falkland Is (U.K.)
Stanley

Rio Gallegos
Punta Arenas
Tierra del Fuego

S.Georgia (U.K.)

❻ Emperor penguins in the Antarctic

S.Shetland Is (U.K.)
S.Orkney Is (U.K.)

S.Sandwich Is (U.K.)

❻ ANTARCTICA

NORTH AMERICA
AFRICA
SOUTH AMERICA
Pacific Ocean
Atlantic Ocean

U.S.A.

VIII

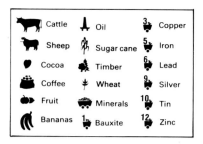

🐄 Cattle	⚒ Oil	**3** Copper
🐑 Sheep	🌿 Sugar cane	**5** Iron
Cocoa	🌲 Timber	**6** Lead
Coffee	🌾 Wheat	**9** Silver
Fruit	⛏ Minerals	**10** Tin
🍌 Bananas	**1** Bauxite	**12** Zinc

FACTS ABOUT SOUTH AMERICA

1 The Angel Falls, Venezuela, are the highest waterfalls in the world, at 979 m (3212 feet).

2 Deforestation is a major problem in South America. About 1 per cent of the total area of forest is lost each year. Often trees are cut down to clear land for agriculture. On hillsides, the soil soon becomes too poor to grow crops and the land is abandoned. Trees cannot grow again, and so soil is eroded away by rain and wind. Trees are also lost when lakes are made for hydro-electric dams; when new towns are built; and as a result of the way people live – they take too much wood for fuel and timber, allow animals to graze on foliage, and light fires which get out of control.

3 In the Andes Mountains, in the north-west of South America, there are ruins of cities built by the Incas. They ruled the Indians in the area 500 years ago. The Incas had well-developed political and religious systems. They built their cities on terraces engineered from the mountain side. The Spanish, the first Europeans to discover these cities, killed the Incas to seize the gold and silver which they had mined, and their cities were abandoned.

4 The highest navigable lake in the world is Lake Titicaca, on the Peru/Bolivia border. It is no less than 3811 m (12 503 feet) above sea level. The local Indian people make boats from bundles of reeds tied together, to use for fishing. The reeds grow around the edge of the lake.

5 Although in the rain forests of the Amazon Basin it rains every day, in the Atacama Desert, Chile, hundreds of years can pass between one rain storm and the next. A storm in 1971 was the first for 400 years. The desert is the driest place in the world.

6 The Emperor Penguin, found in the Antarctic, does not make a nest. Instead, a single egg is carried on top of the male penguin's feet. It is kept warm by a fold of skin which hangs down and covers it. The penguin does not eat during the two months it takes for the egg to hatch out.

NATURAL VEGETATION/PRODUCTS

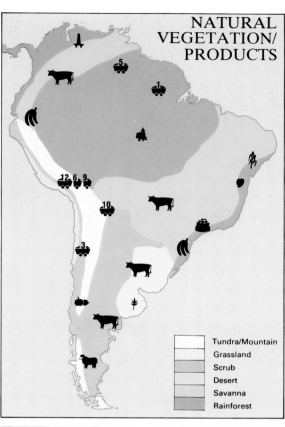

☐	Tundra/Mountain
☐	Grassland
☐	Scrub
☐	Desert
☐	Savanna
☐	Rainforest

POPULATION

☐	over 200 persons per km²
☐	40 to 200 persons per km²
☐	1 to 40 persons per km²
☐	under 1 person per km²

ARGENTINA

Area: 2 777 815 sq km (1 072 514 sq miles)
Population: 32 300 000
Capital: Buenos Aires
Language: Spanish
Currency: Argentine Peso

BOLIVIA

Area: 1 098 575 sq km (424 160 sq miles)
Population: 7 300 000
Capital: La Paz
Languages: Spanish, Aymara, Quechua
Currency: Bolivian Peso

BRAZIL

Area: 8 511 968 sq km (3 286 471 sq miles)
Population: 150 400 000
Capital: Brasilia
Language: Portuguese
Currency: Cruzeiro

CHILE

Area: 756 943 sq km (292 256 sq miles)
Population: 13 200 000
Capital: Santiago
Language: Spanish
Currency: Chilean Peso

COLOMBIA

Area: 1 138 907 sq km (439 732 sq miles)
Population: 33 000 000
Capital: Bogota
Language: Spanish
Currency: Colombian Peso

ECUADOR

Area: 455 502 sq km (175 869 sq miles)
Population: 10 600 000
Capital: Quito
Language: Spanish
Currency: Sucre

GUYANA

Area: 214 969 sq km (83 000 sq miles)
Population: 800 000
Capital: Georgetown
Language: English
Currency: Guyanese Dollar

PERU

Area: 1 285 215 sq km (496 222 sq miles)
Population: 21 600 000
Capital: Lima
Languages: Spanish, Aymara, Quechua
Currency: Sol

VENEZUELA

Area: 912 047 sq km (352 141 sq miles)
Population: 19 700 000
Capital: Caracas
Language: Spanish
Currency: Bolivar

EUROPE

1:15M

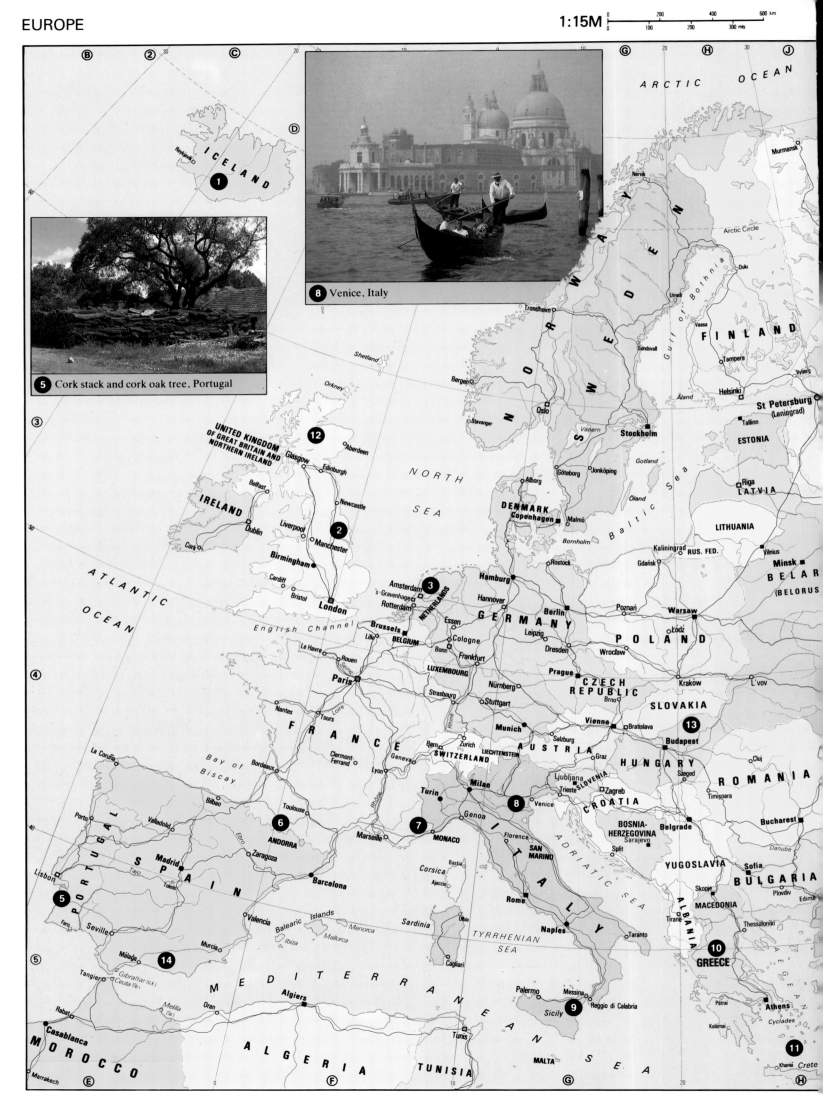

5 Cork stack and cork oak tree, Portugal

8 Venice, Italy

ARCTIC OCEAN

Arctic Circle

Murmansk

Narvik

N O R W A Y

S W E D E N

FINLAND

Ouku

Trondheim

Umeå

Vaasa

Tampere

Bergen

Gulf of Bothnia

Sundsvall

Helsinki

Åland

Stavanger

Oslo

Vänern

Stockholm

Gotland

ESTONIA

Tallinn

Riga

LATVIA

Göteborg

Jönköping

Öland

LITHUANIA

Ålborg

Bornholm

Vilnius

DENMARK

Copenhagen

Malmö

Kaliningrad

RUS. FED.

Minsk

Rostock

Gdańsk

B E L A R

(BELORUS

Hamburg

Poznań

Warsaw

Łódź

P O L A N D

Shetland

NORTH SEA

12

Orkney

UNITED KINGDOM OF GREAT BRITAIN AND NORTHERN IRELAND

Glasgow

Aberdeen

Edinburgh

Belfast

Newcastle

IRELAND

Liverpool

2

Manchester

Dublin

Cork

Birmingham

Cardiff

Bristol

London

Le Havre

English Channel

Rouen

Lille

Brussels

BELGIUM

Amsterdam

3

's-Gravenhage

Rotterdam

NETHERLANDS

Hamburg

Hannover

G E R M A N Y

Essen

Berlin

Leipzig

Dresden

Wrocław

Cologne

Bonn

Frankfurt

LUXEMBOURG

Prague

CZECH REPUBLIC

Kraków

L'vov

Brno

SLOVAKIA

ATLANTIC OCEAN

Paris

Strasbourg

Nürnberg

Stuttgart

F R A N C E

Nantes

Loire

Tours

Clermont-Ferrand

Lyon

Bordeaux

Bay of Biscay

Bilbao

La Coruña

Munich

Bern

Zurich

SWITZERLAND

LIECHTENSTEIN

Salzburg

Vienna

Bratislava

Graz

A U S T R I A

13

Budapest

H U N G A R Y

Cluj

R O M A N I A

Geneva

Ljubljana

SLOVENIA

Trieste

Zagreb

Szeged

Timişoara

Turin

8

Milan

Venice

CROATIA

Toulouse

Marseille

7

Genoa

MONACO

SAN MARINO

Florence

BOSNIA-HERZEGOVINA

Sarajevo

Split

Belgrade

Bucharest

Danube

Porto

Valladolid

6

ANDORRA

Zaragoza

I T A L Y

ADRIATIC SEA

YUGOSLAVIA

Sofia

PORTUGAL

Madrid

Toledo

Tajo

Barcelona

S P A I N

Ebro

Corsica

Bastia

Ajaccio

Rome

BULGARIA

Skopje

Plovdiv

Edirne

Lisbon

5

Valencia

Balearic Islands

Menorca

Sardinia

Olbia

Naples

Taranto

MACEDONIA

Tirane

Thessaloniki

ALBANIA

Faro

Seville

Málaga

14

Murcia

Ibiza

Mallorca

TYRRHENIAN SEA

Cagliari

10

GREECE

Tangier

Gibraltar

Ceuta (Sp.)

Melilla (Sp.)

M E D I T E R R A N E A N

Pátrai

Athens

Casablanca

Rabat

Oran

Algiers

S E A

Palermo

Messina

9

Reggio di Calabria

Sicily

Cyclades

11

M O R O C C O

Marrakech

A L G E R I A

Tunis

TUNISIA

MALTA

Khaniá

Crete

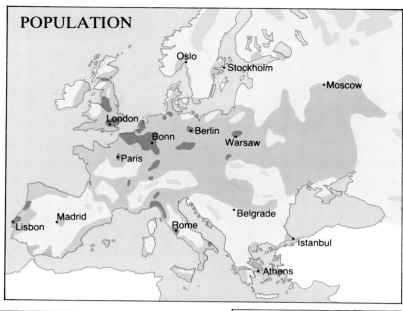

POPULATION

Oslo
• Stockholm
• Moscow
London
Bonn • Berlin
• Paris Warsaw
Madrid
Lisbon Rome • Belgrade
• Istanbul
• Athens

	over 500 persons per km²
	100-500 persons per km²
	5-100 persons per km²
	under 5 persons per km²

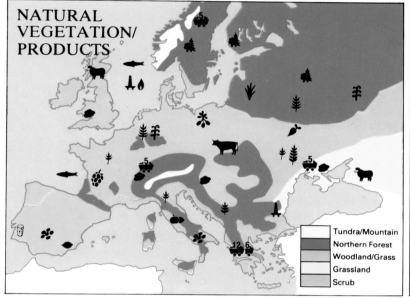

NATURAL VEGETATION/ PRODUCTS

	Tundra/Mountain
	Northern Forest
	Woodland/Grass
	Grassland
	Scrub

	Cattle		Oil
	Sheep		Coal
	Fish		Gas
	Fruit		Oats
	Citrus fruit		Wheat
	Grapes		Maize
	Yams		Rye
	Sugar beet		Barley
	Potatoes	5	Iron
	Timber	6	Lead
	Cork	12	Zinc

FACTS ABOUT EUROPE

1 In Iceland, ice and fire exist side by side. Many active volcanoes and geysers (hot springs which shoot a column of water into the air at intervals) can be seen, while glaciers (continually moving 'rivers' of ice) and ice sheets cover much of the land. One volcano – Vatnajokull – is particularly dangerous for an unusual reason: it is underneath a glacier and when it erupts, the ice melts very quickly, causing terrible floods.

2 The Humber Bridge, England, has one of the longest single spans of any bridge in the world. It stretches for 1410 m (4626 feet).

3 More than a third of the land area of the Netherlands has been reclaimed from the sea. These lands (the *polders*) are below sea level and the sea is kept out by dykes. Drainage ditches divide the fertile fields. The water from them is pumped into canals and rivers, then out to sea.

4 The longest river in Europe is the Volga, which runs for 3690 km (2292 miles) from the forests north west of Moscow in Russia all the way to the Caspian Sea.

5 Portugal is an important source of cork, which is actually the bark of a tree. The cork oak produces cork bark up to 15 cm (6 inches) thick and this is stripped off the trees every 10 to 15 years. Cork oaks grow throughout the western and central Mediterranean region.

6 The Pierre Saint Martin Cavern in the Pyrenees mountains, France, is the deepest cave system yet discovered in the world. It goes 1330 m (4364 feet) into the heart of the mountains.

7 The principality of Monaco is one of the most crowded countries in the world: 28 000 people live on 1.9 sq km (467 acres) of land! By contrast, most of Scandinavia has fewer than 40 people per square kilometre.

8 Venice, Italy, is built on no less than 118 islands. Instead of roads, there are canals, and boats are used for transport. Venice is sinking at a rate of 12 inches each century. Some of the reasons for this include water being extracted from wells, and the compression of the mud on the floor of the lagoon.

9 Mount Etna, Sicily, is the highest volcano in Europe (about 3323 m, 10 902 ft) and is still very active. Despite this, many people live on its lower slopes. This is because the soil there is very fertile and grows good produce.

2 The Humber Bridge, England

ALBANIA

Area: 28 748 sq km
(11 079 sq miles)
Population: 3 200 000
Capital: Tirana
Language: Albanian
Currency: Lek

AUSTRIA

Area: 83 848 sq km
(32 374 sq miles)
Population: 7 600 000
Capital: Vienna
Language: German
Currency: Schilling

BELARUS

Area: 208 000 sq km
(80 309 sq miles)
Population: 10 278 000
Capital: Minsk
Language: Belorussian
Currency: Rouble

BELGIUM

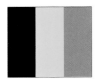

Area: 30 512 sq km
(11 781 sq miles)
Population: 9 900 000
Capital: Brussels
Languages: Flemish, French
Currency: Belgian Franc

BULGARIA

Area: 110 911 sq km
(42 822 sq miles)
Population: 9 000 000
Capital: Sofia
Language: Bulgarian
Currency: Lev

CZECH REPUBLIC

Area: 78 864 sq km
(30 449 sq miles)
Population: 10 300 000
Capital: Prague
Language: Czech
Currency: Koruna

DENMARK

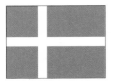

Area: 43 030 sq km
(16 614 sq miles)
Population: 5 100 000
Capital: Copenhagen
Language: Danish
Currency: Krone

ESTONIA

Area: 45 100 sq km
(17 413 sq miles)
Population: 1 600 000
Capital: Tallinn
Language: Estonian
Currency: Kroon

FINLAND

Area: 337 032 sq km
(130 128 sq miles)
Population: 5 000 000
Capital: Helsinki
Languages: Finnish, Swedish
Currency: Markka

FRANCE

Area: 543 965 sq km
(210 025 sq miles)
Population: 56 100 000
Capital: Paris
Language: French
Currency: French Franc

GERMANY

Area: 356 854 sq km
(137 781 sq miles)
Population: 79 000 000
Capital: Berlin
Language: German
Currency: Deutschmark

GREECE

Area: 131 955 sq km
(50 948 sq miles)
Population: 10 000 000
Capital: Athens
Language: Greek
Currency: Drachma

HUNGARY

Area: 93 030 sq km
(35 919 sq miles)
Population: 10 600 000
Capital: Budapest
Language: Magyar
Currency: Forint

ICELAND

Area: 102 828 sq km
(39 702 sq miles)
Population: 259 577
Capital: Reykjavik
Language: Icelandic
Currency: Króna

IRELAND

Area: 70 282 sq km
(27 136 sq miles)
Population: 3 700 000
Capital: Dublin
Language: Irish (Gaelic),
English
Currency: Irish Pound (Punt)

10 Monasteries on rock pillars, Greece

10 Near Kalabaka, Greece, are a group of monasteries built for monks with no fear of heights! They are perched on top of pillars of rock, called meteora, 300 m (1 000 ft) high. The only way up was by ladders or baskets slung on the end of ropes. Now stairways have been constructed so that tourists can visit the buildings.

11 The island of Santorini (Thira) in Greece is the site of the world's largest natural disaster. About 1500 BC this volcanic island erupted leaving a *caldera* (hollow basin shape where the top of the volcano had been) about 13 km (8 miles) across. Many people believe that the destruction of this island is the origin of the story of Atlantis. The people of Atlantis are mentioned by the Greek writer Plato. Crime and corruption spread throughout their island as they became wealthier, until finally the Athenians conquered them. Later the island disappeared into the sea in a single day and night.

7 Monte Carlo, Monaco

12 Loch Ness, in the Highlands of Scotland, is one of the most famous freshwater expanses in the world. Its length and depth are so great that it could accommodate the population of the earth three times over. Its greatest mystery is the world-famous Loch Ness Monster which was first recorded in the 6th century by the Abbot of Iona. 'Nessie', as the monster is affectionately known, has been sighted by many people but evidence of the monster's existence is inconclusive. If it does exist, the most popular theory is that the monster is one of a small colony of unknown creatures which have descended from marine animals trapped in the loch at the end of the last Ice Age 12,000 years ago.

12 Loch Ness, Scotland

13 The stalactite caves of Aggtelek in Hungary form one of the largest cave systems in Europe. They are 23km (14 miles) long and extend over the border into Slovakia. The stalactites and stalagmites in the cave make a spectacular impact. Stalagmites on the floor of the Aggtelek caves bear a clear resemblance to the human form. Others resemble animals, temples, waterfalls, a 'Great Organ' and even a 'Butcher's Shop'.

14 The spectacularly beautiful Alhambra in Spain is situated on a hill overlooking Granada. From the outside, the fortress walls look plain but they belie the complex and colourful interior. Visitors find the intricate stonework, the sumptuous halls and the attractive gardens with their many fountains quite breathtaking. The Palace of the Alhambra was built as a home for the Moorish rulers in the 14th century and is a well-preserved example of the very best of Moorish art.

14 The Alhambra, Spain

ITALY

Area: 301 245 sq km
(116 311 sq miles)
Population: 57 100 000
Capital: Rome
Language: Italian
Currency: Lira

NETHERLANDS

Area: 33 940 sq km
(13 104 sq miles)
Population: 15 000 000
Capital: Amsterdam & The Hague
Language: Dutch
Currency: Guilder

PORTUGAL

Area: 91 671 sq km
(35 394 sq miles)
Population: 10 300 000
Capital: Lisbon
Language: Portuguese
Currency: Escudo

SPAIN

Area: 504 745 sq km
(194 882 sq miles)
Population: 39 200 000
Capital: Madrid
Language: Spanish
Currency: Peseta

UKRAINE

Area: 603 700 sq km
(233 089 sq miles)
Population: 51 857 000
Capital: Kiev
Languages: Ukrainian, Russian
Currency: Rouble

LATVIA

Area: 63 700 sq km
(24 595 sq miles)
Population: 2 700 000
Capital: Riga
Language: Latvian
Currency: Lat

NORWAY

Area: 324 218 sq km
(125 180 sq miles)
Population: 4 200 000
Capital: Oslo
Language: Norwegian
Currency: Krone

ROMANIA

Area: 237 500 sq km
(91 699 sq miles)
Population: 23 300 000
Capital: Bucharest
Language: Romanian
Currency: Leu

SWEDEN

Area: 449 791 sq km
(173 664 sq miles)
Population: 8 400 000
Capital: Stockholm
Language: Swedish
Currency: Krona

UNITED KINGDOM

Area: 244 104 sq km
(94 249 sq miles)
Population: 57 200 000
Capital: London
Language: English
Currency: Pound Sterling

LITHUANIA

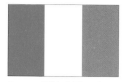

Area: 65 200 sq km
(25 170 sq miles)
Population: 3 700 000
Capital: Vilnius
Language: Lithuanian
Currency: Litas

POLAND

Area: 312 683 sq km
(120 727 sq miles)
Population: 38 400 000
Capital: Warsaw
Language: Polish
Currency: Zloty

RUSSIAN FEDERATION

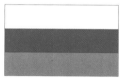

Area: 17 078 000 sq km
(6 593 816 sq miles)
Population: 148 263 000
Capital: Moscow
Language: Russian
Currency: Rouble

SWITZERLAND

Area: 41 287 sq km
(15 941 sq miles)
Population: 6 600 000
Capital: Bern
Languages: German, French Italian, Romansch
Currency: Swiss Franc

YUGOSLAVIA

Area: 91 285 sq km
(35 245 sq miles)
Population: 10 300 000
Capital: Belgrade
Language: Serbo-Croatian
Currency: Dinar

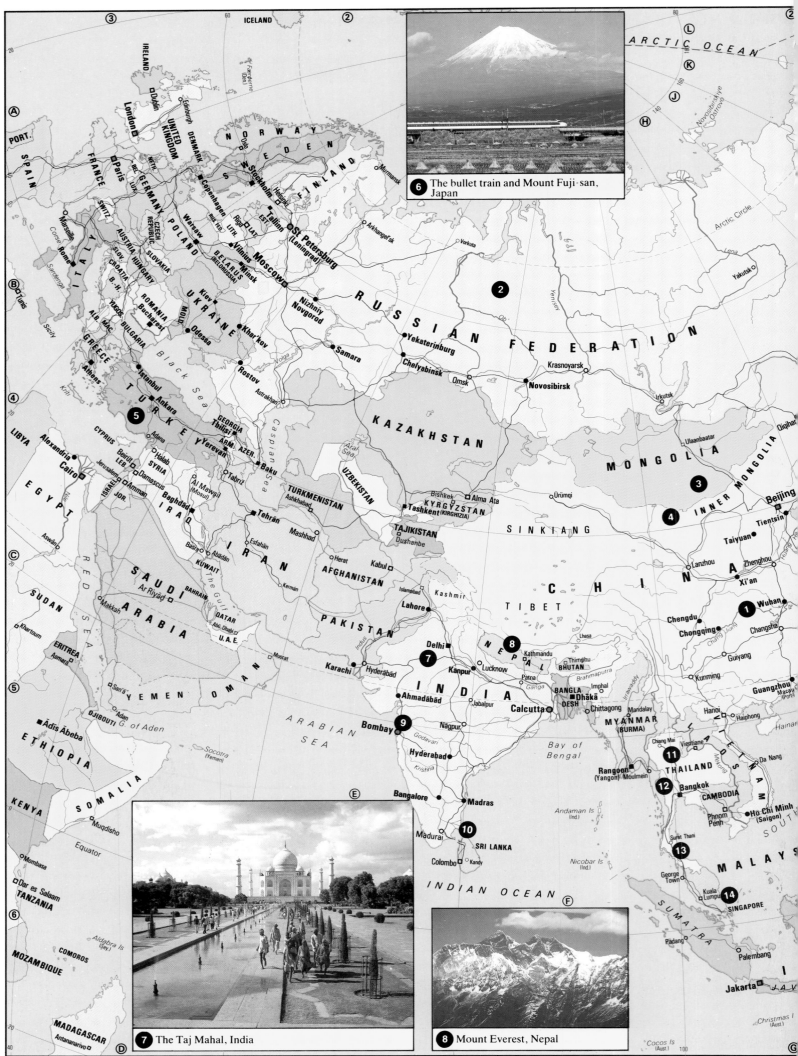

400   800   1200   1600 km
400   800 mls

ICELAND

ARCTIC OCEAN

L
K
J
H

Arctic Circle

PORT.

SPAIN

IRELAND

Dublin
London

UNITED KINGDOM

Edinburgh

DENMARK

NETH.
BEL.
Paris
FRANCE
GERMANY
LUX.

SWITZ.

AUSTRIA

ITALY

Marseille

Corse (Fr.)

Rome

Sardegna

Sicily

Tunis

ALB.
MAC.

GREECE

Athens

Kriti

N O R W A Y
Oslo
S W E D E N
Stockholm
Helsinki

FINLAND

Tallinn
EST.
Riga
LITH.
LAT.

CZECH REPUBLIC
SLOVAKIA
HUNGARY
SLOV.
CROATIA
B.-H.
YUGOS.
ROMANIA
Bucharest
BULGARIA
MOLD.

POLAND
Warsaw
BELARUS
(BELORUSSIA)
Minsk
Vilnius
RUS. FED.

UKRAINE
Kiev
Odessa
Khar'kov

Black Sea

Istanbul
Ankara
T U R K E Y

Murmansk

St Petersburg
(Leningrad)
Moscow
Nizhniy Novgorod
Rostov
Samara
Volga
Astrakhan'

GEORGIA
Tbilisi
ARM. AZER.
Yerevan
Baku

Caspian Sea

Arkhangel'sk

Vorkuta

Yekaterinburg
Chelyabinsk
Omsk

R U S S I A N   F E D E R A T I O N

Ob'
Yenisey

Krasnoyarsk
Novosibirsk
Irkutsk

Lena
Yakutsk

2

2

LIBYA

Alexandria
Cairo

EGYPT

Aswān

SUDAN

Khartoum

ERITREA
Asmara

Ādīs Ābeba

ETHIOPIA

Nile

RED SEA

CYPRUS
LEB.
Beirut
Jerusalem
ISRAEL
JOR.
Damascus
Amman
SYRIA
Halab
(Mosul) Al Mawsil
Baghdad
IRAQ
Basra
Abādān
KUWAIT

SAUDI ARABIA
Makkah
Ar Riyāḍ
BAHRAIN
QATAR
Abu Dhabi
U.A.E.

The Gulf

Adana

Tabrīz

Tehrān
Mashhad
Esfahān
Kermān
I R A N

TURKMENISTAN
Ashkhabad

Herat

Aral Sea

KAZAKHSTAN

UZBEKISTAN

Bishkek
Alma Ata
Tashkent
KYRGYZSTAN
(KIRGHIZIA)

TAJIKISTAN
Dushanbe

Ūrümqi

M O N G O L I A

Ulaanbaatar

Qiqihar

INNER MONGOLIA

Beijing
Tientsin

SINKIANG

Taiyuan

Lanzhou
Zhengzhou
Xi'an

Huang He

2

3

4

OMAN

YEMEN
San'ā
Aden
G. of Aden
DJIBOUTI
Muscat

SOMALIA

KENYA

Mombasa

TANZANIA
Dar es Salaam

MOZAMBIQUE

COMOROS
Aldabra Is (Sey.)

MADAGASCAR
Antananarivo

Socotra (Yemen)

ARABIAN SEA

AFGHANISTAN
Kabul
Islamabad
Kashmir

PAKISTAN
Lahore
Karachi
Hyderābād

INDIA
Delhi
Ahmadābād
Bombay
Hyderabad
Godavari
Krishna
Bangalore
Madras
Madurai
Kanpur
Lucknow
Jabalpur
Nāgpur
Indus

NEPAL
Kathmandu
Patna
Ganga
Patna

Thimphu
BHUTAN

Brahmaputra

TIBET
Lhasa

C H I N A

Chengdu
Chongqing

Wuhan
Chang Jiang
Changsha

Guiyang

Kunming

Guangzhou
Macau (Port.)

1

SRI LANKA
Colombo
Kandy

BANGLA-DESH
Dhākā
Chittagong
Imphal

Calcutta

Bay of Bengal

Andaman Is (Ind.)

Nicobar Is (Ind.)

MYANMAR
(BURMA)
Mandalay
Irrawaddy
Rangoon
(Yangon)
Moulmein

Chiang Mai
Vientiane
THAILAND
Bangkok

LAOS

Hanoi
Haiphong
VIETNAM
Da Nang
Hainan

CAMBODIA
Phnom Penh
Ho Chi Minh
(Saigon)
Mekong
Surat Thani

MALAYS
George Town
Kuala Lumpur
SINGAPORE
SUMATRA
Padang
Palembang
Jakarta   JAV

INDIAN OCEAN

Equator

Mogadishu

Christmas I.
Cocos Is (Aust.)

5

6

A

B

C

D

E

F

7
8
9
10
11
12
13
14

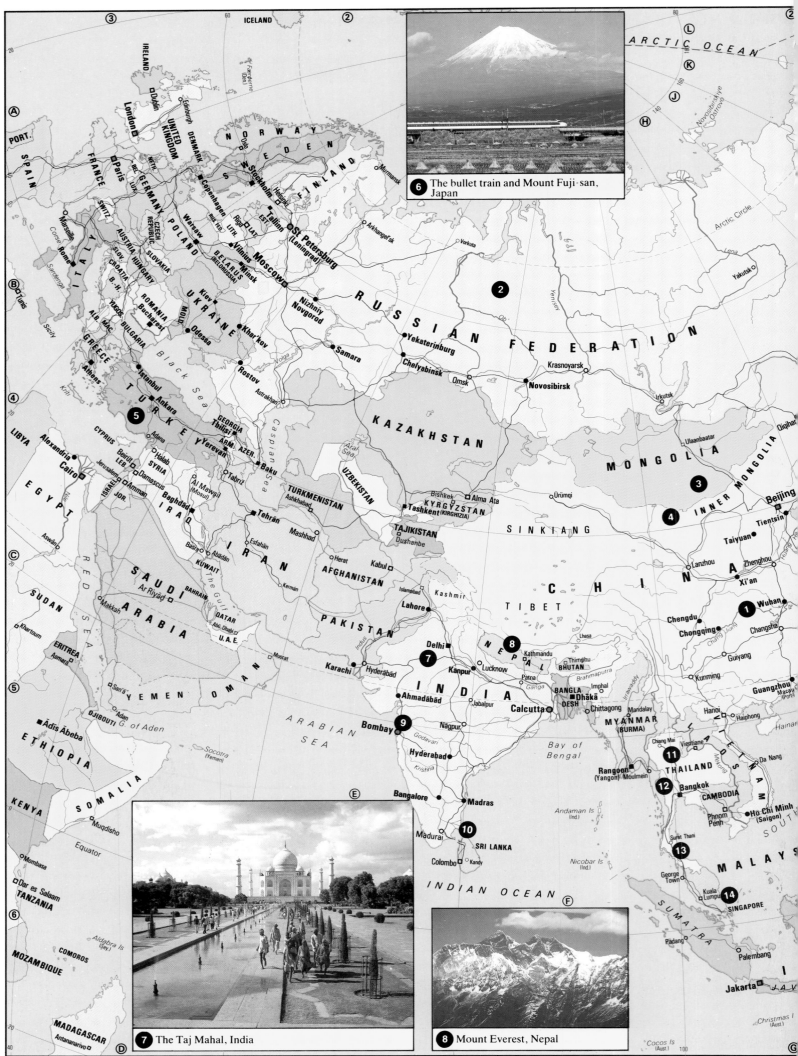
6 The bullet train and Mount Fuji-san, Japan

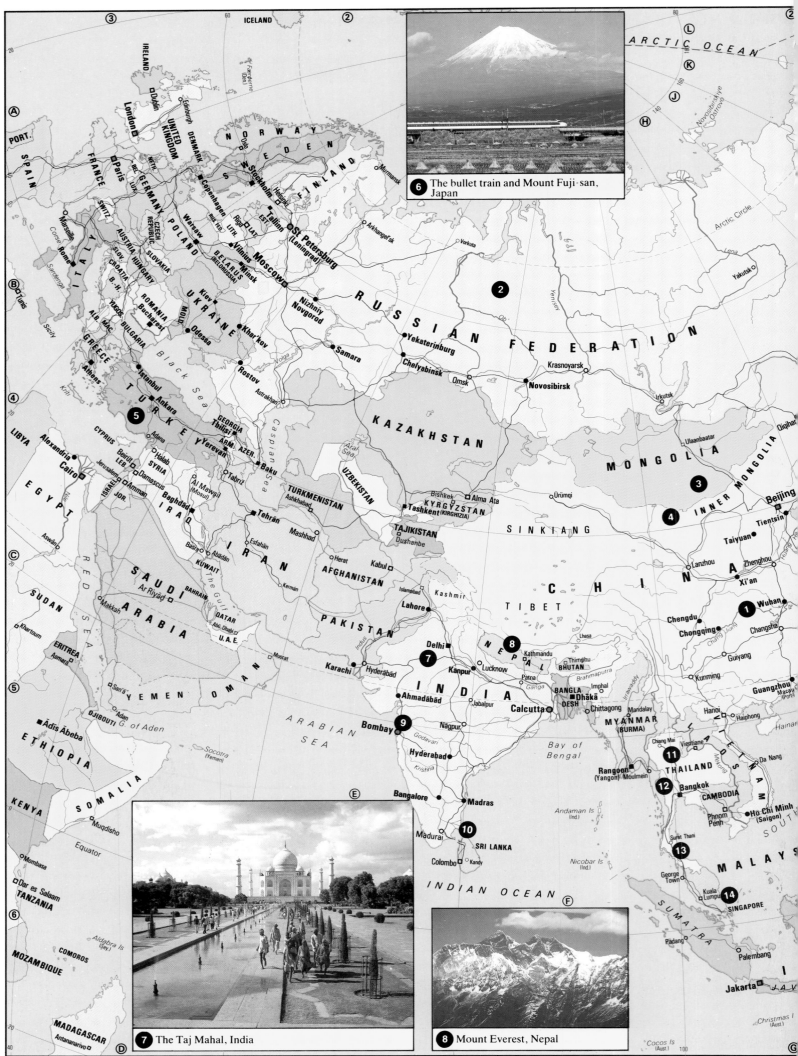
7 The Taj Mahal, India

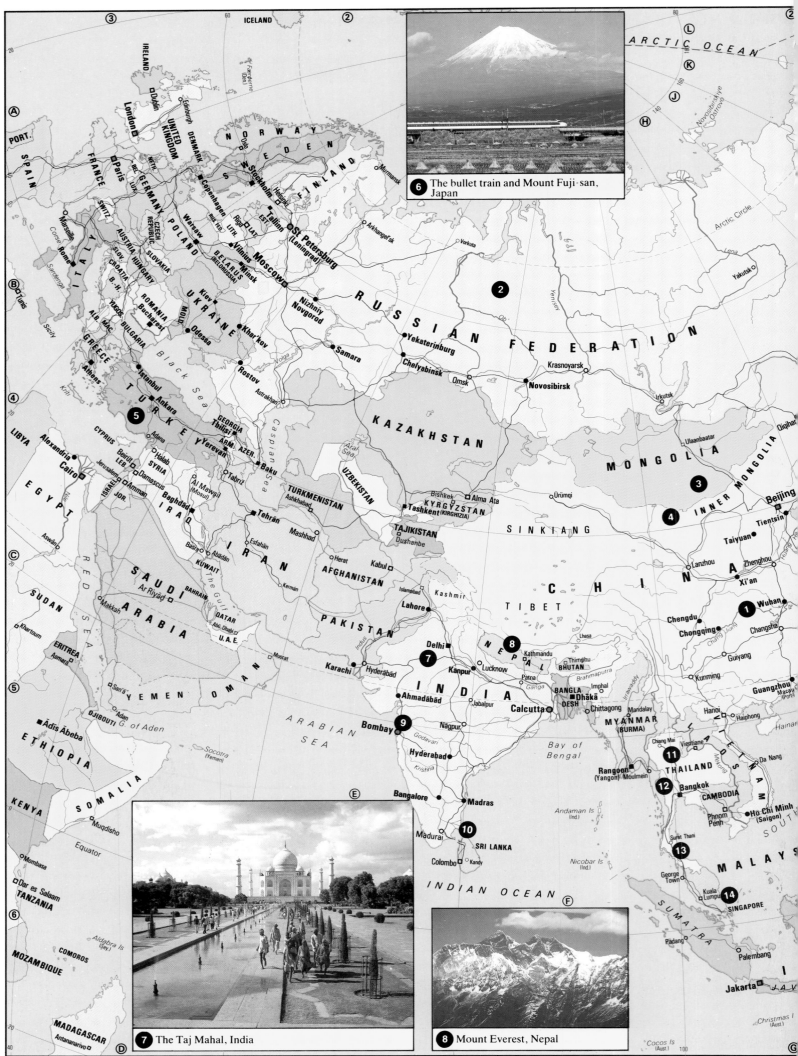
8 Mount Everest, Nepal

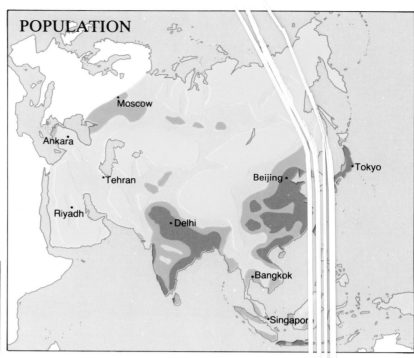

POPULATION

Moscow

Ankara

Tehran

Beijing

Tokyo

Riyadh

Delhi

Bangkok

Singapore

	over 500 persons per km^2
	100-500 persons per km^2
	5-100 persons per km^2
	under 5 persons per km^2

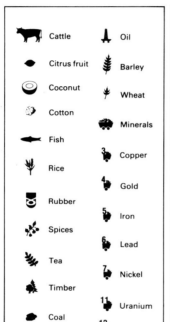

Cattle		Oil	
Citrus fruit		Barley	
Coconut		Wheat	
Cotton		Minerals	
Fish		Copper	3
Rice		Gold	4
Rubber		Iron	5
Spices		Lead	6
Tea		Nickel	7
Timber		Uranium	11
Coal		Zinc	12

NATURAL VEGETATION/PRODUCTS

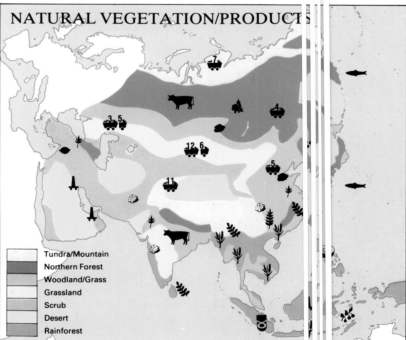

	Tundra/Mountain
	Northern Forest
	Woodland/Grass
	Grassland
	Scrub
	Desert
	Rainforest

FACTS ABOUT ASIA

1 The Chang Jiang river (formerly known as the Yangtze Kiang) is the longest river in Asia. Rising in the Tibetan hills, it flows across southern China to the East China Sea. The river has a length of over 5550 km (3450 miles).

2 In Siberia, there is a huge forest called the *taiga*, which makes up a quarter of the total area of forest in the world. The trees are mostly coniferous - pine and larch. Few people used to live in the taiga, as it is a very cold area, but because it is rich in minerals more people are moving into the forest. They live in industrial towns being built deep in its heart, to exploit the minerals.

3 The huge Gobi Desert covers much of Mongolia. The Gobi is a cold, barren region of rocky plains and hills. Water is very scarce and only a few nomads live here. They exist mainly by cattle raising and live in an unusual tent called a *yurt*, which is shaped like an upside-down bowl.

4 The Great Wall of China stretches for 3460 km (2150 miles), making it the longest in the world. It was built for defence in the 3rd century BC and kept in good repair until 400 years ago. Although part of the wall was blown up to make a dam in 1979, the many remaining sections of the wall are still impressive.

11 Floating vegetable market, Thailand

14 Singapore

12 Bangkok, Thailand

5 Cliff dwellings in Cappadocia, Turkey

13 Water buffalo ploughing Chinese paddy fields

FACTS ABOUT ASIA

5 In central Turkey, near Urgup in the region called Cappadocia, an extraordinary landscape can be seen. There was once a plateau here, made up of layers of rock, some hard and some much softer. Over thousands of years the softer rocks have been eroded by the weather, by streams and even by men digging out caves to live in. The rocks are now shaped into strange cones, towers and 'mushrooms', with 'hats' of harder rock balancing on top. There are also complete 'villages' of caves connected to each other by passageways cut through the rock. Each cave has 'cupboards' and 'shelves' cut into its walls. Here many centuries ago people hid from religious persecution. Over 300 churches which they dug out of the rock have been found. Some people still live in caves in this region, today.

6 The Seikan Tunnel in Japan is the longest tunnel in the world. It is an underwater tunnel, stretching for 54 km (34 miles). It was built for Japan's famous *bullet train*, the first passenger train to travel at 200 kph.

7 There should have been two Taj Mahals in India – a black one and a white one. In 1648, Emperor Shah Jahan completed the present Taj Mahal. It was a tomb for his wife, and made of white marble. He then began building a tomb of black marble for himself. Before work had got very far, he was overthrown.

8 At 8848 m (29 028 ft) the peak of Mt Everest in the Himalayas is the Earth's highest point. In May 1953, New Zealander Sir Edmund Hillary was the first man to climb Everest. Twenty two years later, in 1975, the first woman to reach the summit was Junko Tabei of Japan.

9 In India cows are sacred animals and are allowed to wander freely, even in the centre of big cities! Drivers are used to going round cows lying peacefully in the middle of the road.

10 Banyan trees can be seen in India and Sri Lanka. They are very unusual to look at, because what seems to be several trees growing close together, is actually just one tree! Aerial roots grow down from the banyan's branches and root in the ground. They become extra 'trunks' and support a huge canopy of leaves, which gives a lot of shade, very useful in such a hot climate.

11 Throughout Asia there are areas where many people live on boats – because there is not enough room for them to live in houses on land (or they cannot afford to) or because they just prefer to live on water. In these places, even the shops are on boats.

4 The Great Wall, China

10 Banyan tree, India

9 Street in India

12 Bangkok, Thailand, once had many canals, called *klongs*, instead of roads. (The city was called the 'Venice of the East' because the klongs reminded visitors of the canals in Venice, Italy.) They were used for transport and also helped to drain the land during the rainy season. After cars and lorries began to be used for transport, many of the klongs were filled in to make roads. Now Bangkok has problems with flooding when the monsoons come.

13 Paddy fields, the irrigated fields in which rice is grown, get their name from *padi*, the Malayan word for rice. Rice is grown throughout Asia in the fertile lowlands near the equator. Millions of people live in these areas, and rice is very important to them as it yields more food per acre than any other crop.

14 Over half the population of the world lives in Asia – that is 3 113 000 000 people. Some parts of Asia have many people living in a small area. One of the most densely populated countries is Singapore, which has an average of 4 420 people for each square kilometre of ground.

AFGHANISTAN

Area: 674 500 sq km
(260 424 sq miles)
Population: 16 600 000
Capital: Kabul
Languages: Pashtu, Dari, Uzbek
Currency: Afghani

CHINA

Area: 9 561 000 sq km
(3 691 502 sq miles)
Population: 1 118 800 000
Capital: Beijing
Language: Chinese (Mandarin)
Currency: Yuan

INDIA

Area: 3 287 593 sq km
(1 269 340 sq miles)
Population: 853 100 000
Capital: Delhi
Languages: Hindi, English
Currency: Indian Rupee

INDONESIA

Area: 1 919 263 sq km
(741 027 miles)
Population: 185 000 000
Capital: Jakarta
Language: Bahasa (Indonesian)
Currency: Rupiah

IRAN

Area: 1 648 184 sq km
(636 364 sq miles)
Population: 54 600 000
Capital: Tehran
Language: Persian (Farsi)
Currency: Rial

IRAQ

Area: 434 924 sq km
(167 924 sq miles)
Population: 18 900 000
Capital: Baghdad
Language: Arabic
Currency: Iraqi Dinar

ISRAEL

Area: 20 770 sq km
(8019 sq miles)
Population: 4 600 000
Capital: Jerusalem
Languages: Hebrew, Arabic
Currency: Shekel

JAPAN

Area: 371 000 sq km
(143 243 sq miles)
Population: 123 500 000
Capital: Tokyo
Language: Japanese
Currency: Yen

MALAYSIA

Area: 330 669 sq km
(127 671 sq miles)
Population: 17 900 000
Capital: Kuala Lumpur
Language: Malay
Currency: Ringgit (Malaysian Dollar)

PAKISTAN

Area: 803 941 sq km
(310 402 sq miles)
Population: 122 600 000
Capital: Islamabad
Language: Urdu
Currency: Pakistan Rupee

PHILIPPINES

Area: 299 765 sq km
(115 739 sq miles)
Population: 62 400 000
Capital: Manila
Language: Philipino
Currency: Philippine Peso

SAUDI ARABIA

Area: 2 400 930 sq km
(927 000 sq miles)
Population: 14 100 000
Capital: Riyadh
Language: Arabic
Currency: Riyal

SINGAPORE

Area: 616 sq km
(238 sq miles)
Population: 2 700 000
Capital: Singapore
Languages: Chinese, Malay, Tamil, English
Currency: Singapore Dollar

THAILAND

Area: 513 517 sq km
(198 269 sq miles)
Population: 55 700 000
Capital: Bangkok
Languages: Thai, Chinese
Currency: Baht

TURKEY

Area: 780 576 sq km
(301 380 sq miles)
Population: 55 900 000
Capital: Ankara
Language: Turkish
Currency: Turkish Lira

1:40M

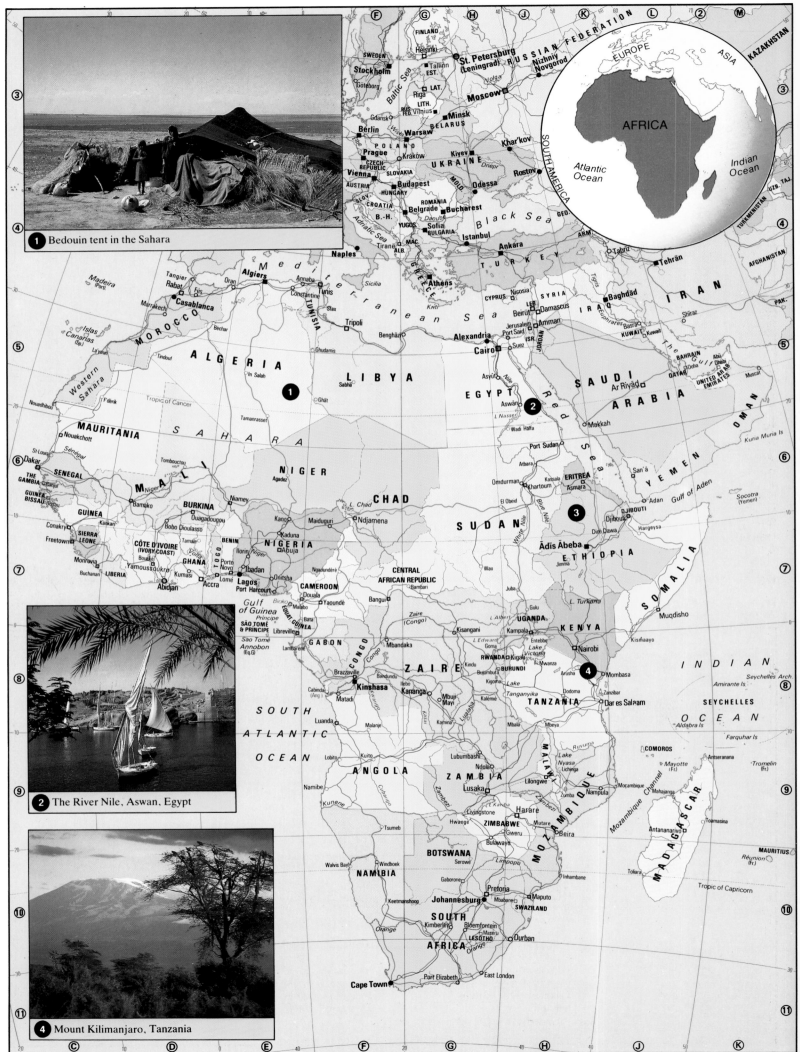

1 Bedouin tent in the Sahara

2 The River Nile, Aswan, Egypt

4 Mount Kilimanjaro, Tanzania

POPULATION

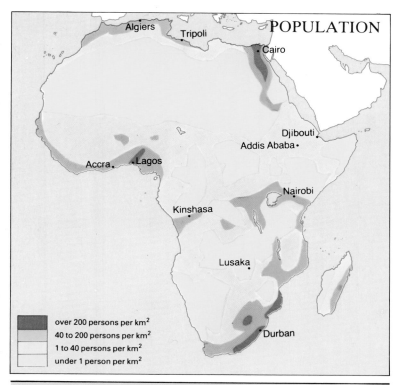

over 200 persons per km²
40 to 200 persons per km²
1 to 40 persons per km²
under 1 person per km²

NATURAL VEGETATION/PRODUCTS

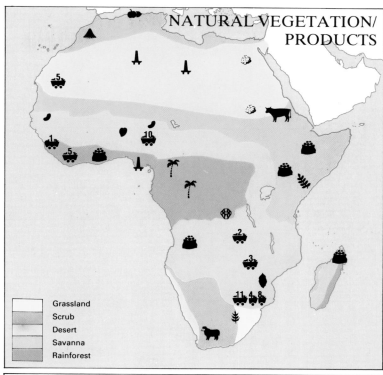

Grassland
Scrub
Desert
Savanna
Rainforest

Cattle	Peanuts	Phosphates	**4** Gold	
Sheep	Palm oil	Maize	**5** Iron	
Cocoa	Tea	Minerals	**8** Platinum	
Coffee	Tobacco	**1** Bauxite	**10** Tin	
Cotton	Diamonds	**2** Cobalt	**11** Uranium	
Fruit	Oil	**3** Copper		

FACTS ABOUT AFRICA

1 The largest desert in the world is the Sahara, but only about 30% of it is sand. The rest is rocky waste. People live mainly near oases, where the land is watered by springs rising to the surface and crops can be grown. The desert is very hot and dry, but there are a few plants and animals (like camels) specially adapted to these conditions.

2 The Nile is the longest river in the world and flows for 6650 km (4160 miles) through North Africa to the Mediterranean Sea. The Nile used to flood its banks each year, but now the High Dam at Aswan controls the floods. When the dam was built, the temples of Abu Simbel (3000 years old) were moved to a higher site to stop them being flooded.

3 Some parts of Africa have had no rain, or very little, for several years. Food crops have failed and many people have died from malnutrition and starvation. A further problem has been wars, which have driven many people from their homes and fields. Even if part of a country can grow food, it is difficult to move that food into areas where none can be grown. There are few lorries and, where people are at war, transporting food may be dangerous. Although western countries have sent food supplies, there is still not enough to feed the hundreds of thousands of people who are starving. Governments are trying to find ways of growing more food and distributing it more quickly.

4 Kilimanjaro (now renamed Uhuru, meaning 'freedom') is the highest mountain in Africa (5895 m; 19 340 feet) and its peaks are always covered in snow.

EGYPT
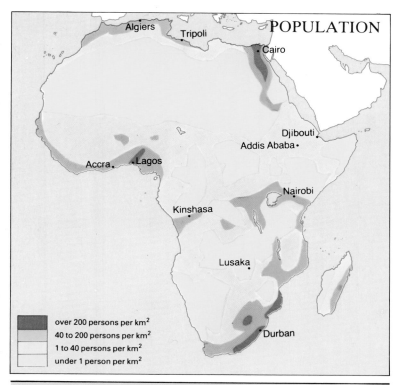
Area: 1 000 250 sq km (386 197 sq miles)
Population: 52 400 000
Capital: Cairo
Language: Arabic
Currency: Egyptian Pound

ETHIOPIA
Area: 1 104 318 sq km (426 377 sq miles)
Population: 46 626 000
Capital: Addis Ababa
Language: Amharic
Currency: Birr

KENYA
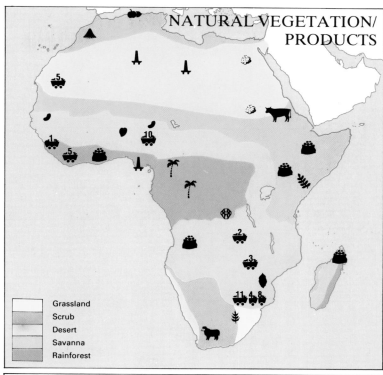
Area: 582 644 sq km (224 959 sq miles)
Population: 24 000 000
Capital: Nairobi
Languages: English, Swahili
Currency: Kenya Shilling

LIBYA
Area: 1 759 530 sq km (679 355 sq miles)
Population: 4 500 000
Capital: Tripoli
Language: Arabic
Currency: Libyan Dinar

NIGERIA
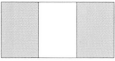
Area: 923 769 sq km (356 667 sq miles)
Population: 108 500 000
Capital: Lagos
Language: English
Currency: Naira

SOUTH AFRICA

Area: 1 221 038 sq km (471 443 sq miles)
Population: 35 300 000
Capital: Pretoria
Languages: Afrikaans, English
Currency: Rand

SUDAN

Area: 2 505 792 sq km (967 486 sq miles)
Population: 25 200 000
Capital: Khartoum
Language: Arabic
Currency: Sudanese Pound

ZAIRE

Area: 2 344 885 sq km (905 360 sq miles)
Population: 35 600 000
Capital: Kinshasa
Language: French
Currency: Zaire

AUSTRALASIA

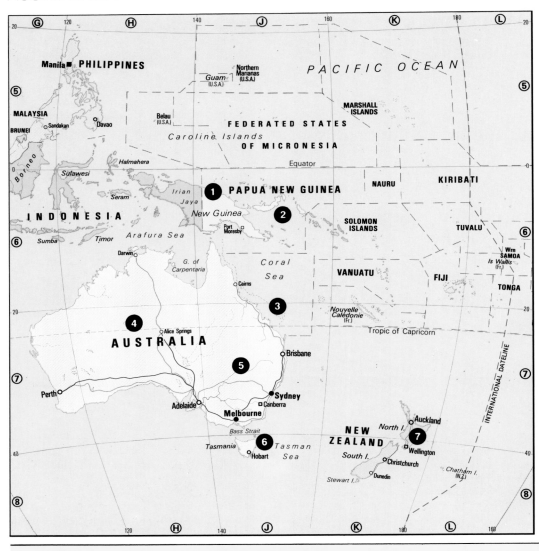

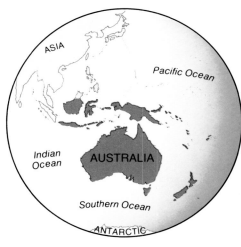

7 Geysers at Whakarewarewa, New Zealand

FACTS ABOUT AUSTRALASIA

1 Over 700 languages are spoken in Papua New Guinea. That is more than a quarter of all the languages spoken in the world. Papua New Guinea's mountains, thick forests and islands meant that different tribes did not mix, so they did not share a common language, but instead each developed its own. Today, Pidgin English and Police Motu have become the languages which the different tribes use to talk to each other.

2 No less than 38 different species of the beautiful Bird of Paradise are to be seen in Papua New Guinea. Another 5 species are found on neighbouring islands and in northern Australia. Their tail feathers are a traditional part of Papua New Guinea tribal costume, although the birds are now protected from hunting to a great extent.

3 Australia's Great Barrier Reef is formed from the shells of millions of tiny sea creatures. It is 2300 km (1430 miles) long and is the world's biggest coral reef. There are many thousands of coral islands or *atolls* in the Pacific region.

4 Ayers Rock is a huge sandstone rock formation which rears up abruptly from the desert in central Australia. The rock is special because it changes colour with the light. To Australia's native *aborigine* people the rock has a very deep spiritual meaning.

5 Australia is a very dry continent. Rainfall is also very unevenly distributed throughout the island: even though some parts of the tropical north receive about 2000 millimetres (79 inches) a year, the central deserts receive less than 150 millimetres (6 inches). Irrigation is very important for agriculture, with rivers and artesian wells being used as sources of water. The Snowy Mountains reservoir and irrigation scheme has brought water from the mountains to irrigate farmland in the east of Australia.

6 A Tasmanian Devil is a little bear-like creature found only in Tasmania. It is just 60 cm (2 ft) long, with a big bushy tail. It has very sharp teeth and eats other

4 Ayers Rock, Australia

6 Tasmanian Devil

POPULATION

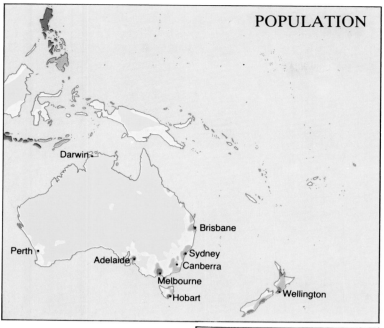

Darwin
Perth
Adelaide
Brisbane
Sydney
Canberra
Melbourne
Hobart
Wellington

NATURAL VEGETATION/PRODUCTS

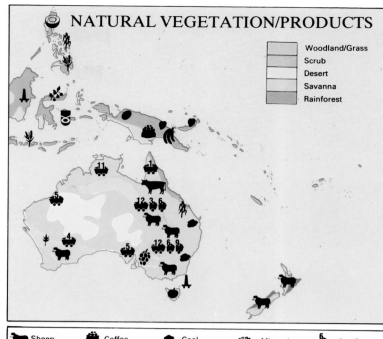

Woodland/Grass
Scrub
Desert
Savanna
Rainforest

2 Traditional dress, Papua New Guinea

over 500 persons per km²
100-500 persons per km²
5-100 persons per km²
under 5 persons per km²

Sheep | Coffee | Coal | Minerals | **6** Lead
Apples | Cocoa | Oil | **1** Bauxite | **9** Silver
Bananas | Rubber | Spices | **3** Copper | **11** Uranium
Grapes | Yams | Sugar cane | **4** Gold | **12** Zinc
Coconut | Rice | Wheat | **5** Iron

animals and small birds when it comes out at night. The Tasmanian Devil is a *marsupial*. This means it carries its young in a pouch.

7 The tallest geyser ever to have erupted was the Waimangu Geyser in New Zealand. Waimangu geyser played to a height of 490 m (1608 ft) between 1900 and 1904. Today, steam from New Zealand's hot springs and geysers is harnessed to generate electricity.

AUSTRALIA

Area: 7 682 300 sq km (2 966 136 sq miles)
Population: 17 658 700
Capital: Canberra
Language: English
Currency: Australian Dollar

NEW ZEALAND

Area: 268 675 sq km (103 735 sq miles)
Population: 3 450 000
Capital: Wellington
Language: English
Currency: New Zealand Dollar

TONGA

Area: 699 sq km (270 sq miles)
Population: 100 000
Capital: Nuku'alofa
Languages: English, Tongan
Currency: Pa'anga

FIJI

Area: 18 272 sq km (7055 sq miles)
Population: 800 000
Capital: Suva
Languages: English, Fijian
Currency: Fiji Dollar

PAPUA NEW GUINEA

Area: 461 692 sq km (178 259 sq miles)
Population: 3 900 000
Capital: Port Moresby
Languages: English, Melanesian Pidgin
Currency: Kina

VANUATU

Area: 14 763 sq km (5700 sq miles)
Population: 160 000
Capital: Vila
Languages: Bislama, English, French
Currency: Australian Dollar, Vatu

KIRIBATI

Area: 800 sq km (309 sq miles)
Population: 66 000
Capital: Tarawa
Languages: English, I Kiribati
Currency: Australian Dollar

SOLOMON ISLANDS

Area: 29 785 sq km (11 500 sq miles)
Population: 320 000
Capital: Honiara
Languages: English, Pidgin
Currency: Solomon Islands Dollar

WESTERN SAMOA

Area: 2831 sq km (1093 sq miles)
Population: 170 000
Capital: Apia
Languages: Samoan, English
Currency: Tala

3 The Great Barrier Reef, Australia

WORLD ENVIRONMENT

The world can be divided into 8 broad 'climatic zones' (these are areas with a particular sort of weather). The natural types of plants and animals found in each zone are different and depend on the weather the zone has. This map shows which parts of the world are in each zone. The colour of the strip at the top of each zone description (for example, Desert, Rainforest) is the same as the colour used for the zone on the big map. The little map beside each zone description pinpoints where that type of habitat is found in the world. (For example, the Desert strip is orange/yellow. The little sketch map shows you where on the big map to look for this colour. You will find this colour in the north of Africa, the west of North America and in parts of Asia and Australia. All these places have deserts. The description tells you what the natural countryside looks like and what plants and animals live there.)

SCRUB OR MEDITERRANEAN

Areas of long, hot, dry summers and short, warm winters. The land used to be covered with trees, but man cleared it for crops and grazed his animals on it. Now there is evergreen scrub – vines and olive trees.

TUNDRA OR MOUNTAIN

Polar areas which are usually frozen over. During the short summers the top layer of soil thaws, creating vast marshes. Compact, wind-resistant plants and lichens and mosses are found here. Animals include lemmings and reindeer.

NORTHERN FOREST (TAIGA)

Forests of conifers growing over a large area. Winters are very cold and long. Summers are short. Trees include spruce and fir. Animals found here include beavers, squirrels and red deer.

WOODLAND AND GRASS

Temperate areas (where the weather is seldom very cold or very hot). Deciduous trees (which lose their leaves in winter) grow in the woodlands. They include oak, beech and maple. Man uses these areas most of all, for farming, building towns and villages, and industry.

GRASSLAND

Hot summers, cold winters and moderate rainfall. Huge area of grassland and 'black' (very fertile) soils. Grain crops grow well, and so does rich pasture for beef cattle. Names for this kind of grassland include steppe, veld, pampas and prairie.

SAVANNA

Tall grasses with thick stems, and flat-topped thorny trees grow here. Animals grazing here include giraffes and zebras. There is a short rainy season. Often it does not rain for a long time (a drought). Fires burn the dried out plants but they have adapted to survive this and grow again.

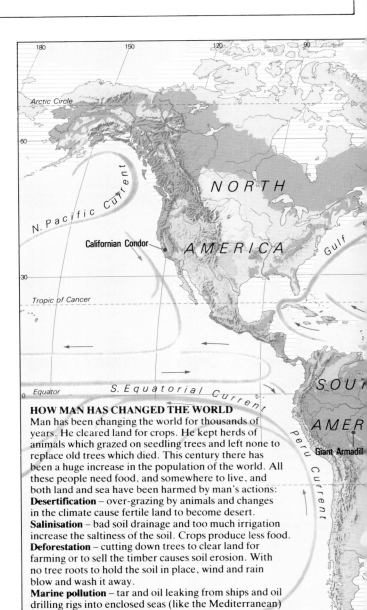

HOW MAN HAS CHANGED THE WORLD
Man has been changing the world for thousands of years. He cleared land for crops. He kept herds of animals which grazed on seedling trees and left none to replace old trees which died. This century there has been a huge increase in the population of the world. All these people need food, and somewhere to live, and both land and sea have been harmed by man's actions:
Desertification – over-grazing by animals and changes in the climate cause fertile land to become desert.
Salinisation – bad soil drainage and too much irrigation increase the saltiness of the soil. Crops produce less food.
Deforestation – cutting down trees to clear land for farming or to sell the timber causes soil erosion. With no tree roots to hold the soil in place, wind and rain blow and wash it away.
Marine pollution – tar and oil leaking from ships and oil drilling rigs into enclosed seas (like the Mediterranean) harm their plants and animals.

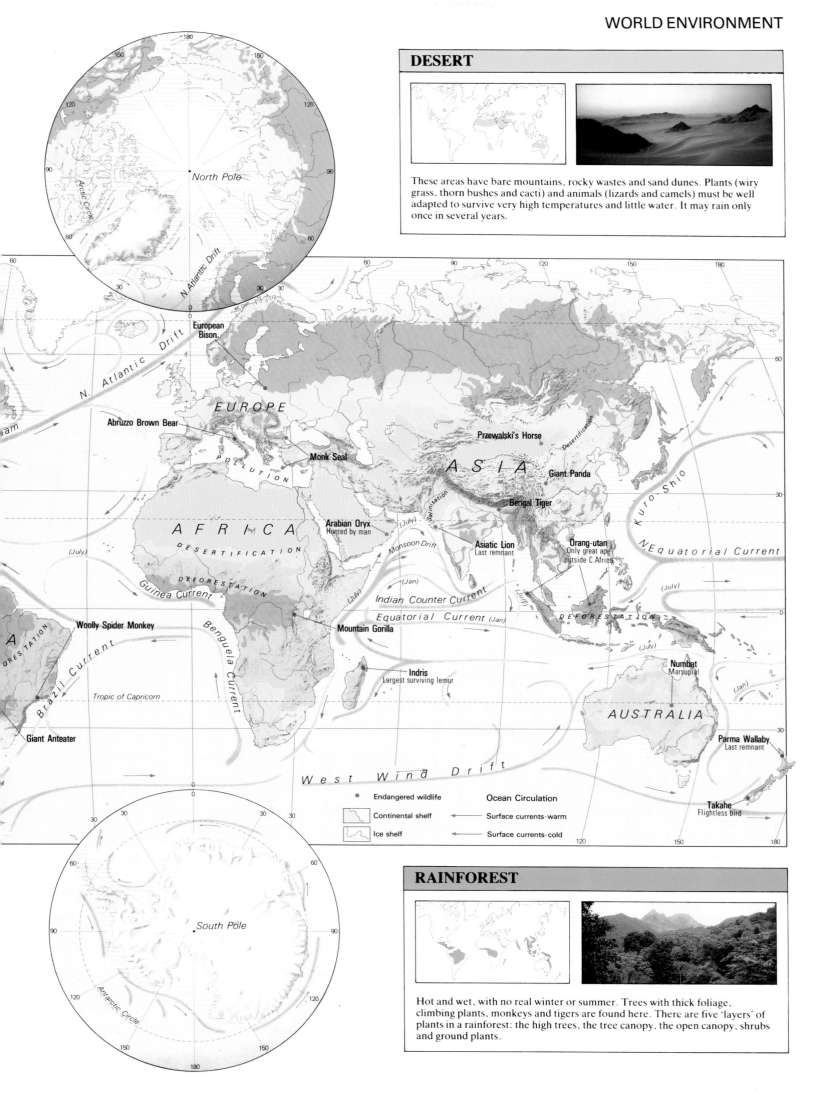

DESERT

These areas have bare mountains, rocky wastes and sand dunes. Plants (wiry grass, thorn bushes and cacti) and animals (lizards and camels) must be well adapted to survive very high temperatures and little water. It may rain only once in several years.

North Pole

Arctic Circle

South Pole

Antarctic Circle

European Bison

Abruzzo Brown Bear

Monk Seal

EUROPE

N. Atlantic Drift

N. Atlantic Drift

ASIA

Przewalski's Horse

Giant Panda

Bengal Tiger

Desertification

AFRICA

DESERTIFICATION

DEFORESTATION

Arabian Oryx
Hunted by man

Salinisation

(July)

Monsoon Drift

Asiatic Lion
Last remnant

Orang-utan
Only great ape
outside C. Africa

Kuro-Shio

(July)

N Equatorial Current

(July)

(July)

(Jan)

Indian Counter Current

Equatorial Current *(Jan)*

Guinea Current

Benguela Current

Brazil Current

(July)

POLLUTION

Woolly Spider Monkey

Mountain Gorilla

DEFORESTATION

Indris
Largest surviving lemur

Numbat
Marsupial

(July)

AUSTRALIA

(Jan)

Tropic of Capricorn

Giant Anteater

Parma Wallaby
Last remnant

West Wind Drift

Takahe
Flightless bird

• Endangered wildlife

Ocean Circulation

☐ Continental shelf

⟵ Surface currents-warm

Ice shelf

⟵ Surface currents-cold

RAINFOREST

Hot and wet, with no real winter or summer. Trees with thick foliage, climbing plants, monkeys and tigers are found here. There are five 'layers' of plants in a rainforest: the high trees, the tree canopy, the open canopy, shrubs and ground plants.

WORLD CLIMATE

World climate has a profound influence upon mankind. Everything is affected by it, from our environment and ability to grow food to our mobility and health. The most important characteristics of climate are rainfall patterns and temperature variations. As the earth revolves around the sun the tilt of its axis causes each hemisphere in turn to be closer than the other to the sun for half a year. The hemisphere facing the overhead sun enjoys a warm summer season while the other experiences winter. Solar radiation, winds, ocean currents, latitude, altitude and land relief also determine types of climate, examples of which are illustrated by the graphs below.

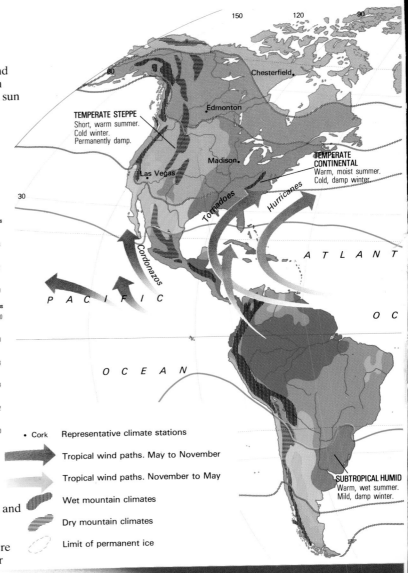

TEMPERATE STEPPE
Short, warm summer.
Cold winter.
Permanently damp.

TEMPERATE CONTINENTAL
Warm, moist summer.
Cold, damp winter.

SUBTROPICAL HUMID
Warm, wet summer.
Mild, damp winter.

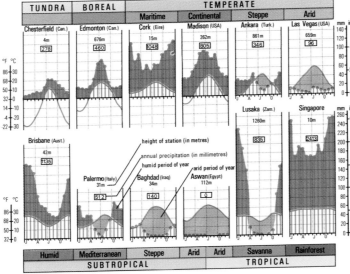

TUNDRA	BOREAL	TEMPERATE				
		Maritime	Continental	Steppe	Arid	
Chesterfield (Can.)	Edmonton (Can.)	Cork (Eire)	Madison (USA)	Ankara (Turk.)	Las Vegas (USA)	
4m / 278	676m / 460	15m / 1048	262m / 905	861m / 346	659m / 98	

Brisbane (Aust.) 42m / 1135

height of station (in metres)
annual precipitation (in millimetres)
humid period of year
arid period of year

Palermo (Italy) 31m / 512
Baghdad (Iraq) 34m / 140
Aswan (Egypt) 112m / 0
Lusaka (Zam.) 1260m / 835
Singapore 10m / 2413

Humid	Mediterranean	Steppe	Arid	Arid	Savanna	Rainforest
SUBTROPICAL				TROPICAL		

- • Cork   Representative climate stations
- → Tropical wind paths. May to November
- → Tropical wind paths. November to May
- Wet mountain climates
- Dry mountain climates
- Limit of permanent ice

THE RESTLESS ATMOSPHERE

As people who travel by aeroplane at altitude soon discover, all weather is confined to the lower part of the atmosphere, where the air is in a continuous state of unrest. This movement can have tremendous force, eroding land and depositing rain and snow. The map shows the intertropical convergence zone which is where trade winds meet, forcing air to rise upwards and causing torrential rainfall. Circulation of air forms three separate 'cells' in each hemisphere where warm air rises and cold air sinks. These are called the Polar, Ferrel and Hadley cells.

JANUARY

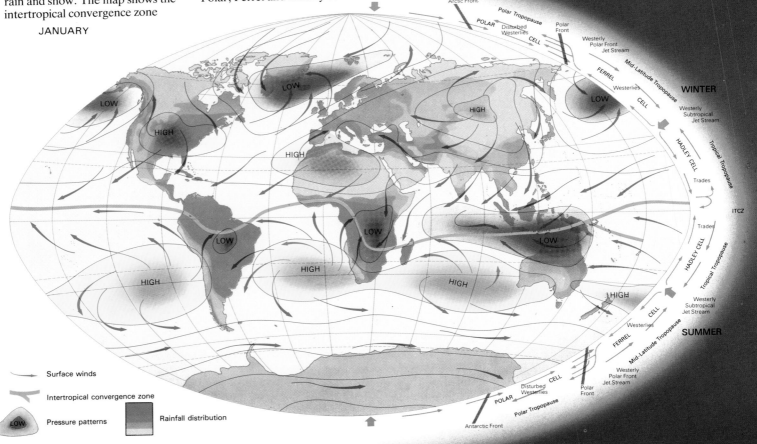

- → Surface winds
- ► Intertropical convergence zone
- LOW Pressure patterns
- Rainfall distribution

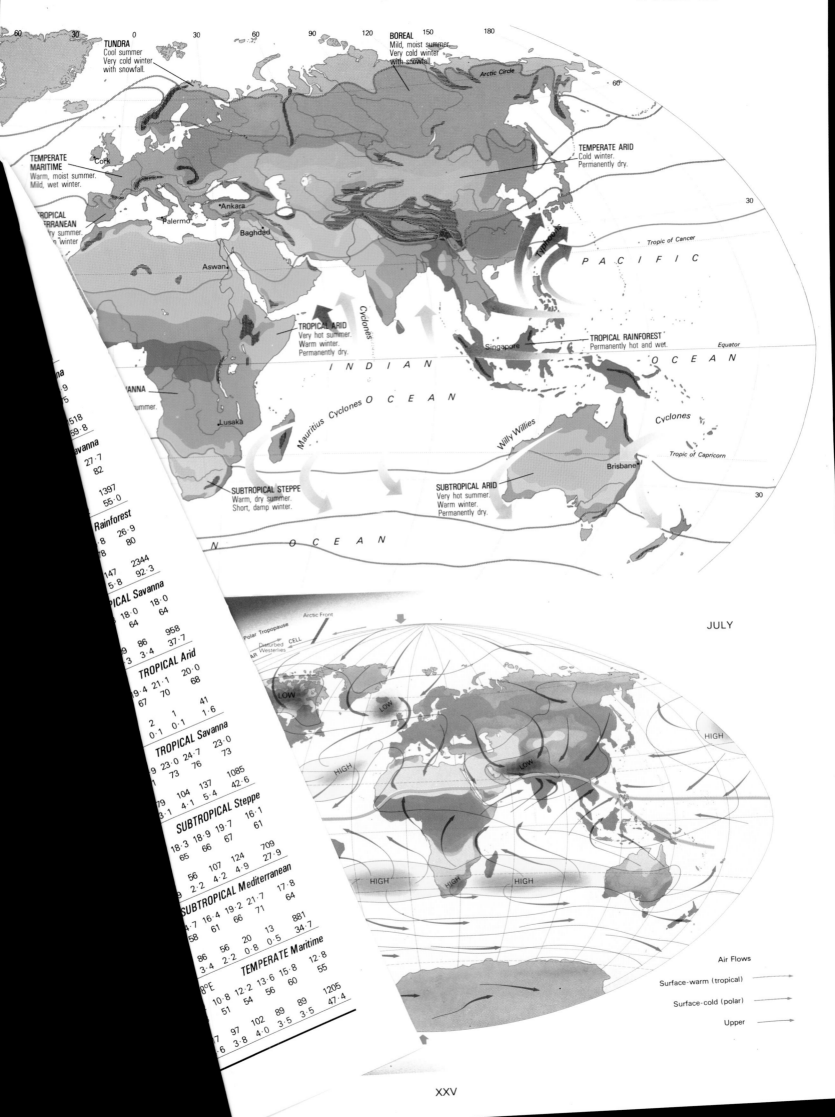

CLIMATE INDICATORS

Listed from north to south, is selection of places from different climate zones of the world (see p xxiv/xxv), indicating their mean monthly temperatures (in °C and °F) and precipitation (in mm and inches). Also shown are their average temperatures and total precipitation for the year.

REYKJAVIK Iceland 64·1°N 21·9°W *TUNDRA*

	J	F	M	A	M	J	J	A	S	O	N	D	Year
°C	-0·2	0·2	1·5	3·5	6·7	9·7	11·3	10·8	8·5	5·2	3·0	0·4	5·0
°F	32	32	35	38	44	49	52	51	47	41	37	33	41
mm	89	64	62	56	42	42	50	56	67	94	78	79	779
ins	3·5	2·5	2·4	2·2	1·6	1·6	2·0	2·2	2·6	3·7	3·1	3·1	30·7

ANCHORAGE U.S.A. 61·2°N 150·0°W *BOREAL*

	J	F	M	A	M	J	J	A	S	O	N	D	Year
°C	-10·4	-7·6	-4·8	2·0	7·7	12·2	14·1	13·1	8·7	1·8	-5·6	-10·2	1·7
°F	13	18	23	36	46	54	57	56	48	35	22	14	29
mm	20	18	13	11	13	25	47	65	63	47	26	24	372
ins	0·8	0·7	0·5	0·4	0·5	1·0	1·8	2·6	2·5	1·8	1·0	0·9	14·6

STOCKHOLM Sweden 59·3°N 18·1°E *TEMPERATE Continental*

	J	F	M	A	M	J	J	A	S	O	N	D	Year
°C	-3·0	-3·1	-0·5	4·6	10·2	15·0	18·5	16·6	12·3	7·1	2·7	0·0	6·6
°F	27	26	31	40	50	59	65	62	54	45	37	32	44
mm	43	30	25	31	34	45	61	76	60	48	53	48	554
ins	1·7	1·2	1·0	1·2	1·3	1·8	2·4	3·0	2·4	1·9	2·1	1·9	21·8

EDINBURGH U.K. 55·9°N 3·2°W *TEMPERATE Maritime*

	J	F	M	A	M	J	J	A	S	O	N	D	Year
°C	3·3	3·5	5·1	7·4	9·9	12·9	14·8	14·4	12·5	9·4	6·4	4·6	8·6
°F	38	38	41	45	50	55	59	58	54	49	43	40	47
mm	57	39	39	39	54	47	83	77	57	65	62	57	676
ins	2·2	1·5	1·5	1·5	2·1	1·8	3·3	3·0	2·2	2·6	2·4	2·2	26·6

MOSKVA Russian Federation 55·7°N 37·6°E *TEMPERATE Continental*

	J	F	M	A	M	J	J	A	S	O	N	D	Year
°C	-12·7	-9·6	-3·8	5·7	13·3	15·8	17·8	16·9	11·8	5·9	-0·9	-7·0	4·4
°F	9	15	25	42	56	60	64	62	54	43	30	19	40
mm	39	38	36	37	53	58	88	71	58	45	47	54	624
ins	1·5	1·5	1·4	1·5	2·1	2·3	3·5	2·8	2·3	1·8	1·8	2·1	24·6

VANCOUVER Canada 49·2°N 123·2°W *TEMPERATE Maritime*

	J	F	M	A	M	J	J	A	S	O	N	D	Year
°C	2·8	4·1	6·4	9·4	12·6	15·5	17·8	17·2	14·4	10·3	6·3	4·2	10·0
°F	37	39	43	49	55	60	64	63	58	50	43	40	50
mm	214	161	151	90	69	65	39	44	83	172	198	243	1529
ins	8·4	6·3	5·9	3·5	2·7	2·6	1·5	1·7	3·3	6·8	7·8	9·6	60·2

PARIS France 48·8°N 2·3°E *TEMPERATE Maritime*

	J	F	M	A	M	J	J	A	S	O	N	D	Year
°C	3·4	4·3	7·9	11·0	14·6	17·8	19·5	19·1	16·5	11·7	7·2	4·3	11·5
°F	38	40	46	52	58	64	67	66	62	53	45	40	53
mm	56	46	35	42	57	54	59	64	55	50	51	50	619
ins	2·2	1·8	1·4	1·6	2·2	2·1	2·3	2·5	2·2	2·0	2·0	2·0	24·3

BUCUREŞTI Romania 44·5°N 26·0°E *TEMPERATE Steppe*

	J	F	M	A	M	J	J	A	S	O	N	D	Year
°C	-4·2	-1·5	6·2	12·4	17·3	21·2	23·5	22·9	18·2	13·0	6·4	0·6	8·2
°F	24	29	43	54	63	70	74	73	65	55	43	33	47
mm	46	26	28	59	77	121	53	45	45	29	36	27	592
ins	1·8	1·0	1·1	2·3	3·0	4·8	2·1	1·8	1·8	1·1	1·4	1·1	23·4

NEW YORK U.S.A. 40·7°N 74·0°W *TEMPERATE Continental*

	J	F	M	A	M	J	J	A	S	O	N	D	Year
°C	0·7	0·8	4·7	10·5	16·3	21·2	24·1	23·3	19·8	14·3	8·1	2·2	12·2
°F	33	33	40	51	61	70	75	74	68	58	47	36	54
mm	89	74	104	89	91	86	102	119	89	84	89	84	1100
ins	3·5	2·9	4·1	3·5	3·6	3·4	4·0	4·7	3·5	3·3	3·5	3·3	43·3

TŌKYŌ Japan 35·7°N 139·8°E *TEMPERATE Continental*

	J	F	M	A	M	J	J	A	S	O	N	D	Year
°C	3·3	4·2	7·2	12·5	16·9	20·8	24·7	26·1	22·5	16·7	10·8	5·8	14·4
°F	38	40	45	54	62	69	76	79	72	62	51	42	58
mm	48	74	107	135	147	165	142	152	234	208	96	56	1565
ins	1·9	2·9	4·2	5·3	5·8	6·5	5·6	6·0	9·2	8·2	3·8	2·2	61·6

TANGER Morocco 35·8°N 5·8°W *SUBTROPICAL Mediterranean*

	J	F	M	A	M	J	J	A	S	O	N	D	Year
°C	11·9	12·5	13·6	14·4	17·2	20·0	22·2	23·0	21·4	18·6	14·7	12·4	16·7
°F	53	54	56	58	63	68	72	73	70	65	58	54	62
mm	114	107	122	89	43	15	2	2	23	99	147	137	897
ins	4·5	4·2	4·8	3·5	1·7	0·6	0·1	0·1	0·9	3·9	5·8	5·4	35·3

JERUSALEM Israel 31·8°N 35·2°E *SUBTROPICAL Steppe*

	J	F	M	A	M	J	J	A	S	O	N	D	Year
°C	8·9	9·4	13·0	16·4	20·5	22·5	23·9	24·1	23·0	21·1	16·4	11·1	17·2
°F	48	49	55	61	69	72	75	75	73	70	61	52	63
mm	132	132	63	28	2	1	0	0	1	13	71	87	528
ins	5·2	5·2	2·5	1·1	0·1	0·1	0·0	0·0	0·1	0·5	2·8	3·4	20·8

NEW ORLEANS U.S.A. 30·0°N 90·2°W *SUBTROPICAL Humid*

	J	F	M	A	M	J	J	A	S	O	N	D	Year
°C	12·5	13·9	16·3	19·9	23·5	26·7	27·6	27·7	25·7	21·3	15·6	13·0	20·3
°F	54	57	61	68	74	80	82	82	78	70	60	55	68
mm	97	102	135	114	112	112	170	135	127	71	84	104	1363
ins	3·8	4·0	5·3	4·5	4·4	4·4	6·7	5·3	5·0	2·8	3·3	4·1	53·7

BAHRAIN 26·2°N 50·5°E *SUBTROPICAL Arid*

	J	F	M	A	M	J	J	A	S	O	N	D	Year
°C	16·9	18·0	20·5	25·0	29·4	31·7	33·3	33·6	31·4	28·0	24·2	18·6	25·8
°F	62	64	69	77	85	89	92	92	88	82	75	65	78
mm	8	18	13	8	1	0	0	0	0	0	18	18	79
ins	0·3	0·7	0·5	0·3	0·1	0·0	0·0	0·0	0·0	0·0	0·7	0·7	3·2

HONG KONG 22·3°N 114·2°E *SUBTROPICAL Humid*

	J	F	M	A	M	J	J	A	S	O	N	D	Year
°C	15·5	15·0	17·5	21·7	25·5	27·5	28·0	28·0	27·2	25·0	20·8	17·5	22·5
°F	60	59	63	71	78	81	82	82	81	77	69	63	72
mm	33	46	74	137	292	394	381	361	256	114	43	30	2161
ins	1·3	1·8	2·9	5·4	11·5	15·5	15·0	14·2	10·1	4·5	1·7	1·2	85·

MIAMI U.S.A. 25·8°N 80·3°W *TROPICAL Savan...*

	J	F	M	A	M	J	J	A	S	O	N	D	Year
°C	19·3	19·9	21·4	23·4	25·3	27·1	27·6	27·9	27·4	25·4	22·4	20·1	23
°F	67	68	70	74	77	81	82	82	81	78	72	68	
mm	51	48	58	99	163	188	170	178	241	208	71	43	
ins	2·0	1·9	2·3	3·9	6·4	7·4	6·7	7·0	9·5	8·2	2·8	1·7	

BANGKOK Thailand 13·7°N 100·5°E *TROPICAL S...*

	J	F	M	A	M	J	J	A	S	O	N	D	Year
°C	25·8	27·5	28·9	30·0	29·4	28·6	28·3	28·3	28·0	27·5	26·4	25·3	
°F	78	81	84	86	85	83	83	83	82	81	79	77	
mm	8	20	36	58	198	160	160	175	305	206	66	5	
ins	0·3	0·8	1·4	2·3	7·8	6·3	6·3	6·9	12·0	8·1	2·6	0·2	

COLOMBO Sri Lanka 6·9°N 79·9°E *TROPICAL*

	J	F	M	A	M	J	J	A	S	O	N	D	Year
°C	26·1	26·4	27·2	27·7	28·0	27·2	27·2	27·2	27·2	26·6	26·1	25	
°F	79	80	81	82	82	81	81	81	81	80	79		
mm	89	69	147	231	371	223	135	109	160	348	315		
ins	3·5	2·7	5·8	9·1	14·6	8·8	5·3	4·3	6·3	13·7	12·4		

NAIROBI Kenya 1·3°S 36·8°E *TRO...*

	J	F	M	A	M	J	J	A	S	O	N	D	Year
°C	18·6	19·4	19·4	19·2	17·7	16·4	15·5	16·1	17·5	18·6	18·		
°F	65	67	67	67	64	61	60	61	63	65	65		
mm	38	63	124	211	157	46	15	23	30	53	10		
ins	1·5	2·5	4·9	8·3	6·2	1·8	0·6	0·9	1·2	2·1	4		

LIMA Peru 12·1°S 77·0°W

	J	F	M	A	M	J	J	A	S	O	N	D	Year
°C	23·3	23·8	23·6	21·9	19·4	17·2	16·7	16·1	16·9	18·0			
°F	74	75	74	71	67	63	62	61	64				
mm	1	1	1	1	5	5	8	8	8	2			
ins	0·1	0·1	0·1	0·1	0·2	0·2	0·3	0·3	0·3	0·3			

RIO DE JANEIRO Brazil 22·9°S 43·2°W

	J	F	M	A	M	J	J	A	S	O	N	D	Year
°C	25·8	26·1	25·3	23·6	21·9	21·1	20·5	21·1	21·1	21			
°F	78	79	77	74	71	70	69	70	70				
mm	124	122	130	107	79	53	41	43	66				
ins	4·9	4·8	5·1	4·2	3·1	2·1	1·6	1·7	2·6				

JOHANNESBURG S. Africa 26·2°S 28·1°E

	J	F	M	A	M	J	J	A	S	O	N	D	Year
°C	20·0	19·7	18·3	16·1	12·5	10·3	10·5	13·0	15·8				
°F	68	67	65	61	54	50	51	55	60				
mm	114	109	89	38	25	8	8	8					
ins	4·5	4·3	3·5	1·5	1·0	0·3	0·3	0·3	0				

PERTH Australia 31·9°S 115·8°E

	J	F	M	A	M	J	J	A	S	O	N	D	Year
°C	23·3	23·3	21·7	19·2	16·1	13·9	13·0	13·3	1				
°F	74	74	71	66	61	57	55	56					
mm	8	10	20	43	130	180	170	145					
ins	0·3	0·4	0·8	1·7	5·1	7·1	6·7	5·7					

WELLINGTON New Zealand 41·3°S 174...

	J	F	M	A	M	J	J	A	S	O	N	D	Year
°C	16·9	16·9	15·8	13·9	11·4	9·7	8·6	9					
°F	62	62	60	57	52	49	47	4					
mm	81	81	81	97	117	117	137	1					
ins	3·2	3·2	3·2	3·8	4·6	4·6	5·4						

Civilisation depends on trade for growth and travel makes this possible.
Shipping is the most important method of world transport but economic
progress and moblity are constantly being improved by the
development of new routes and new modes of transport.

ROAD AND RAIL

Integrated road and rail networks are the basis of
industrial society. Extended highway systems and
improved containerisation techniques have made the
whole road and rail system much more flexible.

Roads – comparative lengths (Log scale)

68/277	(24) USA 6366
49/23	(1) India 1604
16/115	(7) Brazil 1399
296/95	(34) Japan 1118
9/9	(1) China 890
9/324	(14) Canada 884
11/552	(9) Australia 817
146/149	(27) France 803
28/24	(11) Russian Federation 620
172/78	(54) Germany 613
154/63	(49) UK 353
96/83	(10) Poland 299
98/51	(64) Italy 294
7/74	(20) Argentina 208 — (000's km)

Network Densities

◯ Vehicles/km of road

— Motorways (bar length = 1% of network)

| High | Medium | Low |

km/100km^2
100km/million popl.
km/100km^2

3/8	UK 18 ——— (000's km)
4/7	Italy 20
7/8	Poland 24
2/7	Japan 26
3/0·4	Brazil 31
6/6	France 34
12/2	Argentina 35
27/0·5	Australia 40
5/13	Germany 41
1/0·5	China 50
1/2	India 61
6/0·5	Russian Federation 86
33/0·9	Canada 91
14/3	USA 320

Railways – comparative lengths (Log scale)

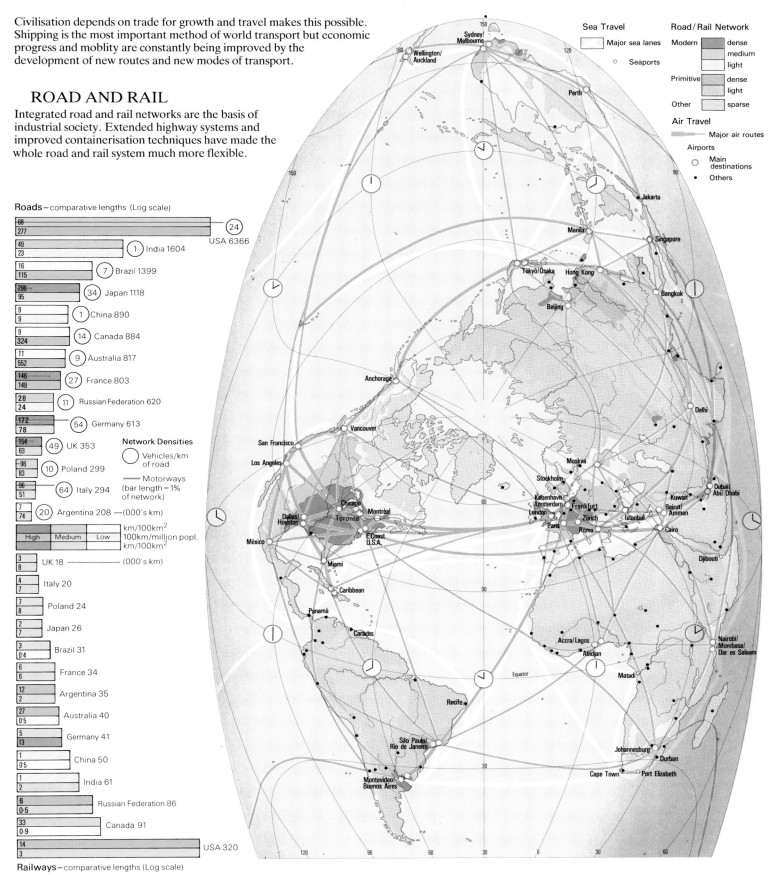

Sea Travel

▢ Major sea lanes
◦ Seaports

Road/Rail Network

Modern — dense / medium / light
Primitive — dense / light
Other — sparse

Air Travel

〰 Major air routes

Airports
◯ Main destinations
• Others

AIR AND SEA ROUTES

JOURNEY TIME

The Suez canal cuts 3600 miles off the
London-Singapore route, while Concorde
halves the London-New York journey time.

A complex network of primary air routes
centred on the Northern Hemisphere
provides rapid transit across the world for
mass travel, mail and urgent freight. Ships

also follow these principal routes, plying
the oceans between major ports and
transporting the commodities of world
trade in bulk.

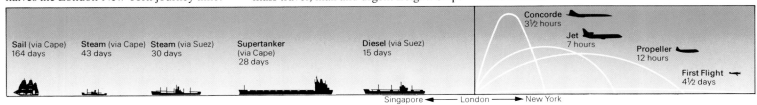

Sail (via Cape) 164 days
Steam (via Cape) 43 days
Steam (via Suez) 30 days
Supertanker (via Cape) 28 days
Diesel (via Suez) 15 days

Concorde 3½ hours
Jet 7 hours
Propeller 12 hours
First Flight 4½ days

Singapore ◄— London —► New York

1:60M

600　　　1200　　　1800　　　2400 km

600　　　　1200 mls

A　　B　　C　　D　　E　　F　　G　　H　　J
40　　　20　　　0　　　20　　　40　　　60　　　80　　　100　　　120　　　140　　　160

Ar

① *Barents Sea*

Arctic Circle

*Norwegian
Basin*

ICELAND

60

*North
Sea*

*Sea
of
Okhotsk*

Sakhalin

② EUROPE

A S I A

*Vityaz Depth
10542*

Black Sea

Caspian Sea

Aral Sea

40

*Sea
of
Japan*

③ *Mediterranean
Sea*

The Gulf

Chang Jiang

Huang He

TAIWAN

Ganga

*Red
Sea*

20

Arabian Sea

*Bay
of
Bengal*

Hainan

South China Sea

*Northern
Mariana
Islands*

Guam

④ AFRICA

*Arabian
Basin*

Raas Caseyr

MALDIVES

Carlsberg Ridge

Maldives Ridge

SRI
LANKA
(CEYLON)

Andaman Is

Nicobar
Is

Mekong

PHILIPPINES

*C. Johnson
Depth
10497*

*11022
Challenger
Depth*

Philippine Trench

Kyushu-Palau Ridge

S. Honshu Ridge

Japan Trench

Kuril Trench

Mariana Trench

M I C R O N

Palau
(Belau)

Caroline Is

*Celebes
Sea*

0

*Somali
Basin*

SEYCHELLES

Mascarene Ridge

Chagos Arch.

Borneo

Celebes

INDONESIA

New
Guinea

6920

*Planet Deep
9140*

M E L A

COMOROS

*Mid
Indian
Basin*

Sumatra

Java

Mid-Indian Ridge

Ninety-East Ridge

I N D I A N

⑤ *Mozambique Channel*

MADAGASCAR

Réunion

MAURITIUS

1737

Java Trench
7450

Christmas I.

Cocos Is

*West
Australian
Basin*

Timor

Arafura Sea

*Coral Sea
Basin*

1924

Natal Basin

S. Madagascar Ridge

*Madagascar
Basin*

O C E A N

2067

W. Australian Ridge

Tropic of Capricorn

AUSTRALIA

Tas ma

⑥ C.Agulhas

*Agulhas
Plateau*

1198

South West Indian Ridge

*Crozet
Basin*

I.Amsterdam
I.St Paul

7102

*South
Australia
Basin*

Tasmania
Sea

40

*Agulhas
Basin*

Is Crozet

Indian-Antarctic Ridge

⑦ *Atlantic-Indian Ridge*

Pr.Edward Is

Îs Kerguelen

1922

Macquarie Is

Kerguelen Ridge

Heard I.

60

Atlantic-Indian Antarctic Basin

*Banzare Seamount
186*

Indian-Antarctic Basin

⑧

A N T A R C T I C A

40　　　20　　　A　　B　　20　　C　　40　　D　　60　　E　　80　　F　　100　　G　　120　　H　　140　　J　　160

XXVIII

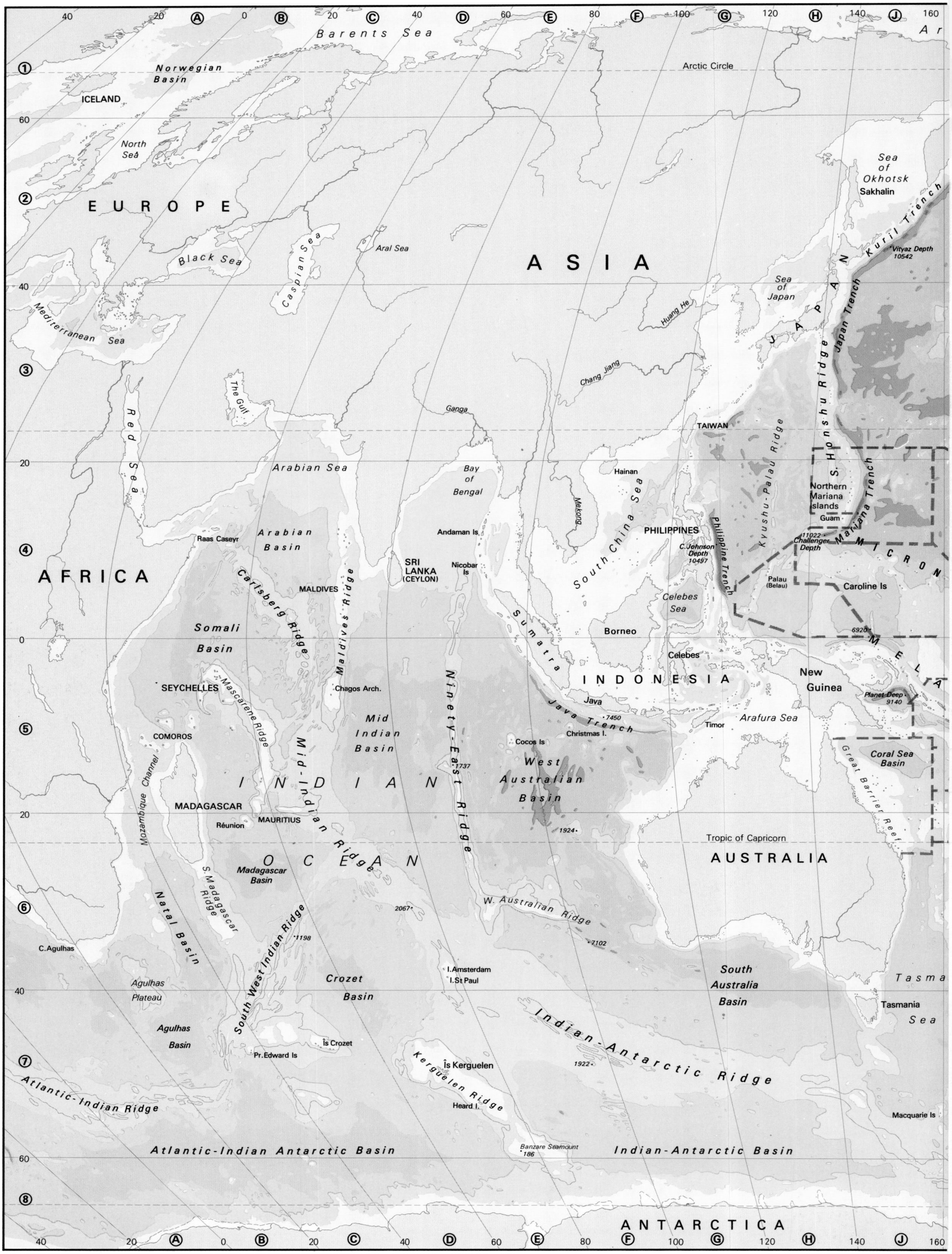

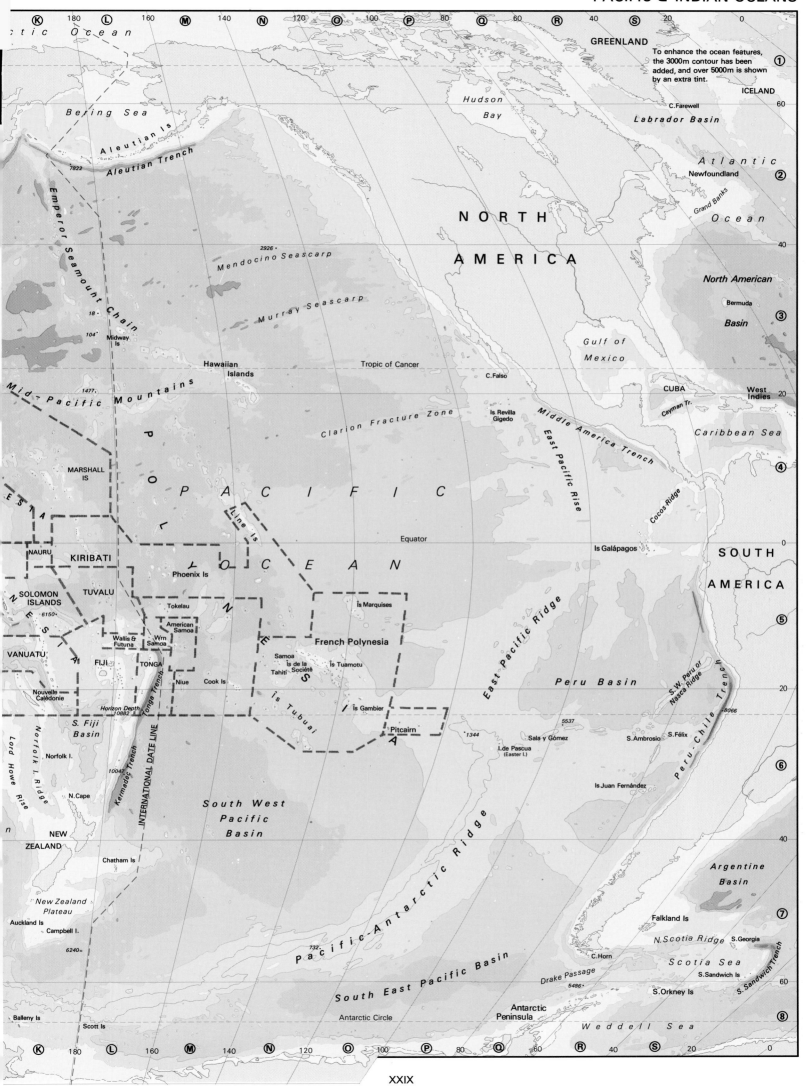

K 180 L 160 M 140 N 120 O 100 P 80 Q 60 R 40 S 20 0

ctic Ocean

GREENLAND

To enhance the ocean features,
the 3000m contour has been
added, and over 5000m is shown
by an extra tint.

ICELAND ①

Bering Sea

C.Farewell

60

Labrador Basin ②

Aleutian Is

Atlantic

Aleutian Trench

7822

Newfoundland ②

Emperor Seamount Chain

N O R T H

Ocean

A M E R I C A

Grand Banks

18•

2926•

40

Mendocino Seascarp

North American

104•

Bermuda ③

Midway
Is

Murray Seascarp

Gulf of

Basin

1477•

Mexico

Tropic of Cancer

20

Hawaiian
Islands

C.Falso

CUBA

West
Indies

Mid-Pacific Mountains

Cayman Tr.

P

Clarion Fracture Zone

Is Revilla
Gigedo

Caribbean Sea

MARSHALL
IS

O

East Pacific Rise

Middle America Trench

④

P A C I F I C

L

Cocos Ridge

Equator

Is Galápagos

S O U T H

0

A

NAURU

KIRIBATI

Y

O C E A N

A M E R I C A

Phoenix Is

TUVALU

N

Line Is

6150•

TOKELAU

Î s Marquises

SOLOMON
ISLANDS

E

American
Samoa

French Polynesia

⑤

S

Wallis &
Futuna

Wrn
Samoa

Samoa

Î s de la
Société

East Pacific Ridge

Peru Basin

VANUATU

I

FIJI

Tahiti

Î s Tuamotu

S.W. Peru or
Nasca Ridge

A

TONGA

Nouvelle
Calédonie

Niue

Cook Is

Î s Gambier

5537

20

S.Ambrosio

S.Félix

*S. Fiji
Basin*

Horizon Depth
10882

Î s Tubuai

A

Pitcairn

•1344

Sala y Gómez

8066

Norfolk I.

10047

I.de Pascua
(Easter I.)

⑥

NEW

Is Juan Fernández

Norfolk I. Ridge

Kermadec Trench

INTERNATIONAL DATE LINE

N.Cape

Lord Howe Rise

Tonga Trench

ZEALAND

*South West
Pacific
Basin*

40

Chatham Is

*Argentine
Basin*

*New Zealand
Plateau*

Falkland Is ⑦

Auckland Is

Pacific-Antarctic Ridge

N.Scotia Ridge

S.Georgia

Campbell I.

732

C.Horn

Scotia Sea

6240•

S.Sandwich Is

Balleny Is

South East Pacific Basin

Drake Passage

S.Orkney Is

S. Sandwich Trench

60

Scott Is

Antarctic Circle

Antarctic
Peninsula

5486•

Weddell Sea ⑧

K 180 L 160 M 140 N 120 O 100 P 80 Q 60 R 40 S 20 0

0 600 1200 1800 2400 km
0 600 1200 mls

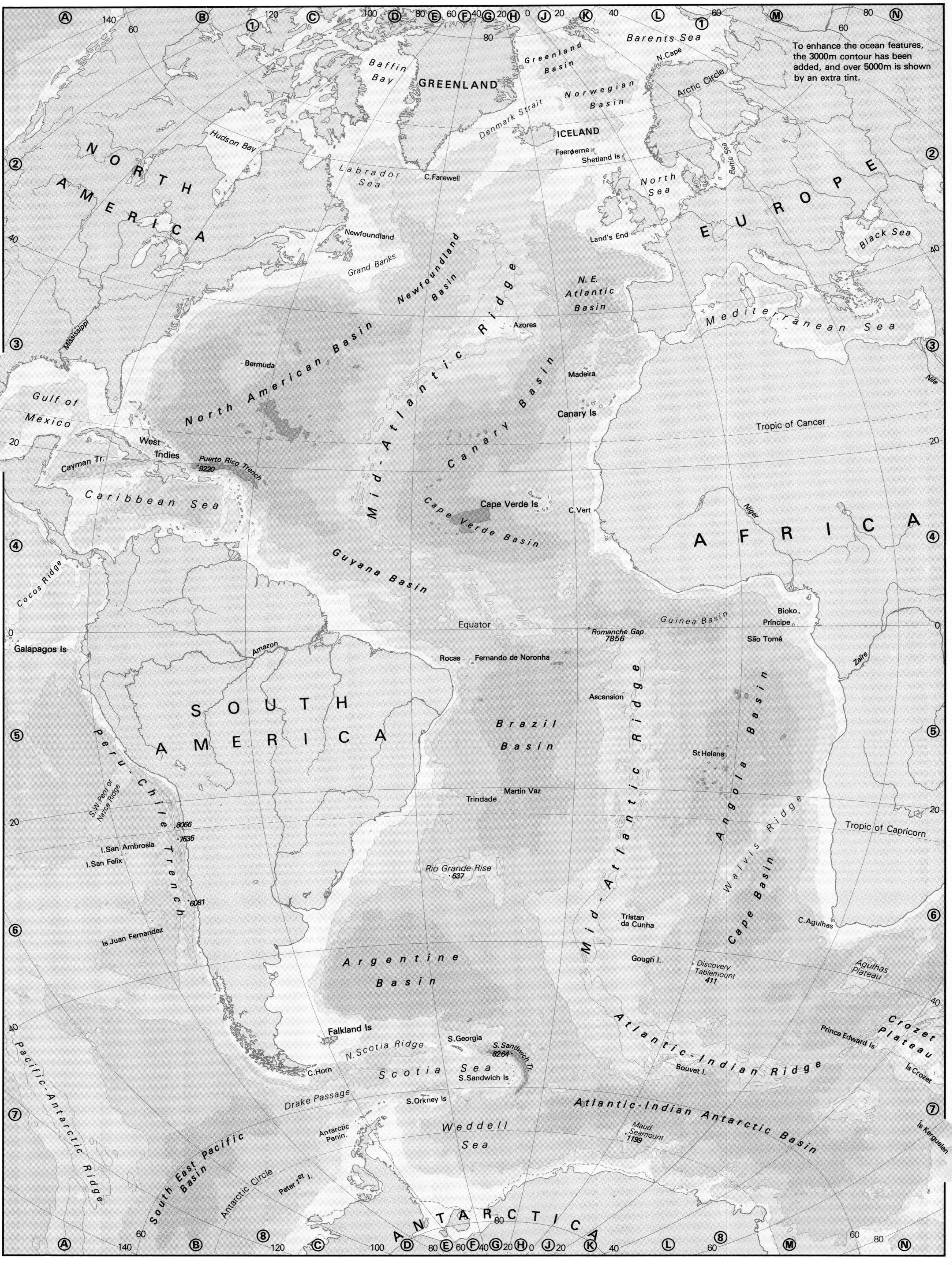

To enhance the ocean features, the 3000m contour has been added, and over 5000m is shown by an extra tint.

NORTH AMERICA

SOUTH AMERICA

EUROPE

AFRICA

ANTARCTICA

GREENLAND

ICELAND

Baffin Bay

Hudson Bay

Labrador Sea

Newfoundland

Grand Banks

Newfoundland Basin

North American Basin

Bermuda

Gulf of Mexico

Mississippi

West Indies

Cayman Tr.

Puerto Rico Trench '9220

Caribbean Sea

Cocos Ridge

Galapagos Is

Amazon

Mid-Atlantic Ridge

Azores

Madeira

Canary Is

Canary Basin

Cape Verde Is

C.Vert

Cape Verde Basin

Guyana Basin

Guinea Basin

Equator

Rocas Fernando de Noronha

Romanche Gap 7856

Bioko
Príncipe
São Tomé

Zaire

Niger

Brazil Basin

Ascension

St Helena

Angola Basin

Mid-Atlantic Ridge

Walvis Ridge

Cape Basin

Trindade Martin Vaz

Rio Grande Rise ·637

Peru-Chile Trench
S.W. Peru or Nazca Ridge
·8066
·7635
I.San Ambrosia
I.San Felix
·6081
Is Juan Fernandez

Tristan da Cunha

Gough I.

Discovery Tablemount 411

C.Agulhas

Agulhas Plateau

Argentine Basin

Falkland Is

N.Scotia Ridge

S.Georgia

S.Sandwich Tr. 8264

S.Sandwich Is

Scotia Sea

C.Horn

Drake Passage

S.Orkney Is

Atlantic-Indian Ridge

Bouvet I.

Atlantic-Indian Antarctic Basin

Prince Edward Is

Crozet Plateau

Is Crozet

Is Kerguelen

Pacific-Antarctic Ridge

South East Pacific Basin

Antarctic Circle

Peter I st I.

Antarctic Penin.

Weddell Sea

Maud Seamount 1199

N.Cape

Barents Sea

Greenland Basin

Norwegian Basin

Denmark Strait

Faerøerne
Shetland Is

North Sea

Land's End

N.E. Atlantic Basin

Mediterranean Sea

Black Sea

Baltic Sea

Nile

Tropic of Cancer

Tropic of Capricorn

Arctic Circle

C.Farewell

Equator

MOUNTAIN HEIGHTS

Metres	Feet		Metres	Feet	
8848	29 028	Everest (Qomolangma Feng) *Nepal-Tibet*	6870	22 541	Bonete *Bolivia*
8611	28 250	K2 (Godwin Austen) *Kashmir-Sinkiang*	6800	22 310	Tupungato *Argentina-Chile*
8598	28 209	Kangchenjunga *Nepal-India*	6770	22 211	Mercedario *Argentina*
8475	27 805	Makalu *Tibet-Nepal*	6768	22 205	Huascarán *Peru*
8172	26 810	Dhaulagiri *Nepal*	6723	22 057	Llullaillaco *Argentina-Chile*
8126	26 660	Nanga Parbat *Kashmir*	6714	22 028	Kangrinboqê Feng (Kailas) *Tibet*
8078	26 504	Annapurna *Nepal*	6634	21 765	Yerupaja *Peru*
8068	26 470	Gasherbrum *Kashmir*	6542	21 463	Sajama *Bolivia*
8013	26 291	Xixabangma Feng (Gosainthan) *Tibet*	6485	21 276	Illampu *Bolivia*
7890	25 885	Distaghil Sar *Kashmir*	6425	21 079	Coropuna *Peru*
7820	25 656	Masherbrum *Kashmir*	6402	21 004	Illimani *Bolivia*
7817	25 645	Nanda Devi *India*	6388	20 958	Ancohuma *Bolivia*
7780	25 550	Rakaposhi *Kashmir*	6310	20 702	Chimborazo *Ecuador*
7756	25 447	Kamet *India-Tibet*	6194	20 320	McKinley *USA*
7756	25 447	Namcha Barwa *Tibet*	5959	19 550	Logan *Canada*
7728	25 355	Gurla Mandhata *Tibet*	5895	19 340	Kilimanjaro *Tanzania*
7723	25 338	Muztag (Ulugh Muztagh) *Sinkiang*	5700	18 700	Citlaltepetl *Mexico*
7719	25 325	Kongur Shan (Kungur) *Sinkiang*	5642	18 510	El'bruz *Russian Federation*
7690	25 230	Tirich Mir *Pakistan*	5452	17 887	Popocatepetl *Mexico*
7590	24 903	Gongga Shan (Minya Konka) *China*	5199	17 057	Kirinyaga (Kenya) *Kenya*
7546	24 757	Muztagata (Muztagh Ata) *Sinkiang*	5165	16 946	Ararat *Turkey*
7495	24 590	Pik Kommunizma *Tajikistan*	5110	16 763	Stanley *Zaire-Uganda*
7439	24 407	Pik Pobedy (Tomur Feng) *Kyrgyzstan-Sinkiang*	5030	16 500	Jaya (Carstensz) *Indonesia*
7313	23 993	Chomo Lhari *Bhutan-Tibet*	4897	16 066	Vinson Massif *Antarctica*
7134	23 406	Pik Lenina *Kyrgyzstan-Tajikistan*	4808	15 774	Mont Blanc *France*
6960	22 834	Aconcagua *Argentina*	4508	14 790	Wilhelm *Papua New Guinea*
6908	22 664	Ojos del Salado *Chile-Argentina*	4201	13 784	Mauna Kea *USA*

RIVER LENGTHS

Km	Miles		Km	Miles	
6695	4160	Nile *Africa*	2850	1770	Danube *Europe*
6570	4080	Amazon *South America*	2820	1750	Salween *Asia*
6380	3964	Yangtze *Asia*	2780	1730	São Francisco *South America*
6020	3740	Mississippi-Missouri *North America*	2655	1650	Zambezi *Africa*
5410	3360	Ob-Irtysh *Asia*	2570	1600	Nelson-Saskatchewan *North America*
4840	3010	Huang He (Yellow River) *Asia*	2510	1560	Ganges *Asia*
4630	2880	Zaïre (Congo) *Africa*	2430	1510	Euphrates *Asia*
4500	2796	Paraná *South America*	2330	1450	Arkansas *North America*
4440	2760	Irtysh *Asia*	2330	1450	Colorado *North America*
4416	2745	Amur *Asia*	2285	1420	Dnieper *Europe*
4400	2730	Lena *Asia*	2090	1300	Irrawaddy *Asia*
4240	2630	Mackenzie *North America*	2060	1280	Orinoco *South America*
4180	2600	Mekong *Asia*	2000	1240	Negro *South America*
4100	2550	Niger *Africa*	1870	1160	Don *Europe*
4090	2540	Yenisey *Asia*	1859	1155	Orange *Africa*
3969	2466	Missouri *North America*	1799	1118	Pechora *Europe*
3779	2348	Mississippi *North America*	1609	1000	Marañón *South America*
3750	2330	Murray-Darling *Australia*	1410	876	Dniester *Europe*
3688	2292	Volga *Europe*	1320	820	Rhine *Europe*
3240	2013	Madeira *South America*	1183	735	Donets *Europe*
3058	1900	St. Lawrence *North America*	1159	720	Elbe *Europe*
3030	1880	Rio Grande *North America*	1094	680	Gambia *Africa*
3020	1870	Yukon *North America*	1080	671	Yellowstone *North America*
2960	1840	Brahmaputra *Asia*	1014	630	Vistula *Europe*
2896	1800	Indus *Asia*	1006	625	Tagus *Europe*

LAKE AND INLAND SEA AREAS

Areas are average and some are subject to seasonal variations.

Sq. Km	Sq. Miles		Sq. Km	Sq. Miles	
371 000	142 240	Caspian *Central Asia (salt)*	22 490	8680	Nyasa (Malawi) *Malawi-Mozambique*
82 900	32 010	Superior *USA-Canada*	19 400	7490	Ontario *USA-Canada*
68 800	26 560	Victoria *Kenya-Uganda-Tanzania*	18 390	7100	Ladoga *Russian Federation*
59 580	23 000	Huron *USA-Canada*	17 400	6700	Balkhash *Kazakhstan*
58 020	22 480	Michigan *USA*	10-26 000	4-10 000	Chad *Nigeria-Niger-Chad-Cameroon*
36 500	14 100	Aral *Central Asia (salt)*	9600	3710	Onega *Russian Federation*
32 900	12 700	Tanganyika *Tanzania-Zambia-Zaire-Burundi*	0-8900	0-3430	Eyre *Australia*
31 330	12 100	Great Bear *Canada*	8340	3220	Titicaca *Peru-Bolivia*
30 500	11 800	Baykal *Russian Federation*	8270	3190	Nicaragua *Nicaragua*
28 570	11 030	Great Slave *Canada*	6410	2470	Turkana (Rudolf) *Kenya-Ethiopia*
25 680	9910	Erie *USA-Canada*	5780	2230	Torrens *Australia (salt)*
24 390	9420	Winnipeg *Canada*	5580	2160	Vänern *Sweden*

GREATEST OCEAN DEPTHS

Metres	Feet	Location	Metres	Feet	Location
		PACIFIC OCEAN			**ATLANTIC OCEAN**
11 022	36 160	Marianas Trench	9220	30 249	Puerto Rico Trench
10 882	35 702	Tonga Trench	8264	27 113	South Sandwich Trench
10 542	34 586	Kuril Trench	7856	25 774	Romanche Gap
10 497	34 439	Philippine Trench	7500	24 600	Cayman Trench
10 047	32 962	Kermadec Trench			
9810	32 185	Izu-Bonin Trench			**INDIAN OCEAN**
9165	30 069	New Hebrides Trench	7450	24 442	Java Trench
9140	29 987	South Solomon Trench	7440	24 409	Weber Basin
8412	27 598	Japan Trench	7102	23 300	Diamantina Trench
8066	26 463	Peru-Chile Trench			
7822	25 662	Aleutian Trench			**ARCTIC OCEAN**
6662	21 857	Middle America	5570	18 274	Nansen Fracture Zone

STATES AND DEPENDENCIES

COUNTRY	Area (sq. km)	Population ('000)	Capital
North and Central America			
Anguilla (UK)	91	7	The Valley
Antigua and Barbuda	442	76	St. John's
The Bahamas	13 864	253	Nassau
Barbados	430	255	Bridgetown
Belize	22 965	187	Belmopan
Bermuda (UK)	53	58	Hamilton
Canada	9 976 147	27 296	Ottawa
Cayman Is. (UK)	259	25	George Town
Costa Rica	50 899	3 015	San José
Cuba	114 524	10 608	La Habana (Havana)
Dominica	751	82	Roseau
Dominican Republic	48 441	7 170	Santo Domingo
El Salvador	20 865	5 252	San Salvador
Grenada	344	85	St. George's
Guadeloupe (Fr.)	1 779	343	Basse Terre
Guatemala	108 888	9 197	Guatemala
Haiti	27 749	6 513	Port-au-Prince
Honduras	112 087	5 138	Tegucigalpa
Jamaica	11 425	2 456	Kingston
Martinique (Fr.)	1 101	341	Fort-de-France
Mexico	1 967 180	107 233	Mexico
Montserrat (UK)	102	12	Plymouth
Netherlands Antilles (Neth.)	993	188	Willemstad
Nicaragua	139 000	3 871	Managua
Panama	75 648	2 418	Panamá
Puerto Rico (USA)	8 897	3 480	San Juan
St. Kitts-Nevis	260	44	Basseterre
St. Lucia	616	150	Castries
St. Vincent	389	116	Kingstown
Trinidad and Tobago	5 128	1 281	Port of Spain
United States of America	9 363 130	248 700	Washington
South America			
Argentina	2 777 815	32 322	Buenos Aires
Bolivia	1 098 575	7 314	La Paz
Brazil	8 511 968	150 368	Brasília
Chile	756 943	13 173	Santiago
Colombia	1 138 907	32 978	Bogotá
Ecuador	455 502	10 587	Quito
French Guiana (Fr.)	91 000	98	Cayenne
Guyana	214 969	796	George Town
Paraguay	406 750	4 277	Asunción
Peru	1 285 215	21 550	Lima
Surinam	163 820	422	Paramribo
Uruguay	186 925	3 094	Montevideo
Venezuela	912 047	19 735	Caracas
Europe			
Albania	28 752	3 245	Tiranë (Tirana)
Andorra	453	47	Andorra-la-Vella
Austria	83 848	7 583	Wien (Vienna)
Belarus (Belorussia)	207 600	10 278	Minsk
Belgium	30 512	9 845	Bruxelles (Brussels)
Bosnia-Herzegovina	51 130	4 400	Sarajevo
Bulgaria	110 911	9 010	Sofiya (Sofia)
Croatia	56 540	4 700	Zagreb
Cyprus	9 251	701	Nicosia
Czech Republic	78 864	10 300	Praha (Prague)
Denmark	43 030	5 143	København (Copenhagen)
Estonia	45 100	1 573	Tallinn
Faroes (Den.)	1 399	47	Tórshavn
Finland	337 032	4 975	Helsinki
France	551 000	56 138	Paris
Germany	356 854	79 070	Berlin
Gibraltar (UK)	6	30	Gibraltar
Great Britain and N. Ireland, see United Kingdom			
Greece	131 955	10 047	Athinai (Athens)
Greenland (Den.)	2 175 600	56	Godthâb
Hungary	93 030	10 552	Budapest
Iceland	102 828	260	Reykjavik
Ireland	70 282	3 720	Dublin
Italy	301 245	57 061	Roma (Rome)
Latvia	63 700	2 681	Riga
Liechtenstein	161	28	Vaduz
Lithuania	65 200	3 690	Vilnius
Luxembourg	2 587	373	Luxembourg
Macedonia	25 713	2 090	Skopje
Malta	316	353	Valletta
Moldova	33 700	4 341	Kishinev
Monaco	1.8	28	Monaco
Netherlands	33 940	14 951	Amsterdam/'s-Gravenhage
Norway	324 218	4 212	Oslo
Poland	312 683	38 423	Warszawa (Warsaw)
Portugal	91 671	10 285	Lisboa (Lisbon)
Romania	237 500	23 272	Bucuresti (Bucharest)
Russian Federation	17 075 000	148 263	Moskva (Moscow)
San Marino	61	23	San Marino
Slovakia	49 035	5 300	Bratislava
Slovenia	7 815	1 900	Ljubljana
Spain	504 745	39 187	Madrid
Sweden	449 791	8 444	Stockholm
Switzerland	41 287	6 609	Bern
Ukraine	603 700	51 857	Kiyev
United Kingdom	244 104	57 237	London
Vatican City	.4	1	Vatican City
Yugoslavia	255 803	23 807	Beograd (Belgrade)
Asia			
Afghanistan	674 500	16 557	Kabul
Armenia	29 800	3 283	Yerevan
Azerbaijan	86 600	7 029	Baku
Bahrain	660	516	Al Manämah
Bangladesh	144 020	115 593	Dhaka (Dacca)
Bhutan	46 620	1 516	Thimphu
Brunei	5 765	266	Bandar Seri Begawan
Cambodia	181 035	8 246	Phnom Penh
China	9 561 000	1 118 760	Beijing (Peking)
Georgia	69 700	5 449	Tbilisi
Hong Kong (UK)	1 062	5 851	
India	3 287 593	853 094	New Delhi
Indonesia	1 919 263	185 020	Jakarta
Iran	1 648 184	54 607	Tehrän
Iraq	434 924	18 920	Baghdâd
Israel	20 770	4 600	Jerusalem
Japan	371 000	123 460	Tōkyō
Jordan	97 740	4 009	Amman
Kazakhstan	2 717 300	16 538	Alma Ata
Korea, North	121 248	21 773	P'yŏngyang
Korea, South	98 447	42 793	Sŏul (Seoul)
Kuwait	24 300	2 039	Kuwait
Kyrgyzstan (Kirghizia)	198 500	4 291	Bishkek (Frunze)
Laos	236 798	4 139	Vientiane
Lebanon	10 399	2 701	Beirut
Macau (Port)	16	479	Macao
Malaysia	330 669	17 891	Kuala Lumpur
Maldives	298	215	Malé
Mongolia	1 565 000	2 190	Ulaanbaatar (Ulan Bator)
Myanmar (Burma)	678 031	41 675	Yangon (Rangoon)
Nepal	141 414	19 143	Kathmandu
Oman	212 379	1 502	Masqat (Muscat)
Pakistan	803 941	122 626	Islamabad
Philippines	299 765	62 413	Manila
Qatar	11 437	368	Ad Dawḩah
Saudi Arabia	2 400 930	14 134	Ar Riyāḍ
Singapore	616	2 723	Singapore
Sri Lanka	65 610	17 217	Colombo
Syria	185 179	12 530	Dimashq (Damascus)
Taiwan	35 980	20 300	T'ai-pei
Tajikistan	143 100	5 112	Dushanbe
Thailand	513 517	55 702	Bangkok
Turkey	780 576	55 868	Ankara
Turkmenistan	488 100	3 534	Ashkhabad
United Arab Emirates	83 600	1 589	Abū Ẓabī
Uzbekistan	447 400	19 906	Tashkent
Vietnam	329 566	66 693	Hanoi
Yemen	528 038	11 687	San'ä'
Africa			
Algeria	2 381 731	24 960	Alger (El Djezair)
Angola	1 246 694	10 020	Luanda
Benin	112 622	4 630	Porto Novo
Botswana	582 000	1 304	Gaborone
Burkina	274 122	8 996	Ouagadougou
Burundi	27 834	5 472	Bujumbura
Cameroon	475 499	11 833	Yaoundé
Cape Verde	4 033	370	Praia
Central African Republic	622 996	3 039	Bangui
Chad	1 284 000	5 678	N'Djamena
Comoros	1 862	550	Moroni
Congo	342 000	2 271	Brazzaville
Côte d'Ivoire (Ivory Coast)	322 463	11 997	Yamoussoukro
Djibouti	21 699	409	Djibouti
Egypt	1 000 250	52 426	Cairo
Equatorial Guinea	28 051	352	Malabo
Eritrea	117 600	2 614	Âsmera (Asmara)
Ethiopia	1 104 318	46 626	Âdis Âbeba
Gabon	267 667	1 172	Libreville
The Gambia	10 688	861	Banjul
Ghana	238 538	15 028	Accra
Guinea	245 855	5 755	Conakry
Guinea-Bissau	36 125	964	Bissau
Kenya	582 644	24 031	Nairobi
Lesotho	30 344	1 774	Maseru
Liberia	111 370	2 575	Monrovia
Libya	1 759 530	4 545	Tripoli
Madagascar	587 042	12 004	Antananarivo
Malawi	94 100	8 754	Lilongwe
Mali	1 240 142	9 214	Bamako
Mauritania	1 030 700	2 024	Nouakchott
Mauritius	1 865	1 082	Port Louis
Morocco	459 000	25 061	Rabat
Mozambique	784 961	15 656	Maputo
Namibia	824 293	1 781	Windhoek
Niger	1 267 000	7 731	Niamey
Nigeria	923 769	108 542	Abuja
Réunion (Fr.)	2 510	598	Saint-Denis
Rwanda	26 338	7 237	Kigali
São Tomé and Principe	964	121	São Tomé
Senegal	196 722	7 327	Dakar
Seychelles	443	69	Victoria
Sierra Leone	71 740	4 151	Freetown
Somalia	637 539	7 497	Muqdisho (Mogadishu)
South Africa	1 221 038	35 282	Pretoria/Cape Town
Sudan	2 505 792	25 203	Khartoum
Swaziland	17 366	788	Mbabane
Tanzania	942 000	27 318	Dodoma
Togo	56 785	3 531	Lomé
Tunisia	164 148	8 180	Tunis
Uganda	236 036	18 794	Kampala
Western Sahara	266 000	178	-
Zaire	2 344 885	35 568	Kinshasa
Zambia	752 617	8 452	Lusaka
Zimbabwe	390 308	9 709	Harare
Oceania			
American Samoa (USA)	197	38	Fagatogo
Australia	7 682 300	17 659	Canberra
Fiji	18 272	764	Suva
French Polynesia (Fr.)	4 198	206	Papeete
Guam (USA)	549	118	Agaña
Kiribati	800	66	Tarawa
Marshall Islands	181	40	Dalap-Uliga-Darrit
Nauru	21	9	Yaren
New Caledonia (Fr.)	19 104	167	Nouméa
New Zealand	268 675	3 450	Wellington
Niue (NZ)	259	3	Alofi
Federated States of Micronesia	1 300	99	Kolonia
Papua New Guinea	461 692	3 874	Port Moresby
Solomon Islands	29 785	320	Honiara
Tonga	699	95	Nuku'alofa
Tuvalu	25	9	Funafuti
Vanuatu	14 763	158	Vila
Western Samoa	2 831	168	Apai

This page explains the main symbols, lettering style and height/depth colours used on the reference maps on pages 2 to 79. The scale of each map is indicated at the top of each page. Abbreviations used on the maps appear at the beginning of the index.

BOUNDARIES

————————	International
▬▬ ▬▬ ▬▬ ▬▬	International under Dispute
▪ ▪ ▪ ▪ ▪ ▪ ▪ ▪	Cease Fire Line
———————	Autonomous or State
··············	Administrative
▬▬ ▬▬ ▬▬ ▬▬	Maritime (National)
— — — — —	International Date Line

COMMUNICATIONS

════════	Motorway/Express Highway
========	Under Construction
————————	Major Highway
———————	Other Roads
– – – – –	Under Construction
· · · · · · · ·	Track
→====←	Road Tunnel
– – – – –	Car Ferry
————————	Main Railway
———————	Other Railway
– – – – –	Under Construction
→–––←	Rail Tunnel
– – – – –	Rail Ferry
╾┼┼┼┼╼	Canal
⊕	International Airport
✈	Other Airport

LAKE FEATURES

	Freshwater
	Saltwater
	Seasonal
	Salt Pan

LANDSCAPE FEATURES

	Glacier, Ice Cap
	Marsh, Swamp
	Sand Desert, Dunes

OTHER FEATURES

	River
	Seasonal River
⊃⊂	Pass, Gorge
	Dam, Barrage
	Waterfall, Rapid
	Aqueduct
	Reef
▲ 4231	Summit, Peak
· 217	Spot Height, Depth
⌣	Well
△	Oil Field
▲	Gas Field
Gas / Oil	Oil/Natural Gas Pipeline
Gemsbok Nat. Pk	National Park
∴UR	Historic Site

LETTERING STYLES

CANADA	Independent Nation
FLORIDA	State, Province or Autonomous Region
Gibraltar (U.K.)	Sovereignty of Dependent Territory
Lothian	Administrative Area
LANGUEDOC	Historic Region
Loire ***Vosges***	Physical Feature or Physical Region

TOWNS AND CITIES

Square symbols denote capital cities. Each settlement is given a symbol according to its relative importance, with type size to match.

▣	◉	**New York**	Major City
■	●	**Dallas**	City
▫	○	Memphis	Small City
▪	•	Oakland	Large Town
▫	○	Boise	Town
▫	○	Durango	Small Town
▫	○	Marshfield	Village
			Built-up-area

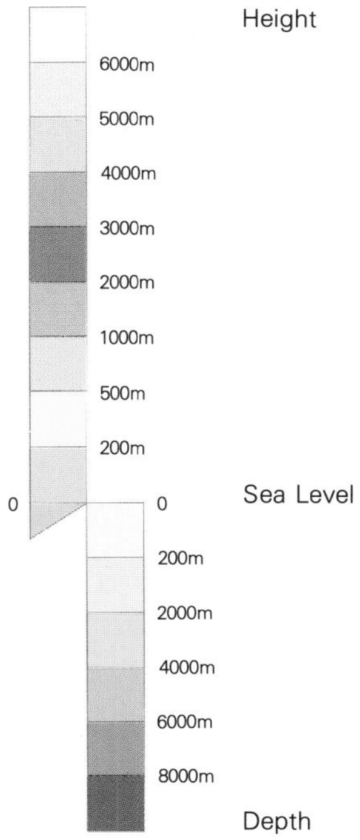

Height

	6000m
	5000m
	4000m
	3000m
	2000m
	1000m
	500m
	200m
0	0 Sea Level
	200m
	2000m
	4000m
	6000m
	8000m

Depth

1:35M

0 250 500 750 1000 1250 km
0 250 500 750 mls

RUS. FED.

Arctic Ocean

ⒶⒷⒸⒹⒺⒻⒼⒽ Ⓙ Ⓚ Ⓛ Ⓜ Ⓝ Ⓞ Ⓟ Ⓠ Ⓡ

① ② ③

Bering Sea

Bering Strait

Beaufort Sea

Aleutian Islands

A L A S K A

Yukon

Anchorage
Fairbanks
Nome

Whitehorse

Banks I.

Victoria I.

Queen Elizabeth Islands

Ellesmere I.

Thule

Devon I.
Resolute

Baffin Bay

Baffin I.

Davis Strait

G R E E N L A N D
(KALAALLIT NUNAAT)
(Denmark)

Goethåb
(Nuuk)

Denmark Strait

ICELAND
Reykjavik

Alexander Arch.
Juneau

Q. Charlotte Is

Prince Rupert

Vancouver I.
Prince George

Mackenzie

Yellowknife

Great Bear L.

Great Slave L.
Hay River

Arctic Circle

C A N A D A

Athabasca

Churchill

Hudson Bay

Inukjuak

Schefferville

Southampton I.

Hudson Strait

Churchill Falls

Sept-Îles

Newfoundland

Anticosti I.

St John's

Charlottetown

Victoria
Vancouver
Seattle
Portland

Spokane

Butte

Edmonton

Calgary

Saskatoon

Regina

Winnipeg

L. Winnipeg

James Bay

Moosonee

Thunder Bay

Fargo
Duluth

L. Superior

Sault Ste Marie

Québec

Montréal

Moncton
Fredericton

Halifax

San Francisco

Salt Lake City

U N I T E D   S T A T E S

Minneapolis   St Paul

Milwaukee
Chicago

L. Michigan

L. Huron

Detroit

L. Erie

Toronto
Ottawa

L. Ontario

Buffalo

Cleveland

Boston

New York

Omaha

Denver

Colorado

O F   A M E R I C A

Kansas City
St Louis

Indianapolis

Ohio

Baltimore
Washington

Philadelphia

A T L A N T I C

O C E A N

Los Angeles
San Diego

Phoenix
Tucson

Albuquerque

El Paso

Dallas
Fort Worth

Mississippi

Memphis

Nashville

Birmingham

Atlanta

Norfolk

Charleston

Bermuda (U.K.)

Guadalupe (Mex.)

San Antonio

Chihuahua

Houston

New Orleans

Jacksonville

Tropic of Cancer

G. de California

M E X I C O

Rio Grande

Monterrey
Torreón

Mazatlán

Tampa

Miami

Gulf of Mexico

Nassau

THE BAHAMAS

Habana

CUBA

Guantánamo

HAITI

DOMINICAN REP.

Pto Rico (U.S.A.)

Is Revilla Gigedo (Mex.)

Guadalajara

México

Tampico

Veracruz

Mérida

BELIZE
Belmopan

Acapulco

GUATEMALA
Guatemala
S.Salvador
EL SALVADOR

HONDURAS
Tegucigalpa

NICARAGUA
Managua

JAMAICA
Kingston

Port au Prince

Sto Domingo

ST KITTS-NEVIS

ANTIGUA & BARBUDA

DOMINICA

ST LUCIA

BARBADOS

ST VINCENT & THE GRENADINES

GRENADA

TRINIDAD & TOBAGO

CARIBBEAN SEA

Netherlands Antilles

P A C I F I C

Clipperton (Fr.)

O C E A N

COSTA RICA
S.José

PANAMA
Panamá

Sta Marta

Barranquilla

Maracaibo

Caracas

VENEZUELA

I.del Coco (C.R)

Malpelo (Col.)

Medellín

Bogotá

C O L O M B I A

B R A Z I L

Negro

Equator

Galapagos Is (Ecu.)

Quito
ECUADOR

PERU

① ② ③ ④ ⑤ ⑥ ⑦ ⑧

Ⓖ Ⓗ Ⓙ Ⓚ Ⓛ Ⓜ

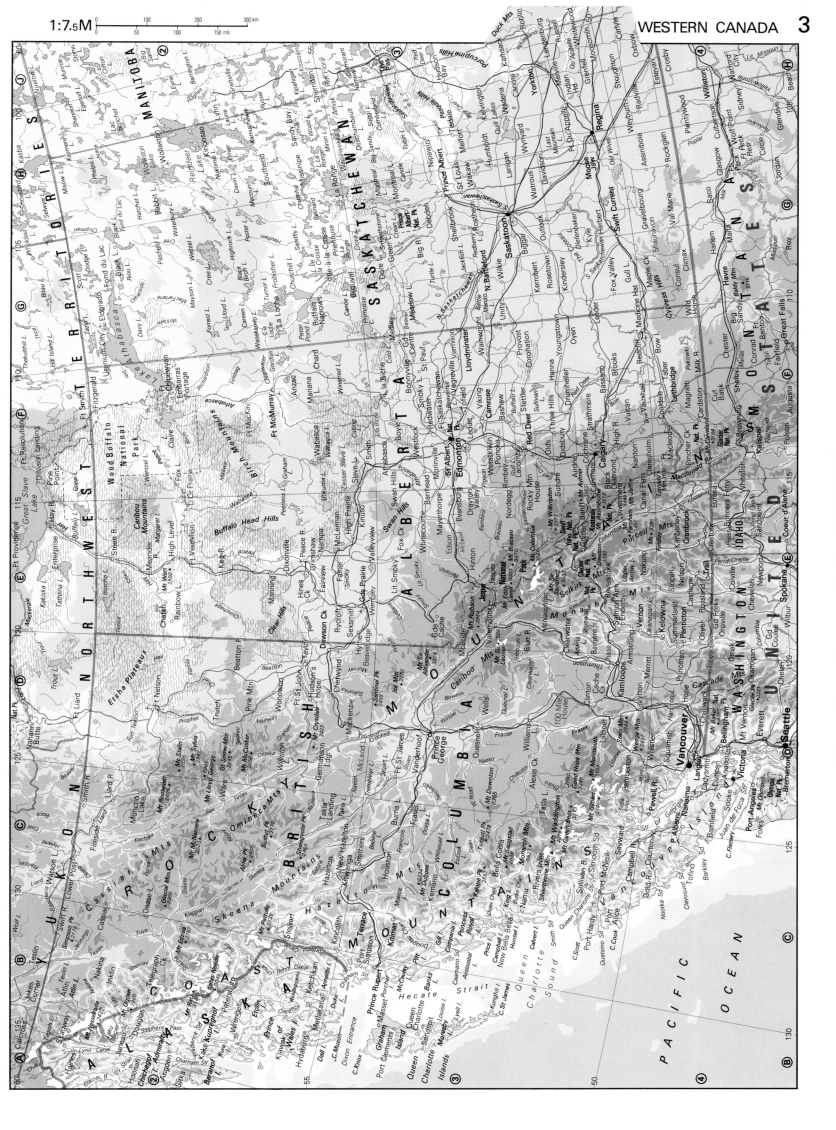

HUDSON BAY

MANITOBA

ONTARIO

JAMES BAY

MINNESOTA

WISCONSIN

MICHIGAN

IOWA

ILLINOIS

UNITED STATES

NEW YORK

LAKE SUPERIOR

LAKE MICHIGAN

LAKE HURON

LAKE ERIE

LAKE ONTARIO

Georgian Bay

Belcher Islands

Polar Bear Provincial Park

Winnipeg

Thunder Bay

Duluth

St. Paul
Minneapolis

Milwaukee

Chicago

Detroit

Cleveland

Sudbury

North Bay

Ottawa

Toronto

Hamilton

Buffalo

Sault Ste. Marie

Timmins

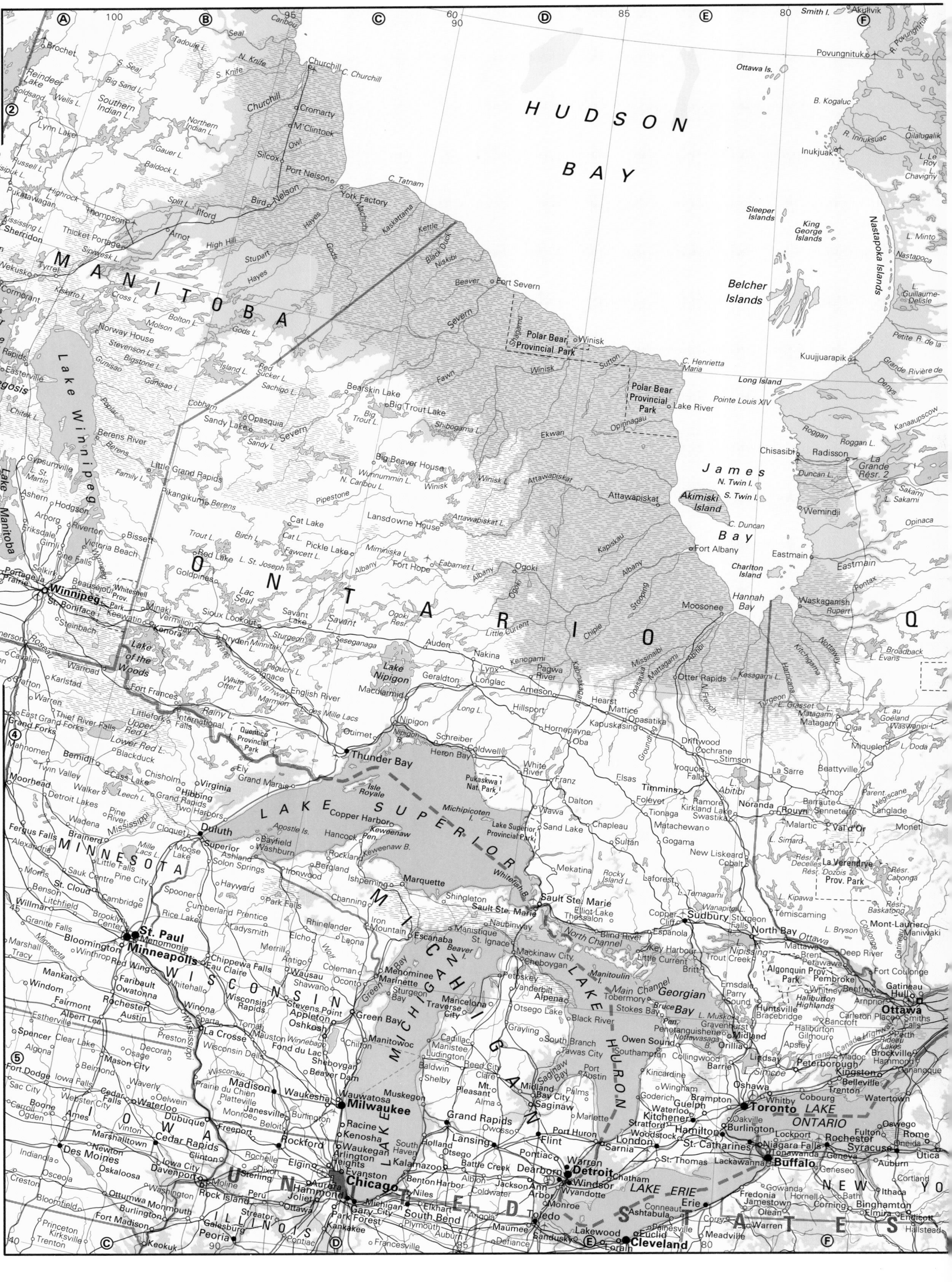

1:15M

| 200 | 400 | 600 km |
| 100 | 200 | 300 mls |

ARCTIC OCEAN

BEAUFORT SEA

PACIFIC OCEAN

Gulf of Alaska

BERING SEA

ALASKA

ALASKA RANGE

Brooks Range

De Long Mts

Endicott Mts

YUKON TERRITORY

NORTHWEST TERRITORIES

BRITISH COLUMBIA

COAST MOUNTAINS

ALBERTA

SASKATCHEWAN

MANITOBA

ROCKY MOUNTAINS

WASHINGTON

OREGON

IDAHO

MONTANA

WYOMING

NORTH DAKOTA

SOUTH DAKOTA

U.S.A.

Queen Charlotte Islands

Vancouver Island

Banks Island

Victoria Island

Prince of Wales Island

Melville Island

Parry Islands

Kodiak Island

Aleutian Ra.

Great Bear Lake

Great Slave Lake

Lake Athabasca

Reindeer Lake

Lake Winnipeg

Vancouver

Victoria

Seattle

Tacoma

Olympia

Portland

Salem

Spokane

Calgary

Edmonton

Saskatoon

Regina

Winnipeg

Whitehorse

Yellowknife

Prince George

Prince Rupert

Kamloops

Kelowna

Medicine Hat

Lethbridge

Moose Jaw

Brandon

Helena

Butte

Billings

Great Falls

Bismarck

Fargo

Pierre

Rapid City

Boise

Twin Falls

Pocatello

Wood Buffalo Nat. Pk.

St. Lawrence I.

Bering Str.

Dixon Entrance

Queen Charlotte Sound

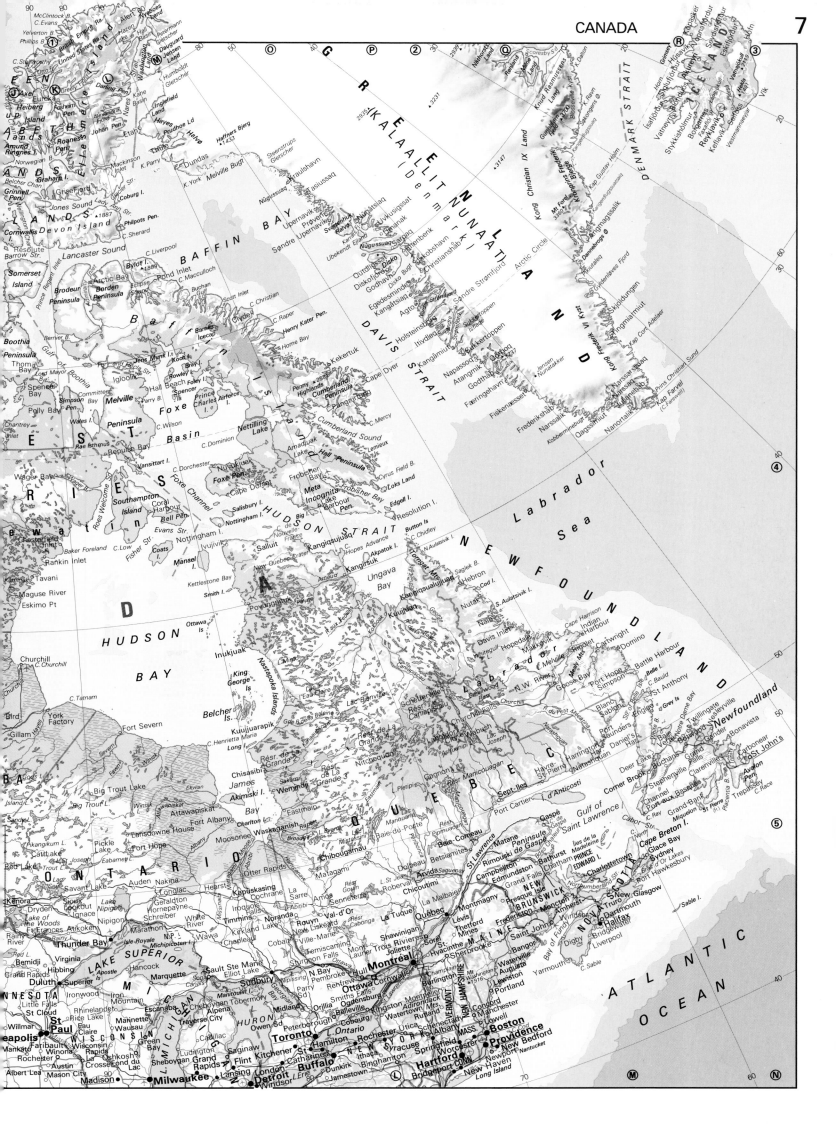

1:12.5M

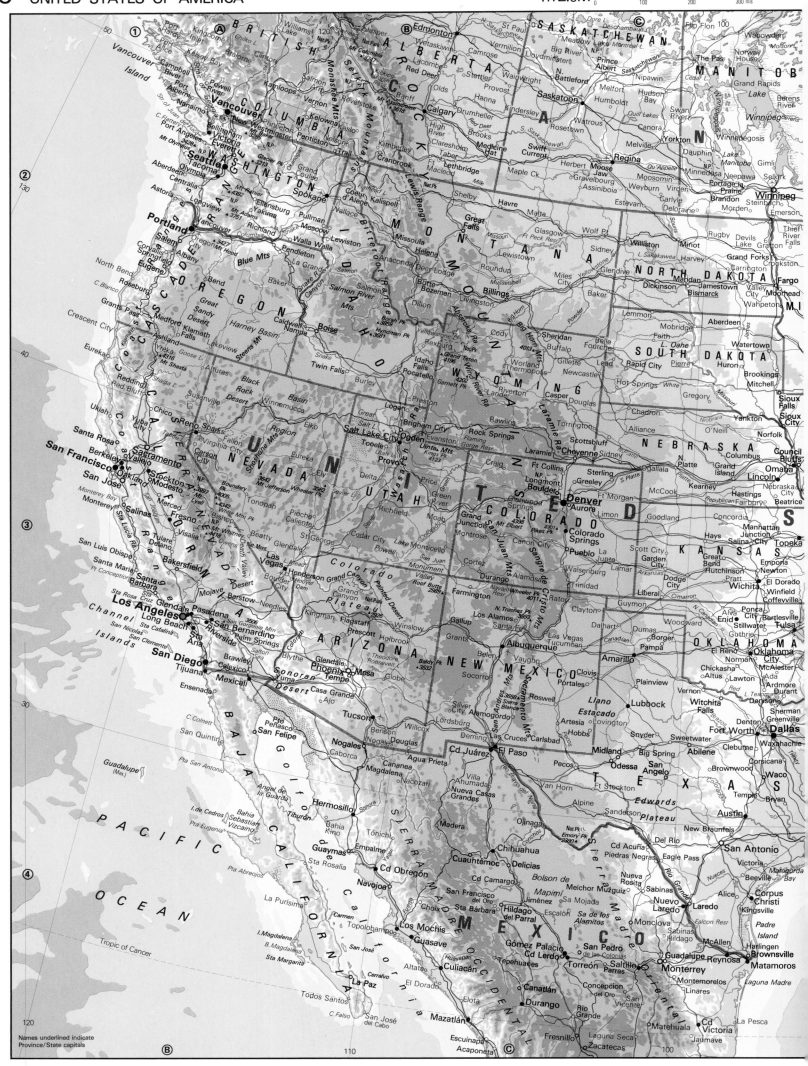

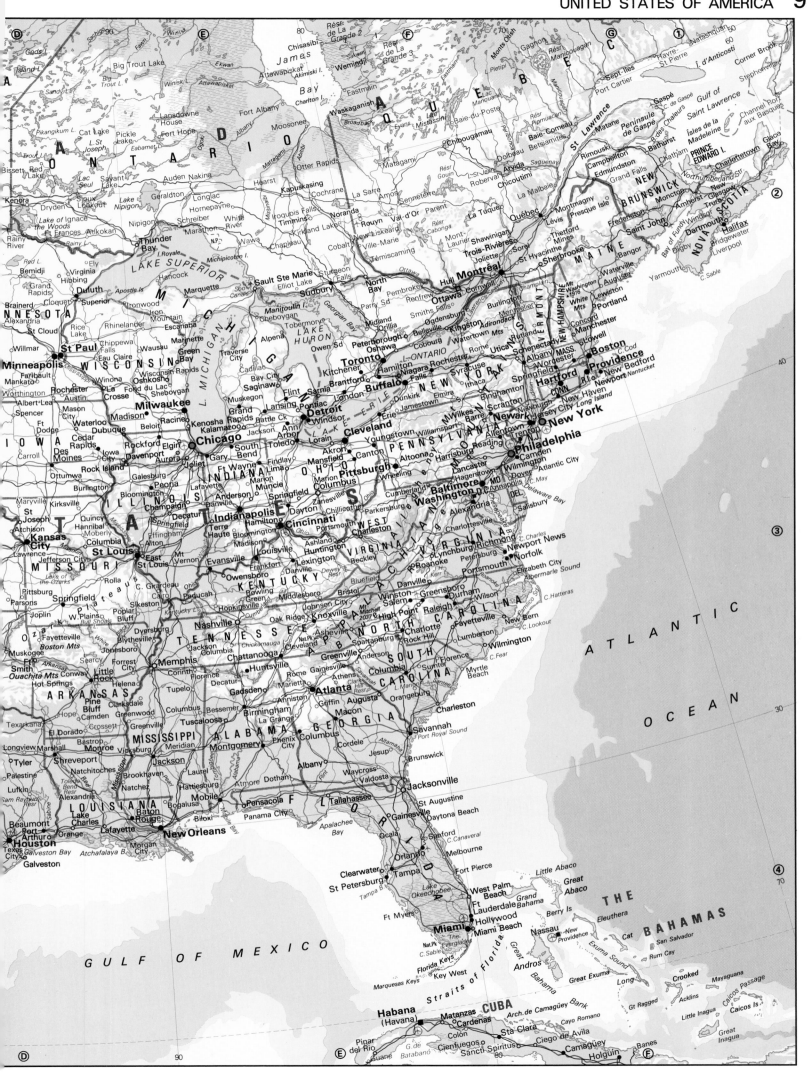

1:10M

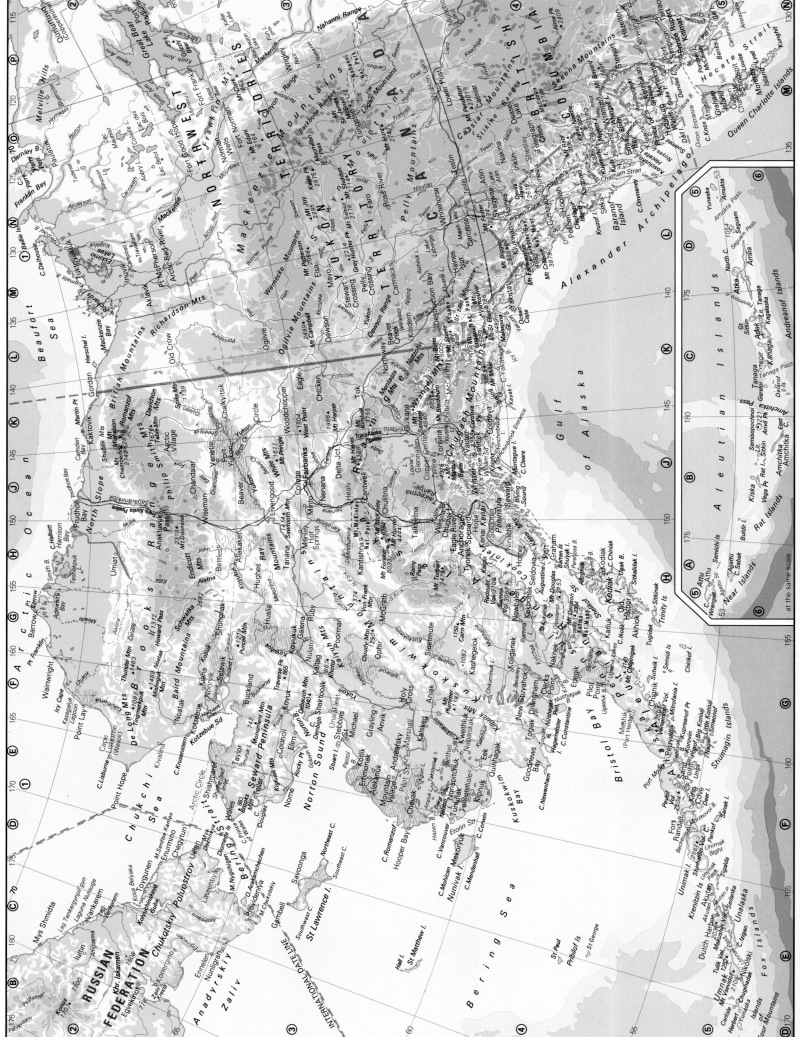

1:5M

50 100 150 200 km
50 100 mls

States / Provinces: ONTARIO, MANITOBA, SASKATCHEWAN, MINNESOTA, WISCONSIN, IOWA, NORTH DAKOTA, SOUTH DAKOTA, NEBRASKA, MONTANA, WYOMING

Selected places:

Thunder Bay, Kakabeka Falls, Grand Marais, Silver Bay, Two Harbors, Duluth, Superior, Ashland, Hurley, Ironwood, Gurney, Prentice, Ladysmith, Park Falls, Chippewa Falls, Eau Claire, Augusta, Neillsville, Tomah, Sparta, La Crosse, Viroqua, Prairie du Chien, Platteville, Dubuque, Bettendorf, Davenport, Rock Island

Kenora, Keewatin, Minaki, Sioux Lookout, Savant Lake, Fort Frances, International Falls, Baudette, Warroad, Roseau, Bemidji, Cass Lake, Grand Rapids, Hibbing, Virginia, Chisholm, Babbitt, Ely

Winnipeg, Steinbach, St Boniface, Transcona, Selkirk, Portage la Prairie, Brandon, Morris, Emerson, Pembina, Cavalier, Grafton, Grand Forks, East Grand Forks, Crookston, Warren, Thief River Falls, Bagley, Fosston, Mahnomen, Detroit Lakes, Moorhead, Fargo

St Paul, Minneapolis, Bloomington, Shakopee, Anoka, Elk River, Cambridge, Mora, Hinckley, Pine City, Stillwater, Hastings, Red Wing, Zumbrota, Rochester, Winona, Chatfield, Caledonia, Decorah, New Hampton, Charles City, Mason City, Waverly, Waterloo, Cedar Falls, Cedar Rapids, Iowa City, Muscatine, Washington, Des Moines, Ames, Boone, Marshalltown, Newton, Grinnell, Knoxville

Aberdeen, Watertown, Huron, Pierre, Mitchell, Sioux Falls, Yankton, Vermillion, Brookings, Sioux City, Le Mars, Cherokee, Storm Lake, Spencer, Estherville, Fort Dodge, Webster City

Bismarck, Mandan, Jamestown, Valley City, Devils Lake, Rugby, Minot, Williston, Dickinson, Watford City, Hettinger, Lemmon, Mobridge

Regina, Moose Jaw, Swift Current, Weyburn, Estevan, Glasgow, Wolf Point, Miles City, Glendive, Baker, Bowman, Buffalo, Rapid City, Black Hills, Lead, Deadwood, Spearfish, Sturgis, Custer, Hot Springs, Edgemont, Chadron, Alliance, Scottsbluff, Casper, Bighorn Mts, Laramie Mts, Sheridan, Buffalo, Gillette, Douglas, Rawlins, Saratoga

Lake of the Woods, Lake Winnipeg, Lake Manitoba, Rainy Lake, Upper Red L., Lower Red L., Leech L., Mille Lacs, Lake Superior, Mississippi, Minnesota R., Missouri, Big Sioux, James, Cheyenne, Lake Oahe, Lake Sakakawea, Little Missouri, Fort Peck Reservoir, Yellowstone, Powder River, Belle Fourche, Badlands, North Platte, Bighorn L., Cloud Peak 4016

50   100   150   200 km
50   100 mls

LAKE SUPERIOR

LAKE MICHIGAN

LAKE HURON

LAKE ERIE

ONTARIO

MINNESOTA

WISCONSIN

IOWA

MISSOURI

ILLINOIS

INDIANA

OHIO

KENTUCKY

TENNESSEE

WEST VIRGINIA

CUMBERLAND PLATEAU

ALLEGHENY

Principal cities and towns:

Thunder Bay, Duluth, Superior, St Paul, St Louis, Milwaukee, Chicago, Madison, Indianapolis, Cincinnati, Columbus, Cleveland, Detroit, Windsor, Grand Rapids, Lansing, Flint, Saginaw, Bay City, Toledo, Akron, Canton, Youngstown, Fort Wayne, Peoria, Springfield, Louisville, Lexington, Evansville, Sudbury, Sault Ste Marie, Kitchener, London, Guelph, Nashville

Isle Royale Nat. Pk.
Apostle Is.
Keweenaw Pen.
Straits of Mackinac
Georgian Bay
Manitoulin I.
Saginaw Bay
Green Bay
Ozark Plateau
Mammoth Cave Nat. Pk.
Mississippi
Ohio
Wabash

Mt Rogers 1743
Bathawana Mtn 653

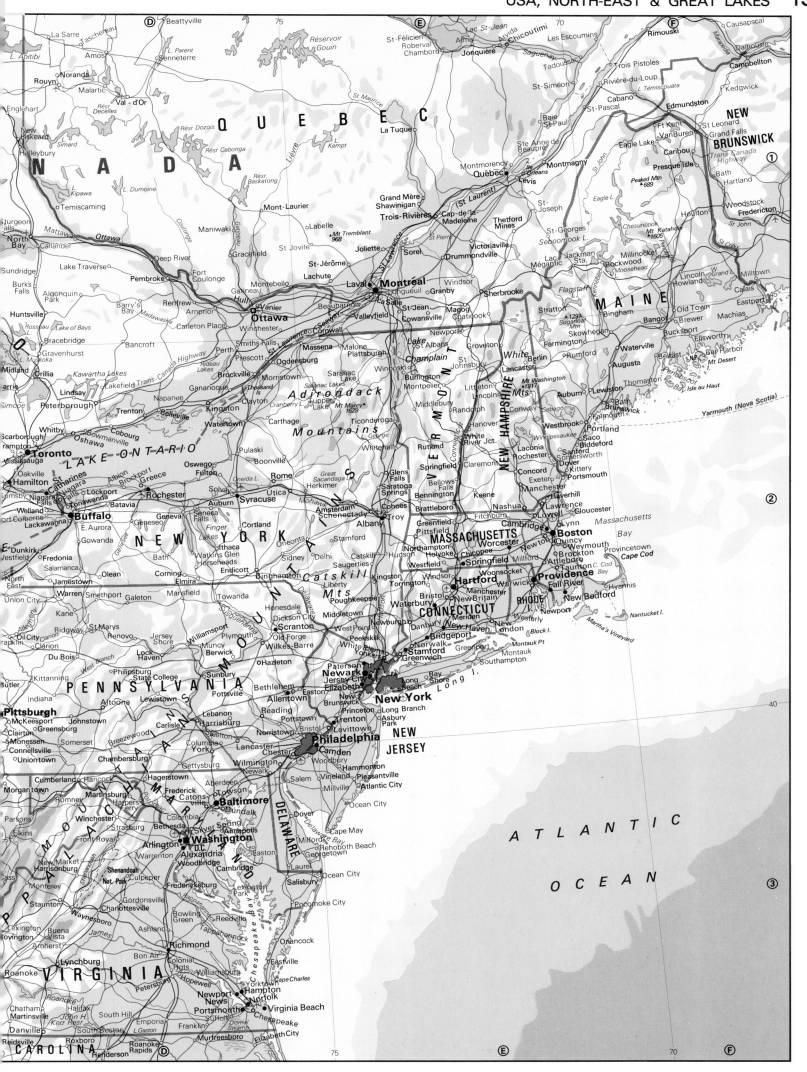

1:2.5M

25 50 75 100 km
25 50 mls

MASSACHUSETTS
NEW HAMPSHIRE
VERMONT
CONNECTICUT
RHODE ISLAND
NEW YORK
PENNSYLVANIA
NEW JERSEY
DELAWARE
MARYLAND
VIRGINIA
WEST VIRGINIA

Boston
New York
Philadelphia
Baltimore
Washington D.C.
Buffalo
Rochester
Syracuse
Albany
Providence
Hartford
New Haven
Bridgeport
Newark
Trenton
Camden
Allentown
Scranton
Wilkes-Barre
Harrisburg
Arlington
Alexandria

ATLANTIC OCEAN

Long Island
Long Island Sound
Cape Cod
Cape Cod Bay
Massachusetts Bay
Nantucket Island
Martha's Vineyard
Delaware Bay
Chesapeake Bay
Lake Ontario

Cape May
Cape Henlopen

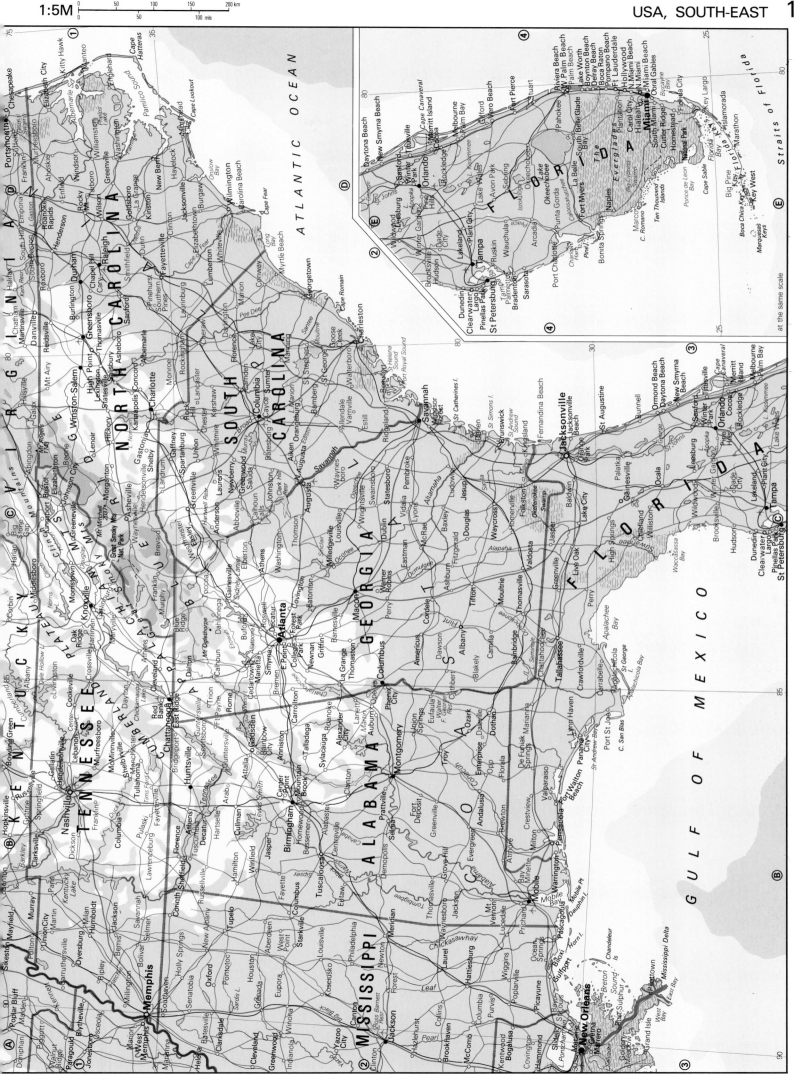

1:5M

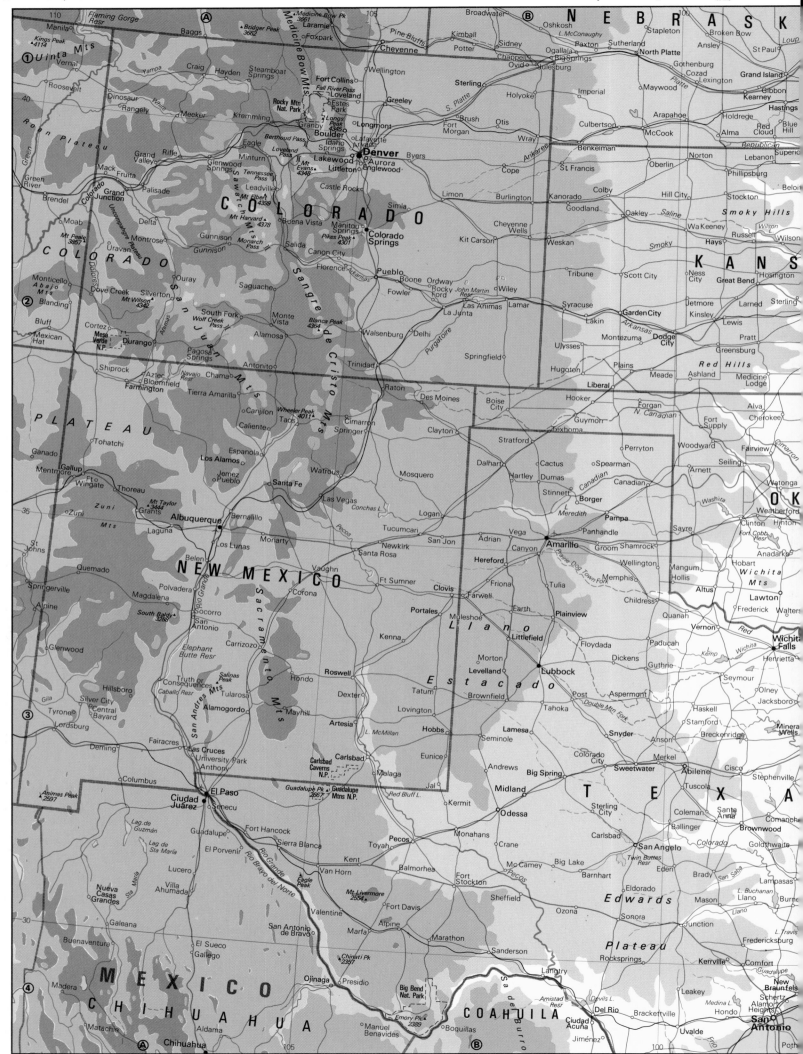

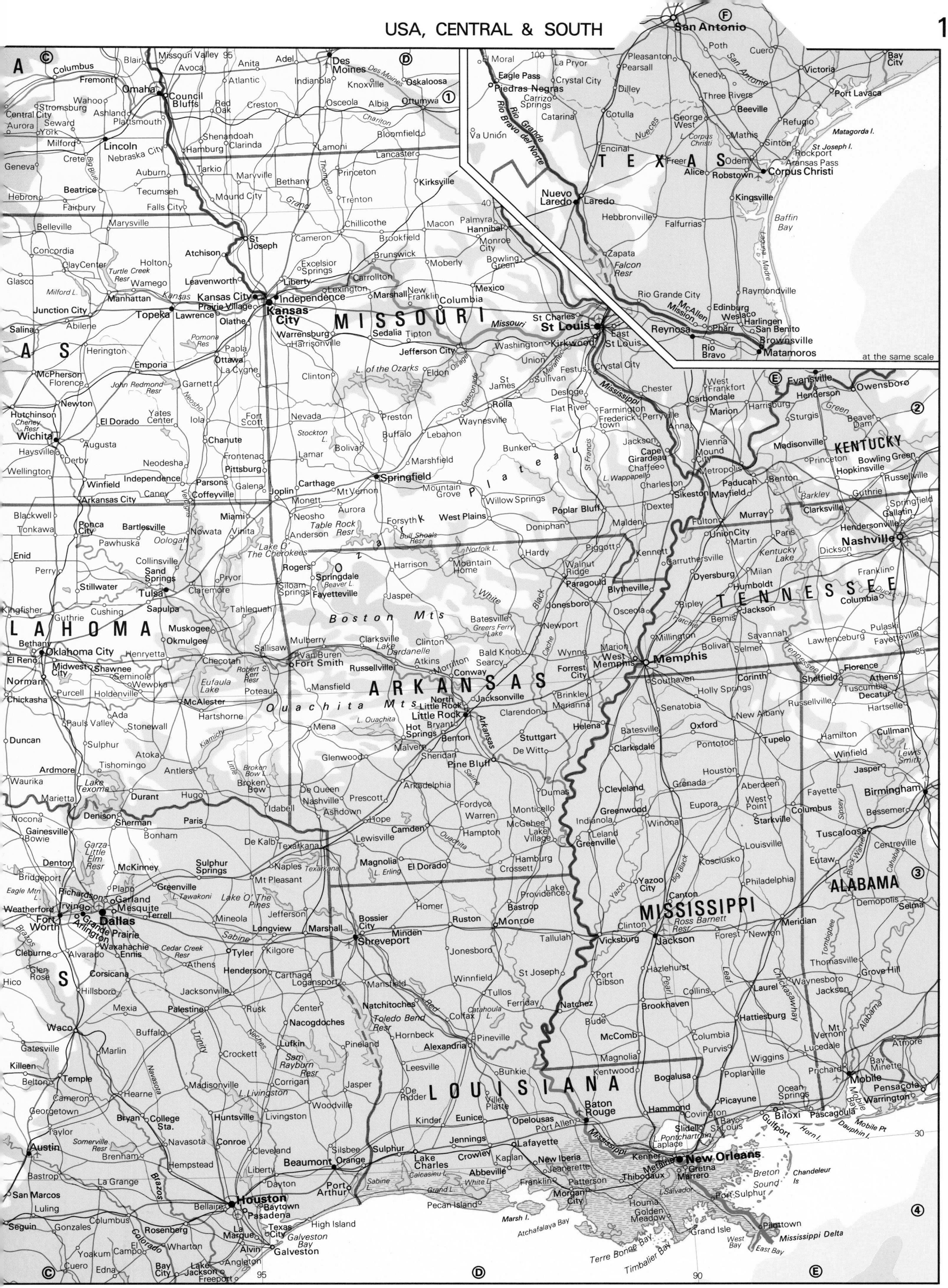

MISSOURI

TEXAS

KENTUCKY

TENNESSEE

OKLAHOMA

LAHOMA

ARKANSAS

Ouachita Mts

Boston Mts

MISSISSIPPI

ALABAMA

LOUISIANA

at the same scale

Columbus · Fremont · Blair · Missouri Valley 95 · Avoca · Anita · Adel · Des Moines · Knoxville · Oskaloosa · Ottumwa · Indianola · Albia · Bloomfield

Omaha · Council Bluffs · Red Oak · Creston · Osceola · Chariton · Lamoni · Lancaster

Wahoo · Ashland · Plattsmouth · Shenandoah · Clarinda · Princeton · Trenton · Kirksville

Lincoln · Nebraska City · Hamburg · Tarkio · Maryville · Bethany · Chillicothe · Macon · Palmyra · Hannibal

St Joseph · Cameron · Brookfield · Brunswick · Moberly · Monroe City · Bowling Green · Mexico

Kansas City · Independence · Lexington · Marshall · New Franklin · Columbia

Kansas City · Olathe · Warrensburg · Sedalia · Tipton · Jefferson City · Washington · Kirkwood · St Louis · East St Louis

Topeka · Lawrence · Harrisonville · Clinton · Eldon · St James · Sullivan · Festus · Crystal City

Springfield · Rolla · Waynesville · Lebanon · Marshfield · Mountain Grove · Willow Springs · West Plains

Joplin · Carthage · Mt Vernon · Aurora · Neosho · Forsyth · Mountain Home · Harrison

Tulsa · Claremore · Siloam Springs · Fayetteville · Springdale · Jasper

Oklahoma City · Fort Smith · Van Buren · Russellville · Clarksville · Dardanelle · Conway

Little Rock · North Little Rock · Hot Springs · Benton · Malvern · Sheridan · Pine Bluff · Stuttgart

Memphis · West Memphis · Southaven

Nashville · Jackson · Columbia · Pulaski · Lawrenceburg · Fayetteville

Birmingham · Tuscaloosa · Bessemer

Dallas · Fort Worth · Arlington · Garland · Mesquite · Grand Prairie · Plano · Richardson

Texarkana · Shreveport · Bossier City · Minden · Monroe · Ruston

Waco · Austin · San Antonio · Houston · Pasadena · Baytown · Galveston

Baton Rouge · New Orleans · Lafayette · Lake Charles · Beaumont · Port Arthur · Orange

Biloxi · Gulfport · Mobile · Pensacola · Pascagoula

San Antonio · Eagle Pass · Piedras Negras · Nuevo Laredo · Laredo · Reynosa · Matamoros · Brownsville · Corpus Christi · Victoria

1:5M

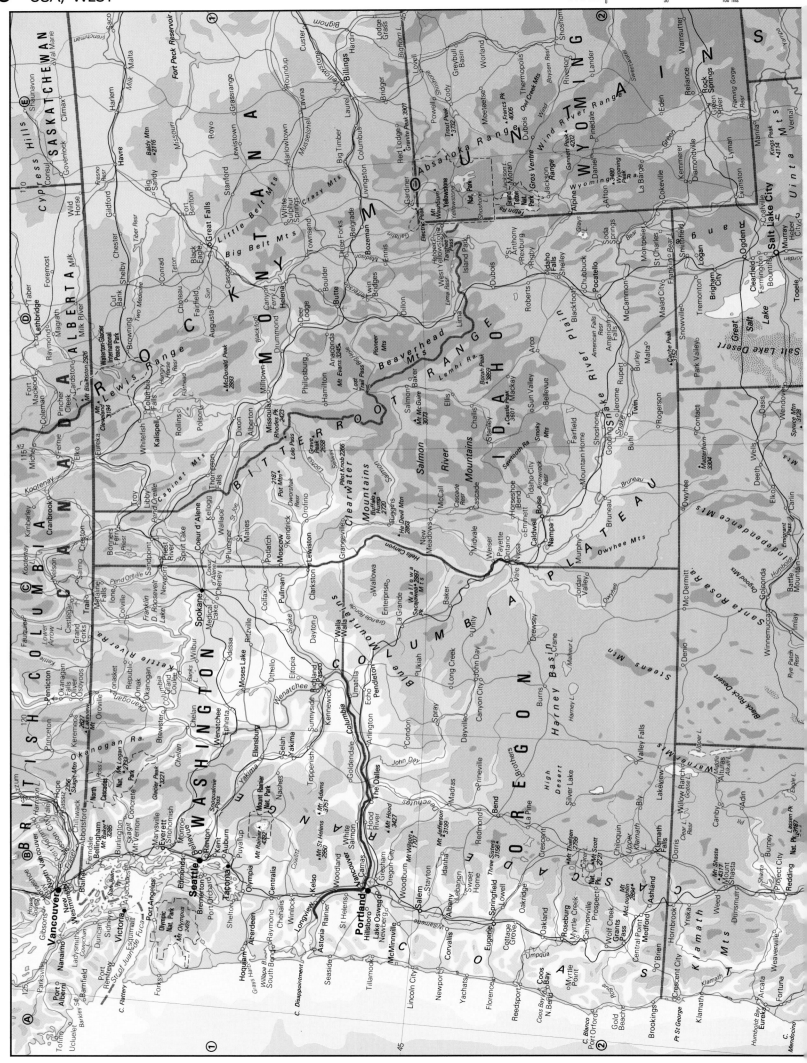

1:2.5M

USA, HAWAII

1:5M

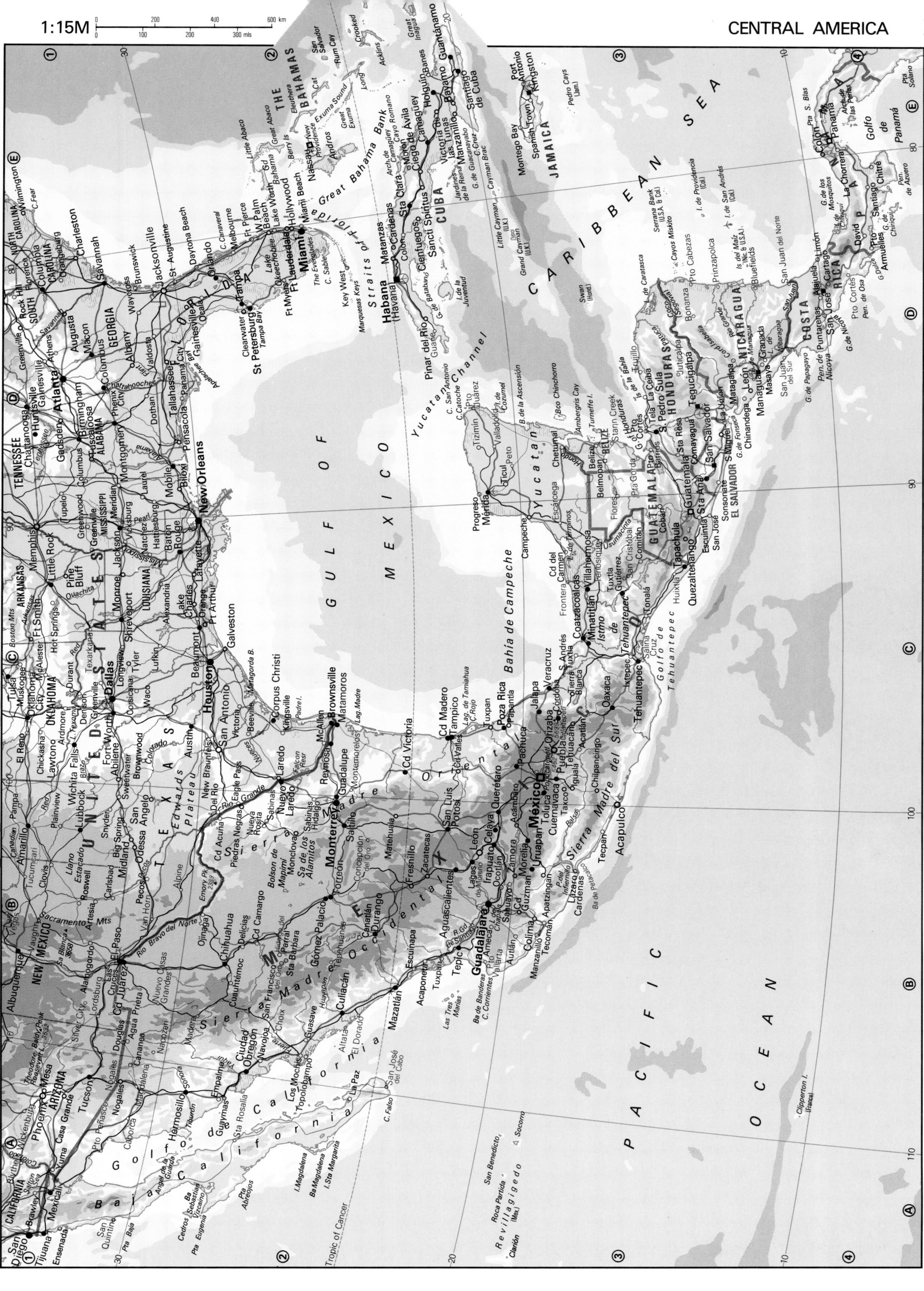

1:15M

200 400 600 km
100 200 300 mls

THE BAHAMAS

CUBA

JAMAICA

CARIBBEAN SEA

GULF OF MEXICO

MEXICO

UNITED STATES

TEXAS

LOUISIANA

GEORGIA

ALABAMA

MISSISSIPPI

ARKANSAS

OKLAHOMA

TENNESSEE

NORTH CAROLINA

SOUTH CAROLINA

FLORIDA

NEW MEXICO

ARIZONA

CALIFORNIA

Baja California

Golfo de California

Sierra Madre Occidental

Sierra Madre Oriental

Sierra Madre del Sur

Bahía de Campeche

Yucatán

BELIZE

GUATEMALA

EL SALVADOR

HONDURAS

NICARAGUA

COSTA RICA

PANAMÁ

PACIFIC OCEAN

Straits of Florida

Yucatán Channel

Great Bahama Bank

Tropic of Cancer

1:5M

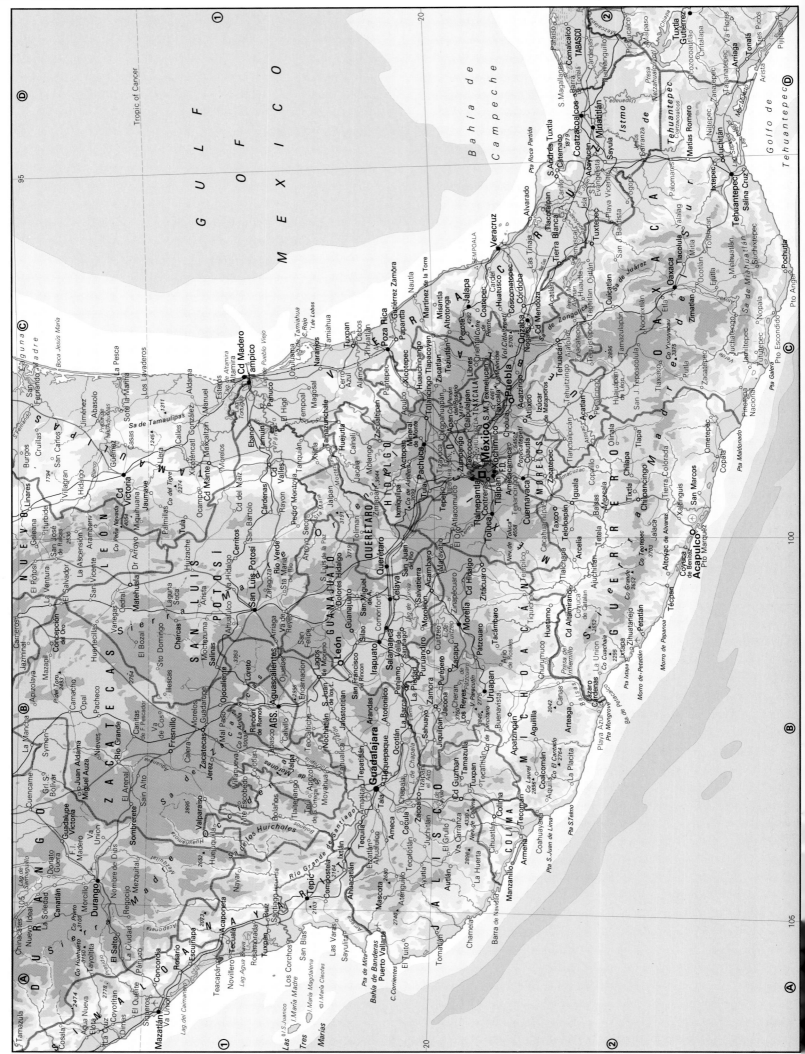

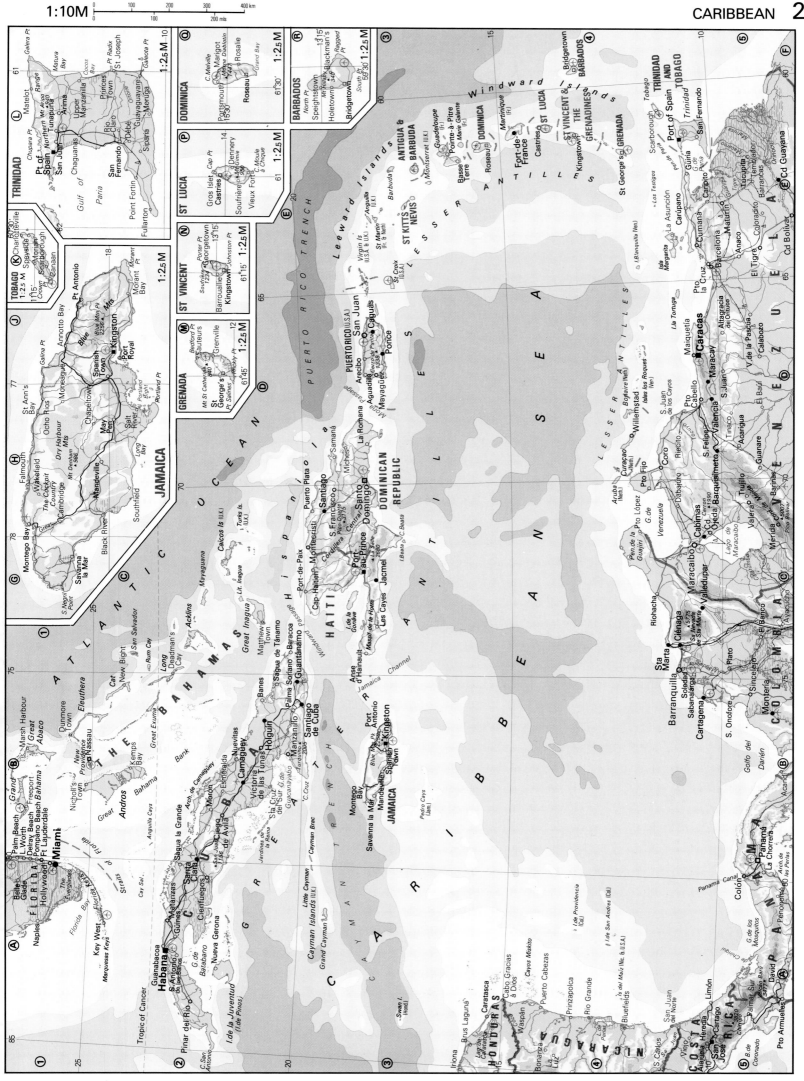

1:35M

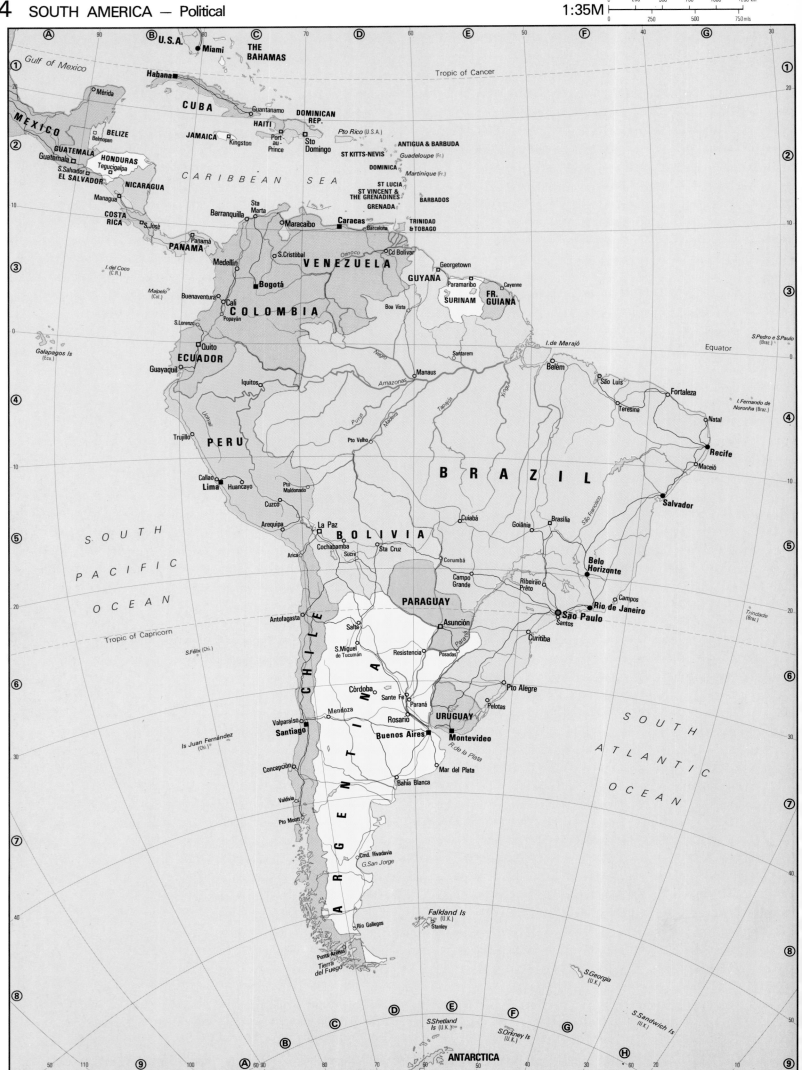

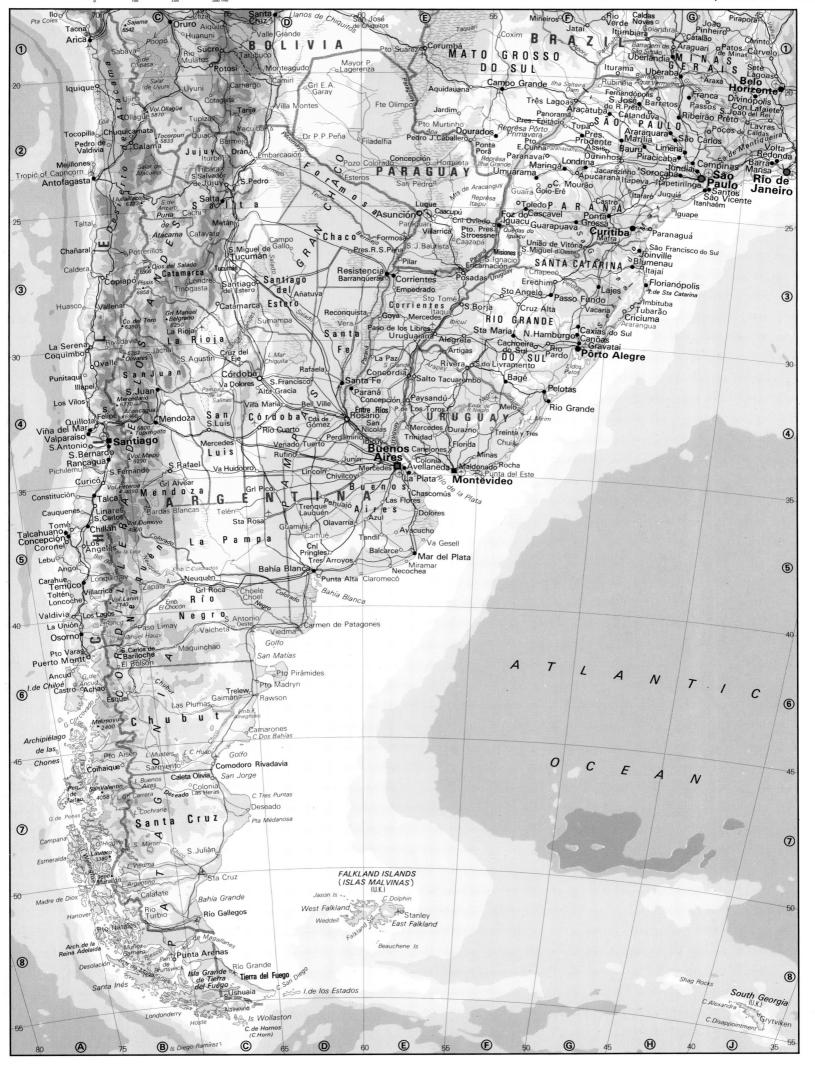

1:15M

200   400   600 km
100   200   300 mls

Roseau
Fort-de-France Martinique (Fr.)
ST LUCIA Castries
Kingstown ST VINCENT & THE GRENADINES
GRENADA St George's
Tobago
Port of Spain Trinidad San Fernando

200 400 600 km
100 200 300 mls

NICARAGUA
Siguatepeque Comayagua Tegucigalpa
San Miguel La Unión Choluteca Chinandega Estelí Matagalpa León Managua Masaya Granada Rivas S. Carlos
Puntarenas San José Cartago Heredia Limón
COSTA RICA
Pen. de Nicoya
Pto Cabezas
I. de Providencia (Col)
I. de San Andrés (Col)
L. de Perlas
Bluefields
Colón Panamá La Chorrera
PANAMA
Santiago David Chitré Arch. de las Perlas La Palma
G. de Panamá
Turbo Quibdó
G. de Uraba
Sta Marta Ciénaga Barranquilla Cartagena
Maracaibo Cabimas Cd Ojeda
Valledupar Machiques
Riohacha Maicao Pto Fijo Coro
Pta Gallinas Pen. de Guajira
G. de Venezuela
Curaçao Bonaire Aruba Willemstad Neth. Antilles
Los Roques (Ven.)
La Tortuga
Pto Cabello Valencia Maracay Maiquetía **Caracas** Pto la Cruz Barcelona
La Asunción I. de Margarita
Cumaná Carúpano Pen. de Paria Güiria
VENEZUELA
Barquisimeto Acarigua S. Juan Zárara V. de la Pascua El Tigre
Maturín Tucupita Barrancas
Cd Guayana Upata
San Cristóbal Cúcuta Pamplona Bucaramanga Málaga
Mérida Barinas
Bolívar 5775
Trujillo Valera
Guanare
Apure
Orinoco
S. Fernando
Cd Bolívar Cd Piar
Sincelejo El Banco Magangué Montería Caucasia Yarumal Barrancabermeja Bello Itagüi **Medellín** Manizales Pereira Cartago Armenia Ibagué Tuluá Buga Palmira **Cali** Santander Popayán Neiva Huila 5750
COLOMBIA
Bogotá Villavicencio Granada
Tolima 5215
Chocontá Tunja Sogamoso
Ocaña Pto Berrio Barbosa
Meta Orocué
Pto Carreño Pto Ayacucho
Vichada
La Gran Sabana Sta Elena Roraima 2870
RORAIMA
Boa Vista Caracaraí
Buenaventura Tumaco Esmeraldas Cojimies Jama Manta Jipijapa La Libertad Playas I. Puná **Guayaquil** Milagro Cuenca Azogues Machala Tumbes Zaruma Loja Zamora
El Diviso Pasto Ipiales Tulcán Ibarra Otavalo Chone Ambato **Quito** Cotopaxi 5896 Chimborazo 6310 Riobamba Guaranda Babahoyo Macas
ECUADOR
Pto Rico Pitalito Florencia Belén Mocoa Pto Asís Leguizamo Pto Legizamo
Calamar Mitú Cucuí Icana
Inírida Guainía
Negro
Boa Vista
Manacapuru
Tefé
AMAZONAS
SELVAS
Iquitos Leticia Tabatinga Caxias
Yurimaguas Moyobamba Tarapoto Chachapoyas
Cruzeiro do Sul Feijó
Bôca do Acre
Lábrea Humaitá Prainha
ACRE
Sena Madureira Rio Branco Brasiléia Cobija Abunã Pôrto Velho
RONDÔNIA
Guajará-Mirim Riberalta
Talara Negritos Paita Piura Catacaos Sullana Chulucanas Huancabamba Jaén Lambayeque Chiclayo Chepén Pacasmayo Cajamarca Cajabamba Huamachuco Trujillo Otuzco Chimbote Huaraz Huascarán 6768 Casma Huarmey Pativilca Barranca Huacho Ancón Callao **Lima** Huancavelica
PERU
Pucallpa Tingo Maria Huánuco La Unión Pomabamba Oxapampa Cerro de Pasco La Merced La Oroya Tarma Jauja Acobamba Huancayo Ayacucho Andahuaylas Abancay Cuzco
MACHU PICCHU
Quillabamba Parque Nac. de Manú Pto Maldonado Pto Heath
Madre de Dios
Rurrenabaque Trinidad
Pôrto Velho
B
Chincha Alta Pisco Ica Nazca
Pen. de Paracas
Chala Camaná
Coropuna 6425
Juliaca Sicuani Ayaviri Puno **Arequipa** Misti 5822 Mollendo Moquegua Ilo Tacna Arica
L. Titicaca Ancohuma 6388 Coroico Chulumani **La Paz**
BOLIVIA
Quillacollo Cochabamba Oruro Sajama 6542 Huanuni **Santa Cruz** Montero San José de Chiquitos Llanos de Chiquitos Valle Grande
Sucre Potosí Tarabuco Monteagudo
Iquique Tocopilla Pedro de Valdivia Chuquicamata Tocorpuri 5833 Calama Vol. Ollague 5870 Ollagüe Ujina
Salar de Uyuni Uyuni Cotagaita Camargo Tarija Villa Montes Dr P.P. Peña
Mejillones Antofagasta
Tropic of Capricorn
S. Salvador de Jujuy Jujuy
CHILE **ARGENTINA**
Salta

PACIFIC OCEAN

BARBADOS
○ Bridgetown

TRINIDAD
AND
TOBAGO

ATLANTIC

OCEAN

Equator

I. Fernando
de Noronha

Rocas

GUYANA
Mabaruma
Charity
Suddie
V. en Hoop
Bartica
Georgetown
New Amsterdam
Linden
Paramaribo
Nieuw
Nickerie
Totness
Albina
Marienburg
Sinnamary
Kourou
Cayenne
I. du Diable (Devil's I.)
Cabo Orange
Oiapoque

SURINAM
Julianatop
1280

FRENCH
GUIANA

Bonfim
Lethem
Kaieteur
Falls

Serra Tumucumaque

AMAPÁ
Amapá
Ilha de Maracá

Sa do Navio

Macapá
Pto Santana

I. de Marajó
B. de Marajó
C. Maguarinho
Salinópolis
Bragança
Capanema
Belém
Abaetetuba
Pinheiro
Alcântara
Cametá
B. de São Marcos
São Luís
Rosário Parnaíba
Monção
Chapadinha
Camocim
Acaraú

Oriximiná
Óbidos
Monte
Alegre
Santarém
Altamira
Amazonas
Pará
Bacabal
Coroatá
Codó
Caxias
Itapipoca
Caucaia
Fortaleza (Ceará)

Manaus
Careiro
Itacoatiara
Aveiro
Itaituba
Parque Nacional
Amazônia
Pimenta

PARÁ
Tucuruí
Represa
Tucuruí
MARANHÃO
Teresina
Castelo
Crateús
Quixeramobim
CEARÁ
Mombaça
Tauá
Iguatu
Acopiara
Patu
Caicó
RIO GRANDE DO NORTE
Mossoró
Macau
Areia Branca
Natal
Pta do Calcanhar

Jacareacanga
Marabá
Imperatriz
S. Félix
Grajaú
Pto Franco
Araguaína
Carolina
Balsas
Floriano
Oeiras
Picos
J. do Norte
Crato
Salgueiro
Ouricuri
PARAÍBA
Campina Grande
Cabedelo
João Pessoa

Serra do Cachimbo
C. do Araguaia
PIAUÍ
S. Raimundo
Nonato
Paulistana
Petrolina
Juàzeiro
PERNAMBUCO
Caruaru
Palmares
Olinda
Recife (Pernambuco)
Jaboatão
Barreiros

Teles Pires
Cachimbo

TOCANTINS
Represa de
Sobradinho
Barra
Jacobina
ALAGOAS
Maceió
SERGIPE
Aracaju

BRAZIL

São Félix
Ilha do Bananal
Barreiras
Ibotirama
Barra
Propriá
Penedo
Lagarto
Estância

Jucurua
Aripuanã
Sa dos Caiabis
Sa Formosa
Pto Artur
GOIÁS
BAHIA
Iacu
Feira de S.
Alagoinhas
Serrinha
R. de Jacuípe
Cachoeira
Castro
Alves
Salvador (Bahia)

Vilhena
Parecis
MATO GROSSO
Mato Grosso
Planalto de
Mato Grosso
Cuiabá
Fátima du Sul
Rondonópolis
Ceres
Jaraguá
Formosa
Goiás
Uruaçu
Aruanã
Januária
Porteirinha
Vitória da
Conquista
Caetité
Contas
Jequié
Ipiaú
Itabuna
Ilhéus

San Matias
Cáceres
Cuiabá
Pto Suárez
Corumbá
MATO GROSSO
DO SUL
Pirenópolis
Anápolis
Brasília
São Francisco
Goiânia
Montes Claros
Salinas
Araçuaí
Sa do Chifre
Itapetinga
Canavieiras
Belmonte
Pôrto Seguro

Fte Olimpo
Aquidauana
Campo Grande
Ilha Solteira
Dam
Caldas
Novas
Iporá
Paracatu
Piripora
Corinto
Curvelo
Diamantina
Gov.
Valadares
Teófilo Otôni
Nanuque
Itamaraju
São Mateus

Pozo Colorado
Jardim
Três Lagoas
Fernandópolis
S. José
do R. Prêto
Rio Verde
Mineiros
Jataí
Coxim
Itumbiara
Goiandira
João
Pinheiro
Patos
de Minas
Araxá
MINAS GERAIS
Serra do Espinhaço
Itabira
Cnl
Fabriciano
Caratinga
Linhares
ESPÍRITO
SANTO
Vitória
Vila Velha

PARAGUAY
San Pedro
Asunción
Lugue
Filadelfia
Pedro J. Caballero
Pto Murtinho
Dourados
Represa Pôrto
Primavera
Pto
E. Cunha
Paranapanema
SÃO PAULO
Araçatuba
Tupã
Pres.
Prudente
Assis
Marília
Bauru
Araraquara
São Carlos
Catanduva
Ribeirão Prêto
Franca
Passos
Divinópolis
Belo
Horizonte
Sete Lagoas
Lafaiete
Barbacena
Ponte Nova
Manhuaçu
Carangola
Cariacica
Cachoeiro de Itapemirim

Pozo Concepción
Hoqueta
Ponta
Porã
Maringá
Londrina
Ourinhos
Piracicaba
Limeira
Campinas
Sorocaba
Jundiaí
Poços de Caldas
Lavras
S. João del Rei
Juiz
de Fora
Petrópolis
Nova
Friburgo
Campos
S. João da Barra

Colorado
Filadelfia
Umuarama
Apucarana
Jacarezinho
PARANÁ
Itapeva
Itapetininga
São Paulo
Santos
São Vicente
Itanhaém
Magé
Niterói
Rio
de Janeiro
Volta
Redonda
Barra
Mansa

San Pedro
Asunción
Cascavel
Toledo
Goio-Erê
C. Mourão
Guaíra
Castro
Itararé
Juquiá
Iguape

BRAZIL

URUGUAY

ARGENTINA

CHILE

ATLANTIC OCEAN

PACIFIC OCEAN

Buenos Aires

Montevideo

Santiago

Córdoba

Rosario

Mar del Plata

Bahía Blanca

Mendoza

Santa Fe

Corrientes

Resistencia

Pôrto Alegre

Catamarca

La Rioja

Santiago del Estero

San Juan

San Luis

La Pampa

Río Negro

Neuquén

Entre Ríos

Buenos Aires

Misiones

Chaco

Andes

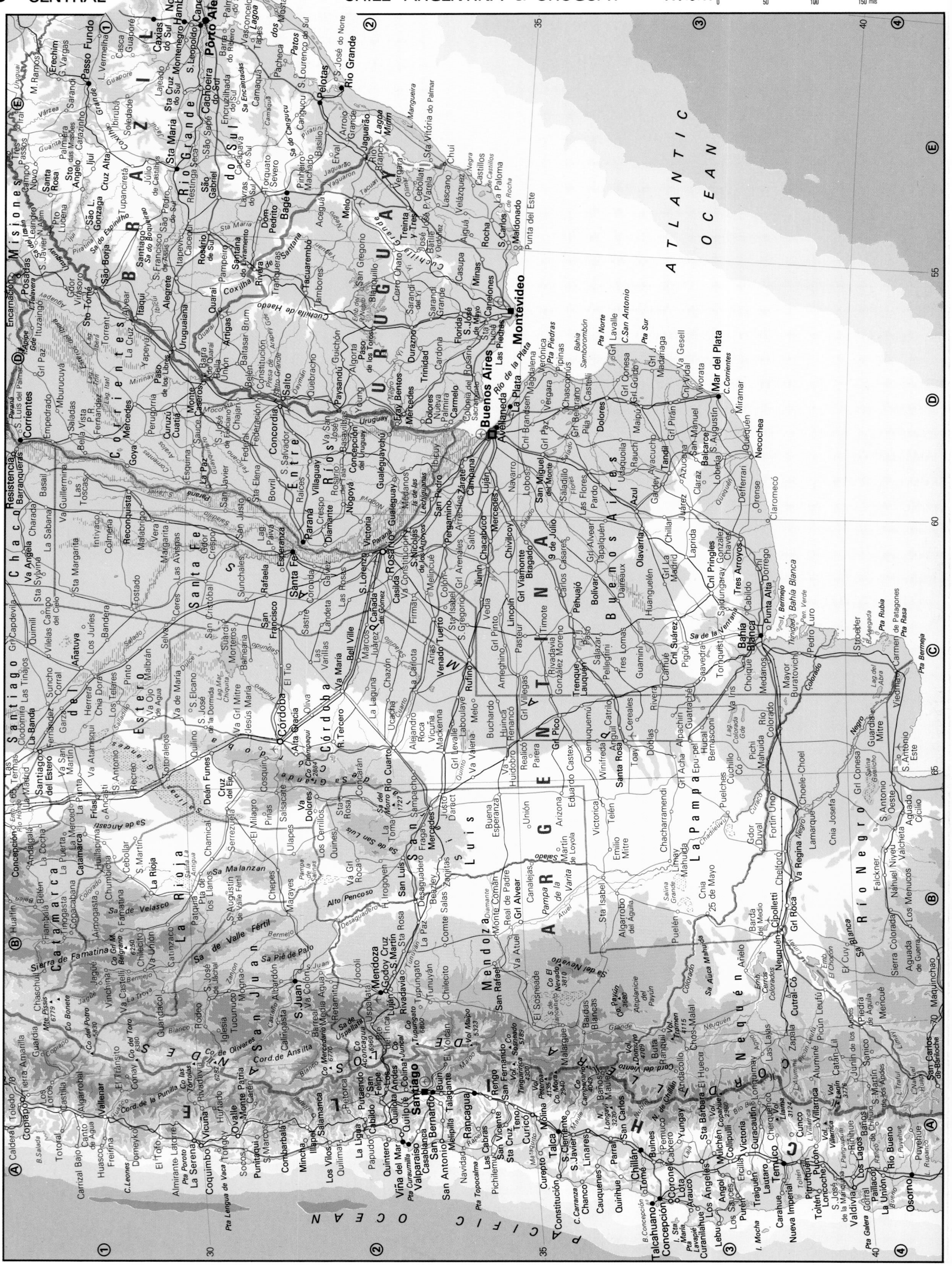

1:7.5M

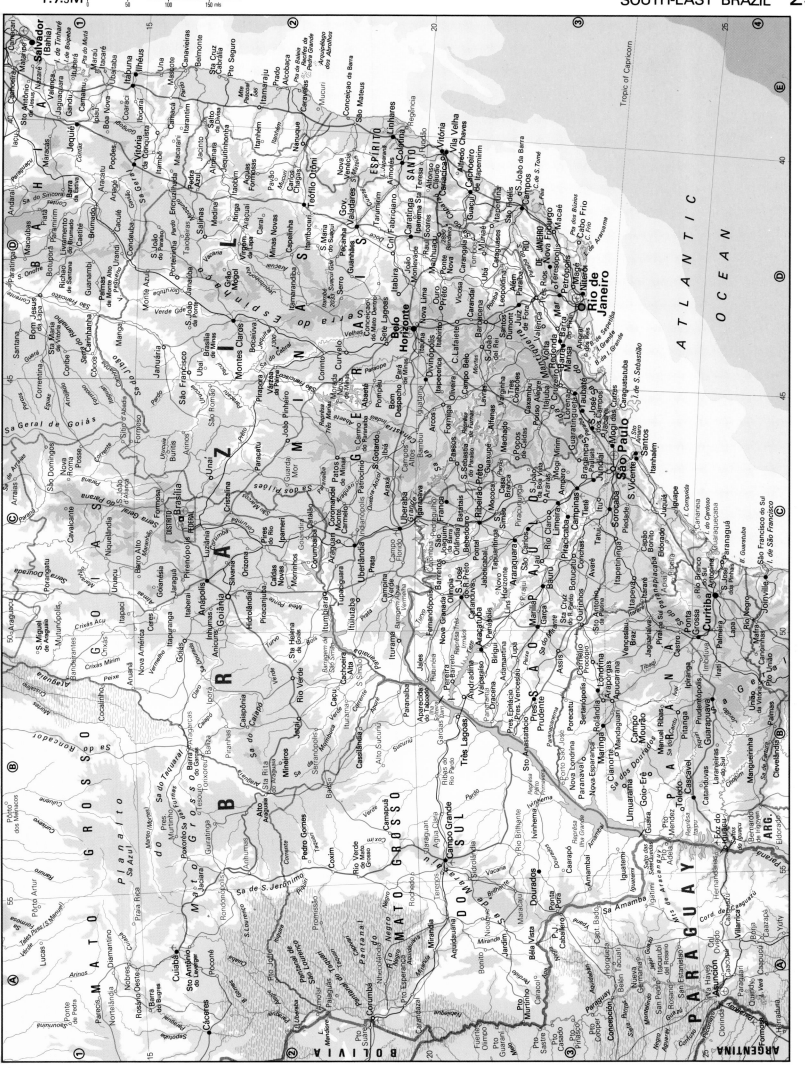

1:15M

200 400 600 km
0 100 200 300 mls

A 40 B 2 30 C 20 D 10 E 0 F 10 G

Greenland (Den.)
Kap Farvel

Jan Mayen (Nor.)

ARCTIC

Reykjavik

ICELAND

Arctic Circle

NORWEGIAN

SEA

Vesterålen
Lofoten
Narvik

NORWAY

SWEDEN

Trondheim

Sundsvall

Færøerne (Den.)

Shetland

Bergen
Stavanger
Oslo

Vänern

Stockholm

Orkney

Göteborg
Jönköping

Gotland

Ålborg

Öland

3

ATLANTIC

OCEAN

50

UNITED KINGDOM
OF GREAT BRITAIN AND
NORTHERN IRELAND

Aberdeen

Glasgow
Edinburgh

NORTH

SEA

DENMARK
København
Malmö

Bornholm

Baltic

Rostock

Gdańsk

Belfast

IRELAND

Newcastle

Liverpool
Manchester

Hamburg

Poznań

Dublin

Cork

Birmingham

GERMANY

Berlin

POL

Cardiff

Amsterdam
's-Gravenhage
Rotterdam

Hannover

4

40

Bristol

London

NETHERLANDS

Essen

Leipzig

Dresden

Wrocław

English Channel

Bruxelles

Lille

BELGIUM

Köln
Bonn
Frankfurt

Praha

CZECH
REPUBLIC

Brno

Le Havre
Rouen

LUXEMBOURG

Nürnberg

SLO

Seine

Paris

Strasbourg

Stuttgart

Wien

Nantes
Tours

Loire

München

Bratislava

HUNG

FRANCE

Bern
Genève

Zurich

Salzburg

AUSTRIA

Graz

La Coruña

Bay of
Biscay

Clermont-
Ferrand

SWITZERLAND

LIECHTENSTEIN

Ljubljana

SLOVENIA

Bordeaux

Lyon

Torino

Milano

Trieste

Zagreb

CROATIA

Porto

Bilbao

Rhône

Venezia

PORTUGAL

Valladolid

Toulouse

Genova

ADRIATIC

BOSNIA-
HERZEGOVINA

Ebro

ANDORRA

Marseille

MONACO

Firenze

SAN
MARINO

Split

Sarajevo

SPAIN

Madrid

Zaragoza

Lisboa

Tajo

Toledo

Barcelona

Bastia

Corse

ITALY

SEA

5

Faro

Sevilla

Valencia

Balearic Islands

Menorca

Sardegna

Olbia

Ajaccio

Roma

Madeira
(Port.)

Málaga

Murcia

Ibiza

Mallorca

TYRRHENIAN

SEA

Napoli

Taranto

Tanger

Gibraltar (U.K.)
Ceuta (Sp.)

Cagliari

Islas Canarias
(Sp.)

MEDITERRANEAN

Palermo

Messina

Reggio di Calabria

Casablanca

Rabat

Melilla
(Sp.)

Oran

Alger

SEA

Sicilia

30

MOROCCO

ALGERIA

Tunis

MALTA

Marrakech

TUNISIA

D 10 E F 10 G

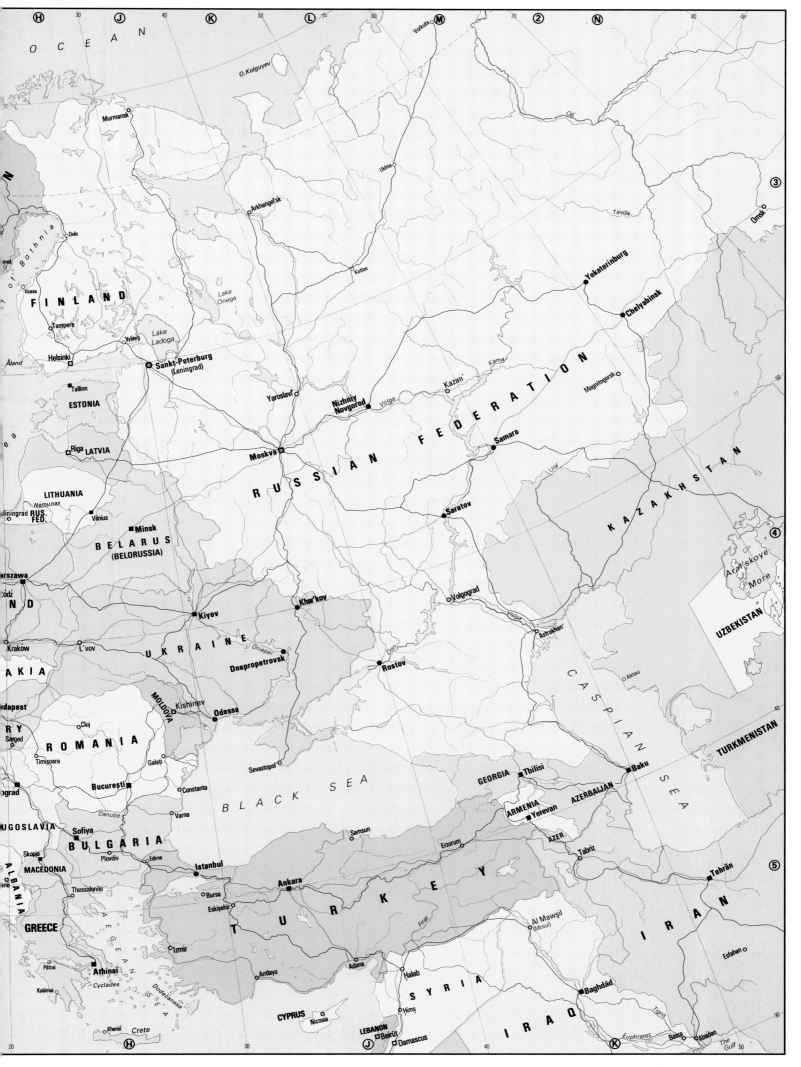

100   200   300 km
50   100   150 mls

Inset — ICELAND (at the same scale)

Bolungarvík, Ísafjörður, Drangajökull, Siglufjörður, Ólafsfjörður, Grímsey, Bakkaflói, Húsavík, Dalvík, Akureyri, Njarðvík, Sauðárkrókur, Blönduós, Seyðisfjörður, Neskaupstaður, Eskifjörður, Biargtangar, Húnaflói, Glama 845, Hofsjökull, Snæfell 1833, ICELAND, Stykkishólmur, Breiðafjörður, Langjökull, Tungnafellsjökull, Óðáðahraun, Faxaflói, Akranes, Reykjavík, Kópavogur, Hafnarfjörður, Selfoss, Þórsá, Ölfusá, Vatnajökull, Öræfajökull 2119, Grindavík, Keflavík, Vestmannaeyjar, Myrdalsjökull, Ingólfshöfði, Surtsey

Inset — Føroyar (Den.) (at the same scale 7W)
Streymoy, Vágar, Tórshavn, Sandoy, Suðuroy

ARCTIC OCEAN
NORWEGIAN SEA
BARENTS SEA
BALTIC SEA
North Sea

NORWAY: Nordkapp, Honningsvåg, Hammerfest, Vardø, Tromsø, Narvik, Bodø, Trondheim, Bergen, Stavanger, Kristiansand, Oslo, Drammen, Lillehammer, Ålesund, Molde, Kristiansund, Lofoten, Vesterålen

SWEDEN: Kiruna, Gällivare, Luleå, Skellefteå, Umeå, Östersund, Sundsvall, Gävle, Uppsala, Stockholm, Västerås, Örebro, Norrköping, Linköping, Jönköping, Göteborg, Borås, Malmö, Helsingborg, Kalmar, Karlskrona, Gotland, Öland

FINLAND: Helsinki (Helsingfors), Turku, Tampere, Oulu, Vaasa, Pori, Jyväskylä, Kuopio, Joensuu, Lappeenranta, Kotka, Rovaniemi, Kemi, Kajaani

DENMARK: København, Ålborg, Århus, Odense, Esbjerg, Kolding, Vejle, Randers

RUSSIAN FEDERATION: Murmansk, Sankt-Peterburg (Leningrad), Novgorod, Pskov, Kaliningrad, Polyarnyy, Monchegorsk, Apatity, Kandalaksha, Vyborg

ESTONIA: Tallinn, Tartu, Pärnu, Narva, Kuressaare

LATVIA: Riga, Jūrmala, Liepāja, Ventspils, Daugavpils

LITHUANIA: Vilnius, Kaunas, Klaipėda, Šiauliai, Panevėžys

BELARUS (BELORUSSIA): Minsk, Borisov, Bobruisk

POLAND: Warszawa, Gdańsk, Gdynia, Szczecin, Bydgoszcz, Poznań, Toruń, Białystok, Olsztyn, Koszalin, Słupsk

GERMANY: Berlin, Hamburg, Bremen, Hannover, Lübeck, Rostock, Kiel, Schwerin, Oldenburg, Bremerhaven, Wilhelmshaven, Braunschweig, Osnabrück

Gulf of Bothnia, Gulf of Finland, Gulf of Riga, Gulf of Gdańsk, Skagerrak, Kattegat, Arctic Circle, Bornholm (Den.), Lake Ladoga, Lake Peipus

Halti 1328, Kebnekaise 2111, Sarektjåkka 2090, Glittertind 2470, Snøhetta 2286, Galdhøpiggen

1:5M

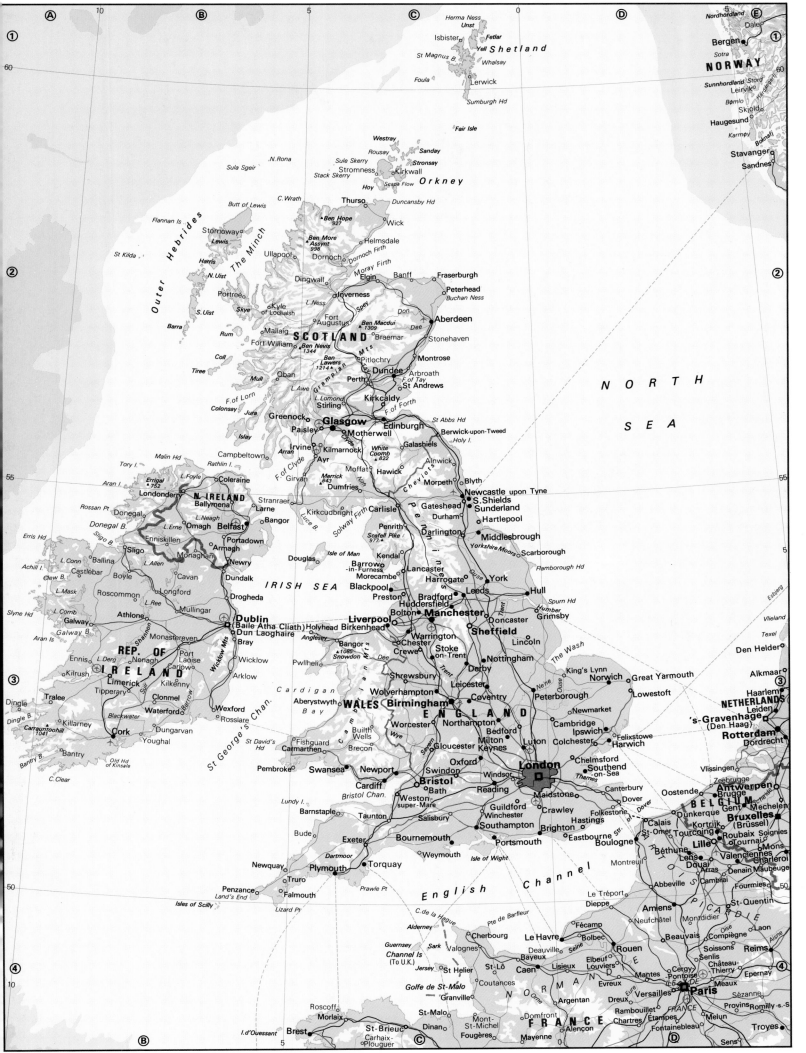

1:2.5M

25   50   75   100 km
25   50 mls

at the same scale

Shetland

Herma Ness · Unst · Fetlar · Yell · Whalsay · Muckle Roe · Brae · Magnus Bay · Bressay · St Magnus Bay · Hillswick · The Faither · Isbister · Mainland · Lerwick · Scalloway · Papa Stour · Fitful Hd · Sumburgh Hd · Gruthess · Fair Isle · Foula

Tórshavn-Seyðisfjörður
Harstad-Bergen
Aberdeen
Bergen · Stavanger
Stromness
Strannraer

N O R T H   S E A

Norway · U.K. · Edda · Nor. Gas · Albuskjell · Duncan · Argyll · Cod · Josephine · Clyde · Fulmar · Auk · Lomond · Montrose · S.E. Forties · Forties · Long Forties · Buchan · Devil's Hole · Piper · Tartan · Petronella · Claymore · Scapa · Highlander · Beatrice

Buchan Deep · Little Halibut Bank · Net. Gas · Net. Gas

O r k n e y

N. Ronaldsay · Sanday · Stronsay · Eday · Shapinsay · Westray · Papa Westray · Rousay · Kirkwall · Hoy · Mainland · Stromness · Pentland Firth · S. Ronaldsay · Dunnet Hd · Duncansby Hd

Lerwick · Tórshavn · Oil

S C O T L A N D

C. Wrath · Durness · Tongue · Ben Hope 927 · Ben Loyal · Ben Klibreck 961 · Stack Skerry · Sule Skerry · Strathy Pt · Thurso · John o' Groats · Wick · Lybster · Helmsdale · Brora · Dornoch Firth · Lairg · L. Shin · Ben More Assynt 998 · Edrachillis Bay · Enard Bay · Ullapool · Lochinver · Dingwall · Ben Wyvis 1045 · Ben Dearg 1081 · Alness · Tain · Black Isle · Cromarty · Dornoch · Loch Broom · Gairloch · L. Maree · L. Torridon · Rhassa · Applecross · Kyle of Lochalsh · Fort Augustus · Loch Ness · Inverness · Nairn · Forres · Elgin · Lossiemouth · Buckie · Keith · Dufftown · Huntly · Banff · Macduff · Fraserburgh · Peterhead · Buchan Ness · Kinnairds Hd · Girdle Ness · Aberdeen · Stonehaven · Montrose

G r a m p i a n · **H i g h l a n d** · **T a y s i d e** · **C e n t r a l** · **F i f e** · **L o t h i a n** · **B o r d e r s** · **S t r a t h c l y d e** · **Dumfries and Galloway**

Monadhliath Mts · Kingussie · Aviemore · Cairngorms · Grantown-on-Spey · Ballater · Braemar · Ben Macdui 1310 · Ben Attow 1031 · Ben Nevis 1344 · Fort William · Glencoe · Rannoch · L. Rannoch · L. Ericht · L. Laggan · L. Treig · Blair Atholl · Pitlochry · Blairgowrie · Aberfeldy · L. Tay · Crieff · Comrie · Callander · Perth · Dundee · Cupar · St Andrews · Glenrothes · Methil · Kirkcaldy · Dunfermline · Firth of Forth · Edinburgh · Livingston · Falkirk · Stirling · Coatbridge · Motherwell · Hamilton · Glasgow · Paisley · Dumbarton · Greenock · Gourock · Helensburgh · Arrochar · Inveraray · Oban · Lorn · L. Awe · L. Etive · L. Linnhe · Sound of Mull · Tobermory · Mull · Iona · Staffa · Colonsay · Jura · Islay · Port Askaig · Port Ellen · Mull of Oa · Gigha · Kintyre · Campbeltown · Mull of Kintyre · Firth of Clyde · Kilmarnock · Irvine · Troon · Prestwick · Ayr · Maybole · Girvan · Ballantrae · Stranraer · Corsewall Pt · Newton Stewart · Wigtown · Merrick 843 · Kells Ra. · New Galloway · Dumfries · Castle Douglas · Kirkcudbright · Thornhill · Sanquhar · Cumnock · Lanark · Peebles · Galashiels · Selkirk · Hawick · Jedburgh · Kelso · Duns · Berwick-upon-Tweed · St Abb's Hd · Eyemouth · Haddington · North Berwick · Dunbar

Cheviot Hills · The Cheviot 816 · Northumberland · Morpeth · Alnwick · Bamburgh · Holy I. · Farne Deep · Blyth · Tynemouth · Newcastle upon Tyne · Gateshead · Sth Shields · Tyne and Wear · Sunderland · Hexham · Haltwhistle · Carlisle · Lockerbie · Moffat · Annan · Gretna · Maryport · Solway Firth

W e s t e r n   I s l e s · **O u t e r   H e b r i d e s**

Butt of Lewis · Port of Ness · Lewis · Stornoway · Carloway · Loch Roag · Tarbert · Harris · Taransay · Sd. of Harris · North Uist · Benbecula · Monach Is. · South Uist · Lochboisdale · Barra · Castlebay · Barra Hd · St Kilda · Flannan Is · N. Rona · Sula Sgeir

Isle of Skye · Portree · Cuillin Hills · L. Snizort · Uig · Rubha Hunish · Raasay · Sd. of Raasay · Broadford · Kyleakin · Sleat · Canna · Rum · Eigg · Muck · Coll · Tiree · Ardnamurchan Pt · Morvern · Lochaline

North Minch · Little Minch · The Minch

NORTHERN IRELAND · **Londonderry** · **Antrim** · **Tyrone** · Coleraine · Portrush · Ballycastle · Ballymoney · Ballymena · Limavady · Strabane · Magherafelt · Cookstown · Omagh · Larne · Antrim Hills · Sperrin Mts · Belfast · Rathlin I. · Fair Hd · Torr Hd

Donegal · Letterkenny · L. Swilly · Malin Hd · Inishowen · Errigal Mts · Blue Stack Mts 676 · Sheep Haven · Buncrana

North Channel · Firth of Clyde · Arran · Brodick · Ardrossan · Holy I. · Sd. of Bute · Bute · Rothesay · Cowal · L. Fyne · Tarbert · Ardrishaig · Sd. of Jura · Scarba

Stanton Banks · Dogger Bank · Edbjerg-Göteborg

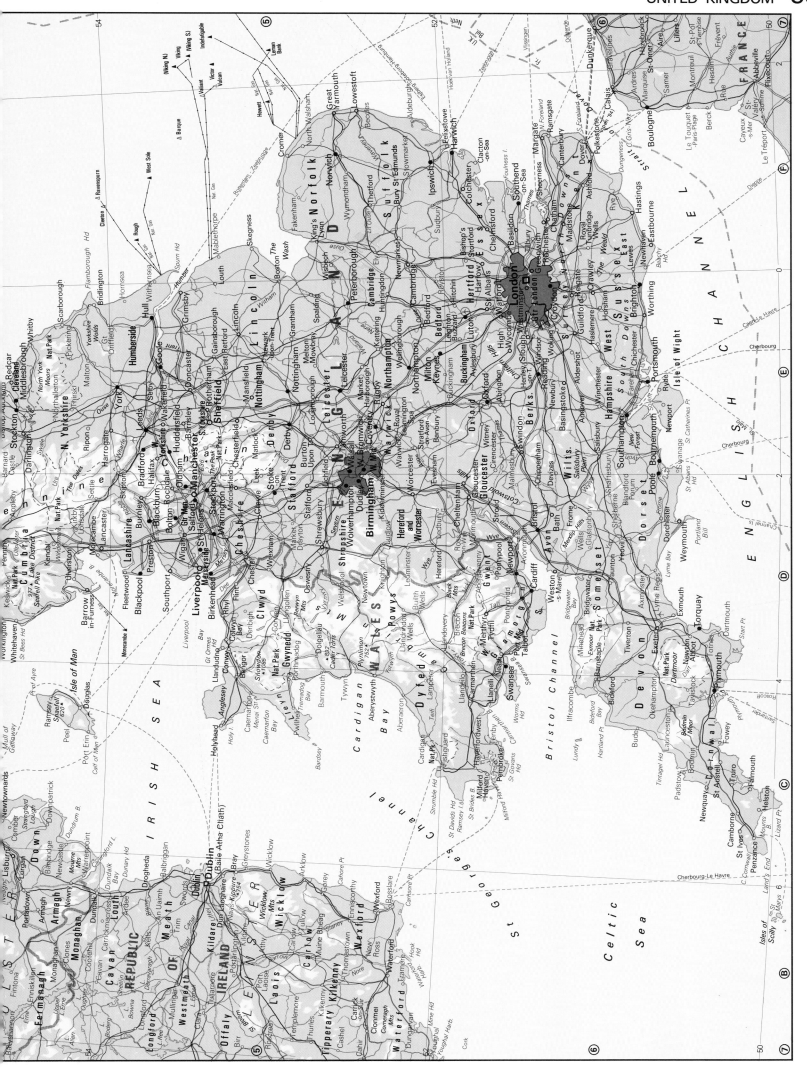

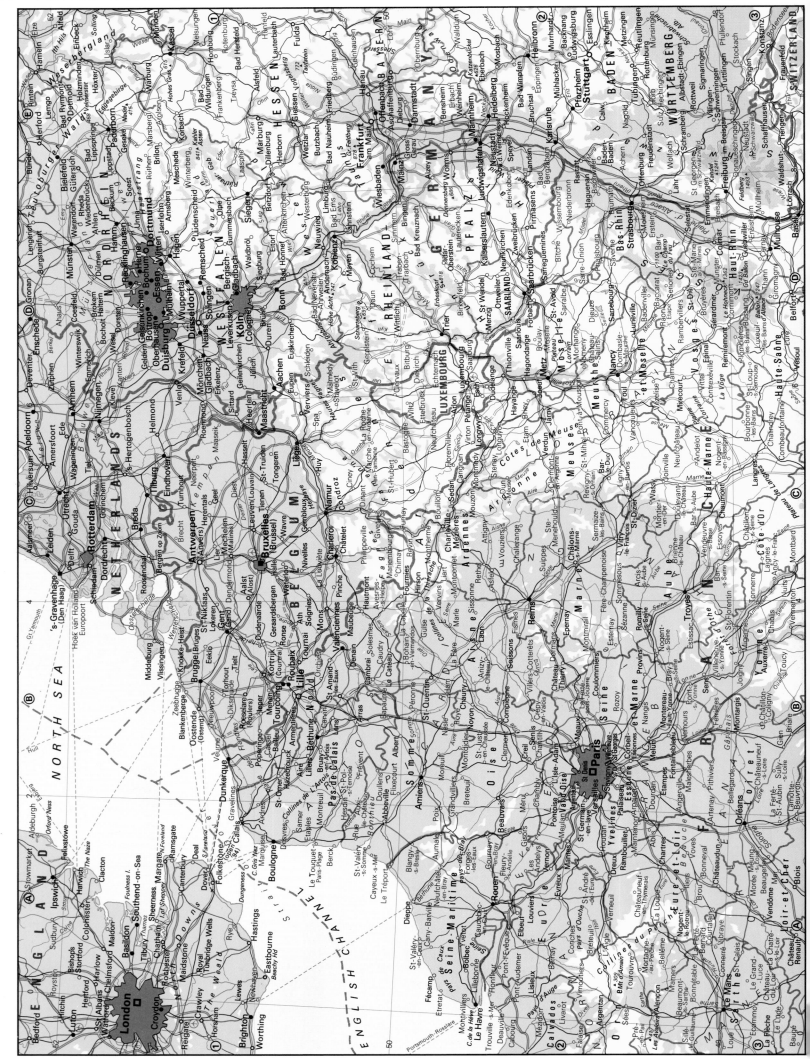

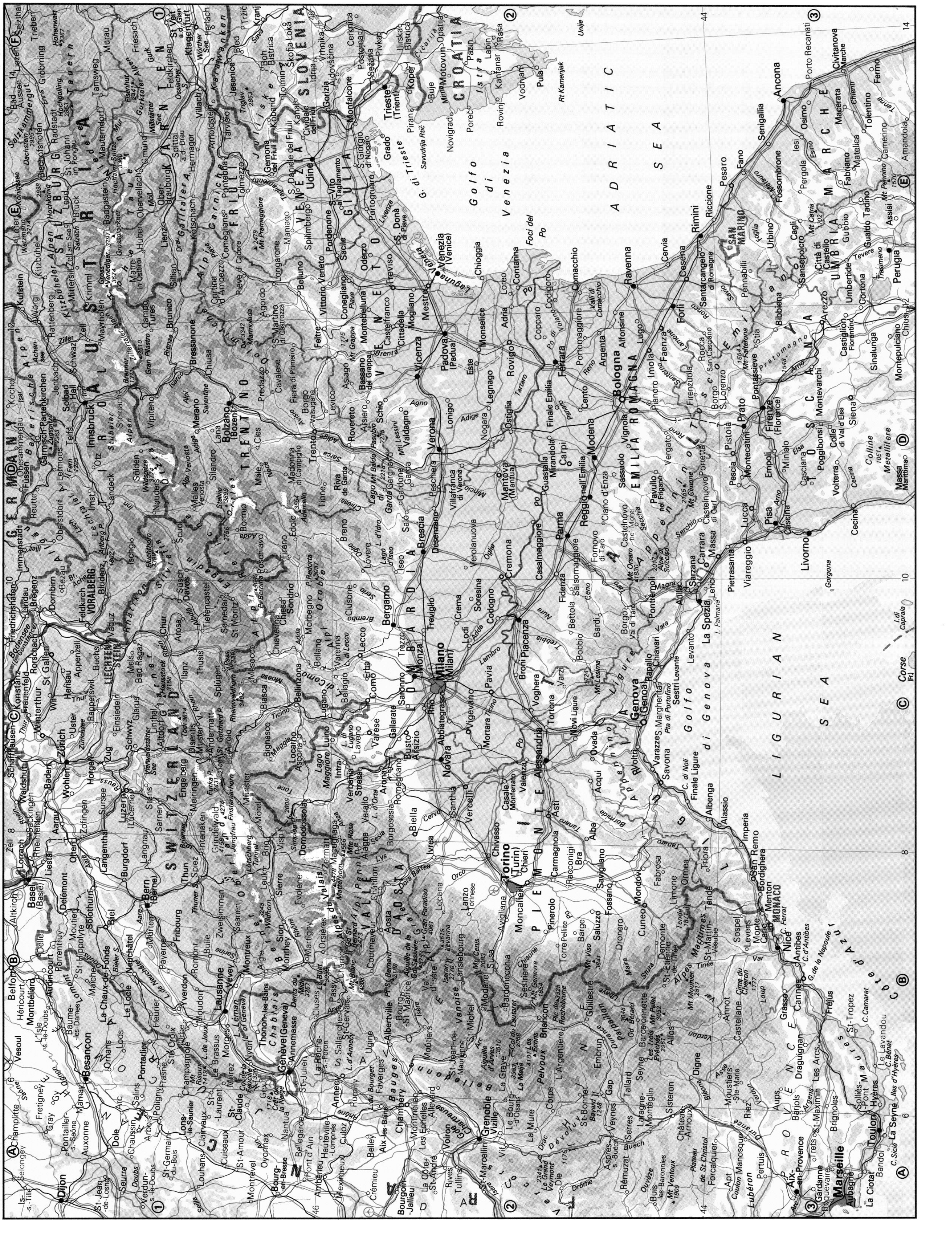

1:2.5M

0 25 50 75 100 km
25 50 mls

GERMANY

AUSTRIA

SWITZERLAND

SLOVENIA

CROATIA

ADRIATIC SEA

LIGURIAN SEA

Golfo di Venezia

Golfo di Genova

KÄRNTEN

SALZBURG

TIROL

VORALBERG

LIECHTENSTEIN

FRIULI

VENEZIA GIULIA

VENETO

TRENTINO

LOMBARDIA

PIEMONTE

VALLE D'AOSTA

EMILIA ROMAGNA

TOSCANA

UMBRIA

MARCHE

SAN MARINO

MONACO

PROVENCE

Côte d'Azur

Corse (Fr)

Milano (Milan)

Torino (Turin)

Genova (Genoa)

Venezia (Venice)

Bologna

Trieste (Trient)

Innsbruck

Bern (Berne)

Basel (Basle)

Zürich

Genève (Geneva)

Lausanne

Marseille

Toulon

Grenoble

Besançon

Dijon

Bern

Padova (Padua)

Verona

Brescia

Bergamo

Parma

Modena

Ferrara

Ravenna

Rimini

Ancona

Perugia

Firenze (Florence)

Pisa

Livorno

La Spezia

Nice

Cannes

1:5M

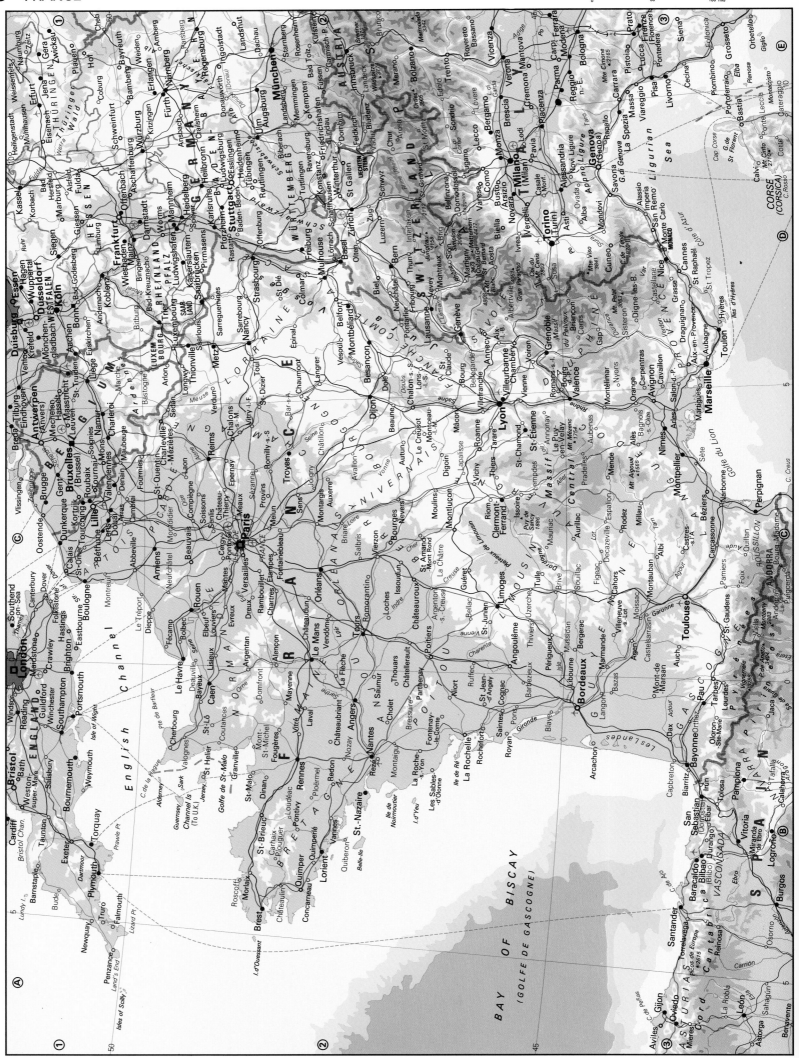

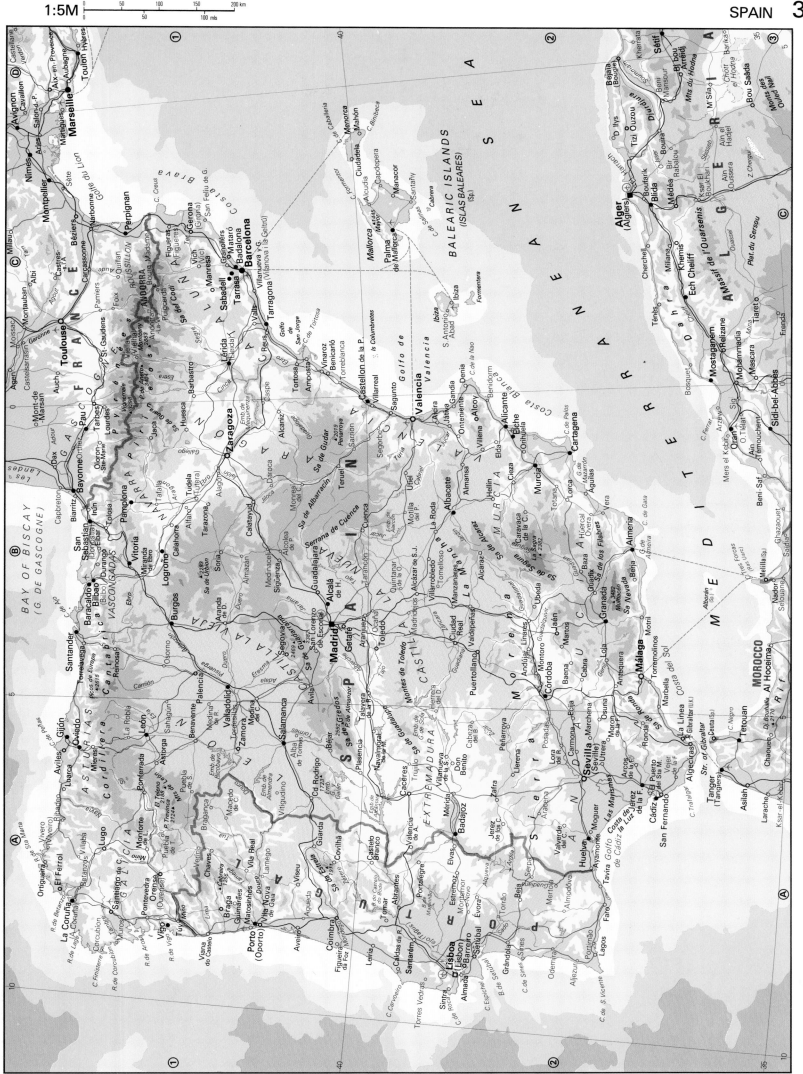

1:5M

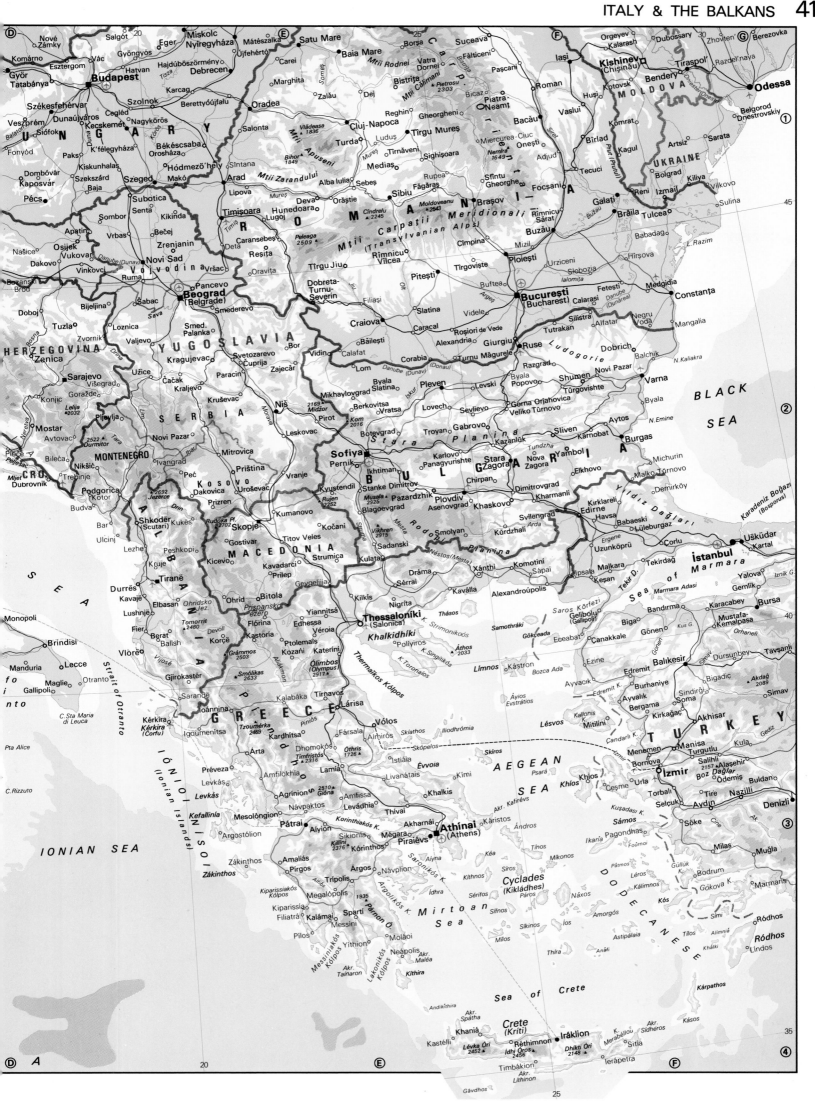

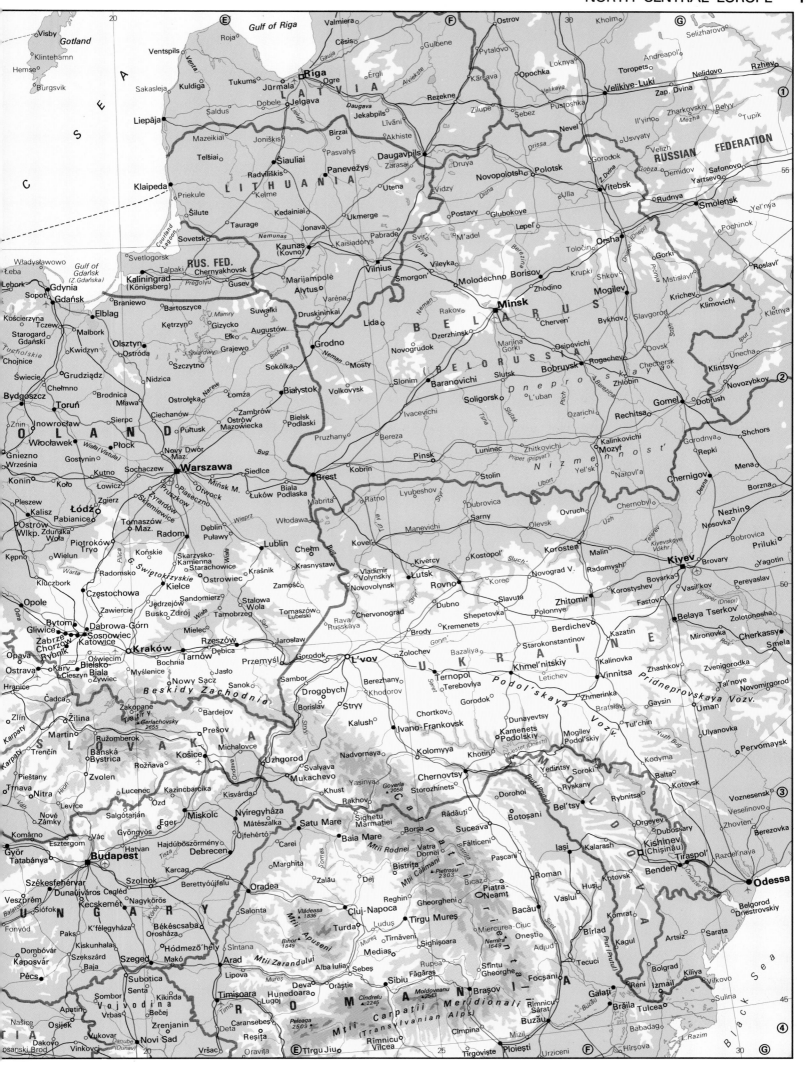

1:10M

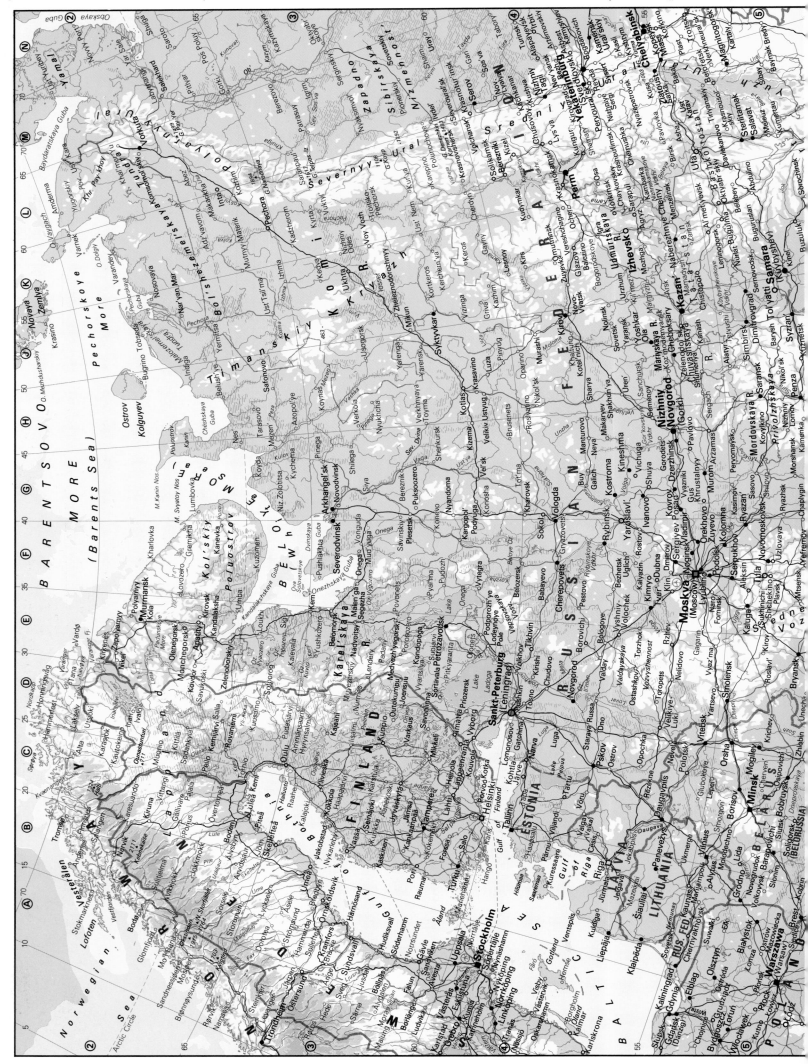

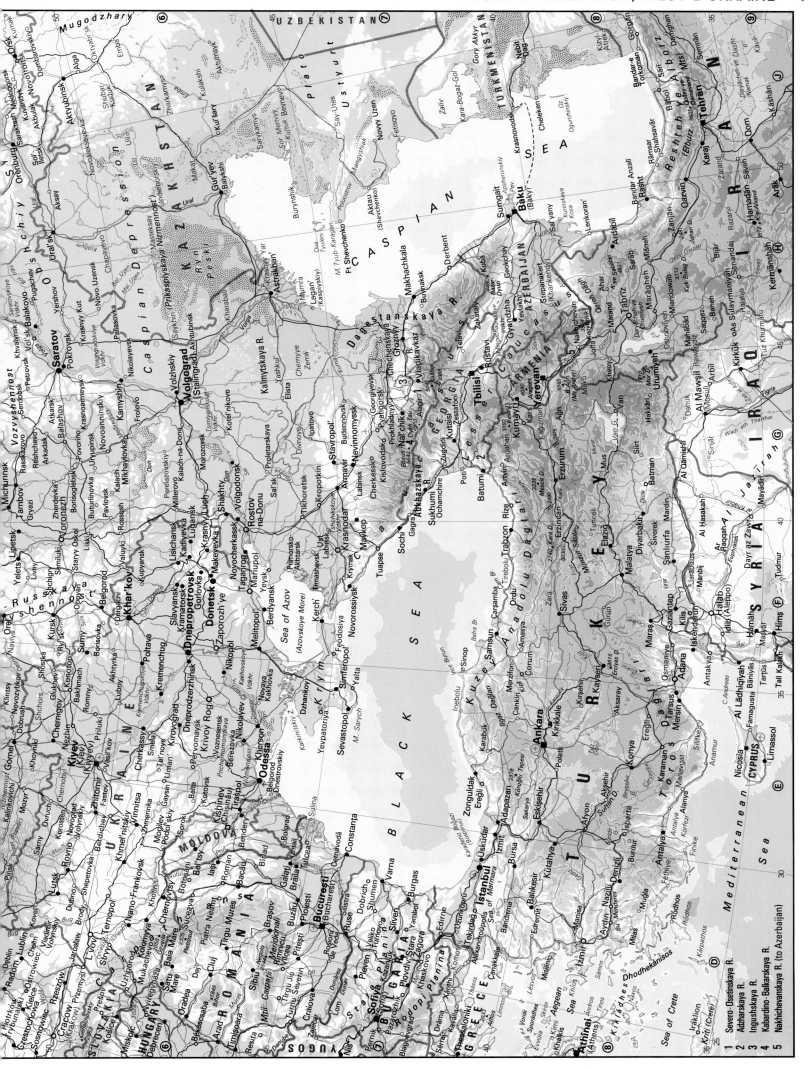

400 800 1200 1600 km
400 800 mls

ARCTIC OCEAN

ICELAND
Greenland (Den.)
IRELAND
Dublin
London
UNITED KINGDOM
Edinburgh
NETH.
DENMARK
København
NORWAY
Oslo
SWEDEN
Stockholm
FINLAND
Helsinki
Murmansk
Barents Sea
Svalbard (Nor.)
Novaya Zemlya
Franz Josef Land (Zemlya Frantsa Iosifa)
Severnaya Zemlya
Novosibirskiye Ostrova

PORT.
SPAIN
FRANCE
Paris
BEL.
GERMANY
SWITZ.
CZECH REP.
AUSTRIA
SLOV.
Warszawa
POLAND
Tallinn
EST.
LAT.
Riga
LITH.
Vilnius
BELARUS
Minsk
Moskva
Sankt-Peterburg (Leningrad)
Arkhangel'sk
Vorkuta
RUSSIAN FEDERATION
Lena
Yakutsk

ITALY
Roma
Corse (Fr.)
Sardegna
Marseille
CROATIA
BOSNIA HERZ.
YUGOSLAVIA
HUNGARY
SLOVAKIA
ROMANIA
București
MOLD.
UKRAINE
Kiyev
Khar'kov
Odessa
Black Sea
Nizhniy Novgorod
Yekaterinburg
Chelyabinsk
Omsk
Krasnoyarsk
Novosibirsk
Irkutsk

Tunis
ALB.
MAC.
GREECE
Athinai
BULGARIA
İstanbul
TURKEY
Ankara
Adana
CYPRUS
Crete
Sicilia
Samara
Rostov
Astrakhan'
Volga
Caspian Sea
Aral Sea
KAZAKHSTAN
Ulaanbaatar
MONGOLIA
INNER MONGOLIA
Beijing
Tianjin

LIBYA
Alexandria
Cairo
EGYPT
Aswân
Nile
RED SEA
SUDAN
Khartoum
ERITREA
Asmera
ETHIOPIA
Adis Abeba
LEB.
Beirut
Halab
Damascus
SYRIA
ISRAEL
Jerusalem
JOR.
Amman
Al Mawsil (Mosul)
Baghdad
IRAQ
KUWAIT
Başra
Abâdân
Eşfahân
Tehrân
Tabrîz
GEORGIA
Tbilisi
ARM.
Yerevan
AZER.
Baku
TURKMENISTAN
Ashkhabad
UZBEKISTAN
Mashhad
Herat
Kabul
Kermân
IRAN
AFGHANISTAN
Tashkent
Bishkek
Alma Ata
KYRGYZSTAN (KIRGHIZIA)
TAJIKISTAN
Dushanbe
Ürümqi
SINKIANG
CHINA
Lanzhou
Zhengzhou
Xi'an
Taiyuan
Huang He

SAUDI ARABIA
Makkah
Ar Riyâḍ
BAHRAIN
QATAR
Abu Dhabi
U.A.E.
Muscat
The Gulf
OMAN
YEMEN
San'a
Aden
G. of Aden
DJIBOUTI
Socotra (Yemen)
SOMALIA
Muqdisho
KENYA
Mombasa
Dar es Salaam
TANZANIA

Islamabad
Kashmir
Lahore
PAKISTAN
Indus
Karachi
Hyderâbâd
Delhi
Kânpur
Lucknow
Patna
Ganga
INDIA
Ahmadâbâd
Jabalpur
Nâgpur
Godavari
Bombay
Hyderabad
Krishna
Bangalore
Madras
Madurai
SRI LANKA
Colombo
Kandy
Lakshadweep (Ind.)
MALDIVES
ARABIAN SEA

TIBET
Lhasa
Kathmandu
NEPAL
Thimphu
BHUTAN
Brahmaputra
Imphal
BANGLA-DESH
Dhâkâ
Calcutta
Chittagong
Mandalay
MYANMAR (BURMA)
Irrawaddy
Chiang Mai
Chengdu
Chongqing
Changsha
Guiyang
Kunming
Wuhan
Chang Jiang
Guangzhou
Hanoi
Haiphong
Hainan
Da Nang
Mekong
LAOS
Vientiane
VIETNAM
THAILAND
Bangkok
Yangon (Rangoon)
Moulmein
CAMBODIA
Phnom Penh
Ho Chi Minh (Saigon)
Surat Thani
Bay of Bengal
Andaman Is (Ind.)
Nicobar Is (Ind.)

MOZAMBIQUE
COMOROS
Aldabra Is (Sey.)
SEYCHELLES
MADAGASCAR
Antananarivo
Equator
INDIAN OCEAN
Chagos Arch. (U.K.)
Cocos Is (Aust.)
Christmas I (Aust.)
George Town
Kuala Lumpur
SINGAPORE
MALAYSIA
SUMATERA
Padang
Palembang
Jakarta
Hai Nan
SOUTH

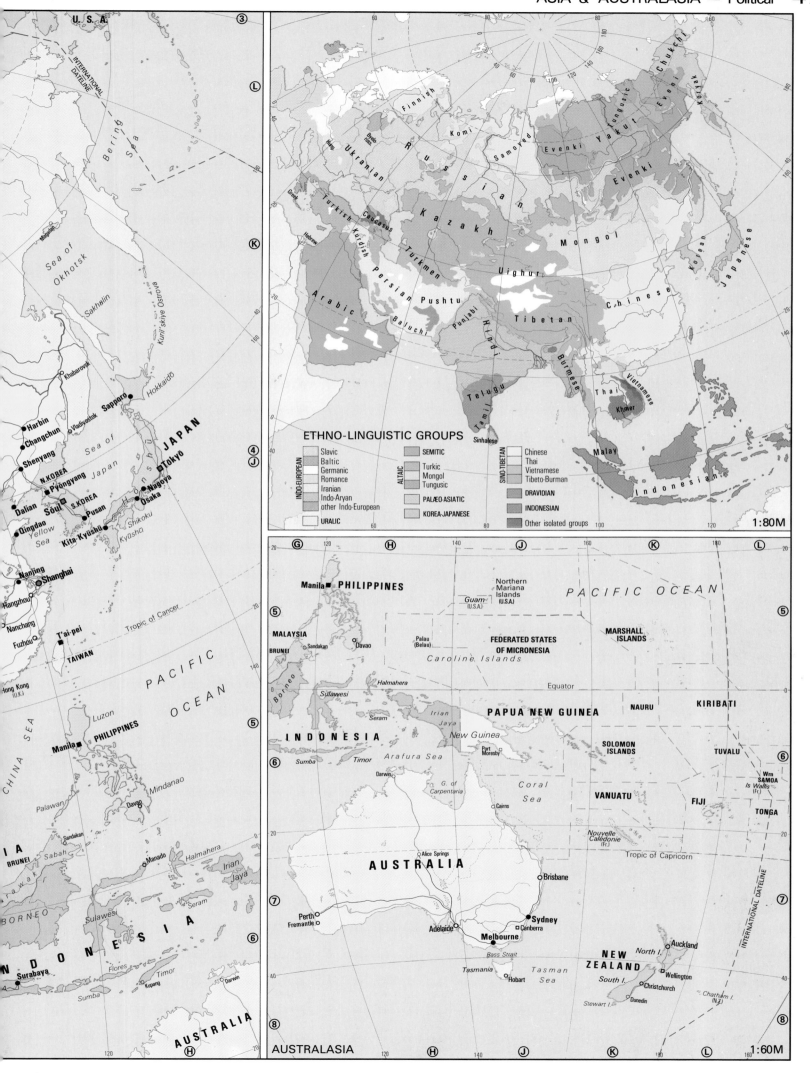

U.S.A.

③

INTERNATIONAL DATELINE

Ⓛ

Bering Sea

Ⓚ

Sea of Okhotsk

Sakhalin

Khabarovsk

Kuril'skiye Ostrova

Hokkaidō

Harbin

Changchun

Sapporo

Vladivostok

Shenyang

JAPAN

Ⓙ

N.KOREA

Pyongyang

Sea of Japan

Nagoya

Tōkyō

Dalian

Sŏul

S.KOREA

Osaka

Honshū

Qingdao

Pusan

Yellow Sea

Kita-Kyūshū

Shikoku

Kyūshū

Nanjing

Shanghai

Hangzhou

Nanchang

Tropic of Cancer

20

T'ai-pei

Fuzhou

140

TAIWAN

Hong Kong (U.K.)

PACIFIC

CHINA SEA

Luzon

OCEAN

⑤

PHILIPPINES

Manila

Mindanao

Palawan

Davao

BRUNEI

Sandakan

Sabah

Manado

Halmahera

SARAWAK

Irian Jaya

BORNEO

Seram

Sulawesi

⑥

INDONESIA

Surabaya

Flores

Timor

Sumba

Kupang

Darwin

120

AUSTRALIA

Ⓗ

ETHNO-LINGUISTIC GROUPS

Finnish

Ukranian

R u s s i a n

Komi

Hung.

Belo. russ.

Samoyed

Evenki

Yakut

Tungusic

Evenki

Chukchi

Koryak

Greek

Turkish

Caucasus

K a z a k h

M o n g o l

Evenki

Hebrew

Kurdish

Turkmen

Uighur

Korean

Japanese

Arabic

P e r s i a n

Pushtu

Chinese

Baluchi

Punjabi

T i b e t a n

Burmese

Thai

Vietnamese

H i n d i

Telugu

Khmer

Tamil

Malay

Sinhalese

I n d o n e s i a n

	INDO-EUROPEAN		ALTAIC		SINO-TIBETAN
	Slavic		SEMITIC		Chinese
	Baltic		Turkic		Thai
	Germanic		Mongol		Vietnamese
	Romance		Tungusic		Tibeto-Burman
	Iranian		PALÆO-ASIATIC		DRAVIDIAN
	Indo-Aryan		KOREA-JAPANESE		INDONESIAN
	other Indo-European				Other isolated groups
	URALIC				

1:80M

Ⓖ 120 Ⓗ 140 Ⓙ 160 Ⓚ 180 Ⓛ 20

Manila ■ **PHILIPPINES**

Northern Mariana Islands (U.S.A.)

PACIFIC OCEAN

⑤

Guam (U.S.A.)

MARSHALL ISLANDS

MALAYSIA

Palau (Belau)

FEDERATED STATES OF MICRONESIA

BRUNEI

Sandakan

Davao

Caroline Islands

Borneo

Sulawesi

Halmahera

Equator

0

Seram

Irian Jaya

PAPUA NEW GUINEA

NAURU

KIRIBATI

I N D O N E S I A

New Guinea

SOLOMON ISLANDS

TUVALU

⑥

Sumba

Timor

Arafura Sea

Port Moresby

Wrn **SAMOA**

Is Wallis (Fr.)

Darwin

G. of Carpentaria

Coral Sea

VANUATU

FIJI

TONGA

Cairns

Nouvelle Calédonie (Fr.)

Tropic of Capricorn

20

Alice Springs

AUSTRALIA

Brisbane

⑦

Perth

Fremantle

Sydney

Canberra

Adelaide

Melbourne

North I.

Auckland

NEW ZEALAND

Wellington

Bass Strait

Tasmania

Tasman Sea

South I.

Christchurch

Hobart

Chatham I. (N.Z.)

Dunedin

Stewart I.

40

⑧

RUSSIAN FEDERATION
1 Ingushskaya R.
2 Chechenskaya R.
3 Severo-Osetinskaya R.
4 Kabardino- Balkarskaya R.
GEORGIA
5 Abkhazskaya R.
6 Adzharskaya R.
AZERBAIJAN
7 Nakhichevanskaya R.

ARCTIC OCEAN

Ostrov Komsomolets
SEVERNAYA ZEMLYA (NORTH LAND)
Ostrov Bol'shevik
O. Oktyabr'skoy Revolyutsii
O. Russkiy
Arkipelag Nordenshelda

NOVOSIBIRSKYE OSTROVA (NEW SIBERIAN ISLANDS)
Ostrova De Longa
O. Bennetta
O. Novaya Sibir'
Ostrov Faddeyevskiy
O. Malyy Lyakhovskiy
O. Bol'shoy Lyakhovskiy
Ostrov Kotel'nyy
O. Bel'kovskiy

LAPTEV SEA
EAST SIBERIAN SEA
CHUKCHI SEA
BERING SEA
SEA OF OKHOTSK
SEA OF JAPAN
YELLOW SEA

Proliv Longa
O. Vrangelya
Medvezh'i Ova
Mys Shmidta
Bering Str.
Mys Shelagskiy
Uelen
Chukotskiy Poluostrov
M. Chaplino
St Lawrence (U.S.A.)
St Matthew (U.S.A.)

RUSSIAN FEDERATION

Gory Byrranga
Poluostrov Taymyr
Gory Putorana
Sredne Sibirskoye Ploskogor'ye

Nordvik
Khatanga
Volochanka
Dudypta
Novorybnoye
Saskylakh
Udzha
Olenek
Zhigansk
Tiksi
Polyarnyy
Chokurdakh
Kazach'ye
Deputatskiy

Khrebet Orulgan
Verkhoyanskiy Khrebet
Khrebet Cherskogo
Kolymskoye Nagor'ye
Koryakskoye Nagor'ye
Sredinnyy Khrebet
KAMCHATKA

Yakutsk
Zhatay
Namtsy
Pokrovsk
Vilyuysk
Verkhnevilyuysk
Nyurba
Suntar
Mirnyy
Lensk
Olekminsk
Aldan
Tommot
Chulman
Stanovoy Khrebet
Aldanskoye Nagor'ye

Magadan
Okhotsk
Petropavlovsk-Kamchatskiy
Ust'-Kamchatsk

SAKHALIN
Yuzhno-Sakhalinsk
Aleksandrovsk-Sakhalinskiy
Okha
Nikolayevsk
Komsomol'sk na-Amure
Kuril'skiye Ostrova (Kuril Islands)

Krasnoyarsk
Achinsk
Kansk
Bratsk
Ust'-Kut
Tulun
Cheremkhovo
Irkutsk
Ulan Ude
Chita
Angarsk
Slyudyanka
Petrovsk
Nerchinsk
Shilka
Skovorodino
Belogorsk
Svobodnyy
Blagoveshchensk
Khabarovsk
Birobidzhan
Vladivostok
Nakhodka
Ussuriysk

HOKKAIDO
Sapporo
Otaru
Muroran
Hakodate
Asahikawa
Wakkanai

HONSHU
JAPAN
Tōkyō
Yokohama
Nagoya
Kyōto
Ōsaka
Kōbe
Hiroshima
Fukuoka
KYUSHU
SHIKOKU
Nagasaki
Kumamoto
Kagoshima
Akita
Sendai
Niigata
Morioka
Aomori
Hirosaki
Yamagata
Fukushima

MONGOLIA
Ulaanbaatar
Darhan
Erdenet
Hovd
Ölgiy
Uliastay
Bayanhongor
Choybalsan
Sühbaatar
Altanbulag

INNER MONGOLIA
Hohhot
Baotou
Erenhot

CHINA
Beijing (Peking)
Tianjin (Tientsin)
Datong
Taiyuan
Baoding
Shijiazhuang
Handan
Anyang
Jinan
Qingdao
Yantai
Zhengzhou
Xuzhou
Xi'an
Linfen
Changzhi
Yan'an
Yinchuan
Yumen
Dunhuang
Hami
Turpan
Lop Nur
Ala Shan
Qilian Shan
Altun Shan
GREAT WALL
GOBI
Ordos

MANCHURIA
Harbin
Changchun
Shenyang
Qiqihar
Jilin
Mudanjiang
Jiamusi
Dalian
Anshan
Fushun
Benxi
Dandong
Jinzhou
Chengde
Zhangjiakou

NORTH KOREA
P'yŏngyang
Hamhŭng
Wŏnsan
Sinŭiju
Ch'ŏngjin

SOUTH KOREA
Sŏul (Seoul)
Inch'ŏn
Taejŏn
Taegu
Pusan
Kwangju
Mokp'o
Cheju Do

1:20M

PHILIPPINES
LUZON
MINDANAO
Manila
Quezon City
FEDERATED STATES OF MICRONESIA
CAROLINE ISLANDS
PAPUA NEW GUINEA
IRIAN JAYA
Port Moresby
Jayapura
MOLUCCAS
CERAM SEA
BANDA SEA
ARAFURA SEA
TIMOR SEA
CELEBES SEA
SULU SEA
SOUTH CHINA SEA
JAVA SEA
FLORES SEA
INDONESIA
BORNEO
SULAWESI
JAWA
SUMATERA
MALAYSIA
SINGAPORE
BRUNEI
THAILAND
CAMBODIA
VIETNAM
Bangkok (Krung Thep)
Ho Chi Minh (Saigon)
Phnom Penh
Yangon (Rangoon)
Jakarta
Surabaya
Bandung
Kuala Lumpur
Medan
Palembang
Ujung Pandang (Makassar)
Manado
Ambon
Darwin
AUSTRALIA
INDIAN OCEAN
Equator
Gulf of Carpentaria
Great Barrier Reef
Cape York Peninsula
Arnhem Land
Kimberley Plateau
TIMOR
Kupang
Dili
Cairns
Davao
Zamboanga
Cebu
Palau
Guam
Hainan
Andaman Sea
Isthmus of Kra
Gulf of Thailand
Makassar Str.
Molucca Sea
Halmahera
Seram
Buru
Flores
Sumba
Sumbawa
Lombok
Bali
Madura
Bangka
Belitung
Mindoro
Palawan
Samar
Leyte
Negros
Panay
Mentawai
Nias
Siberut
Christmas I. (Aust.)
Cocos Is (Aust.)
Torres Strait
Gulf of Papua
Coral Sea
Mariana Islands
Manus
100
110
120
130
140

1:10M

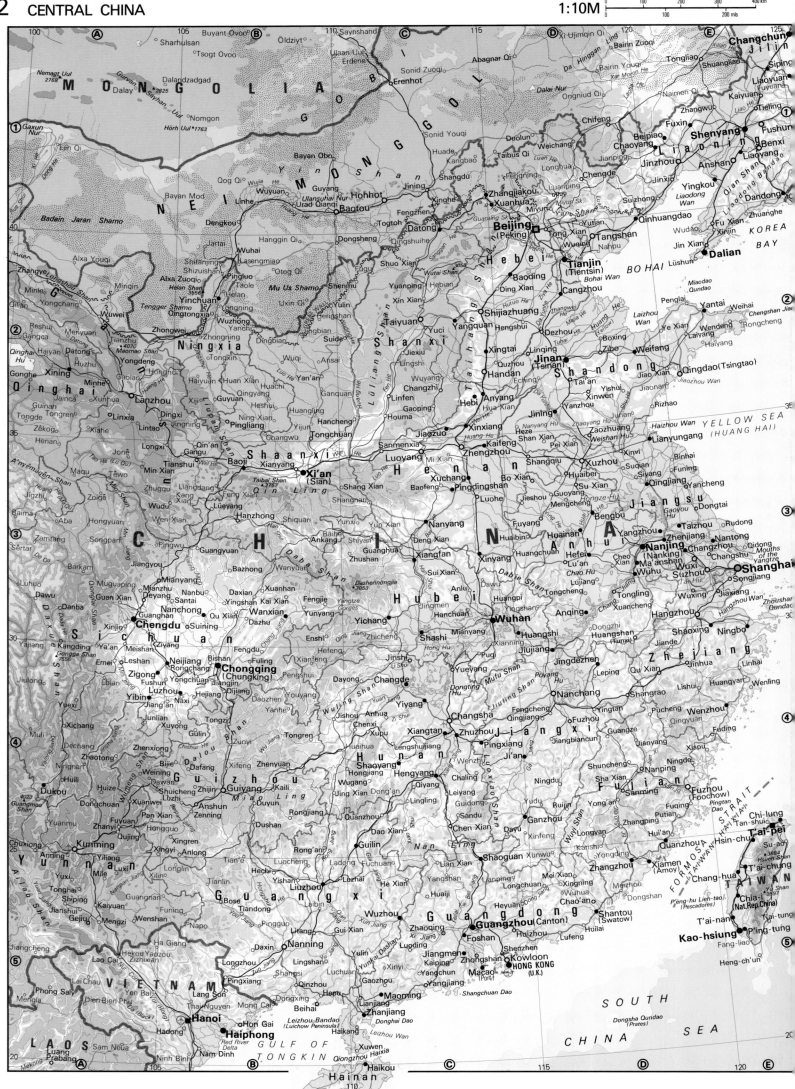

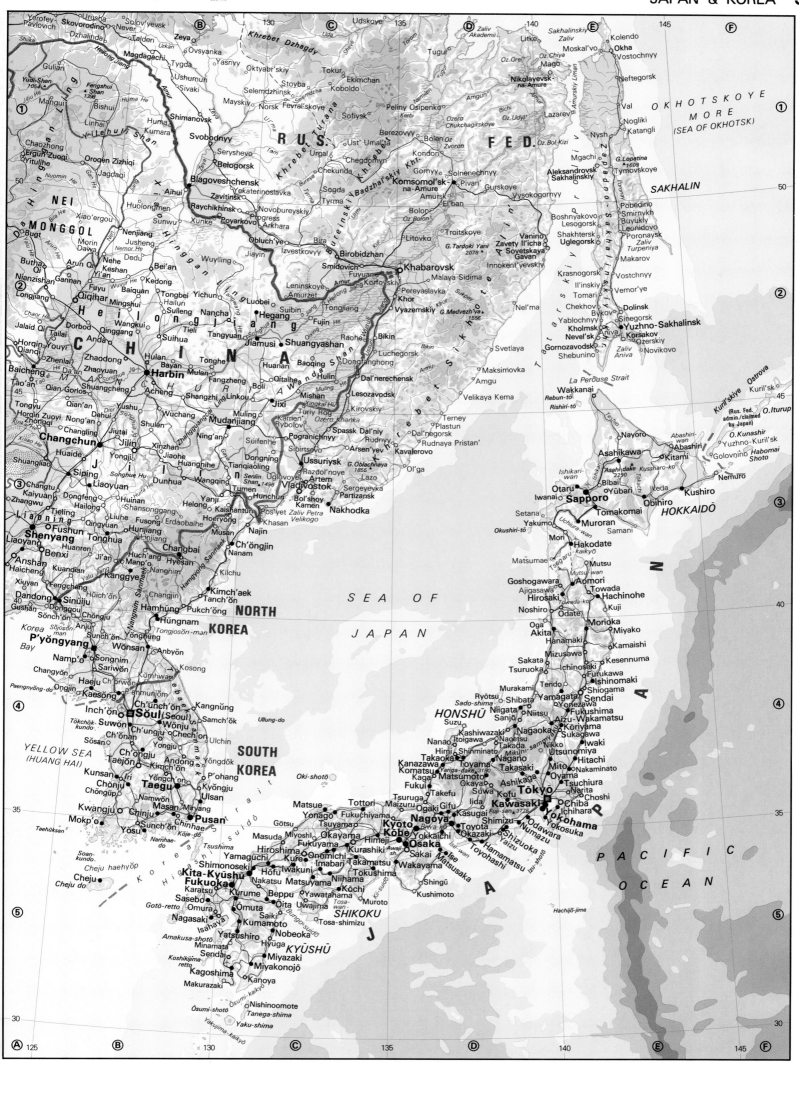

1:5M

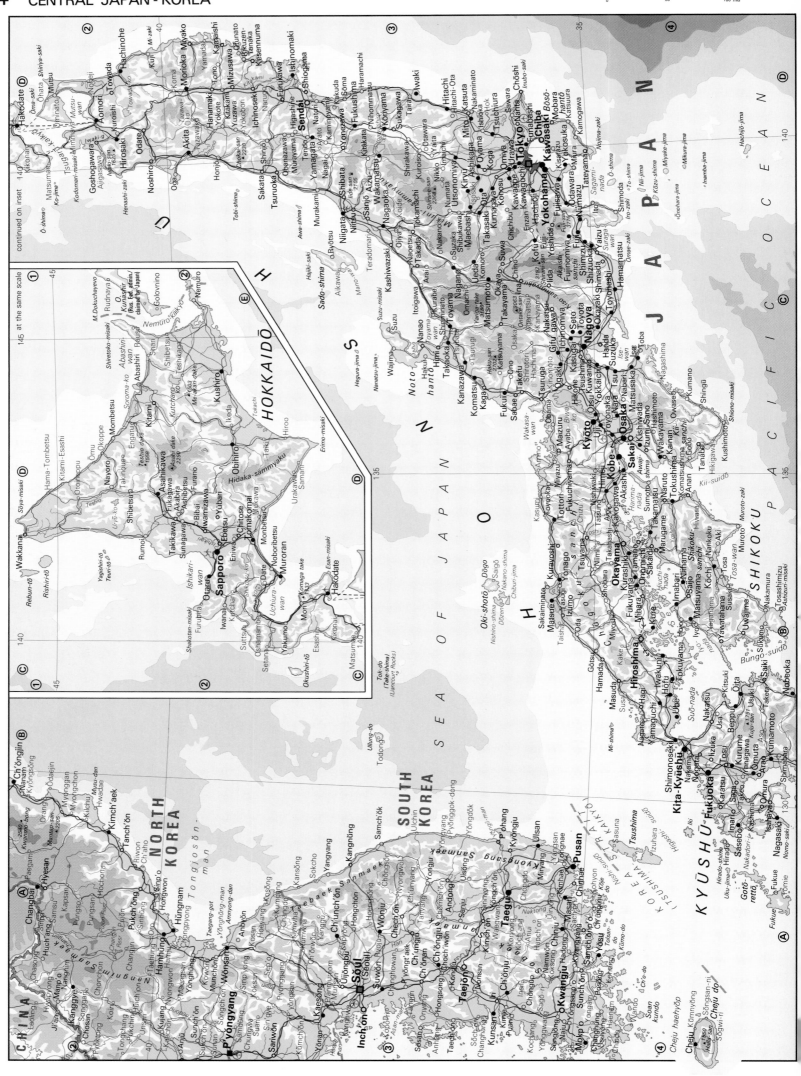

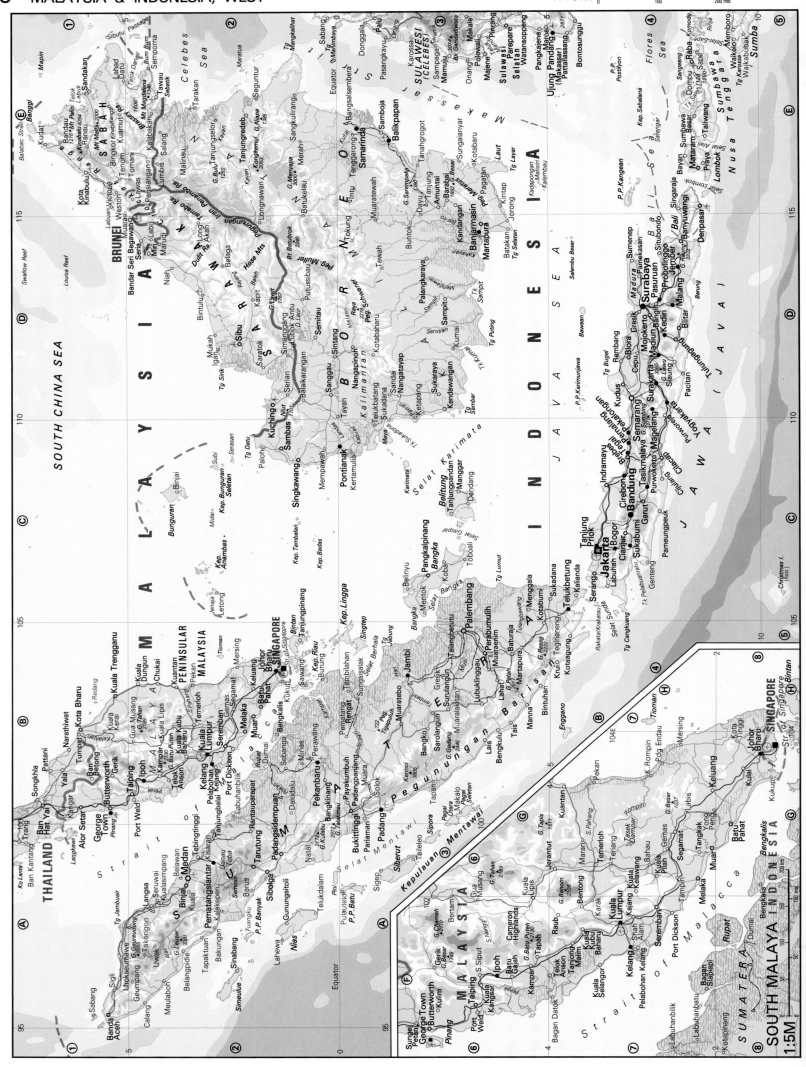

200 400 600 800 km
200 400 mils

Seas & Water Bodies: BLACK SEA, MEDITERRANEAN SEA, CASPIAN SEA, ARABIAN SEA, Aral Sea (Aral'skoye More), Sea of Marmara, Aegean Sea, The Gulf, Gulf of Oman, Gulf of Aden, L. Nasser, Lake Victoria, L. Tana, L. Rudolf, L. Turkana, L. Albert, L. Kyoga

Countries: ROMANIA, MOLDOVA, YUGOSLAVIA, BULGARIA, MACEDONIA, GREECE, TURKEY, CYPRUS, SYRIA, LEBANON, ISRAEL, JORDAN, IRAQ, IRAN, SAUDI ARABIA, KUWAIT, BAHRAIN, QATAR, UNITED ARAB EMIRATES, OMAN, YEMEN, EGYPT, LIBYA, SUDAN, ERITREA, ETHIOPIA, DJIBOUTI, SOMALIA, KENYA, UGANDA, TANZANIA, RWANDA, BURUNDI, ZAIRE, RUS. FED., GEORGIA, ARMENIA, AZERBAIJAN, TURKMENISTAN, UZBEKISTAN, KAZAKHSTAN, AFGHANISTAN, PAKISTAN, INDIA

Cities & Towns:
Beograd, Split, Sarajevo, Dubrovnik, Skopje, Sofiya, Tiranë, Thessaloniki, Plovdiv, Burgas, Varna, Edirne, Istanbul, Bursa, Eskişehir, Ankara, Konya, Kayseri, Sivas, Erzurum, İzmir, Denizli, Antalya, Adana, Gaziantep, Diyarbakir, Van, Athínai, Pátrai, Kalamai, Ródhos, Kríti

Odessa, Nikolayev, Mariupolo, Melitopol, Zaporozh'ye, Donetsk, Rostov-na-Donu, Taganrog, Shakhty, Volgograd, Astrakhan', Gur'yev, Krasnodar, Novorossiysk, Sochi, Maykop, Stavropol', Groznyy, Makhachkala, Sukhumi, Batumi, Kutaisi, Tbilisi, Yerevan, Kumayri, Gyandzha, Baku (Baky), Nakhichevan, Lenkoran', Rasht, Ardabil, Tabriz

Halab, Al Lādhiqīyah, Hamāh, Hims, Beirut, Damascus, Dar'ā, Amman, Jerusalem, Tel Aviv, Haifa, Nicosia, Famagusta, Al Mawsil (Mosul), Al Hasakah, Dayr az Zawr, Arbil, As Sulaymānīyah, Kirkūk, Zanjān, Qazvin, Tehrān, Hamadān, Kermānshāh, Khorramābād, Arāk, Qom, Kāshān, Esfahān, Yazd, Mashhad, Herat, Kandahar

Baghdad, Karbalā', An Najaf, Ad Diwāniyah, Al Amārah, Basra, Kuwait, Abādān, Ahvāz, Dezful, Shiraz, Kermān, Zāhedān, Bandar 'Abbas, Dubai, Abū Dhabi, Doha, Manāmah, Al Hufūf, Ar Riyāḍ, Buraydah, Dhahran, Bushehr, Muscat

Alexandria, Cairo, Tanta, Port Said, Ismā'īlīya, Suez, El Faiyûm, Beni Suef, El Minya, Asyût, El Khârga, Luxor, Aswân, Hurghada, Wadi Halfa, Port Sudan, Medina, Jiddah, Makkah, Aţ Ţā'if, Yanbu' al Bahr, Tabūk, Ḥā'il, 'Unayzah

Omdurman, Khartoum, Kassala, Wad Medani, El Obeid, Ed Dueim, Kosti, Malakal, Juba, Asmera, Mits'iwa (Massawa), Adīs Abeba, Nazrēt, Jima, Gonder, Dese, Debre Markos, Dire Dawa, Harēr, Djibouti, Hargeysa, Berbera, Muqdisho (Mogadishu), Marka, Kismaayo, Socotra (Suqutra), Kampala, Nairobi, Kigali, Bujumbura

Deserts & Physical Features: An Nafūd, Ad Dahna, Rub' al Khali, Libyan Desert, Nubian Desert, Qattâra Depression, Farafra Oasis, El-Khârga Oasis, Dasht-e Kavir, Dasht-e Lūt, Baluchistan, Makran, Tihamah, Hadramawt, Elburz, Zagros, Büyük Ağrı, Damavand

Tropic of Cancer, Equator

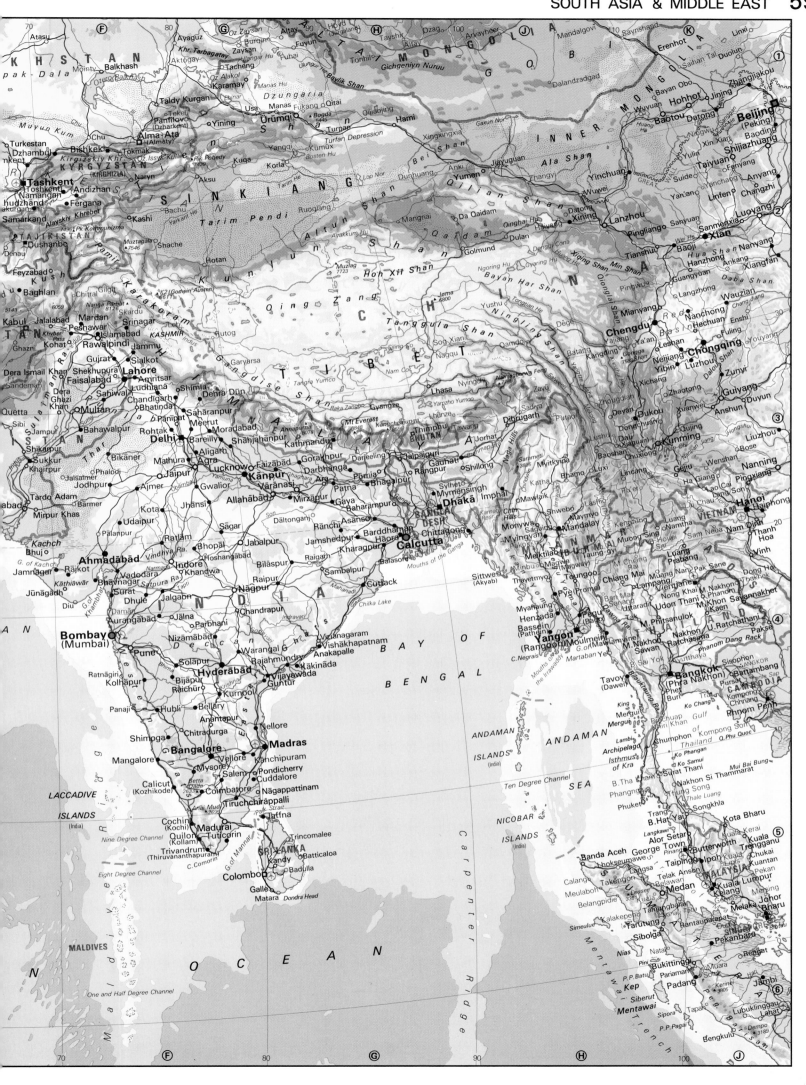

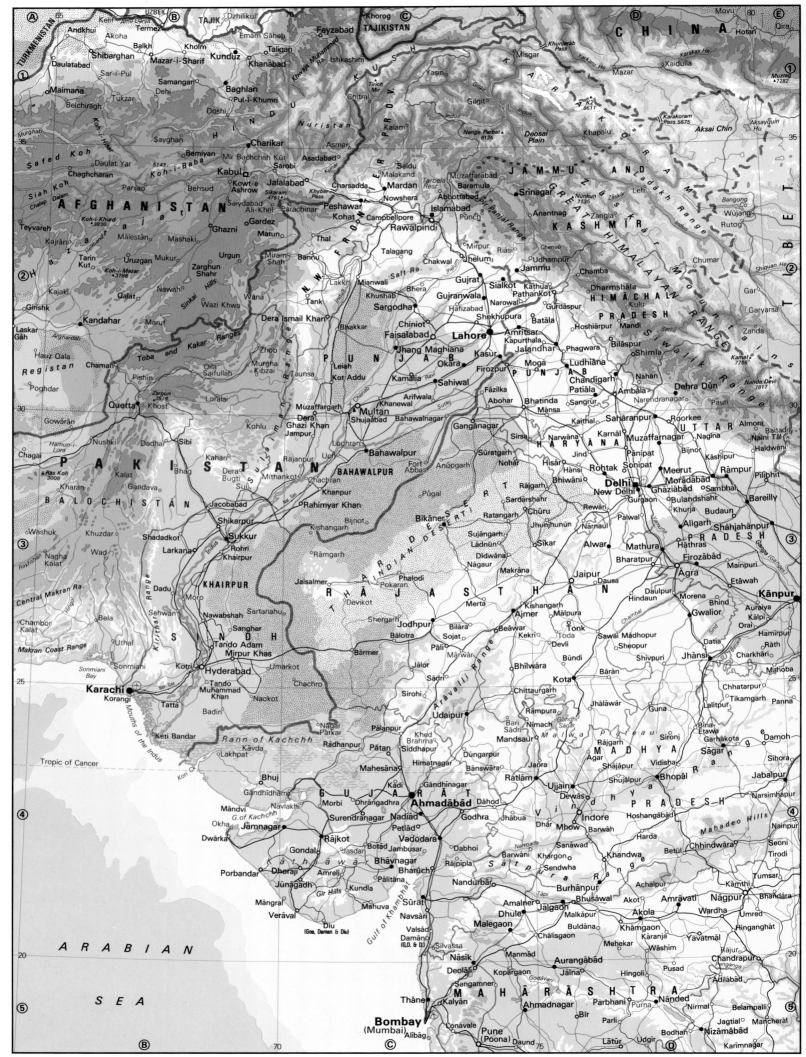

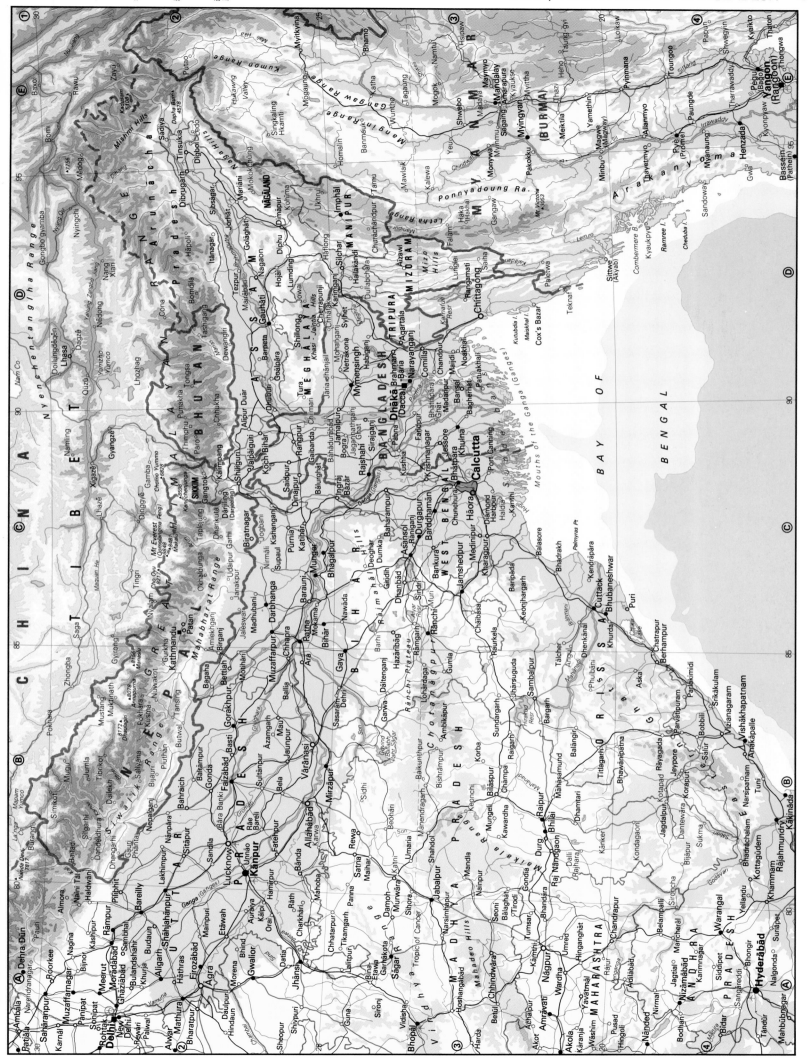

1:7.5M

100   200   300 km
50   100   150 mls

1:7.5M

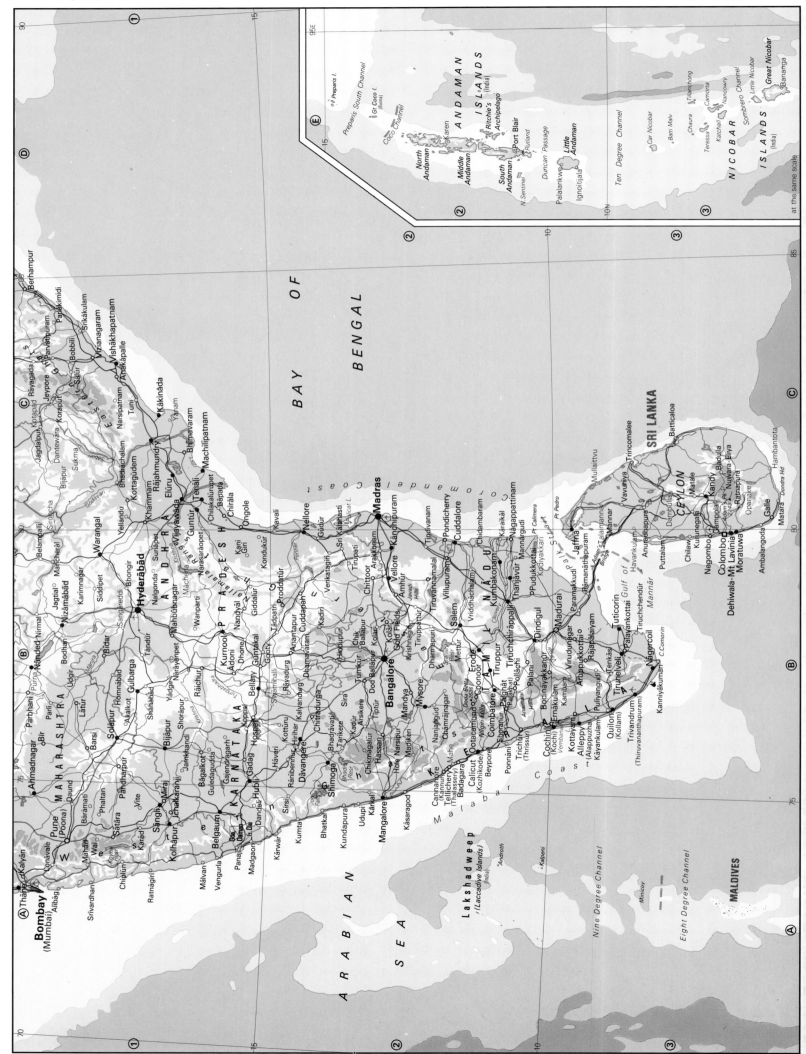

BAY OF BENGAL

ANDAMAN ISLANDS (India)

NICOBAR ISLANDS

North Andaman
Middle Andaman
Ritchie's Archipelago
South Andaman
Port Blair
Little Andaman

Great Nicobar

Car Nicobar
Little Nicobar

Ten Degree Channel

ARABIAN SEA

Lakshadweep (Laccadive Islands) (India)

Nine Degree Channel
Eight Degree Channel

MALDIVES

Bombay (Mumbai)

MAHARASHTRA

ANDHRA PRADESH

KARNATAKA

Hyderabad

Bangalore

TAMIL NADU

Madras

KERALA

SRI LANKA

CEYLON

Colombo

Coromandel Coast

Malabar Coast

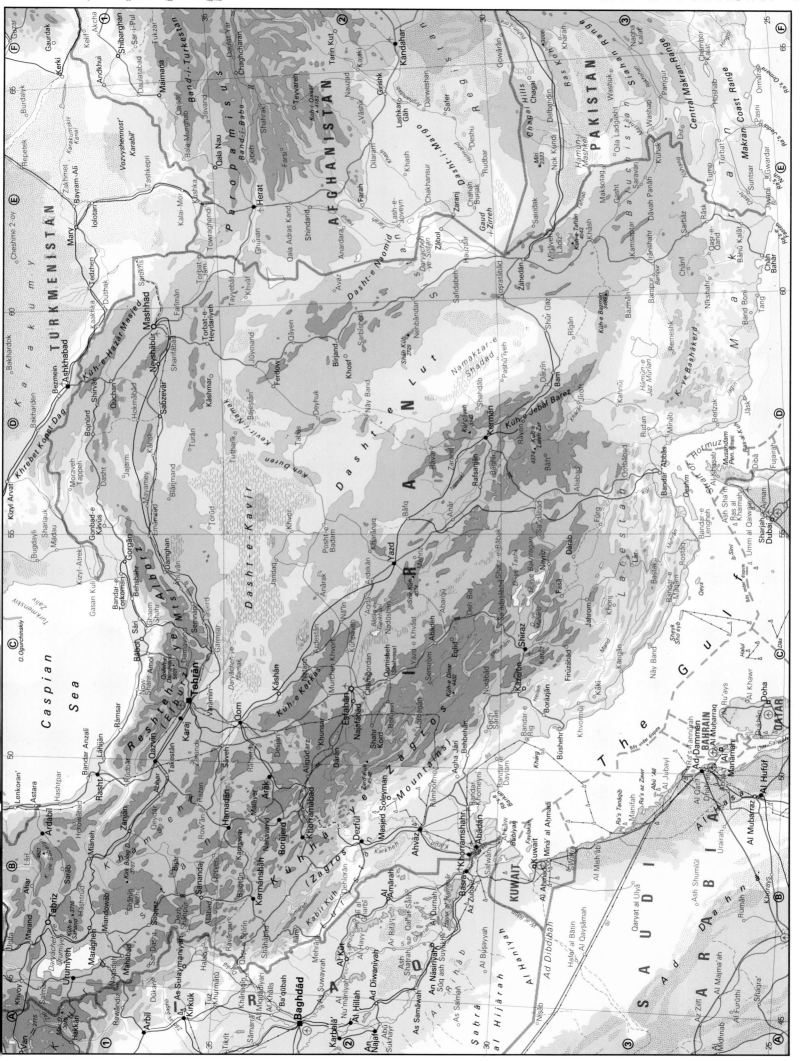

100 200 300 km
50 100 150 mls

Countries / Regions: AZERBAIJAN · GEORGIA · ARMENIA · AZER. · IRAN · IRAQ · SYRIA · TURKEY · LEBANON · ISRAEL · JORDAN · SAUDI ARABIA · KUWAIT · EGYPT · CYPRUS · GREECE

Seas: Caspian Sea · BLACK SEA · Sea of Marmara · Mediterranean Sea · Gulf of Suez · Gulf of Aqaba

Selected place names:

Baku · Sumgait · Shemakha · Masally · Lenkoran · Astara · Ardabil · Herowābād · Zanjan · Hamadān · Malāyer · Borūjerd · Khorramābād · Dezfūl · Ahvāz · Khorramshahr · Abādān · Al Faw · KUWAIT · Mīnā' al Ahmadī

Tbilisi · Rustavi · Gyandzha · Kirovakan · Yerevan · ARMENIA · Nakhichevan · Tabriz · Marand · Miāndowāb · Mahābād · Saqqez · Sanandaj · Bijar · Qazvīn · Kermānshāh · Kangāvar · Nahāvand · Al 'Amārah · Al Qurnah · Az Zubayr · Basra · Al Ahmadī

Batumi · Artvin · Ardahan · Kars · Iğdır · Erzurum · Ağrı · Doğubayazıt · Van · Ercis · Bitlis · Siirt · Zakho · Al Mawsil (Mosul) · Tall 'Afar · Al Hadr · Kirkūk · Arbīl · As Sulaymānīyah · Khānaqīn · Ba'qūbah · Baghdād · Al Kūt · Al 'Amārah

Trabzon · Gümüşhane · Bayburt · Erzincan · Tunceli · Elazığ · Diyarbakır · Siverek · Mardin · Nusaybin · Al Qāmishlī · Al Hasakah · Sinjār · Dayr az Zawr · Ar Ramādī · Al Fallūjah · Al Hillah · Karbalā' · An Najaf · Ad Dīwānīyah · As Samāwah · An Nāsirīyah

Giresun · Ordu · Samsun · Sivas · Malatya · Adıyaman · Şanlıurfa · Ceylanpınar · Ar Raqqah · As Sabkhah · Tudmur · Ar Rutbah

Sinop · Kastamonu · Çankırı · Yozgat · Kırşehir · Kayseri · Kahramanmaraş · Gaziantep · Kilis · Halab (Aleppo) · Hamāh · Hims · Ma'arret an Nu'mān

Ankara · Kırıkkale · Kırşehir · Aksaray · Niğde · Adana · Tarsus · Mersin · İskenderun · Antakya · Al Lādhiqīyah · Tartūs · Tripoli (Tarābulus) · Beirut (Beyrouth) · Saïda · Tyr · Damascus (Dimashq) · An Nabk · Zahle

Eskişehir · Afyon · Konya · Karaman · Ereğli · Silifke · Anamur · Famagusta · Nicosia · Larnaca · Limassol · CYPRUS

İstanbul · Üsküdar · İzmit · Bursa · Balıkesir · Manisa · İzmir · Aydın · Denizli · Muğla · Antalya · Alanya · Fethiye

Rodhos · Kriti · GREECE · Dhodhekánisos

Amman · Irbid · Zarqa · Mafraq · Jerusalem · Nablus · Hebron · Bethlehem · Al Karak · Ma'ān · Al 'Aqabah · Dead Sea

Haifa · 'Akko · Nazareth · Netanya · Tel Aviv Yafo · ISRAEL · Ashdod · Gaza · Beersheba · Negev · Elat · El 'Arīsh · El Tīh · SINAI · EGYPT

Alexandria (El Iskandarīya) · El Alamein · Matrūh · Port Said (Būr Sa'īd) · Dumyāt · El Mansūra · Tanta · Benha · Zagazig · Ismā'īlīya · Suez (El Suweis) · Cairo (El Qāhira) · El Gīza · Helwān · El Faiyūm · Beni Suef · El Minya · Mallawi · Nile

Physical features: Kaukasus · Van Gölü · Tuz Gölü · Euphrates · Tigris · Toros Dağları · Kuzey Anadolu Dağları · Libyan Plateau · Qattara Depression · An Nafūd · Badiyat ash Shām · Al Widyān

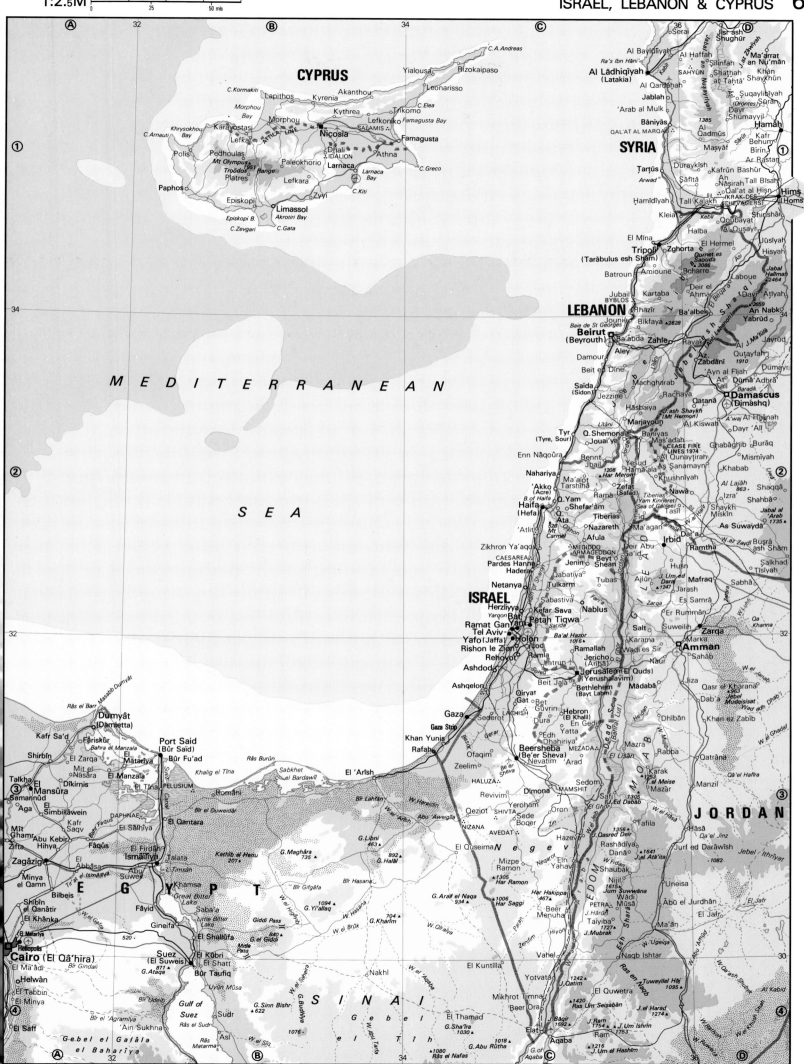

1:2.5M

25 50 75 100 km
25 50 mls

1:7.5M

100 200 300 km
50 100 150 mls

A · B · C · D

JORDAN

El Gîza · Cairo (El Qâ'hira) · Suez (El Suweis) · Ma'ân · El Jafr · As Salmañ
Helwân · W. el Brûk · El Kuntilla · Naqb Ishtar · Sahrâ
30 · Ain Sukhna · Nakhl · Elat · Al Jawf · Sakâkah · Ad Duwayd · al Hijâ
El Faiyûm · Birkat Qârun · El Tîh · Aqaba · Al Mudawwara · At Tubayq · Mughayra · Rafha · Nişâ
Beni Suef · Haql · Al Bi'r · Al Hawjâ' · Al Jumaymah
El Fashn · Biba · SINAI · El'Igma · Dahab · Al 'Uwayrid
Beni Mazar · Maghâgha · Râs Ghârib · G. Katharîna 2637 · Tabûk · Al Qallbah · An Nafûd · Al Taysîyah
El Harra · El Minya · Dairût · El Tûr · Al Muwaylih · J. al Lawz 2578 · Jubbah
Mallawi · Râs Muhammad · Dubâ · Taymâ' · Hâ'il
① Manfalût · Hurghada · Al 'Ulâ · Jabal Shammar
Asyût · Al Kahfah
Abu Tîg · Bur Safâga · Al Wajh · Hulayfah · Ad Dawâdimî
Tahta · Akhmîm · Khaybar · 'Uglat aş Suqûr · Ar Rass · Buraydah
Sohâg · Dishna · Qena · Quseir · Az Zilfî
Girga · El Balyana · Luxor · Umm Lajj · Unayzah · Al Midhnab
Balât · El Khârga · Qus · Marsa Alam · Ra's Abu Madd · Medina (Al Madînah) · 'Afif · Ar Ruwaydah
Isna · Al Qasîm
25 · El-Khârga Oasis · Idfu · Badr Hunayn · Tropic of Cancer
Bârîs · Libyan · W. Sha'it · G. Hamâta 1977 · Berenice · Yanbu'al Bahr
Saad el Aali (Aswân High Dam) · Aswân · Râs Banâs · Zalim
② Desert · Khazzan an-Nasr (Lake Nasser) · Ras Abû Dâra · Râbigh · Harrat Rahat · Harrât Kishb
Wadi Halfa · Halaib · Tuwwal
Akasha · Allâqi · 2217 J.Asoteriba · Râs Hadarba · As Suq
Abri · El Ku · Dungunab · Jiddah · Makkah (Mecca)
Hafir · Abu Fatima 3rd Cataract · Nubian Desert · Muhammad Qol · Ras Abu Shagara · At Tâ'if · Turabah · Ar Rawdah
Delgo · Keheili · Abu Hamed · J.Oda 2260 · Al Khamâsîn
20 · Dongola · 'Amur · Port Sudan · Qishrân · Al Lîth · Baljurshî · Al Khamâsîn · Tathlith
El Khandaq · 4th Cataract · Shereik · Suakin · Al Qunfidhah · An Nimâs
Ed Debba · Karima · Merowe · Baiyuda Desert · Sinkat · Al Birk · Abhâ · Khamis Mushayt
30 · Korti · 5th Cataract · El Bauga · Musmar · Tokar · Ra's Asis · Ad Darb · Haraja
③ El Milh · Berber · Togni · Tohamiyam · Ra's Kasar · Ash Shuqayq · Najrân
Atbara · Derudeb · J.Hamoyet 2780 · Karora
Ed Damer · Ez Zeidab · Eriba · Ra's at Tarfa · Jîzân · Abû Arish · Sa'dah
Kabushiya · Adarama · Nak'fa · Jazâ'ir Farasân · Mîdî · Harad · Khamir
Shendi · Goz Regeb · Dahlak Arch. · Amrân
Omdurman · Khartoum North · Abu Deleiq · Keren · Mits'iwa (Massawa) · Kamarân · Raydah
Umm Inderaba · Khartoum · Kassala · Sebderat · Biskia · Agordat · Massawa Ch. · Sûq 'Abs · Hajjah
15 · El Kamlin · New Haifa · Tessenei · Barentu · Asmera · Ra's 'Isâ · San'â
Kagmar · Umm Saiyala · El Geteina · Khashm el Girba · Decamere · Al Hudaydah · Bâjil
El Homra · Hasaheisa · Rufa'a · Showak · Adi Ugri · Adi Kaie · Mersa Fatma · 3760
Bara · El Manaqil · Wad Medani · Gedaref · Om Hâjer · Aratali · Ras Andadda · Bayt al Faqîh · Dhamâr · Radâ'
Hag 'Abdullah · Mokada 2295 · Adigrat · Kululli · L.Assale · Zabîd · Yarîm
④ Er Rahad · Ed Dueim · Doka · Enda Salassie · Aksum · Adwa · Danakil · Ed · Hanish · Hays · Ibb
Umm Ruwaba · Kosti · Rabak · Singa · El Hawata · Abi Addi · Ta'izz
Bahr el Abiad · Sennar · Gallabat · Metemma · Mek'ele · Al Mukhâ · Lahij
White Nile · Jebelein · Dinder · Rahad · Ras Dashan 4620 · Maichew · Chercher · Aseb · Shaykh 'Uthmân · Little Aden
Rashad · Renk · Ed Damasin · Er Roseires · Dabat · Sek'ota 3935 Sarenga · Moussa Ali 2063 · Daddato · Perim I.
Doleib · J.Belaia 3131 · Bahir Dar · Gogora · Gonder · Guna 4231 · Weldiya · Tendaho · Raheita · Balho
ETHIOPIA · L.Tana · Addis Zemen · Lalibela · Awash · Obock · de Tadjoura
Debre Tabor · Tadjoura · DJIBOUTI · Djibouti

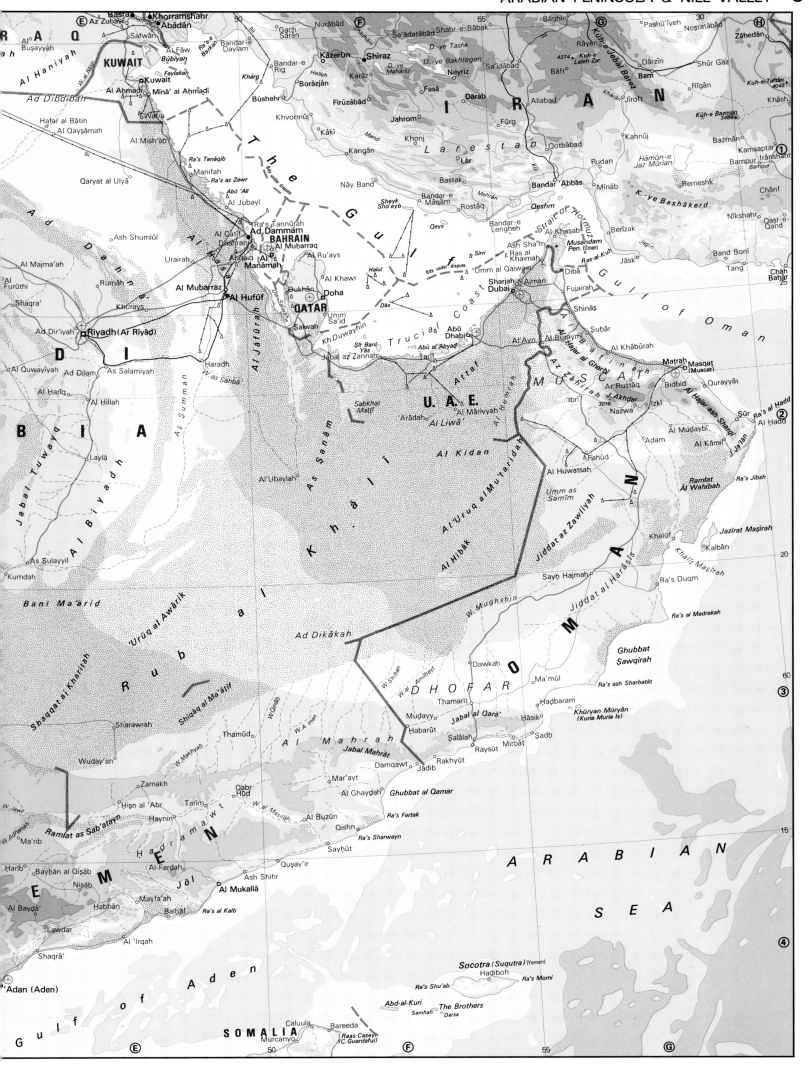

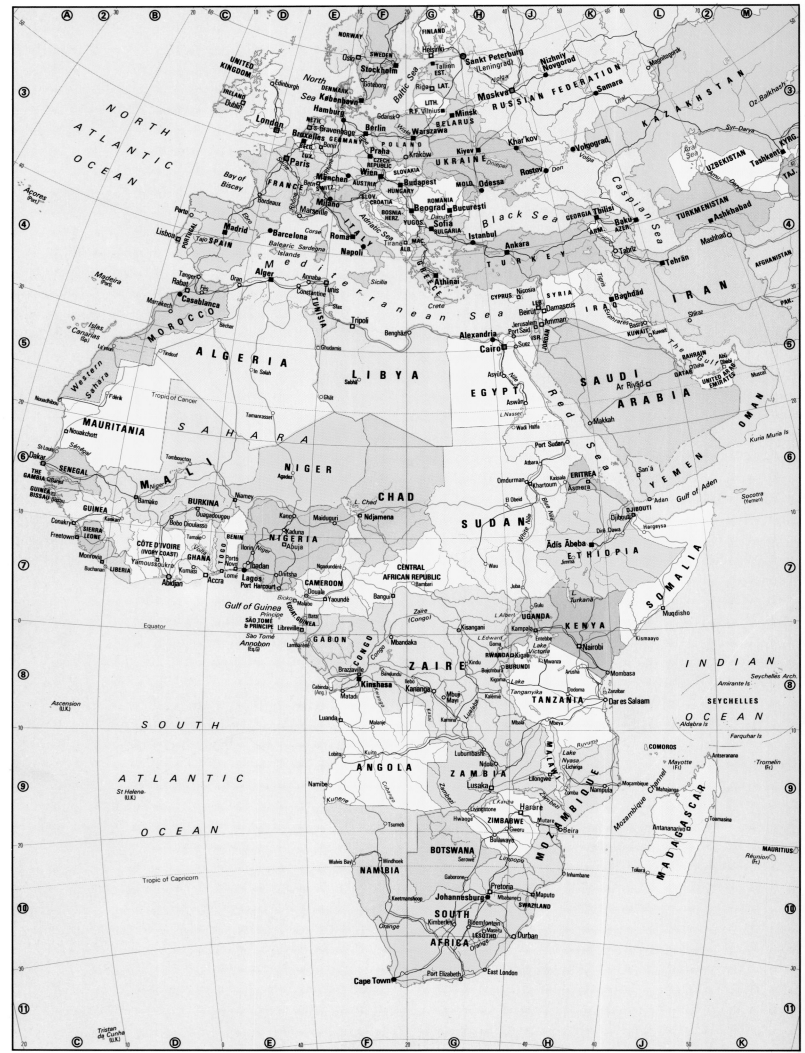

1:15M

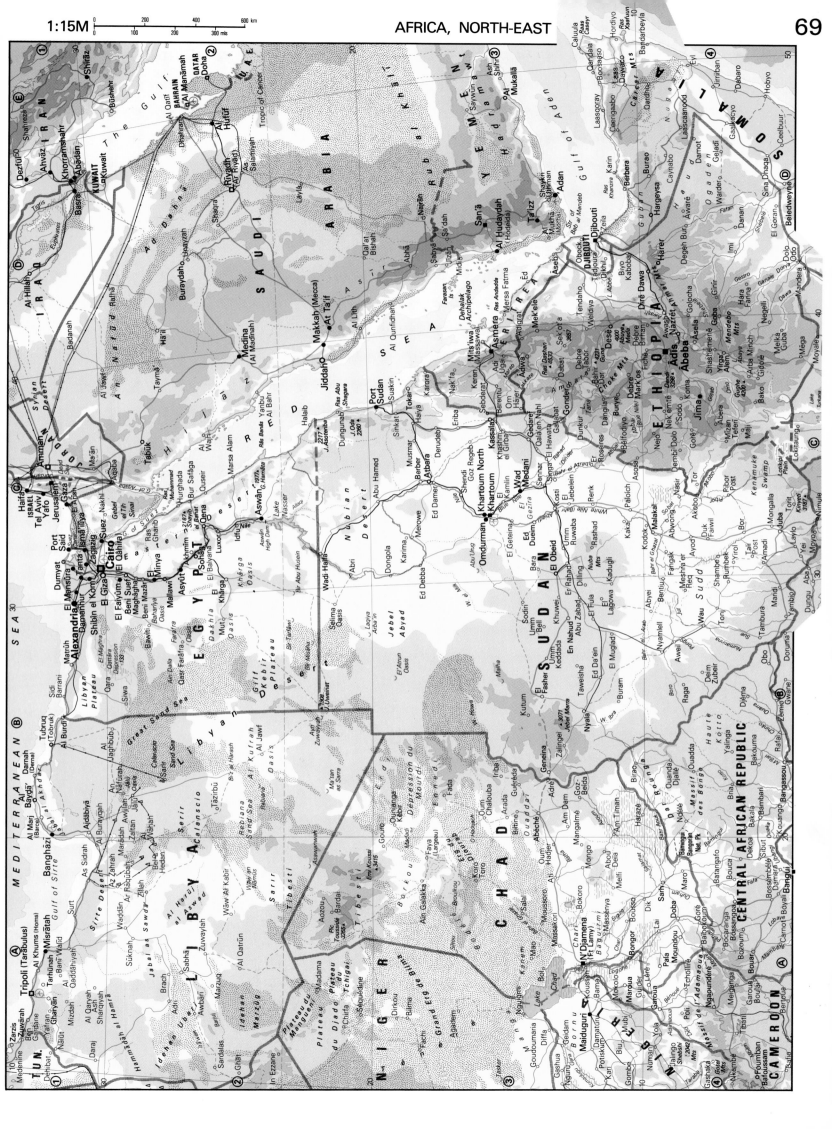

1:15M

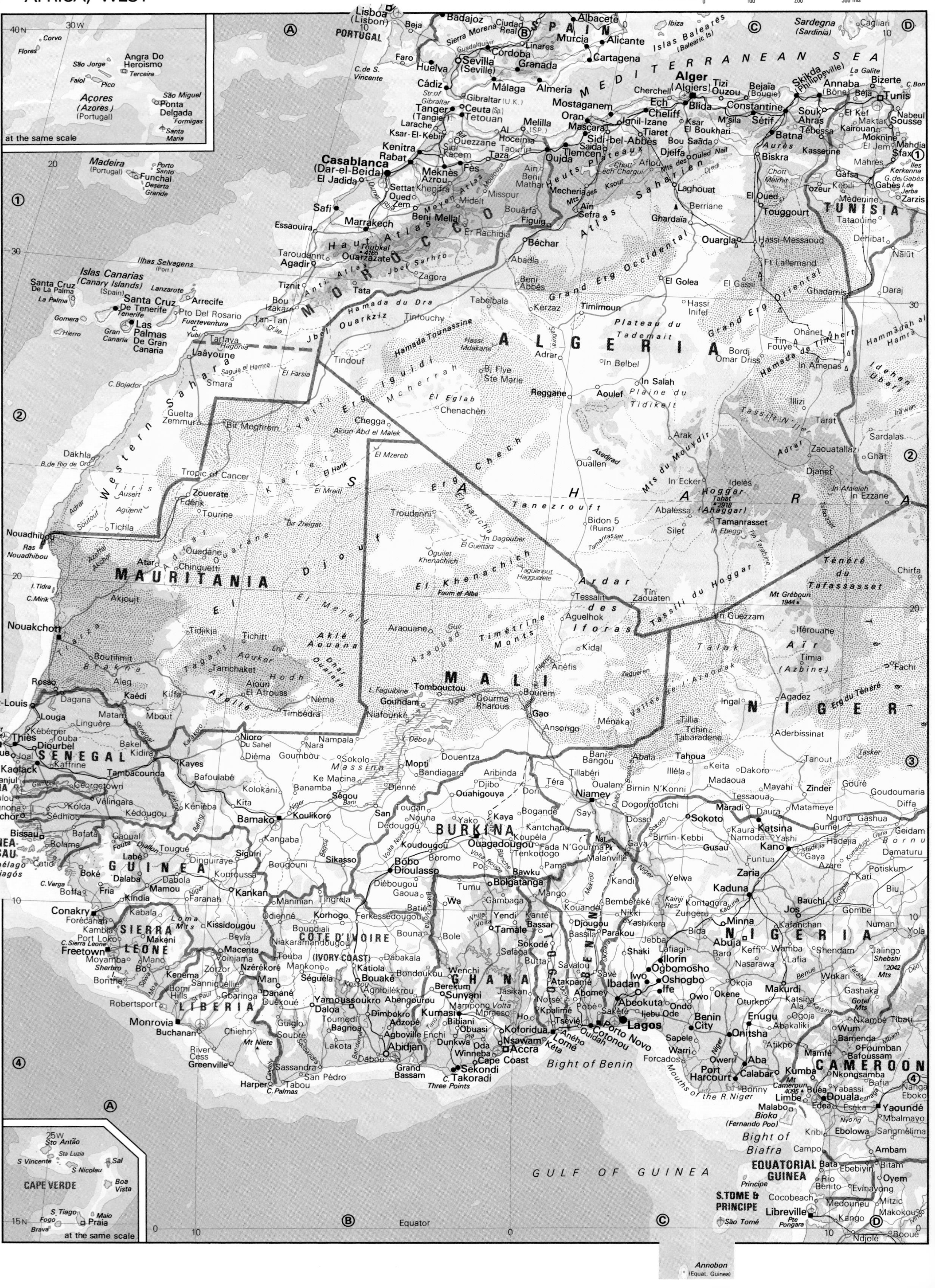

200   400   600 km
100   200   300 mls

MEDITERRANEAN SEA

SPAIN
PORTUGAL
MOROCCO
ALGERIA
TUNISIA
WESTERN SAHARA
MAURITANIA
MALI
NIGER
SENEGAL
THE GAMBIA
GUINEA-BISSAU
GUINEA
SIERRA LEONE
LIBERIA
CÔTE D'IVOIRE (IVORY COAST)
GHANA
BURKINA
BENIN
TOGO
NIGERIA
CAMEROON
EQUATORIAL GUINEA
S. TOME & PRINCIPE

SAHARA

Açores (Azores) (Portugal)
at the same scale

Islas Canarias (Canary Islands) (Spain)
Madeira (Portugal)

CAPE VERDE
at the same scale

GULF OF GUINEA
Bight of Benin
Bight of Biafra

1:7.5M 0 100 200 300 km / 0 50 100 150 mls

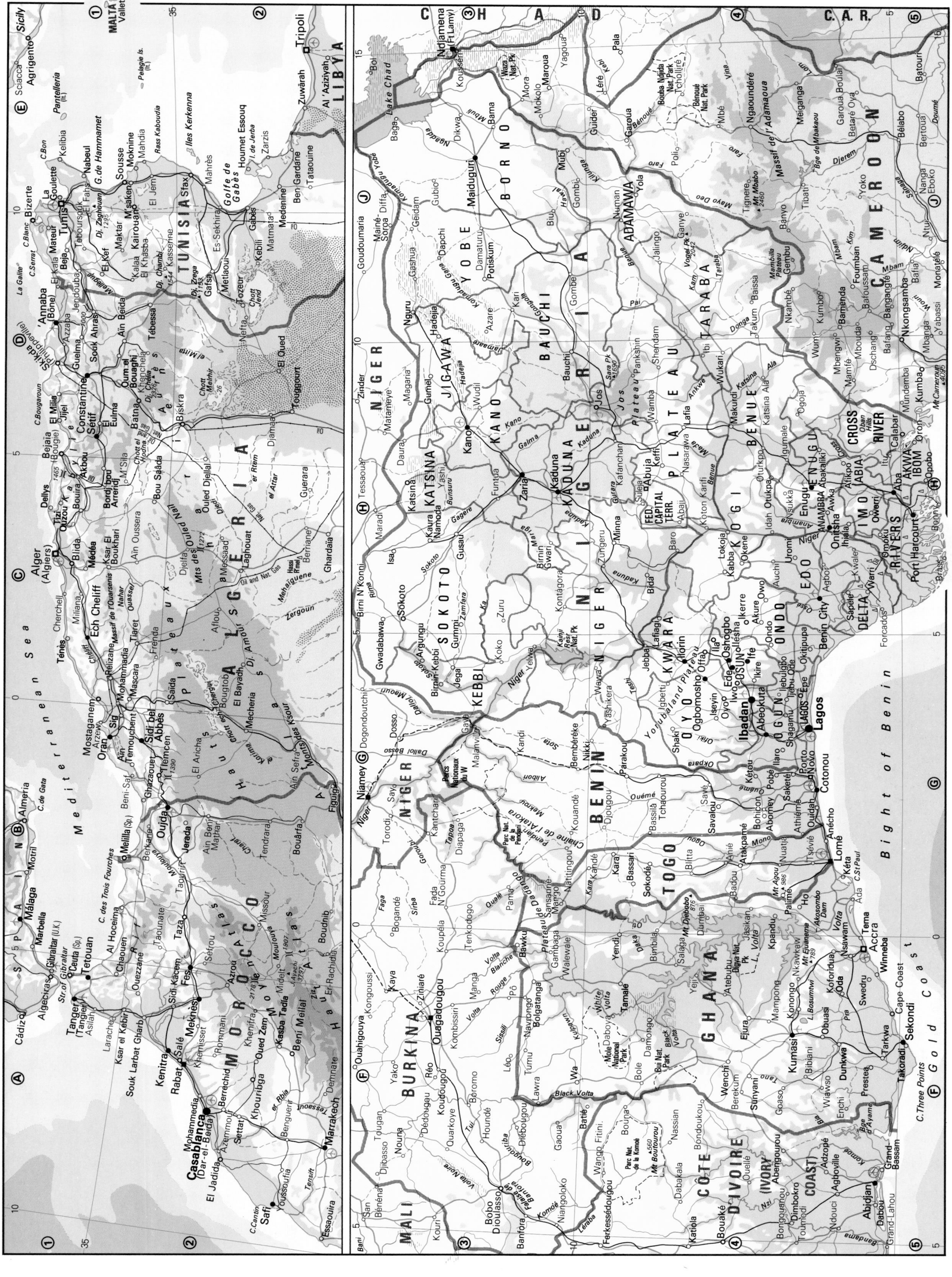

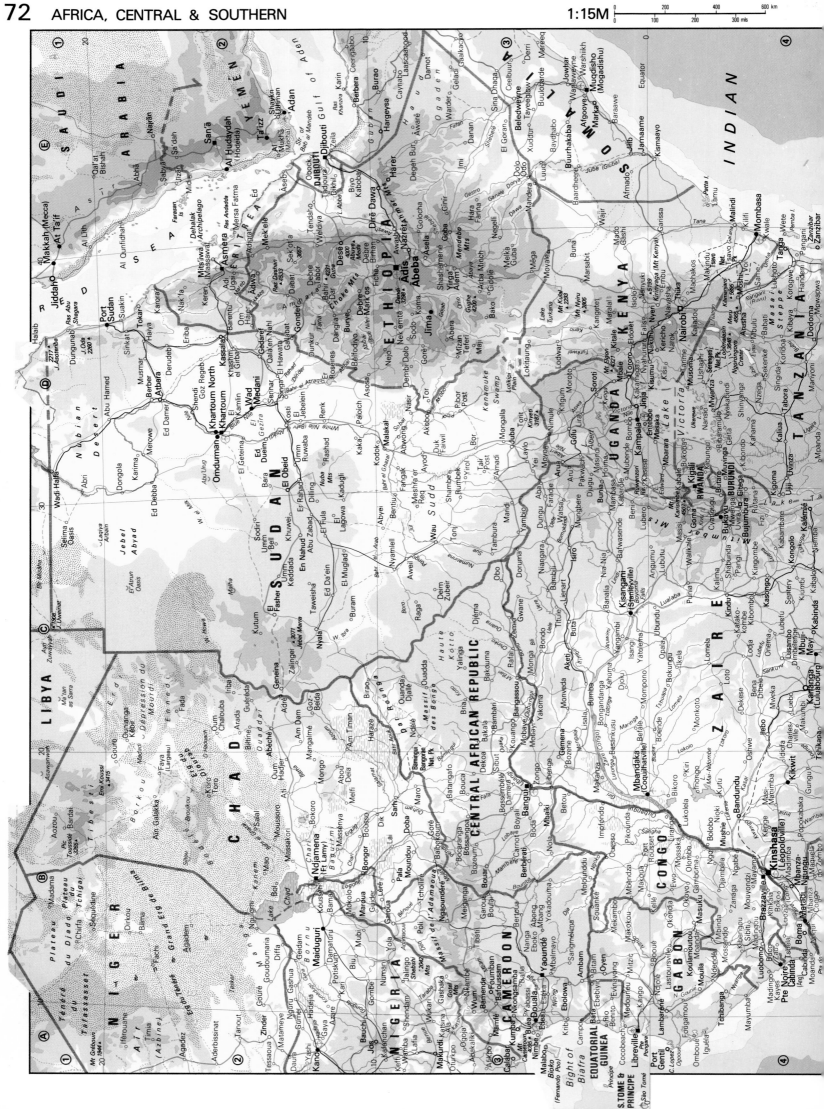

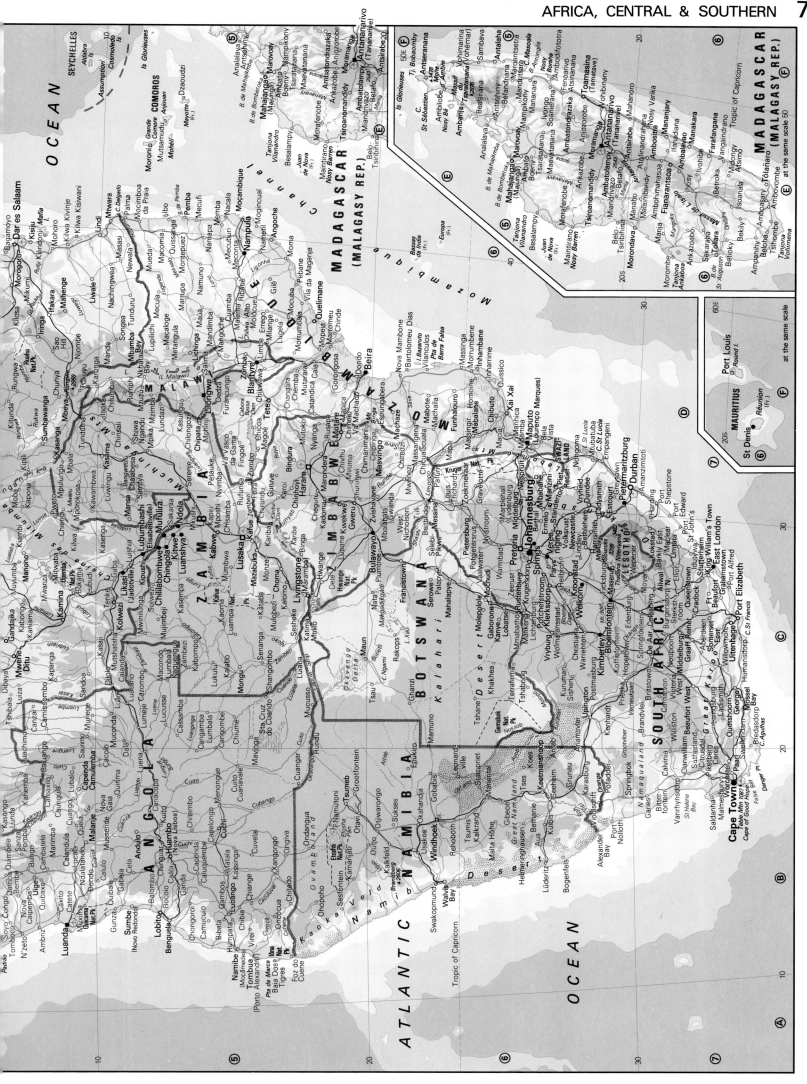

1:7.5M

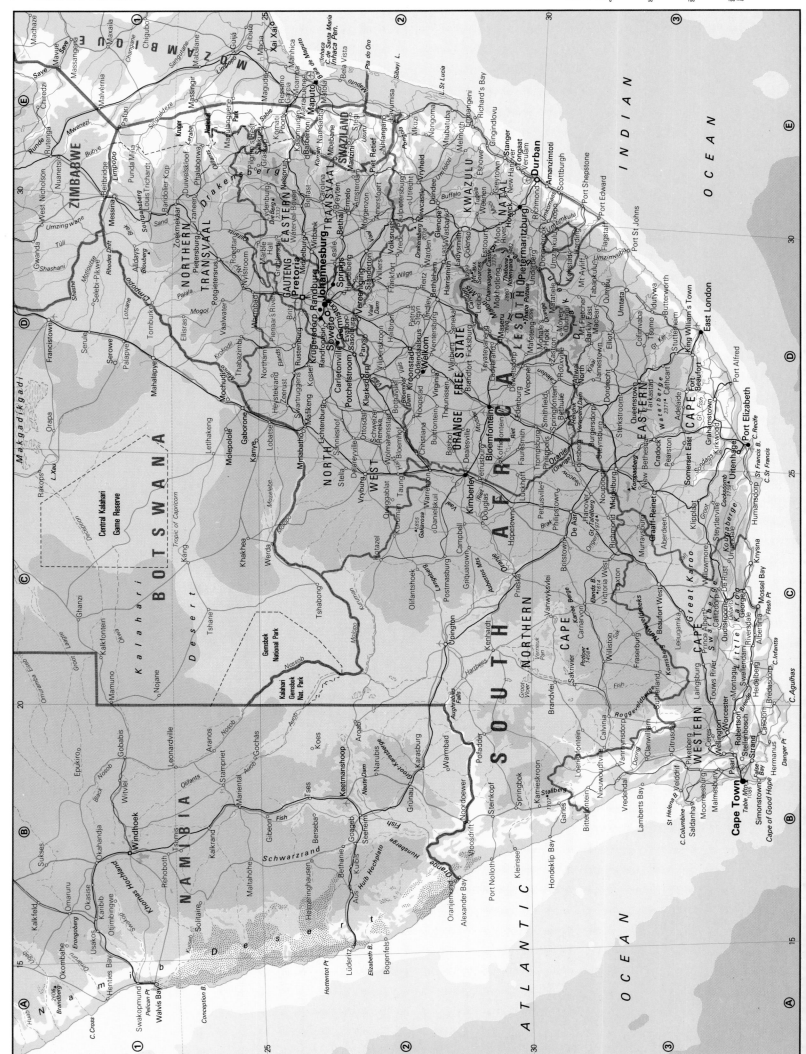

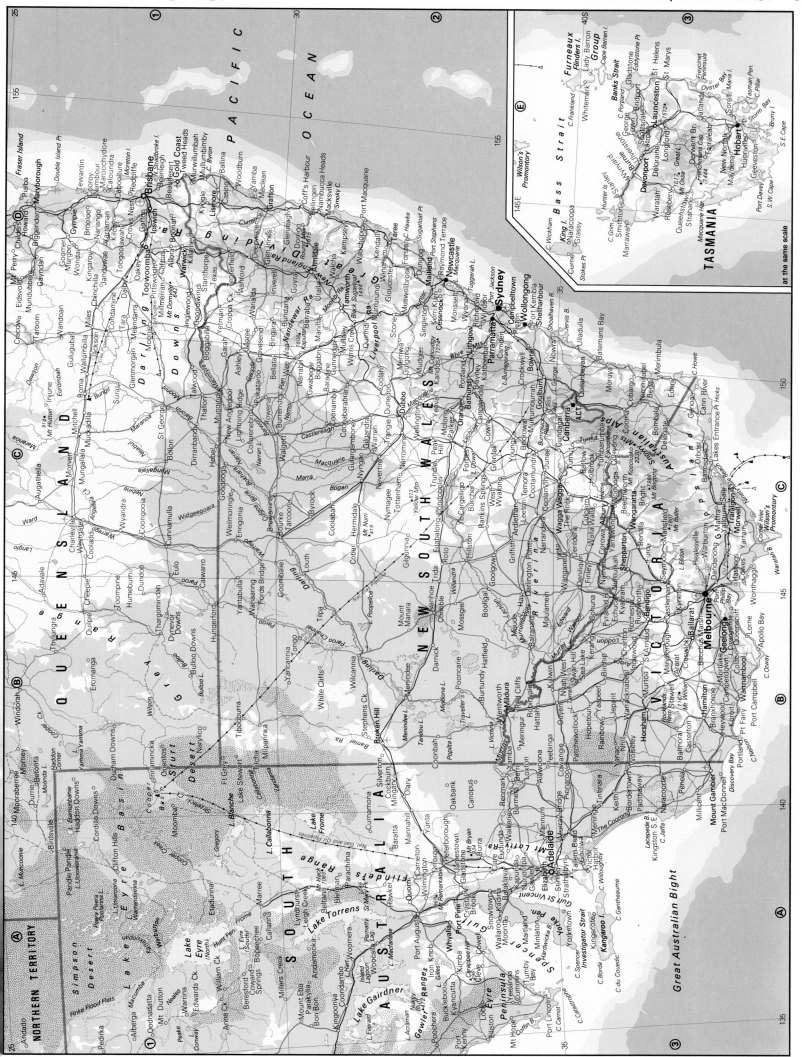

1:20M

200 400 600 800 km
0 200 400 mils

BORNEO

INDONESIA

SULAWESI (CELEBES)

MOLUCCAS

Belang Sea
Molucca Sea
Ceram Sea
Banda Sea
Flores Sea

IRIAN JAYA

NEW GUINEA

PAPUA NEW GUINEA

Bismarck Archipelago
Admiralty Is
Bismarck Sea
New Ireland
New Britain

Pk. Jaya 5025
Pegunungan Maoke

Jayapura
Sorong
Manokwari
Sarmi
Wewak
Madang
Mt Hagen
Goroka
Lae
Morobe
Port Moresby
Gulf of Papua
Owen Stanley Ra
Samarai

Manado
Gorontalo
Tolitoli
Ternate
Halmahera
Morotai
Tubelo

Samarinda
Balikpapan
Banjarmasin
Ujung Pandang (Makassar)
Palu
Poso
Kendari
Ambon
Buru
Ceram

Makassar Strait

Java Trench

INDIAN OCEAN

Timor Sea

Timor
Dili
Kupang

Arafura Sea

Darwin
Rum Jungle
Adelaide River
Pine Creek
Katherine
Arnhem Land
Nhulunbuy
Groote Eylandt

Gulf of Carpentaria

Cape York Peninsula
Weipa
Coen
Cooktown
Cairns
Innisfail
Townsville
Charters Towers
Bowen
Mackay
Rockhampton

Great Barrier Reef

Coral Sea

NORTHERN TERRITORY

Wyndham
Derby
Broome
L. Argyle
Victoria River Downs
Wave Hill
Daly Waters
Tennant Creek
Newcastle Waters
Barkly Tableland
Camooweal
Mount Isa
Cloncurry
Richmond
Hughenden
Croydon
Forsayth
Ingham
Ayr

Great Sandy Desert

Port Hedland
Roebourne
Dampier
Marble Bar
Newman
Paraburdoo

Gibson Desert

WESTERN AUSTRALIA

Macdonnell Ranges
Mt Ziel 1510
Alice Springs
Simpson Desert
Lake Eyre Basin

QUEENSLAND

Longreach
Barcaldine
Blackall
Windorah
Charleville
Quilpie
Roma
Toowoomba

Great Victoria Desert

Coober Pedy

SOUTH AUSTRALIA

Lake Eyre
Oodnadatta
Marree
Woomera
Port Augusta
Port Pirie
Whyalla

Nullarbor Plain

Kalgoorlie
Coolgardie
Norseman
Eyre
Ceduna

Great Australian Bight

Port Lincoln

Carnarvon
Geraldton
Perth
Fremantle
Bunbury
Albany
Esperance

Adelaide
Murray Bridge
Mildura
Broken Hill
Bourke

NEW SOUTH WALES

Dubbo
Orange
Bathurst
Sydney
Wollongong
Newcastle
Canberra
A.C.T.
Wagga Wagga
Albury

VICTORIA

Bendigo
Ballarat
Geelong
Melbourne
Mount Gambier
Portland
Warrnambool

Bass Strait

TASMANIA

Burnie
Devonport
Launceston
Queenstown
Hobart

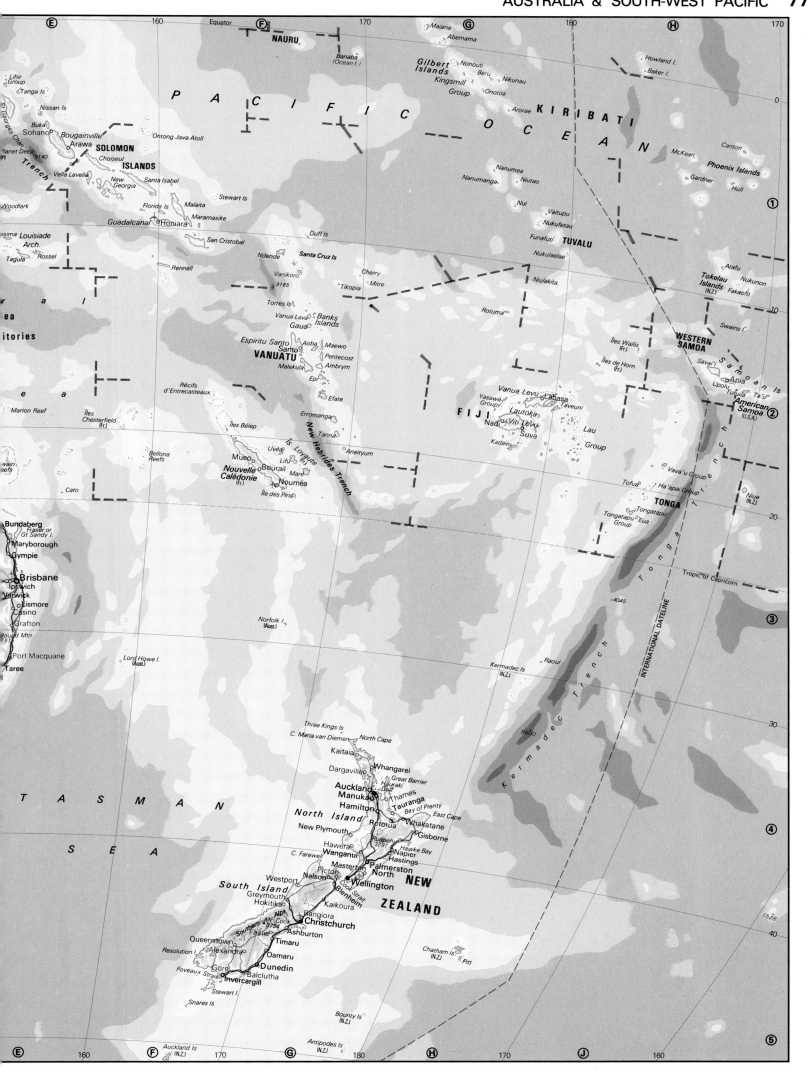

PACIFIC OCEAN

Equator

NAURU

Banaba
(Ocean I.)

Maiana
Abemama

Lihir
Group

Tanga Is

Nissan Is

Gilbert
Islands

Nonouti
Beru
Nikunau

Kingsmill
Group

Onotoa

Arorae

KIRIBATI

Howland I.
Baker I.

Canton

McKean

Phoenix Islands

Gardner

Hull

St George's Chan

Buka
Sohano

Bougainville
Arawa

SOLOMON

Ontong Java Atoll

Choiseul

Planet Deep 9140

Trench

Vella Lavella

New
Georgia

Santa Isabel

ISLANDS

Woodlark

Florida Is

Malaita

Maramasike

Guadalcanal   Honiara

Nanumea

Nanumanga

Niutao

Nui

Vaitupu

Nukufetau

Funafuti   TUVALU

Nukulaelae

Niulakita

Tokelau
Islands
(N.Z.)

Atafu

Nukunon

Fakaofo

Swains I.

isima Louisiade
Arch.

Rossel

Tagula

San Cristobal

Duff Is

Santa Cruz Is

Vanikoro
9165

Rennell

Ndende

Tikopia

Cherry

Mitre

Rotuma

WESTERN
SAMOA

Savai'i

Apia

Upolu

Tutuila   Ta'ū

Samoan Is

itories

Torres Is

Vanua Lava
Gaua

Banks
Islands

Îles Wallis
(Fr.)

Îles de Horn
(Fr.)

American
Samoa
(U.S.A.)

Marion Reef

Espiritu Santo
Santo

Aoba   Maewo

Pentecost

VANUATU

Malekula

Ambrym

Epi

Îles Chesterfield
(Fr.)

Récifs
d'Entrecasteaux

Erromanga

Efate

FIJI

Vanua Levu
Labasa

Yasawa
Group

Taveuni

Lautoka

Vatu

Nadi   Viti Levu

Suva

Lau
Group

Bellona
Reefs

Îles Bélep

Tanna

New Hebrides Trench

Uvéa

Lifu

Kadavu

Vava'u Group

ain
efs

Cato

Nouvelle
Calédonie
(Fr.)

Mueo

Bourail

Nouméa

Île des Pins

Lifou

Maré

Aneityum

Tofua
Ha'apai Group

Niue
(N.Z.)

Tonga
Trench

TONGA

Tongatapu   'Eua
Tongatapu
Group

Bundaberg
Fraser or
Gt Sandy I.

Maryborough

Gympie

Brisbane
Ipswich

Warwick

Lismore

Casino

Grafton

oud Mtn

Norfolk I.
(Aust.)

4045

Tropic of Capricorn

INTERNATIONAL DATELINE

Port Macquarie

Taree

Lord Howe I.
(Aust.)

Kermadec Is
(N.Z.)

Raoul

Kermadec Trench

8600

1528

Three Kings Is

C. Maria van Diemen   North Cape

Kaitaia

Whangarei

Dargaville

Great Barrier

Auckland

Manukau

Hauraki
Gulf

Thames

Hamilton

Tauranga

Bay of Plenty

East Cape

North Island

Rotorua

TASMAN

New Plymouth

Whakatane

Gisborne

Ruapehu
2797

Hawera

Wanganui

C. Farewell

Masterton

Napier
Hawke Bay

Hastings

Palmerston
North

NEW

SEA

Westport

Nelson

Picton

Wellington

Cook Strait

Greymouth

Blenheim

ZEALAND

Hokitika

South Island

Kaikoura

Alps

Rangiora

Mt Cook
3764

Christchurch

Queenstown

Fairlie

Ashburton

Resolution I.

Alexandra

Timaru

Southern

Oamaru

Gore

Dunedin

Foveaux Strait

Balclutha

Invercargill

Stewart I.

Snares Is

Chatham Is
(N.Z.)

Pitt

Bounty Is
(N.Z.)

Auckland Is
(N.Z.)

Antipodes Is
(N.Z.)

1:5M

50 100 150 200 km
50 100 mils

Three Kings Is

C. Maria van Diemen
North Cape
Tanganunu B.
Ninety Mile Beach
Doubtless B.
Ahipara B.
Tauroa Pt
Kaitaia
Kaikohe
Bay of Islands
C. Brett
Russell
Kawakawa
Hikurangi
Hokianga Har.
Whangarei
Hen & Chickens Is
Dargaville
Bream B.
Little Barrier I.
Great Barrier I.
Wellsford
C. Colville
Kaipara Har.
Hauraki Gulf
Mercury Is
Manly
Mercury Bay
Takapuna
Coromandel Peninsula
Auckland
Papatoetoe Manukau
Papakura
Thames
Coromandel Ra.
Mayor I.
Pukekohe
Waiuku
Waihi
Paeroa
C. Runaway
Hicks Bay
Huntly Te Aroha
Matakana I.
Morrinsville
Tauranga Har.
East C.

NORTH
Glen Afton
Ngaruawahia
Tauranga
Bay of Plenty
ISLAND
Hamilton Cambridge
Te Puke
Whakatane
Te Awamutu
Putaruru Rotoma
Opotiki
Kawhia
Otorohanga
Rotorua
Kawerau
T+ Teaneatua
Raukumara Ra.
Waitomo
Te Kuiti
Mangakino
Tolaga Bay
Murupara
Tokomaru Bay

N. Taranaki Bight
Ohura
L. Taupo
Taupo
Tarawera
Gisborne
Waitara
Taumarunui
Poverty Bay
New Plymouth
Inglewood
Mt Ngauruhoe 2291
Mt Makorako 1724
Mohaka
C. Egmont
Mt Egmont 2518
Stratford
Mt Ruapehu 2797
Hawke Bay
Opunake
Eltham
Ohakune
Waiouru
Eskdale
Mahia Peninsula
Hawera
Raetihi
Taihape
Taradale
Napier
Portland I.
S. Taranaki Bight
Patea
Hastings
C. Kidnappers
Havelock North
Wanganui
Marton
Waipukurau
Feilding
Dannevirke

Palmerston N.
Foxton
Woodville
Levin
Pahiatua
C. Turnagain
Otaki
Eketahuna
Herbertville

C. Farewell
Farewell Spit
C. Stephens
Collingwood
Golden Bay
Separation Pt
Paraparaumu
Masterton
Rocks Pt
Takaka
Tasman Bay
Carterton
Tasman Mts
Motueka
Porirua Upper Hutt
The Twins 1826
Tawa
Martinborough
Karamea
Nelson
Picton
Wellington Lower Hutt
Karamea Bight
Richmond
Palliser Bay
Mt Ross 983
Seddonville
Richmond Ra.
Blenheim
C. Palliser
Wairau
C. Campbell
Westport
Murchison
C. Foulwind
L. Rotoroa
Awatere Ra.
Buller
Victoria Ra.
Mt Travers 2338
Tapuaenuku 2865
Reefton
Spenser Mts
Kaikoura Ra.
Clarence
Runanga
Lewis Pass
Hanmer Springs
Kaikoura
Greymouth
Grey
Waiau
Kaikoura Pen.
Hokitika
L. Brunner
Waiau
Ross
L. Sumner
Culverden

SOUTH
Arthurs Pass
Hurunui
Cheviot
Waipara
ISLAND
Abut Hd
Rangiora
Pegasus Bay
Franz Josef Gl.
L. Coleridge
Kaiapoi
Mt Cook 3754
Methven
Christchurch
Mt Sefton 3157
Hornby
Lyttelton
Hermitage
Lincoln
Banks Peninsula
Jackson Hd
L. Tekapo
Geraldine
Akaroa
Cascade Pt
Pollux 2542
Fairlie
L. Ellesmere
L. Pukaki
Ashburton
Ohau
Canterbury Bight
Mt Aspiring 3027
Wanaka
L. Benmore
Temuka
Awarua Pt
Hawea
Timaru
Milford Sd
L. Aviemore
Mt Pyramid 2326
Wanaka
Kurow
Homer Tunnel
Arrowtown
Waimate
George Sd
Caswell Sd
Queenstown
Cromwell
Ranfurly
Oamaru
Secretary I.
Fiordland
Wakatipu
Clyde
Hampden
Doubtful Sd
Te Anau
Alexandra
Nat. Park
L. Te Anau
Roxburgh
Palmerston
Breaksea Sd
Manapouri
Waikouaiti
Resolution I.
Mt Ward
Lumsden
Port Chalmers
Dusky Sd
Manapouri
Riversdale
Heriot
Otago Peninsula
Ohai
Lawrence
Mosgiel
Oreti
Tapanui
Dunedin
Puysegur Pt
Gore
Clutha
Winton
Mataura
Milton
Te Waewae Bay
Edendale
Balclutha
Riverton
Owaka
Kaitangata
Invercargill
Bluff
Foveaux Strait
Solander I.
Codfish I.
Oban
Paterson Inlet
Stewart Island
Mt Allen 730
Shelter Pt
Port Pegasus

TASMAN SEA

PACIFIC OCEAN

COOK STRAIT

1:40M

400   800   1200   1600 km
400   800 mls

Northern Polar Region (top map)

USA
Portland
Seattle
Vancouver I.
Vancouver
Prince Rupert
Calgary
Edmonton
Saskatoon
Flin Flon
L. Winnipeg
Churchill
Juneau
Vaduz
Anchorage
Mt McKinley 6194
Yukon
Fairbanks
Dawson
Teller
Vankarem
Bering Str.
Chukchi Sea
Pevek
Ambarchik
Kolyma
Ust'Nera
Ayan
Blagoveshchensk
CHINA
Skovorodino
Chu'l'man
Amur
Ulan-Ude
Chita
Oz. Baykal
Irkutsk
Ust'-Kut
Yakutsk
Aldan
Verkhoyansk
Zhigansk
Tiksi
Lena
Nordvik
Khatanga
Tree Limit
RUSSIAN FEDERATION
Krasnoyarsk
Noril'sk
Turukhansk
Yenisey
Dikson
Dudinka
Nadym
Salekhard
Berezovo
Ob'
Vorkuta
Tobol'sk
Ob'
Novosibirsk
Barnaul
Omsk
Tselinograd
Ekaterinburg
Ural'skiy Khrebet
Perm'
Ufa
Magnitogorsk
Orsk
KAZAKHSTAN
Aktyubinsk
Kazan'
Samara
Yaroslavl
Nizhniy Novgorod
Sankt-Peterburg (Leningrad)
Kirov
Serov
Syktyvkar
Mezen'
Arkhangel'sk
Kotlas
Sev. Dvina
Murmansk
Nordkapp
Tromsø
Narvik
NORWAY
SWEDEN
FINLAND
Oulu
Umeå
ICELAND
Reykjavik
Jan Mayen (Nor.)
Bjørnøya (Bear I.) (Nor.)
Barents Sea
Novaya Zemlya
Kara Sea
Severnaya Zemlya
Zemlya Frantsa Iosifa
Svalbard (Spitsbergen) (Nor.)
Greenland Sea
Nord
Norwegian Sea
Denmark Strait
Scoresbysund
Angmagssalik
Watkins Bjerge 3700
Julianehåb
K. Farvel
Godthåb (Nuuk)
Søndre Strømfjord
Godhavn
Upernavik
Greenland (Kalaallit Nunaat) (Den.)
Thule
Nares Str.
Lincoln Sea
Alert
Eureka
Ellesmere I.
Queen Elizabeth Islands
N. Magnetic Pole (1990)
Resolute
Pond Inlet
G. of Boothia
Baffin Bay
Baffin I.
Davis Str.
Hudson Str.
Foxe Basin
Southampton I.
Hudson Bay
James B.
Chisasibi
Inukjuak
Schefferville
Hebron
Nain
Gulf of St Lawrence
Newfoundland
Gander
L. Winnipeg
Churchill
Tree Limit
CANADA
Qurlurtuuq
Yellowknife
Gt Slave L.
Gt Bear L.
Great Bear
Norman Wells
Inuvik
Mackenzie
Banks I.
Victoria I.
McClure Str.
Beaufort Sea
Prudhoe Bay
Barrow
Alaska (U.S.A.)
ROCKY MTS
Polyarnyy
Kazach'ye
Laptev Sea
Novosibirskiye Ostrova
E. Siberian Sea
O. Vrangelya
North Pole
ATLANTIC OCEAN
Arctic Circle
average minimum extent of sea ice

Southern Polar Region (bottom map)

ATLANTIC OCEAN
Antarctic Circle
Falkland Is (U.K.)
Scotia Sea
Orcadas (Arg.)
S. Orkney Is (U.K.)
Signy (U.K.)
S. Shetland Is (U.K.)
ARGENTINA
Tierra del Fuego
CHILE
Drake Passage
PACIFIC OCEAN
Graham Land
Antarctic Peninsula
Palmer Arch.
Palmer Land
Alexander I.
Charcot I.
Bellingshausen Sea
Ellsworth Land
Peter I Øy (Nor.)
Thurston I.
Amundsen Sea
Siple I.
Marie Byrd Land
Mt Sidley 4181
Mt Seelig 3022
LESSER ANTARCTICA
Walgreen Coast
Ronne Ice Shelf
Berkner I.
Pensacola Mts
Vinson Massif 4897
Weddell Sea
Coats Land
Halley (U.K.)
Grl Belgrano (Arg.)
C. Norvegia
Georg von Neumayer (Germany)
Sanae (S.A.)
Maitri (India)
Novolozarevskaya (Rus. Fed.)
Prinsesse Astrid Kyst
Prinsesse Ragnhild Kyst
Asuka (Jap.)
Dronning Maud Land
Syowa (Jap.)
Molodezhnaya (Rus. Fed.)
Enderby Land
INDIAN OCEAN
Heard I. (Aust.)
Mawson (Aust.)
Mac. Robertson Land
3355
Pr. Charles Mts
Lambert Gl.
Amery Ice Shelf
Zhongshan (China)
Davis (Aust.)
C. Darnley
GREATER ANTARCTICA
American Highland
South Pole
Amundsen-Scott (U.S.)
Transantarctic Mts
Q. Maud Mts
Mt Kirkpatrick 4528
Mt Markham 4351
Vostok (Rus. Fed.)
Queen Mary Land
Mirnyy (Rus. Fed.)
Shackleton Ice Shelf
Knox Coast
Wilkes Land
Casey (Aust.)
C. Poinsett
Ross Ice Shelf
Roosevelt I.
Scott (U.S.)
McMurdo (U.S.)
C. Colbeck
Ross Sea
Victoria Land
George V Land
Terre Adélie
Dumont d'Urville (Fr.)
S. Magnetic Pole (1990)
C. Adare
Oates Land
Sturge I.
Balleny Is
Scott I.
average minimum extent of sea ice

Antarctic Research Stations
1 Artigas (Uruguay)
2 Teniente Rodolfo Marsh Martin (Chile)
3 Bellingshausen (Rus. Fed.)
4 Chang Cheng (Great Wall) (China)
5 Comandante Ferraz (Brazil)
6 Henryk Arctowski (Poland)
7 Teniente Jubany (Arg.)
8 King Sejong (Korea)
9 Capitán Arturo Prat (Chile)
10 General Bernardo O'Higgins (Chile)
11 Esperanza (Arg.)
12 Vicecomodoro Marambio (Arg.)
13 Palmer (USA)
14 Farady (UK)
15 Rothera
16 General San Martin (Arg.)
17 Václav Voytêch (Czech Rep.)

Abbreviations

Abbreviations used in Reference Map Section

	Full Form	English Form	Language
A			
a.d.	an der	on the	German
Akr.	Akra, Akrotírion	cape	Greek
Appno	Appennino	mountain range	Italian
Arch.	Archipelago	archipelago	English
B			
B.	1. Baai, Bahía, Baía, Baie, Bay, Bucht, Bukhta, Bugt	bay	Dutch, Spanish, Portuguese, French, English, German, Russian, Danish
	2. Ban	village	Indo-Chinese
	3. Barrage	dam	French
Bol.	Bol'sh/aya, -oy, -oye	big	Russian
Br.	1. Branch	branch	English
	2. Bridge, Brücke	bridge	English, German
	3. Burun	cape	Turkish
Brj	Baraj,-i	dam	Turkish
C			
C.	Cabo, Cap, Cape	cape	Spanish, French, English
Can.	Canal	canal	English
Cd	Ciudad	town	Spanish
Chan.	Channel	channel	English
Ck	Creek	creek	English
Cord.	Cordillera	mountain range	Spanish
D			
D.	1. Dağ, Dāgh, Daği, Dağlari	mountain, range	Persian, Turkish
	2. Daryācheh	lake	Persian
Dj.	Djebel	mountain	Arabic
E			
E.	East	east	English
Emb.	Embalse	reservoir	Spanish
Escarp.	Escarpment	escarpment	English
Estr.	Estrecho	strait	Spanish
F			
F.	Firth	estuary	Gaelic
Fj.	1. Fjell	mountain	Norwegian
	2. Fjord, Fjorður	fjord	Norwegian, Icelandic
Ft	Fort	fort	English
G			
G.	1. Gebel	mountain	Arabic
	2. Göl, Gölü	lake	Turkish
	3. Golfe, Golfo, Gulf	gulf	French, Italian, Portuguese, Spanish, English
	4. Gora, -gory	mountain, range	Russian
	5. Gunung	mountain	Malay, Indonesian
Gd, Gde	Grand, Grande	grand	English, French
Geb.	Gebirge	mountain range	German
Gl.	Glacier	glacier	French, English
Grl	General	general	Spanish
Gt, Gtr	Great, Groot, -e, Greater	greater	English, Dutch
H			
Har.	Harbour	harbour	English
Hd	Head	head	English
I			
I.	Ile, Ilha, Insel, Isla, Island Isle, Isola, Isole	island	French, Portuguese, German, Spanish, English, Italian
In.	1. Indre, Inner	inner	Norwegian, English
	2. Inlet	inlet	English
Is	Iles, Ilhas, Islands, Isles, Islas	islands	French, Portuguese, English, Spanish
Isth.	Isthmus	isthmus	English
J			
J.	Jabal, Jebel, Jibal	mountain	Arabic
K			
K.	1. Kaap, Kap, Kapp	cape	Dutch, German, Norwegian, Swedish
	2. Koh, Kuh, Kuhha	mountain	Persian
	3. Kolpos	gulf	Greek
Kep.	Kepulauan	islands	Indonesian
Khr.	Khrebet	mountain range	Russian
Kör.	Körfez, -i	gulf, bay	Turkish
L			
L.	1. Lac, Lago, Lagoa, Lake, Liman, Limni, Loch, Lough	lake	French, Italian, Spanish, Portuguese, English, Russian, Greek, Gaelic
Lag.	Lagoon, Laguna, -e, Lagôa	lagoon	English, Spanish, French, Portuguese
Ld	Land	land	English
Lit.	Little	little	English
M			
M.	1. Muang	town	Thai
	2. Mys	cape	Russian
m	metre, -s	metre(s)	English, French
Mal.	Mali, -o, -yy	small	Russian
Mf	Massif	mountain group	French
Mgne	Montagne(s)	mountain(s)	French
Mont	Monument	monument	English
Mt	Mont, Mount	mountain	French, English
Mte	Monte	mountain	Italian, Portuguese, Spanish
Mti	Monti	mountain, range	Italian
Mtn	Mountain	mountain	English
Mts	Monts, Mountains Montañas, Montes	mountains	French, English, Spanish, Italian, Portuguese
N			
N.	1. Neu, Ny	new	German
	2. Nevado	snow capped mtns	Spanish
	3. Noord, Nord, Norte Nørre, North	north	Danish, French, Portuguese, Spanish, Danish, English
Nat.	National	national	English
Nat. Pk	National Park	national park	English
Ndr	Neder, Nieder	lower	Dutch, Swedish, German
N.E.	North East	north east	English
N.M.	National Monument	national monument	English
N.P.	National Park	national park	English
N.W.	North West	north west	English
O			
O.	1. Oost, Ost	east	Dutch, German
	2. Ostrov	island	Russian
Ø	Øy	island	Norwegian
Oz.	Ozero, Ozera	lake(s)	Russian
P			
P.	1. Pass, Passo	pass	English, German, Italian
	2. Pic, Pico, Pizzo	peak	French, Portuguese, Spanish, Italian
	3. Pulau	island	Malay, Indonesian
P.P.	Pulau-pulau	islands	Indonesian
Pass.	Passage	passage	English
Peg.	Pegunungan	mountains	Indonesian
Pen.	Peninsula, Peninsola	peninsula	English, Italian
Pk	1. Park	park	English
	2. Peak, Pik	peak	English, Russian
Plat.	Plateau, Planalto	plateau	English, French, Portuguese
Pov	Poluostrov	peninsula	Russian
Pr.	Prince	prince	English
Pres.	President, Presidente	president	English, Spanish, Portuguese
Promy	Promontory	promontory	English
Pt	Point	point	English
Pta	1. Ponta, Punta	point	Portuguese, Italian, Spanish
	2. Puerta	pass	Spanish
Pte	Pointe	point	French
Pto	Porto, Puerto	port	Spanish
R			
R.	1. Rio, River, Rivière,	river	Portuguese, Spanish, English, French
	2. Ría	river mouth	Spanish
Ra.	Range	range	English
Rap.	Rapids	rapids	English
Res.	Reserve, Reservation	reserve, reservation	English
Resr	Reservoir	reservoir	English
Résr	Réservoir	reservoir	French
S			
S.	1. Salar, Salina	salt marsh	Spanish
	2. San, São	saint	Spanish, Portuguese
	3. See	sea, lake	German
	4. South, Sud	south	English, French
s.	sur	on	French
Sa	Serra, Sierra	mountain range	Portuguese, Spanish
Sd	Sound, Sund	sound	English, German, Swedish
S.E.	South East	south east	English
Sev.	Sever, Severnaya	north	Russian
Sp.	Spitze	peak	German
Spr.	Spring,(s)	spring(s)	English
St	Saint	saint	English
Sta	Santa	saint	Spanish
Sta.	Station	station	English
Ste	Sainte	saint	French
Sto	Santo	saint	Portuguese, Spanish
Str.	Strait	strait	English
S.W.	South West	south west	English
T			
T.	Tall, Tel	hill, mountain	Arabic, Hebrew
Tg	Tanjong, Tandjong	cape	Malay, Indonesian
Tk	Têluk, Têlok	bay	Indonesian
Tr.	Trench, Trough	trench, trough	English
U			
U.	Uad	wadi	Arabic
Ug	Ujung	cape	Malay
Upr	Upper	upper	English
V			
V.	1. Val, Valle	valley	French, Italian, Spanish
	2. Ville	town	French
Va	Villa	town	Spanish
Vdkhr.	Vodokhranilishche	reservoir	Russian
Vol.	Volcán, Volcano	volcano	Spanish, English
Vozv.	Vozvyshennost'	upland	Russian
W			
W.	1. Wadi	wadi	Arabic
	2. Water	water	English
	3. Well	well	English
	4. West	west	English
Y			
Yuzh.	Yuzhnaya, Yuzhno, Yuzhnyy	south	Russian
Z			
Z.	Zaliv	gulf, bay	Russian
Zap.	Zapadnyy, -aya, -o, -oye	western	Russian
Zem.	Zemlya	country, land	Russian

Index
Introduction to the index

In the index, the first number refers to the page, and the following letter and number to the section of the map in which the index entry can be found. For example, 38C2 **Paris** means that Paris can be found on page 38 where column C and row 2 meet.

Abbreviations used in the index

Afghan	Afghanistan	Hung	Hungary	Par	Paraguay	Arch	Archipelago
Alb	Albania	Ind	Indonesia	Phil	Philippines	B	Bay
Alg	Algeria	Irish Rep	Irish Republic	Pol	Poland	C	Cape
Ant	Antarctica	Kyrg	Kyrgyzstan	Port	Portugal	Chan	Channel
Arg	Argentina	Leb	Lebanon	Rom	Romania	Gl	Glacier
Aust	Australia	Lib	Liberia	Russian Fed	Russian Federation	I(s)	Island(s)
Bang	Bangladesh	Liech	Liechtenstein	S Africa	South Africa	Lg	Lagoon
Belg	Belgium	Lux	Luxembourg	S Arabia	Saudi Arabia	L	Lake
B-H	Bosnia-Herzegovina	Mac	Macedonia	Scot	Scotland	Mt(s)	Mountain(s)
Bol	Bolivia	Madag	Madagascar	Sen	Senegal	O	Ocean
Bulg	Bulgaria	Malay	Malaysia	Sl	Slovakia	P	Pass
Camb	Cambodia	Maur	Mauritania	Switz	Switzerland	Pass	Passage
Can	Canada	Mor	Morocco	Tanz	Tanzania	Pen	Peninsula
CAR	Central African Republic	Mozam	Mozambique	Thai	Thailand	Plat	Plateau
Cz. R	Czech Republic	Neth	Netherlands	Turk	Turkey	Pt	Point
Den	Denmark	Nic	Nicaragua	USA	United States of America	Res	Reservoir
Dom Rep	Dominican Republic	Nig	Nigeria	Urug	Uruguay	R	River
El Sal	El Salvador	N Ire	Ireland, Northern	Ven	Venezuela	S	Sea
Eng	England	Nor	Norway	Viet	Vietnam	Sd	Sound
Eq Guinea	Equatorial Guinea	NZ	New Zealand	Yugos	Yugoslavia	Str	Strait
Eth	Ethiopia	Pak	Pakistan	Zim	Zimbabwe	V	Valley
Fin	Finland	PNG	Papua New Guinea				

A

42B2 **Aachen** Germany
36C1 **Aalst** Belg
32K6 **Äänekoski** Fin
37C1 **Aarau** Switz
37B1 **Aare** R Switz
52A3 **Aba** China
71H4 **Aba** Nig
72D3 **Aba** Zaïre
63B2 **Ābādān** Iran
63C2 **Ābādeh** Iran
70B1 **Abadla** Alg
29C2 **Abaeté** Brazil
29C2 **Abaeté** R Brazil
27J4 **Abaetetuba** Brazil
52D1 **Abagnar Qi** China
71H4 **Abaji** Nig
19E3 **Abajo Mts** USA
71H4 **Abakaliki** Nig
49L4 **Abakan** Russian Fed
70C3 **Abala** Niger
70C2 **Abalessa** Alg
26D6 **Abancay** Peru
63C2 **Abarqū** Iran
53E3 **Abashiri** Japan
53E3 **Abashiri-wan** B Japan
22C1 **Abasolo** Mexico
51H7 **Abau** PNG
72D3 **Abaya** L Eth
72D2 **Abbai** R Eth
72E2 **Abbe** L Eth
38C1 **Abbeville** France
17D4 **Abbeville** Louisiana, USA
15C2 **Abbeville** S Carolina, USA
37C2 **Abbiategrasso** Italy
18B1 **Abbotsford** Can
12A2 **Abbotsford** USA
60C2 **Abbottabad** Pak
67F4 **Abd-al-Kuri** I Yemen
44J5 **Abdulino** Russian Fed
72C2 **Abéché** Chad
71F4 **Abengourou** Côte d'Ivoire
32F7 **Åbenrå** Den
42B1 **Åbenra** Den
71G4 **Abeokuta** Nig
72D3 **Abera** Eth
35C5 **Aberaeron** Wales
20C2 **Aberdeen** California, USA
13D3 **Aberdeen** Maryland, USA
15B2 **Aberdeen** Mississippi, USA
74C3 **Aberdeen** S Africa
34D3 **Aberdeen** Scot
8D2 **Aberdeen** S Dakota, USA

8A2 **Aberdeen** Washington, USA
6J3 **Aberdeen** L Can
34D3 **Aberfeldy** Scot
35D6 **Abergavenny** Wales
35C5 **Aberystwyth** Wales
44L2 **Abez'** Russian Fed
66D3 **Abhā** S Arabia
63B1 **Abhar** Iran
71H4 **Abia** State Nigeria
66C4 **Abi Addi** Eth
71F4 **Abidjan** Côte d'Ivoire
17C2 **Abilene** Kansas, USA
16C3 **Abilene** Texas, USA
35E6 **Abingdon** Eng
12C3 **Abingdon** USA
7K4 **Abitibi** R Can
7L5 **Abitibi,L** Can
45G7 **Abkhazskaya** Respublika, Georgia
36A2 **Ablis** France
60C2 **Abohar** India
71G4 **Abomey** Benin
72B3 **Abong Mbang** Cam
57E9 **Aborlan** Phil
72B2 **Abou Deïa** Chad
67E1 **Abqaiq** S Arabia
39A2 **Abrantes** Port
72D1 **'Abri** Sudan
76A3 **Abrolhos** Is Aust
8B2 **Absaroka Range** Mts USA
67F2 **Abū al Abyad** I UAE
67E1 **Abū 'Ali** I S Arabia
66D3 **Abū Arish** S Arabia
66B3 **Abu Deleiq** Sudan
67F2 **Abu Dhabi** UAE
66B3 **'Abu Dom** Watercourse Sudan
65C3 **Ābū el Jurdhān** Jordan
66B3 **Abu Fatima** Sudan
72D2 **Abu Hamed** Sudan
68E7 **Abuja** Nigeria
65A3 **Abu Kebir Hihya** Egypt
26E5 **Abunã** Brazil
26E6 **Abuna** R Bol
64D3 **Abū Sukhayr** Iraq
65B3 **Abu Suweir** Egypt
78B2 **Abut Head** C NZ
66B1 **Abu Tig** Egypt
72D2 **Abu'Urug** Well Sudan
72D2 **Abuye Meda** Mt Eth
72C2 **Abu Zabad** Sudan
72D3 **Abwong** Sudan
42B1 **Åby** Den

65C3 **Aby 'Aweigîla** Well Egypt
72C3 **Abyei** Sudan
13F2 **Acadia Nat Pk** USA
21B2 **Acambaro** Mexico
23B5 **Acandi** Colombia
21B2 **Acaponeta** Mexico
21B3 **Acapulco** Mexico
27L4 **Acaraú** Brazil
26E2 **Acarigua** Ven
21C3 **Acatlán** Mexico
22C2 **Acatlan** Mexico
22C2 **Acatzingo** Mexico
22D2 **Acayucan** Mexico
71F4 **Accra** Ghana
28E2 **Aceguá** Urug
60D4 **Achalpur** India
25B6 **Achao** Chile
53B2 **Acheng** China
37D1 **Achensee** L Austria
36E2 **Achern** Germany
33A3 **Achill** I Irish Rep
49L4 **Achinsk** Russian Fed
40D3 **Acireale** Italy
11D3 **Ackley** USA
23C2 **Acklins** I Caribbean
26D6 **Acobamba** Peru
25B4 **Aconcagua** Mt Chile
27L5 **Acopiara** Brazil
68B4 **A'cores** Is Atlantic O
A Coruña = La Coruña
37C2 **Acqui** Italy
75A2 **Acraman,L** Aust
Acre = 'Akko
26D5 **Acre** State, Brazil
20C3 **Acton** USA
22C1 **Actopan** Mexico
71G4 **Ada** Ghana
17C3 **Ada** USA
39B1 **Adaja** R Spain
10C6 **Adak** I USA
67G2 **Adam** Oman
72D3 **Adama** Eth
29B3 **Adamantina** Brazil
72B3 **Adamaoua** Region, Nig/Cam
71J4 **Adamawa** State, Nigeria
37D1 **Adamello** Mt Italy
14D1 **Adams** USA
62B3 **Adam's Bridge** India/Sri Lanka
3E3 **Adams L** Can
8A2 **Adams,Mt** USA
62C3 **Adam's Peak** Mt Sri Lanka

67E4 **'Adan** Yemen
45F8 **Adana** Turk
45E7 **Adapazari** Turk
66B3 **Adarama** Sudan
79F7 **Adare,C** Ant
57D4 **Adaut** Indon
75B1 **Adavale** Aust
37C2 **Adda** R Italy
67E1 **Ad Dahna'** Region, S Arabia
66D4 **Ad Dāli'** Yemen
67F1 **Ad Damman** S Arabia
66D3 **Ad Darb** S Arabia
66D2 **Ad Dawādimī** S Arabia
67E1 **Ad Dibdibah** Region, S Arabia
67F3 **Ad Dikākah** Region, S Arabia
67E2 **Ad Dilam** S Arabia
67E2 **Ad Dir'iyah** S Arabia
66C4 **Addis Zeman** Eth
64D3 **Ad Dīwanīyah** Iraq
64D3 **Ad Duwayd** S Arabia
11D3 **Adel** USA
76C4 **Adelaide** Aust
6J3 **Adelaide Pen** Can
51G8 **Adelaide River** Aust
20D3 **Adelanto** USA
Aden = 'Adan
58C4 **Aden,G of** Yemen/Somalia
70C3 **Aderbissinat** Niger
65D2 **Adhra** Syria
51G7 **Adi** I Indon
40C1 **Adige** R Italy
72D2 **Adigrat** Eth
66C4 **Adi Kale** Eth
60D5 **Adilābād** India
18B2 **Adin** USA
13E2 **Adirondack Mts** USA
72D3 **Ādis Abeba** Eth
72D2 **Adi Ugai** Eritrea
64C2 **Adiyaman** Turk
41F1 **Adjud** Rom
10G1 **Admiralty B** USA
6E4 **Admiralty I** USA
7K2 **Admiralty Inlet** B Can
76D1 **Admiralty Is** PNG
57B4 **Adonara** I Indon
62B1 **Ādoni** India
38B3 **Adour** R France
70A2 **Adrar** Region, Maur
70C2 **Adrar** Mts Alg
70A2 **Adrar Soutouf** Region, Mor
72C2 **Adré** Chad

69A2 **Adri** Libya
37E2 **Adria** Italy
12C2 **Adrian** Michigan, USA
16B2 **Adrian** Texas, USA
40C2 **Adriatic S** Italy/Yugos
72D2 **Adwa** Eth
49P3 **Adycha** R Russian Fed
71F4 **Adzopé** Côte d'Ivoire
44K2 **Adz'va** R Russian Fed
44K2 **Adz'vavom** Russian Fed
41E3 **Aegean S** Greece
58E2 **Afghanistan** Republic, Asia
72E3 **Afgooye** Somalia
66D2 **'Afif** S Arabia
71H4 **Afikpo** Nig
32G6 **Åfjord** Nor
71C2 **Aflou** Alg
72E3 **Afmado** Somalia
70A3 **Afollé** Region, Maur
14C1 **Afton** New York, USA
18D2 **Afton** Wyoming, USA
65C2 **Afula** Israel
45E8 **Afyon** Turk
65A3 **Aga** Egypt
72B2 **Agadem** Niger
70C3 **Agadez** Niger
70B1 **Agadir** Mor
60D4 **Agar** India
61D3 **Agartala** India
18B1 **Agassiz** Can
10A6 **Agattu** I USA
10A5 **Agattu Str** USA
71H4 **Agbor** Nig
71F4 **Agboville** Côte d'Ivoire
64E1 **Agdam** Azerbaijan
54C3 **Agematsu** Japan
38C3 **Agen** France
63B2 **Agha Jārī** Iran
45G8 **Aghri** Turk
37D2 **Agno** R Italy
66C3 **Agordat** Eth
37E1 **Agordo** Italy
71G4 **Agou,Mt** Togo
38C3 **Agout** R France
60D3 **Agra** India
64D2 **Ağrı** Turk
40D2 **Agri** R Italy
40C3 **Agrigento** Italy
41E3 **Agrinion** Greece
28A3 **Agrio** R Chile
40C2 **Agropoli** Italy
44J4 **Agryz** Russian Fed
7N3 **Agto** Greenland
29B3 **Agua Clara** Brazil

1

Aguada de Guerra Al Qalībah

28B4 **Aguada de Guerra** Arg
23D3 **Aguadilla** Puerto Rico
28B4 **Aguado Cicilio** Arg
22B1 **Aguanava** *R* Mexico
5J3 **Aguanish** Can
5J3 **Aguanus** *R* Can
28D1 **Aguapey** *R* Arg
21B1 **Agua Prieta** Mexico
29A3 **Aguaray Guazu** Par
21B2 **Aguascalientes** Mexico
22B1 **Aguascalientes** State, Mexico
29D2 **Aguas Formosas** Brazil
25G1 **Agua Vermelha, Barragem** *Res* Brazil
39A1 **Agueda** Port
70C3 **Aguelhok** Mali
70A2 **Agüenit** *Well* Mor
39B2 **Aguilas** Spain
22B2 **Aguililla** Mexico
xxviiiC7 **Agulhas Basin** Indian O
73C7 **Agulhas,C** S Africa
xxviiiC6 **Agulhas Plat** Indian O
57G9 **Agusan** *R* Phil
Ahaggar = Hoggar
45H8 **Ahar** Iran
78B1 **Ahipara B** NZ
36D1 **Ahlen** Germany
60C4 **Ahmadābād** India
62A1 **Ahmadnagar** India
72E3 **Ahmar** *Mts* Eth
15D1 **Ahoskie** USA
36D1 **Ahr** *R* Germany
36D1 **Ahrgebirge** Region, Germany
22B1 **Ahuacatlán** Mexico
22B1 **Ahualulco** Mexico
32G7 **Åhus** Sweden
63C1 **Āhuvān** Iran
63B2 **Ahvāz** Iran
23A4 **Aiajuela** Costa Rica
37B1 **Aigle** Switz
28E2 **Aiguá** Urug
37B2 **Aiguille d'Arves** *Mt* France
37B2 **Aiguille de la Grand Sassière** *Mt* France
53B1 **Aihui** China
54C3 **Aikawa** Japan
15C2 **Aiken** USA
52A5 **Ailao Shan** *Upland* China
28B1 **Aimogasta** Arg
29D2 **Aimorés** Brazil
37A1 **Ain** *R* France
71D1 **Aïn Beïda** Alg
71B2 **Ain Beni Mathar** Mor
69B2 **Ain Dalla** *Well* Egypt
39C2 **Aïn el Hadjel** Alg
72B2 **Aïn Galakka** Chad
71C1 **Aïn Oussera** Alg
71B2 **Aïn Sefra** Alg
64B4 **'Ain Sukhna** Egypt
11C3 **Ainsworth** USA
71B1 **Aïn Temouchent** Alg
54B4 **Aioi** Japan
70B2 **Aioun Abd el Malek** *Well* Maur
70B3 **Aïoun El Atrouss** Maur
26E7 **Aiquile** Bol
70C3 **Aïr** *Desert Region* Niger
3F3 **Airdrie** Can
36B1 **Aire** France
35E5 **Aire** *R* Eng
36C2 **Aire** *R* France
7L3 **Airforce I** Can
37C1 **Airolo** Switz
6E3 **Aishihik** Can
10L3 **Aishihik L** Can
36B2 **Aisne** Department, France
38C2 **Aisne** *R* France
76D1 **Aitape** PNG
43F1 **Aiviekste** *R* Latvia
52B2 **Aixa Zuogi** China
38D3 **Aix-en-Provence** France
37A2 **Aix-les-Bains** France
61C3 **Aiyar Res** India
41E3 **Aíyion** Greece
41E3 **Aíyna** *I* Greece
61D3 **Āīzawl** India
73B6 **Aizeb** *R* Namibia
53E4 **Aizu-Wakamatsu** Japan
40B2 **Ajaccio** Corse
22C2 **Ajalpan** Mexico
69B1 **Ajdabiyah** Libya
37E2 **Ajdovščina** Slovenia
53E3 **Ajigasawa** Japan
65C2 **Ajlūn** Jordan
67G1 **Ajman** UAE
60C3 **Ajmer** India
19D4 **Ajo** USA
41F2 **Ajtos** Bulg
22B2 **Ajuchitan** Mexico
41F3 **Ak** *R* Turk
54D2 **Akabira** Japan
54C3 **Akaishi-sanchi** *Mts* Japan
62B1 **Akalkot** India
65B1 **Akanthou** Cyprus
78B2 **Akaroa** NZ
66B2 **Akasha** Sudan
54B4 **Akashi** Japan
71C1 **Akbou** Alg
45K5 **Akbulak** Russian Fed
64C2 **Akçakale** Turk
70A2 **Akchar** *Watercourse* Maur
41F3 **Ak Dağ** *Mt* Turk
57C2 **Akelamo** Indon
72C3 **Aketi** Zaïre
64D1 **Akhalkalaki** Georgia
64D1 **Akhalsikhe** Georgia
41E3 **Akharnái** Greece
10H4 **Akhiok** USA
64A2 **Akhisar** Turk
43F1 **Akhiste** Latvia
69C2 **Akhmîm** Egypt
45H6 **Akhtubinsk** Russian Fed
45E5 **Akhtyrka** Ukraine
54B4 **Aki** Japan
7K4 **Akimiski I** Can
53E4 **Akita** Japan
70A3 **Akjoujt** Maur
65C2 **'Akko** Israel
10L2 **Aklavik** Can
70B3 **Aklé Aouana** *Desert Region* Maur
72D3 **Akobo** Sudan
72D3 **Akobo** *R* Sudan
60B1 **Akoha** Afghan
60D4 **Akola** India
71G4 **Akosombo Dam** Ghana
60D4 **Akot** India
7M3 **Akpatok I** Can
41E3 **Ákra Kafirévs** *C* Greece
41E4 **Ákra Líthinon** *C* Greece
41E3 **Ákra Maléa** *C* Greece
32A2 **Akranes** Iceland
41F3 **Ákra Sídheros** *C* Greece
41E3 **Ákra Spátha** *C* Greece
41E3 **Ákra Taínaron** *C* Greece
9E2 **Akron** USA
65B1 **Akrotiri B** Cyprus
60D1 **Aksai Chin** *Mts* China
45E8 **Aksaray** Turk
45J5 **Aksay** Kazakhstan
60D1 **Aksayquin Hu** *L* China
64B2 **Akşehir** Turk
64B2 **Akseki** Turk
49N4 **Aksenovo Zilovskoye** Russian Fed
50E1 **Aksha** Russian Fed
59G1 **Aksu** China
66C4 **Aksum** Eth
45J7 **Aktau** Kazakhstan
48J5 **Aktogay** Kazakhstan
45K5 **Aktumsyk** Kazakhstan
45K5 **Aktyubinsk** Kazakhstan
4F1 **Akulivik** Can
71H4 **Akure** Nig
32B1 **Akureyri** Iceland
10E5 **Akutan** USA
10E5 **Akutan** *I* USA
10E5 **Akutan Pass** USA
71H5 **Akwa Ibom** *State* Nigeria
Akyab = Sittwe
48K5 **Akzhal** Kazakhstan
9E3 **Alabama** State, USA
15B2 **Alabama** *R* USA
15B2 **Alabaster** USA
64C2 **Ala Dağlari** *Mts* Turk
45G7 **Alagir** Russian Fed
37B2 **Alagna** Italy
27L5 **Alagoas** State, Brazil
27L6 **Alagoinhas** Brazil
39B1 **Alagón** Spain
64E4 **Al Ahmadi** Kuwait
21D3 **Alajuela** Costa Rica
10F3 **Alakanuk** USA
48K5 **Alakol, Ozero** *L* Russian Fed/Kazakhstan
32L5 **Alakurtti** Russian Fed
64E3 **Al Amārah** Iraq
19B3 **Alameda** USA
22C1 **Alamo** Mexico
19C3 **Alamo** USA
16A3 **Alamogordo** USA
16C4 **Alamo Heights** USA
16A2 **Alamosa** USA
32H6 **Åland** *I* Fin
45E8 **Alanya** Turk
15C2 **Alapaha** *R* USA
44L4 **Alapayevsk** Russian Fed
Alappuzha = Alleppey
56A2 **Alas** *R* Indon
64A2 **Alaşehir** Turk
50D3 **Ala Shan** *Mts* China
6C3 **Alaska** State, USA
6D4 **Alaska,G of** USA
10G4 **Alaska Pen** USA
6C3 **Alaska Range** *Mts* USA
40B2 **Alassio** Italy
37C3 **Alássio** Region, Italy
10H2 **Alatna** *R* USA
44H5 **Alatyr'** Russian Fed
75B2 **Alawoona** Aust
67G2 **Al'Ayn** UAE
59F2 **Alayskiy Khrebet** *Mts* Tajikistan
49R3 **Alazeya** *R* Russian Fed
71E2 **Al'Azīzīyah** Libya
38D3 **Alba** Italy
64C2 **Al Bāb** Syria
39B2 **Albacete** Spain
39A1 **Alba de Tormes** Spain
64D2 **Al Badi** Iraq
41E1 **Alba Iulia** Rom
41D2 **Albania** Republic, Europe
76A4 **Albany** Aust
15C2 **Albany** Georgia, USA
12B3 **Albany** Kentucky, USA
13E2 **Albany** New York, USA
8A2 **Albany** Oregon, USA
4E3 **Albany** *R* Can
7K4 **Albany** *R* Can
66C4 **Albara** *R* Sudan
28B2 **Albardón** Arg
67G2 **Al Batinah** Region, Oman
51H8 **Albatross B** Aust
69B1 **Al Bayḍā** Libya
67E4 **Al Baydā'** Yemen
65C1 **Al Baylūlīyah** Syria
15C1 **Albemarle** USA
15D1 **Albemarle Sd** USA
37C2 **Albenga** Region, Italy
39B1 **Alberche** *R* Spain
75A1 **Alberga** Aust
36B1 **Albert** France
6G4 **Alberta** Province, Can
51H7 **Albert Edward** *Mt* PNG
74C3 **Albertinia** S Africa
72D3 **Albert,L** Uganda/Zaïre
9D2 **Albert Lea** USA
72D3 **Albert Nile** *R* Uganda
18D1 **Alberton** USA
5J4 **Alberton** Can
38D2 **Albertville** France
38C3 **Albi** France
17D1 **Albia** USA
27H2 **Albina** Suriname
12C2 **Albion** Michigan, USA
11C3 **Albion** Nebraska, USA
13D2 **Albion** New York, USA
64C4 **Al Bi'r** S Arabia
66D3 **Al Birk** S Arabia
67E2 **Al Biyadh** Region, S Arabia
39B2 **Alborán** *I* Spain
32G7 **Ålborg** Den
36E2 **Albstadt-Ebingen** Germany
64D3 **Al Bū Kamāl** Syria
37C1 **Albula** *R* Switz
8C3 **Albuquerque** USA
67G2 **Al Buraymi** Oman
69A1 **Al Burayqah**
69B1 **Al Burdī** Libya
76D4 **Albury** Aust
64E3 **Al Buşayyah** Iraq
34G3 **Albuskjell** *Oilfield* N Sea
67F3 **Al Buzūn** Yemen
39B1 **Alcalá de Henares** Spain
40C3 **Alcamo** Italy
39B1 **Alcaniz** Spain
27K4 **Alcântara** Brazil
39B2 **Alcaraz** Spain
39B2 **Alcázar de San Juan** Spain
39B2 **Alcira** Spain
29E2 **Alcobaça** Brazil
39B1 **Alcolea de Pinar** Spain
39B2 **Alcoy** Spain
39C2 **Alcudia** Spain
68J8 **Aldabra** *Is* Indian O
16A4 **Aldama** Mexico
22C1 **Aldama** Mexico
49O4 **Aldan** Russian Fed
49P4 **Aldan** *R* Russian Fed
49O4 **Aldanskoye Nagor'ye** *Upland* Russian Fed
35F5 **Aldeburgh** Eng
38B2 **Alderney** *I* UK
35E6 **Aldershot** Eng
70A3 **Aleg** Maur
29A2 **Alegre** *R* Brazil
25E3 **Alegrete** Brazil
28C2 **Alejandro Roca** Arg
49Q4 **Aleksandrovsk Sakhalinskiy** Russian Fed
48J4 **Alekseyevka** Kazakhstan
44F5 **Aleksin** Russian Fed
42D1 **Älem** Sweden
29D3 **Além Paraíba** Brazil
38C2 **Alençon** France
20E5 **Alenuihaha Chan** Hawaiian Is
Aleppo = Ḥalab
7M1 **Alert** Can
38C3 **Alès** France
40B2 **Alessandria** Italy
48B3 **Ålesund** Nor
10B5 **Aleutian Is** USA
10G4 **Aleutian Range** *Mts* USA
xxixL2 **Aleutian Trench** Pacific O
6E4 **Alexander Arch** USA
74B2 **Alexander Bay** S Africa
15B2 **Alexander City** USA
79G3 **Alexander I** Ant
78A3 **Alexandra** NZ
25J8 **Alexandra,C** South Georgia
7L2 **Alexandra Fjord** Can
69B1 **Alexandria** Egypt
9D3 **Alexandria** Louisiana, USA
9D2 **Alexandria** Minnesota, USA
9F3 **Alexandria** Virginia, USA
41F2 **Alexandroúpolis** Greece
5K3 **Alexis** *R* Can
3D3 **Alexis Creek** Can
65C2 **Aley** Leb
48K4 **Aleysk** Russian Fed
64D3 **Al Fallūjah** Iraq
67E4 **Al Fardah** Yemen
39B1 **Alfaro** Spain
41F2 **Alfatar** Bulg
64E3 **Al Fāw** Iraq
36E1 **Alfeld** Germany
29C3 **Alfensas** Brazil
41E3 **Alfiós** *R* Greece
37D2 **Alfonsine** Italy
29D3 **Alfonzo Cláudio** Brazil
29D3 **Alfredo Chaves** Brazil
67E1 **Al Furūthi** S Arabia
45K6 **Alga** Kazakhstan
28A1 **Algarrobal** Chile
28B3 **Algarrobo del Águila** Arg
39A2 **Algeciras** Spain
71C1 **Alger** Alg
70B2 **Algeria** Republic, Africa
67F3 **Al Ghaydah** Yemen
40B2 **Alghero** Sardegna
Algiers = Alger
11D3 **Algona** USA
13D1 **Algonquin Park** Can
4F4 **Algonquin Prov Park** Can
28D2 **Algorta** Urug
67G2 **Al Hadd** Oman
64D3 **Al Hadithah** Iraq
64C3 **Al Hadīthah** S Arabia
64D2 **Al Haḍr** Iraq
65D1 **Al Haffah** Syria
67G2 **Al Hajar al Gharbī** *Mts* Oman
67G2 **Al Hajar ash Sharqī** *Mts* Oman
64C3 **Al Hamad** *Desert Region* Jordan/S Arabia
64E4 **Al Haniyah** *Desert Region* Iraq
67E2 **Al Harīq** S Arabia
64C3 **Al Harrah** *Desert Region* S Arabia
69A2 **Al Harūj al Aswad** *Upland* Libya
67E1 **Al Hasa** Region, S Arabia
64D2 **Al Hasakah** Syria
64C4 **Al Hawjā'** S Arabia
64E3 **Al Hayy** Iraq
67F2 **Al Hibāk** Region, S Arabia
65D2 **Al Hījānah** Syria
64D3 **Al Hillah** Iraq
67E2 **Al Hillah** S Arabia
71B1 **Al Hoceima** Mor
66D4 **Al Hudaydah** Yemen
67E1 **Al Hufūf** S Arabia
67F2 **Al Humrah** Region, UAE
67G2 **Al Huwatsah** Oman
63B1 **Alīābad** Iran
63D3 **Aliabad** Iran
41E2 **Aliákmon** *R* Greece
64E3 **Alī al Gharbī** Iraq
62A1 **Alībāg** India
71B3 **Alibori** *R* Benin
39B2 **Alicante** Spain
8D4 **Alice** USA
76C3 **Alice Springs** Aust
40C3 **Alicudi** *I* Italy
60D3 **Aligarh** India
63B2 **Alīgūdarz** Iran
60B2 **Ali-Khel** Afghan
41F3 **Alimniá** *I* Greece
61C2 **Alīpur Duār** India
12C2 **Aliquippa** USA
67E4 **Al'Irqah** Yemen
64C3 **Al'Īsawiyah** S Arabia
74D3 **Aliwal North** S Africa
69B2 **Al Jaghbūb** Libya
64D3 **Al Jālamīd** S Arabia
69B2 **Al Jawf** Libya
64C4 **Al Jawf** S Arabia
45G8 **Al Jazīrah** Syria
64D2 **Al Jazīrah** *Desert* Region Syria/Iraq
39A2 **Aljezur** Port
67E1 **Al Jubayl** S Arabia
65D4 **Al Kabid** *Desert* Jordan
66D1 **Al Kahfah** S Arabia
67G2 **Al Kāmil** Oman
64D2 **Al Khābūr** *R* Syria
67G2 **Al Khābūrah** Oman
64D3 **Al Khālis** Iraq
66D2 **Al Khamāsīn** S Arabia
67G1 **Al Khasab** Oman
67F1 **Al Khawr** Qatar
69A1 **Al Khums** Libya
67F2 **Al Kidan** Region, S Arabia
65D2 **Al Kiswah** Syria
42A2 **Alkmaar** Neth
69B2 **Al Kufrah Oasis** Libya
64E3 **Al Kūt** Iraq
64C2 **Al Lādhiqīyah** Syria
61B2 **Allahābād** India
65D2 **Al Lajāh** *Mt* Syria
10H2 **Allakaket** USA
55B2 **Allanmyo** Myanmar
66B2 **'Allaqi** *Watercourse* Egypt
15C2 **Allatoona L** USA
74D1 **Alldays** S Africa
13D2 **Allegheny** *R* USA
9F3 **Allegheny Mts** USA
14A2 **Allegheny Res** USA
15C2 **Allendale** USA
78A3 **Allen,Mt** NZ
13D2 **Allentown** USA
62B3 **Alleppey** India
38C2 **Aller** *R* France
37D1 **Allgäu** *Mts* Germany
11B3 **Alliance** USA
66D2 **Al Līth** S Arabia
67F2 **Al Liwā** Region, UAE
75D1 **Allora** Aust
37B2 **Allos** France
12C2 **Alma** Michigan, USA
16C1 **Alma** Nebraska, USA
59F1 **Alma Ata** Kazakhstan
39A2 **Almada** Port
Al Madinah = Medina
51H5 **Almagan** I Pacific O
67F3 **Al Mahrah** Region, Yemen
67E1 **Al Majma'ah** S Arabia
67F1 **Al Manāmah** Bahrain
64D3 **Al Ma'nīyah** Iraq
19B2 **Almanor,L** USA
39B2 **Almansa** Spain
3C2 **Alma Peak** *Mt* Can
67F2 **Al Māriyyah** UAE
5G4 **Alma** Can
69B1 **Al Marj** Libya
Almaty = Alma Ata
39B1 **Almazán** Spain
36E1 **Alme** *R* Germany
29D2 **Almenara** Brazil
39B2 **Almeria** Spain
29C2 **Almes** *R* Brazil
44J5 **Al'met'yevsk** Russian Fed
42C1 **Älmhult** Sweden
66D1 **Al Midhnab** S Arabia
64E3 **Al Miqdādīyah** Iraq
79G3 **Almirante Brown** *Base* Ant
28A1 **Almirante Latorre** Chile
41E3 **Almirós** Greece
67E1 **Al Mish'ab** A Arabia
39A2 **Almodôvar** Port
60D3 **Almora** India
64D2 **Al Mawşil** Iraq
67E1 **Al Mubarraz** S Arabia
64C4 **Al Mudawwara** Jordan
67G2 **Al Mudaybi** Oman
67F1 **Al Muharraq** Bahrain
67E4 **Al Mukallā** Yemen
66D4 **Al Mukhā** Yemen
64D3 **Al Musayyib** Iraq
66C1 **Al Muwaylih** S Arabia
34C3 **Alness** Scot
64E3 **Al Nu'mānīyah** Iraq
34E4 **Alnwick** Eng
4B3 **Alonsa** Can
57B4 **Alor** *I* Indon
55C4 **Alor Setar** Malay
Alost = Aalst
76E2 **Alotau** PNG
76B3 **Aloysius,Mt** Aust
28C3 **Alpachiri** Arg
37D2 **Alpe di Succiso** *Mt* Italy
12C1 **Alpena** USA
37B1 **Alpes du Valais** *Mts* Switz
37B2 **Alpes Maritimes** *Mts* France
37E1 **Alpi Carniche** *Mts* Italy
40C1 **Alpi Dolomitiche** *Mts* Italy
37B2 **Alpi Graie** *Mts* Italy
19E4 **Alpine** Arizona, USA
16B3 **Alpine** Texas, USA
18D2 **Alpine** Wyoming, USA
37C1 **Alpi Orobie** *Mts* Italy
37B2 **Alpi Penine** *Mts* Italy
37C1 **Alpi Retiche** *Mts* Switz
37D1 **Alpi Venoste** *Mts* Italy
40B1 **Alps** *Mts* Europe
69A1 **Al Qaddāhiyah** Libya
65D1 **Al Qadmūs** Syria
64D3 **Al Qā'im** Iraq
64C4 **Al Qalībah** S Arabia

Al Qāmishlī **Arad**

64D2 **Al Qāmishlī** Syria
65D1 **Al Qardāhah** Syria
69A1 **Al Qaryah Ash Sharqiyah** Libya
64C3 **Al Qaryatayn** Syria
66D1 **Al Qasīm** Region, S Arabia
67E1 **Al Qātif** S Arabia
69A2 **Al Qatrūn** Libya
67E1 **Al Qayṣāmah** S Arabia
65D2 **Al Quatayfah** Syria
39A2 **Alquera** *Res* Port/Spain
64C3 **Al Qunayṭirah** Syria
66D3 **Al Qunfidhah** S Arabia
64E3 **Al Qurnah** Iraq
65D1 **Al Quṣayr** Syria
64C3 **Al Quṭayfah** Syria
67E2 **Al Quwayīyah** S Arabia
42B1 **Als** *I* Den
38D2 **Alsace** Region, France
42B2 **Alsfeld** Germany
34D4 **Alston** Eng
32J5 **Alta** Nor
25D4 **Alta Gracia** Arg
23D5 **Altagracia de Orituco** Ven
50B2 **Altai** *Mts* Mongolia
15C2 **Altamaha** *R* USA
27H4 **Altamira** Brazil
22C1 **Altamira** Mexico
40D2 **Altamura** Italy
50D1 **Altanbulag** Mongolia
49M5 **Altanbulag** Russian Fed
51H7 **Altape** PNG
21B2 **Altata** Mexico
48K5 **Altay** China
49L5 **Altay** Mongolia
48K4 **Altay** *Mts* Russian Fed
37C1 **Altdorf** Switz
36D1 **Altenkirchen** Germany
28B3 **Altiplanicie del Payún** *Plat* Arg
37B1 **Altkirch** France
29B2 **Alto Araguaia** Brazil
73D5 **Alto Molócue** Mozam
12A3 **Alton** USA
13D2 **Altoona** USA
28B2 **Alto Pencoso** *Mts* Arg
29B2 **Alto Sucuriú** Brazil
22C2 **Altotonga** Mexico
22B2 **Altoyac de Alvarez** Mexico
59G2 **Altun Shan** *Mts* China
18B2 **Alturas** USA
16C3 **Altus** USA
67F2 **Al'Ubaylah** S Arabia
66C1 **Al'Ulā** S Arabia
28A3 **Aluminé** Arg
64C4 **Al Urayq** *Desert Region* S Arabia
67F2 **Al'Uruq al Mu'taridah** Region, S Arabia
16C2 **Alva** USA
22C2 **Alvarado** Mexico
17C3 **Alvarado** USA
32G6 **Älvdalen** Sweden
28D1 **Alvear** Arg
17C4 **Alvin** USA
32J5 **Alvsbyn** Sweden
69A2 **Al Wāha** Libya
66C1 **Al Wajh** S Arabia
60D3 **Alwar** India
64D3 **Al Widyān** *Desert Region* Iraq/S Arabia
52A2 **Alxa Yougi** China
64E2 **Alyat** Azerbaijan
32J8 **Alytus** Lithuania
36E2 **Alzey** Germany
22C2 **Amacuzac** *R* Mexico
72D3 **Amadi** Sudan
64D2 **Amādīyah** Iraq
7L3 **Amadjuak L** Can
57C3 **Amahai** Indon
53B5 **Amakusa-shotō** *I* Japan
32G7 **Åmål** Sweden
49N4 **Amalat** *R* Russian Fed
41E3 **Amaliás** Greece
60C4 **Amalner** India
29A3 **Amambai** Brazil
29B3 **Amambai** *R* Brazil
50F4 **Amami** *I* Japan
50F4 **Amami gunto** *Arch* Japan
27H3 **Amapá** Brazil
27H3 **Amapá** State, Brazil
4B3 **Amaranth** Can
61E3 **Amarapura** Myanmar
16B2 **Amarillo** USA
45F7 **Amasya** Turk
22B1 **Amatitan** Mexico
22C1 **Amaulipas** Mexico
Amazonas = Solimões
27H4 **Amazonas** Brazil
26E4 **Amazonas** State, Brazil
24D4 **Amazonas** *R* Brazil
60D2 **Ambāla** India
62C3 **Ambalangoda** Sri Lanka
73E6 **Ambalavao** Madag
72B3 **Ambam** Cam
73E5 **Ambanja** Madag
49S3 **Ambarchik** Russian Fed
26C4 **Ambato** Ecuador
73E5 **Ambato-Boeny** Madag
73E5 **Ambatolampy** Madag
73E5 **Ambatondrazaka** Madag
42C3 **Amberg** Germany
21D3 **Ambergris Cay** *I* Belize
37A2 **Ambérieu** France
61B3 **Ambikāpur** India
73E5 **Ambilobe** Madag
73E6 **Amboasary** Madag
73E5 **Ambodifototra** Madag
73E6 **Ambohimahasoa** Madag
57C3 **Ambon** Indon
57C3 **Ambon** *I* Indon
73E6 **Ambositra** Madag
73E6 **Ambovombe** Madag
73B4 **Ambriz** Angola
77F2 **Ambrym** *I* Vanuatu
10B6 **Amchitka** USA
10B6 **Amchitka** *I* USA
10C6 **Amchitka Pass** USA
72C2 **Am Dam** Chad
44L2 **Amderma** Russian Fed
21B2 **Ameca** Mexico
22A1 **Ameca** *R* Mexico
22C2 **Amecacameca** Mexico
28C2 **Ameghino** Arg
42B2 **Ameland** *I* Neth
14D2 **Amenia** USA
18D2 **American Falls** USA
18D2 **American Falls Res** USA
19D2 **American Fork** USA
79F10 **American Highland** *Upland* Ant
xxixL5 **American Samoa** *Is* Pacific O
15C2 **Americus** USA
42B2 **Amersfoort** Neth
74D2 **Amersfoort** S Africa
11D2 **Amery** USA
79G10 **Amery Ice Shelf** Ant
11D3 **Ames** USA
14E1 **Amesbury** USA
4E4 **Ameson** Can
41E3 **Amfilokhía** Greece
41E3 **Amfissa** Greece
49P3 **Amga** Russian Fed
49P3 **Amgal** *R* Russian Fed
53D2 **Amgu** Russian Fed
10C2 **Amguema** *R* Russian Fed
53D1 **Amgun'** *R* Russian Fed
72D2 **Amhara** *Region* Eth
Amherst = Kyaikkami Myanmar
7M5 **Amherst** Can
14D1 **Amherst** Massachusetts, USA
13D3 **Amherst** Virginia, USA
62B2 **Amhūr** India
38C2 **Amiens** France
54C3 **Amino** Japan
65C1 **Amioune** Leb
68K8 **Amirante Is** Indian O
3H3 **Amisk L** Can
16B4 **Amistad Res** Mexico
61C2 **Amlekhgan** Nepal
10D6 **Amlia** *I* USA
64C3 **Amman** Jordan
32K6 **Ämmänsaario** Fin
54A3 **Amnyong-dan** *C* N Korea
63C1 **Amol** Iran
7L5 **Amos** Can
Amoy = Xiamen
57B3 **Ampana** Indon
73E6 **Ampanihy** Madag
29C3 **Amparo** Brazil
39C1 **Amposta** Spain
5H4 **Amqui** Can
66D3 **Amrān** Yemen
60D4 **Amrāvati** India
60C4 **Amreli** India
60C2 **Amritsar** India
42A2 **Amsterdam** Neth
74E2 **Amsterdam** S Africa
13E2 **Amsterdam** USA
72C2 **Am Timan** Chad
48H5 **Amu Darya** *R* Uzbekistan
10D6 **Amukta** *I* USA
10D6 **Amukta Pass** USA
7J2 **Amund Ringnes I** Can
6F2 **Amundsen G** Can
79F4 **Amundsen S** Ant
79E **Amundsen-Scott** *Base* Ant
56E3 **Amuntai** Indon
49O4 **Amur** *R* Russian Fed
66C3 **Amur** *Watercourse* Sudan
57B2 **Amurang** Indon
53D1 **Amursk** Russian Fed
53E1 **Amurskiy Liman** *Str* Russian Fed
53C2 **Amurzet** Russian Fed
49N2 **Anabar** *R* Russian Fed
26F2 **Anaco** Ven
8B2 **Anaconda** USA
18B1 **Anacortes** USA
16C2 **Anadarko** USA
49T3 **Anadyr'** Russian Fed
49T3 **Anadyr'** *R* Russian Fed
49U3 **Anadyrskiy Zaliv** *S* Russian Fed
49T3 **Anadyrskoye Ploskogor'ye** *Plat* Russian Fed
41F3 **Anáfi** *I* Greece
29D1 **Anagé** Brazil
64D3 **'Ānah** Iraq
19C4 **Anaheim** USA
62B2 **Anaimalai Hills** India
62C1 **Anakāpalle** India
10J2 **Anaktuvuk P** USA
73E5 **Analalaya** Madag
71H4 **Anambra** *State* Nig
71H4 **Anambra** *R* Nig
12A2 **Anamosa** USA
45E8 **Anamur** Turk
54B4 **Anan** Japan
62B2 **Anantapur** India
60D2 **Anantnag** India
27J7 **Anápolis** Brazil
63D2 **Anār** Iran
63C2 **Anārak** Iran
63E2 **Anardara** Afghan
51H5 **Anatahan** *I* Pacific O
25D3 **Añatuya** Arg
53B4 **Anbyŏn** N Korea
20C4 **Ancapa Is** USA
28B1 **Ancasti** Arg
6D3 **Anchorage** USA
26E7 **Ancohuma** *Mt* Bol
26C6 **Ancón** Peru
40C2 **Ancona** Italy
14D1 **Ancram** USA
25B6 **Ancud** Chile
36C3 **Ancy-le-Franc** France
26D6 **Andabuaylas** Peru
28A3 **Andacollo** Arg
75A1 **Andado** Aust
28B1 **Andagalá** Arg
32F6 **Andalsnes** Nor
39A2 **Andalucia** Region, Spain
15B2 **Andalusia** USA
59H4 **Andaman Is** Myanmar
59H4 **Andaman S** Myanmar
75A2 **Andamooka** Aust
29D1 **Andaraí** Brazil
35B5 **Andee** Irish Rep
36C2 **Andelot** France
32H5 **Andenes** Nor
37C1 **Andermatt** Switz
42B2 **Andernach** Germany
12B2 **Anderson** Indiana, USA
17D2 **Anderson** Missouri, USA
15C2 **Anderson** S Carolina, USA
6F3 **Anderson** *R* Can
62B1 **Andhra Pradesh** State, India
41E3 **Andikíthira** *I* Greece
48J5 **Andizhan** Uzbekistan
48H6 **Andkhui** Afghan
53B4 **Andong** S Korea
39C1 **Andorra** Principality, SW Europe
39C1 **Andorra-La-Vella** Andorra
35E6 **Andover** Eng
14E1 **Andover** New Hampshire, USA
14B1 **Andover** New York, USA
29B3 **Andradina** Brazil
10F3 **Andreafsky** USA
10C6 **Andreanof Is** USA
43G1 **Andreapol'** Russian Fed
64B2 **Andreas,C** Cyprus
16B3 **Andrews** USA
40D2 **Andria** Italy
9F4 **Andros** *I* Bahamas
41E3 **Ándros** *I* Greece
62A2 **Androth** *I* India
39B2 **Andújar** Spain
73B5 **Andulo** Angola
71G4 **Anécho** Togo
70C3 **Anéfis** Mali
77F3 **Aneityum** *I* Vanuatu
28B3 **Añelo** Arg
66C4 **Angareb** *Watercourse* Eth
49M4 **Angarsk** Russian Fed
44A3 **Ånge** Sweden
21A2 **Angel de la Guarda** *I* Mexico
57F7 **Angeles** Phil
32G7 **Angelholm** Sweden
75C1 **Angellala Creek** *R* Aust
20B1 **Angels Camp** USA
51G7 **Angemuk** *Mt* Indon
38B2 **Angers** France
36B2 **Angerville** France
55C3 **Angkor** *Hist Site* Camb
33C3 **Anglesey** *I* Wales
17C4 **Angleton** USA
7P3 **Angmagssalik** Greenland
73E5 **Angoche** Mozam
25B5 **Angol** Chile
12C2 **Angola** Indiana, USA
14A1 **Angola** New York, USA
68F9 **Angola** Republic, Africa
73B5 **Angola** Republic, Africa
xxxJ5 **Angola Basin** Atlantic O
10M4 **Angoon** USA
38C2 **Angoulême** France
70A1 **Angra do Heroismo** Açores
29D3 **Angra dos Reis** Brazil
28C3 **Anguil** Arg
23E3 **Anguilla** *I* Caribbean
23B2 **Anguilla Cays** *Is* Caribbean
61C3 **Angul** India
72C4 **Angumu** Zaïre
42C1 **Anholt** *I* Den
52C4 **Anhua** China
52D3 **Anhui** Province, China
29B2 **Anhumas** Brazil
54A3 **Anhŭng** S Korea
10G3 **Aniak** USA
29C2 **Anicuns** Brazil
71G4 **Anié** Togo
16A2 **Animas** *R* USA
16A3 **Animas Peak** *Mt* USA
11D3 **Anita** USA
36B2 **Anizy-le-Château** France
38B2 **Anjou** Republic, France
73E5 **Anjouan** *I* Comoros
73E5 **Anjozorobe** Madag
53B4 **Anju** N Korea
52B3 **Ankang** China
45E8 **Ankara** Turk
73E5 **Ankaratra** *Mt* Madag
73E6 **Ankazoabo** Madag
73E5 **Ankazobe** Madag
11D3 **Ankeny** USA
42C2 **Anklam** Germany
71H4 **Ankwe** *R* Nig
55D3 **An Loc** Viet
52B4 **Anlong** China
52C3 **Anlu** China
12B3 **Anna** USA
68E4 **Annaba** Alg
71D1 **'Annaba** Alg
64C3 **An Nabk** S Arabia
64C3 **An Nabk** Syria
75A1 **Anna Creek** Aust
69B2 **An Nāfūrah** Libya
64D3 **An Najaf** Iraq
34D4 **Annan** Scot
13D3 **Annapolis** USA
61B2 **Annapurna** *Mt* Nepal
12C2 **Ann Arbor** USA
65D1 **An Nāsirah** Syria
64E3 **An Nāsirīyah** Iraq
37B2 **Annecy** France
37B1 **Annemasse** France
3B2 **Annette I** USA
55D3 **An Nhon** Viet
66D3 **An Nimās** S Arabia
52A5 **Anning** China
15B2 **Anniston** USA
70C4 **Annobon, I** Eq Guinea
38C2 **Annonay** France
37B3 **Annot** France
23J1 **Annotto Bay** Jamaica
52D3 **Anqing** China
52B2 **Ansai** China
42C3 **Ansbach** Germany
23C3 **Anse d'Hainault** Haiti
52E1 **Anshan** China
52B4 **Anshun** China
16C1 **Ansley** USA
16C3 **Anson** USA
51F8 **Anson B** Aust
70C3 **Ansongo** Mali
12C1 **Ansonville** Can
12C3 **Ansted** USA
45F8 **Antakya** Turk
73F5 **Antalaha** Madag
45E8 **Antalya** Turk
45E8 **Antalya Körfezi** *B* Turk
73E5 **Antananarivo** Madag
79G1 **Antarctic Circle** Ant
79G3 **Antarctic Pen** Ant
39B2 **Antequera** Spain
16A3 **Anthony** USA
70B1 **Anti-Atlas** *Mts* Mor
37B3 **Antibes** France
7M5 **Anticosti, Î d'** Can
5J4 **Anticosti Prov Park** Can
12B1 **Antigo** USA
23E3 **Antigua** *I* Caribbean
Anti Lebanon = Jebel esh Sharqi
19B3 **Antioch** USA
77G5 **Antipodes Is** NZ
17C3 **Antlers** USA
25B2 **Antofagasta** Chile
29C4 **Antonina** Brazil
16A2 **Antonito** USA
34B4 **Antrim** County, N Ire
34B4 **Antrim** N Ire
14E1 **Antrim** USA
34B4 **Antrim Hills** N Ire
73E5 **Antseranana** Madag
73E5 **Antsirabe** Madag
73E5 **Antsohiny** Madag
55D3 **An Tuc** Viet
28C1 **Añtuya** Arg
36C1 **Antwerpen** Belg
35B5 **An Uaimh** Irish Rep
54A3 **Anui** S Korea
60C3 **Anupgarh** India
62C3 **Anuradhapura** Sri Lanka
Anvers = Antwerpen
6B3 **Anvik** USA
10B6 **Anvil Pk** *Mt* USA
49L5 **Anxi** China
52C2 **Anyang** China
52A3 **A'nyêmaqên Shan** *Upland* China
49S3 **Anyuysk** Russian Fed
37C2 **Anza** *R* Italy
3F2 **Anzac** Can
48K4 **Anzhero-Sudzhensk** Russian Fed
40C2 **Anzio** Italy
77F2 **Aoba** *I* Vanuatu
53E3 **Aomori** Japan
40B1 **Aosta** Italy
70B3 **Aoukar** *Desert Region* Maur
70C2 **Aoulef** Alg
72B1 **Aozou** Chad
25E2 **Apa** *R* Brazil/Par
9E4 **Apalachee B** USA
15C3 **Apalachicola** USA
15B3 **Apalachicola B** USA
22C2 **Apan** Mexico
26D3 **Apaporis** *R* Colombia
29B3 **Aparecida do Taboado** Brazil
57F7 **Aparri** Phil
41D1 **Apatin** Croatia, Yugos
44E2 **Apatity** Russian Fed
21B3 **Apatzingan** Mexico
42B2 **Apeldoorn** Neth
77H2 **Apia** Western Samoa
29C3 **Apiai** Brazil
22B1 **Apizolaya** Mexico
27G2 **Apoera** Suriname
75B3 **Apollo Bay** Aust
57G9 **Apo,Mt** Phil
15C3 **Apopka,L** USA
27H7 **Aporé** *R* Brazil
12A1 **Apostle Is** USA
22B1 **Apozol** Mexico
9E3 **Appalachian Mts** USA
37D2 **Appenino Tosco-Emiliano** *Mts* Italy
40C2 **Appennino Abruzzese** *Mts* Italy
40B2 **Appennino Ligure** *Mts* Italy
40D2 **Appennino Lucano** *Mts* Italy
40D2 **Appennino Napoletano** *Mts* Italy
40C2 **Appennino Tosco-Emilliano** *Mts* Italy
40C2 **Appennino Umbro-Marchigiano** *Mts* Italy
37C1 **Appenzell** Switz
35D4 **Appleby** Eng
11C2 **Appleton** Minnesota, USA
12B2 **Appleton** Wisconsin, USA
45J7 **Apsheronskiy Poluostrov** *Pen* Azerbaijan
4F5 **Apsley** Can
37A3 **Apt** France
25F2 **Apucarana** Brazil
22C1 **Apulco** Mexico
26E2 **Apure** *R* Ven
26D6 **Apurimac** *R* Peru
64C4 **'Aqaba** Jordan
64B4 **'Aqaba,G of** Egypt/S Arabia
63C2 **'Aqdā** Iran
27G8 **Aqidauana** Brazil
22A1 **Aqua Nueva** Mexico
29A3 **Aquidabán** *R* Par
25E2 **Aquidauana** Brazil
29A2 **Aquidauana** *R* Brazil
22B2 **Aquila** Mexico
61B2 **Ara** India
15B2 **Arab** USA
65C1 **'Arab al Mulk** Syria
58E4 **Arabian** *S* Asia/Arabian Pen
xxviiiE4 **Arabian Basin** Indian O
27L6 **Aracajú** Brazil
25E2 **Aracanguy, Mts de** *Mts* Brazil
29A3 **Aracanguy, Mts de** Par
27L4 **Aracati** Brazil
29D1 **Aracatu** Brazil
27H8 **Araçatuba** Brazil
39A2 **Aracena** Spain
27K7 **Araçuai** Brazil
65C3 **Arad** Israel
45C6 **Arad** Rom

Arada Augustów

72C2 Arada Chad
67F2 'Arādah UAE
76C1 Arafura S Indon/Aust
27H7 Aragarças Brazil
45G7 Aragats *Mt* Armenia
39B1 Aragón Region, Spain
39B1 Aragon *R* Spain
29C1 Araguaçu Brazil
27H6 Araguaia *R* Brazil
27J5 Araguaína Brazil
27J7 Araguari Brazil
29C2 Araguari *R* Brazil
54C3 Arai Japan
70C2 Arak Alg
63B2 Arāk Iran
10D3 Arakamchechen, Ostrov *Is* Russian Fed
55A2 Arakan Yoma *Mts* Myanmar
62B2 Arakkonam India
48G5 Aral Sea Kazakhstan/Uzbekistan
48H5 Aral'sk Kazakhstan
Aral'skoye More = Aral Sea
22C1 Aramberri Mexico
33B2 Aran *I* Irish Rep
33B3 Aran *Is* Irish Rep
39B1 Aranda de Duero Spain
22B1 Arandas Mexico
39B1 Aranjuez Spain
74B1 Aranos Namibia
17F4 Aransas Pass USA
54B4 Arao Japan
70B3 Araouane Mali
16C1 Arapahoe USA
25E4 Arapey *R* Urug
28D2 Arapey Grande *R* Urug
27L6 Arapiraca Brazil
29B3 Araporgas Brazil
25G3 Ararangua Brazil
27J8 Araraquara Brazil
29C3 Araras Brazil
76D4 Ararat Aust
64D2 Ararat Armenia
64D1 Aras *R* Turk
45H8 Aras *R* Azerbaijan/Iran
66C3 Aratali Eth
54D3 Arato Japan
26E2 Arauca *R* Ven
28A3 Arauco Chile
26D2 Arauea Colombia
60C3 Arāvalli Range *Mts* India
77E1 Arawa PNG
27J7 Araxá Brazil
45G8 Araxes *R* Iran
72D3 Arba Minch Eth
40B3 Arbatax Sardegna, Italy
45G8 Arbīl Iraq
37A1 Arbois France
4B3 Arborg Can
32H6 Arbrå Sweden
34D3 Arbroath Scot
37A3 Arc *R* France
37B2 Arc *R* France
38B3 Arcachon France
14A1 Arcade USA
15E4 Arcadia USA
18B2 Arcata USA
20D1 Arc Dome, Mt USA
22B2 Arcelia Mexico
14C2 Archbald USA
20E3 Arches Nat Pk USA
23B2 Archipiélago de Camaguey *Arch* Cuba
25B8 Archipiélago de la Reina Adelaida *Arch* Chile
25B6 Archipiélago de las Chones *Arch* Chile
26C2 Archipiélago de las Perlas *Arch* Panama
36C2 Arcis-sur-Aube France
18D2 Arco USA
29C3 Arcos Brazil
39A2 Arcos de la Frontera Spain
37A1 Arc Senans France
79C1 Arctic Circle
6E3 Arctic Red Can
6E3 Arctic Red River Can
6D3 Arctic Village USA
79G2 Arctowski *Base* Ant
41F2 Arda *R* Bulg
45H8 Ardabīl Iran
45G7 Ardahan Turk
70C2 Ardar des Iforas *Upland* Alg/Mali
63C2 Ardekān Iran
32F6 Ardel Nor
36C2 Ardennes Department, France
42B2 Ardennes Region, Belg
63C2 Ardestan Iran
64C3 Ardh es Suwwan *Desert Region* Jordan
39A2 Ardila *R* Port
75C2 Ardlethan Aust
8D3 Ardmore USA
34B3 Ardnamurchan *Pt* Scot
35F6 Ardres France
36A1 Ardres France
34C3 Ardrishaig Scot
34C4 Ardrossan Scot
23D3 Arecibo Puerto Rico
27L4 Areia Branca Brazil
19B3 Arena,Pt USA
32F7 Arendal Nor
26D7 Arequipa Peru
40C2 Arezzo Italy
37B3 Argens *R* France
40C2 Argenta Italy
38C2 Argentan France
36B2 Argenteuil France
5L4 Argentia Can
24D7 Argentina Republic, S America
xxxF7 Argentine Basin Atlantic O
38C2 Argenton-sur-Creuse France
41F2 Argeşul *R* Rom
60B2 Arghardab *R* Afghan
41E3 Argolikós Kólpos *G* Greece
36C2 Argonne Region, France
41E3 Árgos Greece
41E3 Argostólion Greece
20B3 Arguello,Pt USA
71G3 Argungu Nig
20D3 Argus Range *Mts* USA
76B2 Argyle,L Aust
34G3 Argyll *Oilfield* N Sea
42C1 Århus Den
73C6 Ariamsvlei Namibia
39B1 Arian zón *R* Spain
28C2 Arias Venado Arg
70B3 Aribinda Burkina
25B1 Arica Chile
60C2 Arifwala Pak
Arihā = Jericho
16B2 Arikaree, R USA
23L1 Arima Trinidad
29C2 Arinos Brazil
27G6 Arinos *R* Brazil
22B2 Ario de Rosales Mexico
23L1 Aripo,Mt Trinidad
26F5 Aripuana Brazil
26F5 Aripuaná *R* Brazil
34C3 Arisaig Scot
62B2 Ariskere India
22B1 Arista Mexico
22D2 Arista Mexico
3C3 Aristazabal I Can
28B3 Arizona Arg
8B3 Arizona State, USA
32G7 Årjäng Sweden
49Q4 Arka Russian Fed
45G5 Arkadak Russian Fed
17D3 Arkadelphia USA
48H4 Arkalyk Kazakhstan
9D3 Arkansas State, USA
9D3 Arkansas *R* USA
17C2 Arkansas City USA
44G3 Arkhangel'sk Russian Fed
53C2 Arkhara Russian Fed
49K2 Arkipelag Nordenshelda *Arch* Russian Fed
33B3 Arklow Irish Rep
5G5 Arkville USA
37D1 Arlberg P Austria
38C3 Arles France
11C3 Arlington S Dakota, USA
17C3 Arlington Texas, USA
13D3 Arlington Virginia, USA
18B1 Arlington Washington, USA
12B2 Arlington Heights USA
42B3 Arlon Belg
Armageddon = Megido
35B4 Armagh County, N Ire
35B4 Armagh N Ire
41F3 Armagós *I* Greece
36B3 Armançon *R* France
45G7 Armavir Russian Fed
22B2 Armena Mexico
45G7 Armenia Republic, Asia
26C3 Armenia Colombia
76E4 Armidale Aust
53E3 Armstrong Can
53D2 Armu *R* Russian Fed
7L3 Arnaud *R* Can
64B2 Arnauti *C* Cyprus
16C2 Arnett USA
42B2 Arnhem Neth
76C2 Arnhem,C Aust
76C2 Arnhem Land Aust
37D3 Arno *R* Italy
20B1 Arnold USA
37E1 Arnoldstein Austria
4B2 Arnot Can
4F4 Arnprior Can
36E1 Arnsberg Germany
74B2 Aroab Namibia
36E1 Arolsen Germany
37C2 Arona Italy
10F3 Aropuk L USA
77G1 Arorae *I* Kiribati
40B1 Arosa Switz
36B2 Arpajon France
29E2 Arquipélago dos Abrolhos *Arch* Brazil
70A3 Arquipélago dos Bijagós *Arch* Guinea-Bissau
29C1 Arraias Brazil
64D3 Ar Ramādī Iraq
34C4 Arran *I* Scot
64C2 Ar Raqqah Syria
69A2 Ar Rāqūbah Libya
38C1 Arras France
66D1 Ar Rass S Arabia
65D1 Ar Rastan Syria
66D2 Ar Rawdah S Arabia
70A2 Arrecife Canary Is
28C2 Arrecifes Arg
22B1 Arriaga Mexico
22D2 Arriaga Mexico
64E3 Ar Rifā't Iraq
64E3 Ar Rihāb *Desert Region* Iraq
Ar Rīyād = Riyadh
34C3 Arrochar Scot
28E2 Arroio Grande Brazil
29C1 Arrojado *R* Brazil
18C2 Arrowrock Res USA
78A2 Arrowtown NZ
20B3 Arroyo Grande USA
22C1 Arroyo Seco Mexico
67F1 Ar Ru'ays Qatar
67G2 Ar Rustaq Oman
64D3 Ar Rutbah Iraq
66D2 Ar Ruwaydah S Arabia
53C3 Arsen'yev Russian Fed
37D2 Arsiero Italy
38D2 Arsizio Italy
44H4 Arsk Russian Fed
41E3 Árta Greece
22B2 Arteaga Mexico
53C3 Artem Russian Fed
49L4 Artemovsk Russian Fed
49N4 Artemovskiy Russian Fed
36A2 Artenay France
8C3 Artesia USA
78B2 Arthurs P NZ
32G7 Århus Den
7K2 Artic Bay Can
25E4 Artigas Urug
28D2 Artigas Urug
6H3 Artillery L Can
38C1 Artois Region, France
43F3 Artsiz Ukraine
79G2 Arturo Prat *Base* Ant
45G7 Artvin Turk
72D3 Aru Zaïre
27H6 Aruanã Brazil
23C4 Aruba *I* Caribbean
61C2 Arun *R* Nepal
61D2 Arunāchal Pradesh Union Territory, India
53A2 Arun He *R* China
53A2 Arun Qi China
62B3 Aruppukkottai India
72D4 Arusha Tanz
72C3 Aruwimi *R* Zaïre
16A2 Arvada USA
50D2 Arvayheer Mongolia
37B2 Arve *R* France
7L5 Arvida Can
32H5 Arvidsjaur Sweden
44B2 Arvidsjaur Sweden
32G7 Arvika Sweden
19C3 Arvin USA
65C1 Arwad *I* Syria
57C4 Arwala Indon
44G4 Arzamas Russian Fed
71B1 Arzew Alg
60C2 Asadabad Afghan
54B4 Asahi *R* Japan
53E3 Asahi dake *Mt* Japan
53E3 Asahikawa Japan
54A3 Asan-man *B* S Korea
61C3 Asansol India
69A2 Asawanwah *Well* Libya
44L4 Asbest Russian Fed
74C2 Asbestos Mts S Africa
13E2 Asbury Park USA
xxxH5 Ascension *I* Atlantic O
42B3 Aschaffenburg Germany
42C2 Aschersleben Germany
40C2 Ascoli Piceno Italy
37C1 Ascona Switz
72E2 Āseb Eritrea
70C2 Asedjirad *Upland* Alg
72D3 Asela Eth
32H6 Åsele Sweden
41E2 Asenovgrad Bulg
36C2 Asfeld France
44K4 Asha Russian Fed
15C2 Ashburn USA
77G5 Ashburton NZ
76A3 Ashburton *R* Aust
64B3 Ashdod Israel
17D3 Ashdown USA
15D1 Asheboro USA
4B3 Ashern Can
9E3 Asheville USA
75D1 Ashford Aust
35F6 Ashford Eng
19D3 Ash Fork USA
Ashgabat = Ashkhabad
54D2 Ashibetsu Japan
53D4 Ashikaga Japan
54B4 Ashizuri-misaki *Pt* Japan
48G6 Ashkhabad Turkmenistan
16C2 Ashland Kansas, USA
9E3 Ashland Kentucky, USA
11A2 Ashland Montana, USA
17C1 Ashland Nebraska, USA
12C2 Ashland Ohio, USA
8A2 Ashland Oregon, USA
13D3 Ashland Virginia, USA
11D2 Ashland Wisconsin, USA
75C1 Ashley Aust
11C2 Ashley USA
14C2 Ashokan Res USA
65C3 Ashqelon Israel
64D3 Ash Shabakh Iraq
67G1 Ash Sha'm UAE
66D3 Ash Sh'ār S Arabia
64D2 Ash Sharqāt Iraq
64E3 Ash Shatrah Iraq
67E4 Ash Shihr Yemen
67E1 Ash Shumlul S Arabia
66D3 Ash Shuqayq S Arabia
12C2 Ashtabula USA
7M4 Ashuanipi L Can
5G4 Ashuapmushuan Prov Park Can
45F8 'Āsī *R* Syria
37D2 Asiago Italy
71A1 Asilah Mor
40B2 Asinara *I* Medit S
48K4 Asino Russian Fed
66D2 Asir Region, S Arabia
61B4 Aska India
64D2 Aşkale Turk
32G7 Askersund Sweden
65B4 Asl Egypt
60C1 Asmar Afghan
72D2 Asmera Eth
54B4 Aso Japan
72D2 Asosa Eth
16B3 Aspermont USA
78A2 Aspiring,Mt NZ
37A2 Aspres-sur-Buëch France
64C2 As Sabkhah Syria
67E2 As Salamiyah S Arabia
64C2 As Salamīyah Syria
66D4 Assale,L Eth
64D3 As Salmān Iraq
61D2 Assam State, India
64E3 As Samāwah Iraq
67F2 AsŞanām Region, S Arabia
65D2 As Sanamayn Syria
37B3 Asse *R* France
42B2 Assen Neth
42C1 Assens Den
69A1 As Sidrah Libya
6H5 Assiniboia Can
6G4 Assiniboine,Mt Can
4B4 Assiniboine *R* Can
5G3 Assinica Prov Park Can
37E3 Assisi Italy
64C3 As Sukhnah Syria
64E3 As Sulaymanīyāh Iraq
67E2 As Sulayyil S Arabia
67E2 As Summan Region, S Arabia
73E4 Assumption *I* Seychelles
66D2 As Suq S Arabia
64C3 As Suwaydā' Syria
64D3 As Suwayrah Iraq
64E2 Astara Azerbaijan
40B2 Asti Italy
41F3 Astipálaia *I* Greece
39A1 Astorga Spain
8A2 Astoria USA
45H6 Astrakhan' Russian Fed
39A1 Asturias Region, Spain
25E3 Asunción Par
72D3 Aswa *R* Uganda
66B2 Aswân Egypt
69C2 Aswân High Dam Egypt
69C2 Asyût Egypt
64C3 As Zilaf Syria
77H1 Atafu *I* Tokelau Is
71G4 Atakpamé Togo
57B5 Atambua Indon
7N3 Atangmik Greenland
57B4 Atapupu Indon
70A2 Atar Maur
20B3 Atascadero USA
48J5 Atasu Kazakhstan
57C4 Atauro *I* Indon
72D2 Atbara Sudan
48H4 Atbasar Kazakhstan
9D4 Atchafalaya B USA
9D3 Atchison USA
14C3 Atco USA
71F4 Atebubu Ghana
22B1 Atenguillo Mexico
40C2 Atessa Italy
36B1 Ath Belg
3F3 Athabasca Can
6G4 Athabasca *R* Can
6H4 Athabasca, L Can
Athens = Athínai
15B2 Athens Alabama, USA
9E3 Athens Georgia, USA
12C3 Athens Ohio, USA
14B2 Athens Pennsylvania, USA
15C1 Athens Tennessee, USA
17C3 Athens Texas, USA
71G4 Athiémé Benin
41E3 Athínai Greece
33B3 Athlone Irish Rep
65B1 Athna Cyprus
14D1 Athol USA
41E2 Áthos *Mt* Greece
35B5 Athy Irish Rep
72B2 Ati Chad
7J5 Atikoken Can
5J3 Atikonak L Can
49R3 Atka Russian Fed
10D6 Atka *I* USA
45G5 Atkarsk Russian Fed
17D2 Atkins USA
22C2 Atlacomulco Mexico
9E3 Atlanta Georgia, USA
12C2 Atlanta Michigan, USA
17C1 Atlantic USA
9F3 Atlantic City USA
14C2 Atlantic Highlands USA
xxxH8 Atlantic Indian Basin Atlantic O
xxxH7 Atlantic Indian Ridge Atlantic O
70C1 Atlas Saharien *Mts* Alg
6E4 Atlin Can
6E4 Atlin L Can
65C2 'Atlit Israel
22C2 Atlixco Mexico
9E3 Atmore USA
73E6 Atofinandrahana Madag
10H4 Atognak I USA
17C3 Atoka USA
22B1 Atotonilco Mexico
22C2 Atoyac *R* Mexico
26C2 Atrato *R* Colombia
67F2 Attaf Region, UAE
66D2 At Tā'if S Arabia
65D2 At Tall Syria
15B2 Attalla USA
7K4 Attawapiskat Can
4D3 Attawapiskat L Can
7K4 Attawapiskat *R* Can
64D3 At Taysīyah *Desert Region* S Arabia
12B2 Attica Indiana, USA
14A1 Attica New York, USA
36C2 Attigny France
5H2 Attikamagen L Can
65B1 Attila Line Cyprus
13E2 Attleboro Massachusetts, USA
55D3 Attopeu Laos
10A5 Attu USA
10A5 Attu *I* USA
64C4 At Tubayq *Upland* S Arabia
28B3 Atuel *R* Arg
32H7 Atvidaberg Sweden
20B2 Atwater USA
38D3 Aubagne France
36C2 Aube Department, France
36C2 Aube *R* France
38C3 Aubenas France
10N2 Aubry L Can
15B2 Auburn Alabama, USA
19B3 Auburn California, USA
12B2 Auburn Indiana, USA
13E2 Auburn Maine, USA
17C1 Auburn Nebraska, USA
13D2 Auburn New York, USA
18B1 Auburn Washington, USA
38C3 Auch France
71H4 Auchi Nig
77G4 Auckland NZ
xxixK7 Auckland Is NZ
38C3 Aude *R* France
7K4 Auden Can
37B1 Audincourt France
11D3 Audubon USA
75C1 Augathella Aust
74B2 Aughrabies Falls S Africa
42C3 Augsburg Germany
76A4 Augusta Aust
9E3 Augusta Georgia, USA
17C2 Augusta Kansas, USA
9G2 Augusta Maine, USA
18D1 Augusta Montana, USA
12A2 Augusta Wisconsin, USA
10H4 Augustine I USA
43E2 Augustów Pol

Banes Beja

21E2 **Banes** Cuba
3E3 **Banff** Can
34D3 **Banff** Scot
6G4 **Banff** *R* Can
3E3 **Banff Nat Pk** Can
71F3 **Banfora** Burkina
62B2 **Bangalore** India
71J4 **Bangangté** Cam
72C3 **Bangassou** CAR
56E1 **Banggi** *I* Malay
55D2 **Bang Hieng** *R* Laos
56C3 **Bangka** *I* Indon
56B2 **Bangkinang** Indon
56B3 **Bangko** Indon
55C3 **Bangkok** Thai
59H3 **Bangladesh** Republic, Asia
60D2 **Bangong Co** *L* China
9G2 **Bangor** Maine, USA
34B4 **Bangor** N Ire
14C2 **Bangor** Pennsylvania, USA
35C5 **Bangor** Wales
56E3 **Bangsalsembera** Indon
55B3 **Bang Saphan Yai** Thai
57F7 **Bangued** Phil
72B3 **Bangui** CAR
73D5 **Bangweulu** *L* Zambia
55C4 **Ban Hat Yai** Thai
55C2 **Ban Hin Heup** Laos
55C1 **Ban Houei Sai** Laos
55B3 **Ban Hua Hin** Thai
70B3 **Bani** *R* Mali
70C3 **Bani Bangou** Niger
67E3 **Banī Ma'arid** Region, S Arabia
69A1 **Banī Walīd** Libya
64C2 **Bāniyās** Syria
65C2 **Baniyas** Syria
40D2 **Banja Luka** Bosnia-Herzegovina
56D3 **Banjarmasin** Indon
70A3 **Banjul** The Gambia
55B4 **Ban Kantang** Thai
55D2 **Ban Khemmarat** Laos
55B4 **Ban Khok Kloi** Thai
77F2 **Banks** *Is* Vanuatu
51H8 **Banks I** Aust
6E4 **Banks I** British Columbia, Can
6F2 **Banks I** Northwest Territories, Can
18C1 **Banks L** USA
78B2 **Banks Pen** NZ
75E3 **Banks Str** Aust
61C3 **Bankura** India
55B2 **Ban Mae Sariang** Thai
55B2 **Ban Mae Sot** Thai
61E3 **Banmauk** Myanmar
55D3 **Ban Me Thuot** Viet
34B4 **Bann** *R* N Ire
55B4 **Ban Na San** Thai
60C2 **Bannu** Pak
28A4 **Baños de Chihuio** Chile
28A3 **Baños Maule** Chile
55C2 **Ban Pak Neun** Laos
55C4 **Ban Pak Phanang** Thai
55D3 **Ban Ru Kroy** Camb
55B3 **Ban Sai Yok** Thai
55C3 **Ban Sattahip** Thai
43D3 **Banská Bystrica** Slovakia
60C4 **Bānswāra** India
57B4 **Bantaeng** Indon
55B4 **Ban Tha Kham** Thai
55D2 **Ban Thateng** Laos
55C2 **Ban Tha Tum** Thai
33B3 **Bantry** Irish Rep
33A3 **Bantry** *B* Irish Rep
55D3 **Ban Ya Soup** Viet
71J4 **Banyo** Cam
56D4 **Banyuwangi** Indon
xxviiiE7 **Banzare Seamount** Indian O
52C3 **Baofeng** China
55C1 **Bao Ha** Viet
52B3 **Baoji** China
55D3 **Bao Loc** Viet
53C2 **Baoqing** China
50C4 **Baoshan** China
52C1 **Baotou** China
62C1 **Bāpatla** India
36B1 **Bapaume** France
64D3 **Ba'Qūbah** Iraq
41D2 **Bar** Montenegro, Yugos
57C3 **Bara** Indon
72D2 **Bara** Sudan
72E3 **Baraawe** Somalia
56E3 **Barabai** Indon
61B2 **Bāra Banki** India
48J4 **Barabinsk** Russian Fed
48J4 **Barabinskaya Step** *Steppe* Kazakhstan/Russian Fed
39B1 **Baracaldo** Spain
23C2 **Baracoa** Cuba
65D2 **Baradá** *R* Syria
75C2 **Baradine** Aust
66C3 **Baraka** *Watercourse* Eth
62A1 **Bārāmati** India
60C2 **Baramula** Pak
60D3 **Bārān** India
57F8 **Barangas** Phil
6E4 **Baranof I** USA
44D5 **Baranovichi** Belarus
75A2 **Baratta** Aust
61C2 **Barauni** India
27K8 **Barbacena** Brazil
23F4 **Barbados** *I* Caribbean
39C1 **Barbastro** Spain
74E2 **Barberton** S Africa
38B2 **Barbezieux** France
26D2 **Barbòsa** Colombia
23E3 **Barbuda** *I* Caribbean
76D3 **Barcaldine** Aust
Barce = Al Marj
40D3 **Barcellona** Italy
39C1 **Barcelona** Spain
26F1 **Barcelona** Ven
37B2 **Barcelonnette** France
76D3 **Barcoo** *R* Aust
28B3 **Barda del Medio** Arg
72B1 **Bardai** Chad
25C5 **Bardas Blancas** Arg
61C3 **Barddhamān** India
43E3 **Bardejov** Slovakia
37C2 **Bardi** Italy
37B2 **Bardonecchia** Italy
35C5 **Bardsey** *I* Wales
12B3 **Bardstown** USA
67F4 **Bareeda** Somalia
60D3 **Bareilly** India
44F1 **Barentsovo More** *S* Russian Fed
48D2 **Barentsøya** *I* Barents S
Barents S = Barentsovo More
72D2 **Barentu** Eritrea
61B3 **Bargarh** India
37B2 **Barge** Italy
49M4 **Barguzin** Russian Fed
49N4 **Barguzin** *R* Russian Fed
13F2 **Bar Harbor** USA
61C3 **Barhi** India
40D2 **Bari** Italy
39D2 **Barika** Alg
26D2 **Barinas** Ven
61C3 **Baripāda** India
66B2 **Bârîs** Egypt
60C4 **Bari Sādri** India
61D3 **Barisal** Bang
56D3 **Barito** *R* Indon
37B3 **Barjols** France
69A2 **Barjuj** *Watercourse* Libya
52A3 **Barkam** China
12B3 **Barkley,L** USA
17E2 **Barkley,L** USA
3C4 **Barkley Sd** Can
74D3 **Barkly East** S Africa
76C2 **Barkly Tableland** *Mts* Aust
36C2 **Bar-le-Duc** France
76A3 **Barlee,L** Aust
76A3 **Barlee Range** *Mts* Aust
40D2 **Barletta** Italy
60C3 **Barmer** India
75B2 **Barmera** Aust
35C5 **Barmouth** Wales
35E4 **Barnard Castle** Eng
48K4 **Barnaul** Russian Fed
14C3 **Barnegat** USA
14C3 **Barnegat B** USA
14A2 **Barnesboro** USA
7L2 **Barnes Icecap** Can
15C2 **Barnesville** Georgia, USA
12C3 **Barnesville** Ohio, USA
16B3 **Barnhart** USA
35E5 **Barnsley** Eng
35C6 **Barnstaple** Eng
71H4 **Baro** Nig
61D2 **Barpeta** India
26E1 **Barquisimeto** Ven
35F5 **Barqe** *Oilfield* N Sea
36D2 **Barr** France
27K6 **Barra** Brazil
34B3 **Barra** *I* Scot
75D2 **Barraba** Aust
29D1 **Barra da Estiva** Brazil
22B2 **Barra de Navidad** Mexico
29D3 **Barra de Piraí** Brazil
22D2 **Barra de Tonalá** Mexico
29A2 **Barra do Bugres** Brazil
29B2 **Barra do Garças** Brazil
28D2 **Barra do Quarai** Brazil
28E2 **Barra do Ribeiro** Brazil
71F4 **Barrage d'Ayama** Côte d'Ivoire
71J4 **Barrage de Mbakaou** *Dam* Cam
27K6 **Barragem de Sobradinho** Brazil
39A2 **Barragem do Castelo do Bode** *Res* Port
39A2 **Barragem do Maranhão** Port
34B3 **Barra Head** *Pt* Scot
27K8 **Barra Mansa** Brazil
26C6 **Barranca** Peru
26D2 **Barrancabermeja** Colombia
26F2 **Barrancas** Ven
105E3 **Barranqueras** Arg
26D1 **Barranquilla** Colombia
34B3 **Barra,Sound of** *Chan* Scot
4F4 **Barraute** Can
14D1 **Barre** USA
28B2 **Barreal** Arg
27K6 **Barreiras** Brazil
39A2 **Barreiro** Port
27L5 **Barreiros** Brazil
76D5 **Barren,C** Aust
10H4 **Barren Is** USA
27J8 **Barretos** Brazil
3F3 **Barrhead** Can
4F5 **Barrie** Can
3D3 **Barrière** Can
75B2 **Barrier Range** *Mts* Aust
3H2 **Barrington L** Can
76E4 **Barrington,Mt** Aust
29C2 **Barro Alto** Brazil
51G8 **Barroloola** Aust
12A1 **Barron** USA
23N2 **Barrouaillie** St Vincent
6C2 **Barrow** USA
33B3 **Barrow** *R* Irish Rep
35B5 **Barrow** *R* Irish Rep
76C3 **Barrow Creek** Aust
76A3 **Barrow I** Aust
35D4 **Barrow-in-Furness** Eng
6C2 **Barrow,Pt** USA
7J2 **Barrow Str** Can
13D1 **Barry's Bay** Can
14C2 **Barryville** USA
62B1 **Barsi** India
8B3 **Barstow** USA
38C2 **Bar-sur-Aube** France
36C2 **Bar-sur-Seine** France
27G2 **Bartica** Guyana
64B1 **Bartın** Turk
76D2 **Bartle Frere,Mt** Aust
8D3 **Bartlesville** USA
11C3 **Bartlett** USA
73D6 **Bartolomeu Dias** Mozam
43E2 **Bartoszyce** Pol
26B2 **Barú** Panama
56D4 **Barung** *I* Indon
56A2 **Barus** Indon
60D4 **Barwāh** India
60C4 **Barwāni** India
75C1 **Barwon** *R* Aust
44H5 **Barysh** Russian Fed
28D1 **Basail** Arg
20C1 **Basalt** USA
72B3 **Basankusu** Zaïre
28D2 **Basavilbas** Arg
57F6 **Basco** Phil
36D3 **Basel** France
40B1 **Basel** Switz
40D2 **Basento** *R* Italy
3F3 **Bashaw** Can
57F6 **Bashi Chan** Phil
44J5 **Bashkortostan** Respublika, Russian Fed
57B3 **Basiano** Indon
57F9 **Basilan** *I* Phil
35F6 **Basildon** Eng
28E2 **Basilio** Brazil
18E2 **Basin** USA
35E6 **Basingstoke** Eng
8B2 **Basin Region** USA
64E3 **Basra** Iraq
36D2 **Bas-Rhin** Department, France
55D3 **Bassac** *R* Camb
3F3 **Bassano** Can
40C1 **Bassano** Italy
37D2 **Bassano del Grappa** Italy
71G4 **Bassari** Togo
73D6 **Bassas da India** *I* Mozam Chan
55A2 **Bassein** Myanmar
23E3 **Basse Terre** Guadeloupe
11C3 **Bassett** USA
71G4 **Bassila** Benin
20C2 **Bass Lake** USA
76D5 **Bass Str** Aust
32G7 **Båstad** Sweden
63C3 **Bastak** Iran
61B2 **Basti** India
40B2 **Bastia** Corse
42B3 **Bastogne** Belg
17D3 **Bastrop** Louisiana, USA
17C3 **Bastrop** Texas, USA
72A3 **Bata** Eq Guinea
56D3 **Batakan** Indon
60D2 **Batala** India
50C3 **Batang** China
72B3 **Batangafo** CAR
57F6 **Batan Is** Phil
57D3 **Batanta** *I* Indon
29C3 **Batatais** Brazil
13D2 **Batavia** USA
75D3 **Batemans Bay** Aust
15C2 **Batesburg** USA
17D2 **Batesville** Arkansas, USA
17E3 **Batesville** Mississippi, USA
5H4 **Bath** Can
35D6 **Bath** Eng
13F2 **Bath** Maine, USA
13D2 **Bath** New York, USA
72B2 **Batha** *R* Chad
12C1 **Bathawana Mt** Can
76D4 **Bathurst** Aust
7M5 **Bathurst** Can
6F2 **Bathurst,C** Can
76C2 **Bathurst I** Aust
6H2 **Bathurst I** Can
6H3 **Bathurst Inlet** *B* Can
71F4 **Batié** Burkina
63C2 **Bātlāq-e-Gavkhūnī** *Salt Flat* Iran
75C3 **Batlow** Aust
64D2 **Batman** Turk
71D1 **Batna** Alg
9D3 **Baton Rouge** USA
65C1 **Batroun** Leb
55C3 **Battambang** Camb
62C3 **Batticaloa** Sri Lanka
62E3 **Batti Malv** *I* Indian O
3G3 **Battle** *R* Can
9E2 **Battle Creek** USA
7N4 **Battle Harbour** Can
18C2 **Battle Mountain** USA
56F6 **Batu Gajah** Malay
56E2 **Batukelau** Indon
45G7 **Batumi** Georgia
55C5 **Batu Pahat** Malay
56B3 **Baturaja** Indon
65C2 **Bat Yam** Israel
76B1 **Baubau** Indon
71H3 **Bauchi** Nig
71H3 **Bauchi** State, Nig
11D2 **Baudette** USA
37B2 **Bauges** *Mts* France
7N4 **Bauld,C** Can
37B1 **Baumes-les-Dames** France
49N4 **Baunt** Russian Fed
27J8 **Bauru** Brazil
29B2 **Baus** Brazil
42C2 **Bautzen** Germany
56D4 **Baween** *I* Indon
69B2 **Bawîti** Egypt
71F3 **Bawku** Ghana
55B2 **Bawlake** Myanmar
75A2 **Bawlen** Aust
15C2 **Baxley** USA
61E1 **Baxoi** China
21E2 **Bayamo** Cuba
53B2 **Bayan** China
56E4 **Bayan** Indon
50D2 **Bayandzürh** Mongolia
50C3 **Bayan Har Shan** *Mts* China
52A1 **Bayan Mod** China
52B1 **Bayan Obo** China
11B3 **Bayard** Nebraska, USA
16A3 **Bayard** New Mexico, USA
37B2 **Bayard** *P* France
10N4 **Bayard,Mt** Can
49N5 **Bayasgalant** Mongolia
57F8 **Baybay** Phil
64D1 **Bayburt** Turk
9E2 **Bay City** Michigan, USA
17C4 **Bay City** Texas, USA
64B2 **Bay Dağlari** Turk
44M2 **Baydaratskaya Guba** *B* Russian Fed
72E3 **Baydhabo** Somalia
38B2 **Bayeaux** France
37D1 **Bayerische Alpen** *Mts* Germany
42C3 **Bayern** State, Germany
12A1 **Bayfield** USA
67E4 **Bayhan al Qisāb** Yemen
64C3 **Bāyir** Jordan
49M6 **Baykal, Ozero** *L* Kazakhstan
50D1 **Baykalskiy Khrebet** *Mts* Russian Fed
49L3 **Baykit** Russian Fed
49L5 **Baylik Shan** *Mts* China/Mongolia
44K5 **Baymak** Russian Fed
15B2 **Bay Minette** USA
57F7 **Bayombang** Phil
38B3 **Bayonne** France
63E1 **Bayram Ali** Turkmenistan
42C3 **Bayreuth** Germany
17E3 **Bay St Louis** USA
13E2 **Bay Shore** USA
13D1 **Bays,L of** Can
66D4 **Bayt al Faqīh** Yemen
50B2 **Baytik Shan** *Mts* China
Bayt Lahm = Bethlehem
17D4 **Baytown** USA
39B2 **Baza** Spain
43F3 **Bazaliya** Ukraine
45H7 **Bazar-Dyuzi** *Mt* Azerbaijan
38B3 **Bazas** France
52B3 **Bazhong** China
63E3 **Bazmān** Iran
65D1 **Bcharre** Leb
11B2 **Beach** USA
14C3 **Beach Haven** USA
35F6 **Beachy Head** Eng
14D2 **Beacon** USA
73E5 **Bealanana** Madag
18D2 **Bear** *R* USA
12A2 **Beardstown** USA
Bear I = Bjørnøya
18D2 **Bear L** USA
4C3 **Bearskin Lake** Can
20B1 **Bear Valley** USA
8D2 **Beatrice** USA
34D2 **Beatrice** *Oilfield* N Sea
3D2 **Beatton** *R* Can
6F4 **Beatton River** Can
8B3 **Beatty** USA
4F4 **Beattyville** Can
36A2 **Beauce** Region, France
25E8 **Beauchene Is** Falkland Is
75D1 **Beaudesert** Aust
79B5 **Beaufort S** Can
74C3 **Beaufort West** S Africa
36A3 **Beaugeney** France
13E1 **Beauharnois** Can
34C3 **Beauly** Scot
19C4 **Beaumont** California, USA
9D3 **Beaumont** Texas, USA
36A2 **Beaumont-sur-Sarthe** France
38C2 **Beaune** France
4B3 **Beauséjour** Can
38C2 **Beauvais** France
3G2 **Beauval** Can
10J2 **Beaver** Alaska, USA
19D3 **Beaver** Utah, USA
4D2 **Beaver** *R* Can
3G3 **Beaver** *R* Saskatchewan, Can
3C1 **Beaver** *R* Yukon, Can
6D3 **Beaver Creek** Can
10J2 **Beaver Creek** USA
12B3 **Beaver Dam** Kentucky, USA
12B2 **Beaver Dam** Wisconsin, USA
18D1 **Beaverhead Mts** USA
3F3 **Beaverhill L** Can
12B1 **Beaver I** USA
17D2 **Beaver L** USA
3E2 **Beaverlodge** Can
60C3 **Beawar** India
28B2 **Beazley** Arg
29C3 **Bebedouro** Brazil
35F5 **Beccles** Eng
41E1 **Bečej** Serbia, Yugos
70B1 **Béchar** Alg
10G4 **Becharof L** USA
10F4 **Bechevin B** USA
9E3 **Beckley** USA
36E1 **Beckum** Germany
35E5 **Bedford** County, Eng
35E5 **Bedford** Eng
12B3 **Bedford** Indiana, USA
14A3 **Bedford** Pennsylvania, USA
23M2 **Bedford Pt** Grenada
14B2 **Beech Creek** USA
6D2 **Beechey Pt** USA
75C3 **Beechworth** Aust
75D1 **Beenleigh** Aust
65C3 **Beer Menuha** Israel
65C4 **Beer Ora** Israel
64B3 **Beersheba** Israel
Beèr Sheva = Beersheba
65C3 **Beér Sheva,** *R* Israel
8D4 **Beeville** USA
72C3 **Befale** Zaïre
73E5 **Befandriana** Madag
75C3 **Bega** Aust
49N2 **Begicheva, Ostrov** *I* Russian Fed
63C2 **Behbehān** Iran
10M4 **Behm Canal** *Sd* USA
63C1 **Behshahr** Iran
60B2 **Behsud** Afghan
53B2 **Bei'an** China
52B5 **Beihai** China
55D1 **Beihai** China
52D2 **Beijing** China
55E1 **Beiliu** China
52B4 **Beipan Jiang** *R* China
52E1 **Beipiao** China
73D5 **Beira** Mozam
64C3 **Beirut** Leb
50C2 **Bei Shan** *Mts* China
74E1 **Beitbridge** Zim
65C2 **Beit ed Dīne** Leb
65C3 **Beit Jala** Israel
39A2 **Beja** Port
71D1 **Beja** Tunisia

Bejaïa
Birch Mts

71D1 Bejaïa Alg
39A1 Béjar Spain
63D2 Bejestān Iran
43E3 Békéscsaba Hung
73E6 Bekily Madag
61B2 Bela India
60B3 Bela Pak
56D2 Belaga Malay
14B3 Bel Air USA
62B1 Belamoalli India
57B2 Belang Indon
56A2 Belangpidie Indon
44D5 Belarus Republic, Europe
Belau = Palau
74E2 Bela Vista Mozam
29A3 Béla Vista Par/Brazil
56A2 Belawan Indon
44K4 Belaya *R* Ukraine
43G3 Belaya Tserkov' Russian Fed
7J2 Belcher Chan Can
7L4 Belcher Is Can
60B1 Belchiragh Afghan
44J5 Belebey Russian Fed
72E3 Beled Weyne Somalia
27J4 Belém Brazil
28B1 Belén Arg
26C3 Belén Colombia
29A3 Belén Par
28D2 Belén Urug
8C3 Belen USA
28B1 Belén *R* Arg
34B4 Belfast N Ire
74E2 Belfast S Africa
5H5 Belfast USA
34B4 Belfast Lough *Estuary* N Ire
11B2 Belfield USA
72D2 Bēlfodiyo Eth
34E4 Belford Eng
38D2 Belfort France
62A1 Belgaum India
42A2 Belgium Kingdom, N W Europe
45F5 Belgorod Russian Fed
45E6 Belgorod Dnestrovskiy Ukraine
Belgrade = Beograd
18D1 Belgrade USA
69A2 Bel Hedan Libya
56C3 Belinyu Indon
56C3 Belitung *I* Indon
21D3 Belize Belize
21D3 Belize Republic, C America
49P2 Bel'kovskiv, Ostrov *I* Russian Fed
38C2 Bellac France
6F4 Bella Coola Can
37C2 Bellagio Italy
17C4 Bellaire USA
37C1 Bellano Italy
62B1 Bellary India
75C1 Bellata Aust
28D2 Bella Union Urug
28D1 Bella Vista Arg
37B2 Belledonne *Mts* France
14B2 Bellefonte USA
8C2 Belle Fourche USA
11B3 Belle Fourche *R* USA
38D2 Bellegarde France
15E4 Belle Glade USA
7N4 Belle I Can
38B2 Belle-Ile *I* France
7N4 Belle Isle,Str of Can
36A2 Bellême France
5K4 Belleoram Can
7L5 Belleville Can
12B3 Belleville Illinois, USA
17C2 Belleville Kansas, USA
18D2 Bellevue Idaho, USA
12A2 Bellevue Iowa, USA
18B1 Bellevue Washington, USA
37A2 Belley France
75D2 Bellingen Aust
8A2 Bellingham USA
79G2 Bellingshausen *Base* Ant
79G3 Bellingshausen S Ant
40B1 Bellinzona Switz
26C2 Bello Colombia
77E3 Bellona Reefs Nouvelle Calédonie
20B1 Bellota USA
13E2 Bellows Falls USA
7K3 Bell Pen Can
40C1 Belluno Italy
25D4 Bell Ville Arg
4C5 Belmond USA
14B1 Belmont USA
27L7 Belmonte Brazil
21D3 Belmopan Belize
53B1 Belogorsk Russian Fed
73E6 Beloha Madag
27K7 Belo Horizonte Brazil
16C2 Beloit Kansas, USA
9E2 Beloit Wisconsin, USA
44E3 Belomorsk Russian Fed
44K5 Beloretsk Russian Fed
Belorusssia = Belarus
73E5 Belo-Tsiribihina Madag
44F2 Beloye More *S*
44F3 Beloye Ozero *L* Russian Fed
44F3 Belozersk Russian Fed
12C3 Belpre USA
75A2 Beltana Aust
17C3 Belton USA
43F3 Bel'tsy Moldova
48K5 Belukha *Mt* Russian Fed
44H2 Belush'ye Russian Fed
12B2 Belvidere Illinois, USA
14C2 Belvidere New Jersey, USA
48J2 Belyy, Ostrov *I* Russian Fed
73B4 Bembe Angola
71G3 Bembéréke Benin
9D2 Bemidji USA
15B1 Bemis USA
32G6 Bena Nor
72C4 Bena Dibele Zaïre
75C3 Benalla Aust
34C2 Ben Attow *Mt* Scot
39A1 Benavente Spain
34B3 Benbecula *I* Scot
76A4 Bencubbin Aust
8A2 Bend USA
69E3 Bendarbeyla Somalia
34C3 Ben Dearg *Mt* Scot
43F3 Bendery Moldova
76D4 Bendigo Aust
71F3 Bénéna Mali
42C3 Benešov Czech Republic
40C2 Benevento Italy
59G4 Bengal,B of Asia
69A1 Ben Gardane Libya
71E2 Ben Gardane Tunisia
52D3 Bengbu China
57B3 Benggai *I* Indon
69B1 Benghāzī Libya
56B2 Bengkalis Indon
56B3 Bengkulu Indon
73B5 Benguela Angola
71A2 Benguerir Mor
64B3 Benha Egypt
34C2 Ben Hope *Mt* Scot
72C3 Beni Zaïre
26E6 Béni *R* Bol
70B1 Beni Abbes Alg
39C1 Benicarló Spain
39B2 Benidorm Spain
39C2 Beni Mansour Alg
69C2 Beni Mazar Egypt
71A2 Beni Mellal Mor
70C4 Benin Republic, Africa
71H4 Benin City Nig
71B1 Beni-Saf Alg
69C2 Beni Suef Egypt
16B2 Benkelman USA
34C2 Ben Kilbreck *Mt* Scot
33C2 Ben Lawers *Mt* Scot
34D3 Ben Macdui *Mt* Scot
34C2 Ben More Assynt *Mt* Scot
78B2 Benmore,L NZ
49R2 Bennetta, Ostrov *I* Russian Fed
34C3 Ben Nevis *Mt* Scot
13E2 Bennington USA
65C2 Bennt Jbail Leb
72B3 Bénoué *R* Cam
71J4 Bénoué Nat Pk Cam
36E2 Bensheim Germany
8B3 Benson Arizona, USA
11C2 Benson Minnesota, USA
72C3 Bentiu Sudan
29A2 Bento Gomes *R* Brazil
17D3 Benton Arkansas, USA
20C2 Benton California, USA
12B3 Benton Kentucky, USA
12B2 Benton Harbor USA
71H4 Benue State, Nig
71H4 Benue *R* Nig
34C3 Ben Wyvis *Mt* Scot
52E1 Benxi China
57C2 Beo Indon
41E2 Beograd Serbia, Yugos
61B3 Beohāri India
53C5 Beppu Japan
41D2 Berat Alb
72D2 Berber Sudan
72E2 Berbera Somalia
72B3 Berbérati CAR
36A1 Berck France
43F3 Berdichev Ukraine
45F6 Berdyansk Ukraine
12C3 Berea USA
57C2 Berebere Indon
71F4 Berekum Ghana
20B2 Berenda USA
66C2 Berenice Egypt
4C3 Berens *R* Can
6J4 Berens *R* Can
6J4 Berens River Can
75A1 Beresford Aust
11C3 Beresford USA
43E3 Berettyóújfalu Hung
43E2 Bereza Belarus
43E3 Berezhany Ukraine
43F2 Berezina *R* Belarus
44G3 Bereznik Russian Fed
44K4 Berezniki Russian Fed
45E6 Berezovka Ukraine
44L3 Berezovo Russian Fed
53D1 Berezovyy Russian Fed
64A2 Bergama Turk
40B1 Bergamo Italy
32F6 Bergen Nor
14B1 Bergen USA
36C1 Bergen op Zoom Neth
38C3 Bergerac France
36D1 Bergisch-Gladbach Germany
4D4 Bergland USA
62C1 Berhampur India
49S4 Beringa, Ostrov *I* Russian Fed
10K3 Bering Gl USA
49T3 Beringovskiy Russian Fed
xxixK2 Bering S Russian Fed/USA
79C6 Bering Str Russian Fed/ USA
63D3 Berīzak Iran
39B2 Berja Spain
71B2 Berkane Mor
8A3 Berkeley USA
14A3 Berkeley Spring USA
79F2 Berkner I Ant
41E2 Berkovitsa Bulg
35E6 Berkshire County, Eng
14D1 Berkshire Hills USA
3E3 Berland *R* Can
42C2 Berlin Germany
13E2 Berlin New Hampshire, USA
14A3 Berlin Pennsylvania, USA
42C2 Berlin State, Germany
26F8 Bermejo Bol
25E3 Bermejo *R* Arg
2M5 Bermuda *I* Atlantic O
40B1 Bern Switz
16A2 Bernalillo USA
29B4 Bernardo de Irigoyen Arg
14C2 Bernardsville USA
28C3 Bernasconi Arg
36A2 Bernay France
42C2 Bernburg Germany
37B1 Berner Orberland *Mts* Switz
7K2 Bernier B Can
42C3 Berounka *R* Czech Republic
71A2 Berrechid Mor
75B2 Berri Aust
71C2 Berriane Alg
38C2 Berry Region, France
20A1 Berryessa,L USA
9F4 Berry Is Bahamas
14B3 Berryville USA
74B2 Berseba Namibia
56F6 Bertam Malay
16A2 Berthoud P USA
72B3 Bertoua Cam
77G1 Beru *I* Kiribati
13D2 Berwick USA
34D4 Berwick-upon-Tweed Eng
35D5 Berwyn *Mts* Wales
73E5 Besalampy Madag
38D2 Besançon France
43E3 Beskidy Zachodnie *Mts* Pol
3G2 Besnard L Can
64C2 Besni Turk
65C3 Besor *R* Israel
15B2 Bessemer Alabama, USA
12B1 Bessemer Michigan, USA
73E5 Betafo Madag
39A1 Betanzos Spain
71J4 Betaré Oya Cam
65C3 Bet Guvrin Israel
74D2 Bethal S Africa
74B2 Bethanie Namibia
17D1 Bethany Missouri, USA
17C2 Bethany Oklahoma, USA
6B3 Bethel Alaska, USA
14D2 Bethel Connecticut, USA
12C2 Bethel Park USA
13D3 Bethesda USA
65C3 Bethlehem Israel
74D2 Bethlehem S Africa
13D2 Bethlehem USA
74D3 Bethulie S Africa
38C1 Bethune France
36A2 Béthune *R* France
73E6 Betioky Madag
75B1 Betoota Aust
72B3 Betou Congo
59E1 Betpak Dala *Steppe* Kazakhstan
73E6 Betroka Madag
7M5 Betsiamites Can
12A2 Bettendorf USA
61B2 Bettiah India
10H2 Bettles USA
37C2 Bēttola Italy
60D4 Bētul India
36C1 Betuwe Region, Neth
60D3 Betwa *R* India
36D1 Betzdorf Germany
10G4 Beverley,L USA
14E1 Beverly USA
20C3 Beverly Hills USA
70B4 Beyla Guinea
62B2 Beypore India
Beyrouth = Beirut
64B2 Beyşehir Turk
45E8 Beysehir Gölü *L* Turk
65C2 Beyt Shean Israel
37C1 Bezan Austria
44F4 Bezhetsk Russian Fed
38C3 Béziers France
63D1 Bezmein Turkmenistan
50D1 Beznosova Russian Fed
61C2 Bhadgaon Nepal
62C1 Bhadrāchalam India
61C3 Bhadrakh India
62B2 Bhadra Res India
62B2 Bhadrāvati India
60B3 Bhag Pak
61C2 Bhāgalpur India
60C2 Bhakkar Pak
61E3 Bhamo Myanmar
60D4 Bhandāra India
60D3 Bharatpur India
60C4 Bharūch India
61C3 Bhātiāpāra Ghat Bang
60C2 Bhatinda India
62A2 Bhatkal India
61C3 Bhātpāra India
60C4 Bhāvnagar India
61B4 Bhawānipatna India
60C2 Bhera Pak
61B2 Bheri *R* Nepal
61B3 Bhilai India
60C3 Bhīlwāra India
62C1 Bhīmavaram India
60D3 Bhind India
60D3 Bhiwāni India
62B1 Bhongir India
60D4 Bhopāl India
61C3 Bhubaneshwar India
60B4 Bhuj India
60D4 Bhusāwal India
46F4 Bhutan Kingdom, Asia
59H3 Bhutan Kingdom, Asia
71F4 Bia *R* Ghana
51G7 Biak *I* Indon
43E2 Biala Podlaska Pol
42D2 Bialograd Pol
43E2 Bialystok Pol
32A1 Biargtangar *C* Iceland
63D1 Bīarjmand Iran
57C2 Biaro *I* Indon
38B3 Biarritz France
37C1 Biasca Switz
64B4 Biba Egypt
53E3 Bibai Japan
73B5 Bibala Angola
37D3 Bibbiena Italy
42B3 Biberach Germany
71F4 Bibiani Ghana
5H4 Bic Can
41F1 Bicaz Rom
53D1 Bichi *R* Russian Fed
19D3 Bicknell USA
71H4 Bida Nig
62B1 Bīdar India
67G2 Bidbid Oman
13E2 Biddeford USA
35C6 Bideford Eng
35C6 Bideford B Eng
70C2 Bidon 5 Alg
43E2 Biebrza Pol
40B1 Biel Switz
42D2 Bielawa Pol
42B2 Bielefeld Germany
37B1 Bieler See *L* Switz
40B1 Biella Italy
43E2 Bielsk Podlaski Pol
55D3 Bien Hoa Viet
40C2 Biferno *R* Italy
64A1 Biga Turk
41F3 Bigadiç Turk
5H4 Big Bald Mt Can
4D3 Big Beaver House Can
16B4 Big Bend Nat Pk USA
18D1 Big Belt Mts USA
17E3 Big Black *R* USA
17C1 Big Blue *R* USA
15E4 Big Cypress Swamp USA
6D3 Big Delta USA
38D2 Bigent Germany
3G3 Biggar Can
75D1 Biggenden Aust
10L4 Bigger,Mt Can
18D1 Big Hole *R* USA
11A2 Bighorn *R* USA
11A2 Bighorn L USA
11A3 Bighorn Mts USA
55C3 Bight of Bangkok *B* Thai
70C4 Bight of Benin *B* W Africa
70C4 Bight of Biafra *B* Cam
7L3 Big I Can
10G4 Big Koniuji *I* USA
16B3 Big Lake USA
37C1 Bignasco Switz
70A3 Bignona Sen
19C3 Big Pine USA
15E4 Big Pine Key USA
20C3 Big Pine Mt USA
12B2 Big Rapids USA
6H4 Big River Can
4B2 Big Sand L Can
18D1 Big Sandy USA
3H3 Big Sandy L Can
11C3 Big Sioux *R* USA
20D1 Big Smokey V USA
8C3 Big Spring USA
16B1 Big Springs USA
11C2 Big Stone City USA
12C3 Big Stone Gap USA
4B3 Bigstone L Can
20B2 Big Sur USA
18E1 Big Timber USA
7J4 Big Trout L Can
4D3 Big Trout Lake Can
7K4 Big Trout Lake Can
40D2 Bihać Bosnia-Herzegovina
61C2 Bihār India
61C3 Bihar State, India
72D4 Biharamulo Tanz
45C6 Bihor *Mt* Rom
62B1 Bījāpur India
62C1 Bījāpur India
63B1 Bījār Iran
61B2 Bijauri Nepal
41D2 Bijeljina Bosnia-Herzegovina
52B4 Bijie China
60D3 Bijnor India
60C3 Bijnot Pak
60C3 Bikāner India
65C2 Bikfaya Leb
53C2 Bikin Russian Fed
53D2 Bikin *R* Russian Fed
72B4 Bikoro Zaïre
53A2 Bila He *R* China
60C3 Bilara India
60D2 Bilaspur India
61B3 Bilāspur India
55B3 Bilauktaung Range *Mts* Thai
39B1 Bilbao Spain
65A3 Bilbeis Egypt
Bilbo = Bilbao
42D3 Bílé *R* Czech Republic/ Slovakia
41D2 Bileća Bosnia-Herzegovina
64B1 Bilecik Turk
72C3 Bili *R* Zaïre
49S3 Bilibino Russian Fed
57F8 Biliran *I* Phil
8C2 Billings USA
72B2 Bilma Niger
9E3 Biloxi USA
72C2 Biltine Chad
71F4 Bimbita Ghana
60D4 Bina-Etawa India
57F8 Binalbagan Phil
73D5 Bindura Zim
73C5 Binga Zim
73D5 Binga *Mt* Zim
75D1 Bingara Aust
42B3 Bingen Germany
13F1 Bingham USA
9F2 Binghamton USA
56E1 Bingkor Malay
64D2 Bingöl Turk
52D3 Binhai China
56A2 Binjai Indon
56C2 Binjai Indon
57B4 Binongko *I* Indon
56B2 Bintan *I* Indon
56B3 Bintuhan Indon
56D2 Bintulu Malay
25B5 Bío Bío *R* Chile
xxxJ4 Bioko *I* Atlantic O
62B1 Bīr India
53C2 Bira Russian Fed
69B2 Bīr Abu Husein *Well* Egypt
69B2 Bi'r al Harash *Well* Libya
72C2 Birao CAR
61C2 Biratnagar Nepal
3F2 Birch *R* Can
10J2 Birch Creek USA
75B3 Birchip Aust
11D2 Birch L USA
4C3 Birch L Can
6G4 Birch Mts Can

Bouvet I **Busuanga**

xxxJ7 **Bouvet I** Atlantic O
28D2 **Bovril** Arg
3F3 **Bow** *R* Can
11B2 **Bowbells** USA
76D2 **Bowen** Aust
19E4 **Bowie** Arizona, USA
17C3 **Bowie** Texas, USA
3F4 **Bow Island** Can
9E3 **Bowling Green** Kentucky, USA
17D2 **Bowling Green** Missouri, USA
12C2 **Bowling Green** Ohio, USA
13D3 **Bowling Green** Virginia, USA
11B2 **Bowman** USA
13D2 **Bowmanville** Can
75D2 **Bowral** Aust
3D3 **Bowron** *R* Can
52D3 **Bo Xian** China
52D2 **Boxing** China
64B1 **Boyabat** Turk
72B3 **Boyali** CAR
43G2 **Boyarka** Ukraine
6J4 **Boyd** Can
14C2 **Boyertown** USA
3F3 **Boyle** Can
33B3 **Boyle** Irish Rep
35B5 **Boyne** *R* Irish Rep
15E4 **Boynoton Beach** USA
72C3 **Boyoma Falls** Zaïre
18E2 **Boysen Res** USA
41F3 **Bozcaada** *I* Turk
41F3 **Boz Dağlari** *Mts* Turk
8B2 **Bozeman** USA
Bozen = Bolzano
72B3 **Bozene** Zaïre
72B3 **Bozoum** CAR
37B2 **Bra** Italy
40D2 **Brač** *I* Croatia, Yugos
4F4 **Bracebridge** Can
69A2 **Brach** Libya
32H6 **Bräcke** Sweden
16B4 **Brackettville** USA
15E4 **Bradenton** USA
35E5 **Bradford** Eng
14A2 **Bradford** USA
20B3 **Bradley** USA
16C3 **Brady** USA
34E1 **Brae** Scot
34D3 **Braemar** Scot
39A1 **Braga** Port
28C3 **Bragado** Arg
39A1 **Bragana** Port
27J4 **Bragança** Brazil
29C3 **Bragança Paulista** Brazil
61D3 **Brahman-Baria** Bang
61C3 **Brāhmani** *R* India
61D2 **Brahmaputra** *R* India
45D6 **Brăila** Rom
9D2 **Brainerd** USA
74C3 **Brak** *R* S Africa
74D1 **Brak** *R* S Africa
70A3 **Brakna** Region, Maur
6F4 **Bralorne** Can
4F5 **Brampton** Can
26F3 **Branco** *R* Brazil
73B6 **Brandberg** *Mt* Namibia
42C2 **Brandenburg** Germany
42C2 **Brandenburg** State, Germany
74D2 **Brandfort** S Africa
8D2 **Brandon** Can
11C3 **Brandon** USA
74C3 **Brandvlei** S Africa
42C2 **Brandys nad Lebem** Czech Republic
43D2 **Braniewo** Pol
9E2 **Brantford** Can
75B3 **Branxholme** Aust
7M5 **Bras d'Or L** Can
29D2 **Brasíla de Minas** Brazil
26E6 **Brasiléia** Brazil
27J7 **Brasilia** Brazil
41F1 **Brasov** Rom
56E2 **Brassay Range** *Mts* Malay
42D3 **Bratislava** Slovakia
49M4 **Bratsk** Russian Fed
43F3 **Bratslav** Ukraine
13E2 **Brattleboro** USA
42C2 **Braunschweig** Germany
70A4 **Brava** *I* Cape Verde
8B3 **Brawley** USA
35B5 **Bray** Irish Rep
7L3 **Bray I** Can
36B2 **Bray-sur-Seine** France
3E3 **Brazeau** *R* Can
3E3 **Brazeau,Mt** Can
24E5 **Brazil** Republic, S America
xxxG5 **Brazil Basin** Atlantic O
8D3 **Brazos** *R* USA
72B4 **Brazzaville** Congo
42C3 **Brdy** *Upland* Czech Republic
78A3 **Breaksea Sd** NZ
78B1 **Bream B** NZ
56C4 **Brebes** Indon
34D3 **Brechin** Scot
36C1 **Brecht** Belg
11C2 **Breckenridge** Minnesota, USA
16C3 **Breckenridge** Texas, USA
42D3 **Břeclav** Czech Republic
35D6 **Brecon** Wales
35D6 **Brecon Beacons** *Mts* Wales
35C5 **Brecon Beacons Nat Pk** Wales
42A2 **Breda** Neth
74C3 **Bredasdorp** S Africa
32H6 **Bredby** Sweden
44B3 **Bredbyn** Sweden
44K5 **Bredy** Russian Fed
74B3 **Breede** *R* S Africa
13D2 **Breezewood** USA
37C1 **Bregenz** Austria
37C1 **Bregenzer Ache** *R* Austria
32A1 **Breiðafjörður** *B* Iceland
36D2 **Breisach** Germany
37C2 **Brembo** Italy
37C2 **Brembo** *R* Italy
15B2 **Bremen** USA
42B2 **Bremen** Germany
42B2 **Bremerhaven** Germany
18B1 **Bremerton** USA
19E3 **Brendel** USA
17C3 **Brenham** USA
38E2 **Brenner** *Mt* Austria
42C3 **Brenner** *P* Austria/Italy
37D2 **Breno** Italy
4F4 **Brent** Can
37D2 **Brenta** *R* Italy
20B2 **Brentwood** USA
40C1 **Brescia** Italy
Breslau = Wrocław
37D1 **Bressanone** Italy
34E1 **Bressay** *I* Scot
38B2 **Bressuire** France
38B2 **Brest** France
43E2 **Brest** Belarus
38B2 **Bretagne** Region, France
36B2 **Breteuil** France
36A2 **Bretevil** France
15B3 **Breton Sd** USA
14C2 **Breton Woods** USA
78B1 **Brett,C** NZ
15C1 **Brevard** USA
75C1 **Brewarrina** Aust
13F2 **Brewer** USA
14D2 **Brewster** New York, USA
18C1 **Brewster** Washington, USA
15B2 **Brewton** USA
74D2 **Breyten** S Africa
40D1 **Brežice** Slovenia, Yugos
72C3 **Bria** CAR
38D3 **Briancon** France
38C2 **Briare** France
15B2 **Bridgeport** Alabama, USA
19C3 **Bridgeport** California, USA
13E2 **Bridgeport** Connecticut, USA
11B3 **Bridgeport** Nebraska, USA
17C3 **Bridgeport** Texas, USA
20C1 **Bridgeport Res** USA
18E1 **Bridger** USA
16A1 **Bridger Peak** USA
14C3 **Bridgeton** USA
23F4 **Bridgetown** Barbados
5H5 **Bridgetown** Can
7M5 **Bridgewater** Can
14E2 **Bridgewater** USA
35D6 **Bridgwater** Eng
35D6 **Bridgwater B** Eng
35E4 **Bridlington** Eng
75E3 **Bridport** Aust
36C2 **Brienne-le-Château** France
37B1 **Brienzer See** *L* Switz
36C2 **Briey** France
40B1 **Brig** Switz
8B2 **Brigham City** USA
75C3 **Bright** Aust
35E6 **Brighton** Eng
37B3 **Brignoles** France
29A3 **Brilhante** *R* Brazil
36E1 **Brilon** Germany
41D2 **Brindisi** Italy
17D3 **Brinkley** USA
77E3 **Brisbane** Aust
13E2 **Bristol** Connecticut, USA
35D6 **Bristol** Eng
13E2 **Bristol** Pennsylvania, USA
14E2 **Bristol** Rhode Island, USA
9E3 **Bristol** Tennessee, USA
10F4 **Bristol B** USA
35C6 **Bristol Chan** Eng/Wales
6F4 **British Columbia** Province, Can
7K1 **British Empire Range** *Mts* Can
10K2 **British Mts** USA/Can
74D2 **Brits** S Africa
74C3 **Britstown** S Africa
4E4 **Britt** Can
11C2 **Britton** USA
38C2 **Brive** France
42D3 **Brno** Czech Republic
15C2 **Broad** *R* USA
14C1 **Broadalbin** USA
7L4 **Broadback** *R* Can
34B2 **Broad Bay** *Inlet* Scot
34C3 **Broadford** Scot
11A2 **Broadus** USA
11B1 **Broadview** Can
11B3 **Broadwater** USA
6H4 **Brochet** Can
6G2 **Brock I** Can
13D2 **Brockport** USA
14E1 **Brockton** USA
4F5 **Brockville** Can
14A2 **Brockway** USA
7K2 **Brodeur Pen** Can
34C4 **Brodick** Scot
43D2 **Brodnica** Pol
45D5 **Brody** Ukraine
36D1 **Brokem Haltern** Germany
16C1 **Broken Bow** Nebraska, USA
17D3 **Broken Bow** Oklahoma, USA
17D3 **Broken Bow L** USA
76D4 **Broken Hill** Aust
37C2 **Broni** Italy
32G5 **Brønnøysund** Nor
14D2 **Bronx** *Borough* New York, USA
57E9 **Brooke's Point** Phil
17D2 **Brookfield** Missouri, USA
12B2 **Brookfield** Wisconsin, USA
9D3 **Brookhaven** USA
18B2 **Brookings** Oregon, USA
8D2 **Brookings** South Dakota, USA
14E1 **Brookline** USA
11D3 **Brooklyn** USA
14D2 **Brooklyn** *Borough* New York, USA
11D2 **Brooklyn Center** USA
6G4 **Brooks** Can
10G4 **Brooks,L** USA
10E2 **Brooks Mt** USA
6C3 **Brooks Range** *Mts* USA
15C3 **Brooksville** USA
13E2 **Brookton** USA
75D1 **Brooloo** Aust
76B2 **Broome** Aust
34D2 **Brora** Scot
18B2 **Brothers** USA
67F4 **Brothers,The** *Is* Yemen
36A2 **Brou** France
72B2 **Broulkou** *Well* Chad
43G2 **Brovary** Ukraine
11D2 **Browerville** USA
16B3 **Brownfield** USA
3F4 **Browning** USA
8D4 **Brownsville** USA
8D3 **Brownwood** USA
51F8 **Browse** *I* Aust
36B1 **Bruay-en-Artois** France
76A3 **Bruce,Mt** Aust
4E5 **Bruce Pen** Can
36E2 **Bruchsal** Germany
37E1 **Bruck** Austria
42D3 **Bruck an der Mur** Austria
Bruges = Brugge
36B1 **Brugge** Belg
36D1 **Brühl** Germany
29D1 **Brumado** Brazil
36D2 **Brumath** France
18C2 **Bruneau** USA
18C2 **Bruneau** *R* USA
56D2 **Brunei** Sultanate, S E Asia
40C1 **Brunico** Italy
78B2 **Brunner,L** NZ
9E3 **Brunswick** Georgia, USA
13F2 **Brunswick** Maine, USA
17D2 **Brunswick** Mississippi, USA
25B8 **Brunswick,Pen de** Chile
75E3 **Bruny I** Aust
44G3 **Brusenets** Russian Fed
16B1 **Brush** USA
23A3 **Brus Laguna** Honduras
Brussel = Bruxelles
42A2 **Bruxelles** Belg
36D2 **Bruyères** France
8D3 **Bryan** USA
75A2 **Bryan,Mt** Aust
44E5 **Bryansk** Russian Fed
17D3 **Bryant** USA
20D3 **Bryce Canyon Nat Pk** USA
42D2 **Brzeg** Pol
64E4 **Būbīyan** *I* Kuwait/Iraq
72D4 **Bubu** *R* Tanz
74E1 **Bubye** *R* Zim
26D2 **Bucaramanga** Colombia
34E3 **Buchan** *Oilfield* N Sea
70A4 **Buchanan** Lib
16C3 **Buchanan,L** USA
34E3 **Buchan Deep** N Sea
7L2 **Buchan G** Can
33C2 **Buchan Ness** *Pen* Scot
7N5 **Buchans** Can
28C2 **Buchardo** Arg
Bucharest = Bucureşti
20B3 **Buchon, Pt** USA
37C1 **Buchs** Switz
19D4 **Buckeye** USA
35E5 **Buckingham** Eng
10F2 **Buckland** USA
10F2 **Buckland** *R* USA
75A2 **Buckleboo** Aust
13F2 **Bucksport** USA
72B4 **Buco Zau** Congo
5J4 **Buctouche** Can
41F2 **Bucureşti** Rom
43D3 **Budapest** Hung
60D3 **Budaun** India
35C6 **Bude** Eng
17D3 **Bude** USA
45G7 **Budennovsk** Russian Fed
36E1 **Büdingen** Germany
41D2 **Budva** Montenegro, Yugos
72A3 **Buéa** Cam
37A2 **Buech** *R* France
20B3 **Buellton** USA
28B2 **Buena Esperanza** Arg
26C3 **Buenaventura** Colombia
16A4 **Buenaventura** Mexico
16A2 **Buena Vista** Colorado, USA
22B2 **Buenavista** Mexico
13D3 **Buena Vista** Virginia, USA
20C3 **Buena Vista L** USA
28A4 **Bueno** *R* Chile
25E4 **Buenos Aires** Arg
25E5 **Buenos Aires** State, Arg
17D2 **Buffalo** Missisippi, USA
9F2 **Buffalo** New York, USA
11B2 **Buffalo** South Dakota, USA
17C3 **Buffalo** Texas, USA
8C2 **Buffalo** Wyoming, USA
74E2 **Buffalo** *R* S Africa
3E2 **Buffalo Head Hills** *Mts* Can
18C1 **Buffalo Hump** USA
3F3 **Buffalo L** Alberta, Can
3E1 **Buffalo L** Northwest Territories, Can
6H4 **Buffalo Narrows** Can
15C2 **Buford** USA
41F2 **Buftea** Rom
43E2 **Bug** *R* Pol/Ukraine
26C3 **Buga** Colombia
63C1 **Bugdayli** Turkmenistan
44H2 **Bugrino** Russian Fed
53A2 **Bugt** China
44J5 **Bugulma** Russian Fed
44J5 **Buguruslan** Russian Fed
64C2 **Buhayrat al Asad** *Res* Syria
18D2 **Buhl** Idaho, USA
11D2 **Buhl** Minnesota, USA
71F4 **Bui Dam** Ghana
35D5 **Builth Wells** Wales
28A2 **Buin** Chile
37A2 **Buis-les-Baronnies** France
37E2 **Buje** Croatia
72C4 **Bujumbura** Burundi
77E1 **Buka** *I* PNG
73C4 **Bukama** Zaïre
72C4 **Bukavu** Zaïre
58E2 **Bukhara** Uzbekistan
56D2 **Bukit Batubrok** *Mt* Indon
56B3 **Bukittinggi** Indon
72D4 **Bukoba** Tanz
57B3 **Buku Gandadiwata** *Mt* Indon
57C2 **Buku Saolat** *Mt* Indon
51G7 **Bula** Indon
57F8 **Bulan** Phil
60D3 **Bulandshahr** India
73C6 **Bulawayo** Zim
41F3 **Buldan** Turk
60D4 **Buldāna** India
10B6 **Buldir I** USA
50D2 **Bulgan** Mongolia
41E2 **Bulgaria** Republic, Europe
57C2 **Buli** Indon
37B1 **Bulle** Switz
78B2 **Buller** *R* NZ
75C3 **Buller,Mt** Aust
76A4 **Bullfinch** Aust
75B1 **Bulloo** *R* Aust
75B1 **Bulloo Downs** Aust
75B1 **Bulloo L** Aust
17D2 **Bull Shoals Res** USA
28A3 **Bulnes** Chile
76D1 **Bulolo** PNG
74D2 **Bultfontein** S Africa
57B4 **Bulukumba** Indon
72C3 **Bumba** Zaïre
56E2 **Bum Bum** *I* Malay
45D8 **Bu Menderes** *R* Turk
55B2 **Bumphal Dam** Thai
72D3 **Buna** Kenya
76A4 **Bunbury** Aust
34B4 **Buncrana** Irish Rep
77E3 **Bundaberg** Aust
75D2 **Bundarra** Aust
60D3 **Būndi** India
75C1 **Bungil** *R* Aust
73B4 **Bungo** Angola
54B4 **Bungo-suidō** *Str* Japan
56C2 **Bunguran** *I* Indon
72D3 **Bunia** Zaïre
17D2 **Bunker** USA
17D3 **Bunkie** USA
15C3 **Bunnell** USA
71H3 **Bunsuru** *R* Nig
56D3 **Buntok** Indon
57B2 **Buol** Indon
65D2 **Burāg** Syria
72C2 **Buram** Sudan
61B1 **Burang** China
72E3 **Burao** Somalia
57G8 **Burauen** Phil
66D1 **Buraydah** S Arabia
19C4 **Burbank** USA
75C2 **Burcher** Aust
63E1 **Burdalyk** Turkmenistan
45E8 **Burdur** Turk
53C1 **Bureinskiy Khrebet** *Mts* Russian Fed
50F2 **Bureya** Russian Fed
53C1 **Bureya** *R* Russian Fed
65B3 **Bûr Fu'ad** Egypt
42C2 **Burg** Germany
41F2 **Burgas** Bulg
15D2 **Burgaw** USA
37B1 **Burgdorf** Switz
5K4 **Burgeo** Can
74D3 **Burgersdorp** S Africa
48K5 **Burgin** China
22C1 **Burgos** Mexico
39B1 **Burgos** Spain
43D1 **Burgsvik** Sweden
41F3 **Burhaniye** Turk
60D4 **Burhānpur** India
57F8 **Burias** *I* Phil
5K4 **Burin Pen** Can
55C2 **Buriram** Thai
29C2 **Buritis** Brazil
3C3 **Burke Chan** Can
76C2 **Burketown** Aust
70B3 **Burkina** Republic, Africa
13D1 **Burk's Falls** Can
8B2 **Burley** USA
4F5 **Burlington** Can
16B2 **Burlington** Colorado, USA
9D2 **Burlington** Iowa, USA
14C2 **Burlington** New Jersey, USA
15D1 **Burlington** North Carolina, USA
9F2 **Burlington** Vermont, USA
18B1 **Burlington** Washington, USA
4D5 **Burlington** Wisconsin, USA
Burma = Myanmar
16C3 **Burnet** USA
18B2 **Burney** USA
14B2 **Burnham** USA
76D5 **Burnie** Aust
35D5 **Burnley** Eng
18C2 **Burns** USA
6F4 **Burns Lake** Can
59G1 **Burqin** China
75A2 **Burra** Aust
75D2 **Burragorang,L** Aust
34D2 **Burray** *I* Scot
75C2 **Burren Junction** Aust
75C2 **Burrinjuck Res** Aust
51G8 **Burrundie** Aust
45D7 **Bursa** Turk
66B1 **Bur Safâga** Egypt
Bûr Sa'îd = Port Said
65B4 **Bûr Taufiq** Egypt
12C2 **Burton** USA
35E5 **Burton upon Trent** Eng
32J6 **Burtrask** Sweden
75B2 **Burtundy** Aust
57C3 **Buru** Indon
72C4 **Burundi** Republic, Africa
56B2 **Burung** Indon
11C3 **Burwell** USA
49N4 **Buryatskaya** Respublika, Russian Fed
72D2 **Burye** Eth
45J6 **Burynshik** Kazakhstan
35F5 **Bury St Edmunds** Eng
63C3 **Būshehr** Iran
72B4 **Busira** *R* Zaïre
43E2 **Busko Zdrój** Pol
65D2 **Busrā ash Shām** Syria
36D3 **Bussang** France
76A4 **Busselton** Aust
38D2 **Busto** Italy
40B1 **Busto Arsizio** Italy
57E8 **Busuanga** *I* Phil

Buta Cap Rosso

72C3 **Buta** Zaïre
28B3 **Buta Ranquil** Arg
72C4 **Butare** Rwanda
34C4 **Bute** *I* Scot
53A2 **Butha Qi** China
13D2 **Butler** USA
8B2 **Butte** USA
55C4 **Butterworth** Malay
74D3 **Butterworth** S Africa
33B2 **Butt of Lewis** *C* Scot
7M3 **Button Is** Can
20C3 **Buttonwillow** USA
57G9 **Butuan** Phil
57B4 **Butung** *I* Indon
76B1 **Butung** *I* Indon
45G5 **Buturlinovka** Russian Fed
61B2 **Butwal** Nepal
36E1 **Butzbach** Germany
72E3 **Buulobarde** Somalia
72E3 **Buurhaakaba** Somalia
44G4 **Buy** Russian Fed
52B1 **Buyant Ovvo** Mongolia
45H7 **Buynaksk** Russian Fed
49N5 **Buyr Nuur** *L* Mongolia
45G8 **Büyük Ağri Daği** *Mt* Turk
53E2 **Buyukly** Russian Fed
64A2 **Büyük Menderes** *R* Turk
41F1 **Buzău** Rom
41F1 **Buzău** *R* Rom
44J5 **Buzuluk** Russian Fed
14E2 **Buzzards B** USA
41F2 **Byala** Bulg
41E2 **Byala Slatina** Bulg
6H2 **Byam Martin Chan** Can
6H2 **Byam Martin I** Can
65C1 **Byblos** *Hist. Site* Leb
43D2 **Bydgoszcz** Pol
16B2 **Byers** USA
32F7 **Bygland** Nor
43G2 **Bykhov** Belarus
53E2 **Bykov** Russian Fed
7K2 **Bylot I** Can
75C2 **Byrock** Aust
20B2 **Byron** USA
75D1 **Byron,C** Aust
49P3 **Bytantay** *R* Russian Fed
43D2 **Bytom** Pol

C

25E3 **Caacupé** Par
29A4 **Caaguazú** Par
73B5 **Caála** Angola
3C3 **Caamano Sd** Can
29A4 **Caapucú** Par
29B3 **Caarapó** Brazil
25E3 **Caazapá** Par
16A3 **Caballo Res** USA
57F7 **Cabanatuan** Phil
13F1 **Cabano** Can
27M5 **Cabedelo** Brazil
39A2 **Cabeza del Buey** Spain
28C3 **Cabildo** Arg
28A2 **Cabildo** Chile
26D1 **Cabimas** Ven
72B4 **Cabinda** Angola
72B4 **Cabinda** Province, Angola
18C1 **Cabinet Mts** USA
23C3 **Cabo Beata** Dom Rep
39C2 **Cabo Binibeca** *C* Spain
71A2 **Cabo Cantin** *C* Mor
40B3 **Cabo Carbonara** *C* Sardegna
28A3 **Cabo Carranza** *C* Chile
39A2 **Cabo Carvoeiro** *C* Port
8B3 **Cabo Colnett** *C* Mexico
28D3 **Cabo Corrientes** *C* Arg
26C2 **Cabo Corrientes** *C* Colombia
21B2 **Cabo Corrientes** *C* Mexico
23B3 **Cabo Cruz** *C* Cuba
39B1 **Cabo de Ajo** *C* Spain
39C1 **Cabo de Caballeria** *C* Spain
39C1 **Cabo de Creus** *C* Spain
25C9 **Cabo de Hornos** *C* Chile
39C2 **Cabo de la Nao** *C* Spain
39A1 **Cabo de Peñas** *C* Spain
39A2 **Cabo de Roca** *C* Port
39C2 **Cabo de Salinas** *C* Spain
74E2 **Cabo de Santa Maria** *C* Mozam
29D3 **Cabo de São Tomé** *C* Brazil
39A2 **Cabo de São Vicente** *C* Port
39B2 **Cabo de Sata** *C* Spain
39A2 **Cabo de Sines** *C* Port
39C1 **Cabo de Tortosa** *C* Spain
25C6 **Cabo Dos Bahias** *C* Arg
39A2 **Cabo Espichel** *C* Port
8B4 **Cabo Falso** *C* Mexico
39B2 **Cabo Ferrat** *C* Alg
39A1 **Cabo Finisterre** *C* Spain
39C1 **Cabo Formentor** *C* Spain
29D3 **Cabo Frio** Brazil
29D3 **Cabo Frio** *C* Brazil
23A4 **Cabo Gracias à Dios** Honduras
28A1 **Cabo Leones** *C* Chile
27J4 **Cabo Maguarinho** *C* Brazil
39A2 **Cabo Negro** *C* Mor
75D1 **Caboolture** Aust
27H3 **Cabo Orange** *C* Brazil
19C4 **Cabo Punta Banda** *C* Mexico
73D5 **Cabora Bassa Dam** Mozam
21A1 **Caborca** Mexico
21C2 **Cabo Rojo** *C* Mexico
22C1 **Cabos** Mexico
28D3 **Cabo San Antonio** *C* Arg
23A2 **Cabo San Antonio** *C* Cuba
25C8 **Cabo San Diego** *C* Arg
26B4 **Cabo San Lorenzo** *C* Ecuador
40B3 **Cabo Teulada** *C* Sardegna
39A2 **Cabo Trafalgar** *C* Spain
39B2 **Cabo Tres Forcas** *C* Mor
25C7 **Cabo Tres Puntas** *C* Arg
7M5 **Cabot Str** Can
39B2 **Cabra** Spain
39A1 **Cabreira** *Mt* Port
39C2 **Cabrera** *I* Spain
28A3 **Cabrero** Chile
39B2 **Cabriel** *R* Spain
22C2 **Cacahuamilpa** Mexico
41E2 **Čačak** Serbia, Yugos
28E2 **Cacapava do Sul** Brazil
14A3 **Cacapon** *R* USA
22C2 **C A Carillo** Mexico
28E1 **Caceoul** Brazil
27G7 **Cáceres** Brazil
39A2 **Caceres** Spain
17D2 **Cache** *R* USA
3D3 **Cache Creek** Can
20A1 **Cache Creek, R** USA
18D2 **Cache Peak** *Mt* USA
25C3 **Cachi** Arg
27G5 **Cachimbo** Brazil
27L6 **Cachoeira** Brazil
29B2 **Cachoeira Alta** Brazil
27L5 **Cachoeira de Paulo Afonso** *Waterfall* Brazil
25F4 **Cachoeira do Sul** Brazil
27K8 **Cachoeiro de Itapemirim** Brazil
20C3 **Cachuma, L** USA
73B5 **Cacolo** Angola
73B5 **Caconda** Angola
16B2 **Cactus** USA
29B2 **Caçu** Brazil
29D1 **Caculé** Brazil
73B5 **Caculuvar** *R* Angola
43D3 **Čadca** Slovakia
35D5 **Cader Idris** *Mts* Wales
11A2 **Cadillac** Can
9E2 **Cadillac** USA
57F8 **Cadiz** Phil
39A2 **Cadiz** Spain
27K6 **Caeité** Brazil
38B2 **Caen** France
35C5 **Caernarfon** Wales
35C5 **Caernarfon B** Wales
65C2 **Caesarea** *Hist Site* Israel
29D1 **Caetité** Brazil
25C3 **Cafayate** Arg
64B2 **Caga Tepe** Turk
57F7 **Cagayan** *R* Phil
57F9 **Cagayan de Oro** Phil
57F9 **Cagayan Is** Phil
37E3 **Cagli** Italy
40B3 **Cagliari** Sardegna
23D3 **Caguas** Puerto Rico
15B2 **Cahaba** *R* USA
35B5 **Cahir** Irish Rep
35B5 **Cahone Pt** Irish Rep
38C3 **Cahors** France
73D5 **Caia** Mozam
73C5 **Caianda** Angola
29B2 **Caiapó** *R* Brazil
29B2 **Caiapônia** Brazil
27L5 **Caicó** Brazil
23C2 **Caicos Is** Caribbean
9F4 **Caicos Pass** Bahamas
10G3 **Cairn Mt** USA
76D2 **Cairns** Aust
64B3 **Cairo** Egypt
9E3 **Cairo** USA
75B1 **Caiwarro** Aust
26C5 **Cajabamba** Peru
26C5 **Cajamarca** Peru
23D5 **Calabozo** Ven
41E2 **Calafat** Rom
25B8 **Calafate** Arg
57F8 **Calagua Is** Phil
39B1 **Calahorra** Spain
38C1 **Calais** France
13F1 **Calais** USA
25C2 **Calama** Chile
26D3 **Calamar** Colombia
57E8 **Calamian Group** *Is* Phil
73B4 **Calandula** Angola
56A2 **Calang** Indon
69B2 **Calanscio Sand Sea** Libya
57F8 **Calapan** Phil
41F2 **Calarasi** Rom
39B1 **Calatayud** Spain
20B2 **Calaveras Res** USA
57F8 **Calbayog** Phil
17D4 **Calcasieu L** USA
61C3 **Calcutta** India
39A2 **Caldas da Rainha** Port
27J7 **Caldas Novas** Brazil
25B3 **Caldera** Chile
8B2 **Caldwell** USA
74B3 **Caledon** S Africa
74D3 **Caledon** *R* S Africa
12A2 **Caledonia** Minnesota, USA
14B1 **Caledonia** New York, USA
5H4 **Caledonia Hills** Can
22B1 **Calera** Mexico
25C7 **Caleta Olivia** Arg
8B3 **Calexico** USA
6G4 **Calgary** Can
15C2 **Calhoun** USA
15C2 **Calhoun Falls** USA
26C3 **Cali** Colombia
62B2 **Calicut** India
20C3 **Caliente** California, USA
8B3 **Caliente** Nevada, USA
16A2 **Caliente** New Mexico, USA
20C3 **California Aqueduct** USA
8A3 **California** State, USA
62B2 **Calimera,Pt** India
28B2 **Calingasta** Arg
19C4 **Calipatria** USA
74C3 **Calitzdorp** S Africa
75B1 **Callabonna** *R* Aust
75A1 **Callabonna,L** Aust
13D1 **Callander** Can
34C3 **Callander** Scot
75A1 **Callanna** Aust
26C6 **Callao** Peru
22C1 **Calles** Mexico
14C2 **Callicoon** USA
3F2 **Calling L** Can
22C1 **Calnali** Mexico
15E4 **Caloosahatchee** *R* USA
75D1 **Caloundra** Aust
22C2 **Calpulalpan** Mexico
40C3 **Caltanissetta** Italy
73B4 **Caluango** Angola
73B5 **Calulo** Angola
73B5 **Caluquembe** Angola
67F4 **Caluula** Somalia
3C3 **Calvert I** Can
40B2 **Calvi** Corse
22B1 **Calvillo** Mexico
74B3 **Calvinia** S Africa
36E2 **Calw** Germany
29E1 **Camacari** Brazil
22B1 **Camacho** Mexico
28E2 **Camaguã** Brazil
28E2 **Camaguã** *R* Brazil
21E2 **Camagüey** Cuba
21E2 **Camagüey,Arch de** *Is* Cuba
29E1 **Camamu** Brazil
26D7 **Camaná** Peru
10N5 **Camania** *I* Can
29B2 **Camapuã** Brazil
26E8 **Camargo** Bol
20C3 **Camarillo** USA
25C6 **Camarones** Arg
18B1 **Camas** USA
73B4 **Camaxilo** Angola
73B4 **Cambatela** Angola
55C3 **Cambodia** Republic, S E Asia
35C6 **Camborne** Eng
38C1 **Cambrai** France
20B3 **Cambria** USA
35D5 **Cambrian Mts** Wales
12C2 **Cambridge** Can
35E5 **Cambridge** County, Eng
35F5 **Cambridge** Eng
23H1 **Cambridge** Jamaica
13D3 **Cambridge** Maryland, USA
13E2 **Cambridge** Massachussets, USA
11D2 **Cambridge** Minnesota, USA
78C1 **Cambridge** NZ
12C2 **Cambridge** Ohio, USA
6H3 **Cambridge Bay** Can
51F8 **Cambridge G** Aust
45F7 **Cam Burun** *Pt* Turk
9D3 **Camden** Arkansas, USA
75D2 **Camden** Aust
13E3 **Camden** New Jersey, USA
14C1 **Camden** New York, USA
15C2 **Camden** South Carolina, USA
10J1 **Camden B** USA
37E3 **Camerino** Italy
17D2 **Cameron** Missouri, USA
17C3 **Cameron** Texas, USA
56F6 **Cameron Highlands** Malay
6H2 **Cameron I** Can
78A3 **Cameron Mts** NZ
72B3 **Cameroon** Federal Republic, Africa
72A3 **Cameroun** *Mt* Cam
27J4 **Cametá** Brazil
57F9 **Camiguin** *I* Phil
57F7 **Camiling** Phil
15C2 **Camilla** USA
20B1 **Camino** USA
26F8 **Camiri** Bol
73C4 **Camissombo** Angola
27K4 **Camocim** Brazil
76C2 **Camooweal** Aust
62E3 **Camorta** *I* Indian O
28D2 **Campana** Arg
25A7 **Campana** *I* Chile
3C3 **Campania I** Can
74C2 **Campbell** S Africa
78B2 **Campbell,C** NZ
3C3 **Campbell I** Can
xxixN7 **Campbell I** NZ
10M2 **Campbell L** Can
6E3 **Campbell,Mt** Can
60C2 **Campbellpore** Pak
6F5 **Campbell River** Can
12B3 **Campbellsville** USA
7M5 **Campbellton** Can
75D2 **Campbelltown** Aust
34C4 **Campbeltown** Scot
21C3 **Campeche** Mexico
75B3 **Camperdown** Aust
27L5 **Campina Grande** Brazil
27J8 **Campinas** Brazil
29C2 **Campina Verde** Brazil
57B5 **Camplong** Indon
20C2 **Camp Nelson** USA
72A3 **Campo** Cam
40C2 **Campobasso** Italy
29C3 **Campo Belo** Brazil
28C1 **Campo del Cielo** Arg
29C2 **Campo Florido** Brazil
25D3 **Campo Gallo** Arg
25F2 **Campo Grande** Brazil
27K4 **Campo Maior** Brazil
25F2 **Campo Mourão** Brazil
28E1 **Campo Novo** Brazil
29D3 **Campos** Brazil
29C2 **Campos Altos** Brazil
37D1 **Campo Tures** Italy
19D4 **Camp Verde** USA
55D3 **Cam Ranh** Viet
6G4 **Camrose** Can
73B5 **Camucuio** Angola
23K1 **Canaan** Tobago
14D1 **Canaan** USA
73B5 **Canacupa** Angola
2F3 **Canada** Dominion, N America
25D4 **Cañada de Gomez** Arg
14C2 **Canadensis** USA
16B2 **Canadian** USA
8C3 **Canadian** *R* USA
45D7 **Canakkale** Turk
28B3 **Canalejas** Arg
3E3 **Canal Flats** Can
14B1 **Canandaigua** USA
14B1 **Canandaigua L** USA
21A1 **Cananea** Mexico
29C4 **Cananeia** Brazil
xxxG3 **Canary Basin** Atlantic O
Canary Is = Islas Canarias
22B2 **Canas** Mexico
21B2 **Canatlán** Mexico
9E4 **Canaveral,C** USA
27L7 **Canavieiras** Brazil
76D4 **Canberra** Aust
18B2 **Canby** California, USA
11C3 **Canby** Minnesota, USA
41F3 **Çandarli Körfezi** *B* Turk
3G3 **Candle L** Can
14D2 **Candlewood,L** USA
11C2 **Cando** USA
14B1 **Candor** USA
25E4 **Canelones** Urug
17C2 **Caney** USA
73C5 **Cangamba** Angola
73C5 **Cangombe** Angola
28E2 **Canguçu** Brazil
52D2 **Cangzhou** China
7M4 **Caniapiscau** *R* Can
7M4 **Caniapiscau, Réservoir** *Res* Can
40C3 **Canicatti** Italy
27L4 **Canindé** Brazil
14B1 **Canisteo** USA
14B1 **Canisteo** *R* USA
22B1 **Canitas de Felipe Pescador** Mexico
16A2 **Canjilon** USA
64B1 **Çankırı** Turk
3E3 **Canmore** Can
34B3 **Canna** *I* Scot
62B2 **Cannanore** India
38D3 **Cannes** France
11B2 **Cannonball** *R* USA
75C3 **Cann River** Aust
25F3 **Canõas** Brazil
3G2 **Canoe L** Can
29B4 **Canoinhas** Brazil
16A2 **Canon City** USA
75B2 **Canopus** Aust
6H4 **Canora** Can
75C2 **Canowindra** Aust
5J4 **Canso** Can
35B5 **Cansore Pt** Irish Rep
35F6 **Canterbury** Eng
78B2 **Canterbury Bight** *B* NZ
78B2 **Canterbury Plains** NZ
55D4 **Can Tho** Viet
20D3 **Cantil** USA
28A1 **Canto de Augua** Chile
Canton = Guangzhou
17E3 **Canton** Mississippi, USA
12A2 **Canton** Missouri, USA
9E2 **Canton** Ohio, USA
14B2 **Canton** Pensylvania, USA
11C3 **Canton** S Dakota, USA
77H1 **Canton** *I* Phoeniz Is
10J3 **Cantwell** USA
36A2 **Cany-Barville** France
16B3 **Canyon** USA
18C2 **Canyon City** USA
18D1 **Canyon Ferry L** USA
19D3 **Canyonlands Nat Pk** USA
10N3 **Canyon Range** *Mts* Can
18B2 **Canyonville** USA
73C4 **Canzar** Angola
55D1 **Cao Bang** Viet
27J4 **Capanema** Brazil
29C3 **Capão Bonito** Brazil
37B3 **Cap Bénat** *C* France
71D1 **Cap Blanc** *C* Tunisia
71E1 **Cap Bon** *C* Tunisia
71D1 **Cap Bougaron** *C* Alg
38B3 **Capbreton** France
37B3 **Cap Camarat** *C* France
5H4 **Cap Chat** Can
22A1 **Cap Corrientes** *C* Mexico
40B2 **Cap Corse** *C* Corse
73E5 **Cap d'Ambre** *C* Madag
37B3 **Cap d'Antibes** *C* France
5J4 **Cap de Gaspé** *C* Can
38B2 **Cap de la Hague** *C* France
5G4 **Cap-de-la-Madeleine** Can
7L3 **Cap de Nouvelle-France** *C* Can
39C2 **Capdepera** Spain
22B2 **Cap de Tancitiario** *C* Mexico
71B1 **Cap des Trois Fourches** *C* Mor
75E3 **Cape Barren I** Aust
xxxJ6 **Cape Basin** Atlantic O
7N5 **Cape Breton I** Can
71F4 **Cape Coast** Ghana
13E2 **Cape Cod B** USA
7M3 **Cape Dyer** Can
79F7 **Cape Evans** *Base* Ant.
15D2 **Cape Fear** *R* USA
17E2 **Cape Girardeau** USA
Cape Horn = Cabo de Hornos
xxviiiH4 **Cape Johnston Depth** Pacific O
29D2 **Capelinha** Brazil
10E2 **Cape Lisburne** USA
73B5 **Capelongo** Angola
13E3 **Cape May** USA
73B4 **Capenda Camulemba** Angola
6F2 **Cape Parry** Can
74B3 **Cape Town** S Africa
xxxG4 **Cape Verde** *Is* Atlantic O
xxxG4 **Cape Verde Basin** Atlantic O
10K4 **Cape Yakataga** USA
76D2 **Cape York Pen** Aust
37B3 **Cap Ferrat** *C* France
36A1 **Cap Gris Nez** *C* France
23C3 **Cap-Haitien** Haiti
27J4 **Capim** *R* Brazil
29A3 **Capitán Bado** Par
20D3 **Capitol Reef Nat Pk** USA
29A2 **Capivari** *R* Brazil
5K3 **Cap Mécatina** *C* Can
23P2 **Cap Moule à Chique** *C* St Lucia
37C2 **Capo di Noli** *C* Italy
40D3 **Capo Isola de Correnti** *C* Italy
40D3 **Capo Rizzuto** *C* Italy
41D3 **Capo Santa Maria di Leuca** *C* Italy
40C3 **Capo San Vito** Italy
40D3 **Capo Spartivento** *C* Italy
23P2 **Cap Pt** St Lucia
40C2 **Capri** *I* Italy
73C5 **Caprivi Strip** Region, Namibia
40B2 **Cap Rosso** *C* Corse

Cap Serrat

Chandrapur

71D1 **Cap Serrat** *C* Tunisia
37A3 **Cap Sicié** *C* France
70A3 **Cap Vert** *C* Sen
26D4 **Caquetá** *R* Colombia
41E2 **Caracal** Rom
26F3 **Caracaraí** Brazil
26E1 **Caracas** Ven
29A3 **Caracol** Brazil
29C3 **Caraguatatuba** Brazil
25B5 **Carahue** Chile
29D2 **Caraí** Brazil
29D3 **Carandaí** Brazil
29A2 **Carandazal** Brazil
27K8 **Carangola** Brazil
41E1 **Caransebeş** Rom
75A2 **Carappee Hill** *Mt* Aust
23A3 **Caratasca** Honduras
29D2 **Caratinga** Brazil
39B2 **Caravaca** Spain
29E2 **Caravelas** Brazil
28E1 **Carazinho** Brazil
12B3 **Carbondale** Illinois, USA
14C2 **Carbondale** Pennsylvania, USA
7N5 **Carbonear** Can
40B3 **Carbonia** Sardegna
6G4 **Carcajou** Can
69D3 **Carcar Mts** Somalia
38C3 **Carcassonne** France
6E3 **Carcross** Can
22C2 **Cardel** Mexico
21D2 **Cardenas** Cuba
22C1 **Cárdenas** Mexico
22D2 **Cárdenas** Mexico
35D6 **Cardiff** Wales
35C5 **Cardigan** Wales
35C5 **Cardigan B** Wales
28D2 **Cardóna** Urug
3F4 **Cardston** Can
3G2 **Careen L** Can
41E1 **Carei** Rom
27G4 **Careiro** Brazil
28A2 **Carén** Chile
12C2 **Carey** USA
38B2 **Carhaix-Plouguer** France
25D5 **Carhué** Arg
27K8 **Cariacica** Brazil
24C2 **Caribbean S** C America
4B2 **Caribou** Can
6J4 **Caribou** Can
13F1 **Caribou** USA
10N3 **Caribou** *R* Can
6G4 **Caribou Mts** Alberta, Can
6F4 **Caribou Mts** British Columbia, Can
57F8 **Carigara** Phil
36C2 **Carignan** France
36B1 **Carin** France
29D1 **Carinhanha** Brazil
29D1 **Carinhanha** *R* Brazil
26F1 **Caripito** Ven
4F4 **Carleton Place** Can
74D2 **Carletonville** S Africa
18C2 **Carlin** USA
12B3 **Carlinville** USA
34D4 **Carlisle** Eng
13D2 **Carlisle** USA
10D5 **Carlisle** *I* USA
28C3 **Carlos** Arg
29D2 **Carlos Chagas** Brazil
35B5 **Carlow** County, Irish Rep
35B5 **Carlow** Irish Rep
19C4 **Carlsbad** California, USA
8C3 **Carlsbad** New Mexico, USA
16B3 **Carlsbad Caverns Nat Pk** USA
xxviiiE4 **Carlsberg Ridge** Indian O
6H5 **Carlyle** Can
10L3 **Carmacks** Can
37B2 **Carmagnola** Italy
35C6 **Carmarthen** Wales
35C6 **Carmarthen B** Wales
20B2 **Carmel** California, USA
14D2 **Carmel** New York, USA
65C2 **Carmel,Mt** Israel
28D2 **Carmelo** Urug
20B2 **Carmel Valley** USA
8B4 **Carmen** *I* Mexico
25D6 **Carmen de Patagones** Arg
12B3 **Carmi** USA
19B3 **Carmichael** USA
29C2 **Carmo do Paranaiba** Brazil
39A2 **Carmona** Spain
76A3 **Carnarvon** Aust
74C3 **Carnarvon** S Africa
29E2 **Carncacá** Brazil
34B4 **Carndonagh** Irish Rep
76B3 **Carnegi,L** Aust
34D3 **Carngorms** *Mts* Scot
62E3 **Car Nicobar** *I* Indian O
72B3 **Carnot** CAR
75A2 **Carnot,C** Aust
10N2 **Carnwath** *R* Can
15E4 **Carol City** USA
27J5 **Carolina** Brazil
74E2 **Carolina** S Africa
15D2 **Carolina Beach** USA
xxviiiJ4 **Caroline Is** Pacific O
45C6 **Carpathians** *Mts* E Europe
43F3 **Carpatii Orientali** *Mts* Rom
76C2 **Carpentaria,G of** Aust
59H5 **Carpenter Ridge** Indian O
38D3 **Carpentras** France
40C2 **Carpi** Italy
20C3 **Carpinteria** USA
15C3 **Carrabelle** USA
40C2 **Carrara** Italy
33B3 **Carrauntoohill** *Mt* Irish Rep
35B5 **Carrickmacross** Irish Rep
35B5 **Carrick-on-Suir** Irish Rep
75A2 **Carrieton** Aust
6J5 **Carrington** USA
8D2 **Carrington** USA
39B1 **Carrión** *R* Spain
28A1 **Carrizal Bajo** Chile
17F4 **Carrizo Spring** USA
16A3 **Carrizozo** USA
9D2 **Carroll** USA
15B2 **Carrollton** Georgia, USA
12B3 **Carrollton** Kentucky, USA
17D2 **Carrollton** Missouri, USA
3H3 **Carrot** *R* Can
17E2 **Carruthersville** USA
45F7 **Carsamba** Turk
45E8 **Carsamba** *R* Turk
8B3 **Carson City** USA
12C3 **Carsonville** USA
23B4 **Cartagena** Colombia
39B2 **Cartagena** Spain
26C3 **Cartago** Colombia
21D4 **Cartago** Costa Rica
20C2 **Cartago** USA
26D1 **Cartegena** Colombia
78C2 **Carterton** NZ
17D2 **Carthage** Missouri, USA
13D2 **Carthage** New York, USA
17D3 **Carthage** Texas, USA
76B2 **Cartier I** Timor S
7N4 **Cartwright** Can
27L5 **Caruaru** Brazil
26F1 **Carúpano** Ven
15D1 **Cary** USA
28A2 **Casablanca** Chile
71A2 **Casablanca** Mor
29C3 **Casa Branca** Brazil
8B3 **Casa Grande** USA
40B1 **Casale Monferrato** Italy
37D2 **Casalmaggiore** Italy
28C3 **Casares** Arg
22C1 **Casas** Mexico
28E1 **Casca** Brazil
18D1 **Cascade** USA
3D4 **Cascade Mts** Can/USA
78A2 **Cascade Pt** NZ
8A2 **Cascade Range** *Mts* USA
18C2 **Cascade Res** USA
25F2 **Cascavel** Brazil
37D3 **Casciana** Italy
37D3 **Cascina** Italy
40C2 **Caserta** Italy
79G9 **Casey** *Base* Ant
35B5 **Cashel** Irish Rep
28C2 **Casilda** Arg
77E3 **Casino** Aust
26C5 **Casma** Peru
20B3 **Casmalia** USA
39C1 **Caspe** Spain
8C2 **Casper** USA
45H6 **Caspian Depression** *Region* Kazakhstan
45H7 **Caspian S** Asia/Europe
13D3 **Cass** USA
73C5 **Cassamba** Angola
36B1 **Cassel** France
11C2 **Casselton** USA
3C2 **Cassiar** Can
6E3 **Cassiar Mts** Can
29B2 **Cassilândia** Brazil
40C2 **Cassino** Italy
11D2 **Cass Lake** USA
20C3 **Castaic** USA
28B2 **Castaño** *R* Arg
37D2 **Castelfranco** Italy
38D3 **Castellane** France
28D3 **Castelli** Arg
39C1 **Castellon de la Plana** Spain
37D2 **Castelnovo ne'Monti** Italy
37D2 **Castelnuovo di Garfagnana** Italy
27K5 **Castelo** Brazil
39A2 **Castelo Branco** Port
38C3 **Castelsarrasin** France
40C3 **Castelvetrano** Italy
75B3 **Casterton** Aust
37D3 **Castiglion Fiorentino** Italy
28A1 **Castilla** Chile
39B2 **Castilla La Nueva** Region, Spain
39B1 **Castilla La Vieja** Region, Spain
28E2 **Castillos** Urug
33B3 **Castlebar** Irish Rep
34B3 **Castlebay** Scot
19D3 **Castle Dale** USA
34D4 **Castle Douglas** Scot
18C1 **Castlegar** Can
75B3 **Castlemain** Aust
20B3 **Castle,Mt** USA
18D2 **Castle Peak** USA
75C2 **Castlereagh** Aust
16B2 **Castle Rock** USA
38C3 **Castres-sur-l'Agout** France
23E4 **Castries** St Lucia
25B6 **Castro** Arg
25F2 **Castro** Brazil
27L6 **Castro Alves** Brazil
40D3 **Castrovillari** Italy
20B2 **Castroville** USA
28D2 **Casupa** Urug
78A2 **Caswell Sd** NZ
21E2 **Cat** *I* Bahamas
57F8 **Catabalogan** Phil
26B5 **Catacaos** Peru
29D3 **Cataguases** Brazil
17D3 **Catahoula L** USA
29C2 **Catalão** Brazil
39C1 **Cataluña** Region, Spain
25C3 **Catamarca** Arg
25C3 **Catamarca** State, Arg
73D5 **Catandica** Mozam
57F8 **Catanduanes** *I* Phil
25G2 **Catanduva** Brazil
29B4 **Catanduvas** Brazil
40D3 **Catania** Italy
28A3 **Catan-Lil** Arg
40D3 **Catanzaro** Italy
17F4 **Catarina** USA
57F8 **Catarman** Phil
75A2 **Catastrophe,C** Aust
23C5 **Catatumbo** *R* Ven
14B2 **Catawissa** USA
22C2 **Catemaco** Mexico
38D3 **Cater** Corse
40B2 **Cateraggio** Corse
73B4 **Catete** Angola
74D3 **Cathcart** S Africa
28B1 **Catinzaco** Arg
70A3 **Catio** Guinea-Bissau
4C3 **Cat L** Can
4C3 **Cat Lake** Can
7J4 **Cat Lake** Can
77E3 **Cato** *I* Aust
21D2 **Catoche,C** Mexico
14B3 **Catoctin Mt** USA
13D3 **Catonsville** USA
28C3 **Catrilo** Arg
13E2 **Catskill** USA
13E2 **Catskill Mts** USA
5J2 **Caubvick,Mt** Can
26D2 **Cauca** *R* Colombia
27L4 **Caucaia** Brazil
26C2 **Caucasia** Colombia
45G7 **Caucasus** *Mts* Georgia
36A2 **Caudebec-en-Caux** France
36B1 **Caudry** France
73B4 **Caungula** Angola
25B5 **Cauquenes** Chile
13F1 **Causapscal** Can
62B2 **Cauvery** *R* India
38D3 **Cavaillon** France
29C1 **Cavalcanta** Brazil
37D1 **Cavalese** italy
11C2 **Cavalier** USA
70B4 **Cavally** *R* Lib
35B5 **Cavan** County, Irish Rep
35B5 **Cavan** Irish Rep
57F8 **Cavite** Phil
26D4 **Caxias** Brazil
27K4 **Caxias** Brazil
25F3 **Caxias do Sul** Brazil
73B4 **Caxito** Angola
15C2 **Cayce** USA
64D1 **Çayeli** Turk
27H3 **Cayenne** French Guiana
36A1 **Cayeux-sur-Mer** France
21E3 **Cayman Brac** *I* Caribbean
23A3 **Cayman Is** Caribbean
23A3 **Cayman Trench** Caribbean
72E3 **Caynabo** Somalia
20B3 **Cayncos** USA
21E2 **Cayo Romana** *I* Cuba
21D3 **Cayos Mistikos** *Is* Nic
23A2 **Cay Sal** *I* Caribbean
14B1 **Cayuga L** USA
14C1 **Cazenovia** USA
73C5 **Cazombo** Angola
5J4 **C Breton Highlands** Can
Ceará = Fortaleza
27K5 **Ceara** State, Brazil
28B1 **Cebollar** Arg
28E2 **Cebollati** Urug
57F8 **Cebu** Phil
57F8 **Cebu** *I* Phil
14C3 **Cecilton** USA
40C2 **Cecina** Italy
37D3 **Cecina** *R* Italy
11D3 **Cedar** *R* USA
8B3 **Cedar City** USA
17C3 **Cedar Creek Res** USA
11D3 **Cedar Falls** USA
6H4 **Cedar L** Can
20D1 **Cedar Mts** USA
9D2 **Cedar Rapids** USA
15B2 **Cedartown** USA
22B1 **Cedral** Mexico
21A2 **Cedros** *I* Mexico
76C4 **Ceduna** Aust
72E3 **Ceelbuur** Somalia
69D3 **Ceerigaabo** Somalia
40C3 **Cefalù** Italy
43D3 **Cegléd** Hung
73B5 **Cela** Angola
21B2 **Celaya** Mexico
Celebes = Sulawesi
51F6 **Celebes S** S E Asia
12C2 **Celina** USA
40D1 **Celje** Slovenia
42C2 **Celle** Germany
35B6 **Celtic S** UK
51G7 **Cendrawasih** *Pen* Indon
37C2 **Ceno** *R* Italy
17D3 **Center** USA
15B1 **Center Hill L** USA
14D2 **Center Moriches** USA
37D2 **Cento** Italy
34C3 **Central** Region, Scot
16A3 **Central** USA
72B3 **Central African Republic** Africa
17C1 **Central City** Nebraska, USA
14A2 **Central City** Pennsylvania, USA
12B3 **Centralia** Illinois, USA
8A2 **Centralia** Washington, USA
74C1 **Central Kalahari Game Res** Botswana
63E3 **Central Makran Range** *Mts* Pak
18B2 **Central Point** USA
51H7 **Central Range** *Mts* PNG
14B1 **Central Square** USA
15B2 **Centre Point** USA
15B2 **Centreville** Alabama, USA
14B3 **Centreville** Maryland, USA
56D4 **Cepu** Indon
Ceram = Seram
51F7 **Ceram Sea** Indonesia
28C3 **Cereales** Arg
28C1 **Ceres** Arg
27J7 **Ceres** Brazil
74B3 **Ceres** S Africa
20B2 **Ceres** USA
38C2 **Cergy-Pontoise** France
40D2 **Cerignola** Italy
45D7 **Cernavodă** Rom
36D3 **Cernay** France
8C4 **Cerralvo** *I* Mexico
22B1 **Cerritos** Mexico
28B2 **Cerro Aconcagua** *Mt* Arg
22C1 **Cerro Azul** Mexico
28B1 **Cerro Boneta** *Mt* Arg
28A3 **Cerro Campanario** *Mt* Chile
28C2 **Cerro Champaqui** *Mt* Arg
28D2 **Cerro Chatto** Urug
22B2 **Cerro Cuachaia** *Mt* Mexico
22C1 **Cerro de Astillero** Mexico
28B1 **Cerro del Potro** *Mt* Chile/Arg
22C1 **Cerro del Tigre** *Mt* Mexico
28B1 **Cerro del Toro** *Mt* Chile/Arg
28B2 **Cerro de Olivares** *Mt* Arg
26C6 **Cerro de Pasco** Peru
23D3 **Cerro de Punta** *Mt* Puerto Rico
22B2 **Cerro El Cantado** *Mt* Mexico
28B3 **Cerro El Nevado** Arg
28B1 **Cerro General M Belgrano** *Mt* Arg
22B2 **Cerro Grande** *Mts* Mexico
22A1 **Cerro Huehueto** *Mt* Mexico
28A2 **Cerro Juncal** *Mt* Arg/Chile
22B1 **Cerro la Ardilla** *Mts* Mexico
28A1 **Cerro las Tortolas** *Mt* Chile
22B2 **Cerro Laurel** *Mt* Mexico
28A2 **Cerro Mercedario** *Mt* Arg
28A3 **Cerro Mora** *Mt* Chile
23C4 **Cerron** *Mt* Ven
28B3 **Cerro Payún** *Mt* Arg
22C1 **Cerro Peña Nevada** *Mt* Mexico
22C2 **Cerro Penón del Rosario** *Mt* Mexico
28B2 **Cerro Sosneado** *Mt* Arg
22B2 **Cerro Teotepec** *Mt* Mexico
28B2 **Cerro Tupungato** *Mt* Arg
22C2 **Cerro Yucuyacau** *Mt* Mexico
37E2 **Cervia** Italy
37C2 **Cervo** *R* Italy
40C2 **Cesena** Italy
44D4 **Cēsis** Latvia
42C3 **České Budějovice** Czech Republic
42D3 **Českomoravská Vysočina** *U* Czech Republic
41F3 **Çeşme** Turk
76E4 **Cessnock** Aust
40D2 **Cetina** *R* Croatia
71A1 **Ceuta** N W Africa
64C2 **Ceyham** Turk
64C2 **Ceyhan** *R* Turk
64C2 **Ceylanpınar** Turk
Ceylon = Sri Lanka
49L4 **Chaa-Khol** Russian Fed
38C2 **Chaâteaudun** France
37B1 **Chablais** Region, France
36B3 **Chablis** France
28C2 **Chacabuco** Arg
26C5 **Chachapoyas** Peru
28B3 **Chacharramendi** Arg
60C3 **Chachran** Pak
25D3 **Chaco** State, Arg
72B2 **Chad** Republic, Africa
72B2 **Chad** *L* C Africa
28B3 **Chadileuvu** *R* Arg
8C2 **Chadron** USA
17E2 **Chaffee** USA
60A3 **Chagai** Pak
63E3 **Chagai Hills** Pak
49P4 **Chagda** Russian Fed
60B2 **Chaghcharan** Afghan
xxviiiE5 **Chagos Arch** Indian O
23L1 **Chaguanas** Trinidad
63E2 **Chahah Burjak** Afghan
63E3 **Chāh Bahār** Iran
54A2 **Ch'aho** N Korea
55C2 **Chai Badan** Thai
71G3 **Chaîne de l'Atakor** *Mts* Benin
55C3 **Chaîne des Cardamomes** *Mts* Camb
73C4 **Chaine des Mitumba** *Mts* Zaïre
55C2 **Chaiyaphum** Thai
28D2 **Chajari** Arg
63E2 **Chakhansur** Afghan
60C2 **Chakwal** Pak
26D7 **Chala** Peru
73D5 **Chalabesa** Zambia
60A2 **Chalap Dalam** *Mts* Afghan
36C3 **Chalindrey** France
52C4 **Chaling** China
60D4 **Chālisgaon** India
10K2 **Chalkyitsik** USA
36C2 **Challerange** France
18D2 **Challis** USA
36C2 **Châlons sur Marne** France
38C2 **Chalon sur Saône** France
42C3 **Cham** Germany
16A2 **Chama** USA
60B2 **Chaman** Pak
60D2 **Chamba** India
60D3 **Chambal** *R* India
11C3 **Chamberlain** USA
10J2 **Chamberlin,Mt** USA
13D3 **Chambersburg** USA
38D2 **Chambéry** France
36B2 **Chambly** France
13E1 **Chambord** Can
60A3 **Chambor Kalat** Pak
22A2 **Chamela** Mexico
63C2 **Chamgordan** Iran
28B2 **Chamical** Arg
37B2 **Chamonix** France
61B3 **Champa** India
38C2 **Champagne** Region, France
74D2 **Champagne Castle** *Mt* Lesotho
37A1 **Champagnole** France
9E2 **Champaign** USA
55D3 **Champassak** Laos
9F2 **Champlain,L** USA
37A1 **Champlitte** France
62B2 **Chāmrājnagar** India
25B3 **Chañaral** Chile
28A3 **Chanco** Chile
6D3 **Chandalar** USA
6D3 **Chandalar** *R* USA
15B3 **Chandeleur Is** USA
60D2 **Chandīgarh** India
5J4 **Chandler** Can
19D4 **Chandler** USA
61D3 **Chandpur** Bang
60D5 **Chandrapur** India

Chungwa

Cooma

54A3 **Chungwa** N Korea
73D4 **Chunya** Tanz
49M3 **Chunya** *R* Russian Fed
54A3 **Ch'unyang** S Korea
23L1 **Chupara Pt** Trinidad
25C2 **Chuquicamata** Chile
40B1 **Chur** Switz
61D3 **Churāchāndpur** India
49P3 **Churapcha** Russian Fed
7J4 **Churchill** Can
7M4 **Churchill** *R* Labrador, Can
7J4 **Churchill** *R* Manitoba, Can
7J4 **Churchill,C** Can
7M4 **Churchill Falls** Can
6H4 **Churchill L** Can
60C3 **Chūru** India
22B2 **Churumuco** Mexico
44K4 **Chusovoy** Russian Fed
44H4 **Chuvashskaya** Respublika, Russian Fed
50C4 **Chuxiong** China
55D3 **Chu Yang Sin** *Mt* Viet
56C4 **Cianjur** Indon
37D2 **Ciano d'Enza** Italy
29B3 **Cianorte** Brazil
43E2 **Ciechanów** Pol
22B2 **Ciedad Altamirano** Mexico
26D1 **Ciedad Ojeda** Ven
21E2 **Ciego de Avila** Cuba
26D1 **Ciénaga** Colombia
21D2 **Cienfuegos** Cuba
43D3 **Cieszyn** Pol
39B2 **Cieza** Spain
64B2 **Cihanbeyli** Turk
22B2 **Cihuatlán** Mexico
56C4 **Cijulang** Indon
56C4 **Cilacap** Indon
16B2 **Cimarron** USA
16C2 **Cimarron** *R* USA
37B3 **Cime du Cheiron** *Mt* France
41F1 **Cîmpina** Rom
39C1 **Cinca** *R* Spain
40D2 **Činčer** *Mt* Bosnia-Herzegovina, Yugos
9E3 **Cincinnati** USA
41E1 **Cindrelu** *Mt* Rom
41F3 **Cine** *R* Turk
36C1 **Ciney** Belg
22D2 **Cintalapa** Mexico
28B3 **Cipolletti** Arg
6D3 **Circle** Alaska, USA
11A2 **Circle** Montana, USA
12C3 **Circleville** USA
56C4 **Cirebon** Indon
35E6 **Cirencester** Eng
16C3 **Cisco** USA
37D2 **Citadella** Italy
21C3 **Citlaltepetl** *Mt* Mexico
74B3 **Citrusdal** S Africa
40C2 **Citta del Vaticano** Italy
40C2 **Città di Castello** Italy
21B2 **Ciudad Acuña** Mexico
26F2 **Ciudad Bolivar** Ven
21B2 **Ciudad Camargo** Mexico
21C3 **Ciudad del Carmen** Mexico
39C2 **Ciudadela** Spain
26F2 **Ciudad Guayana** Ven
21B3 **Ciudad Guzman** Mexico
22B2 **Ciudad Hidalgo** Mexico
21B1 **Ciudad Juárez** Mexico
8C4 **Ciudad Lerdo** Mexico
21C2 **Ciudad Madero** Mexico
22C2 **Ciudad Mendoza** Mexico
21B2 **Ciudad Obregon** Mexico
23C4 **Ciudad Ojeda** Ven
26F2 **Ciudad Piar** Ven
39B2 **Ciudad Real** Spain
39A1 **Ciudad Rodrigo** Spain
21C2 **Ciudad Valles** Mexico
21C2 **Ciudad Victoria** Mexico
37E1 **Cividale del Friuli** Italy
37E3 **Civitanova Marche** Italy
40C2 **Civitavecchia** Italy
64D2 **Cizre** Turk
35F6 **Clacton-on-Sea** Eng
6G4 **Claire,L** Can
13D2 **Clairton** USA
37A1 **Clairvaux** France
15B2 **Clanton** USA
74B3 **Clanwilliam** S Africa
35B5 **Clara** Irish Rep
28D3 **Claraz** Arg
12C2 **Clare** USA
13E2 **Claremont** USA
17C2 **Claremore** USA
75D1 **Clarence** *R* Aust
78B2 **Clarence** *R* NZ
76C2 **Clarence Str** Aust
10M4 **Clarence Str** USA
17D3 **Clarendon** USA
5L4 **Clarenville** Can
7N5 **Clarenville** Can
6G4 **Claresholm** Can
17C1 **Clarinda** USA
11D3 **Clarion** Iowa, USA
13D2 **Clarion** Pennsylvania, USA
21A3 **Clarión** *I* Mexico
13D2 **Clarion** *R* USA
xxixM4 **Clarion Fracture Zone** Pacific O
9E3 **Clark Hill Res** USA
10O3 **Clark,Mt** Can
19C3 **Clark Mt** USA
12C2 **Clark,Pt** Can
12C3 **Clarksburg** USA
9D3 **Clarksdale** USA
10G4 **Clarks Point** USA
18C1 **Clarkston** USA
17D2 **Clarksville** Arkansas, USA
15B1 **Clarksville** Tennessee, USA
29B2 **Claro** *R* Brazil
25E5 **Claromecó** Arg
17C2 **Clay Center** USA
34E2 **Claymore** *Oilfield* N Sea
3C4 **Clayoquot Sd** Can
8C3 **Clayton** New Mexico, USA
13D2 **Clayton** New York, USA
33B3 **Clear** *C* Irish Rep
10J4 **Cleare,C** USA
14A2 **Clearfield** Pennsylvania, USA
18D2 **Clearfield** Utah, USA
3E2 **Clear Hills** *Mts* Can
19B3 **Clear L** USA
11D3 **Clear Lake** USA
18B2 **Clear Lake Res** USA
11A3 **Clearmont** USA
3D3 **Clearwater** Can
9E4 **Clearwater** USA
3F2 **Clearwater** *R* Can
3D3 **Clearwater L** Can
18C1 **Clearwater Mts** USA
8D3 **Cleburne** USA
35F4 **Cleeton** *Oilfield* N Sea
20B1 **Clements** USA
57E8 **Cleopatra Needle** *Mt* Phil
76D3 **Clermont** Aust
36B2 **Clermont** France
36C2 **Clermont-en-Argonne** France
38C2 **Clermont-Ferrand** France
36D1 **Clervaux** Germany
37D1 **Cles** Italy
75A2 **Cleve** Aust
35E4 **Cleveland** County, Eng
17D3 **Cleveland** Mississippi, USA
9E2 **Cleveland** Ohio, USA
15C1 **Cleveland** Tennessee, USA
17C3 **Cleveland** Texas, USA
29B4 **Clevelândia** Brazil
18D1 **Cleveland,Mt** USA
33B3 **Clew** *B* Irish Rep
19E4 **Clifton** Arizona, USA
75D1 **Clifton** Aust
14C2 **Clifton** New Jersey, USA
75A1 **Clifton Hills** Aust
3J2 **Clifton L** Can
3G4 **Climax** Can
15C1 **Clinch** *R* USA
15C1 **Clinch Mts** USA
17D2 **Clinton** Arkansas, USA
6F4 **Clinton** Can
14D2 **Clinton** Connecticut, USA
12A2 **Clinton** Iowa, USA
14E1 **Clinton** Massachusetts, USA
17D3 **Clinton** Mississippi, USA
17D2 **Clinton** Missouri, USA
15D2 **Clinton** N Carolina, USA
14C2 **Clinton** New Jersey, USA
16C2 **Clinton** Oklahoma, USA
6H3 **Clinton-Colden L** Can
21B3 **Clipperton I** Pacific O
26E7 **Cliza** Bol
28C1 **Clodomira** Arg
76D3 **Cloncurry** Aust
35B4 **Clones** Irish Rep
35B5 **Clonmel** Irish Rep
9D2 **Cloquet** USA
29A4 **Clorinda** Arg
11A3 **Cloud Peak** *Mt* USA
10G3 **Cloudy Mt** USA
20A1 **Cloverdale** USA
20C2 **Clovis** California, USA
8C3 **Clovis** New Mexico, USA
45C6 **Cluj** Rom
41E1 **Cluj-Napoca** Rom
37B1 **Cluses** France
37C2 **Clusone** Italy
78A3 **Clutha** *R* NZ
35D5 **Clwyd** County, Wales
7M2 **Clyde** Can
78A3 **Clyde** NZ
14B1 **Clyde** USA
34C4 **Clyde** *R* Scot
19C4 **Coachella** USA
22B2 **Coahuayana** Mexico
16B4 **Coahuila** State, Mexico
10N3 **Coal** *R* Can
22B2 **Coalcomán** Mexico
3F4 **Coaldale** Can
19C3 **Coaldale** USA
19B3 **Coalinga** USA
18D2 **Coalville** USA
29E1 **Coaraci** Brazil
26F5 **Coari** *R* Brazil
15B2 **Coastal Plain** USA
6E4 **Coast Mts** Can
8A2 **Coast Ranges** *Mts* USA
34C4 **Coatbridge** Scot
22C2 **Coatepec** Mexico
14C3 **Coatesville** USA
13E1 **Coaticook** Can
7K3 **Coats I** Can
79F1 **Coats Land** Region, Ant
21C3 **Coatzacoalcas** Mexico
22D2 **Coatzacoalcos** *R* Mexico
7L5 **Cobalt** Can
21C3 **Cobán** Guatemala
76D4 **Cobar** Aust
75C3 **Cobargo** Aust
4C3 **Cobham** *R* Can
26E6 **Cobija** Bol
14C1 **Cobleskill** USA
39B2 **Cobo de Palos** *C* Spain
7L5 **Cobourg** Can
76C2 **Cobourg Pen** Aust
42C2 **Coburg** Germany
26C4 **Coca** Ecuador
15C3 **Coca** USA
29B1 **Cocalinho** Brazil
26E7 **Cochabamba** Bol
36D1 **Cochem** Germany
62B3 **Cochin** India
3F3 **Cochrane** Alberta, Can
7K5 **Cochrane** Ontario, Can
3H2 **Cochrane** *R* Can
75B2 **Cockburn** Aust
14B3 **Cockeysville** USA
23H1 **Cockpit Country,The** Jamaica
74C3 **Cockscomb** *Mt* S Africa
21D3 **Coco** *R* Honduras/Nic
72A3 **Cocobeach** Gabon
62E2 **Coco Channel** Andaman Is
29D1 **Côcos** Brazil
23L1 **Cocos B** Trinidad
xxviiiF5 **Cocos Is** Indian O
xxixP4 **Cocos Ridge** Pacific O
22B1 **Cocula** Mexico
34G3 **Cod** *Oilfield* N Sea
9F2 **Cod,C** USA
78A3 **Codfish I** NZ
7M4 **Cod I** Can
37E2 **Codigoro** Italy
27K4 **Codó** Brazil
37C2 **Codogno** Italy
8C2 **Cody** USA
51H8 **Coen** Aust
42B2 **Coesfeld** Germany
3E4 **Coeur d'Alene** USA
8D3 **Coffeyville** USA
75A2 **Coffin B** Aust
75D2 **Coff's Harbour** Aust
74D3 **Cofimvaba** S Africa
22C2 **Cofre de Perote** *Mt* Mexico
38B2 **Cognac** France
14B1 **Cohocton** USA
14B1 **Cohocton** *R* USA
13E2 **Cohoes** USA
75B3 **Cohuna** Aust
25B7 **Coihaique** Chile
62B2 **Coimbatore** India
39A1 **Coimbra** Port
26B3 **Cojimies** Ecuador
18D2 **Cokeville** USA
76D4 **Colac** Aust
27K7 **Colatina** Brazil
79F6 **Colbeck,C** Ant
16B2 **Colby** USA
35F6 **Colchester** Eng
14D2 **Colchester** USA
37B1 **Col de la Faucille** France
3F3 **Cold L** Can
40B1 **Col du Grand St Bernard** *P* Switz/Italy
37B2 **Col du Lautaret** *P* France
40B1 **Col du Mont Cenis** *P* Italy/France
38D2 **Col du Mt Cenis** *P* Italy
12C2 **Coldwater** USA
4D4 **Coldwell** Can
10K2 **Coleen** *R* USA
18D1 **Coleman** Can
12C2 **Coleman** Michigan, USA
16C3 **Coleman** Texas, USA
74D2 **Colenso** S Africa
34B4 **Coleraine** N Ire
78B2 **Coleridge,L** NZ
74D3 **Colesberg** S Africa
20C1 **Coleville** USA
19B3 **Colfax** California, USA
17D3 **Colfax** Louisiana, USA
18C1 **Colfax** Washington, USA
21B3 **Colima** Mexico
22B2 **Colima** State, Mexico
28A2 **Colina** Chile
34B3 **Coll** *I* Scot
75C1 **Collarenebri** Aust
40B2 **Colle de Tende** *P* Italy/France
37D3 **Colle di Val d'Elsa** Italy
10J3 **College** USA
15C2 **College Park** Georgia, USA
14B3 **College Park** Washington, USA
17C3 **College Station** USA
76A4 **Collie** Aust
76B2 **Collier B** Aust
37D3 **Colline Metallifere** *Mts* Italy
36A1 **Collines de L'Artois** *Mts* France
36B2 **Collines De Thiérache** France
36A2 **Collines du Perche** *Mts* France
4E5 **Collingwood** Can
78B2 **Collingwood** NZ
17E3 **Collins** Mississippi, USA
14A1 **Collins** New York, USA
6H2 **Collinson Pen** Can
76D3 **Collinsville** Aust
12B3 **Collinsville** Illinois, USA
17C2 **Collinsville** Oklahoma, USA
28A3 **Collipulli** Chile
38D2 **Colmar** France
28C1 **Colmena** Arg
36A1 **Colne** *R* Eng
Cologne = Köln
29C3 **Colômbia** Brazil
26D3 **Colombia** Republic, S America
13D3 **Colombia** USA
62B3 **Colombo** Sri Lanka
25E4 **Colón** Arg
21D2 **Colon** Cuba
26C2 **Colón** Panama
25E4 **Colonia** Urug
28D2 **Colonia del Sacramento** Urug
28B3 **Colonia 25 de Mayo** Arg
28C1 **Colonia Dora** Arg
28B3 **Colonia Josefa** Arg
25C7 **Colonia Las Heras** Arg
13D3 **Colonial Heights** USA
34B3 **Colonsay** *I* Scot
23E5 **Coloradito** Ven
8C3 **Colorado** State, USA
8B3 **Colorado** *R* Arizona, USA
25D5 **Colorado** *R* Buenos Aires, Arg
28B1 **Colorado** *R* La Rioja, Arg
8D3 **Colorado** *R* Texas, USA
16B3 **Colorado City** USA
8B3 **Colorado Plat** USA
8C3 **Colorado Springs** USA
22B1 **Colptlán** Mexico
14B3 **Columbia** Maryland, USA
17E3 **Columbia** Mississippi, USA
9D3 **Columbia** Missouri, USA
13D2 **Columbia** Pennsylvania, USA
9E3 **Columbia** S Carolina, USA
9E3 **Columbia** Tennessee, USA
3E3 **Columbia** *R* Can
8A2 **Columbia** *R* USA
18D1 **Columbia Falls** USA
6G4 **Columbia,Mt** Can
18C1 **Columbia Plat** USA
74B3 **Columbine,C** S Africa
9E3 **Columbus** Georgia, USA
12B3 **Columbus** Indiana, USA
9E3 **Columbus** Mississippi, USA
18E1 **Columbus** Montana, USA
8D2 **Columbus** Nebraska, USA
16A3 **Columbus** New Mexico, USA
9E2 **Columbus** Ohio, USA
17C4 **Columbus** Texas, USA
12B2 **Columbus** Wisconsin, USA
18C1 **Colville** USA
6C3 **Colville** *R* USA
78C1 **Colville,C** NZ
6F3 **Colville L** Can
35D5 **Colwyn Bay** Wales
37E2 **Comacchio** Italy
22D2 **Comalcalco** Mexico
16C3 **Comanche** USA
20B1 **Comanche Res** USA
21D3 **Comayagua** Honduras
28A2 **Combarbalá** Chile
35C4 **Comber** N Ire
61D4 **Combermere B** Myanmar
36C3 **Combeufontaine** France
37E1 **Comeglians** Italy
35B5 **Comeragh** *Mts* Irish Rep
16C3 **Comfort** USA
61D3 **Comilla** Bang
21C3 **Comitán** Mexico
36C2 **Commercy** France
7K3 **Committee B** Can
40B1 **Como** Italy
25C7 **Comodoro Rivadavia** Arg
22B1 **Comonfort** Mexico
62B3 **Comorin,C** India
73E5 **Comoros** *Is* Indian O
38C2 **Compiègne** France
22B1 **Compostela** Mexico
28B2 **Comte Salas** Arg
61D2 **Cona** China
70A4 **Conakry** Guinea
28A1 **Conay** Chile
28B2 **Concarán** Arg
38B2 **Concarneau** France
29E2 **Conceiçao da Barra** Brazil
27J5 **Conceição do Araguaia** Brazil
29D2 **Conceiçao do Mato Dentro** Brazil
28B1 **Concepción** Arg
29A3 **Concepción** Brazil/Par
25B5 **Concepción** Chile
25E2 **Concepción** Par
25E4 **Concepción** *R* Arg
21B2 **Concepcion del Oro** Mexico
28D2 **Concepcion del Uruguay** Arg
74A1 **Conception B** Namibia
8A3 **Conception,Pt** USA
29C3 **Conchas** Brazil
16B2 **Conchas** *L* USA
36A2 **Conches** France
8C4 **Conchos** *R* Mexico
19B3 **Concord** California, USA
9F2 **Concord** New Hampshire, USA
15C1 **Concord** North Carolina, USA
25E4 **Concordia** Arg
22A1 **Concordia** Mexico
8D3 **Concordia** USA
18B1 **Concrete** USA
75D1 **Condamine** Aust
29D1 **Condeuba** Brazil
76D4 **Condobolin** Aust
18B1 **Condon** USA
36C1 **Condroz, Mts** Belg
27H8 **Condrina** Brazil
15B2 **Conecuh** *R* USA
37E2 **Conegliano** Italy
14B1 **Conesus L** USA
29A3 **Confuso** *R* Par
68F8 **Congo** Republic, Africa
68F8 **Congo** *R* Congo
Congo,R = Zaïre,R
12C1 **Coniston** Can
12C2 **Conneaut** USA
9F2 **Connecticut** State, USA
13E2 **Connecticut** *R* USA
13D2 **Connellsville** USA
36A2 **Connerré** France
12B3 **Connersville** USA
75B2 **Conoble** Aust
18D1 **Conrad** USA
17C3 **Conroe** USA
29D3 **Conselheiro Lafaiete** Brazil
55D4 **Con Son** *Is* Viet
Constance,L = Bodensee
45D7 **Constanta** Rom
71D1 **Constantine** Alg
10G4 **Constantine,C** USA
25B5 **Constitución** Chile
28D2 **Constitución** Urug
3G4 **Consul** Can
18D2 **Contact** USA
37E2 **Contarina** Italy
27K6 **Contas** *R* Brazil
22C2 **Contreras** Mexico
36C2 **Contrexéville** France
6H3 **Contwoyto L** Can
9D3 **Conway** Arkansas, USA
13E2 **Conway** New Hampshire, USA
15D2 **Conway** South Carolina, USA
75A1 **Conway,L** Aust
35D5 **Conwy** Wales
76C3 **Coober Pedy** Aust
3C3 **Cook,C** Can
15B1 **Cookeville** USA
6C3 **Cook Inlet** *B* USA
xxixL5 **Cook Is** Pacific O
78B2 **Cook,Mt** NZ
77G5 **Cook Str** NZ
76D2 **Cooktown** Aust
75C2 **Coolabah** Aust
75C1 **Cooladdi** Aust
75C2 **Coolah** Aust
75C2 **Coolamon** Aust
76B4 **Coolgardie** Aust
19D4 **Coolidge** USA
75C3 **Cooma** Aust

Dihang Dzhambul

61D2 **Dihang** *R* India
Dijlah = Tigris
37A1 **Dijon** France
72B3 **Dik** Chad
72E2 **Dikhil** Djibouti
65A3 **Dîkirnis** Egypt
36B1 **Diksmuide** Belg
48K2 **Dikson** Russian Fed
71J3 **Dikwa** Nig
63E2 **Dilaram** Afghan
57C4 **Dili** Indon
55D3 **Di Linh** Viet
36E1 **Dillenburg** Germany
17F4 **Dilley** USA
72C2 **Dilling** Sudan
10G4 **Dillingham** USA
8B2 **Dillon** USA
14B2 **Dillsburg** USA
73C5 **Dilolo** Zaïre
22A1 **Dimas** Mexico
Dimashq = Damascus
72C4 **Dimbelenge** Zaïre
71F4 **Dimbokro** Côte d'Ivoire
41F2 **Dimitrovgrad** Bulg
44H5 **Dimitrovgrad** Russian Fed
65C3 **Dimona** Israel
61D2 **Dimpāpur** India
57G8 **Dinagat** *I* Phil
61C2 **Dinajpur** India
38B2 **Dinan** France
36C1 **Dinant** Belg
64B2 **Dinar** Turk
72D2 **Dinder** *R* Sudan
62B2 **Dindigul** India
52B2 **Dingbian** China
61C2 **Dinggyê** China
33A3 **Dingle** Irish Rep
33A3 **Dingle** *B* Irish Rep
70A3 **Dinguiraye** Guinea
34C3 **Dingwall** Scot
52A2 **Dingxi** China
52D2 **Ding Xian** China
55D1 **Dinh Lap** Viet
11D2 **Dinorwic L** Can
16A1 **Dinosaur** USA
20C2 **Dinuba** USA
10E2 **Diomede Is** Russian Fed/ USA
70A3 **Diouloulou** Sen
61D2 **Diphu** India
72E3 **Diredawa** Eth
76A3 **Dirk Hartog** *I* Aust
72B2 **Dirkou** Niger
75C1 **Dirranbandi** Aust
25J8 **Disappointment,C** South Georgia
18B1 **Disappointment,C** USA
76B3 **Disappointment,L** Aust
75B3 **Discovery B** Aust
xxxJ6 **Discovery Tablemount** Atlantic O
37C1 **Disentis Muster** Switz
66B1 **Dishna** Egypt
7N3 **Disko** *I* Greenland
7N3 **Disko Bugt** *B* Greenland
7N3 **Diskofjord** Greenland
13D3 **Dismal Swamp** USA
43F1 **Disna** *R* Belarus
29C2 **Distrito Federal** Federal District, Brazil
60C4 **Diu** India
57G9 **Diuat Mts** Phil
36A2 **Dives** *R* France
27K8 **Divinópolis** Brazil
45G6 **Divnoye** Russian Fed
64C2 **Divriği** Turk
20B1 **Dixon** California, USA
12B2 **Dixon** Illinois, USA
18D1 **Dixon** Montana, USA
6E4 **Dixon Entrance** *Sd* Can/ USA
3E2 **Dixonville** Can
64E3 **Diyālā** *R* Iraq
45G8 **Diyarbakir** Turk
63E3 **Diz** Pak
63B2 **Diz** *R* Iran
72B3 **Dja** *R* Cam
71C2 **Djadi** *R* Alg
72B1 **Djado,Plat du** Niger
71D2 **Djamaa** Alg
72B4 **Djambala** Congo
70C2 **Djanet** Alg
71C2 **Djebel Amour** *Mts* Alg
39A2 **Djebel Bouhalla** *Mt* Mor
71D1 **Djebel Chambi** *Mt* Tunisia
71D1 **Djebel Chélia** *Mts* Alg
71E1 **Djebel Zaghouan** *Mt* Tunisia
71D2 **Djebel Zrega** *Mt* Tunisia
71G4 **Djebobo** *Mt* Ghana
71C2 **Djelfa** Alg
72C3 **Djéma** CAR
70B3 **Djenné** Mali
71J4 **Djerem** *R* Cam
71F3 **Djibasso** Burkina
70B3 **Djibo** Burkina
72E2 **Djibouti** Djibouti
72E2 **Djibouti** Republic, E Africa
72C3 **Djolu** Zaïre
71G4 **Djougou** Benin
72D3 **Djugu** Zaïre
32C2 **Djúpivogur** Iceland
39C2 **Djurdjura** *Mts* Alg
44F4 **Dmitrov** Russian Fed
Dnepr = Dnieper
45E6 **Dneprodzerzhinsk** Ukraine
45F6 **Dnepropetrovsk** Ukraine
44D5 **Dneprovskaya Nizmennost'** Region, Belarus
Dnestr = Dniester
45E6 **Dnieper** *R* Ukraine
45C6 **Dniester** *R* Ukraine
44E4 **Dno** Russian Fed
72B3 **Doba** Chad
43E1 **Dobele** Latvia
28C3 **Doblas** Arg
76C1 **Dobo** Indon
41D2 **Doboj** Bosnia-Herzegovina
41F2 **Dobrich** Bulg
45E5 **Dobrush** Belarus
27K7 **Doce** *R* Brazil
25D2 **Doctor R P Peña** Arg
62B2 **Dod** India
62B2 **Doda Betta** *Mt* India
41F3 **Dodecanese** *Is* Greece
8C3 **Dodge City** USA
3G2 **Dodge L** Can
12A2 **Dodgeville** USA
72D4 **Dodoma** Tanz
34G4 **Dogger Bank** *Sand-bank* N Sea
12B1 **Dog L** Can
12C1 **Dog L** Can
54B3 **Dōgo** *I* Japan
70C3 **Dogondoutchi** Niger
64D2 **Doğubayazit** Turk
67F1 **Doha** Qatar
61D2 **Doilungdêqên** China
66C4 **Doka** Sudan
76C1 **Dolak** *I* Indon
11C3 **Doland** USA
7L5 **Dolbeau** Can
38D2 **Dole** France
66B4 **Doleib** *Watercourse* Sudan
35D5 **Dolgellau** Wales
14C1 **Dolgeville** USA
44K2 **Dolgiy, Ostrov** *I* Russian Fed
53E2 **Dolinsk** Russian Fed
37D1 **Dolomitche** *Mts* Italy
72E3 **Dolo Odo** Eth
25E5 **Dolores** Arg
28D2 **Dolores** Urug
16A2 **Dolores** *R* USA
22B1 **Dolores Hidalgo** Mexico
6G3 **Dolphin and Union Str** Can
25E8 **Dolphin,C** Falkland Is
51G7 **Dom** *Mt* Indon
45K5 **Dombarovskiy** Russian Fed
32F6 **Dombas** Nor
36D2 **Dombasle-sur-Meurthe** France
41D1 **Dombóvár** Hung
28A1 **Domeyko** Chile
38B2 **Domfront** France
23E3 **Dominica** *I* Caribbean
23C3 **Dominican Republic** Caribbean
7L3 **Dominion,C** Can
7N4 **Domino** Can
50E1 **Domna** Russian Fed
40B1 **Domodossola** Italy
28E2 **Dom Pedrito** Brazil
56E4 **Dompu** Indon
25B5 **Domuyo** *Mt* Arg
75D1 **Domville,Mt** Aust
34D3 **Don** *R* Scot
45G6 **Don** *R* Russian Fed
34B4 **Donaghadee** N Ire
22B1 **Donato Guerta** Mexico
Donau = Dunav
42C3 **Donau, R** Austria
42C3 **Donau** *R* Germany
36E3 **Donaueschingen** Germany
42C3 **Donauwörth** Germany
39A2 **Don Benito** Spain
35E5 **Doncaster** Eng
73B4 **Dondo** Angola
73D5 **Dondo** Mozam
62C3 **Dondra Head** *C* Sri Lanka
34B4 **Donegal** County, Irish Rep
33B3 **Donegal** Irish Rep
33B3 **Donegal** *B* Irish Rep
34A4 **Donegal** *Mts* Irish Rep
45F6 **Donetsk** Ukraine
71J4 **Donga** *R* Nig
52C4 **Dong'an** China
76A3 **Dongara** Aust
52A4 **Dongchuan** China
55D2 **Dongfang** China
53B3 **Dongfeng** China
76A1 **Donggala** Indon
50C3 **Donggi Cona** *L* China
53A4 **Donggou** China
52C5 **Donghai Dao** *I* China
52A1 **Dong He** *R* China
55D2 **Dong Hoi** Viet
52C5 **Dong Jiang** *R* China
53C2 **Donglanghong** China
53C3 **Dongning** China
72D2 **Dongola** Sudan
52D5 **Dongshan** China
50E4 **Dongsha Qundao** *I* China
52C2 **Dongsheng** China
52E3 **Dongtai** China
52C4 **Dongting Hu** *L* China
52B5 **Dongxing** China
52D3 **Dongzhi** China
17D2 **Doniphan** USA
40D2 **Donji Vakuf** Bosnia-Herzegovina
32G5 **Dönna** *I* Nor
19B3 **Donner** *P* USA
36D2 **Donnersberg** *Mt* Germany
74D2 **Donnybrook** S Africa
38B3 **Donostia** Spain
20B2 **Don Pedro Res** USA
10H2 **Doonerak,Mt** USA
57F9 **Dopolong** Phil
52A3 **Do Qu** *R* China
37B2 **Dora Baltea** *R* Italy
38D2 **Dorbirn** Austria
53A2 **Dorbod** China
35D6 **Dorchester** Eng
7L3 **Dorchester,C** Can
38C2 **Dordogne** *R* France
42A2 **Dordrecht** Neth
74D3 **Dordrecht** S Africa
3G3 **Doré L** Can
3G3 **Doré Lake** Can
14D1 **Dorest Peak** *Mt* USA
70B3 **Dori** Burkina
74B3 **Doring** *R* S Africa
36B2 **Dormans** France
42B3 **Dornbirn** Austria
34C3 **Dornoch** Scot
34C3 **Dornoch Firth** *Estuary* Scot
32H6 **Dorotea** Sweden
75D2 **Dorrigo** Aust
18B2 **Dorris** USA
35D6 **Dorset** County, Eng
36D1 **Dorsten** Germany
42B2 **Dortmund** Germany
72C3 **Doruma** Zaïre
49N4 **Dosatuy** Russian Fed
60B1 **Doshi** Afghan
20B2 **Dos Palos** USA
71G3 **Dosso** Niger
48G5 **Dossor** Kazakhstan
9E3 **Dothan** USA
38C1 **Douai** France
72A3 **Douala** Cam
75D1 **Double Island Pt** Aust
5K3 **Double Mer** *B* Can
16B3 **Double Mountain Fork** *R* USA
20C3 **Double Mt** USA
38D2 **Doubs** *R* France
78A3 **Doubtful Sd** NZ
70B3 **Douentza** Mali
3B2 **Douglas** Alaska, USA
8C3 **Douglas** Arizona, USA
35C4 **Douglas** Eng
15C2 **Douglas** Georgia, USA
74C2 **Douglas** S Africa
8C2 **Douglas** Wyoming, USA
10E2 **Douglas,C** USA
3C3 **Douglas Chan** Can
15C1 **Douglas L** USA
10H4 **Douglas,Mt** USA
36C2 **Doulevant-le-Château** France
36B1 **Doullens** France
35B4 **Doun** County, N Ire
27H8 **Dourados** Brazil
29B3 **Dourados** *R* Brazil
36B2 **Dourdan** France
39A1 **Douro** *R* Port
16A2 **Dove Creek** USA
13D3 **Dover** Delaware, USA
35F6 **Dover** Eng
13E2 **Dover** New Hampshire, USA
14C2 **Dover** New Jersey, USA
12C2 **Dover** Ohio, USA
35E5 **Dover** *R* Eng
35F6 **Dover,Str of** Eng/France
43G2 **Dovsk** Belarus
14C3 **Downington** USA
35C4 **Downpatrick** N Ire
14C1 **Downsville** USA
3D3 **Downton,Mt** Can
14C2 **Doylestown** USA
54B3 **Dōzen** *I* Japan
70A2 **Dr'aa** *R* Mor
37A2 **Drac** *R* France
29B3 **Dracena** Brazil
14E1 **Dracut** USA
38D3 **Draguignan** France
11B2 **Drake** USA
73D6 **Drakensberg** *Mts* S Africa
74D2 **Drakensberg** *Mt* S Africa
xxxE7 **Drake Pass** Pacific/ Atlantic O
41E2 **Dráma** Greece
32G6 **Drammen** Nor
32A1 **Drangajökull** Iceland
22B1 **Dr Arroyo** Mexico
37E1 **Drau** *R* Austria
40D1 **Drava** *R* Slovenia
3F3 **Drayton Valley** Can
38C2 **Dreaux** France
42C2 **Dresden** Germany
36A2 **Dreux** France
18C2 **Drewsey** USA
4E4 **Driftwood** Can
14A2 **Driftwood** USA
41E2 **Drin** *R* Alb
41D2 **Drina** *R* Bosnia-Herzegovina/Serbia, Yugos
43F1 **Drissa** *R* Belarus
35B5 **Drogheda** Irish Rep
43E3 **Drogobych** Ukraine
37A2 **Drôme** *R* France
37B2 **Dronera** Italy
79F12 **Dronning Maud Land** Region, Ant
26F8 **Dr P.P. Pená** Par
6G4 **Drumheller** Can
18D1 **Drummond** USA
12C1 **Drummond I** USA
5G4 **Drummondville** Can
43E2 **Druskininksi** Lithuania
49Q3 **Druzhina** Russian Fed
10L4 **Dry B** USA
11D2 **Dryberry L** Can
7J5 **Dryden** Can
14B1 **Dryden** USA
23H1 **Dry Harbour Mts** Jamaica
71J4 **Dschang** Cam
55B3 **Duang** *I* Myanmar
66C1 **Dubā** S Arabia
67G1 **Dubai** UAE
6H3 **Dubawnt** *R* Can
6H3 **Dubawnt L** Can
76D4 **Dubbo** Aust
35B5 **Dublin** County, Irish Rep
35B5 **Dublin** Irish Rep
15C2 **Dublin** USA
44F4 **Dubna** Russian Fed
45D5 **Dubno** Ukraine
18D2 **Dubois** Idaho, USA
13D2 **Du Bois** USA
18E2 **Dubois** Wyoming, USA
3C3 **Dubose,Mt** Can
43F3 **Dubossary** Moldova
43F2 **Dubrovica** Ukraine
41D2 **Dubrovnik** Croatia
9D2 **Dubuque** USA
19D2 **Duchesne** USA
15B1 **Duck** *R* USA
3H3 **Duck Mts** Can
20C3 **Ducor** USA
36D2 **Dudelange** Lux
48K3 **Dudinka** Russian Fed
35D5 **Dudley** Eng
49L2 **Dudypta** *R* Russian Fed
70B4 **Duekoué** Côte d'Ivoire
39B1 **Duero** *R* Spain
77F1 **Duff Is** Solomon Is
34D3 **Dufftown** Scot
40C2 **Dugi Otok** *I* Croatia
5G2 **Du Gué** *R* Can
42B2 **Duisburg** Germany
74E1 **Duiwelskloof** S Africa
64E3 **Dūkan** Iraq
10M5 **Duke I** USA
72D3 **Duk Faiwil** Sudan
67F1 **Dukhān** Qatar
52A4 **Dukou** China
50C3 **Dulan** China
28C2 **Dulce** *R* Arg
56D2 **Dulit Range** *Mts* Malay
61D3 **Dullabchara** India
36D1 **Dülmen** Germany
9D2 **Duluth** USA
65D2 **Dūmā** Syria
56B2 **Dumai** Indon
57E8 **Dumaran** *I* Phil
8C3 **Dumas** USA
65D2 **Dumayr** Syria
71G4 **Dumbai** Ghana
34C4 **Dumbarton** Scot
34D4 **Dumfries** Scot
34C4 **Dumfries and Galloway** Region, Scot
61C3 **Dumka** India
57B2 **Dumoga Kecil** Indon
13D1 **Dumoine,L** Can
79G8 **Dumont d'Urville** *Base* Ant
69C1 **Dumyât** Egypt
Dunărea = Danube *R* Rom
35B5 **Dunary Head** *Pt* Irish Rep
Dunav = Danube
43F3 **Dunayevtsy** Ukraine
3D4 **Duncan** Can
17C3 **Duncan** USA
4E3 **Duncan,C** Can
4F3 **Duncan L** Can
14B2 **Duncannon** USA
62E2 **Duncan Pass** Andaman Is
34D2 **Duncansby Head** *Pt* Scot
35B4 **Dundalk** Irish Rep
14B3 **Dundalk** USA
35B5 **Dundalk B** Irish Rep
7M2 **Dundas** Greenland
10M5 **Dundas I** Can
6G2 **Dundas Pen** Can
51G8 **Dundas Str** Aust
74E2 **Dundee** S Africa
34D3 **Dundee** Scot
14B1 **Dundee** USA
75B1 **Dundoo** Aust
35C4 **Dundrum** *B* N Ire
77G5 **Dunedin** NZ
15C3 **Dunedin** USA
75C2 **Dunedoo** Aust
34D3 **Dunfermline** Scot
60C4 **Dungarpur** India
35B5 **Dungarvan** Irish Rep
35F6 **Dungeness** Eng
75D2 **Dungog** Aust
72C3 **Dungu** Zaïre
72D1 **Dungunab** Sudan
53B3 **Dunhua** China
50C2 **Dunhuang** China
36B1 **Dunkerque** France
9F2 **Dunkirk** USA
72D2 **Dunkur** Eth
71F4 **Dunkwa** Ghana
33B3 **Dun Laoghaire** Irish Rep
14C2 **Dunmore** USA
23B1 **Dunmore Town** Bahamas
15D1 **Dunn** USA
34D2 **Dunnet Head** *Pt* Scot
11B3 **Dunning** USA
34D4 **Duns** Scot
11B2 **Dunseith** USA
18B2 **Dunsmuir** USA
78A2 **Dunstan Mts** NZ
36C2 **Dun-sur-Meuse** France
52D1 **Duolun** China
11B2 **Dupree** USA
73B4 **Duque de Braganca** Angola
12B3 **Du Quoin** USA
65C3 **Dura** Israel
38D3 **Durance** *R* France
12A2 **Durand** USA
21B2 **Durango** Mexico
39B1 **Durango** Spain
22A1 **Durango** State, Mexico
8C3 **Durango** USA
8D3 **Durant** USA
65D1 **Duraykīsh** Syria
25E4 **Durazho** Urug
74E2 **Durban** S Africa
36D1 **Duren** Germany
61B3 **Durg** India
61C3 **Durgapur** India
34E4 **Durham** County, Eng
34E4 **Durham** Eng
9F3 **Durham** N Carolina, USA
14E1 **Durham** New Hampshire, USA
75B1 **Durham Downs** Aust
41D2 **Durmitor** *Mt* Montenegro, Yugos
34C2 **Durness** Scot
41D2 **Durrës** Alb
75B1 **Durrie** Aust
41F3 **Dursunbey** Turk
78B2 **D'Urville I** NZ
63E1 **Dushak** Turkmenistan
52B4 **Dushan** China
59E2 **Dushanbe** Tajikistan
14B2 **Dushore** USA
78A3 **Dusky Sd** NZ
42B2 **Düsseldorf** Germany
10E5 **Dutch Harbor** USA
19D3 **Dutton,Mt** USA
52B4 **Duyun** China
64B1 **Düzce** Turk
44F2 **Dvinskaya Guba** *B* Russian Fed
60B4 **Dwārka** India
18C1 **Dworshak Res** USA
9E3 **Dyersburg** USA
35C5 **Dyfed** County, Wales
45G7 **Dykh Tau** *Mt* Russian Fed
75B1 **Dynevor Downs** Aust
50C2 **Dzag** Mongolia
50D2 **Dzamïn Üüd** Mongolia
73E5 **Dzaoudzi** Mayotte
50C2 **Dzavhan Gol** *R* Mongolia
44G4 **Dzerzhinsk** Russian Fed
49O4 **Dzhalinda** Russian Fed
48J5 **Dzhambul** Kazakhstan

F

G

Karamay Khaskovo

48K5 **Karamay** China
78B2 **Karamea** NZ
78B2 **Karamea Bight** *B* NZ
45E8 **Karanhk** *R* Turk
60D4 **Kāranja** India
64B2 **Karapınar** Turk
48J2 **Kara S** Russian Fed
74B2 **Karasburg** Namibia
32K5 **Karasjok** Nor
48J4 **Karasuk** Russian Fed
64C2 **Karataş** Turk
48H5 **Kara Tau** *Mts* Kazakhstan
55B3 **Karathuri** Myanmar
53B5 **Karatsu** Japan
48K2 **Karaul** Russian Fed
65B1 **Karavostasi** Cyprus
37E1 **Karawanken** *Mts* Austria
63C3 **Karāz** Iran
64D3 **Karbalā'** Iraq
43E3 **Karcag** Hung
41E3 **Kardhítsa** Greece
44E3 **Karel'skaya** Respublika, Russian Fed
62E2 **Karen** Andaman Is
44K3 **Karepino** Russian Fed
32J5 **Karesvando** Sweden
70B2 **Karet** *Desert Region* Maur
48K4 **Kargasok** Russian Fed
44F3 **Kargopol'** Russian Fed
45G8 **Karh** *R* Turk
71J3 **Kari** Nig
73C5 **Kariba** Zim
73C5 **Kariba** *L* Zim/Zambia
73C5 **Kariba Dam** Zim/Zambia
74B1 **Karibib** Namibia
72D2 **Karima** Sudan
56C3 **Karimata** *I* Indon
61D3 **Karimganj** Bang
62B1 **Karīmnagar** India
72E2 **Karin** Somalia
32J6 **Karis** Fin
72C4 **Karishimbe** *Mt* Zaïre
41E3 **Káristos** Greece
62A2 **Kārkal** India
51H7 **Karkar** *I* PNG
63B2 **Karkheh** *R* Iran
45E6 **Karkinitskiy Zaliv** *B* Ukraine
49L5 **Karlik Shan** *Mt* China
42D2 **Karlino** Pol
40D2 **Karlobag** Croatia
40D1 **Karlovac** Croatia
41E2 **Karlovo** Bulg
42C2 **Karlovy Vary** Czech Republic
32G7 **Karlshamn** Sweden
32G7 **Karlskoga** Sweden
32H7 **Karlskrona** Sweden
42B3 **Karlsruhe** Germany
32G7 **Karlstad** Sweden
11C2 **Karlstad** USA
10H4 **Karluk** USA
61D3 **Karnafuli Res** Bang
60D3 **Karnal** India
62A1 **Karnataka** State, India
41F2 **Karnobat** Bulg
37E1 **Kärnten** Province, Austria
73C5 **Karoi** Zim
73D4 **Karonga** Malawi
72D2 **Karora** Sudan
57A3 **Karossa** Indon
41F3 **Kárpathos** *I* Greece
7N2 **Karrats Fjord** Greenland
74C3 **Karree Berge** S Africa
45G7 **Kars** Turk
48H5 **Karsakpay** Kazakhstan
43F1 **Kārsava** Latvia
58E2 **Karshi** Uzbekistan
32J6 **Karstula** Fin
65C1 **Kartaba** Leb
41F2 **Kartal** Turk
44L5 **Kartaly** Russian Fed
14A2 **Karthaus** USA
63B2 **Kārūn** *R* Iran
61B2 **Karwa** India
62A2 **Kārwār** India
50E1 **Karymskoye** Russian Fed
72B4 **Kasai** *R* Zaïre
73C5 **Kasaji** Zaïre
73D5 **Kasama** Zambia
73D4 **Kasanga** Tanz
62A2 **Kāsaragod** India
6H3 **Kasba L** Can
71A2 **Kasba Tadla** Mor
10F1 **Kasegaluk Lg** USA
73C5 **Kasempa** Zambia
73C5 **Kasenga** Zaïre
72D3 **Kasese** Uganda
63C2 **Kāshān** Iran
10G3 **Kashegelok** USA
59F2 **Kashi** China
54B4 **Kashima** Japan
60D3 **Kāshipur** India
53D4 **Kashiwazaki** Japan
63D1 **Kashmar** Iran
46E4 **Kashmir** State, India
44G5 **Kasimov** Russian Fed
57C3 **Kasiruta** *I* Indon
12B3 **Kaskaskia** *R* USA
4C2 **Kaskattama** *R* Can
32J6 **Kasko** Fin
44L4 **Kasli** Russian Fed
6G5 **Kaslo** Can
3H2 **Kasmere L** Can
72C4 **Kasonga** Zaïre
73B4 **Kasongo-Lunda** Zaïre
41F3 **Kásos** *I* Greece
Kaspiyskiy = Lagan'
72D2 **Kassala** Sudan
42B2 **Kassel** Germany
71D1 **Kasserine** Tunisia
73B5 **Kassinga** Angola
64B1 **Kastamonou** Turk
41E3 **Kastélli** Greece
64A2 **Kastellorizon** *I* Greece
41E2 **Kastoría** Greece
41F3 **Kástron** Greece
53D4 **Kasugai** Japan
54B3 **Kasumi** Japan
73D5 **Kasungu** Malawi
60C2 **Kasur** Pak
73C5 **Kataba** Zambia
13F1 **Katahdin,Mt** USA
72C4 **Katako-kombe** Zaïre
10M3 **Katalla** USA
49Q4 **Katangli** Russian Fed
76A4 **Katanning** Aust
62E3 **Katchall** *I* Indian O
41E2 **Kateríni** Greece
6E4 **Kates Needle** *Mt* Can/USA
61E3 **Katha** Myanmar
76C2 **Katherine** Aust
60C4 **Kāthiāwār** *Pen* India
65B3 **Kathib El Henu** Egypt
61C2 **Kathmandu** Nepal
60D2 **Kathua** India
61C2 **Katihār** India
73C5 **Katima Mulilo** Namibia
6C4 **Katmai,Mt** USA
10H4 **Katmai Nat Mon** USA
61B3 **Katni** India
75D2 **Katoomba** Aust
43D2 **Katowice** Pol
32H7 **Katrineholm** Sweden
71H3 **Katsina** Nig
71H3 **Katsina** *Region* Nig
71H3 **Katsina** *State* Nig
71H4 **Katsina Ala** Nig
54D3 **Katsuta** Japan
54D3 **Katsuura** Japan
54C3 **Katsuy** Japan
48H6 **Kattakurgan** Uzbekistan
32G7 **Kattegat** *Str* Denmark/Sweden
36E2 **Katzenbuckel** *Mt* Germany
57C2 **Kau** Indon
20E5 **Kauai** *I* Hawaiian Is
20E5 **Kauai Chan** Hawaiian Is
20E5 **Kaulakahi Chan** Hawaiian Is
20E5 **Kaunakaki** Hawaiian Is
44C5 **Kaunas** Lithuania
71H3 **Kaura Namoda** Nig
32J5 **Kautokeino** Nor
41E2 **Kavadarci** Macedonia, Yugos
41D2 **Kavajë** Alb
53D3 **Kavalerovo** Russian Fed
62B2 **Kavali** India
41E2 **Kavála** Greece
60B4 **Kāvda** India
76E1 **Kavieng** PNG
54C3 **Kawagoe** Japan
54C3 **Kawaguchi** Japan
20E5 **Kawaihae** Hawaiian Is
78B1 **Kawakawa** NZ
73C4 **Kawambwa** Zambia
61B3 **Kawardha** India
13D2 **Kawartha Lakes** Can
53D4 **Kawasaki** Japan
20C2 **Kaweah** *R* USA
78C1 **Kawerau** NZ
78B1 **Kawhia** NZ
71F3 **Kaya** Burkina
10K4 **Kayak I** USA
56E2 **Kayan** *R* Indon
62B3 **Kāyankulam** India
11A3 **Kaycee** USA
57C3 **Kayeli** Indon
19D3 **Kayenta** USA
70A3 **Kayes** Mali
45F8 **Kayseri** Turk
49P2 **Kazach'ye** Russian Fed
64E1 **Kazakh** Azerbaijan
48G5 **Kazakhstan** Republic, Asia
44H4 **Kazan'** Russian Fed
41F2 **Kazanlük** Bulg
50H4 **Kazan Retto** *Is* Japan
43F3 **Kazatin** Ukraine
45G7 **Kazbek** *Mt* Georgia
63C3 **Kāzerūn** Iran
44J3 **Kazhim** Russian Fed
64E1 **Kazi Magomed** Azerbaijan
43E3 **Kazincbarcika** Hung
44M3 **Kazym** *R* Russian Fed
44M3 **Kazymskaya** Russian Fed
41E3 **Kéa** *I* Greece
20E5 **Kealaikahiki Chan** Hawaiian Is
8D2 **Kearney** USA
19D4 **Kearny** USA
64C2 **Keban Baraji** *Res* Turk
71G3 **Kebbi** *State* Nig
70A3 **Kébémer** Sen
71J4 **Kebi** *R* Chad
71D2 **Kebili** Tunisia
65D1 **Kebīr** *R* Syria/Leb
32H5 **Kebrekaise** *Mt* Sweden
3C2 **Kechika** *R* Can
43D3 **Kecskemet** Hung
43E1 **Kedainiai** Lithuania
5H4 **Kedgwick** Can
53B2 **Kedong** China
70A3 **Kédougou** Sen
44J3 **Kedva** Russian Fed
10N4 **Keechiga** *R* Can
10N3 **Keele** *R* Can
10M3 **Keele Pk** *Mt* Can
19C3 **Keeler** USA
20C3 **Keene** California, USA
13E2 **Keene** New Hampshire, USA
74B2 **Keetmanshoop** Namibia
12B2 **Keewanee** USA
4C4 **Keewatin** Can
12A1 **Keewatin** USA
6J3 **Keewatin** *Region* Can
41E3 **Kefallinía** *I* Greece
57B4 **Kefamenanu** Indon
65C2 **Kefar Sava** Israel
71H4 **Keffi** Nig
32A2 **Keflavik** Iceland
6G4 **Keg River** Can
66B3 **Keheili** Sudan
55B1 **Kehsi Mansam** Myanmar
75B3 **Keith** Aust
34D3 **Keith** Scot
6F3 **Keith Arm** *B* Can
7M3 **Kekertuk** Can
60D3 **Kekri** India
55C5 **Kelang** Malay
57C3 **Kelang** *I* Indon
55C4 **Kelantan** *R* Malay
71E1 **Kelibia** Tunisia
60B1 **Kelif** Turkmenistan
64C1 **Kelkit** *R* Turk
72B4 **Kellé** Congo
10O3 **Keller L** Can
6F2 **Kellet,C** Can
18C1 **Kellogg** USA
48D3 **Kelloselka** Fin
35B5 **Kells** Irish Rep
34C4 **Kells Range** *Hills* Scot
43E1 **Kelme** Lithuania
6G5 **Kelowna** Can
6F4 **Kelsey Bay** Can
34D4 **Kelso** Scot
18B1 **Kelso** USA
3H3 **Kelvington** Can
44E3 **Kem'** Russian Fed
44E3 **Kem'** *R* Russian Fed
70B3 **Ke Macina** Mali
3C3 **Kemano** Can
48K4 **Kemerovo** Russian Fed
32J5 **Kemi** Fin
32K5 **Kemi** *R* Fin
32K5 **Kemijärvi** Fin
18D2 **Kemmerer** USA
36C1 **Kempen** Region, Belg
16C3 **Kemp,L** USA
23B2 **Kemps Bay** Bahamas
75D2 **Kempsey** Aust
42C3 **Kempten** Germany
10H3 **Kenai** USA
10H4 **Kenai Mts** USA
10H3 **Kenai Pen** USA
72D3 **Kenamuke Swamp** Sudan
35D4 **Kendal** Eng
75D2 **Kendall** Aust
76B1 **Kendari** Indon
56D3 **Kendawangan** Indon
61C3 **Kendrāpāra** India
18C1 **Kendrick** USA
17F4 **Kenedy** USA
70A4 **Kenema** Sierra Leone
72B4 **Kenge** Zaïre
55B1 **Kengtung** Myanmar
74C2 **Kenhardt** S Africa
70A3 **Kéniéba** Mali
71A2 **Kenitra** Mor
11B2 **Kenmare** USA
16B3 **Kenna** USA
13F1 **Kennebec** *R* USA
14E1 **Kennebunk** USA
14A1 **Kennedy** USA
17D4 **Kenner** USA
17E2 **Kennett** USA
14C3 **Kennett Square** USA
18C1 **Kennewick** USA
6F4 **Kenny Dam** Can
4D3 **Kenogami** *R* Can
7J5 **Kenora** Can
9E2 **Kenosha** USA
35F6 **Kent** County, Eng
16B3 **Kent** Texas, USA
18B1 **Kent** Washington, USA
12B2 **Kentland** USA
12C2 **Kenton** USA
6H3 **Kent Pen** Can
9E3 **Kentucky** State, USA
12C3 **Kentucky** *R* USA
9E3 **Kentucky L** USA
5J4 **Kentville** Can
17D3 **Kentwood** Louisiana, USA
12B2 **Kentwood** Michigan, USA
72D3 **Kenya** Republic, Africa
72D4 **Kenya,Mt** Kenya
12A2 **Keokuk** USA
61B3 **Keonchi** India
61C3 **Keonjhargarh** India
51G7 **Kepaluan Tanimbar** *Arch* Indon
43D2 **Kępno** Pol
57C3 **Kepualuan Widi** *Arch* Indon
57B4 **Kepulauan Alor** *Arch* Indon
56C2 **Kepulauan Anambas** *Arch* Indon
51G7 **Kepulauan Aru** *Arch* Indon
76B1 **Kepulauan Babar** *I* Indon
56C2 **Kepulauan Badas** *Is* Indon
51G7 **Kepulauan Banda** *Arch* Indon
76B1 **Kepulauan Banggai** *I* Indon
76B1 **Kepulauan Barat Daya** *Is* Indon
56C2 **Kepulauan Bunguran Seletan** *Arch* Indon
57D3 **Kepulauan Gorong** *Arch* Indon
51G7 **Kepulauan Kai** *Arch* Indon
57C2 **Kepulauan Kawio** *Arch* Indon
76B1 **Kepulauan Leti** *I* Indon
56B3 **Kepulauan Lingga** *Is* Indon
57C2 **Kepulauan Loloda** *Arch* Indon
56A3 **Kepulauan Mentawi** *Arch* Indon
57C2 **Kepulauan Nenusa** *Arch* Indon
57C3 **Kepulauan Obi** *Arch* Indon
56B2 **Kepulauan Riau** *Arch* Indon
56E4 **Kepulauan Sabalana** *Arch* Indon
57C2 **Kepulauan Sangihe** *Arch* Indon
76B1 **Kepulauan Sermata** *I* Indon
76B1 **Kepulauan Sula** *I* Indon
57C2 **Kepulauan Talaud** *Arch* Indon
56C2 **Kepulauan Tambelan** *Is* Indon
76C1 **Kepulauan Tanimbar** *I* Indon
76B1 **Kepulauan Togian** *I* Indon
76B1 **Kepulauan Tukangbesi** *Is* Indon
57D3 **Kepulauan Watubela** *Arch* Indon
57C3 **Kepulauan Yef Fam** *Arch* Indon
57B4 **Kepulaun Solor** *Arch* Indon
62B2 **Kerala** State, India
75B3 **Kerang** Aust
32J6 **Kerava** Fin
53D1 **Kerbi** *R* Russian Fed
45F6 **Kerch'** Ukraine
44J3 **Kerchem'ya** Russian Fed
76D1 **Kerema** PNG
18C1 **Keremeps** Can
72D2 **Keren** Eritrea
xxviiiE7 **Kerguelen Ridge** Indian O
72D4 **Kericho** Kenya
56B3 **Kerinci** *Mt* Indon
72D3 **Kerio** *R* Kenya
58E2 **Kerki** Turkmenistan
41D3 **Kérkira** Greece
41D3 **Kérkira** *I* Greece
77H3 **Kermadec Is** NZ
77H4 **Kermadec Trench** Pacific O
63D2 **Kerman** Iran
20B2 **Kerman** USA
63B2 **Kermānshāh** Iran
41F3 **Kerme Körfezi** *B* Turk
16B3 **Kermit** USA
19C3 **Kern** *R* USA
20C3 **Kernville** USA
44J3 **Keros** Russian Fed
3G3 **Kerrobert** Can
16C3 **Kerrville** USA
15C2 **Kershaw** USA
56C3 **Kertamulia** Indon
49N5 **Kerulen** *R* Mongolia
70B2 **Kerzaz** Alg
4F3 **Kesagami L** Can
41F2 **Keşan** Turk
53E4 **Kesennuma** Japan
53B2 **Keshan** China
45G7 **Kesir Daglari** *Mt* Turk
32L5 **Kesten'ga** Russian Fed
35D4 **Keswick** Eng
71G4 **Kéta** Ghana
56D3 **Ketapang** Indon
6E4 **Ketchikan** USA
70C3 **Ketia** Niger
60B4 **Keti Bandar** Pak
71G4 **Kétou** Benin
43E2 **Kętrzyn** Pol
35E5 **Kettering** Eng
12C3 **Kettering** USA
4D2 **Kettle** *R* Can
18C1 **Kettle** *R* Can
20C2 **Kettleman City** USA
18C1 **Kettle River Range** *Mts* USA
7L3 **Kettlestone B** Can
14B1 **Keuka L** USA
63D2 **Kevir-i Namak** *Salt Flat* Iran
12B2 **Kewaunee** USA
12B1 **Keweenaw B** USA
12B1 **Keweenaw Pen** USA
4E4 **Key Harbour** Can
15E4 **Key Largo** USA
14A3 **Keyser** USA
9E4 **Key West** USA
49M4 **Kezhma** Russian Fed
41D1 **K'félegháza** Hung
10F3 **Kgun L** USA
65D2 **Khabab** Syria
53D2 **Khabarovsk** Russian Fed
45G8 **Khabur** *R* Syria
60B3 **Khairpur** Pak
60B3 **Khairpur** Region, Pak
74C1 **Khakhea** Botswana
65B3 **Khalig El Tina** *B* Egypt
67G2 **Khalīj Maşīrah** *B* Oman
41F3 **Khálki** *I* Greece
41E2 **Khalkidhíki** *Pen* Greece
41E3 **Khalkís** Greece
44L2 **Khal'mer-Yu** Russian Fed
44H4 **Khalturin** Russian Fed
67G2 **Khalūf** Oman
60C4 **Khambhāt,G** of India
60D4 **Khāmgaon** India
66D3 **Khamir** Yemen
66D3 **Khamis Mushayt** S Arabia
55C2 **Kham Keut** Laos
62C1 **Khammam** India
65B3 **Khamsa** Egypt
63B1 **Khamseh** *Mts* Iran
55C2 **Khan** *R* Laos
60B1 **Khanabad** Afghan
64E3 **Khānaqīn** Iraq
60D4 **Khandwa** India
60C2 **Khanewal** Pak
65D3 **Khan ez Zabib** Jordan
55D4 **Khanh Hung** Viet
41E3 **Khaniá** Greece
53C3 **Khanka, Ozero** *L* China
Khankendy = Stepanakert
60C3 **Khanpur** Pak
65D1 **Khān Shaykhūn** Syria
48H3 **Khanty-Mansiysk** Russian Fed
65C3 **Khan Yunis** Egypt
60D1 **Khapalu** India
50E2 **Khapcheranga** Russian Fed
45H6 **Kharabali** Russian Fed
61C3 **Kharagpur** India
63D3 **Khārān** Iran
60B3 **Kharan** Pak
63C2 **Kharānaq** Iran
63C3 **Khārg** *Is* Iran
69C2 **Khârga Oasis** Egypt
60D4 **Khargon** India
45F6 **Khar'kov** Ukraine
44F2 **Kharlovka** Russian Fed
41F2 **Kharmanli** Bulg
44G4 **Kharovsk** Russian Fed
72D2 **Khartoum** Sudan
72D2 **Khartoum North** Sudan
53C3 **Khasan** Russian Fed
63E2 **Khash** Afghan
63E3 **Khāsh** Iran
63E2 **Khash** *R* Afghan
72D2 **Khashm el Girba** Sudan
61D2 **Khasi-Jaīntīa Hills** India
41F2 **Khaskovo** Bulg

Khatanga **Komsomolets, Ostrov**

49M2 **Khatanga** Russian Fed
49N2 **Khatangskiy Zaliv** *Estuary* Russian Fed
49T3 **Khatyrka** Russian Fed
55B3 **Khawsa** Myanmar
66C1 **Khaybar** S Arabia
66B2 **Khazzan an-Nasr** *L* Egypt
55C2 **Khe Bo** Viet
60C4 **Khed Brahma** India
39C2 **Khemis** Alg
71A2 **Khemisset** Mor
71D1 **Khenchela** Alg
71A2 **Khenifra** Mor
39D2 **Kherrata** Alg
45E6 **Kherson** Ukraine
49N4 **Khilok** Russian Fed
41F3 **Khíos** Greece
41F3 **Khíos** *I* Greece
45D6 **Khmel'nitskiy** Ukraine
43E3 **Khodorov** Ukraine
59E1 **Khodzhent** Taji
60B1 **Kholm** Afghan
43G1 **Kholm** Russian Fed
53E2 **Kholmsk** Russian Fed
74B1 **Khomas Hochland, Mts** Namibia
55D3 **Khong** Laos
63C3 **Khonj** Iran
53C2 **Khor** Russian Fed
53D2 **Khor** *R* Russian Fed
63B2 **Khoramshahr** Iran
67F2 **Khōr Duwayhin** *B* UAE
60C1 **Khorog** Tajikistan
63B2 **Khorramābad** Iran
63D2 **Khosf** Iran
60B2 **Khost** Pak
45D6 **Khotin** Ukraine
10G3 **Khotol** *Mt* USA
71A2 **Khouribga** Mor
45D5 **Khoyniki** Belarus
49Q3 **Khrebet Cherskogo** *Mts* Russian Fed
53B1 **Khrebet Dzhagdy** *Mts* Russian Fed
49P4 **Khrebet Dzhugdzhur** *Mts* Russian Fed
10C2 **Khrebet Iskamen** *Mts* Russian Fed
49O3 **Khrebet Orulgan** *Mts* Russian Fed
44L2 **Khrebet Pay-khoy** *Mts* Russian Fed
53D2 **Khrebet Sikhote Alin'** *Mts* Russian Fed
59G1 **Khrebet Tarbagatay** *Mts* Kazakhstan
49O4 **Khrebet Tukuringra** *Mts* Russian Fed
53C1 **Khrebet Turana** *Upland* Russian Fed
65B1 **Khrysokhou B** Cyprus
44L3 **Khulga** *R* Russian Fed
61C3 **Khulna** Bang
60D1 **Khunjerab** *P* China/India
63C2 **Khunsar** Iran
67E1 **Khurays** S Arabia
61C3 **Khurda** India
60D3 **Khurja** India
67G3 **Khūryan Mūryān** *Is* Oman
60C2 **Khushab** Pak
65C2 **Khushnīyah** Syria
43E3 **Khust** Ukraine
72C2 **Khuwei** Sudan
60B3 **Khuzdar** Pak
63E2 **Khvāf** Iran
45H5 **Khvalynsk** Russian Fed
63D2 **Khvor** Iran
63C3 **Khvormūj** Iran
45G8 **Khvoy** Iran
60C1 **Khwaja Muhammad** *Mts* Afghan
60C2 **Khyber P** Afghan/Pak
73C4 **Kiambi** Zaïre
17C3 **Kiamichi** *R* USA
10F2 **Kiana** USA
72B4 **Kibangou** Congo
72D4 **Kibaya** Tanz
72C4 **Kibombo** Zaïre
72D4 **Kibondo** Tanz
72D4 **Kibungu** Rwanda
41E2 **Kičevo** Macedonia
6G4 **Kicking Horse P** Can
70C3 **Kidal** Mali
35D5 **Kidderminster** Eng
70A3 **Kidira** Sen
78C1 **Kidnappers,C** NZ
42C2 **Kiel** Germany
43E2 **Kielce** Pol
42C2 **Kieler Bucht** *B* Germany
Kiev = Kiyev
58E2 **Kifab** Uzbekistan
70A3 **Kiffa** Maur
68H8 **Kigali** Rwanda
5J2 **Kiglapatt,C** Can
10E3 **Kigluaik Mts** USA
72C4 **Kigoma** Tanz
20E5 **Kiholo** Hawaiian Is
54C4 **Kii-sanchi** *Mts* Japan
53C5 **Kii-suido** *B* Japan
49R4 **Kikhchik** Russian Fed
41E1 **Kikinda** Serbia, Yugos
Kikládhes = Cyclades
76D1 **Kikon** PNG
54D2 **Kikonai** Japan
51H7 **Kikori** PNG
72B4 **Kikwit** Zaïre
20E5 **Kilauea Crater** *Mt* Hawaiian Is
6C3 **Kilbuck Mts** USA
53B3 **Kilchu** N Korea
75D1 **Kilcoy** Aust
35B5 **Kildane** County, Irish Rep
35B5 **Kildare** Irish Rep
17D3 **Kilgore** USA
72E4 **Kilifi** Kenya
72D4 **Kilimanjaro** *Mt* Tanz
73D4 **Kilindoni** Tanz
64C2 **Kilis** Turk
43F3 **Kiliya** Ukraine
35B5 **Kilkenny** County, Irish Rep
35B5 **Kilkenny** Irish Rep
41E2 **Kilkís** Greece
75D1 **Killarney** Aust
33B3 **Killarney** Irish Rep
17C3 **Killeen** USA
10H2 **Killik** *R* USA
34C3 **Killin** Scot
5J1 **Killinek I** Can
41E3 **Killíni** *Mt* Greece
34C4 **Kilmarnock** Scot
44J4 **Kil'mez** Russian Fed
73D4 **Kilosa** Tanz
33B3 **Kilrush** Irish Rep
71J4 **Kilunga** *R* Nig
73C4 **Kilwa** Zaïre
73D4 **Kilwa Kisiwani** Tanz
73D4 **Kilwa Kivinje** Tanz
71J4 **Kim** *R* Cam
75A2 **Kimba** Aust
16B1 **Kimball** USA
10K3 **Kimball,Mt** USA
3E4 **Kimberley** Can
74C2 **Kimberley** S Africa
76B2 **Kimberley Plat** Aust
53B3 **Kimch'aek** N Korea
53B4 **Kimch'ŏn** S Korea
54A3 **Kimhae** S Korea
41E3 **Kími** Greece
54A3 **Kimje** S Korea
44F4 **Kimry** Russian Fed
54A3 **Kimwha** N Korea
56E1 **Kinabalu** *Mt* Malay
56E1 **Kinabatangan** *R* Malay
4E5 **Kincardine** Can
3C2 **Kincolith** Can
17D3 **Kinder** USA
3G3 **Kindersley** Can
70A3 **Kindia** Guinea
72C4 **Kindu** Zaïre
44J5 **Kinel'** Russian Fed
44G4 **Kineshma** Russian Fed
75D1 **Kingaroy** Aust
19B3 **King City** USA
6F4 **Kingcome Inlet** Can
10F4 **King Cove** USA
17C2 **Kingfisher** USA
7L4 **King George Is** Can
76D5 **King I** Aust
3C3 **King I** Can
44C4 **Kingissepp** Estonia
76B2 **King Leopold Range** *Mts* Aust
8B3 **Kingman** USA
72C4 **Kingombe** Zaïre
75A2 **Kingoonya** Aust
20C2 **Kingsburg** USA
19C3 **Kings Canyon Nat Pk** USA
75A3 **Kingscote** Aust
76B2 **King Sd** Aust
12B1 **Kingsford** USA
15C2 **Kingsland** USA
35F5 **King's Lynn** Eng
77G1 **Kingsmill Group** *Is* Kiribati
14D2 **Kings Park** USA
8B2 **Kings Peak** *Mt* USA
15C1 **Kingsport** USA
76C4 **Kingston** Aust
7L5 **Kingston** Can
21E3 **Kingston** Jamaica
13E2 **Kingston** New York, USA
78A3 **Kingston** NZ
14C2 **Kingston** Pennsylvania, USA
23E4 **Kingstown** St Vincent
8D4 **Kingsville** USA
5J2 **Kingurutik** *R* Can
34C3 **Kingussie** Scot
6J3 **King William I** Can
74D3 **King William's Town** S Africa
72B4 **Kinkala** Congo
32G7 **Kinna** Sweden
34D3 **Kinnairds Head** *Pt* Scot
54C3 **Kinomoto** Japan
34D3 **Kinross** Scot
72B4 **Kinshasa** Zaïre
16C2 **Kinsley** USA
15D1 **Kinston** USA
56E3 **Kintap** Indon
34C4 **Kintyre** *Pen* Scot
3E2 **Kinuso** Can
72D3 **Kinyeti** *Mt* Sudan
36E1 **Kinzig** *R* Germany
3H2 **Kipahigan L** Can
41E3 **Kiparissía** Greece
41E3 **Kiparissiakós Kólpos** *G* Greece
13D1 **Kipawa,L** Can
73D4 **Kipili** Tanz
10F4 **Kipnuk** USA
35B5 **Kippure** *Mt* Irish Rep
73C5 **Kipushi** Zaïre
36E2 **Kirchheim** Germany
49M4 **Kirensk** Russian Fed
Kirghizia = Kyrgyzstan
59F1 **Kirgizskiy Khrebet** *Mts* Kyrgyzstan
72B4 **Kiri** Zaïre
77G1 **Kiribati** *Is* Pacific O
64B2 **Kırıkkale** Turk
44E4 **Kirishi** Russian Fed
60B3 **Kirithar Range** *Mts* Pak
41F3 **Kirkağaç** Turk
45H8 **Kirk Bulāg Dāgh** *Mt* Iran
35D4 **Kirkby** Eng
34D3 **Kirkcaldy** Scot
34C4 **Kirkcudbright** Scot
32K5 **Kirkenes** Nor
7K5 **Kirkland Lake** Can
64A1 **Kırklareli** Turk
79E **Kirkpatrick,Mt** Ant
9D2 **Kirksville** USA
64D2 **Kirkūk** Iraq
34D2 **Kirkwall** Scot
17D2 **Kirkwood** USA
74D3 **Kirkwood** *R* S Africa
44E5 **Kirov** Russian Fed
44H4 **Kirov** Russian Fed
45H7 **Kirovabad** Azerbaijan
64D1 **Kirovakan** Armenia
44K4 **Kirovgrad** Russian Fed
45E6 **Kirovograd** Ukraine
44E2 **Kirovsk** Russian Fed
49R4 **Kirovskiy** Kamchatka, Russian Fed
53C2 **Kirovskiy** Primorskiykray, Russian Fed
44J4 **Kirs** Russian Fed
64B2 **Kirşehir** Turk
42C2 **Kiruna** Sweden
54C3 **Kiryū** Japan
72C3 **Kisangani** Zaïre
57C4 **Kisar** *I* Indon
56A2 **Kisaran** Indon
54C3 **Kisarazu** Japan
61C2 **Kishanganj** India
60C3 **Kishangarh** India
43F3 **Kishinev** Moldova
54C4 **Kishiwada** Japan
72D4 **Kisii** Kenya
73D4 **Kisiju** Tanz
10B6 **Kiska** *I* USA
4B3 **Kiskitto L** Can
43D3 **Kiskunhalas** Hung
45G7 **Kislovodsk** Russian Fed
72E4 **Kismaayo** Somalia
54C3 **Kiso-sammyaku** *Mts* Japan
70B4 **Kissidougou** Guinea
15C3 **Kissimmee,L** USA
3H2 **Kississing L** Can
72D4 **Kisumu** Kenya
43E3 **Kisvárda** Hung
70B3 **Kita** Mali
48H6 **Kitab** Uzbekistan
54D3 **Kitakami** Japan
54D3 **Kitakami** *R* Japan
54D3 **Kitakata** Japan
53C5 **Kita-Kyūshū** Japan
72D3 **Kitale** Kenya
50H4 **Kitalo** *I* Japan
53E3 **Kitami** Japan
54D2 **Kitami-Esashi** Japan
16B2 **Kit Carson** USA
7K5 **Kitchener** Can
4F3 **Kitchigama** *R* Can
72D3 **Kitgum** Uganda
41E3 **Kithira** *I* Greece
41E3 **Kithnos** *I* Greece
65B1 **Kiti,C** Cyprus
6G2 **Kitikmeot** Region, Can
6F4 **Kitimat** Can
32K5 **Kitnen** *R* Fin
54B4 **Kitsuki** Japan
13D2 **Kittanning** USA
13E2 **Kittery** USA
32J5 **Kittilä** Fin
15D1 **Kitty Hawk** USA
73D4 **Kitunda** Tanz
10N4 **Kitwanga** Can
73C5 **Kitwe** Zambia
42C3 **Kitzbühel** Austria
37E1 **Kitzbühler Alpen** *Mts* Austria
42C3 **Kitzingen** Germany
72C4 **Kiumbi** Zaïre
10F2 **Kivalina** USA
43F2 **Kivercy** Ukraine
72C4 **Kivu,L** Zaïre/Rwanda
6B3 **Kiwalik** USA
45E5 **Kiyev** Ukraine
43G2 **Kiyevskoye Vodokhranilishche** *Res* Ukraine
44K4 **Kizel** Russian Fed
44G3 **Kizema** Russian Fed
64C2 **Kizil** *R* Turk
58D2 **Kizyl-Arvat** Turkmenistan
45J8 **Kizyl-Atrek** Turkmenistan
42C2 **Kladno** Czech Republic
42C3 **Klagenfurt** Austria
44C4 **Klaipėda** Lithuania
18B2 **Klamath** USA
8A2 **Klamath** *R* USA
8A2 **Klamath Falls** USA
18B2 **Klamath Mts** USA
3C2 **Klappan** *R* Can
42C3 **Klatovy** Czech Republic
10M4 **Klawak** USA
65C1 **Kleiat** Leb
74B2 **Kleinsee** S Africa
74D2 **Klerksdorp** S Africa
43G2 **Kletnya** Russian Fed
36D1 **Kleve** Germany
43G2 **Klimovichi** Belarus
44F4 **Klin** Russian Fed
43D1 **Klintehamn** Sweden
45E5 **Klintsy** Russian Fed
74C3 **Klipplaat** S Africa
40D2 **Ključ** Bosnia-Herzegovina
42D2 **Kłodzko** Pol
10L3 **Klondike** *R* USA/Can
6D3 **Klondike Plat** USA/Can
42D3 **Klosterneuburg** Austria
10L3 **Kluane** *R* Can
10L3 **Kluane L** Can
10L3 **Kluane Nat Pk** Can
43D2 **Kluczbork** Pol
10L4 **Klukwan** USA
10J3 **Klutina L** USA
10J3 **Knight I** USA
35D5 **Knighton** Wales
40D2 **Knin** Croatia, Yugos
76A4 **Knob,C** Aust
36B1 **Knokke-Heist** Belg
10M5 **Knox,C** Can
79G9 **Knox Coast** Ant
11D3 **Knoxville** Iowa, USA
9E3 **Knoxville** Tennessee, USA
7Q3 **Knud Ramussens Land** *Region* Greenland
74C3 **Knysna** S Africa
56C3 **Koba** Indon
7O3 **Kobberminebugt** *B* Greenland
53D5 **Kobe** Japan
42C1 **København** Den
37E1 **Kobiard** Slovenia
42B2 **Koblenz** Germany
53C1 **Koboldo** Russian Fed
44C5 **Kobrin** Russian Fed
51G7 **Kobroör** *I* Indon
10G2 **Kobuk** *R* USA
41E2 **Kočani** Macedonia
54A3 **Kochang** S Korea
54A3 **Kŏch'ang** S Korea
55C3 **Ko Chang** *I* Thai
61C2 **Koch Bihār** India
37D1 **Kochel** Germany
36E2 **Kocher** *R* Germany
7L3 **Koch I** Can
Kochi = Cochin
53C5 **Kōchi** Japan
10H4 **Kodiak** USA
10H4 **Kodiak I** USA
62B2 **Kodiyakkari** India
72D3 **Kodok** Sudan
54D2 **Kodomari-misaki** *C* Japan
43F3 **Kodyma** Ukraine
20D3 **Koehn L** USA
74B2 **Koes** Namibia
74D2 **Koffiefontein** S Africa
71F4 **Koforidua** Ghana
53D4 **Kōfu** Japan
54C3 **Koga** Japan
5J2 **Kogaluk** *R* Can
32G7 **Køge** Den
71H4 **Kogi** *State* Nig
60C2 **Kohat** Pak
60B2 **Koh-i-Baba** *Mts* Afghan
60B1 **Koh-i-Hisar** *Mts* Afghan
60B2 **Koh-i-Khurd** *Mt* Afghan
61D2 **Kohīma** India
60B1 **Koh-i-Mazar** *Mt* Afghan
63E2 **Koh-i-Qaisar** *Mt* Afghan
60B3 **Kohlu** Pak
44D4 **Kohtla Järve** Estonia
54A4 **Kohung** S Korea
54A4 **Kohyon** S Korea
54C3 **Koide** Japan
10K3 **Koidern** Can
55A4 **Koihoa** *Is* Nicobar Is
54A2 **Koin** N Korea
53B5 **Kōje-do** *I* S Korea
54C2 **Ko-jima** *I* Japan
48H4 **Kokchetav** Kazakhstan
32J6 **Kokemaki** *L* Fin
32J6 **Kokkola** Fin
71G3 **Koko** Nig
76D1 **Kokoda** PNG
12B2 **Kokomo** USA
51G7 **Kokonau** Indon
50B2 **Kokpekty** Kazakhstan
54A3 **Koksan** N Korea
7M4 **Koksoak** *R* Can
54A3 **Koksŏng** S Korea
74D3 **Kokstad** S Africa
55C3 **Ko Kut** *I* Thai
44E2 **Kola** Russian Fed
57B3 **Kolaka** Indon
55B4 **Ko Lanta** *I* Thai
62B2 **Kolār** India
62B2 **Kolār Gold Fields** India
70A3 **Kolda** Sen
32F7 **Kolding** Den
53E1 **Kolendo** Russian Fed
44H2 **Kolguyev, Ostrov** *I* Russian Fed
62A1 **Kolhāpur** India
10G4 **Koliganek** USA
42D2 **Kolín** Czech Republic
Kollam = Quilon
42B2 **Köln** Germany
43D2 **Kolo** Pol
20E5 **Koloa** Hawaiian Is
42D2 **Kolobrzeg** Pol
70B3 **Kolokani** Mali
44F4 **Kolomna** Russian Fed
45D6 **Kolomyya** Ukraine
57B3 **Kolono** Indon
57B3 **Kolonodale** Indon
49R4 **Kolpakovskiy** Russian Fed
48K4 **Kolpashevo** Russian Fed
41F3 **Kólpos Merabéllou** *B* Greece
41E2 **Kólpos Singitikós** *G* Greece
41E2 **Kólpos Strimonikós** *G* Greece
41E2 **Kólpos Toronaíos** *G* Greece
44F2 **Kol'skiy Poluostrov** *Pen* Russian Fed
44K2 **Kolva** *R* Russian Fed
32G6 **Kolvereid** Nor
73C5 **Kolwezi** Zaïre
49R3 **Kolyma** *R* Russian Fed
49R3 **Kolymskaya Nizmennost** *Lowland* Russian Fed
49S3 **Kolymskoye Nagor'ye** *Mts* Russian Fed
10D2 **Kolyuchinskaya Guba** *B* Russian Fed
41E2 **Kom** *Mt* Bulg/Serbia
72D3 **Koma** Eth
54D3 **Koma** Japan
71J3 **Komaduga Gana** *R* Nig
71J3 **Komadugu Yobé** *R* Nig
54D2 **Komaga take** *Mt* Japan
49S4 **Komandorskiye Ostrova** *I* Russian Fed
43D3 **Komárno** Slovakia
74E2 **Komati,R** S Africa
74E2 **Komati Poort** S Africa
53D4 **Komatsu** Japan
54B4 **Komatsushima** Japan
71F3 **Kombissiri** Burkina
44J3 **Komi** Respublika, Russian Fed
50B1 **Kommunar** Russian Fed
57A4 **Komodo** *I* Indon
71F4 **Komoé** *R* Côte d'Ivoire
51G7 **Komoran** *I* Indon
54C3 **Komoro** Japan
41F2 **Komotiní** Greece
74C3 **Kompasberg** *Mt* S Africa
55D3 **Kompong Cham** Camb
55C3 **Kompong Chhnang** *Mts* Camb
Kompong Som = Sihanoukville
55D3 **Kompong Thom** Camb
55D3 **Kompong Trabek** Camb
43F3 **Komrat** Moldova
74C3 **Komsberg** *Mts* S Africa
49Li **Komsomolets, Ostrov** *I* Russian Fed

Komsomol'skiy Kzyl Orda

44L2 Komsomol'skiy Russian Fed
49P4 Komsomol'sk na Amure Russian Fed
48H4 Konda *R* Russian Fed
61B4 Kondagaon India
72D4 Kondoa Tanz
53D1 Kondon Russian Fed
44E3 Kondopoga Russian Fed
62B1 Kondukūr India
10C2 Konergino Russian Fed
44F3 Konevo Russian Fed
7P3 Kong Christian IX Land *Region* Greenland
7O3 Kong Frederik VI Kyst *Region* Greenland
54A3 Kongju S Korea
48D2 Kong Karls Land *Is* Barents S
56E2 Kongkemul *Mt* Indon
72C4 Kongolo Zaïre
71F3 Kongoussi Burkina
32F7 Kongsberg Den
32G6 Kongsvinger Nor
Königsberg = Kaliningrad
37E1 Königsee, L Germany
43D2 Konin Pol
41D2 Konjic Bosnia-Herzegovina
71F4 Konongo Ghana
44G3 Konosha Russian Fed
54C3 Konosu Japan
45E5 Konotop Ukraine
43E2 Końskie Pol
36E3 Konstanz Germany
71H3 Kontagora Nig
55D3 Kontum Viet
10B2 Konus *Mt* Russian Fed
45E8 Konya Turk
18C1 Kootenay *L* Can
3E4 Kootenay *R* Can
60C5 Kopargaon India
7R3 Kópasker Iceland
32A2 Kópavogur Iceland
40C1 Koper Slovenia
58D2 Kopet Dag *Mts* Iran/Turkmenistan
44L4 Kopeysk Russian Fed
55C4 Ko Phangan *I* Thai
55B4 Ko Phuket *I* Thai
32H7 Köping Sweden
54A3 Kopo-ri S Korea
62B1 Koppal India
40D1 Koprivnica Croatia
60B4 Korangi Pak
62C1 Koraput India
61B3 Korba India
42B2 Korbach Germany
41E2 Korçë Alb
40D2 Korčula *I* Croatia
52E2 Korea B China/Korea
53B5 Korea Str S Korea/Japan
43F2 Korec Ukraine
49S3 Korf Russian Fed
64B1 Körğlu Tepesi *Mt* Turk
70B4 Korhogo Côte d'Ivoire
60B4 Kori Creek India
41E3 Korinthiakós Kólpos *G* Greece
41E3 Kórinthos Greece
53E4 Kōriyama Japan
44L5 Korkino Russian Fed
49R3 Korkodon Russian Fed
49R3 Korkodon *R* Russian Fed
64B2 Korkuteli Turk
59G1 Korla China
65B1 Kormakiti,C Cyprus
40D2 Kornat *I* Croatia
45E7 Köroğlu Tepesi *Mt* Turk
72D4 Korogwe Tanz
75B3 Koroit Aust
51G6 Koror Palau Is, Pacific O
43E3 Körös *R* Hung
45D5 Korosten Ukraine
43F2 Korostyshev Ukraine
72B2 Koro Toro Chad
10F4 Korovin *I* USA
53E2 Korsakov Russian Fed
32G7 Korsør Den
66B3 Korti Sudan
44J3 Kortkeroz Russian Fed
42A2 Kortrijk Belg
49S3 Koryakskoye Nagor'ye *Mts* Russian Fed
54A3 Koryong S Korea
41F3 Kós *I* Greece
10D2 Kosa Belyaka *B* Russian Fed
55C4 Ko Samui *I* Thai
54A3 Kosan N Korea
43D2 Koscierzyna Pol
15B2 Kosciusko USA
76D4 Kosciusko *Mt* Aust
10M4 Kosciusko I USA
53B5 Koshikijima-retto *I* Japan
43E3 Košiče Slovakia
44J2 Kosma *R* Russian Fed
53B4 Kosong N Korea
41E2 Kosovo *Aut Republic* Serbia, Yugos
70B4 Kossou *L* Côte d'Ivoire
74D2 Koster S Africa
72D2 Kosti Sudan
43F2 Kostopol' Ukraine
44G4 Kostroma Russian Fed
42C2 Kostrzyn Pol
44K2 Kos'yu *R* Russian Fed
32H8 Koszalin Pol
60D3 Kota India
56B4 Kotaagung Indon
56D3 Kotabaharu Indon
56E3 Kotabaru Indon
55C4 Kota Bharu Malay
56C3 Kotabum Indon
60C2 Kot Addu Pak
56E1 Kota Kinabulu Malay
57B2 Kotamobagu Indon
62C1 Kotapad India
56F7 Kotapinang *I* Indon
56G8 Kota Tinggi Malay
44H4 Kotel'nich Russian Fed
45G6 Kotel'nikovo Russian Fed
49P2 Kotel'nyy, Ostrov *I* Russian Fed
32K6 Kotka Fin
44H3 Kotlas Russian Fed
10F3 Kotlik USA
71H4 Koton Karifi Nig
41D2 Kotor Montenegro, Yugos
45D6 Kotovsk Ukraine
60B3 Kotri Pak
37E1 Kötschach Austria
62C1 Kottagūdem India
62B3 Kottayam India
72C3 Kotto *R* CAR
62B2 Kottūru India
49L3 Kotuy *R* Russian Fed
10F2 Kotzebue USA
6B3 Kotzebue Sd USA
71G3 Kouande Benin
72C3 Kouango CAR
71F3 Koudougou Burkina
74C3 Kougaberge *Mts* S Africa
72B4 Koulamoutou Gabon
70B3 Koulikoro Mali
71F3 Koupéla Burkina
71F3 Kouri Mali
27H2 Kourou French Guiana
70B3 Kouroussa Guinea
72B2 Kousséri Cam
32K6 Kouvola Fin
32L5 Kovdor Russian Fed
32L5 Kovdozero, Ozero *L* Russian Fed
43E2 Kovel' Ukraine
Kovno = Kaunas
44G4 Kovrov Russian Fed
44G5 Kovylkino Russian Fed
44F3 Kovzha *R* Russian Fed
55C4 Ko Way *I* Thai
52C5 Kowloon Hong Kong
54A3 Kowŏn N Korea
60B2 Kowt-e-Ashrow Afghan
64A2 Köyceğiz Turk
44G2 Koyda Russian Fed
62A1 Koyna Res India
44H3 Koynas Russian Fed
57C2 Koyoa *I* Indon
10F3 Koyuk USA
10F2 Koyuk *R* USA
10G3 Koyukuk USA
10G2 Koyukuk *R* USA
64C2 Kozan Turk
41E2 Kozańi Greece
Kozhikode = Calicut
44K2 Kozhim Russian Fed
44H4 Koz'modemyansk Russian Fed
54C4 Kōzu-shima *I* Japan
71G4 Kpandu Ghana
74D3 Kraai *R* S Africa
32F7 Kragerø Nor
41E2 Kragujevac Serbia, Yugos
55B3 Kra,Isthmus of Myanmar/Malay
Krakatau = Rakata
65D1 Krak des Chevaliers *Hist Site* Syria
43D2 Kraków = Cracow Pol
41E2 Kraljevo Serbia, Yugos
45F6 Kramatorsk Ukraine
32H6 Kramfors Sweden
40C1 Kranj Slovenia, Yugos
44H3 Krasavino Russian Fed
44J1 Krasino Russian Fed
43E2 Kraśnik Pol
45H5 Krasnoarmeysk Russian Fed
45F6 Krasnodar Russian Fed
53E2 Krasnogorsk Russian Fed
44K4 Krasnokamsk Russian Fed
44L4 Krasnotur'insk Russian Fed
44K4 Krasnoufimsk Russian Fed
44K5 Krasnousol'-skiy Russian Fed
44K3 Krasnovishersk Russian Fed
45J7 Krasnovodsk Turkmenistan
49L4 Krasnoyarsk Russian Fed
43E2 Krasnystaw Pol
45H5 Krasnyy Kut Russian Fed
45F6 Krasnyy Luch Ukraine
45H6 Krasnyy Yar Russian Fed
55D3 Kratie Camb
7N2 Kraulshavn Greenland
42B2 Krefeld Germany
45E6 Kremenchug Ukraine
45E6 Kremenchugskoye Vodokhranilische *Res* Ukraine
43F2 Kremenets Ukraine
16A1 Kremming USA
10E5 Krenitzin Is USA
72A3 Kribi Cam
44E5 Krichev Belarus
37E1 Krimml Austria
32J6 Krinstinestad Fin
62B1 Krishna *R* India
62B2 Krishnagiri India
61C3 Krishnangar India
32F7 Kristiansand Nor
32G7 Kristianstad Sweden
48B3 Kristiansund Nor
32G7 Kristineham Sweden
Kríti = Crete
45E6 Krivoy Rog Ukraine
40C1 Krk *I* Croatia
74D1 Krokodil *R* S Africa
49S4 Kronotskaya Sopka *Mt* Russian Fed
7P3 Kronpris Frederik Bjerge *Mts* Greenland
32K7 Kronshtadt Russian Fed
74D2 Kroonstad S Africa
45G6 Kropotkin Russian Fed
74E1 Kruger Nat Pk S Africa
74D2 Krugersdorp S Africa
56B4 Krui Indon
41D2 Kruje Alb
43F2 Krupki Belarus
10F2 Krusenstern,C USA
41E2 Kruševac Serbia
32K7 Krustpils Latvia
10L4 Kruzof I USA
45E6 Krym *Pen* Ukraine
45F7 Krymsk Russian Fed
42D2 Krzyz Pol
71C1 Ksar El Boukhari Alg
71A2 Ksar el Kebir Mor
56A2 Kuala Indon
55C5 Kuala Dungun Malay
56F6 Kuala Kangsar Malay
56G7 Kuala Kelawang Malay
55C4 Kuala Kerai Malay
55C5 Kuala Kubu Baharu Malay
55C5 Kuala Lipis Malay
55C5 Kuala Lumpur Malay
56G7 Kuala Pilah Malay
56F7 Kuala Selangor Malay
56A2 Kualasimpang Indon
55C4 Kuala Trengganu Malay
56E1 Kuamut Malay
53A3 Kuandian China
55C5 Kuantan Malay
45H7 Kuba Azerbaijan
51H7 Kubar PNG
56D2 Kuching Malay
56E1 Kudat Malay
56D4 Kudus Indon
44J4 Kudymkar Russian Fed
42C3 Kufstein Austria
10M2 Kugaluk *R* Can
10M2 Kugmallit B Can
63E3 Kuhak Iran
63D2 Kuh Duren *Upland* Iran
63D3 Kūh e Bazmān *Mt* Iran
63C2 Kūh-e Dinar *Mt* Iran
63D1 Kūh-e-Hazār Masjed *Mts* Iran
63D3 Kūh-e Jebāl Barez *Mts* Iran
63C2 Kūh-e Karkas *Mts* Iran
63D3 Kūh-e Laleh Zar *Mt* Iran
63B1 Kūh-e Sahand *Mt* Iran
63E3 Kuh e Taftān *Mt* Iran
45H9 Kūhhaye Alvand *Mts* Iran
45H8 Kūhhaye Sabalan *Mts* Iran
63B2 Kūhhā-ye Zāgros *Mts* Iran
32K6 Kuhmo Fin
63C2 Kūhpāyeh Iran
63D2 Kūhpāyeh *Mt* Iran
63D3 Kūh ye Bashākerd *Mts* Iran
63B1 Kūh ye Sabalan *Mt* Iran
74B2 Kuibis Namibia
74B1 Kuiseb *R* Namibia
73B5 Kuito Angola
10M4 Kuiu I USA
54A3 Kujang N Korea
53E3 Kuji Japan
54B4 Kuju-san *Mt* Japan
10G4 Kukaklek L USA
41E2 Kukës Alb
10F2 Kukpowruk *R* USA
55C5 Kukup Malay
63D3 Kūl *R* Iran
41F3 Kula Turk
56G8 Kulai Malay
45K6 Kulakshi Kazakhstan
72D3 Kulal,Mt Kenya
41E2 Kulata Bulg
44C4 Kuldīga Latvia
56F6 Kulim Malay
44G2 Kulov *R* Russian Fed
71F3 Kulpawn *R* Ghana
45J6 Kul'sary Kazakhstan
60D2 Kulu India
64B2 Kulu Turk
66D4 Kululli Eth
48J4 Kulunda Russian Fed
75B2 Kulwin Aust
45H7 Kuma *R* Russian Fed
54C3 Kumagaya Japan
56D3 Kumai Indon
45L5 Kumak Russian Fed
53C5 Kumamoto Japan
54C4 Kumano Japan
41E2 Kumanovo Macedonia
53B1 Kumara China
71F4 Kumasi Ghana
45G7 Kumayri Armenia
72A3 Kumba Cam
62B2 Kumbakonam India
71J4 Kumbo Cam
54A3 Kŭmch'ŏn N Korea
67E2 Kumdah S Arabia
44K5 Kumertau Russian Fed
54A3 Kumgang N Korea
53B4 Kŭmhwa S Korea
32H7 Kumla Sweden
54A4 Kŭmnyŏng S Korea
54A4 Kŭmo-do *I* S Korea
61E2 Kumon Range *Mts* Myanmar
62A2 Kumta India
59G1 Kümüx China
60C2 Kunar *R* Afghan
53F3 Kunashir, Ostrov *I* Russian Fed
32K7 Kunda Estonia
62A2 Kundāpura India
60C4 Kundla India
60B1 Kunduz Afghan
68F9 Kunene *R* Angola
10M5 Kunghit *I* Can
32G7 Kungsbacka Sweden
44K4 Kungur Russian Fed
55B1 Kunhing Myanmar
59G2 Kunlun Shan *Mts* China
52A4 Kunming China
44M3 Kunovat *R* Russian Fed
53B4 Kunsan S Korea
32K6 Kuopio Fin
40D1 Kupa *R* Croatia/Bosnia-Herzegovina
76B2 Kupang Indon
76D2 Kupiano PNG
10M4 Kupreanof I USA
10G4 Kupreanof Pt USA
45F6 Kupyansk Ukraine
59G1 Kuqa China
53C2 Kur *R* Russian Fed
45H8 Kura *R* Azerbaijan
54C3 Kurabe Japan
53C5 Kurashiki Japan
54B3 Kurayoshi Japan
63B1 Kurdistan Region, Iran
41F2 Kürdzhali Bulg
53C5 Kure Japan
49L3 Kureyka *R* Russian Fed
48H4 Kurgan Russian Fed
Kuria Muria Is = Khūryan Mūryān
32J6 Kurikka Fin
Kuril Is = Kuril'skiye Ostrova
53F2 Kuril'sk Russian Fed
49Q5 Kuril'skiye Ostrova *Is* Russian Fed
xxviiiJ2 Kuril Trench Pacific O
45H8 Kurinskaya Kosa *Sand Spit* Azerbaijan
62B1 Kurnool India
54D2 Kuroishi Japan
54D3 Kuroiso Japan
78B2 Kurow NZ
75D2 Kurri Kurri Aust
45F5 Kursk Russian Fed
50B2 Kuruktag *R* China
74C2 Kuruman S Africa
74C2 Kuruman *R* S Africa
53C5 Kurume Japan
62C3 Kurunegala Sri Lanka
48K5 Kurunktag *R* China
44K3 Kur'ya Russian Fed
44K4 Kusa Russian Fed
41F3 Kuşadasi Körfezi *B* Turk
41F2 Kus Golü *L* Turk
53D5 Kushimoto Japan
53E3 Kushiro Japan
63E1 Kushka Afghan
61C3 Kushtia Bang
45J5 Kushum *R* Kazakhstan
44K4 Kushva Russian Fed
10F3 Kuskokwim *R* USA
10F4 Kuskokwim B USA
10G3 Kuskokwim Mts USA
61B2 Kusma Nepal
53E3 Kussharo-ko *L* Japan
48H4 Kustanay Kazakhstan
45D8 Kütahya Turk
56E3 Kutai *R* Indon
45G7 Kutaisi Georgia
54D2 Kutchan Japan
42D3 Kutná Hora Czech Republic
43D2 Kutno Pol
72B4 Kutu Zaïre
61D3 Kutubdia I Bang
72C2 Kutum Sudan
7M4 Kuujjuaq Can
7L4 Kuujjuarapik Can
32K5 Kuusamo Fin
45K5 Kuvandyk Russian Fed
64E4 Kuwait Kuwait
58C3 Kuwait Sheikdom, S W Asia
54C3 Kuwana Japan
48J4 Kuybyshev Russian Fed
44H5 Kuybyshevskoye Vodokhranilishche *Res* Russian Fed
44E2 Kuyto, Ozero *L* Russian Fed
49M4 Kuytun Russian Fed
45F7 Kuzey Anadolu Daglari *Mts* Turk
44H5 Kuznetsk Russian Fed
44F2 Kuzomen Russian Fed
44C2 Kvaenangen *Sd* Nor
10G4 Kvichak USA
10G4 Kvichak *R* USA
10G4 Kvichak B USA
32G5 Kvigtind *Mt* Nor
44B2 Kvikkjokk Sweden
72D4 Kwale Kenya
71H4 Kwale Nig
53B4 Kwangju S Korea
72B4 Kwango *R* Zaïre
54A3 Kwangyang S Korea
54A2 Kwanmo-bong *Mt* N Korea
71H4 Kwara State, Nig
74E2 KwaZulu Natal Province, S Africa
73C5 Kwekwe Zim
10F3 Kwethluk USA
10F3 Kwethluk *R* USA
43D2 Kwidzyn Pol
6B4 Kwigillingok USA
51G7 Kwoka *Mt* Indon
75C3 Kyabram Aust
55B2 Kyaikkami Myanmar
55B2 Kyaikto Myanmar
50D1 Kyakhta Russian Fed
75A2 Kyancutta Aust
55B1 Kyaukme Myanmar
55B1 Kyauk-padaung Myanmar
55A2 Kyaukpyu Myanmar
61E3 Kyaukse Myanmar
44G2 Kychema Russian Fed
3G3 Kyle Can
33B2 Kyle of Lochalsh Scot
36D1 Kyll *R* Germany
75B3 Kyneton Aust
72D3 Kyoga *L* Uganda
75D1 Kyogle Aust
53B4 Kyŏngju S Korea
54A3 Kyongsang Sanmaek *Mts* S Korea
54A2 Kyŏngsŏng N Korea
61E4 Kyonpyaw Myanmar
53D4 Kyoto Japan
65B1 Kyrenia Cyprus
48J5 Kyrgyzstan Republic, Asia
44K3 Kyrta Russian Fed
44L4 Kyshtym Russian Fed
65B1 Kythrea Cyprus
53C5 Kyūshū *I* Japan
xxviiiH4 Kyushu-Palau Ridge Pacific O
41E2 Kyustendil Bulg
49O2 Kyusyur Russian Fed
Kyyiv = Kiyev
50C1 Kyzyl Russian Fed
48H5 Kyzylkum *Desert* Uzbekistan
48H5 Kzyl Orda Kazakhstan

Laascaanood La Pesca

L

72E3 Laascaanood Somalia
22C1 La Ascension Mexico
69D3 Laas Dawaco Somalia
36E1 Laasphe Germany
69D3 Laasqoray Somalia
26F1 La Asunción Ven
70A2 Laâyoune Mor
28C1 La Banda Arg
22B1 La Barca Mexico
18D2 La Barge USA
77G2 Labasa Fiji
70A3 Labé Guinea
42D2 Labe R Czech Republic
13E1 Labelle Can
15E4 La Belle USA
10L3 Laberge,L Can
56D2 Labi Brunei
45G7 Labinsk Russian Fed
56G7 Labis Malay
65D1 Laboué Leb
28C2 Laboulaye Arg
7M4 Labrador Region Can
7M4 Labrador City Can
7N4 Labrador S Greenland/Can
26F5 Lábrea Brazil
56E1 Labuan I Malay
57C3 Labuha Indon
56C4 Labuhan Indon
57B4 Labuhanbajo Indon
56F7 Labuhanbatu Indon
56B2 Labuhanbilik Indon
55A2 Labutta Myanmar
44M2 Labytnangi Russian Fed
7L4 Lac à l'Eau Claire Can
4F2 Lac Anuc L Can
36B1 La Capelle France
28C2 La Carlota Arg
57F8 La Carlota Phil
4F4 Lac au Goéland L Can
5G2 Lac aux Feuilles L Can
5J2 Lac aux Goélands L Can
5G2 Lac Bacquerville L Can
5G2 Lac Bécard L Can
10N2 Lac Belot L Can
7L4 Lac Bienville L Can
3H2 Lac Brochet Can
5J3 Lac Brûlé R Can
4F4 Lac Bryson L Can
Laccadive Is = Lakshadweep
59F4 Laccadive Is India
5J2 Lac Champdoré L Can
5G2 Lac Châteauguay L Can
5F2 Lac Chavigny L Can
5H3 Lac Clairambault L Can
4F1 Lac Couture L Can
5G3 Lac Dalmas L Can
37B2 Lac d'Annecy L France
6G3 Lac de Gras L Can
37B1 Lac de Joux L Switz
5G3 Lac Delorme L Can
37B1 Lac de Neuchâtel L Switz
22B2 Lac de Patzcuaro L Mexico
22B2 Lac de Sayula L Mexico
6F3 Lac des Bois L Can
4C4 Lac des Mille Lacs L Can
4F4 Lac Doda L Can
11C1 Lac du Bonnet Can
37A2 Lac du Bourget L France
21D3 La Ceiba Honduras
75A3 Lacepede B Aust
5G2 Lac Faribault L Can
4F3 Lac Grasset L Can
5J2 Lac Gruéard L Can
4F2 Lac Guillaume-Delisle L Can
38C2 La Châtre France
36A3 La Châtre-sur-le-Loir France
37B1 La-Chaux-de-Fonds Switz
65C3 Lachish Hist Site Israel
76D4 Lachlan R Aust
5G3 Lac Holmer L Can
26C2 La Chorrera Panama
13E1 Lachute Can
37A3 La Ciotat France
22A1 La Ciudad Mexico
7M4 Lac Joseph L Can
13D2 Lackawanna USA
5G4 Lac Kempt L Can
4F4 Lac Kipawa L Can
5G1 Lac Klotz L Can
3F3 Lac la Biche Can
6F3 Lac la Martre L Can
5H3 Lac Lapointe L Can
5G2 Lac La Potherie L Can
6H4 Lac la Ronge L Can
40B1 Lac Léman L Switz/France
5F2 Lac Le Roy L Can
5G2 Lac Mannessier L Can
7L4 Lac Manouane Can
4F4 Lac Matagami L Can
10N2 Lac Maunoir L Can
7L4 Lac Mistassini L Can
4F4 Lac Muskoka L Can
5G3 Lac Naocoane L Can
5G3 Lac Néret L Can
5H3 Lac Nouveau L Can
28B1 La Cocha Arg
3F3 Lacombe Can
13E2 Laconia USA
5H3 Lac Opiscotéo L Can
39A1 La Coruña Spain
37A2 La Côte-St-André France
4F4 Lac Parent L Can
5F2 Lac Qilalugalik L Can
5H3 Lac Rambau L Can
5J2 Lac Ramusio L Can
9D2 La Crosse USA
28D1 La Cruz Arg
22A1 La Cruz Mexico
5G4 Lac Saint Jean L Can
4F3 Lac Sakami L Can
7J4 Lac Seul L Can
4F4 Lac Simard L Can
5G3 Lac Sureau L Can
5G3 Lac Taffanel L Can
5G2 Lac Tassialouc L Can
17D2 La Cygne USA
60D2 Ladākh Range India
63E3 Lādīz Iran
60C3 Lādnūn India
52B5 Ladong China
7K2 Lady Ann Str Can
75E3 Lady Barron Aust
74D2 Ladybrand S Africa
3D4 Ladysmith Can
74D2 Ladysmith S Africa
12A1 Ladysmith USA
76D1 Lae PNG
55C3 Laem Ngop Thai
42C1 Laesø I Den
16A2 Lafayette Colorado, USA
9E2 Lafayette Indiana, USA
9D3 Lafayette Louisiana, USA
36B2 La Fène France
36A2 La-Ferté-Barnard France
36B2 La Ferté-St-Aubin France
36B2 La-Ferté-sous-Jouarre France
71H4 Lafia Nig
71H4 Lafiagi Nig
38B2 La Flèche France
4E4 Laforest Can
71D1 La Galite I Tunisia
42C1 Lagan R Sweden
45H6 Lagan' Russian Fed
27L6 Lagarto Brazil
71C2 Laghouat Alg
29D3 Lagoa de Araruama Brazil
28E2 Lagoa de Castillos L Urug
28E2 Lagoa de Rocha Urug
25F4 Lagoa dos Patos Lg Brazil
29D3 Lagoa Feia Brazil
26C4 Lago Agrio Ecuador
29D2 Lagoa Juparanã L Brazil
29A2 Lagoa Mandiore L Brazil
28E2 Lagoa Mangueira L Brazil
25D4 Lagoa mar Chiquita L Arg
25F4 Lagoa Mirim L Urug/Brazil
28E2 Lagoa Negra L Urug
25B8 Lago Argentino L Arg
29A2 Lagoa Uberaba L Brazil
28E1 Lagoa Vermelha Brazil
25B7 Lago Buenos Aries L Arg
25B7 Lago Cochrane L Chile/Arg
25C7 Lago Colhué Huapi L Arg
21B2 Lago de Chapala L Mexico
26B2 Lago de Chiriqui L Panama
22B2 Lago de Cuitzeo L Mexico
25B5 Lago de la Laja L Chile
40B2 Lago del Coghinas L Sardegna
26D2 Lago de Maracaibo L Ven
26A1 Lago de Nicaragua L Nic
26B1 Lago de Perlas L Nic
22B1 Lago de Santiaguillo L Mexico
40C2 Lago di Bolsena L Italy
40C2 Lago di Bracciano L Italy
40B1 Lago di Como L Italy
37D2 Lago d'Idro L Italy
40C1 Lago di Garda L Italy
37C2 Lago di Lecco L Italy
37C2 Lago di Lugano L Italy
37D2 Lago d'Iseo L Italy
37C2 Lago d'Orta L Italy
25B7 Lago General Carrera L Chile
40B1 Lago Maggiore L Italy
25C7 Lago Musters L Arg
38B3 Lagon France
25B6 Lago Nahuel Haupi L Arg
25B7 Lago O'Higgins L Chile
40B2 Lago Omodeo L Sardegna
26E7 Lago Poopó L Bol
25B6 Lago Ranco L Chile
26E6 Lago Rogaguado L Bol
71G4 Lagos Nig
39A2 Lagos Port
71G4 Lagos State, Nig
25B7 Lago San Martin L Chile/Arg
21B2 Lagos de Moreno Mexico
26E7 Lago Titicaca Bol/Peru
37E3 Lago Trasimeno L Italy
71E1 La Goulette Tunisia
25B7 Lago Viedma L Arg
8B2 La Grande USA
4F3 La Grande Réservoir 2 Res Can
5G3 La Grande Réservoir 3 Res Can
5G3 La Grande Réservoir 4 Res Can
76B2 Lagrange Aust
9E3 La Grange Georgia, USA
12B3 La Grange Kentucky, USA
15D1 La Grange N Carolina, USA
17C4 La Grange Texas, USA
26F2 La Gran Sabana Mts Ven
37B2 La Grave France
38B3 Lagronño Spain
16A3 Laguna USA
22A1 Laguna Agua Brava Mexico
28A3 Laguna Aluminé L Arg
19C4 Laguna Beach USA
28C3 Laguna Colorada Grande L Arg
57F8 Laguna de Bay Lg Phil
21D3 Laguna de Caratasca Lg Honduras
21D4 Laguna de Chiriqui L Panama
16A3 Laguna de Guzmán L Mexico
28C4 Laguna del Abra L Arg
22A1 Laguna del Caimanero L Mexico
21D3 Laguna de Managua L Nicaragua
21D3 Laguna de Nicaragua L Nicaragua
23A4 Laguna de Perlas Lg Nic
22C1 Laguna de Pueblo Viejo L Mexico
16A3 Laguna de Santa Maria L Mexico
21C2 Laguna de Tamiahua Lg Mexico
21C3 Laguna de Términos Lg Mexico
22B1 Laguna de Yuriria L Mexico
28D1 Laguna Iberá Arg
28D1 Laguna Itati L Arg
22C1 Laguna le Altamira Mexico
21C2 Laguna Madre Lg Mexico
17F4 Laguna Madre Lg USA
28C2 Laguna Mar Chiquita L Arg
28A4 Laguna Nahuel Huapi L Arg
10C2 Laguna Nutauge Lg Russian Fed
28C2 Laguna Paiva Arg
28A3 Laguna Panguipulli L Chile
28A4 Laguna Puyehue L Chile
28A4 Laguna Ranco Chile
28A4 Laguna Repanco L Chile
19C4 Laguna Salada L Mexico
8C4 Laguna Seca Mexico
22C2 Laguna Superior L Mexico
10C2 Laguna Tenkergynpil'gyn Lg Russian Fed
22C1 Laguna Tortugas L Mexico
28A4 Laguna Traful L Arg
28D1 Laguna Trin L Arg
10C2 Laguna Vankarem Lg Russian Fed
37E2 Laguna Veneta Lg Italy
28A3 Laguna Villarrica L Chile
22B1 Lagund Seca Mexico
56E1 Lahad Datu Malay
56B3 Lahat Indon
56A2 Lahewa Indon
32J6 Lahia Fin
66D4 Lahij Yemen
63C1 Lāhījān Iran
36D1 Lahn R Germany
36D1 Lahnstein Germany
60C2 Lahore Pak
36D2 Lahr France
32K6 Lahti Fin
22B2 La Huerta Mexico
72B3 Lai Chad
52B5 Laibin China
55C1 Lai Chau Viet
36A2 L'Aigle France
74C3 Laingsburg S Africa
34C2 Lairg Scot
56B3 Lais Indon
57G9 Lais Phil
57C3 Laiwui Indon
52E2 Laiyang China
52D2 Laizhou Wan B China
28A3 Laja R Chile
28E1 Lajeado Brazil
25F3 Lajes Brazil
20D4 La Jolla USA
8C3 La Junta USA
11C3 Lake Andes USA
75C2 Lake Cargelligo Aust
9D3 Lake Charles USA
15C2 Lake City Florida, USA
11D3 Lake City Minnesota, USA
15D2 Lake City S Carolina, USA
35D4 Lake District Region Eng
20D4 Lake Elsinore USA
76C3 Lake Eyre Basin Aust
13D2 Lakefield Can
12B2 Lake Geneva USA
14D1 Lake George USA
7M3 Lake Harbour Can
19D4 Lake Havasu City USA
20C3 Lake Hughes USA
14C2 Lakehurst USA
20C3 Lake Isabella USA
17C4 Lake Jackson USA
3F3 Lake la Biche Can
44F3 Lake Onega Russian Fed
15C3 Lakeland USA
7J5 Lake of the Woods Can
44E3 Lake Ladoga Ukraine
18B1 Lake Oswego USA
5G5 Lake Placid USA
19B3 Lakeport USA
17D3 Lake Providence USA
78B2 Lake Pukaki NZ
4E3 Lake River Can
75C3 Lakes Entrance Aust
20C2 Lakeshore USA
75B1 Lake Stewart Aust
4E4 Lake Superior Prov Park Can
13D1 Lake Traverse Can
8A2 Lakeview USA
18B1 Lakeview Mt Can
17D3 Lake Village USA
15C3 Lake Wales USA
20C4 Lakewood California, USA
16A2 Lakewood Colorado, USA
14C2 Lakewood New Jersey, USA
12C2 Lakewood Ohio, USA
15E4 Lake Worth USA
61B2 Lakhīmpur India
60B4 Lakhpat India
16B2 Lakin USA
60C2 Lakki Pak
41E3 Lakonikós Kólpos G Greece
57C4 Lakor I Indon
70B4 Lakota Côte d'Ivoire
32K4 Laksefjord Inlet Nor
32K4 Lakselv Nor
62A2 Lakshadweep Is India
28C2 La Laguna Arg
66C4 Lalibela Eth
26B4 La Libertad Ecuador
28A2 La Ligua Chile
57B5 Lalindi Indon
57B3 Lalindu R Indon
39A2 La Linea Spain
60D4 Lalitpur India
57B3 Laloa Indon
6H4 La Loche Can
3G2 La Loche,L Can
36A2 La Loupe France
36C1 La Louvière Belg
23A4 La Luz Nic
28B1 La Madrid Arg
7L5 La Malbaie Can
22C2 La Malinche Mt Mexico
22B1 La Mancha Mexico
39B2 La Mancha Region, Spain
8C3 Lamar Colorado, USA
17D2 Lamar Missouri, USA
28B3 Lamarque Arg
17C4 La Marque USA
72B4 Lambaréné Gabon
26B5 Lambayeque Peru
79F10 Lambert Gl Ant
74B3 Lamberts Bay S Africa
14C2 Lambertville USA
37C2 Lambro R Italy
6F2 Lambton,C Can
55C2 Lam Chi R Thai
39A1 Lamego Port
37B2 La Meije Mt France
28B1 La Merced Arg
26C6 La Merced Peru
16B3 Lamesa USA
19C4 La Mesa USA
41E3 Lamía Greece
34D4 Lammermuir Hills Scot
32G7 Lammhult Sweden
57F8 Lamon B Phil
37D2 Lamone R Italy
17D1 Lamoni USA
20C3 Lamont California, USA
11A3 Lamont Wyoming, USA
51H6 Lamotrek I Pacific O
36B3 Lamotte Beuvron France
11C2 La Moure USA
16C3 Lampasas USA
35C5 Lampeter Wales
72E4 Lamu Kenya
37A2 La Mure France
37D1 Lana Italy
20E5 Lanai I Hawaiian Is
20E5 Lanai City Hawaiian Is
34D4 Lanark Scot
55B3 Lanbi I Myanmar
55C1 Lancang R China
35D5 Lancashire County, Eng
19C4 Lancaster California, USA
35D4 Lancaster Eng
17D1 Lancaster Mississippi, USA
13E2 Lancaster New Hampshire, USA
14A1 Lancaster New York, USA
12C3 Lancaster Ohio, USA
9F3 Lancaster Pennsylvania, USA
15C2 Lancaster S Carolina, USA
7K2 Lancaster Sd Can
56C3 Landak R Indon
36E2 Landan Germany
42C3 Landeck Austria
8C2 Lander USA
28C2 Landeta Arg
15C1 Landrum USA
42C3 Landsberg Germany
6F2 Lands End C Can
35C6 Land's End Pt Eng
42C3 Landshut Germany
32G7 Landskrona Sweden
15B2 Lanett USA
61B1 La'nga Co L China
11C2 Langdon USA
66C3 Langeb Watercourse Sudan
74C2 Langeberg Mt S Africa
3H3 Langenburg Can
42B2 Langenhagen Germany
37B1 Langenthal Switz
34D4 Langholm Scot
32A2 Langjökull Mts Iceland
55B4 Langkawi I Malay
4F4 Langlade Can
3D4 Langley Can
75C1 Langlo R Aust
37B1 Langnau Switz
38D2 Langres France
56A2 Langsa Indon
50D2 Lang Shan Mts China
55D1 Lang Son Viet
16B4 Langtry USA
38C3 Languedoc Region, France
3G3 Lanigan Can
25B5 Lanin Mt Arg
57F9 Lanoa,L Phil
14C2 Lansdale USA
4D3 Lansdowne House Can
7K4 Lansdowne House Can
5K3 L'Anse au Loup Can
14C2 Lansford USA
9E2 Lansing USA
37B2 Lanslebourg France
70A2 Lanzarote I Canary Is
52A2 Lanzhou China
37B2 Lanzo Torinese Italy
57F7 Laoag Phil
55C1 Lao Cai Viet
52D1 Laoha He R China
35B5 Laois County, Irish Rep
35B5 Laoise Port Irish Rep
54A2 Laoling China
36B2 Laon France
4D4 Laona USA
26C6 La Orova Peru
55C2 Laos Republic, S E Asia
29C4 Lapa Brazil
38C2 Lapalisse France
70A2 La Palma I Canary Is
26C2 La Palmas Panama
28E2 La Paloma Urug
28B3 La Pampa State, Arg
20B3 La Panza Range Mts USA
26F2 La Paragua Ven
25E4 La Paz Arg
28B2 La Paz Arg
26E7 La Paz Bol
21A2 La Paz Mexico
53E2 La Perouse Str Russian Fed/Japan
22C1 La Pesca Mexico

Linapacan Str **Lucena**

57E8 **Linapacan Str** Phil
25B5 **Linares** Chile
8D4 **Linares** Mexico
39B2 **Linares** Spain
50C4 **Lincang** China
25D4 **Lincoln** Arg
17C1 **Lincoln** California, USA
35E5 **Lincoln** County, Eng
35E5 **Lincoln** Eng
12B2 **Lincoln** Illinois, USA
13F1 **Lincoln** Maine, USA
8D2 **Lincoln** Nebraska, USA
13E2 **Lincoln** New Hampshire, USA
78B2 **Lincoln** NZ
79A **Lincoln** *S* Greenland
18B2 **Lincoln City** USA
12C2 **Lincoln Park** USA
40B2 **L'Incudine** *Mt* Corse, France
42B3 **Lindau** Germany
27G2 **Linden** Guyana
32F7 **Lindesnes** *C* Nor
73D4 **Lindi** Tanz
72C3 **Lindi** *R* Zaïre
74D2 **Lindley** S Africa
41F3 **Lindos** Greece
4F5 **Lindsay** Can
20C2 **Lindsay** California, USA
11A2 **Lindsay** Montana, USA
xxixM4 **Line Is** Pacific O
52C2 **Linfen** China
55D2 **Lingao** China
57F7 **Lingayen** Phil
42B2 **Lingen** Germany
11B3 **Lingle** USA
52C4 **Lingling** China
52B5 **Lingshan** China
52C2 **Lingshi** China
70A3 **Linguère** Sen
53A1 **Linhai** Heilongjiang, China
52E4 **Linhai** Rhejiang, China
27L7 **Linhares** Brazil
52B1 **Linhe** China
53B3 **Linjiang** China
32H7 **Linköping** Sweden
53C2 **Linkou** China
52D2 **Linqing** China
29C3 **Lins** Brazil
52A2 **Lintao** China
37C1 **Linthal** Switz
11B2 **Linton** USA
50E2 **Linxi** China
52A2 **Linxia** China
42C3 **Linz** Austria
57F8 **Lipa** Phil
40C3 **Lipari** *I* Italy
45F5 **Lipetsk** Russian Fed
41E1 **Lipova** Rom
42B2 **Lippe** *R* Germany
36E1 **Lippstadt** Germany
72D3 **Lira** Uganda
72B4 **Liranga** Congo
72C3 **Lisala** Zaïre
39A2 **Lisboa** Port
Lisbon = Lisboa
11C2 **Lisbon** USA
35B4 **Lisburn** N Ire
10E2 **Lisburne,C** USA
52D4 **Lishui** China
52C4 **Li Shui** *R* China
45F6 **Lisichansk** Ukraine
38C2 **Lisieux** France
45F5 **Liski** Russian Fed
36B2 **L'Isle-Adam** France
37B1 **L'Isle-sur-le-Doubs** France
77E3 **Lismore** Aust
52B5 **Litang** China
65C2 **Lītanī** *R* Leb
27H3 **Litani** *R* Suriname
12B3 **Litchfield** Illinois, USA
11D2 **Litchfield** Minnesota, USA
76E4 **Lithgow** Aust
44C4 **Lithuania** Republic, Europe
14B2 **Lititz** USA
53E1 **Litke** Russian Fed
53D2 **Litovko** Russian Fed
17C3 **Little** *R* USA
9F4 **Little Abaco** *I* Bahamas
66D4 **Little Aden** Yemen
62E2 **Little Andaman** *I* Andaman Is
78C1 **Little Barrier I** NZ
18D1 **Little Belt Mts** USA
65B3 **Little Bitter L** Egypt
3F3 **Little Bow** *R* Can
21D3 **Little Cayman** *I* Caribbean
4D3 **Little Current** Can
4E4 **Little Current** Can
14C3 **Little Egg Harbor** *B* USA
11D2 **Little Falls** Minnesota, USA
14C1 **Little Falls** New York, USA
16B3 **Littlefield** USA
11D2 **Littlefork** USA
11D2 **Little Fork** *R* USA
4B3 **Little Grand Rapids** Can
34E2 **Little Halibut Bank** *Sandbank* Scot
23C2 **Little Inagua** *I* Caribbean
74C3 **Little Karroo** *R* S Africa
10G4 **Little Koniuji** *I* USA
20D3 **Little Lake** USA
11B2 **Little Missouri** *R* USA
55A4 **Little Nicobar** *I* Nicobar Is
9D3 **Little Rock** USA
20D3 **Littlerock** USA
10B6 **Little Sitkin** *I* USA
3E3 **Little Smoky** Can
3E3 **Little Smoky** *R* Can
14B3 **Littlestown** USA
10C6 **Little Tanaga** *I* USA
16A2 **Littleton** Colorado, USA
13E2 **Littleton** New Hampshire, USA
53B3 **Liuhe** China
52B5 **Liuzhou** China
41E3 **Livanátais** Greece
43F1 **Līvāni** Latvia
36A2 **Livarot** France
10J2 **Livengood** USA
37E2 **Livenza** *R* Italy
15C2 **Live Oak** USA
19B3 **Livermore** USA
16B3 **Livermore,Mt** USA
7M5 **Liverpool** Can
35D5 **Liverpool** Eng
6E2 **Liverpool B** Can
35D5 **Liverpool B** Eng
7L2 **Liverpool,C** Can
75D2 **Liverpool Range** *Mts* Aust
8B2 **Livingston** Montana, USA
15B1 **Livingston** Tennessee, USA
17D3 **Livingston** Texas, USA
73C5 **Livingstone** Zambia
17C3 **Livingston,L** USA
40D2 **Livno** Bosnia-Herzegovina
45F5 **Livny** Russian Fed
12C2 **Livonia** USA
40C2 **Livorno** Italy
29D1 **Livramento do Brumado** Brazil
73D4 **Liwale** Tanz
35C7 **Lizard Pt** Eng
40C1 **Ljubljana** Slovenia
32G6 **Ljungan** *R* Sweden
32G7 **Ljungby** Sweden
32H6 **Ljusdal** Sweden
44B3 **Ljusnan** *R* Sweden
35D6 **Llandeilo** Wales
35D6 **Llandovery** Wales
35D5 **Llandrindod Wells** Wales
35D5 **Llandudno** Wales
35C6 **Llanelli** Wales
35D5 **Llangollen** Wales
16C3 **Llano** USA
16C3 **Llano** *R* USA
8C3 **Llano Estacado** *Plat* USA
Z4D2 **Llanos** Region, Colombia/ Ven
26F7 **Llanos de Chiquitos** Region, Bol
Lleida = Láerida
22C1 **Llera** Mexico
39A2 **Llerena** Spain
35C5 **Lleyn** *Pen* Wales
68E7 **Llorin** Nigeria
3C2 **Lloyd George,Mt** Can
3G2 **Lloyd L** Can
6H4 **Lloydminster** Can
25C2 **Llullaillaco** *Mt* Chile/Arg
25C2 **Loa** *R* Chile
38C2 **Loan** France
72B4 **Loange** *R* Zaïre
74D2 **Lobatse** Botswana
72B3 **Lobaye** *R* CAR
28D3 **Loberia** Arg
73B5 **Lobito** Angola
28D3 **Lobos** Arg
37B2 **Locano** Italy
37C1 **Locarno** Switz
34C3 **Loch Awe** *L* Scot
34B3 **Lochboisdale** Scot
34B3 **Loch Bracadale** *Inlet* Scot
34C3 **Loch Broom** *Estuary* Scot
34C4 **Loch Doon** *L* Scot
34C3 **Loch Earn** *L* Scot
34C2 **Loch Eriboll** *Inlet* Scot
34C3 **Loch Ericht** *L* Scot
38C2 **Loches** France
34C3 **Loch Etive** *Inlet* Scot
34C3 **Loch Ewe** *Inlet* Scot
34C3 **Loch Fyne** *Inlet* Scot
34C3 **Loch Hourn** *Inlet* Scot
34B4 **Loch Indaal** *Inlet* Scot
34C2 **Lochinver** Scot
34C3 **Loch Katrine** *L* Scot
34D3 **Loch Leven** *L* Scot
34C3 **Loch Linnhe** *Inlet* Scot
34C3 **Loch Lochy** *L* Scot
34C3 **Loch Lomond** *L* Scot
34C3 **Loch Long** *Inlet* Scot
34B3 **Lochmaddy** Scot
34C3 **Loch Maree** *L* Scot
34C3 **Loch Morar** *L* Scot
34D3 **Lochnagar** *Mt* Scot
34C3 **Loch Ness** *L* Scot
34C3 **Loch Rannoch** *L* Scot
34B2 **Loch Roag** *Inlet* Scot
18C1 **Lochsa** *R* USA
34C3 **Loch Sheil** *L* Scot
34C2 **Loch Shin** *L* Scot
34B3 **Loch Snizort** *Inlet* Scot
34C3 **Loch Sunart** *Inlet* Scot
34C3 **Loch Tay** *L* Scot
34C3 **Loch Torridon** *Inlet* Scot
75A2 **Lock** Aust
5H5 **Lockeport** Can
34D4 **Lockerbie** Scot
13D2 **Lock Haven** USA
13D2 **Lockport** USA
55D3 **Loc Ninh** Viet
40D3 **Locri** Italy
65C3 **Lod** Israel
75B3 **Loddon** *R* Aust
44E3 **Lodeynoye Pole** Russian Fed
18E1 **Lodge Grass** USA
60C3 **Lodhran** Pak
40B1 **Lodi** Italy
19B3 **Lodi** USA
72C4 **Lodja** Zaïre
37B1 **Lods** France
72D3 **Lodwar** Kenya
43D2 **Łódź** Pol
74B3 **Loeriesfontein** S Africa
37E1 **Lofer** Austria
32G5 **Lofoten** *Is* Nor
16B2 **Logan** New Mexico, USA
8B2 **Logan** Utah, USA
6D3 **Logan,Mt** Can
10N3 **Logan Mts** Can
12B2 **Logansport** Indiana, USA
17D3 **Logansport** Louisiana, USA
14B2 **Loganton** USA
39B1 **Logroño** Spain
61B3 **Lohārdaga** India
32J6 **Lohja** Fin
36E2 **Lohr** Germany
55B2 **Loikaw** Myanmar
32J6 **Loimaa** Fin
36B2 **Loing** *R* France
38C2 **Loir** *R* France
36A3 **Loir et Cher** Department, France
38C2 **Loire** *R* France
36B3 **Loiret** Department, France
26C4 **Loja** Ecuador
39B2 **Loja** Spain
57C3 **Loji** Indon
32K5 **Lokan Tekojärvi** *Res* Fin
36B1 **Lokeren** Belg
72D3 **Lokitaung** Kenya
43F1 **Loknya** Russian Fed
71H4 **Lokoja** Nig
72C4 **Lokolo** *R* Zaïre
72C4 **Lokoro** *R* Zaïre
7M3 **Loks Land** *I* Can
42C2 **Lolland** *I* Den
57C2 **Loloda** Indon
18D1 **Lolo P** USA
41E2 **Lom** Bulg
71J4 **Lom** *R* Cam
73C4 **Lomami** *R* Zaïre
70A4 **Loma Mts** Sierra Leone/ Guinea
57B2 **Lombagin** Indon
37C2 **Lombardia** Region, Italy
57B4 **Lomblen** *I* Indon
56E4 **Lombok** *I* Indon
71G4 **Lomé** Togo
72C4 **Lomela** Zaïre
72C4 **Lomela** *R* Zaïre
34G3 **Lomond** *Oilfield* N Sea
44D4 **Lomonosov** Russian Fed
37B1 **Lomont** Region, France
19B4 **Lompoc** USA
43E2 **Łomza** Pol
62A1 **Lonāvale** India
25B5 **Loncoche** Chile
7K5 **London** Can
35E6 **London** Eng
12C3 **London** USA
34B4 **Londonderry** County, N Ire
34B4 **Londonderry** N Ire
25B9 **Londonderry** *I* Chile
76B2 **Londonderry,C** Aust
25C3 **Londres** Arg
25F2 **Londrina** Brazil
20D1 **Lone Mt** USA
20C2 **Lone Pine** USA
9F4 **Long** *I* Bahamas
51H7 **Long** *I* PNG
56D2 **Long Akah** Malay
37E1 **Longarone** Italy
28A3 **Longavi** *Mt* Chile
23H2 **Long B** Jamaica
15D2 **Long B** USA
8B3 **Long Beach** California, USA
13E2 **Long Beach** New York, USA
13E2 **Long Branch** USA
52D5 **Longchuan** China
18C2 **Long Creek** USA
75E3 **Longford** Aust
35B5 **Longford** County, Irish Rep
35B5 **Longford** Irish Rep
34E3 **Long Forties** *Region* N Sea
52D1 **Longhua** China
7L4 **Long I** Can
76D1 **Long I** PNG
9F2 **Long I** USA
14D2 **Long Island Sd** USA
53A2 **Longjiang** China
4D4 **Long L** Can
11B2 **Long L** USA
7K5 **Longlac** Can
52B5 **Longlin** China
8C2 **Longmont** USA
56E2 **Longnawan** Indon
36C2 **Longny** France
11D2 **Long Prairie** USA
25B5 **Longquimay** Chile
5K4 **Long Range Mts** Can
76D3 **Longreach** Aust
52A2 **Longshou Shan** *Upland* China
16A1 **Longs Peak** *Mt* USA
34D4 **Longtown** Eng
13E1 **Longueuil** Can
28A3 **Longuimay** Chile
36C2 **Longuyon** France
9D3 **Longview** Texas, USA
8A2 **Longview** Washington, USA
38D2 **Longwy** France
52A3 **Longxi** China
55D3 **Long Xuyen** Viet
52D4 **Longyan** China
52B5 **Longzhou** China
37D2 **Lonigo** Italy
38D2 **Lons-le-Saunier** France
9F3 **Lookout,C** USA
72D4 **Loolmalasin** *Mt* Tanz
3E2 **Loon** *R* Can
55C3 **Lop Buri** Thai
72A4 **Lopez** *C* Gabon
50C2 **Lop Nur** *L* China
39A2 **Lora del Rio** Spain
9E2 **Lorain** USA
60B2 **Loralai** Pak
63C2 **Lordegān** Iran
77E4 **Lord Howe** *I* Aust
xxixK5 **Lord Howe Rise** Pacific O
7J3 **Lord Mayor B** Can
8C3 **Lordsburg** USA
29C3 **Lorena** Brazil
37E2 **Loreo** Italy
22B1 **Loreto** Mexico
38B2 **Lorient** France
75B3 **Lorne** Aust
42B3 **Lörrach** Germany
38D2 **Lorraine** *Region* France
8C3 **Los Alamos** USA
28A2 **Los Andes** Chile
25B5 **Los Angeles** Chile
8B3 **Los Angeles** USA
20C3 **Los Angeles Aqueduct** USA
19B3 **Los Banos** USA
28B2 **Los Cerrillos** Arg
22A1 **Los Corchos** Mexico
19B3 **Los Gatos** USA
40C2 **Lošinj** *I* Croatia
28C1 **Los Juries** Arg
28A3 **Los Lagos** Chile
22C1 **Los Laiaderoz** Mexico
28A1 **Los Loros** Chile
16A3 **Los Luncas** USA
28B4 **Los Menucos** Arg
21B2 **Los Mochis** Mexico
20B3 **Los Olivos** USA
28A3 **Los Sauces** Chile
34D3 **Lossiemouth** Scot
28C1 **Los Telares** Arg
23E4 **Los Testigos** *Is* Ven
20C3 **Lost Hills** USA
18D1 **Lost Trail P** USA
25B4 **Los Vilos** Chile
38C3 **Lot** *R* France
28A3 **Lota** Chile
34D4 **Lothian** Region, Scot
72D3 **Lotikipi Plain** Sudan/Kenya
72C4 **Loto** Zaïre
74D1 **Lotsane** *R* Botswana
37B1 **Lötschberg Tunnel** Switz
32K5 **Lotta** *R* Fin/Russian Fed
38B2 **Loudéac** France
70A3 **Louga** Sen
33B3 **Lough Allen** *L* Irish Rep
35E5 **Loughborough** Eng
33B3 **Lough Conn** *L* Irish Rep
33B3 **Lough Corrib** *L* Irish Rep
33B3 **Lough Derg** *L* Irish Rep
6H2 **Lougheed I** Can
35B5 **Lough Ennell** *L* Irish Rep
33B3 **Lough Erne** *L* N Ire
33B2 **Lough Foyle** *Estuary* N Ire/Irish Rep
33B3 **Lough Neagh** *L* N Ire
33B3 **Lough Ree** *L* Irish Rep
35C4 **Lough Strangford** *L* Irish Rep
34B4 **Lough Swilly** *Estuary* Irish Rep
37A1 **Louhans** France
12C3 **Louisa** USA
56D1 **Louisa Reef** *I* S E Asia
10M5 **Louise** *I* Can
10J3 **Louise,L** USA
77E2 **Louisiade Arch** Solomon Is
9D3 **Louisiana** State, USA
74D1 **Louis Trichardt** S Africa
15C2 **Louisville** Georgia, USA
9E3 **Louisville** Kentucky, USA
15B2 **Louisville** Mississippi, USA
44E2 **Loukhi** Russian Fed
11D1 **Lount L** Can
37B3 **Loup** *R* France
16C1 **Loup** *R* USA
38B3 **Lourdes** France
75C2 **Louth** Aust
35B5 **Louth** County, Irish Rep
35E5 **Louth** Eng
Louvain = Leuven
38C2 **Louviers** France
44E4 **Lovat** *R* Russian Fed
41E2 **Lovech** Bulg
16A1 **Loveland** USA
16A2 **Loveland P** USA
18E2 **Lovell** USA
19C2 **Lovelock** USA
40C1 **Lóvere** Italy
16B3 **Lovington** USA
44F2 **Lovozero** Russian Fed
7K3 **Low,C** Can
9F2 **Lowell** Massachusetts, USA
18B2 **Lowell** Oregon, USA
14E1 **Lowell** USA
18C1 **Lower Arrow L** Can
78B2 **Lower Hutt** NZ
20A1 **Lower Lake** USA
10N4 **Lower Post** Can
11C2 **Lower Red L** USA
35F5 **Lowestoft** Eng
43D2 **Łowicz** Pol
75B2 **Loxton** Aust
74C3 **Loxton** S Africa
14B2 **Loyalsock Creek** *R* USA
41D2 **Loznica** Serbia, Yugos
22B2 **loz Reyes** Mexico
48H3 **Lozva** *R* Russian Fed
73C5 **Luacano** Angola
73C4 **Luachimo** Angola
72C4 **Lualaba** *R* Zaïre
73C5 **Luampa** Zambia
73C5 **Luân** Angola
52D3 **Lu'an** China
73B4 **Luanda** Angola
73B5 **Luando** *R* Angola
73C5 **Luanginga** *R* Angola
55C1 **Luang Namtha** Laos
55C2 **Luang Prabang** Laos
73B4 **Luangue** *R* Angola
73D5 **Luangwa** *R* Zambia
52D1 **Luan He** *R* China
52D1 **Luanping** China
73C5 **Luanshya** Zambia
73C5 **Luapula** *R* Zaïre
39A1 **Luarca** Spain
73B4 **Lubalo** Angola
43F2 **L'uban** Belarus
57F8 **Lubang Is** Phil
73B5 **Lubango** Angola
8C3 **Lubbock** USA
42C2 **Lübeck** Germany
72C4 **Lubefu** Zaïre
72C4 **Lubefu** *R* Zaïre
72C3 **Lubero** Zaïre
37A3 **Lubéron** *R* France
73C4 **Lubilash** *R* Zaïre
43E2 **Lublin** Pol
45E5 **Lubny** Ukraine
56D2 **Lubok Antu** Malay
73C4 **Lubudi** Zaïre
73C4 **Lubudi** *R* Zaïre
56B3 **Lubuklinggau** Indon
73C5 **Lubumbashi** Zaïre
72C4 **Lubutu** Zaïre
29A1 **Lucas** Brazil
57F8 **Lucban** Phil
40C2 **Lucca** Italy
34C4 **Luce** *B* Scot
17E3 **Lucedale** USA
57F8 **Lucena** Phil

Lucenec Malange

43D3 **Lucenec** Slovakia
Lucerne = Luzern
16A3 **Lucero** Mexico
53C2 **Luchegorsk** Russian Fed
52C5 **Luchuan** China
20B2 **Lucia** USA
42C2 **Luckenwalde** Germany
74C2 **Luckhoff** S Africa
61B2 **Lucknow** India
73C5 **Lucusse** Angola
36D1 **Lüdenscheid** Germany
74B2 **Lüderitz** Namibia
60D2 **Ludhiana** India
12B2 **Ludington** USA
19C4 **Ludlow** California, USA
35D5 **Ludlow** Eng
14D1 **Ludlow** Vermont, USA
41F2 **Ludogorie** *Upland* Bulg
15C2 **Ludowici** USA
41E1 **Luduş** Rom
32H6 **Ludvika** Sweden
42B3 **Ludwigsburg** Germany
42B3 **Ludwigshafen** Germany
42C2 **Ludwigslust** Germany
72C4 **Luebo** Zaïre
72C4 **Luema** *R* Zaïre
73C4 **Luembe** *R* Angola
73B5 **Luena** Angola
73C5 **Luene** *R* Angola
52B3 **Lüeyang** China
52D5 **Lufeng** China
9D3 **Lufkin** USA
44D4 **Luga** Russian Fed
44D4 **Luga** *R* Russian Fed
40B1 **Lugano** Switz
73D5 **Lugela** Mozam
73D5 **Lugenda** *R* Mozam
37D2 **Lugo** Italy
39A1 **Lugo** Spain
41E1 **Lugoj** Rom
52A3 **Luhuo** China
73B4 **Lui** *R* Angola
73C5 **Luiana** Angola
73C5 **Luiana** *R* Angola
Luichow Peninsula = Leizhou Bandao
37C2 **Luino** Italy
72B3 **Luionga** *R* Zaïre
52B2 **Luipan Shan** *Upland* China
44D2 **Luiro** *R* Fin
73C5 **Luishia** Zaïre
50C4 **Luixi** China
73C4 **Luiza** Zaïre
28B2 **Luján** Arg
28D2 **Luján** Arg
52D3 **Lujiang** China
72B4 **Lukenie** *R* Zaïre
19D4 **Lukeville** USA
72B4 **Lukolela** Zaïre
43E2 **Łuków** Pol
72C4 **Lukuga** *R* Zaïre
73C5 **Lukulu** Zambia
44C2 **Lule** *R* Sweden
32J5 **Luleå** Sweden
41F2 **Lüleburgaz** Turk
52C2 **Lüliang Shan** *Mts* China
17C4 **Luling** USA
26E8 **Lullaillaco** *Mt* Chile
72C3 **Lulonga** *R* Zaïre
Luluabourg = Kananga
73C5 **Lumbala Kaquengue** Angola
9F3 **Lumberton** USA
56E2 **Lumbis** Indon
44G2 **Lumbovka** Russian Fed
61D2 **Lumding** India
73C5 **Lumeje** Angola
78A3 **Lumsden** NZ
32G7 **Lund** Sweden
11C1 **Lundar** Can
73D5 **Lundazi** Zambia
73D6 **Lundi** *R* Zim
35C6 **Lundy** *I* Eng
42C2 **Lüneburg** Germany
36D2 **Lunéville** France
73C5 **Lunga** *R* Zambia
61D3 **Lunglei** India
73B5 **Lungue Bungo** *R* Angola
43F2 **Luninec** Belarus
20C1 **Luning** USA
53C2 **Luobei** China
72B4 **Luobomo** Congo
52B5 **Luocheng** China
52C5 **Luoding** China
52C3 **Luohe** China
52C3 **Luo He** *R* Henan, China
52B2 **Luo He** *R* Shaanxi, China
52C4 **Luoxiao Shan** *Hills* China
52C3 **Luoyang** China
72B4 **Luozi** Zaïre
73C5 **Lupane** Zim
73D5 **Lupilichi** Mozam
Lu Qu = Tao He
25E3 **Luque** Par
36D3 **Lure** France
35B4 **Lurgan** N Ire
73D5 **Lurio** *R* Mozam
63B2 **Luristan** Region, Iran
73C5 **Lusaka** Zambia
72C4 **Lusambo** Zaïre
41D2 **Lushnjë** Alb
72D4 **Lushoto** Tanz
50C4 **Lushui** China
52E2 **Lüshun** China
11B3 **Lusk** USA
35E6 **Luton** Eng
45D5 **Lutsk** Ukraine
72E3 **Luuq** Somalia
11C3 **Luverne** USA
73C4 **Luvua** *R* Zaïre
73D4 **Luwegu** *R* Tanz
73D5 **Luwingu** Zambia
57B3 **Luwuk** Indon
36D2 **Luxembourg** Grand Duchy, N W Europe
38D2 **Luxembourg** Lux
36D3 **Luxeuil-les-Bains** France
52A5 **Luxi** China
69C2 **Luxor** Egypt
44H3 **Luza** Russian Fed
44H3 **Luza** *R* Russian Fed
40B1 **Luzern** Switz
14D1 **Luzerne** USA
52B5 **Luzhai** China
52B4 **Luzhi** China
52B4 **Luzhou** China
29C2 **Luziânia** Brazil
57F7 **Luzon** *I* Phil
57F6 **Luzon Str** Phil
43E3 **L'vov** Ukraine
34D2 **Lybster** Scot
32H6 **Lycksele** Sweden
73C6 **Lydenburg** S Africa
3B3 **Lyell I** Can
8B3 **Lyell,Mt** USA
14B2 **Lykens** USA
18D2 **Lyman** USA
35D6 **Lyme B** Eng
35D6 **Lyme Regis** Eng
9F3 **Lynchburg** USA
75A2 **Lyndhurst** Aust
13E2 **Lynn** USA
3A2 **Lynn Canal** *Sd* USA
15B2 **Lynn Haven** USA
3H2 **Lynn Lake** Can
4D3 **Lynx** Can
6H3 **Lynx L** Can
38C2 **Lyon** France
10L4 **Lyon Canal** *Sd* USA
15C2 **Lyons** Georgia, USA
14B1 **Lyons** New York, USA
76A3 **Lyons** *R* Aust
37B2 **Lys** *R* Italy
44K4 **Lys'va** Russian Fed
78B2 **Lyttelton** NZ
3D3 **Lytton** Can
20A1 **Lytton** USA
43F2 **Lyubeshov** Ukraine
44F4 **Lyublino** Russian Fed

M

55C1 **Ma** *R* Viet
65C2 **Ma'agan** Jordan
65C2 **Ma'alot Tarshīha** Israel
64C3 **Ma'an** Jordan
52D3 **Ma'anshan** China
65D1 **Ma'arrat an Nu'mān** Syria
36C1 **Maas** *R* Neth
36C1 **Maaseik** Belg
57F8 **Maasin** Phil
42B2 **Maastricht** Neth
74E1 **Mabalane** Mozam
27G2 **Mabaruma** Guyana
35F5 **Mablethorpe** Eng
73D6 **Mabote** Mozam
43E2 **Mabrita** Belarus
43F2 **M'adel** Belarus
29D3 **Macaé** Brazil
8D3 **McAlester** USA
8D4 **McAllen** USA
73D5 **Macaloge** Mozam
52C5 **Macao** Dependency, China
27H3 **Macapá** Brazil
29D2 **Macarani** Brazil
26C4 **Macas** Ecuador
27L5 **Macaú** Brazil
29D1 **Macaúbas** Brazil
72C3 **M'Bari** *R* CAR
3D3 **McBride** Can
18C2 **McCall** USA
16B3 **McCamey** USA
18D2 **McCammon** USA
10K3 **McCarthy** USA
3B3 **McCauley I** Can
35D5 **Macclesfield** Eng
7K1 **McClintock B** Can
6H2 **McClintock Chan** Can
14B2 **McClure** USA
20B2 **McClure,L** USA
6G2 **McClure Str** Can
17D3 **McComb** USA
16B1 **McConaughy,L** USA
14B3 **McConnellsburg** USA
8C2 **McCook** USA
7L2 **Macculloch,C** Can
3D2 **McCusker,Mt** Can
6F4 **McDame** Can
18C2 **McDermitt** USA
4D4 **Macdiarmid** Can
18D1 **Mcdonald Peak** *Mt* USA
76C3 **Macdonnell Ranges** *Mts* Aust
39A1 **Macedo de Cavaleiros** Port
41E2 **Macedonia** Republic, Europe
27L5 **Maceió** Brazil
70B4 **Macenta** Guinea
40C2 **Macerata** Italy
3G2 **Macfarlane** *R* Can
75A2 **Macfarlane,L** Aust
17D3 **McGehee** USA
19D3 **McGill** USA
6C3 **McGrath** USA
18D1 **McGuire,Mt** USA
29C3 **Machado** Brazil
73D6 **Machaíla** Mozam
72D4 **Machakos** Kenya
26C4 **Machala** Ecuador
73D6 **Machaze** Mozam
62B1 **Mācherla** India
65C2 **Machgharab** Leb
13F2 **Machias** USA
4C2 **Machichi** *R* Can
62C1 **Machilīpatnam** India
26D1 **Machiques** Ven
26D6 **Machu-Picchu** *Hist Site* Peru
73D6 **Macia** Mozam
Macias Nguema = Fernando Poo
11B2 **McIntosh** USA
75C1 **MacIntyre** *R* Aust
16A2 **Mack** USA
76D3 **Mackay** Aust
18D2 **Mackay** USA
76B3 **Mackay,L** Aust
77H1 **McKean** *I* Phoenix Is
13D2 **McKeesport** USA
3D2 **Mackenzie** Can
6F3 **Mackenzie** *R* Can
6E3 **Mackenzie B** Can
6G2 **Mackenzie King I** Can
6E3 **Mackenzie Mts** Can
12C1 **Mackinac,Str of** USA
12C1 **Mackinaw City** USA
10H3 **McKinley,Mt** USA
17C3 **McKinney** USA
7L2 **Mackinson Inlet** *B* Can
20C3 **McKittrick** USA
75D2 **Macksville** Aust
18B2 **Mclaoughlin,Mt** USA
11B2 **McLaughlin** USA
75D1 **Maclean** Aust
74D3 **Maclear** S Africa
6G4 **McLennan** Can
3E3 **McLeod** *R* Can
6G3 **McLeod B** Can
76A3 **McLeod,L** Aust
3D2 **McLeod Lake** Can
6E3 **Macmillan** *R* Can
16B3 **McMillan,L** USA
10M3 **Macmillan P** Can
18B1 **McMinnville** Oregon, USA
15B1 **McMinnville** Tennessee, USA
79F7 **McMurdo** *Base* Ant
3C2 **McNamara,Mt** Can
19E4 **McNary** USA
3E3 **McNaughton L** Can
12A2 **Macomb** USA
40B2 **Macomer** Sardegna
73D5 **Macomia** Mozam
38C2 **Mâcon** France
9E3 **Macon** Georgia, USA
17D2 **Macon** Missouri, USA
73C5 **Macondo** Angola
3H2 **Macoun L** Can
17C2 **McPherson** USA
xxviiiJ7 **Macquarie** *Is* Aust
75C2 **Macquarie** *R* Aust
75E3 **Macquarie Harbour** *B* Aust
75D2 **Macquarie,L** Aust
15C2 **McRae** USA
79F11 **Mac Robertson Land** Region, Ant
71E1 **M'saken** Tunisia
71C1 **M'Sila** Alg
6G3 **McTavish Arm** *B* Can
75A1 **Macumba** *R* Aust
37C2 **Macunaga** Italy
6F3 **McVicar Arm** *B* Can
42D3 **M'yaróvár** Hung
71H4 **Mada** *R* Nig
65C3 **Mādabā** Jordan
72C2 **Madadi** *Well* Chad
68J9 **Madagascar** *I* Indian O
xxviiiD6 **Madagascar Basin** Indian O
72B1 **Madama** Niger
76D1 **Madang** PNG
70C3 **Madaoua** Niger
61D3 **Madaripur** Bang
63C1 **Madau** Turkmenistan
5H4 **Madawaska** USA
13D1 **Madawaska** *R* Can
61E3 **Madaya** Myanmar
70A1 **Madeira** *I* Atlantic O
26F5 **Madeira** *R* Brazil
7M5 **Madeleine, Îles de la** Can
11D3 **Madelia** USA
21B2 **Madera** Mexico
19B3 **Madera** USA
62A1 **Madgaon** India
61C2 **Madhubani** India
61B3 **Madhya Pradesh** State, India
62B2 **Madikeri** India
72B4 **Madimba** Zaïre
72B4 **Madingo Kayes** Congo
72B4 **Madingou** Congo
9E3 **Madison** Indiana, USA
11C2 **Madison** Minnesota, USA
11C3 **Madison** Nebraska, USA
11C3 **Madison** S Dakota, USA
9E2 **Madison** Wisconsin, USA
18D1 **Madison** *R* USA
12B3 **Madisonville** Kentucky, USA
17C3 **Madisonville** Texas, USA
56D4 **Madiun** Indon
4F5 **Madoc** Can
72D3 **Mado Gashi** Kenya
37D1 **Madonna Di Campiglio** Italy
62C2 **Madras** India
18B2 **Madras** USA
25A8 **Madre de Dios** *I* Chile
26E6 **Madre de Dios** *R* Bol
39B1 **Madrid** Spain
39B2 **Madridejos** Spain
56D4 **Madura** *I* Indon
62B3 **Madurai** India
54C3 **Maebashi** Japan
55B3 **Mae Khlong** *R* Thai
55B4 **Mae Nam Lunang** *R* Thai
55C2 **Mae Nam Mun** *R* Thai
55B2 **Mae Nam Ping** *R* Thai
54A3 **Maengsan** N Korea
73E5 **Maevatanana** Madag
77F2 **Maewo** *I* Vanuatu
74D2 **Mafeking** S Africa
74D2 **Mafeteng** Lesotho
75C3 **Maffra** Aust
73D4 **Mafia** *I* Tanz
25G3 **Mafra** Brazil
64C3 **Mafraq** Jordan
49R4 **Magadan** Russian Fed
26D2 **Magargué** Colombia
71H3 **Magaria** Niger
53B1 **Magdagachi** Russian Fed
28D3 **Magdalena** Arg
8B3 **Magdalena** Mexico
16A3 **Magdalena** USA
23C4 **Magdalena** *R* Colombia
56E2 **Magdalena,Mt** Malay
42C2 **Magdeburg** Germany
26D2 **Magdelena** *R* Colombia
27K8 **Magé** Brazil
56D4 **Magelang** Indon
37C1 **Maggia** *R* Switz
64B4 **Maghâgha** Egypt
34B4 **Magherafelt** N Ire
41D2 **Maglie** Italy
44K5 **Magnitogorsk** Russian Fed
17D3 **Magnolia** USA
53E1 **Mago** Russian Fed
5G4 **Magog** Can
13E1 **Magog** Can
22C1 **Magosal** Mexico
5J3 **Magpie** *R* Can
37C2 **Magra** *R* Italy
3F3 **Magrath** Can
20D2 **Magruder Mt** USA
74E2 **Magude** Mozam
7J3 **Maguse River** Can
Magway = Magwe
55B1 **Magwe** Myanmar
45H8 **Mahābād** Iran
61C2 **Mahabharat Range** *Mts* Nepal
62A1 **Mahād** India
60D4 **Mahadeo Hills** India
14A2 **Mahaffey** USA
73E5 **Mahajanga** Madag
74D1 **Mahalapye** Botswana
61B3 **Mahānadi** *R* India
73E5 **Mahanoro** Madag
14B2 **Mahanoy City** USA
62A1 **Maharashtra** State, India
61B3 **Māhāsamund** India
55C2 **Maha Sarakham** Thai
73E5 **Mahavavy** *R* Madag
62B1 **Mahbūbnagar** India
71E1 **Mahdia** Tunisia
62B2 **Mahe** India
60D4 **Mahekar** India
61B3 **Mahendragarh** India
73D4 **Mahenge** Tanz
60C4 **Mahesāna** India
78C1 **Mahia Pen** NZ
11C2 **Mahnomen** USA
60D3 **Mahoba** India
39C2 **Mahón** Spain
5J5 **Mahone B** Can
10N2 **Mahony L** Can
71E2 **Mahrés** Tunisia
60C4 **Mahuva** India
26D1 **Maicao** Colombia
37B1 **Maîche** France
66C4 **Maichew** Eth
35F6 **Maidstone** Eng
72B2 **Maiduguri** Nig
44B3 **Maigomaj** *R* Sweden
61B3 **Maihar** India
61D3 **Maijdi** Bang
55B3 **Mail Kyun** *I* Myanmar
60A1 **Maimana** Afghan
36E2 **Main** *R* Germany
4E4 **Main Chan** Can
72B4 **Mai-Ndombe** *L* Zaïre
9G2 **Maine** State, USA
36A3 **Maine** *Region* France
71J3 **Mainé-Soroa** Niger
34D2 **Mainland** *I* Scot
60D3 **Mainpuri** India
36A2 **Maintenon** France
73E5 **Maintirano** Madag
42B2 **Mainz** Germany
70A4 **Maio** *I* Cape Verde
25C4 **Maipó** *Mt* Arg/Chile
28D3 **Maipú** Arg
26E1 **Maiquetía** Ven
37B2 **Maira** *R* Italy
61D2 **Mairābāri** India
61D3 **Maiskhal I** Bang
76E4 **Maitland** New South Wales, Aust
75A2 **Maitland** S Australia, Aust
79F12 **Maitri** *Base* Ant
38D1 **Maiz** Germany
53D4 **Maizuru** Japan
76A1 **Majene** Indon
26D7 **Majes** *R* Peru
72D3 **Maji** Eth
52D2 **Majia He** *R* China
Majunga = Mahajanga
72D2 **Makale** Eth
57A3 **Makale** Indon
56B3 **Makalo** Indon
61C2 **Makalu** *Mt* China/Nepal
44K2 **Makarikha** Russian Fed
53E2 **Makarov** Russian Fed
40D2 **Makarska** Croatia
44G4 **Makaryev** Russian Fed
Makassar Ujung Pandang
56E3 **Makassar Str** Indon
45J6 **Makat** Kazakhstan
70A4 **Makeni** Sierra Leone
45F6 **Makeyevka** Ukraine
73C6 **Makgadikgadi** *Salt Pan* Botswana
45H7 **Makhachkala** Russian Fed
64D1 **Makharadze** Georgia
57C2 **Makian** *I* Indon
72D4 **Makindu** Kenya
Makkah = Mecca
7N4 **Makkovik** Can
43E3 **Makó** Hung
72B3 **Makokou** Gabon
78C1 **Makorako,Mt** NZ
72B3 **Makoua** Congo
60C3 **Makrāna** India
60A3 **Makran Coast Range** *Mts* Pak
53D2 **Maksimovka** Russian Fed
63E3 **Maksotag** Iran
71D1 **Maktar** Tunisia
45G8 **Mākū** Iran
72C4 **Makumbi** Zaïre
53C5 **Makurazaki** Japan
71H4 **Makurdi** Nig
10E5 **Makushin V** USA
57F9 **Malabang** Phil
62B2 **Malabar Coast** India
68E7 **Malabo** Bioko
28D1 **Malabrigo** Arg
55C5 **Malacca,Str of** S E Asia
18D2 **Malad City** USA
26D2 **Málaga** Colombia
39B2 **Malaga** Spain
16B3 **Malaga** USA
73E6 **Malaimbandy** Madag
77F1 **Malaita** *I* Solomon Is
72D3 **Malakal** Sudan
60C2 **Malakand** Pak
57B3 **Malamala** Indon
56D4 **Malang** Indon
73B4 **Malange** Angola

Masai Steppe Mexico

72D4 **Masai Steppe** *Upland* Tanz
72D4 **Masaka** Uganda
64E2 **Masally** Azerbaijan
57B3 **Masamba** Indon
53B4 **Masan** S Korea
73D5 **Masasi** Tanz
21D3 **Masaya** Nic
57F8 **Masbate** Phil
57F8 **Masbate** *I* Phil
71C1 **Mascara** Alg
xxviiiD5 **Mascarene Ridge** Indian O
22B1 **Mascota** Mexico
29E2 **Mascote** Brazil
57C4 **Masela** *I* Indon
74D2 **Maseru** Lesotho
60B2 **Mashaki** Afghan
63D1 **Mashhad** Iran
63E3 **Mashkel** *R* Pak
72B4 **Masi-Manimba** Zaïre
72D3 **Masindi** Uganda
72C4 **Masisi** Zaïre
63B2 **Masjed Soleyman** Iran
73F5 **Masoala** *C* Madag
20C1 **Mason** Nevada, USA
16C3 **Mason** Texas, USA
9D2 **Mason City** USA
67G2 **Masqat** Oman
42B2 **Mass** *R* Neth
40C2 **Massa** Italy
9F2 **Massachusetts** State, USA
13E2 **Massachusetts B** USA
72B2 **Massakori** Chad
37D3 **Massa Marittima** Italy
73D6 **Massangena** Mozam
66C3 **Massawa Chan** Eth
13E2 **Massena** USA
72B2 **Massénya** Chad
3B3 **Masset** Can
12C1 **Massey** Can
38C2 **Massif Central** *Mts* France
71C1 **Massif de l'Ouarsenis** *Mts* Alg
72B3 **Massif de l'Adamaoua** *Mts* Cam
23C3 **Massif de la Hotte** *Mts* Haiti
73E6 **Massif de l'Isalo** *Upland* Madag
72C3 **Massif des Bongo** *Upland* CAR
38D2 **Massif du Pelvoux** *Mts* France
73E5 **Massif du Tsaratanana** *Mt* Madag
12C2 **Massillon** USA
70B3 **Massina** Region, Mali
73D6 **Massinga** Mozam
74E1 **Massingir** Mozam
45J6 **Masteksay** Kazakhstan
77G5 **Masterton** NZ
53C5 **Masuda** Japan
72B4 **Masuku** Gabon
64C2 **Maşyāf** Syria
4E4 **Matachewan** Can
16A4 **Matachie** Mexico
72B4 **Matadi** Zaïre
26A1 **Matagalpa** Nic
7L5 **Matagami** Can
8D4 **Matagorda B** USA
17F4 **Matagorda I** USA
78C1 **Matakana I** NZ
73B5 **Matala** Angola
62C3 **Matale** Sri Lanka
70A3 **Matam** Sen
70C3 **Matameye** Niger
21C2 **Matamoros** Mexico
69B2 **Ma'tan as Sarra** *Well* Libya
7M5 **Matane** Can
21D2 **Matanzas** Cuba
13F1 **Matapédia** *R* Can
28A2 **Mataquito** *R* Chile
62C3 **Matara** Sri Lanka
76A1 **Mataram** Indon
26D7 **Matarani** Peru
29E1 **Mataripe** Brazil
39C1 **Mataró** Spain
74D3 **Matatiele** S Africa
78A3 **Mataura** NZ
21B2 **Matehuala** Mexico
37E3 **Matelica** Italy
23L1 **Matelot** Trinidad
40D2 **Matera** Italy
43E3 **Mátészalka** Hung
71D1 **Mateur** Tunisia
20C2 **Mather** USA
12C1 **Matheson** Can
17F4 **Mathis** USA
60D3 **Mathura** India
57G9 **Mati** Phil
22C2 **Matias Romero** Mexico
56E3 **Matisiri** *I* Indon
35E5 **Matlock** Eng
71D2 **Matmatma** Tunisia
27G6 **Mato Grosso** Brazil
27G6 **Mato Grosso** State, Brazil
27G7 **Mato Grosso do Sul** State, Brazil
74E2 **Matola** Mozam
67G2 **Matrah** Oman
37E1 **Matrei im Osttirol** Austria
64A3 **Matrûh** Egypt
53C4 **Matsue** Japan
53E3 **Matsumae** Japan
53D4 **Matsumoto** Japan
53D5 **Matsusaka** Japan
53C5 **Matsuyama** Japan
7K5 **Mattagami** *R* Can
4F4 **Mattawa** Can
5H4 **Mattawamkeag** USA
40B1 **Matterhorn** *Mt* Switz/Italy
18C2 **Matterhorn** *Mt* USA
23C2 **Matthew Town** Bahamas
4E4 **Mattice** Can
14D2 **Mattituck** USA
12B3 **Mattoon** USA
60B2 **Matun** Afghan
23L1 **Matura B** Trinidad
26F2 **Maturin** Ven
61B2 **Mau** India
73D5 **Maúa** Mozam
38C1 **Maubeuge** France
75B2 **Maude** Aust
xxxJ8 **Maud Seamount** Atlantic O
20E5 **Maui** *I* Hawaiian Is
28A3 **Maule** *R* Chile
12C2 **Maumee** USA
12C2 **Maumee** *R* USA
57B4 **Maumere** Indon
73C5 **Maun** Botswana
20E5 **Mauna Kea** *Mt* Hawaiian Is
20E5 **Mauna Loa** *Mt* Hawaiian Is
6F3 **Maunoir,L** Can
37B3 **Maures** *Mts* France
38C2 **Mauriac** France
70A2 **Mauritania** Republic, Africa
68K10 **Mauritius** *I* Indian O
12A2 **Mauston** USA
37E1 **Mauterndorf** Austria
73C5 **Mavinga** Angola
74E1 **Mavue** Mozam
61D3 **Mawlaik** Myanmar
Mawlamyine = Moulmein
79G10 **Mawson** *Base* Ant
11B2 **Max** USA
74E1 **Maxaila** Mozam
22C1 **Maxcaltzin** Mexico
56C3 **Maya** *I* Indon
49P4 **Maya** *R* Russian Fed
64D2 **Mayādīn** Syria
9F4 **Mayaguana** *I* Bahamas
23D3 **Mayagüez** Puerto Rico
70C3 **Mayahi** Niger
72B4 **Mayama** Congo
63D1 **Mayamey** Iran
57D4 **Mayanobab** Indon
34C4 **Maybole** Scot
9F3 **May,C** USA
75E3 **Maydena** Aust
36D1 **Mayen** Germany
38B2 **Mayenne** France
19D4 **Mayer** USA
3E3 **Mayerthorpe** Can
67E4 **Mayfa'ah** Yemen
12B3 **Mayfield** USA
16A3 **Mayhill** USA
45G7 **Maykop** Russian Fed
48H6 **Maymaneh** Afghan
55B1 **Maymyo** Myanmar
6E3 **Mayo** Can
14B3 **Mayo** USA
71J4 **Mayo Deo** *R* Cam
57F8 **Mayon** *Mt* Phil
39C2 **Mayor** *Mt* Spain
28C3 **Mayor Buratovich** Arg
78C1 **Mayor I** NZ
25D1 **Mayor P Lagerenza** Par
73E5 **Mayotte** *I* Indian O
23H2 **May Pen** Jamaica
14C3 **May Point,C** USA
37D1 **Mayrhofen** Austria
53B1 **Mayskiy** Russian Fed
14C3 **Mays Landing** USA
3G2 **Mayson L** Can
12C3 **Maysville** USA
72B4 **Mayumba** Gabon
11C2 **Mayville** USA
16B1 **Maywood** USA
73C5 **Mazabuka** Zambia
22B1 **Mazapil** Mexico
60D1 **Mazar** China
65C3 **Mazār** Jordan
40C3 **Mazara del Vallo** Italy
60B1 **Mazar-i-Sharif** Afghan
21B2 **Mazatlán** Mexico
44C4 **Mazeikiai** Lithuania
65C3 **Mazra** Jordan
73D6 **Mbabane** Swaziland
71J4 **Mbabo,Mt** Cam
72B3 **Mbaïki** CAR
73D4 **Mbala** Zambia
73C6 **Mbalabala** Zim
72D3 **Mbale** Uganda
72B3 **Mbalmayo** Cam
72B3 **Mbam** *R* Cam
73D5 **Mbamba Bay** Tanz
72B3 **Mbandaka** Zaïre
72B4 **Mbanza Congo** Angola
72B4 **Mbanza-Ngungu** Zaïre
72D4 **Mbarara** Uganda
71J4 **Mbé** Cam
71J4 **Mbengwi** Cam
72B3 **Mbènza** Congo
72B3 **Mbére** *R* Cam
73D4 **Mbeya** Tanz
72B4 **Mbinda** Congo
71J4 **Mbouda** Cam
70A3 **Mbout** Maur
72C4 **Mbuji-Mayi** Zaïre
71J3 **Mbuli** *R* Nig
72D4 **Mbulu** Tanz
28D1 **Mburucuyá** Arg
70B2 **Mcherrah** Region, Alg
73D5 **Mchinji** Malawi
4C2 **M'Clintock** Can
55D3 **Mdrak** Viet
16B2 **Meade** USA
10G1 **Meade** *R* USA
8B3 **Mead,L** USA
6H4 **Meadow Lake** Can
12C2 **Meadville** USA
54D2 **Me-akan dake** *Mt* Japan
7N4 **Mealy Mts** Can
75C1 **Meandarra** Aust
6G4 **Meander River** Can
35B5 **Meath** Irish Rep
38C2 **Meaux** France
66C2 **Mecca** S Arabia
19C4 **Mecca** USA
14D1 **Mechanicville** USA
48G2 **Mechdusharskiy, Ostrov** *I* Russian Fed
42A2 **Mechelen** Belg
71B2 **Mecheria** Alg
42C2 **Mecklenburger Bucht** *B* Germany
42C2 **Mecklenburg-Vorpommern** State, Germany
73D5 **Meconta** Mozam
73D5 **Mecuburi** Mozam
73E5 **Mecufi** Mozam
73D5 **Mecula** Mozam
56A2 **Medan** Indon
28C3 **Medanos** Arg
28D2 **Médanos** Arg
71C1 **Médéa** Alg
26C2 **Medellin** Colombia
71E2 **Medenine** Tunisia
8A2 **Medford** USA
41F2 **Medgidia** Rom
28B2 **Media Agua** Arg
41E1 **Mediaş** Rom
18C1 **Medical Lake** USA
11A3 **Medicine Bow** USA
16A1 **Medicine Bow Mts** USA
11A3 **Medicine Bow Peak** *Mt* USA
6G5 **Medicine Hat** Can
16C2 **Medicine Lodge** USA
29D2 **Medina** Brazil
11C2 **Medina** N Dakota, USA
14A1 **Medina** New York, USA
66C2 **Medina** S Arabia
39B1 **Medinaceli** Spain
39A1 **Medina del Campo** Spain
39A1 **Medina de Rio Seco** Spain
16C4 **Medina L** USA
61C3 **Medinīpur** India
68E4 **Mediterranean S** Europe
3F3 **Medley** Can
45K5 **Mednogorsk** Russian Fed
49S4 **Mednyy, Ostrov** *I* Russian Fed
61E2 **Mêdog** China
72B3 **Medouneu** Gabon
45G5 **Medvedista** *R* Russian Fed
49S2 **Medvezh'i Ova** *I* Russian Fed
44E3 **Medvezh'yegorsk** Russian Fed
76A3 **Meekatharra** Aust
16A1 **Meeker** USA
60D3 **Meerut** India
18E2 **Meeteetse** USA
72D3 **Mēga** Eth
41E3 **Megalópolis** Greece
41E3 **Mégara** Greece
61D2 **Meghālaya** State, India
61D3 **Meghna** *R* Bang
65C2 **Megido** *Hist Site* Israel
4F4 **Mégiscane** *R* Can
71C2 **Mehaïguene** *R* Alg
10E3 **Mehoryuk** USA
63C3 **Mehran** *R* Iran
63C2 **Mehriz** Iran
29C2 **Meia Ponte** *R* Brazil
72B3 **Meiganga** Cam
55B1 **Meiktila** Myanmar
37C1 **Meiringen** Switz
52A4 **Meishan** China
42C2 **Meissen** Germany
52D5 **Mei Xian** China
52D5 **Meizhou** China
26D8 **Mejillones** Chile
72B3 **Mekambo** Gabon
4E4 **Mekatina** Can
71C4 **Mek'elē** Eth
71A2 **Meknès** Mor
Mekong = Lancang
55D3 **Mekong, R** Camb
71G3 **Mekrou** *R* Benin
55C5 **Melaka** Malay
xxviiiJ5 **Melanesia** *Region* Pacific O
56D3 **Melawi** *R* Indon
76D4 **Melbourne** Aust
9E4 **Melbourne** USA
8C4 **Melchor Muźguiz** Mexico
44K5 **Meleuz** Russian Fed
72B2 **Melfi** Chad
6H4 **Melfort** Can
71B1 **Melilla** N W Africa
25B6 **Melimoyu** *Mt* Chile
28C2 **Melincué** Arg
28A2 **Melipilla** Chile
11B2 **Melita** Can
45F6 **Melitopol'** Ukraine
7M2 **Meliville Bugt** *B* Greenland
72D3 **Melka Guba** Eth
71D1 **Mellègue** *R* Tunisia
66D4 **Melli** *R* Eth
74E2 **Melmoth** S Africa
28C2 **Melo** Arg
25F4 **Melo** Urug
29A3 **Melo** *R* Brazil
20B2 **Melones Res** USA
10H2 **Melozitna** *R* USA
11D2 **Melrose** USA
37C1 **Mels** Switz
36E1 **Melsungen** Germany
56E1 **Melta,Mt** Malay
35E5 **Melton Mowbray** Eng
38C2 **Melun** France
6H4 **Melville** Can
23Q2 **Melville,C** Dominica
6F3 **Melville Hills** *Mts* Can
76C2 **Melville I** Aust
6G2 **Melville I** Can
7N4 **Melville,L** Can
7K3 **Melville Pen** Can
73E5 **Memba** Mozam
76A1 **Memboro** Indon
42C3 **Memmingen** Germany
56C2 **Mempawan** Indon
9E3 **Memphis** Tennessee, USA
16B3 **Memphis** Texas, USA
17D3 **Mena** USA
43G2 **Mena** Ukraine
35C5 **Menai Str** Wales
70C3 **Ménaka** Mali
12B2 **Menasha** USA
28B4 **Mencué** Arg
56D3 **Mendawai** *R* Indon
38C3 **Mende** France
72D3 **Mendebo** *Mts* Eth
10E4 **Mendenhall,C** USA
76D1 **Mendi** PNG
35D6 **Mendip Hills** *Upland* Eng
18B2 **Mendocino,C** USA
xxixM3 **Mendocino Seascarp** Pacific O
20B2 **Mendota** California, USA
12B2 **Mendota** Illinois, USA
25C4 **Mendoza** Arg
25C5 **Mendoza** State, Arg
41F3 **Menemen** Turk
36B1 **Menen** Belg
52D3 **Mengcheng** China
56C3 **Menggala** Indon
55B1 **Menghai** China
52A5 **Mengla** China
55B1 **Menglian** China
52A5 **Mengzi** China
5H3 **Menihek Lakes** Can
76D4 **Menindee** Aust
75B2 **Menindee L** Aust
75A3 **Meningie** Aust
12B1 **Menominee** USA
12B2 **Menomonee Falls** USA
12A2 **Menomonie** USA
73B5 **Menongue** Angola
39C1 **Menorca** *I* Spain
10K3 **Mentasta Mts** USA
16A2 **Mentmore** USA
56C3 **Mentok** Indon
37B3 **Menton** France
12C2 **Mentor** USA
36B2 **Ménu** France
52A2 **Menyuan** China
44J4 **Menzelinsk** Russian Fed
42B2 **Meppen** Germany
36A3 **Mer** France
56E2 **Merah** Indon
17D2 **Meramec** *R* USA
40C1 **Merano** Italy
76D1 **Merauke** Indon
8A3 **Merced** USA
20B2 **Merced** *R* USA
25B4 **Mercedario** *Mt* Chile
25C4 **Mercedes** Arg
25E4 **Mercedes** Buenos Aires, Arg
25E3 **Mercedes** Corrientes, Arg
25E4 **Mercedes** Urug
78C1 **Mercury B** NZ
78C1 **Mercury Is** NZ
6F2 **Mercy B** Can
7M3 **Mercy,C** Can
16B2 **Meredith,L** *L* USA
55B3 **Mergui** Myanmar
55B3 **Mergui Arch** Myanmar
21D2 **Mérida** Mexico
39A2 **Mérida** Spain
26D2 **Mérida** Ven
9E3 **Meridian** USA
75C3 **Merimbula** Aust
75B2 **Meringur** Aust
16B3 **Merkel** USA
72D2 **Merowe** Sudan
76A4 **Merredin** Aust
34C4 **Merrick** *Mt* Scot
12B1 **Merrill** USA
12B2 **Merrillville** USA
14E1 **Merrimack** *R* USA
11B3 **Merriman** USA
3D3 **Merritt** Can
15C3 **Merritt Island** USA
75D2 **Merriwa** Aust
66D4 **Mersa Fatma** Eth
39B2 **Mers el Kebir** Alg
35D5 **Mersey** *R* Eng
35D5 **Merseyside** County, Eng
45E8 **Mersin** Turk
55C5 **Mersing** Malay
60C3 **Merta** India
35D6 **Merthyr Tydfil** Wales
39A2 **Mertola** Port
72D4 **Meru** *Mt* Tanz
45F7 **Merzifon** Turk
36D2 **Merzig** Germany
8B3 **Mesa** USA
16A2 **Mesa Verde Nat Pk** USA
36E1 **Meschede** Germany
64D1 **Mescit Dağ** *Mt* Turk
10G4 **Meshik** USA
72C3 **Meshra'er Req** Sudan
37C1 **Mesocco** Switz
41E3 **Mesolóngion** Greece
19D3 **Mesquite** Nevada, USA
17C3 **Mesquite** Texas, USA
71C2 **Messaad** Alg
73D5 **Messalo** *R* Mozam
40D3 **Messina** Italy
74D1 **Messina** S Africa
41E3 **Messíni** Greece
41E3 **Messiniakós Kólpos** *G* Greece
Mesta = Néstos
41E2 **Mesta, R** Bulg
40C1 **Mestre** Italy
26D3 **Meta** *R* Colombia
44E4 **Meta** *R* Russian Fed
26E2 **Meta** *R* Ven
7L3 **Meta Incognita Pen** Can
17D4 **Metairie** USA
18C1 **Metaline Falls** USA
25D3 **Metán** Arg
73D5 **Metangula** Mozam
40D2 **Metaponto** Italy
37E3 **Metauro** *R* Italy
66C4 **Metemma** Eth
34D3 **Methil** Scot
14E1 **Methuen** USA
78B2 **Methven** NZ
10M4 **Metlakatla** USA
71D2 **Metlaoui** Tunisia
12B3 **Metropolis** USA
62B2 **Mettūr** India
38D2 **Metz** France
36E2 **Metzingen** Germany
56A2 **Meulaboh** Indon
36A2 **Meulan** France
36A3 **Meung-sur-Loire** France
36D2 **Meurthe** *R* France
36D2 **Meurthe-et-Moselle** Department, France
36C2 **Meuse** Department, France
36C1 **Meuse** *R* Belg
38D2 **Meuse** *R* France
17C3 **Mexia** USA
21A1 **Mexicali** Mexico
19E3 **Mexican Hat** USA
21B2 **Mexico** Federal Republic, Central America

Monroe **Mugadishu**

17D3 **Monroe** Louisiana, USA
12C2 **Monroe** Michigan, USA
15C2 **Monroe** N Carolina, USA
18B1 **Monroe** Washington, USA
12B2 **Monroe** Wisconsin, USA
17D2 **Monroe City** USA
70A4 **Monrovia** Lib
20D3 **Monrovia** USA
42A2 **Mons** Belg
37D2 **Monselice** Italy
14D1 **Monson** USA
42D1 **Mönsterås** Sweden
73E5 **Montagne d'Ambre** *Mt* Madag
71C2 **Montagnes des Ouled Naïl** *Mts* Alg
74C3 **Montagu** S Africa
5J4 **Montague** Can
10J4 **Montague I** USA
38B2 **Montaigu** France
40D3 **Montallo** *Mt* Italy
8B2 **Montana** State, USA
39A1 **Montañas de León** *Mts* Spain
38C2 **Montargis** France
38C3 **Montauban** France
13E2 **Montauk** USA
13E2 **Montauk Pt** USA
36C3 **Montbard** France
38D2 **Montbéliard** France
40B1 **Mont Blanc** *Mt* France/Italy
Montblanc = Montblanch
39C1 **Montblanch** Spain
38C2 **Montceau les Mines** France
39C1 **Montceny** *Mt* Spain
38D3 **Mont Cinto** *Mt* Corse
36C2 **Montcornet** France
36A2 **Mont d'Amain** *Mt* France
38B3 **Mont-de-Marsin** France
38C2 **Montdidier** France
26F7 **Monteagudo** Bol
27H4 **Monte Alegre** Brazil
40C2 **Monte Amiata** *Mt* Italy
29D2 **Monte Azul** Brazil
37D2 **Monte Baldo** *Mt* Italy
13D1 **Montebello** Can
76A3 **Monte Bello Is** Aust
37E2 **Montebelluna** Italy
37B3 **Monte Carlo** France
29C2 **Monte Carmelo** Brazil
28D2 **Monte Caseros** Arg
37D3 **Montecatini** Italy
37E3 **Monte Catria** *Mt* Italy
40C2 **Monte Cimone** *Mt* Italy
40B2 **Monte Cinto** *Mt* Corse
28B2 **Monte Coman** Arg
40C2 **Monte Corno** *Mt* Italy
23C3 **Montecristi** Dom Rep
40C2 **Montecristo** *I* Italy
22B1 **Monte Escobedo** Mexico
37D3 **Monte Falterona** *Mt* Italy
40D2 **Monte Gargano** *Mt* Italy
23B3 **Montego Bay** Jamaica
37D2 **Monte Grappa** *Mt* Italy
37C2 **Monte Lesima** *Mt* Italy
38C3 **Montélimar** France
29A3 **Montelindo** *R* Par
40C2 **Monte Miletto** *Mt* Italy
39A2 **Montemo-o-Novo** Port
21C2 **Montemorelos** Mexico
23B5 **Montená** Colombia
41D2 **Montenegro** Republic, Yugos
28E1 **Montengero** Brazil
37C3 **Monte Orsaro** *Mt* Italy
29E2 **Monte Pascoal** *Mt* Brazil
28A2 **Monte Patria** Chile
37E3 **Monte Pennino** *Mt* Italy
28B1 **Monte Pissis** *Mt* Arg
40D3 **Monte Pollino** *Mt* Italy
37E2 **Monte Pramaggiore** *Mt* Italy
73D5 **Montepuez** Mozam
37D3 **Montepulciano** Italy
36B2 **Montereau-Faut-Yonne** France
8A3 **Monterey** California, USA
13D3 **Monterey** Virginia, USA
8A3 **Monterey B** USA
26C2 **Montería** Colombia
26F7 **Montero** Bol
37B2 **Monte Rosa** *Mt* Italy/Switz
21B2 **Monterrey** Mexico
27K7 **Montes Claros** Brazil
39B2 **Montes de Toledo** *Mts* Spain
37D3 **Montevarchi** Italy
25E4 **Montevideo** Urug
11C3 **Montevideo** USA
35F6 **Montevil** France
40B2 **Monte Viso** *Mt* Italy
16A2 **Monte Vista** USA
16B2 **Montezuma** USA
20D2 **Montezuma Peak** *Mt* USA
23P2 **Mont Gimie** *Mt* St Lucia
9E3 **Montgomery** Alabama, USA
14B2 **Montgomery** Pennsylvania, USA
20C2 **Montgomery P** USA
70C2 **Mont Gréboun** Niger
36C2 **Montherme** France
37B1 **Monthey** Switz
17D3 **Monticello** Arkansas, USA
12A2 **Monticello** Iowa, USA
11D2 **Monticello** Minnesota, USA
14C2 **Monticello** New York, USA
8C3 **Monticello** Utah, USA
40B2 **Monti del Gennargentu** *Mt* Sardegna
36C2 **Montier-en-Der** France
37D2 **Monti Lessini** *Mts* Italy
40C3 **Monti Nebrodi** *Mts* Italy
36A2 **Montivilliers** France
5H4 **Mont Joli** Can
4F4 **Mont-Laurier** Can
7L5 **Mont-Laurier** Can
5H4 **Mont Louis** Can
38C2 **Montluçon** France
7L5 **Montmagny** Can
36C2 **Montmédy** France
36B2 **Montmirail** France
13E1 **Montmorency** Can
37B2 **Mont Mounier** *Mt* France
39B2 **Montoro** Spain
14B2 **Montoursville** USA
38D3 **Mont Pelat** *Mt* France
18D2 **Montpelier** Idaho, USA
12C2 **Montpelier** Ohio, USA
9F2 **Montpelier** Vermont, USA
38C3 **Montpellier** France
7L5 **Montréal** Can
3G3 **Montreal L** Can
3G3 **Montreal Lake** Can
38C1 **Montreuil** France
40B1 **Montreux** Switz
37A1 **Montrevel** France
37B1 **Mont Risoux** *Mt* France
8C3 **Montrose** Colorado, USA
14C2 **Montrose** Pennsylvania, USA
33C2 **Montrose** Scot
34F3 **Montrose** *Oilfield* N Sea
38B2 **Mont-St-Michel** France
71B2 **Monts des Ksour** *Mts* Alg
39C3 **Monts des Ouled Neil** *Mts* Alg
39C2 **Monts du Hodna** *Mts* Alg
23E3 **Montserrat** *I* Caribbean
5H4 **Monts Notre Dame** *Mts* Can
5G3 **Monts Otish** *Mts* Can
5G4 **Mont Tremblant Prov Park** Can
37A2 **Mont Ventoux** *Mt* France
10F2 **Monument Mt** USA
8B3 **Monument V** USA
72C3 **Monveda** Zaïre
55B1 **Monywa** Myanmar
40B1 **Monza** Italy
73C5 **Monze** Zambia
74E2 **Mooi** *R* S Africa
74D2 **Mool River** S Africa
75B1 **Moomba** Aust
75D2 **Moonbi Range** *Mts* Aust
75B1 **Moonda L** Aust
75D1 **Moonie** Aust
75C1 **Moonie** *R* Aust
75A2 **Moonta** Aust
76A4 **Moora** Aust
75B1 **Mooraberree** Aust
11B3 **Moorcroft** USA
76A3 **Moore,L** Aust
34D4 **Moorfoot Hills** Scot
8D2 **Moorhead** USA
20C3 **Moorpark** USA
74B3 **Moorreesburg** S Africa
7K4 **Moose** *R* Can
13F1 **Moosehead L** USA
6H4 **Moose Jaw** Can
11D2 **Moose Lake** USA
6H4 **Moosomin** Can
7K4 **Moosonee** Can
14E2 **Moosup** USA
73D5 **Mopeia** Mozam
70B3 **Mopti** Mali
26D7 **Moquegua** Peru
71J3 **Mora** Cam
32G6 **Mora** Sweden
11D2 **Mora** USA
27L5 **Morada** Brazil
60D3 **Morādābād** India
29C2 **Morada Nova de Minas** *L* Brazil
73E5 **Morafenobe** Madag
73E5 **Moramanga** Madag
18D2 **Moran** USA
23J2 **Morant Bay** Jamaica
23J2 **Morant Pt** Jamaica
62B3 **Moratuwa** Sri Lanka
41E2 **Morava** *R* Serbia, Yugos
63D1 **Moraveh Tappeh** Iran
33C2 **Moray Firth** *Estuary* Scot
37C1 **Morbegno** Italy
60C4 **Morbi** India
22B1 **Morcillo** Mexico
64D2 **Mor Dağ** *Mt* Turk
6J5 **Morden** Can
44G5 **Mordovskaya** Respublika, Russian Fed
11B2 **Moreau** *R* USA
35D4 **Morecambe** Eng
35D4 **Morecambe B** Eng
76D3 **Moree** Aust
36A3 **Morée** France
12C3 **Morehead** USA
15D2 **Morehead City** USA
37C1 **Mörel** Switz
21B3 **Morelia** Mexico
22B1 **Morelos** Mexico
22C1 **Morelos** Mexico
22C2 **Morelos** State, Mexico
60D3 **Morena** India
6E4 **Moresby I** Can
75D1 **Moreton I** Aust
36B2 **Moreuil** France
37B1 **Morez** France
17D4 **Morgan City** USA
20B2 **Morgan Hill** USA
20C2 **Morgan,Mt** USA
15C1 **Morganton** USA
13D3 **Morgantown** USA
74D2 **Morgenzon** S Africa
37B1 **Morges** Switz
36D2 **Morhange** France
53E3 **Mori** Japan
16A3 **Moriarty** USA
23K1 **Moriatio** Tobago
3C3 **Morice L** Can
53A2 **Morin Dawa** China
3F3 **Morinville** Can
53E4 **Morioka** Japan
75D2 **Morisset** Aust
49N3 **Morkoka** *R* Russian Fed
38B2 **Morlaix** France
23Q2 **Morne Diablotin** *Mt* Dominica
75B1 **Morney** Aust
76C2 **Mornington** *I* Aust
60B3 **Moro** Pak
76D1 **Morobe** PNG
70B1 **Morocco** Kingdom, Africa
57F9 **Moro G** Phil
73D4 **Morogoro** Tanz
22B1 **Moroleon** Mexico
73E6 **Morombe** Madag
23B2 **Morón** Cuba
73E6 **Morondava** Madag
39A2 **Moron de la Frontera** Spain
73E5 **Moroni** Comoros
57C2 **Morotai** *I* Indon
72D3 **Moroto** Uganda
45G6 **Morozovsk** Russian Fed
34E4 **Morpeth** Eng
65B1 **Morphou** Cyprus
65B1 **Morphou B** Cyprus
11B3 **Morrill** USA
17D2 **Morrilton** USA
29C2 **Morrinhos** Brazil
78C1 **Morrinsville** NZ
11C2 **Morris** Can
11C2 **Morris** USA
14C2 **Morristown** New Jersey, USA
13D2 **Morristown** New York, USA
15C1 **Morristown** Tennessee, USA
14C1 **Morrisville** New York, USA
14C2 **Morrisville** Pennsylvania, USA
20B3 **Morro Bay** USA
22B2 **Morro de Papanoa** Mexico
22B2 **Morro de Petatlán** Mexico
73D5 **Morrumbala** Mozam
73D6 **Morrumbene** Mozam
44G5 **Morshansk** Russian Fed
36A2 **Mortagne-au-Perche** France
37C2 **Mortara** Italy
28C2 **Morteros** Arg
Mortes = Manso
27H6 **Mortes** *R* Malo Grosso, Brazil
29D3 **Mortes** *R* Minas Gerais, Brazil
75B3 **Mortlake** Aust
16B3 **Morton** USA
23L1 **Moruga** Trinidad
75D3 **Moruya** Aust
75C1 **Morven** Aust
34C3 **Morvern** *Pen* Scot
75C3 **Morwell** Aust
10F4 **Morzhovoi B** USA
36E2 **Mosbach** Germany
55B3 **Moscos Is** Myanmar
Moscow = Moskva
18C1 **Moscow** Idaho, USA
14C2 **Moscow** Pennsylvania, USA
42B2 **Mosel** *R* Germany
74C2 **Moselebe** *R* Botswana
36D2 **Moselle** Department, France
36D2 **Moselle** *R* France
18C1 **Moses Lake** USA
78B3 **Mosgiel** NZ
72D4 **Moshi** Tanz
12B2 **Mosinee** USA
32G5 **Mosjøen** Nor
49Q4 **Moskal'vo** Russian Fed
44F4 **Moskva** Russian Fed
16B2 **Mosquero** USA
29D2 **Mosquito** *R* Brazil
32G7 **Moss** Nor
72B4 **Mossaka** Congo
Mossâmedes = Moçâmedes
74C3 **Mossel Bay** S Africa
72B4 **Mossendjo** Congo
75B2 **Mossgiel** Aust
27L5 **Mossoró** Brazil
42C2 **Most** Czech Republic
71C1 **Mostaganem** Alg
41D2 **Mostar** Bosnia-Herzegovina
28E2 **Mostardos** Brazil
43E2 **Mosty** Belarus
64D2 **Mosul** Iraq
32G7 **Motala** Sweden
34D4 **Motherwell** Scot
61B2 **Motihāri** India
39B2 **Motilla del Palancar** Spain
74D1 **Motloutse** *R* Botswana
37E2 **Motovun** Croatia
39B2 **Motril** Spain
11B2 **Mott** USA
78B2 **Motueka** NZ
78B2 **Motueka** *R* NZ
5H3 **Mouchalagane** *R* Can
37B1 **Moudon** Switz
72B4 **Mouila** Gabon
75B2 **Moulamein** Aust
6G2 **Mould Bay** Can
38C2 **Moulins** France
55B2 **Moulmein** Myanmar
71B2 **Moulouya** *R* Mor
15C2 **Moultrie** USA
15D2 **Moultrie,L** USA
12B3 **Mound City** Illinois, USA
17C1 **Mound City** Missouri, USA
72B3 **Moundou** Chad
12C3 **Moundsville** USA
38C3 **Mount Aigoual** *Mt* France
10N2 **Mountain** *R* Can
15B2 **Mountain Brook** USA
17D2 **Mountain Grove** USA
17D2 **Mountain Home** Arkansas, USA
18C2 **Mountain Home** Idaho, USA
20A2 **Mountain View** USA
10F3 **Mountain Village** USA
14B3 **Mount Airy** Maryland, USA
15C1 **Mount Airy** N Carolina, USA
74D3 **Mount Ayliff** S Africa
14B2 **Mount Carmel** USA
13F2 **Mount Desert I** USA
75A1 **Mount Dutton** Aust
75A2 **Mount Eba** Aust
74D3 **Mount Fletcher** S Africa
75B3 **Mount Gambier** Aust
76D1 **Mount Hagen** PNG
14C3 **Mount Holly** USA
14B2 **Mount Holly Springs** USA
75A2 **Mount Hope** Aust
76C3 **Mount Isa** Aust
14A3 **Mount Jackson** USA
5H4 **Mt Jacques Cartier** Can
14A2 **Mount Jewett** USA
75A2 **Mount Lofty Range** *Mts* Aust
10H3 **Mount McKinley Nat Pk** USA
76A3 **Mount Magnet** Aust
75B2 **Mount Manara** Aust
38C3 **Mount Mézenc** *Mt* France
76E3 **Mount Morgan** Aust
14B1 **Mount Morris** USA
75D1 **Mount Perry** Aust
4E5 **Mt Pleasant** Michigan, USA
17D3 **Mount Pleasant** Texas, USA
19D3 **Mount Pleasant** Utah, USA
14C2 **Mount Pocono** USA
18B1 **Mount Rainier Nat Pk** USA
35C6 **Mounts B** Eng
18B2 **Mount Shasta** USA
14B2 **Mount Union** USA
15B2 **Mount Vernon** Alabama, USA
12B3 **Mount Vernon** Illinois, USA
17C3 **Mount Vernon** Kentucky, USA
18B1 **Mount Vernon** Washington, USA
35B4 **Mourne Mts** N Ire
66D4 **Moussa Ali** *Mt* Djibouti
72B2 **Moussoro** Chad
37B3 **Moustiers Ste Marie** France
60B4 **Mouth of the Indus** Pak
61C3 **Mouths of the Ganga** India/Bang
55D4 **Mouths of the Mekong** Viet
70C4 **Mouths of the Niger** Nigeria
37B1 **Moutier** Switz
37B2 **Moûtiers** France
57B2 **Moutong** Indon
70C2 **Mouydir** *Mts* Alg
72B4 **Mouyondzi** Congo
36C2 **Mouzon** France
22B1 **Moyahua** Mexico
72D3 **Moyale** Kenya
70A4 **Moyamba** Sierra Leone
71A2 **Moyen Atlas** *Mts* Mor
74D3 **Moyeni** Lesotho
49M3 **Moyero** *R* Russian Fed
72D3 **Moyo** Uganda
26C5 **Moyobamba** Peru
60D1 **Moyu** China
73D6 **Mozambique** Republic, Africa
73D6 **Mozambique Chan** Mozam/Madag
44J4 **Mozhga** Russian Fed
32K8 **Mozyr'** Belarus
72D4 **Mpanda** Tanz
73D5 **Mpika** Zambia
73D4 **Mporokosa** Zambia
73C5 **Mposhi** Zambia
73D4 **Mpulungu** Zambia
72D4 **Mpwapwa** Tanz
43G2 **Mstislavl'** Belarus
44F5 **Mtsensk** Russian Fed
74E2 **Mtubatuba** S Africa
73E5 **Mtwara** Tanz
55C2 **Muang Chainat** Thai
55C2 **Muang Chiang Rai** Thai
55C2 **Muang Kalasin** Thai
55C2 **Muang Khon Kaen** Thai
55B2 **Muang Lampang** Thai
55B2 **Muang Lamphun** Thai
55C2 **Muang Loei** Thai
55C2 **Muang Lom Sak** Thai
55C2 **Muang Nakhon Phanom** Thai
55B2 **Muang Nakhon Sawan** Thai
55C2 **Muang Nan** Thai
55C2 **Muang Phayao** Thai
55C2 **Muang Phetchabun** Thai
55C2 **Muang Phichit** Thai
55C2 **Muang Phitsanulok** Thai
55C2 **Muang Phrae** Thai
55C2 **Muang Roi Et** Thai
55C2 **Muang Sakon Nakhon** Thai
55C3 **Muang Samut Prakan** Thai
55C2 **Muang Uthai Thani** Thai
55C2 **Muang Yasothon** Thai
55C5 **Muar** Malay
56D2 **Muara** Brunei
56B3 **Muara** Indon
56B3 **Muaralakitan** Indon
56B3 **Muaratebo** Indon
56E3 **Muaratewah** Indon
56B3 **Muarenim** Indon
55A2 **Muaungmaya** Myanmar
72D3 **Mubende** Uganda
71J3 **Mubi** Nig
73D5 **Muchinga** *Mts* Zambia
34B3 **Muck** *I* Scot
75C1 **Muckadilla** Aust
73C5 **Muconda** Angola
29E2 **Mucuri** Brazil
29D2 **Mucuri** *R* Brazil
73C5 **Mucusso** Angola
53B3 **Mudanjiang** China
67F3 **Mudayy** Oman
11A3 **Muddy Gap P** USA
75C2 **Mudgee** Aust
20D2 **Mud L** USA
55B2 **Mudon** Myanmar
44F3 **Mud'yuga** Russian Fed
77F3 **Mue** Nouvelle Calédonie
73D5 **Mueda** Mozam
73C5 **Mufulira** Zambia
52C4 **Mufu Shan** *Hills* China
Mugadishu = Muqdisho

34D4 **Nith** *R* Scot
57B4 **Nitibe** Indon
43D3 **Nitra** Slovakia
12C3 **Nitro** USA
77J2 **Niue** *I* Pacific O
77G2 **Niulakita** *I* Tuvalu
56D2 **Niut** *Mt* Malay
77G1 **Niutao** *I* Tuvalu
36C1 **Nivelles** Belg
38C2 **Nivernais** Region, France
32L5 **Nivskiy** Russian Fed
62B1 **Nizāmābād** India
65C3 **Nizana** *Hist Site* Israel
44J4 **Nizhnekamskoye Vodokhranilische** *Res* Russian Fed
50C1 **Nizhneudinsk** Russian Fed
44K4 **Nizhniye Sergi** Russian Fed
44G5 **Nizhniy Lomov** Russian Fed
44G4 **Nizhniy Novgorod** Russian Fed
44J3 **Nizhniy Odes** Russian Fed
44K4 **Nizhniy Tagil** Russian Fed
49L3 **Nizhnyaya Tunguska** *R* Russian Fed
44G2 **Nizhnyaya Zolotitsa** Russian Fed
64C2 **Nizip** Turk
73C5 **Njoko** *R* Zambia
73D4 **Njombe** Tanz
72B3 **Nkambé** Cam
71F4 **Nkawkaw** Ghana
73D5 **Nkhata Bay** Malawi
72B3 **Nkongsamba** Cam
70C3 **N'Konni** Niger
61D3 **Noakhali** Bang
10F2 **Noatak** USA
10G2 **Noatak** *R* USA
53C5 **Nobeoka** Japan
54D2 **Noboribetsu** Japan
29A1 **Nobres** Brazil
37D1 **Noce** *R* Italy
22B1 **Nochistlán** Mexico
22C2 **Nochixtlán** Mexico
17C3 **Nocona** USA
21A1 **Nogales** Sonora, Mexico
19D4 **Nogales** USA
22C2 **Nogales** Veracruz, Mexico
37D2 **Nogara** Italy
54B4 **Nogata** Japan
36C2 **Nogent-en-Bassigny** France
36A2 **Nogent-le-Rotrou** France
36B2 **Nogent-sur-Seine** France
44F4 **Noginsk** Russian Fed
53E1 **Nogliki** Russian Fed
28D2 **Nogoyá** Arg
28D2 **Nogoyá** *R* Arg
60C3 **Nohar** India
54D2 **Noheji** Japan
74C1 **Nojane** Botswana
54C4 **Nojima-zaki** *C* Japan
63E3 **Nok Kundi** Pak
3H2 **Nokomis L** Can
72B3 **Nola** CAR
44H4 **Nolinsk** Russian Fed
14E2 **Nomans Land** *I* USA
22B1 **Nombre de Dioz** Mexico
10E3 **Nome** USA
36D2 **Nomeny** France
52B1 **Nomgon** Mongolia
54A4 **Nomo-saki** *Pt* Japan
6H3 **Nonachol L** Can
53B3 **Nong'an** China
55C2 **Nong Khai** Thai
74E2 **Nongoma** S Africa
77G1 **Nonouti** *I* Kiribati
54A3 **Nonsan** S Korea
74B2 **Noordoewer** Namibia
10F2 **Noorvik** USA
3C4 **Nootka Sd** Can
22C2 **Nopala** Mexico
72B4 **Noqui** Angola
7L5 **Noranda** Can
36B1 **Nord** Department, France
48D2 **Nordaustlandet** *I* Barents S
3E3 **Nordegg** Can
32F6 **Nordfjord** *Inlet* Nor
32F8 **Nordfriesische** *Is* Germany
42C2 **Nordhausen** Germany
32J4 **Nordkapp** *C* Nor
7N3 **Nordre Strømfjord** Greenland
42B2 **Nordrhein Westfalen** State, Germany
32G5 **Nord Stronfjället** *Mt* Sweden
49N2 **Nordvik** Russian Fed
35B5 **Nore** *R* Irish Rep
35F5 **Norfolk** County, Eng
11C3 **Norfolk** Nebraska, USA
13D3 **Norfolk** Virginia, USA
77F3 **Norfolk I** Aust
17D2 **Norfolk L** USA
xxixK5 **Norfolk Ridge** Pacific O
49K3 **Noril'sk** Russian Fed
12B2 **Normal** USA
17C2 **Norman** USA
38B2 **Normandie** Region, France
15C1 **Norman,L** USA
76D2 **Normanton** Aust
10N2 **Norman Wells** Can
44B2 **Norra Storfjället** *Mt* Sweden
15C1 **Norris L** USA
13D2 **Norristown** USA
32H7 **Norrköping** Sweden
32H6 **Norrsundet** Sweden
32H7 **Norrtälje** Sweden
76B4 **Norseman** Aust
53C1 **Norsk** Russian Fed
29A1 **Nortelândia** Brazil
xxxJ2 **North** *S* N W Europe
35E4 **Northallerton** Eng
76A4 **Northam** Aust
74D2 **Northam** S Africa
xxxE3 **North American Basin** Atlantic O
76A3 **Northampton** Aust
35E5 **Northampton** County, Eng
35E5 **Northampton** Eng
13E2 **Northampton** USA
62E2 **North Andaman** *I* Indian O
6G3 **North Arm** *B* Can
15C2 **North Augusta** USA
7M4 **North Aulatsivik I** Can
3G3 **North Battleford** Can
7L5 **North Bay** Can
18B2 **North Bend** USA
34D3 **North Berwick** Scot
14E1 **North Berwick** USA
7M5 **North,C** Can
77G4 **North C** NZ
10D5 **North C** USA
16B2 **North Canadian** *R* USA
4C3 **North Caribou L** Can
9E3 **North Carolina** State, USA
18B1 **North Cascade Nat Pk** USA
4E4 **North Chan** Can
34C4 **North Chan** Ire/Scot
14A1 **North Collins** USA
8C2 **North Dakota** State, USA
35F6 **North Downs** Eng
36A1 **North Downs** *Upland* Eng
13D2 **North East** USA
xxxH1 **North East Atlantic Basin** Atlantic O
10E3 **Northeast C** USA
74C2 **Northern Cape** Province, S Africa
4B2 **Northern Indian L** Can
33B3 **Northern Ireland** UK
11D2 **Northern Light L** Can
xxviiiJ3 **Northern Mariana Is** Pacific O
23L1 **Northern Range** *Mts* Trinidad
76C2 **Northern Territory** Aust
74D2 **Northern Transvaal** Province, S Africa
34D3 **North Esk** *R* Scot
14D1 **Northfield** Massachusetts, USA
11D3 **Northfield** Minnesota, USA
35F6 **North Foreland** Eng
36A1 **North Foreland** *Pt* Eng
10H3 **North Fork** *R* USA
4E3 **North French** *R* Can
5K3 **North Head** *C* Can
78B1 **North I** NZ
4B2 **North Knife** *R* Can
53B4 **North Korea** Republic, S E Asia
North Land = Severnaya Zemlya
17D3 **North Little Rock** USA
11B3 **North Loup** *R* USA
79B4 **North Magnetic Pole** Can
15E4 **North Miami** USA
15E4 **North Miami Beach** USA
10O3 **North Nahanni** *R* Can
20C2 **North Palisade** *Mt* USA
16B1 **North Platte** USA
8C2 **North Platte** *R* USA
5J4 **North Pt** *C* Can
79A **North Pole** Arctic
23Q2 **North Pt** Barbados
12C1 **North Pt** USA
11D3 **North Raccoon** *R* USA
33B2 **North Rona** *I* Scot
34D2 **North Ronaldsay** *I* Scot
3G3 **North Saskatchewan** *R* Can
33D2 **North Sea** N W Europe
3H2 **North Seal** *R* Can
62E2 **North Sentinel** Andaman Is
10J2 **North Slope** USA
6D3 **North Slope** *Region* USA
75D1 **North Stradbroke** *I* Aust
14B1 **North Syracuse** USA
78B1 **North Taranaki Bight** *B* NZ
14A1 **North Tonawanda** USA
8C3 **North Truchas Peak** *Mt* USA
4F3 **North Twin I** Can
34B3 **North Uist** *I* Scot
34D4 **Northumberland** County, Eng
76E3 **Northumberland Is** Aust
7M5 **Northumberland Str** Can
18B1 **North Vancouver** Can
14C1 **Northville** USA
35F5 **North Walsham** Eng
10K3 **Northway** USA
74C2 **North West** Province, S Africa
76A3 **North West C** Aust
60C2 **North West Frontier** Province, Pak
7M4 **North West River** Can
6G3 **North West Territories** Can
11C2 **Northwood** USA
35E4 **North York Moors Nat Pk** Eng
16C2 **Norton** *R* USA
10F3 **Norton B** USA
10F3 **Norton Sd** USA
79F1 **Norvegia,C** Ant
14D2 **Norwalk** Connecticut, USA
12C2 **Norwalk** Ohio, USA
32F6 **Norway** Kingdom, Europe
6J4 **Norway House** Can
7J2 **Norwegian B** Can
xxxH1 **Norwegian Basin** Norewegian S
48B3 **Norwegian S** N W Europe
14D2 **Norwich** Connecticut, USA
35F5 **Norwich** Eng
14C1 **Norwich** New York, USA
14E1 **Norwood** Massachusetts, USA
12C3 **Norwood** Ohio, USA
41F2 **Nos Emine** *C* Bulg
53D3 **Noshiro** Japan
41F2 **Nos Kaliakra** *C* Bulg
44J2 **Nosovaya** Russian Fed
43G2 **Nosovka** Ukraine
34E1 **Noss** *I* Scot
74B1 **Nossob** *R* Namibia
63E3 **Nostrābād** Iran
73E5 **Nosy Barren** *I* Madag
73E5 **Nosy Bé** *I* Madag
73F5 **Nosy Boraha** *I* Madag
73E6 **Nosy Varika** Madag
42D2 **Notéc** *R* Pol
6G4 **Notikewin** Can
40D3 **Noto** Italy
32F7 **Notodden** Nor
54C3 **Noto-hantō** *Pen* Japan
7N5 **Notre Dame B** Can
4E5 **Nottawasaga B** Can
4F3 **Nottaway** *R* Can
35E5 **Nottingham** County, Eng
35E5 **Nottingham** Eng
7L3 **Nottingham I** Can
11A2 **Notukeu Creek** *R* Can
70A2 **Nouadhibou** Maur
70A3 **Nouakchott** Maur
77F3 **Nouméa** Nouvelle Calédonie
71F3 **Nouna** Burkina
74C3 **Noupoort** S Africa
77F3 **Nouvelle Calédonie** *I* S W Pacific O
29C2 **Nova América** Brazil
73B4 **Nova Caipemba** Angola
29B3 **Nova Esperança** Brazil
29D3 **Nova Friburgo** Brazil
73B5 **Nova Gaia** Angola
29C3 **Nova Granada** Brazil
29C3 **Nova Herizonte** Brazil
29D3 **Nova Lima** Brazil
Nova Lisboa = Huambo
29B3 **Nova Londrina** Brazil
73D6 **Nova Mambone** Mozam
37C2 **Novara** Italy
29C1 **Nova Roma** Brazil
57C4 **Nova Sagres** Indon
7M5 **Nova Scotia** Province, Can
20A1 **Novato** USA
29D2 **Nova Venécia** Brazil
45E6 **Novaya Kakhovka** Ukraine
49R2 **Novaya Sibir, Ostrov** *I* Russian Fed
48G2 **Novaya Zemlya** *I* Russian Fed
41F2 **Nova Zagora** Bulg
27K4 **Nove Russas** Brazil
41D1 **Nové Zámky** Slovakia
44E4 **Novgorod** Russian Fed
37E2 **Novigrad** Croatia
53E2 **Novikovo** Russian Fed
37C2 **Novi Ligure** Italy
22A1 **Novillero** Mexico
41F2 **Novi Pazar** Bulg
41E2 **Novi Pazar** Serbia, Yugos
41D1 **Novi Sad** Serbia, Yugos
45K5 **Novoalekseyevka** Kazakhstan
45G5 **Novoanninskiy** Russian Fed
53C2 **Novobureyskiy** Russian Fed
45G6 **Novocherkassk** Russian Fed
44G3 **Novodvinsk** Russian Fed
43G2 **Novogorod** Belarus
45D5 **Novograd Volynskiy** Ukraine
43F2 **Novogrudok** Belarus
28E1 **Novo Hamburgo** Brazil
48H5 **Novokazalinsk** Kazakhstan
48K4 **Novokuznetsk** Russian Fed
79F12 **Novolazarevskaya** *Base* Ant
40D1 **Novo Mesto** Slovenia, Yugos
43G3 **Novomirgorod** Ukraine
44F5 **Novomoskovsk** Russian Fed
Novo Redondo = Sumbe
45F7 **Novorossiysk** Russian Fed
49M2 **Novorybnoye** Russian Fed
48K4 **Novosibirsk** Russian Fed
49P2 **Novosibirskye Ostrova** *Is* Russian Fed
45K5 **Novotroitsk** Russian Fed
45H5 **Novo Uzensk** Russian Fed
43E2 **Novovolynsk** Ukraine
44H4 **Novo Vyatsk** Russian Fed
45E5 **Novozybkov** Russian Fed
48J3 **Novvy Port** Russian Fed
43E2 **Novy Dwór Mazowiecki** Pol
44L4 **Novyy Lyalya** Russian Fed
44N2 **Novyy Port** Russian Fed
45J7 **Novyy Uzen** Kazakhstan
42D2 **Nowa Sól** Pol
17C2 **Nowata** USA
10H3 **Nowitna** *R* USA
75D2 **Nowra** Aust
63C1 **Now Shahr** Iran
60C2 **Nowshera** Pak
43E3 **Nowy Sącz** Pol
10M4 **Noyes I** USA
36B2 **Noyon** France
71F4 **Nsawam** Ghana
71H4 **Nsukka** Nig
74E1 **Nuanetsi** Zim
74E1 **Nuanetsi** *R* Zim
71G4 **Nuatja** Togo
72D2 **Nuba** *Mts* Sudan
66B2 **Nubian Desert** Sudan
28A3 **Nuble** *R* Chile
8D4 **Nueces** *R* USA
6J3 **Nueltin L** Can
21B1 **Nueva Casas Grandes** Mexico
29A3 **Nueva Germania** Par
23A2 **Nueva Gerona** Cuba
28A3 **Nueva Imperial** Chile
28D2 **Nueva Palmira** Urug
21B2 **Nueva Rosita** Mexico
23B2 **Nuevitas** Cuba
22B1 **Nuevo** State, Mexico
21B1 **Nuevo Casas Grandes** Mexico
22A1 **Nuevo Ideal** Mexico
21C2 **Nuevo Laredo** Mexico
69D4 **Nugaal** Region, Somalia
7N2 **Nûgâtsiaq** Greenland
7N2 **Nûgussuaq** *Pen* Greenland
7N2 **Nûgussuaq** *I* Greenland
77G1 **Nui** *I* Tuvalu
52A5 **Nui Con Voi** *R* Vietnam
36C3 **Nuits** France
61E2 **Nu Jiang** *R* China
75A2 **Nukey Bluff** *Mt* Aust
64D3 **Nukhayb** Iraq
77G1 **Nukufetau** *I* Tuvalu
77G1 **Nukulaelae** *I* Tuvalu
77H1 **Nukunon** *I* Tokelau Is
48G5 **Nukus** Uzbekistan
10G3 **Nulato** USA
76B4 **Nullarbor Plain** Aust
71J4 **Numan** Nig
54C3 **Numata** Japan
72C3 **Numatinna** *R* Sudan
53D4 **Numazu** Japan
51G7 **Numfoor** *I* Indon
75C3 **Numurkah** Aust
10F3 **Nunapitchuk** USA
14A1 **Nunda** USA
10E3 **Nunivak I** USA
60D2 **Nunkun** *Mt* India
10C3 **Nunligran** Russian Fed
53A1 **Nuomin He** *R* China
40B2 **Nuoro** Sardegna
63C2 **Nurābād** Iran
37C2 **Nure** *R* Italy
75A2 **Nuriootpa** Aust
60C1 **Nuristan** *Upland* Afghan
44J5 **Nurlat** Russian Fed
32K6 **Nurmes** Fin
42C3 **Nürnberg** Germany
75C2 **Nurri,Mt** Aust
56E4 **Nusa Tenggara** *Is* Indon
57B4 **Nusa Tenggara Timor** Province, Indon
64D2 **Nusaybin** Turk
10G4 **Nushagak** *R* USA
10G4 **Nushagak B** USA
10G4 **Nushagak Pen** USA
60B3 **Nushki** Pak
7M4 **Nutak** Can
10K3 **Nutzotin Mts** USA
Nuuk = Godthåb
7L3 **Nuvukjuak** Can
61B2 **Nuwakot** Nepal
62C3 **Nuwara-Eliya** Sri Lanka
74C3 **Nuweveldreeks** *Mts* S Africa
45C3 **Nyac** USA
14D2 **Nyack** USA
72D3 **Nyahururu Falls** Kenya
75B3 **Nyah West** Aust
50C3 **Nyaingentanglha Shan** *Mts* China
72D4 **Nyakabindi** Tanz
44L3 **Nyaksimvol'** Russian Fed
72C2 **Nyala** Sudan
61C2 **Nyalam** China
72C3 **Nyamlell** Sudan
73D6 **Nyanda** Zim
44G3 **Nyandoma** Russian Fed
72B4 **Nyanga** *R* Gabon
61D2 **Nyang Qu** China
73D5 **Nyasa L** Malawi/Mozam
55B2 **Nyaunglebin** Myanmar
44K4 **Nyazepetrovsk** Russian Fed
32G7 **Nyborg** Den
32H7 **Nybro** Sweden
48J3 **Nyda** Russian Fed
7M1 **Nyeboes Land** *Region* Can
61D1 **Nyenchentanglha Range** *Mts* China
72D4 **Nyeri** Kenya
73D5 **Nyimba** Zambia
59H2 **Nyingchi** China
43E3 **Nyiregyháza** Hung
72D3 **Nyiru,Mt** Kenya
32J6 **Nykarleby** Fin
32F7 **Nykøbing** Den
32G8 **Nykøbing** Den
32H7 **Nyköping** Sweden
74D1 **Nyl** *R* S Africa
74D1 **Nylstroom** S Africa
75C2 **Nymagee** Aust
32H7 **Nynäshamn** Sweden
75C2 **Nyngan** Aust
37B1 **Nyon** Switz
72B3 **Nyong** *R* Cam
54A3 **Nyongwol** S Korea
54A3 **Nyongwon** N Korea
38D3 **Nyons** France
42D2 **Nysa** Pol
53E1 **Nysh** Russian Fed
18C2 **Nyssa** USA
44H3 **Nyukhcha** Russian Fed
50F1 **Nyukzha** *R* Russian Fed
49N3 **Nyurba** Russian Fed
72D4 **Nzega** Tanz
70B4 **Nzérékore** Guinea
73B4 **N'zeto** Angola
71F4 **Nzi** *R* Côte d'Ivoire

O

11C3 **Oacoma** USA
11B3 **Oahe,L** *Res* USA
20E5 **Oahu,I** Hawaiian Is
75B2 **Oakbank** Aust
20B2 **Oakdale** USA
11C2 **Oakes** USA
75D1 **Oakey** Aust
19B3 **Oakland** California, USA
11C3 **Oakland** Nebraska, USA
18B2 **Oakland** Oregon, USA
12B3 **Oakland City** USA
12B2 **Oak Lawn** USA
20B2 **Oakley** California, USA
16B2 **Oakley** Kansas, USA
15C1 **Oak Ridge** USA
18B2 **Oakridge** USA
4F5 **Oakville** Can
78B3 **Oamaru** NZ
20D2 **Oasis** California, USA
18D2 **Oasis** Nevada, USA
79F7 **Oates Land** Region, Ant
75E3 **Oatlands** Aust
22C2 **Oaxaca** Mexico
22C2 **Oaxaca** State, Mexico
48H3 **Ob'** *R* Russian Fed
4E4 **Oba** Can
54C3 **Obama** Japan
78A3 **Oban** NZ
34C3 **Oban** Scot

Ostróda
Paropamisus

43D2 **Ostróda** Pol
43E2 **Ostrołęka** Pol
44D4 **Ostrov** Russian Fed
43E2 **Ostrowiec** Pol
43E2 **Ostrów Mazowiecka** Pol
43D2 **Ostrów Wielkopolski** Pol
53C5 **Ōsumi-kaikyō** *Str* Japan
53C5 **Ōsumi-shotō** *Is* Japan
71G4 **Osun** *State* Nigeria
39A2 **Osuna** Spain
14B1 **Oswego** USA
14B1 **Oswego** *R* USA
35D5 **Oswestry** Eng
43D3 **Oświęcim** Pol
54C3 **Ota** Japan
78B3 **Otago Pen** NZ
78C2 **Otaki** NZ
53E3 **Otaru** Japan
26C3 **Otavalo** Ecuador
73B5 **Otavi** Namibia
54D3 **Otawara** Japan
14C1 **Otego** USA
18C1 **Othello** USA
3G2 **Otherside** *R* Can
41E3 **Óthris** *Mt* Greece
71G4 **Oti** *R* Ghana
71G4 **Otiki** *R* Nig
16B1 **Otis** Colorado, USA
14D1 **Otis** Massachusetts, USA
14C2 **Otisville** USA
74B1 **Otjimbingwe** Namibia
73B6 **Otjiwarongo** Namibia
52B2 **Otog Qi** China
54D2 **Otoineppu** Japan
78C1 **Otorohanga** NZ
41D2 **Otranto** Italy
41D2 **Otranto,Str of** *Chan* Italy/Alb
12B2 **Otsego** USA
14C1 **Otsego L** USA
4E5 **Otsego Lake** USA
54C3 **Otsu** Japan
32F6 **Otta** Nor
32F7 **Otta** *R* Nor
4F4 **Ottawa** Can
4F4 **Ottawa** *R* Can
12B2 **Ottawa** Illinois, USA
17C2 **Ottawa** Kansas, USA
7K4 **Ottawa Is** Can
7K4 **Otter Rapids** Can
7K1 **Otto Fjord** Can
74D2 **Ottosdal** S Africa
12A2 **Ottumwa** USA
36D2 **Ottweiler** Germany
71H4 **Otukpa** Nig
71H4 **Oturkpo** Nig
26C5 **Otusco** Peru
75B3 **Otway,C** Aust
43E2 **Otwock** Pol
37D1 **Ötz** Austria
37D1 **Otzal** *Mts* Austria
55C1 **Ou** *R* Laos
17D3 **Ouachita** *R* USA
17D3 **Ouachita,L** USA
17D3 **Ouachita Mts** USA
70A2 **Ouadane** Maur
72C3 **Ouadda** CAR
72C2 **Ouaddai** *Desert Region* Chad
71F3 **Ouagadougou** Burkina
71F3 **Ouahigouya** Burkina
72C3 **Ouaka** CAR
70C3 **Oualam** Niger
71G3 **Oualé** *R* Burkina
70C2 **Ouallen** Alg
72C3 **Ouanda Djallé** CAR
36B3 **Ouanne** *R* France
70A2 **Ouarane** Region, Maur
70C1 **Ouargla** Alg
72C3 **Ouarra** *R* CAR
70B1 **Ouarzazate** Mor
39C2 **Ouassel** *R* Alg
72B3 **Oubangui** *R* Congo
36B1 **Oudenaarde** Belg
74C3 **Oudtshoorn** S Africa
39B2 **Oued Tlêlat** Alg
71A2 **Oued Zem** Mor
71F4 **Ouellé** Côte d'Ivoire
72B3 **Ouesso** Congo
71A2 **Ouezzane** Mor
72B3 **Ouham** *R* Chad
71G4 **Ouidah** Benin
4D4 **Ouimet** Can
71B2 **Oujda** Mor
32J6 **Oulainen** Fin
32K5 **Oulu** Fin
32K6 **Oulu** *R* Fin
32K6 **Oulujärvi** *L* Fin
72C2 **Oum Chalouba** Chad
71D1 **Oum el Bouaghi** Alg
71A2 **Oumer Rbia** *R* Mor
72B2 **Oum Hadjer** Chad
72C2 **Oum Haouach** *Watercourse* Chad
32K5 **Ounas** *R* Fin
44C2 **Ounasjoki** *R* Fin
44C2 **Ounastunturi** *Mt* Fin
72C2 **Ounianga Kebir** Chad
36D1 **Our** *R* Germany
16A2 **Ouray** USA
36C2 **Ource** *R* France
Ourense = Orense
36B2 **Ourcq** *R* France
27K5 **Ouricurí** Brazil
29C3 **Ourinhos** Brazil
29D3 **Ouro Prêto** Brazil
36C1 **Ourthe** *R* Belg
35E4 **Ouse** *R* Eng
35F5 **Ouse** *R* Eng
33B2 **Outer Hebrides** *Is* Scot
20C4 **Outer Santa Barbara** *Chan* USA
73B6 **Outjo** Namibia
3G3 **Outlook** Can
32K6 **Outokumpu** Fin
37A2 **Ouvèze** *R* France
75B3 **Ouyen** Aust
37C2 **Ovada** Italy
28A2 **Ovalle** Chile
73B5 **Ovamboland** Region, Namibia
19D3 **Overton** USA
32J5 **Övertorneå** Sweden
16B1 **Ovid** Colorado, USA
14B1 **Ovid** New York, USA
39A1 **Oviedo** Spain
45D5 **Ovruch** Ukraine
49O4 **Ovsyanka** Russian Fed
78A3 **Owaka** NZ
14B1 **Owasco L** USA
54C4 **Owase** Japan
11D3 **Owatonna** USA
14B1 **Owego** USA
20C2 **Owens** *R* USA
12B3 **Owensboro** USA
20D2 **Owens L** USA
4E5 **Owen Sound** Can
76D1 **Owen Stanley Range** *Mts* PNG
71H4 **Owerri** Nig
4C2 **Owl** *R* Can
18E2 **Owl Creek Mts** USA
71H4 **Owo** Nig
12C2 **Owosso** USA
18C2 **Owyhee** USA
18C2 **Owyhee** *R* USA
18C2 **Owyhee Mts** USA
26C6 **Oxampampa** Peru
3H4 **Oxbow** Can
32H7 **Oxelösund** Sweden
35E6 **Oxford** County, Eng
35E5 **Oxford** Eng
14E1 **Oxford** Massachusetts, USA
17E3 **Oxford** Mississippi, USA
14C1 **Oxford** New York, USA
20C3 **Oxnard** USA
53D4 **Oyama** Japan
3F3 **Oyen** Can
72B3 **Oyen** Gabon
34C3 **Oykel** *R* Scot
49Q3 **Oymyakon** Russian Fed
71G4 **Oyo** Nig
37A1 **Oyonnax** France
32F6 **Øyre** Nor
75E3 **Oyster B** Aust
57F9 **Ozamiz** Phil
43F2 **Ozarichi** Belarus
15B2 **Ozark** USA
17D2 **Ozark Plat** USA
17D2 **Ozarks,L of the** USA
43E3 **Ózd** Hung
53E2 **Ozerskiy** Russian Fed
16B3 **Ozona** USA
22C1 **Ozuluama** Mexico
64D1 **Ozurgeti** Georgia

P

74B3 **Paarl** S Africa
34B3 **Pabbay** *I* Scot
43D2 **Pabianice** Pol
61C3 **Pabna** Bang
43F1 **Pabrade** Lithuania
26C5 **Pacasmayo** Peru
28E2 **Pacheca** Brazil
22B1 **Pacheco** Mexico
22C1 **Pachuca** Mexico
20B1 **Pacific** USA
xxixN7 **Pacific-Antarctic Ridge** Pacific O
20B2 **Pacific Grove** USA
xxixG8 **Pacific O**
56D4 **Pacitan** Indon
29D2 **Pacuí** *R* Brazil
56B3 **Padang** Indon
57B4 **Padang** Indon
56B3 **Padangpanjang** Indon
56A2 **Padangsidempuan** Indon
44E3 **Padany** Russian Fed
42B2 **Paderborn** Germany
6J3 **Padlei** Can
61D3 **Padma** *R* Bang
37D2 **Padova** Italy
8D4 **Padre I** USA
35C6 **Padstow** Eng
75B3 **Padthaway** Aust
Padua = Padova
12B3 **Paducah** Kentucky, USA
16B3 **Paducah** Texas, USA
32L5 **Padunskoye More** *L* Russian Fed
54A2 **Paegam** N Korea
53A4 **Paengnyŏng-do** *I* S Korea
78C1 **Paeroa** NZ
74E1 **Pafuri** Mozam
40C2 **Pag** *I* Croatia
57F9 **Pagadian** Phil
56B3 **Pagai Seletan** *I* Indon
56B3 **Pagai Utara** *I* Indon
51H5 **Pagan** *I* Pacific O
56E3 **Pagatan** Indon
19D3 **Page** USA
51F8 **Pago Mission** Aust
41F3 **Pagondhas** Greece
16A2 **Pagosa Springs** USA
4C4 **Paguchi L** Can
4D3 **Pagwa River** Can
20E5 **Pahala** Hawaiian Is
78C2 **Pahiatua** NZ
20E5 **Pahoa** Hawaiian Is
15E4 **Pahokee** USA
71J4 **Pai** *R* Nig
32K6 **Päijänna** *L* Fin
28A4 **Paillaco** Chile
20E5 **Pailola Chan** Hawaiian Is
12C2 **Painesville** USA
19D3 **Painted Desert** USA
12C3 **Paintsville** USA
34C4 **Paisley** Scot
26B5 **Paita** Peru
32J5 **Pajala** Sweden
57B4 **Pajeti** Indon
58E3 **Pakistan** Republic, Asia
55C2 **Pak Lay** Laos
61E3 **Pakokku** Myanmar
3F4 **Pakowki L** Can
40D1 **Pakrac** Croatia
41D1 **Paks** Hung
55C2 **Pak Sane** Laos
55D2 **Pakse** Laos
72D3 **Pakwach** Uganda
72B3 **Pala** Chad
40D2 **Palagruža** *I* Croatia
36B2 **Palaiseau** France
Palakhat = Pālghāt
74D1 **Palala** *R* S Africa
62E2 **Palalankwe** Andaman Is
49S4 **Palana** Russian Fed
56D3 **Palangkaraya** Indon
62B2 **Palani** India
60C4 **Palanpur** India
74D1 **Palapye** Botswana
15C3 **Palatka** USA
51G6 **Palau Is** Pacific O
55B3 **Palaw** Myanmar
57E9 **Palawan** *I* Phil
57E9 **Palawan Pass** Phil
62B3 **Palayankottai** India
32J7 **Paldiski** Estonia
57B2 **Paleleh** Indon
56B3 **Palembang** Indon
39B1 **Palencia** Spain
65B1 **Paleokhorio** Cyprus
40C3 **Palermo** Italy
17C3 **Palestine** USA
61D3 **Paletwa** Myanmar
62B2 **Pālghāt** India
60C3 **Pāli** India
71G4 **Palimé** Togo
56E1 **Palin,Mt** Malay
16A2 **Palisade** USA
60C4 **Pālitāna** India
62B3 **Palk Str** India/Sri Lanka
45H5 **Pallasovka** Russian Fed
32J5 **Pallastunturi** *Mt* Fin
78B2 **Palliser B** NZ
78C2 **Palliser,C** NZ
73E5 **Palma** Mozam
39C2 **Palma de Mallorca** Spain
27L5 **Palmares** Brazil
28E2 **Palmares do Sul** Brazil
23A5 **Palmar Sur** Costa Rica
29B4 **Palmas** Brazil
70B4 **Palmas,C** Lib
29D1 **Palmas de Monte Alto** Brazil
23B2 **Palma Soriano** Cuba
15C3 **Palm Bay** USA
15E4 **Palm Beach** USA
20C3 **Palmdale** USA
29C4 **Palmeira** Brazil
27L5 **Palmeira dos Indos** Brazil
10J3 **Palmer** USA
79G3 **Palmer** *Base* Ant
79G3 **Palmer Arch** Ant
79F3 **Palmer Land** *Region* Ant
78B3 **Palmerston** NZ
78C2 **Palmerston North** NZ
14C2 **Palmerton** USA
15E4 **Palmetto** USA
40D3 **Palmi** Italy
28E1 **Palmiera das Missões** Brazil
22C1 **Palmillas** Mexico
26C3 **Palmira** Colombia
76D2 **Palm Is** Aust
4E5 **Palms** USA
19C4 **Palm Springs** USA
12A3 **Palmyra** Missouri, USA
14B1 **Palmyra** New York, USA
14B2 **Palmyra** Pennsylvania, USA
61C3 **Palmyras Pt** India
20A2 **Palo Alto** USA
56C2 **Paloh** Indon
72D2 **Paloích** Sudan
22C2 **Palomares** Mexico
19C4 **Palomar Mt** USA
57B3 **Palopo** Indon
57A3 **Palu** Indon
64C2 **Palu** Turk
60D3 **Palwal** India
10B2 **Palyavaam** *R* Russian Fed
71G3 **Pama** Burkina
56D4 **Pamekasan** Indon
56C4 **Pameungpeuk** Indon
38C3 **Pamiers** France
59F2 **Pamir** *Mts* China
48J6 **Pamir** *R* Russian Fed
15D1 **Pamlico** *R* USA
15D1 **Pamlico Sd** USA
16B2 **Pampa** USA
28B2 **Pampa de la Salinas** *Salt pan* Arg
28B3 **Pampa de la Varita** *Plain* Arg
57B3 **Pampanua** Indon
28D2 **Pampeiro** Brazil
26D2 **Pamplona** Colombia
39B1 **Pamplona** Spain
12B3 **Pana** USA
19D3 **Panaca** USA
41E2 **Panagyurishte** Bulg
62A1 **Panaji** India
26C2 **Panamá** Panama
26B2 **Panama** Republic, C America
23B5 **Panama Canal** Panama
15B2 **Panama City** USA
19C3 **Panamint Range** *Mts* USA
20D2 **Panamint V** USA
37D2 **Panaro** *R* Italy
57F8 **Panay** *I* Phil
41E2 **Pancevo** Serbia, Yugos
57F8 **Pandan** Phil
62B1 **Pandharpur** India
75A1 **Pandie Pandie** Aust
43E1 **Panevežys** Lithuania
48K5 **Panfilov** Kazakhstan
55B1 **Pang** *R* Myanmar
72D4 **Pangani** Tanz
72D4 **Pangani** *R* Tanz
72C4 **Pangi** Zaïre
57A3 **Pangkajene** Indon
56C3 **Pangkalpinang** Indon
7M3 **Pangnirtung** Can
55B1 **Pangtara** Myanmar
19D3 **Panguitch** USA
57F9 **Pangutaran Group** *Is* Phil
16B2 **Panhandle** USA
60D3 **Panipat** India
60B2 **Panjao** Afghan
63E3 **Panjgur** Pak
10F5 **Pankof,C** USA
71H4 **Pankshin** Nig
53B4 **P'anmunjŏm** N Korea
61B3 **Panna** India
29B3 **Panorama** Brazil
29A2 **Pantanal de São Lourenço** *Swamp* Brazil
29A2 **Pantanal do Rio Negro** *Swamp* Brazil
29A2 **Pantanal do Taquari** *Swamp* Brazil
57B4 **Pantar** *I* Indon
40C3 **Pantelleria** *I* Medit S
22C1 **Pantepec** Mexico
22C1 **Panuco** Mexico
22C1 **Pánuco** *R* Mexico
52A4 **Pan Xian** China
40D3 **Paola** Italy
17D2 **Paola** USA
12B3 **Paoli** USA
42D3 **Papa** Hung
20E5 **Papaikou** Hawaiian Is
78B1 **Papakura** NZ
22C2 **Papaloapan** *R* Mexico
22C1 **Papantla** Mexico
34E1 **Papa Stour** *I* Scot
78B1 **Papatoetoe** NZ
34D2 **Papa Westray** *I* Scot
65B1 **Paphos** Cyprus
76D1 **Papua,G of** PNG
76D1 **Papua New Guinea** Republic, S E Asia
28A2 **Papudo** Chile
55B2 **Papun** Myanmar
27H4 **Para** State, Brazil
27J4 **Pará** *R* Brazil
76A3 **Paraburdoo** Aust
26C6 **Paracas,Pen de** Peru
29C2 **Paracatu** Brazil
29C2 **Paracatu** *R* Brazil
55E2 **Paracel Is** S E Asia
75A2 **Parachilna** Aust
60C2 **Parachinar** Pak
41E2 **Paracin** Serbia, Yugos
29D2 **Pará de Minas** Brazil
19B3 **Paradise** California, USA
19D3 **Paradise** Nevada, USA
5K3 **Paradise** *R* Can
20D1 **Paradise Peak** *Mt* USA
17D2 **Paragould** USA
26F6 **Paraguá** *R* Bol
26F2 **Paragua** *R* Ven
29D1 **Paraguaçu** *R* Brazil
27G7 **Paraguai** *R* Brazil
29A4 **Paraguari** Par
25E2 **Paraguay** Republic, S America
25E2 **Paraguay** *R* Par
27L5 **Paraiba** State, Brazil
29D3 **Paraiba do Sul** *R* Brazil
22D2 **Paraiso** Mexico
71G4 **Parakou** Benin
75A2 **Parakylia** Aust
62B3 **Paramakkudi** India
27G2 **Paramaribo** Suriname
29D1 **Paramirim** Brazil
49R4 **Paramushir, Ostrov** *I* Russian Fed
29B4 **Paraná** Brazil
25F2 **Paraná** State, Brazil
28C2 **Paraná** Urug
25E4 **Paraná** *R* Arg
27J6 **Paranã** *R* Brazil
29C4 **Paranaguá** Brazil
29B2 **Paranaiba** Brazil
29B2 **Paranaiba** *R* Brazil
29B3 **Paranapanema** *R* Brazil
29B3 **Paranavai** Brazil
57F9 **Parang** Phil
29D2 **Paraope** *R* Brazil
78B2 **Paraparaumu** NZ
29D1 **Paratinga** Brazil
62B1 **Parbhani** India
71G3 **Parc National d'Arly** Burkina
71F4 **Parc National de la Komoé** Côte d'Ivoire
71G3 **Parc National de la Pendjari** Benin
71G3 **Parcs Nationaux du W** Benin
65C2 **Pardes Hanna** Israel
28D3 **Pardo** Arg
29E2 **Pardo** *R* Bahia, Brazil
29B3 **Pardo** *R* Mato Grosso do Sul, Brazil
29C2 **Pardo** *R* Minas Gerais, Brazil
29C3 **Pardo** *R* Sao Paulo, Brazil
42D2 **Pardubice** Czech Republic
50G4 **Parece Vela** *Reef* Pacific O
29A1 **Parecis** Brazil
4G4 **Parent** Can
57A3 **Parepare** Indon
28C3 **Parera** Arg
56B3 **Pariaman** Indon
26F1 **Paria,Pen de** Ven
57B3 **Parigi** Indon
38C2 **Paris** France
12C3 **Paris** Kentucky, USA
15B1 **Paris** Tennessee, USA
17C3 **Paris** Texas, USA
19D4 **Parker** USA
12C3 **Parkersburg** USA
75C2 **Parkes** Aust
14C3 **Parkesburg** USA
12A1 **Park Falls** USA
20B3 **Parkfield** USA
12B2 **Park Forest** USA
11C2 **Park Rapids** USA
11C3 **Parkston** USA
18B1 **Parksville** Can
18D2 **Park Valley** USA
62C1 **Parlākimidi** India
62B1 **Parli** India
37D2 **Parma** Italy
12C2 **Parma** USA
27K4 **Parnaiba** Brazil
27K4 **Parnaiba** *R* Brazil
41E3 **Párnon Óros** *Mts* Greece
44C4 **Pärnu** Estonia
61C2 **Paro** Bhutan
75B1 **Paroo** *R* Aust
75B2 **Paroo Channel** *R* Aust
63E2 **Paropamisus** *Mts* Afghan

Picún Leufú

Portland

28A3 **Picún Leufú** *R* Arg
29C3 **Piedade** Brazil
20C2 **Piedra** USA
28B4 **Piedra de Aguila** Arg
20B3 **Piedras Blancas,Pt** USA
21B2 **Piedras Negras** Mexico
12B1 **Pie I** Can
32K6 **Pieksämäki** Fin
32K6 **Pielinen** *L* Fin
37B2 **Piemonte** Region, Italy
74D2 **Pienaarsrivier** S Africa
11B3 **Pierre** USA
43D3 **Piešťany** Slovakia
74E2 **Pietermaritzburg** S Africa
74D1 **Pietersburg** S Africa
37D3 **Pietrasanta** Italy
74E2 **Piet Retief** S Africa
45C6 **Pietrosu** *Mt* Rom
41F1 **Pietrosul** *Mt* Rom
37E1 **Pieve di Cadore** Italy
51H6 **Pigailoe** *I* Pacific O
3F3 **Pigeon L** Can
17D2 **Piggott** USA
28C3 **Pigüé** Arg
22D2 **Pijijapan** Mexico
4C3 **Pikangikum** Can
7J4 **Pikangikum L** Can
16A2 **Pikes Peak** USA
74B3 **Piketberg** S Africa
12C3 **Pikeville** USA
7O3 **Pikiutaleq** Greenland
59F2 **Pik Kommunizma** *Mt* Tajikistan
72B3 **Pikounda** Congo
59G1 **Pik Pobedy** *Mt* China/ Kyrgyzstan
28D3 **Pila** Arg
42D2 **Pila** Pol
25E3 **Pilar** Par
25D2 **Pilcomayo** *R* Arg/Par
74E1 **Pilgrim's Rest** S Africa
60D3 **Pīlībhīt** India
43D2 **Pilica** *R* Pol
75E3 **Pillar,C** Aust
41E3 **Pílos** Greece
18C1 **Pilot Knob Mt** USA
20D1 **Pilot Peak** *Mt* USA
10G4 **Pilot Point** USA
10F3 **Pilot Station** USA
17E3 **Pilottown** USA
27G4 **Pimenta** Brazil
55C4 **Pinang** *I* Malay
23A2 **Pinar del Rio** Cuba
28B2 **Pinas** Arg
36C1 **Pinche** Belg
3F4 **Pincher Creek** Can
27J4 **Pindaré** *R* Brazil
41E3 **Píndhos** *Mts* Greece
17D3 **Pine Bluff** USA
16B1 **Pine Bluffs** USA
5L4 **Pine,C** Can
11D2 **Pine City** USA
76C2 **Pine Creek** Aust
14B2 **Pine Creek** *R* USA
20C1 **Pinecrest** USA
20C2 **Pinedale** California, USA
18E2 **Pinedale** Wyoming, USA
4B3 **Pine Falls** Can
20C2 **Pine Flat Res** USA
44G3 **Pinega** Russian Fed
44H3 **Pinega** *R* Russian Fed
14B2 **Pine Grove** USA
15C3 **Pine Hills** USA
3G2 **Pinehouse L** Can
15D1 **Pinehurst** USA
15E4 **Pine I** USA
17D3 **Pineland** USA
15C3 **Pinellas Park** USA
20B3 **Pine Mt** USA
3F1 **Pine Point** Can
11B3 **Pine Ridge** USA
4C4 **Pine River** USA
37B2 **Pinerolo** Italy
17D3 **Pines,Lo'the** USA
17D3 **Pineville** USA
52C3 **Pingdingshan** China
52B5 **Pingguo** China
52B2 **Pingliang** China
52B2 **Pingluo** China
52D4 **Pingtan Dao** *I* China
52E5 **P'ing tung** Taiwan
52A3 **Pingwu** China
52B5 **Pingxiang** Guangxi, China
52C4 **Pingxiang** Jiangxi, China
27J4 **Pinheiro** Brazil
28E2 **Pinheiro Machado** Brazil
56A2 **Pini** *I* Indon
41E3 **Piniós** *R* Greece
57B2 **Pinjang** Indon
76A4 **Pinjarra** Aust
3D2 **Pink Mountain** Can
75B3 **Pinnaroo** Aust
Pinos,I de = Isla de la Juventud
20C3 **Pinos,Mt** USA
19B3 **Pinos,Pt** USA
22C2 **Pinotepa Nacional** Mexico
57A3 **Pinrang** Indon
45D5 **Pinsk** Belarus
28C1 **Pinto** Arg
44H3 **Pinyug** Russian Fed
19D3 **Pioche** USA
40C2 **Piombino** Italy
49K2 **Pioner, Ostrov** *I* Russian Fed
18D1 **Pioneer Mts** USA
44L3 **Pionerskiy** Russian Fed
43D2 **Piotrków Trybunalski** Pol
34F2 **Piper** *Oilfield* N Sea
20D2 **Piper Peak** *Mt* USA
11C3 **Pipestone** USA
4C3 **Pipestone** *R* Can
28D3 **Pipinas** Arg
5M4 **Pipmudcan, Réservoir** *Res* Can
12C2 **Piqua** USA
29B4 **Piquiri** *R* Brazil
29C2 **Piracanjuba** Brazil
29C3 **Piracicaba** Brazil
29C3 **Piraçununga** Brazil
29C3 **Pirai do Sul** Brazil
41E3 **Piraiévs** Greece
29C3 **Pirajui** Brazil
37E2 **Piran** Slovenia, Yugos
29B2 **Piranhas** Brazil
29D2 **Pirapora** Brazil
28D1 **Piratina** *R* Brazil
28E2 **Piratini** *R* Brazil
41E2 **Pirdop** Bulg
29C2 **Pirenópolis** Brazil
29C2 **Pires do Rio** Brazil
41E3 **Pírgos** Greece
Pirineos = Pyrénées
38B3 **Pirineos** *Mts* Spain
27K4 **Piripiri** Brazil
36D2 **Pirmasens** Germany
41E2 **Pirot** Serbia, Yugos
60C2 **Pīr Panjāl Range** *Mts* Pak
57C3 **Piru** Indon
20C3 **Piru Creek** *R* USA
37D3 **Pisa** Italy
26C6 **Pisco** Peru
14C1 **Piseco** USA
42C3 **Písek** Czech Republic
60B2 **Pishin** Pak
20B3 **Pismo Beach** USA
25C3 **Pissis** *Mt* Arg
37D3 **Pistoia** Italy
39B1 **Pisuerga** *R* Spain
18B2 **Pit** *R* USA
26C3 **Pitalito** Colombia
xxixN6 **Pitcairn** *I* Pacific O
32H5 **Pite** *R* Sweden
32J5 **Piteå** Sweden
41E2 **Piteşti** Rom
49L4 **Pit Gorodok** Russian Fed
36B2 **Pithiviers** France
44E3 **Pitkyaranta** Russian Fed
34D3 **Pitlochry** Scot
44M2 **Pitlyar** Russian Fed
28A3 **Pitrutquén** Chile
77H5 **Pitt** *I* NZ
3C3 **Pitt I** Can
20B1 **Pittsburg** California, USA
17D2 **Pittsburg** Kansas, USA
5G4 **Pittsburg** New Hampshire, USA
13D2 **Pittsburgh** USA
12A3 **Pittsfield** Illinois, USA
14D1 **Pittsfield** Massachusetts, USA
14C2 **Pittston** USA
75D1 **Pittsworth** Aust
20C3 **Piute Peak** *Mt* USA
61B2 **Piuthan** Nepal
53D1 **Pivan'** Russian Fed
20C3 **Pixley** USA
37D1 **Pizzo Redorta** *Mt* Italy
32B2 **Pjórsá** Iceland
26B5 **Pjura** Peru
5L4 **Placentia** Can
7N5 **Placentia B** Can
20B1 **Placerville** USA
36D2 **Plaine d'Alsace** *Plain* France
36B1 **Plaine des Flandres** *Plain* France/Belg
70C2 **Plaine du Tidikelt** *Desert* Region
36C2 **Plaine Lorraine** Region, France
16B2 **Plains** USA
11C3 **Plainview** Nebraska, USA
16B3 **Plainview** Texas, USA
20B2 **Planada** USA
27H7 **Planalto de Mato Grosso** *Plat* Brazil
27L5 **Planalto do Borborema** *Plat* Brazil
26B1 **Planalto do Mato Grosso** *Mts* Brazil
77E1 **Planet Deep** PNG
11C3 **Plankinton** USA
17C3 **Plano** USA
15E4 **Plantation** USA
15C3 **Plant City** USA
39A1 **Plasencia** Spain
44L5 **Plast** Russian Fed
53D3 **Plastun** Russian Fed
71H4 **Plateau** State, Nig
71G3 **Plateau de Dadango** Togo
36C3 **Plateau de Langres** *Plat* France
37A2 **Plateau De St Christol** Region, France
70C2 **Plateau du Tademait** Alg
36D2 **Plateau Lorrain** *Plat* France
38C2 **Plateaux de Limousin** *Plat* France
39C2 **Plateaux du Sersou** *Plat* Alg
23C5 **Plato** Colombia
45J7 **Plato Ustyurt** *Plat* Kazakhstan
65B1 **Platres** Cyprus
11C3 **Platte** USA
16B1 **Platte** *R* USA
12A2 **Platteville** USA
13E2 **Plattsburgh** USA
17C1 **Plattsmouth** USA
42C2 **Plauen** Germany
44F5 **Plavsk** Russian Fed
22B2 **Playa Azul** Mexico
26B4 **Playas** Ecuador
22C2 **Playa Vincente** Mexico
39A1 **Plaza de Moro Almanzor** *Mt* Spain
20B2 **Pleasanton** California, USA
17F4 **Pleasanton** Texas, USA
14C3 **Pleasantville** USA
12B3 **Pleasure Ridge Park** USA
55D3 **Pleiku** Viet
78C1 **Plenty,B of** NZ
11B2 **Plentywood** USA
44G3 **Plesetsk** Russian Fed
43D2 **Pleszew** Pol
7L4 **Pletipi,L** Can
41E2 **Pleven** Bulg
41D2 **Pljevlja** Montenegro, Yugos
41D2 **Ploče** Croatia
43D2 **Płock** Pol
38B2 **Ploërmel** France
41F2 **Ploieşti** Rom
36D3 **Plombières-les-Bains** France
44C5 **Płońsk** Pol
41E2 **Plovdiv** Bulg
18C1 **Plummer** USA
10G3 **Plummer,Mt** USA
73C6 **Plumtree** Zim
20B1 **Plymouth** California, USA
35C6 **Plymouth** Eng
12B2 **Plymouth** Indiana, USA
14E2 **Plymouth** Massachusetts, USA
14C2 **Plymouth** Pennsylvania, USA
14E2 **Plymouth B** USA
35C6 **Plymouth Sd** Eng
35D5 **Plynlimon** *Mt* Wales
42C3 **Plzeň** Czech Republic
42D2 **Pniewy** Pol
71F3 **Pô** Burkina
37E2 **Po** *R* Italy
71G4 **Pobé** Benin
53E2 **Pobedino** Russian Fed
18D2 **Pocatello** USA
43G2 **Pochinok** Russian Fed
22C2 **Pochutla** Mexico
29D1 **Poções** Brazil
13D3 **Pocomoke City** USA
29A2 **Poconé** Brazil
29C3 **Pocos de Caldas** Brazil
41D2 **Podgorica** Montenegro, Yugos
37D2 **Po di Volano** *R* Italy
49L3 **Podkamennaya Tunguska** *R* Russian Fed
44F4 **Podol'sk** Russian Fed
43F3 **Podol'skaya Vozvyshennost'** *Upland* Ukraine
44E3 **Podporozh'ye** Russian Fed
44G3 **Podyuga** Russian Fed
74B2 **Pofadder** S Africa
37D3 **Poggibonsi** Italy
60A2 **Poghdar** Afghan
53C3 **Pogranichnyy** Russian Fed
57B3 **Poh** Indon
53B4 **P'ohang** S Korea
79G9 **Poinsett,C** Ant
75C2 **Point** Aust
23E3 **Pointe-à-Pitre** Guadeloupe
5H4 **Pointe aux Anglais** Can
38B2 **Pointe de Barfleur** *Pt* France
5J4 **Pointe de l'Est** *C* Can
4F3 **Pointe Louis XIV** *C* Can
72B4 **Pointe Noire** Congo
72A3 **Pointe Pongara** *Pt* Gabon
75B3 **Point Fairy** Aust
23L1 **Point Fortin** Trinidad
10E2 **Point Hope** USA
6G3 **Point L** Can
10F2 **Point Lay** USA
14C2 **Point Pleasant** New Jersey, USA
12C3 **Point Pleasant** W Virginia, USA
37B2 **Point St Bernard** *Mt* France
38C2 **Poitiers** France
38B2 **Poitou** Region, France
36A2 **Poix** France
60C3 **Pokaran** India
75C1 **Pokataroo** Aust
61B2 **Pokhara** Nepal
49O3 **Pokrovsk** Russian Fed
19D3 **Polacca** USA
43D2 **Poland** Republic, Europe
14C1 **Poland** USA
4E3 **Polar Bear Prov Park** Can
45E8 **Polath** Turk
64B2 **Polatli** Turk
57B3 **Poleang** Indon
57A3 **Polewali** Indon
71J4 **Poli** Cam
37A1 **Poligny** France
49P4 **Poliny Osipenko** Russian Fed
65B1 **Polis** Cyprus
41E2 **Políyiros** Greece
62B2 **Pollāchi** India
57F8 **Pololo Is** Phil
43F2 **Polonnye** Ukraine
43F1 **Polotsk** Belarus
18D1 **Polson** USA
45E6 **Poltava** Ukraine
40D1 **Pölten** Austria
44K3 **Polunochoye** Russian Fed
16A3 **Polvadera** USA
44E2 **Polyarnyy** Murmansk, Russian Fed
49Q2 **Polyarnyy** Yakutskaya, Russian Fed
44L2 **Polyarnyy Ural** *Mts* Russian Fed
xxixL4 **Polynesia** *Region* Pacific O
26C5 **Pomabamba** Peru
29D3 **Pomba** *R* Brazil
20D3 **Pomona** USA
17C2 **Pomona Res** USA
15E4 **Pompano Beach** USA
14C2 **Pompton Lakes** USA
17C2 **Ponca City** USA
23D3 **Ponce** Puerto Rico
15E4 **Ponce de Leon B** USA
62B2 **Pondicherry** India
7L2 **Pond Inlet** Can
5K3 **Ponds,I of** Can
39A1 **Ponferrade** Spain
72C3 **Pongo** *R* Sudan
74E2 **Pongola** *R* S Africa
62B2 **Ponnāni** India
61D3 **Ponnyadoung Range** *Mts* Myanmar
3F3 **Ponoka** Can
48F3 **Ponoy** Russian Fed
44G2 **Ponoy** *R* Russian Fed
38B2 **Pons** France
29E2 **Ponta da Baleia** *Pt* Brazil
70A1 **Ponta Delgada** Açores
29E1 **Ponta do Mutá** *Pt* Brazil
72B4 **Ponta do Padrão** *Pt* Angola
29D3 **Ponta dos Búzios** *Pt* Brazil
29B4 **Ponta Grossa** Brazil
37A1 **Pontailler-sur-Saône** France
29C3 **Pontal** Brazil
36C2 **Pont-à-Mousson** France
29A3 **Ponta Pora** Brazil
38D2 **Pontarlier** France
37D3 **Pontassieve** Italy
4F3 **Pontax** *R* Can
17D3 **Pontchartrain,L** USA
37A1 **Pont d'Ain** France
29A1 **Ponte de Pedra** Brazil
40C2 **Pontedera** Italy
40B2 **Ponte Lecca** Corse
39A1 **Pontevedra** Spain
12B2 **Pontiac** Illinois, USA
12C2 **Pontiac** Michigan, USA
56C3 **Pontianak** Indon
38B2 **Pontivy** France
36B2 **Pontoise** France
17E3 **Pontotoc** USA
37C2 **Pontremoli** Italy
36B2 **Pont-sur-Yonne** France
35D6 **Pontypool** Wales
35D6 **Pontypridd** Wales
35E6 **Poole** Eng
Poona = Pune
75B2 **Pooncarie** Aust
75B2 **Poopelloe,L** Aust
10G3 **Poorman** USA
26C3 **Popayán** Colombia
36B1 **Poperinge** Belg
75B2 **Popilta L** Aust
11A2 **Poplar** USA
4B3 **Poplar** *R* Can
3G4 **Poplar** *R* USA
17D2 **Poplar Bluff** USA
17E3 **Poplarville** USA
76D1 **Popndetta** PNG
22C2 **Popocatepetl** *Mt* Mexico
10F4 **Popof** *I* USA
72B4 **Popokabaka** Zaïre
51H7 **Popondetta** PNG
41F2 **Popovo** Bulg
29C3 **Poraiba** *R* Brazil
29C1 **Porangatu** Brazil
60B4 **Porbandar** India
3B3 **Porcher I** Can
29C1 **Porcos** *R* Brazil
10K2 **Porcupine** *R* USA/Can
3H3 **Porcupine Hills** Can
37E2 **Pordenone** Italy
40C1 **Poreč** Croatia
29B3 **Porecatu** Brazil
32J6 **Pori** Fin
78B2 **Porirua** NZ
32H5 **Porjus** Sweden
53E1 **Poronay** *R* Russian Fed
53E2 **Poronaysk** Russian Fed
44E3 **Porosozero** Russian Fed
37B1 **Porrentruy** Switz
37D3 **Porretta** Italy
32K4 **Porsangen** *Inlet* Nor
32F7 **Porsgrunn** Nor
35B4 **Portadown** N Ire
12B2 **Portage** USA
4B4 **Portage la Prairie** Can
11B2 **Portal** USA
3D4 **Port Alberni** Can
39A2 **Portalegre** Port
16B3 **Portales** USA
74D3 **Port Alfred** S Africa
3C3 **Port Alice** Can
14A2 **Port Allegany** USA
17D3 **Port Allen** USA
18B1 **Port Angeles** USA
23B3 **Port Antonio** Jamaica
35B5 **Portarlington** Irish Rep
17D4 **Port Arthur** USA
34B4 **Port Askaig** Scot
36A2 **Port-Audemer** France
75A2 **Port Augusta** Aust
23C3 **Port-au-Prince** Haiti
12C2 **Port Austin** USA
62E2 **Port Blair** Andaman Is
75B3 **Port Campbell** Aust
61C3 **Port Canning** India
7M5 **Port Cartier** Can
78B3 **Port Chalmers** NZ
15E4 **Port Charlotte** USA
14D2 **Port Chester** USA
3B3 **Port Clements** Can
12C2 **Port Clinton** USA
13D2 **Port Colborne** Can
75E3 **Port Davey** Aust
23C3 **Port-de-Paix** Haiti
55C5 **Port Dickson** Malay
74E3 **Port Edward** S Africa
29D2 **Porteirinha** Brazil
12C2 **Port Elgin** Can
74D3 **Port Elizabeth** S Africa
34B4 **Port Ellen** Scot
23N2 **Porter Pt** St Vincent
20C2 **Porterville** USA
76D4 **Port Fairy** Aust
72A4 **Port Gentil** Gabon
17D3 **Port Gibson** USA
10H4 **Port Graham** USA
18B1 **Port Hammond** Can
68E7 **Port Harcourt** Nigeria
3C3 **Port Hardy** Can
7M5 **Port Hawkesbury** Can
76A3 **Port Hedland** Aust
Port Heiden = Meshik
35C5 **Porthmadog** Wales
7N4 **Port Hope Simpson** Can
20C3 **Port Hueneme** USA
12C2 **Port Huron** USA
39A2 **Portimão** Port
75D2 **Port Jackson** *B* Aust
14D2 **Port Jefferson** USA
14C2 **Port Jervis** USA
75D2 **Port Kembla** Aust
12C2 **Portland** Indiana, USA
13E2 **Portland** Maine, USA
75C2 **Portland** New South Wales, Aust
18B1 **Portland** Oregon, USA
75B3 **Portland** Victoria, Aust

Romang **St James,C**

57C4 **Romang** *I* Indon
45C6 **Romania** Republic, E Europe
15E4 **Romano,C** USA
38D2 **Romans sur Isère** France
10E3 **Romanzof,C** USA
10K2 **Romanzof Mts** USA
57F8 **Romblon** Phil
Rome = Roma
15B2 **Rome** Georgia, USA
14C1 **Rome** New York, USA
13D2 **Rome** USA
38C2 **Romilly-sur-Seine** France
71A2 **Rommani** Mor
13D3 **Romney** USA
45E5 **Romny** Ukraine
42B1 **Rømø** *I* Den
37B1 **Romont** Switz
38C2 **Romoratin** France
56G7 **Rompin** Malay
56G7 **Rompin** *R* Malay
37D2 **Ronco** Italy
39A2 **Ronda** Spain
26F6 **Rondônia** Brazil
26F6 **Rondônia** State, Brazil
29B2 **Rondonópolis** Brazil
52B4 **Rong'an** China
52B4 **Rongchang** China
52E2 **Rongcheng** China
52B4 **Rongjiang** China
52B4 **Rong Jiang** *R* China
55A1 **Rongklang Range** *Mts* Myanmar
32G7 **Rønne** Denmark
32H7 **Ronneby** Sweden
79F2 **Ronne Ice Shelf** Ant
36B1 **Ronse** Belg
36A1 **Ronthieu** Region, France
8C3 **Roof Butte** *Mt* USA
60D3 **Roorkee** India
36C1 **Roosendaal** Neth
19D2 **Roosevelt** USA
79E **Roosevelt I** Ant
3C2 **Roosevelt,Mt** Can
10O3 **Root** *R* Can
11D3 **Root** *R* USA
76C2 **Roper** *R* Aust
37A3 **Roquevaire** France
26F3 **Roraima** State, Brazil
26F2 **Roraime** *Mt* Ven
4B3 **Rorketon** Can
32G6 **Røros** Nor
37C1 **Rorschach** Switz
32G6 **Rørvik** Nor
43G3 **Ros'** *R* Ukraine
23Q2 **Rosalie** Dominica
20C3 **Rosamond** USA
20C3 **Rosamond L** USA
22A1 **Rosamorada** Mexico
28C2 **Rosario** Arg
27K4 **Rosário** Brazil
22A1 **Rosario** Mexico
29A3 **Rosario** Par
28D2 **Rosario** Urug
29B2 **Rosario del Tala** Arg
28E2 **Rosário do Sul** Brazil
29A1 **Rosário Oeste** Brazil
14C2 **Roscoe** USA
38B2 **Roscoff** France
33B3 **Roscommon** Irish Rep
35B5 **Roscrea** Irish Rep
23E3 **Roseau** Dominica
4B4 **Roseau** *R* Can/USA
75E3 **Rosebery** Aust
5K4 **Rose Blanche** Can
11A2 **Rosebud** USA
18B2 **Roseburg** USA
17C4 **Rosenberg** USA
42C3 **Rosenheim** Germany
3G3 **Rosetown** Can
20B1 **Roseville** USA
41E2 **Rosiorii de Verde** Rom
32G7 **Roskilde** Den
44E5 **Roslavl'** Russian Fed
44G4 **Roslyatino** Russian Fed
78B2 **Ross** NZ
10M3 **Ross** *R* Can
33B3 **Rossan** *Pt* Irish Rep
40D3 **Rossano** Italy
17E3 **Ross Barnet Res** USA
13D1 **Rosseau L** Can
77E2 **Rossel** *I* Solomon Is
79E **Ross Ice Shelf** Ant
18B1 **Ross L** USA
3E4 **Rossland** Can
35B5 **Rosslare** Irish Rep
78C2 **Ross,Mt** NZ
70A3 **Rosso** Maur
35D6 **Ross-on-Wye** Eng
45F5 **Rossosh** Russian Fed
6E3 **Ross River** Can
79F6 **Ross S** Ant
63C3 **Rostāq** Iran
3G3 **Rosthern** Can
42C2 **Rostock** Germany
44F4 **Rostov** Russian Fed
45F6 **Rostov-na-Donu** Russian Fed
15C2 **Roswell** Georgia, USA
16B3 **Roswell** New Mexico, USA
51H5 **Rota** Pacific O
36E1 **Rotenburg** Hessen, Germany
42B2 **Rotenburg** Niedersachsen, Germany
36E1 **Rothaar-Geb** *Region* Germany
79G3 **Rothera** *Base* Ant
35E5 **Rotherham** Eng
5H4 **Rothesay** Can
34C4 **Rothesay** Scot
57B5 **Roti** *I* Indon
75C2 **Roto** Aust
78B2 **Rotoiti,L** NZ
78B2 **Rotoroa,L** NZ
78C1 **Rotorua** NZ
78C1 **Rotorua,L** NZ
36E2 **Rottenburg** Germany
42A2 **Rotterdam** Neth
36E2 **Rottweil** Germany
77G2 **Rotuma** *I* Fiji
36B1 **Roubaix** France
38C2 **Rouen** France
35F5 **Rough** *Oilfield* N Sea
Roulers = Roeselare
73F6 **Round I** Mauritius
20D1 **Round Mountain** USA
75D2 **Round Mt** Aust
18E1 **Roundup** USA
34D2 **Rousay** *I* Scot
38C3 **Roussillon** Region, France
74D3 **Rouxville** S Africa
4F4 **Rouyn** Can
32K5 **Rovaniemi** Fin
37D2 **Rovereto** Italy
37D2 **Rovigo** Italy
40C1 **Rovinj** Croatia
43F2 **Rovno** Ukraine
63B1 **Row'ān** Iran
75C1 **Rowena** Aust
7L3 **Rowley I** Can
76A2 **Rowley Shoals** Aust
57E8 **Roxas** Palawan, Phil
57F8 **Roxas** Panay, Phil
15D1 **Roxboro** USA
78A3 **Roxburgh** NZ
18E1 **Roy** USA
35B5 **Royal Canal** Irish Rep
35E5 **Royal Leamington Spa** Eng
12C2 **Royal Oak** USA
35F6 **Royal Tunbridge Wells** Eng
38B2 **Royan** France
36B2 **Roye** France
35E5 **Royston** Eng
43E3 **Rožňava** Slovakia
36B2 **Rozoy** France
45G5 **Rtishchevo** Russian Fed
37E2 **Rt Kamenjak** *C* Croatia
73D4 **Ruaha Nat Pk** Tanz
78C1 **Ruahine Range** *Mts* NZ
78C1 **Ruapehu,Mt** NZ
67D3 **Rub al Khālī** *Desert* S Arabia
34B3 **Rubha Hunish** Scot
25F2 **Rubinéia** Brazil
29B3 **Rubinéia** Brazil
48K4 **Rubtsovsk** Russian Fed
10G3 **Ruby** USA
19C2 **Ruby Mts** USA
63D3 **Rudan** Iran
63E2 **Rudbar** Afghan
63B1 **Rūdbār** Iran
53D3 **Rudnaya Pristan'** Russian Fed
43G2 **Rudnya** Russian Fed
53C3 **Rudnyy** Russian Fed
41E2 **Rudoka Planina** *Mt* Macedonia
48G1 **Rudol'fa, Ostrov** *I* Russian Fed
52E3 **Rudong** China
12C1 **Rudyard** USA
36A1 **Rue** France
66B4 **Rufa'a** Sudan
38C2 **Ruffec** France
73D4 **Rufiji** *R* Tanz
28C2 **Rufino** Arg
70A3 **Rufisque** Sen
73C5 **Rufunsa** Zambia
35E5 **Rugby** Eng
11B2 **Rugby** USA
32G8 **Rügen** *I* Germany
42B2 **Ruhr** *R* Germany
52D4 **Ruijin** China
41E2 **Rujen** *Mt* Macedonia, Bulg/Yugos
73D4 **Rukwa** *L* Tanz
34B3 **Rum** *I* Scot
41D1 **Ruma** Serbia, Yugos
67E1 **Rumāh** S Arabia
72C3 **Rumbek** Sudan
23C2 **Rum Cay** *I* Caribbean
13E2 **Rumford** USA
37A2 **Rumilly** France
76C2 **Rum Jungle** Aust
54D2 **Rumoi** Japan
73D5 **Rumphi** Malawi
78B2 **Runanga** NZ
78C1 **Runaway,C** NZ
73B5 **Rundu** Namibia
73D4 **Rungwa** Tanz
73D4 **Rungwa** *R* Tanz
73D4 **Rungwe** *Mt* Tanz
59G2 **Ruoqiang** China
50D2 **Ruo Shui** *R* China
56F7 **Rupat** *I* Indon
41F1 **Rupea** Rom
18D2 **Rupert** USA
7L4 **Rupert** *R* Can
36D1 **Rur** *R* Germany
26E6 **Rurrenabaque** Bol
73D5 **Rusape** Zim
41F2 **Ruse** Bulg
12A2 **Rushville** Illinois, USA
11B3 **Rushville** Nebraska, USA
75B3 **Rushworth** Aust
17C3 **Rusk** USA
15E4 **Ruskin** USA
3H2 **Russel L** Can
3H3 **Russell** Can
78B1 **Russell** NZ
16C2 **Russell** USA
4A2 **Russell L** Can
15B2 **Russellville** Alabama, USA
17D2 **Russellville** Arkansas, USA
12B3 **Russellville** Kentucky, USA
19B3 **Russian** *R* USA
44E4 **Russian Federation**
49L2 **Russkiy, Ostrov** *I* Russian Fed
64E1 **Rustavi** Georgia
74D2 **Rustenburg** S Africa
17D3 **Ruston** USA
72C4 **Rutana** Burundi
57B4 **Ruteng** Indon
74E1 **Rutenga** Zim
19C3 **Ruth** USA
36E1 **Rüthen** Germany
22C2 **Rutla** Mexico
13E2 **Rutland** USA
62E2 **Rutland** *I* Andaman Is
60D2 **Rutog** China
Ruvu = Pangani
73E5 **Ruvuma, R** Tanz/Mozam
72D3 **Ruwenzori Range** *Mts* Uganda/Zaïre
73D5 **Ruya** *R* Zim
43D3 **Ružomberok** Slovakia
72C4 **Rwanda** Republic, Africa
44F5 **Ryazan'** Russian Fed
44G5 **Ryazhsk** Russian Fed
32L5 **Rybachiy, Poluostrov** *Pen* Russian Fed
44F4 **Rybinsk** Russian Fed
44F4 **Rybinskoye Vodokhranilishche** *Res* Russian Fed
43F3 **Rybnitsa** Moldova
3E2 **Rycroft** Can
35E6 **Ryde** Eng
35F6 **Rye** Eng
18C2 **Rye Patch Res** USA
45E5 **Ryl'sk** Russian Fed
45H6 **Ryn Peski** *Desert* Kazakhstan
54A3 **Ryoju** S Korea
53D4 **Ryōtsu** Japan
43F3 **Ryskany** Moldova
50F4 **Ryūkyū Retto** *Arch* Japan
43E2 **Rzeszów** Pol
44E4 **Rzhev** Russian Fed

S

63C2 **Sa'ādatābād** Iran
66B2 **Saad el Aali** *Dam* Egypt
42C2 **Saale** *R* Germany
37B1 **Saanen** Switz
36D2 **Saar** *R* Germany
36D2 **Saarbrücken** Germany
36D2 **Saarburg** Germany
32J7 **Saaremaa** *I* Estonia
36D2 **Saarland** State, Germany
36D2 **Saarlouis** Germany
28C3 **Saavedra** Arg
65B3 **Saba'a** Egypt
41D2 **Šabac** Serbia, Yugos
39C1 **Sabadell** Spain
54C3 **Sabae** Japan
56E1 **Sabah** State, Malay
10A6 **Sabak,C** USA
57B3 **Sabal** Indon
23C4 **Sabanalarga** Colombia
56A1 **Sabang** Indon
57A2 **Sabang** Indon
62C1 **Sabari** *R* India
65C2 **Sabastiya** Israel
26E7 **Sabaya** Bol
64C3 **Sab'Bi'ār** Syria
66C3 **Sabderat** Eth
65D2 **Sabhā** Jordan
69A2 **Sabhā** Libya
73D6 **Sabi** *R* Zim
74E2 **Sabie** *R* S Africa
21B2 **Sabinas** Mexico
21B2 **Sabinas Hidalgo** Mexico
17C3 **Sabine** *R* USA
17D4 **Sabine L** USA
67F2 **Sabkhat Maṭṭi** *Salt Marsh* UAE
65B3 **Sabkhet El Bardawîl** *Lg* Egypt
57F8 **Sablayan** Phil
7M5 **Sable,C** Can
15E4 **Sable,C** USA
7N5 **Sable I** Can
63D1 **Sabzevār** Iran
18C1 **Sacajawea Peak** USA
14C1 **Sacandaga Res** USA
11D3 **Sac City** USA
9D1 **Sachigo** *R* Can
4C3 **Sachigo L** Can
54A3 **Sach'on** S Korea
42C2 **Sachsen** State, Germany
42C2 **Sachsen-Anhalt** State, Germany
6F2 **Sachs Harbour** Can
37E2 **Sacile** Italy
37B1 **Säckingen** Germany
5J4 **Sackville** Can
13E2 **Saco** Maine, USA
11A2 **Saco** Montana, USA
20B1 **Sacramento** USA
20B1 **Sacramento** *R* USA
19B2 **Sacramento** *V* USA
16A3 **Sacramento Mts** USA
66D3 **Sa'dah** Yemen
41E2 **Sadanski** Bulg
67G3 **Sadh** Oman
61E2 **Sadiya** India
39A2 **Sado** *R* Port
53D4 **Sado-shima** *I* Japan
60C3 **Sādri** India
Safad = Zefat
60A2 **Safed Koh** *Mts* Afghan
63E2 **Safer** Afghan
32G7 **Saffle** Sweden
19E4 **Safford** USA
64C3 **Safi** Jordan
71A2 **Safi** Mor
63E2 **Safidabeh** Iran
65D1 **Şāfītā** Syria
43G1 **Safonovo** Russian Fed
44H2 **Safonovo** Russian Fed
64E3 **Safwān** Iraq
61C2 **Saga** China
54B4 **Saga** Japan
55B1 **Sagaing** Myanmar
54C4 **Sagami-nada** *B* Japan
60D4 **Sāgar** India
10J2 **Sagavanirktok** *R* USA
14D2 **Sag Harbor** USA
12C2 **Saginaw** USA
12C2 **Saginaw B** USA
7M4 **Saglek B** Can
54A3 **Sagō-ri** S Korea
16A2 **Saguache** USA
23B2 **Sagua de Tánamo** Cuba
23B2 **Sagua la Grande** Cuba
7L5 **Saguenay** *R* Can
39B2 **Sagunto** Spain
65D3 **Sahāb** Jordan
39A1 **Sahagún** Spain
70C2 **Sahara** *Desert* N Africa
60D3 **Saharanpur** India
60C2 **Sahiwal** Pak
64D3 **Şahrā al Hijārah** *Desert Region* Iraq
66B1 **Sahra esh Sharqiya** *Desert Region* Egypt
22B1 **Sahuayo** Mexico
65D1 **Sahyun** *Hist Site* Syria
76D1 **Saibai I** Aust
71C2 **Saïda** Alg
65C2 **Saïda** Leb
63D3 **Sa'īdabad** Iran
39B2 **Saidia** Mor
61C2 **Saidpur** India
60C2 **Saidu** Pak
54B3 **Saigō** Japan
Saigon = Ho Chi Minh
61D3 **Saiha** India
50E2 **Saihan Tal** China
54B4 **Saijo** Japan
53C5 **Saiki** Japan
44D3 **Saimaa** *L* Fin
22B1 **Sain Alto** Mexico
63E3 **Saindak** Pak
34D4 **St Abb's Head** *Pt* Scot
5G4 **St Agapit** Can
5G4 **Ste Agathe-des-Monts** Can
5K4 **St Albans** Can
35E6 **St Albans** Eng
13E2 **St Albans** Vermont, USA
12C3 **St Albans** West Virginia, USA
35D6 **St Albans Head** *C* Eng
3F3 **St Albert** Can
36B1 **St Amand-les-Eaux** France
38C2 **St Amand-Mont Rond** France
37A1 **St-Amour** France
73E5 **St André** *C* Madag
36A2 **St-André-de-l'Eure** France
15B3 **St Andrew B** USA
34D3 **St Andrews** Scot
15C2 **St Andrew Sd** USA
11C2 **Ste Anne** Can
5G4 **Ste Anne de Beaupré** Can
5H4 **Ste-Anne-des-Monts** Can
23H1 **St Ann's Bay** Jamaica
7N4 **St Anthony** Can
18D2 **St Anthony** USA
75B3 **St Arnaud** Aust
5K3 **St Augustin** *R* Can
15C3 **St Augustine** USA
5K3 **St Augustin-Saguenay** Can
35C6 **St Austell** Eng
36D2 **St-Avold** France
35D4 **St Bees Head** *Pt* Eng
4B4 **St Boniface** Can
37B2 **St-Bonnet** France
35C6 **St Brides B** Wales
38B2 **St-Brieuc** France
36A3 **St-Calais** France
4F5 **St Catharines** Can
23M2 **St Catherine,Mt** Grenada
15C2 **St Catherines I** USA
35E6 **St Catherines Pt** Eng
38C2 **St Chamond** France
18D2 **St Charles** Idaho, USA
17D2 **St Charles** Missouri, USA
12C2 **St Clair** USA
12C2 **St Clair,L** USA/Can
12C2 **St Clair Shores** USA
38D2 **St Claud** France
11D2 **St Cloud** USA
37B1 **Ste Croix** Switz
23E3 **St Croix** *I* Caribbean
12A1 **St Croix** *R* USA
13F1 **St Croix** *R* USA/Can
12A1 **St Croix Falls** USA
35C6 **St Davids Head** *Pt* Wales
36B2 **St Denis** France
73F6 **St Denis** Réunion
36D2 **St-Dié** France
36C2 **St Dizier** France
10K3 **St Elias,Mt** USA
10L3 **St Elias Mts** Can
38B2 **Saintes** France
38C2 **St Étienne** France
37B2 **St Étienne-de-Tinée** France
13E1 **St-Félicien** Can
5K4 **St Fintan's** Can
36B2 **St-Florentin** France
16B2 **St Francis** USA
17D2 **St Francis** *R* USA
74C3 **St Francis B** S Africa
74C3 **St Francis,C** S Africa
37C1 **St Gallen** Switz
38C3 **St-Gaudens** France
75C1 **St George** Aust
15C2 **St George** South Carolina, USA
19D3 **St George** Utah, USA
10E4 **St George** *I* Alaska, USA
15C3 **St George I** Florida, USA
36E2 **St Georgen im Schwarzwald** Germany
18B2 **St George,Pt** USA
5H4 **St George** Can
13E1 **St-Georges** Can
23E4 **St George's** Grenada
5K4 **St George's B** Can
35B5 **St Georges Chan** Irish Rep/ Wales
77E1 **St Georges Chan** PNG
37A1 **St Germain-du-Bois** France
36A2 **St German-en-laye** France
37B2 **St-Gervais** France
37C1 **St Gotthard** *P* Switz
35C6 **St Govans Head** *Pt* Wales
20A1 **St Helena** USA
xxxH5 **St Helena** *I* Atlantic O
74B3 **St Helena B** S Africa
15C2 **St Helena Sd** USA
75E3 **St Helens** Aust
35D5 **St Helens** Eng
18B1 **St Helens** USA
18B1 **St Helens,Mt** USA
38B2 **St Helier** Jersey
37B1 **St Hippolyte** France
36C1 **St-Hubert** Belg
7L5 **St-Hyacinthe** Can
12C1 **St Ignace** USA
12B1 **St Ignace I** Can
35C6 **St Ives** Eng
11D3 **St James** Minnesota, USA
17D2 **St James** Missouri, USA
3B3 **St James,C** Can

Shathah at Tahtā **Sirte,G of**

65D1 **Shathah at Tahtā** Syria
64E3 **Shaţţ al Gharrat** *R* Iraq
65C3 **Shaubak** Jordan
3G4 **Shaunavon** Can
20C2 **Shaver L** USA
14C2 **Shawangunk Mt** USA
12B2 **Shawano** USA
17C2 **Shawnee** Oklahoma, USA
11A3 **Shawnee** Wyoming, USA
5G4 **Shawinigan** Can
52D4 **Sha Xian** China
76B3 **Shay Gap** Aust
65D2 **Shaykh Miskīn** Syria
66D4 **Shaykh 'Uthmān** Yemen
44F5 **Shchekino** Russian Fed
45F5 **Shchigry** Russian Fed
45E5 **Shchors** Ukraine
48J4 **Shchuchinsk** Kazakhstan
12B2 **Sheboygan** USA
72E3 **Shebelē** *R* Eth
72B3 **Shebshi** *Mts* Nig
53E2 **Shebunino** Russian Fed
5J4 **Shediac** Can
10K2 **Sheenjek** *R* USA
34B4 **Sheep Haven** *Estuary* Irish Rep
35F6 **Sheerness** Eng
5J5 **Sheet Harbour** Can
65C2 **Shefar'am** Israel
15B2 **Sheffield** Alabama, USA
35E5 **Sheffield** Eng
14A2 **Sheffield** Pennsylvania, USA
16B3 **Sheffield** Texas, USA
5K3 **Shekalika Bay** Can
60C2 **Shekhupura** Pak
3C2 **Shelagyote Peak** *Mt* Can
5H5 **Shelburne** Can
14D1 **Shelburne Falls** USA
12B2 **Shelby** Michigan, USA
18D1 **Shelby** Montana, USA
15C1 **Shelby** N Carolina, USA
12B3 **Shelbyville** Indiana, USA
15B1 **Shelbyville** Tennessee, USA
11C3 **Sheldon** USA
10M3 **Sheldon,Mt** Can
5J3 **Sheldrake** Can
10H4 **Shelikof Str** USA
3G3 **Shellbrook** Can
18D2 **Shelley** USA
75D2 **Shellharbour** Aust
78A3 **Shelter Pt** NZ
18B1 **Shelton** USA
64E1 **Shemakha** Azerbaijan
17C1 **Shenandoah** USA
13D3 **Shenandoah** *R* USA
14A3 **Shenandoah Mt** USA
13D3 **Shenandoah Nat Pk** USA
71H4 **Shendam** Nig
66B3 **Shendi** Sudan
44G3 **Shenkursk** Russian Fed
52C2 **Shenmu** China
52E1 **Shenyang** China
52C5 **Shenzhen** China
60D3 **Sheopur** India
43F2 **Shepetovka** Ukraine
14B3 **Shepherdstown** USA
75C3 **Shepparton** Aust
36A1 **Sheppey,I of** Eng
7K2 **Sherard,C** Can
35D6 **Sherborne** Eng
70A4 **Sherbro I** Sierra Leone
5G4 **Sherbrooke** Can
14C1 **Sherburne** USA
66B3 **Shereik** Sudan
60C3 **Shergarh** India
17D3 **Sheridan** Arkansas, USA
11A3 **Sheridan** Wyoming, USA
17C3 **Sherman** USA
3H2 **Sherridon** Can
42B2 **s-Hertogenbosh** Neth
10M4 **Sheslay** Can
3B2 **Sheslay** *R* Can
33C1 **Shetland** *Is* Scot
Shevchenko = Aktau
53C1 **Shevli** *R* Russian Fed
11C2 **Sheyenne** USA
11C2 **Sheyenne** *R* USA
63C3 **Sheyk Sho'eyb** *I* Iran
50J2 **Shiashkotan** *I* Russian Fed
60B1 **Shibarghan** Afghan
53D4 **Shibata** Japan
54D2 **Shibetsu** Japan
69C1 **Shibin el Kom** Egypt
65A3 **Shibîn el Qanâtir** Egypt
4D3 **Shibogama L** Can
54C3 **Shibukawa** Japan
14B2 **Shickshinny** USA
52C2 **Shijiazhuang** China
60B3 **Shikarpur** Pak
47H4 **Shikoku,I** Japan
54B4 **Shikoku-sanchi** *Mts* Japan
54D2 **Shikotsu-ko** *L* Japan
44G3 **Shilega** Russian Fed
61C2 **Shiliguri** India
50E1 **Shilka** Russian Fed
50E1 **Shilka** *R* Russian Fed
14C2 **Shillington** USA
61D2 **Shillong** India
44G5 **Shilovo** Russian Fed
54B4 **Shimabara** Japan
54C4 **Shimada** Japan
53B1 **Shimanovsk** Russian Fed
53D4 **Shimizu** Japan
60D2 **Shimla** India
54C4 **Shimoda** Japan
62B2 **Shimoga** India
53C5 **Shimonoseki** Japan
54C3 **Shinano** *R* Japan
67G2 **Shināş** Oman
63E2 **Shindand** Afghan
14A2 **Shinglehouse** USA
4D4 **Shingleton** USA
53D5 **Shingū** Japan
54D3 **Shinjō** Japan
53D4 **Shinminato** Japan
65D1 **Shinshār** Syria
72D4 **Shinyanga** Tanz
53E4 **Shiogama** Japan
54C4 **Shiono-misaki** *C* Japan
52A5 **Shiping** China
5J4 **Shippegan** Can
14B2 **Shippensburg** USA
16A2 **Shiprock** USA
67E3 **Shiqāq al Ma'ātīf** Region, Yemen
52B3 **Shiquan** China
54D3 **Shirakawa** Japan
54C3 **Shirane-san** *Mt* Japan
54C3 **Shirani-san** *Mt* Japan
63C3 **Shīraz** Iran
65A3 **Shirbîn** Egypt
54D2 **Shiriya-saki** *C* Japan
63C2 **Shīr Kūh** Iran
54C3 **Shirotori** Japan
63D1 **Shirvān** Iran
10F5 **Shishaldin V** USA
10E2 **Shishmaref** USA
10E2 **Shishmaref Inlet** USA
52B2 **Shitanjing** China
12B3 **Shively** USA
60D3 **Shivpuri** India
65C3 **Shivta** *Hist Site* Israel
19D3 **Shivwits Plat** USA
73D5 **Shiwa Ngandu** Zambia
52C3 **Shiyan** China
52B2 **Shizuishan** China
54C3 **Shizuoka** Japan
41D2 **Shkodër** Alb
43G2 **Shkov** Belarus
49L1 **Shmidta, Ostrov** *I* Russian Fed
75D2 **Shoalhaven** *R* Aust
54B4 **Shobara** Japan
62B2 **Shoranūr** India
62B1 **Shorāpur** India
19C3 **Shoshone** California, USA
18D2 **Shoshone** Idaho, USA
18E2 **Shoshone** *R* USA
18D2 **Shoshone L** USA
19C3 **Shoshone Mts** USA
18E2 **Shoshoni** USA
45E5 **Shostka** Ukraine
66C4 **Showak** Sudan
19D4 **Show Low** USA
17D3 **Shreveport** USA
35D5 **Shrewsbury** Eng
35D5 **Shropshire** County, Eng
53B2 **Shuangcheng** China
52E1 **Shuanglia** China
53C2 **Shuangyashan** China
45K6 **Shubar-Kuduk** Kazakhstan
5J4 **Shubenacadie** Can
10J2 **Shublik Mts** USA
44N2 **Shuga** Russian Fed
52D2 **Shu He** *R* China
52A4 **Shuicheng** China
60C3 **Shujaabad** Pak
60D4 **Shujālpur** India
53B3 **Shulan** China
50C2 **Shule He** China
10G5 **Shumagin Is** USA
41F2 **Shumen** Bulg
44H4 **Shumerlya** Russian Fed
52D4 **Shuncheng** China
10G2 **Shungnak** USA
52C2 **Shuo Xian** China
63D3 **Shūr Gaz** Iran
73C5 **Shurugwi** Zim
3E3 **Shuswap L** Can
44G4 **Shuya** Russian Fed
10H4 **Shuyak I** USA
61E3 **Shwebo** Myanmar
55B2 **Shwegyin** Myanmar
61E3 **Shweli** *R* Myanmar
63E3 **Siahan Range** *Mts* Pak
60A2 **Siah Koh** *Mts* Afghan
60C2 **Sialkot** Pak
Sian = Xi'an
57G9 **Siarao, I** Phil
57F9 **Siaton** Phil
57C2 **Siau** *I* Indon
43E1 **Šiauliai** Lithuania
44K5 **Sibay** Russian Fed
74E2 **Sibayi L** S Africa
40D2 **Šibenik** Croatia, Yugos
56A3 **Siberut** *I* Indon
60B3 **Sibi** Pak
53C3 **Sibirtsevo** Russian Fed
72B4 **Sibiti** Congo
72D4 **Sibiti** *R* Tanz
41E1 **Sibiu** Rom
11C3 **Sibley** USA
57A2 **Siboa** Indon
56A2 **Sibolga** Indon
61D2 **Sibsāgār** India
56D2 **Sibu** Malay
57F9 **Sibuguay B** Phil
72B3 **Sibut** CAR
56E1 **Sibutu Pass** Malay/Phil
57F8 **Sibuyan** *I* Phil
57F8 **Sibuyan S** Phil
52A3 **Sichuan** Province, China
40C3 **Sicilia** *I* Medit S
40C3 **Sicilian** *Chan* Italy/Tunisia
Sicily = Sicilia
26D6 **Sicuari** Peru
60C4 **Siddhapur** India
62B1 **Siddipet** India
61B3 **Sidhi** India
69B1 **Sidi Barrani** Egypt
71B1 **Sidi bel Abbès** Alg
71A2 **Sidi Kacem** Mor
34D3 **Sidlaw Hills** Scot
79F5 **Sidley,Mt** Ant
18B1 **Sidney** Can
11B2 **Sidney** Montana, USA
16B1 **Sidney** Nebraska, USA
14C1 **Sidney** New York, USA
12C2 **Sidney** Ohio, USA
15C2 **Sidney Lanier,L** USA
Sidon = Saïda
29B3 **Sidrolândia** Brazil
43E2 **Siedlce** Pol
36D1 **Sieg** *R* Germany
36D1 **Siegburg** Germany
36D1 **Siegen** Germany
37A1 **Sielle** *R* France
55C3 **Siem Reap** Camb
40C2 **Siena** Italy
36C3 **Siene** *R* France
43D2 **Sierpc** Pol
22C2 **Sierra Andrés Tuxtla** Mexico
28B3 **Sierra Auca Mahuida** *Mts* Arg
16A3 **Sierra Blanca** USA
28B4 **Sierra Blanca** *Mts* Arg
28B4 **Sierra Colorada** Arg
39B1 **Sierra de Albarracin** *Mts* Spain
39B2 **Sierra de Alcaraz** *Mts* Spain
28B1 **Sierra de Ancasti** *Mts* Arg
28B2 **Sierra de Cordoba** *Mts* Arg
28B1 **Sierra de Famantina** *Mts* Arg
39A1 **Sierra de Gredos** *Mts* Spain
39A2 **Sierra de Guadalupe** *Mts* Spain
39B1 **Sierra de Guadarrama** *Mts* Spain
39B1 **Sierra de Guara** *Mts* Spain
39B1 **Sierra de Gudar** *Mts* Spain
22C2 **Sierra de Juárez** *Mts* Mexico
28C3 **Sierra de la Ventana** *Mts* Arg
39C1 **Sierra del Codi** *Mts* Spain
28D1 **Sierra del Imán** *Mts* Arg
28B2 **Sierra del Morro** *Mt* Arg
28B3 **Sierra del Nevado** *Mts* Arg
21B2 **Sierra de los Alamitos** *Mts* Mexico
39B2 **Sierra de los Filabres** *Mts* Spain
22B1 **Sierra de los Huicholes** *Mts* Mexico
22C2 **Sierra de Miahuatlán** *Mts* Mexico
22B1 **Sierra de Morones** *Mts* Mexico
39A2 **Sierra de Ronda** *Mts* Spain
28B2 **Sierra de San Luis** *Mts* Arg
39B2 **Sierra de Segura** *Mts* Spain
22C1 **Sierra de Tamaulipas** *Mts* Mexico
39B1 **Sierra de Urbion** *Mts* Spain
28B2 **Sierra de Uspallata** *Mts* Arg
28B1 **Sierra de Valasco** *Mts* Arg
28B2 **Sierra de Valle Fértil** *Mts* Arg
22B1 **Sierra de Zacatécas** *Mts* Mexico
22C2 **Sierra de Zongolica** *Mts* Mexico
28C2 **Sierra Grande** *Mts* Arg
70A4 **Sierra Leone** Republic, Africa
70A4 **Sierra Leone,C** Sierra Leone
57F7 **Sierra Madre** *Mts* Phil
22B2 **Sierra Madre del Sur** *Mts* Mexico
20B3 **Sierra Madre Mts** USA
21B2 **Sierra Madre Occidental** *Mts* Mexico
22B1 **Sierra Madre Oriental** *Mts* Mexico
28B2 **Sierra Malanzan** *Mts* Arg
8C4 **Sierra Mojada** Mexico
39A2 **Sierra Morena** *Mts* Spain
39B2 **Sierra Nevada** *Mts* Spain
19B3 **Sierra Nevada** *Mts* USA
26D1 **Sierra Nevada de santa Marta** *Mts* Colombia
28B2 **Sierra Pié de Palo** *Mts* Arg
19D4 **Sierra Vista** USA
37B1 **Sierre** Switz
29A3 **Siete Puntas** *R* Par
41E3 **Sífnos** *I* Greece
71B1 **Sig** Alg
44E2 **Sig** Russian Fed
56A3 **Sigep** Indon
43E3 **Sighetu Marmaţiei** Rom
41E1 **Sighişoara** Rom
56A1 **Sigli** Indon
32B1 **Siglufjörður** Iceland
36E2 **Sigmaringen** Germany
26A1 **Siguatepeque** Honduras
39B1 **Sigüenza** Spain
70B3 **Siguiri** Guinea
55C3 **Sihanoukville** Camb
60D4 **Sihora** India
64D2 **Siirt** Turk
50C3 **Sikai Hu** *L* China
3D2 **Sikanni** *R* Can
60D3 **Sīkar** India
60B2 **Sikaram** *Mt* Afghan
70B3 **Sikasso** Mali
57B4 **Sikeli** Indon
17E2 **Sikeston** USA
41F3 **Síkinos** *I* Greece
41E3 **Sikionía** Greece
61C2 **Sikkim** State, India
49O3 **Siktyakh** Russian Fed
39A1 **Sil** *R* Spain
37D1 **Silandro** Italy
22B1 **Silao** Mexico
57F8 **Silay** Phil
61D3 **Silchar** India
4C2 **Silcox** Can
70C2 **Silet** Alg
61B2 **Silgarhi** Nepal
64B2 **Silifke** Turk
65D1 **Silinfah** Syria
59G2 **Siling Co** *L* China
41F2 **Silistra** Bulg
44A3 **Siljan** *L* Sweden
32F7 **Silkeborg** Den
37E1 **Sillian** Austria
17D2 **Siloam Springs** USA
17D3 **Silsbee** USA
72B2 **Siltou** *Well* Chad
43E1 **Šilute** Lithuania
64D2 **Silvan** Turk
29C2 **Silvania** Brazil
60C4 **Silvassa** India
11D2 **Silver Bay** USA
19C3 **Silver City** Nevada, USA
16A3 **Silver City** New Mexico, USA
18B2 **Silver Lake** USA
20D2 **Silver Peak Range** *Mts* USA
14B3 **Silver Spring** USA
3C3 **Silverthrone Mt** Can
75B2 **Silverton** Aust
16A2 **Silverton** USA
37D1 **Silvretta** *Mts* Austria/Switz
56D2 **Simanggang** Malay
55C1 **Simao** China
63B2 **Simareh** *R* Iran
41F3 **Simav** Turk
41F3 **Simav** *R* Turk
44H5 **Simbirsk** Russian Fed
4F5 **Simcoe,L** Can
10G5 **Simeohof** *I* USA
56A2 **Simeulue** *I* Indon
45E7 **Simferopol'** Ukraine
41F3 **Sími** *I* Greece
61B2 **Simikot** Nepal
16B2 **Simla** USA
36D1 **Simmern** Germany
20C3 **Simmler** USA
74B3 **Simonstown** S Africa
3C3 **Simoom Sound** Can
38D2 **Simplon** *Mt* Switz
37C1 **Simplon** *P* Switz
6C2 **Simpson,C** USA
76C3 **Simpson Desert** Aust
10N2 **Simpson L** Can
3B2 **Simpson Peak** *Mt* Can
7K3 **Simpson Pen** Can
32G7 **Simrishamn** Sweden
50J2 **Simushir** *I* Russian Fed
56A2 **Sinabang** Indon
72E3 **Sina Dhaqa** Somalia
64B4 **Sinai** *Pen* Egypt
22A1 **Sinaloa** State, Mexico
37D3 **Sinalunga** Italy
26C2 **Sincelejo** Colombia
15C2 **Sinclair,L** USA
60D3 **Sind** *R* India
60B3 **Sindh** *Region* Pak
41F3 **Sindirği** Turk
61C3 **Sindri** India
53E2 **Sinegorsk** Russian Fed
39A2 **Sines** Port
72D2 **Singa** Sudan
55C5 **Singapore** Republic, S E Asia
55C5 **Singapore,Str of** S E Asia
56E4 **Singaraja** Indon
36E3 **Singen** Germany
72D4 **Singida** Tanz
61E2 **Singkaling Hkamti** Myanmar
56C2 **Singkawang** Indon
75D2 **Singleton** Aust
56B3 **Singtep** *I* Indon
55B1 **Singu** Myanmar
74E1 **Singuédeze** *R* Mozam
54A3 **Sin'gye** N Korea
54A2 **Sinhŭng** N Korea
40B2 **Siniscola** Sardgena
57B4 **Sinjai** Indon
64D2 **Sinjár** Iraq
60B2 **Sinkai Hills** *Mts* Afghan
66C3 **Sinkat** Sudan
59G1 **Sinkiang** Autonomous Region, China
36E1 **Sinn** *R* Germany
27H2 **Sinnamary** French Guiana
54A3 **Sinnyong** S Korea
64C1 **Sinop** Turk
54A2 **Sinpa** N Korea
54A2 **Sinp'o** N Korea
54A3 **Sinp'yong** N Korea
41E1 **Sintana** Rom
56D2 **Sintang** Indon
17F4 **Sinton** USA
39A2 **Sintra** Port
26C2 **Sinú** *R* Colombia
53A3 **Sinŭiju** N Korea
43D3 **Siofok** Hung
37B1 **Sion** Switz
11C3 **Sioux City** USA
11C3 **Sioux Falls** USA
4C3 **Sioux Lookout** Can
57F9 **Sipalay** Phil
23L1 **Siparia** Trinidad
53A3 **Siping** China
4B3 **Sipiwesk L** Can
79F3 **Siple** *Base* Ant
79F5 **Siple I** Ant
57F8 **Sipocot** Phil
56A3 **Sipora** Indon
15B2 **Sipsey** *R* USA
22A1 **Siqueros** Mexico
57F9 **Siquijor** *I* Phil
62B2 **Sira** India
40D3 **Siracusa** Italy
61C3 **Sirajganj** Bang
3D3 **Sir Alexander,Mt** Can
71G3 **Sirba** *R* Burkina
67F2 **Sīr Banī Yās** *I* UAE
76C2 **Sir Edward Pellew Group** *Is* Aust
41F1 **Siret** *R* Rom
10N3 **Sir James McBrien,Mt** Can
62B2 **Sir Kālahasti** India
3D3 **Sir Laurier,Mt** Can
64D2 **Şirnak** Turk
60C4 **Sirohi** India
62C1 **Sironcha** India
60D4 **Sironj** India
41E3 **Síros** *I* Greece
20C3 **Sirretta Peak,Mt** USA
63C3 **Sirri** *I* Iran
60C3 **Sirsa** India
3E3 **Sir Sandford,Mt** Can
62A2 **Sirsi** India
69A1 **Sirte Desert** Libya
69A1 **Sirte,G of** Libya

Split L **Swale**

4B2 **Split L** Can
40D2 **Split** Croatia
37C1 **Splügen** Switz
18C1 **Spokane** USA
12A1 **Spooner** USA
18C2 **Spray** USA
42C2 **Spree** *R* Germany
74B2 **Springbok** S Africa
5K4 **Springdale** Can
17D2 **Springdale** USA
16B2 **Springer** USA
19E4 **Springerville** USA
16B2 **Springfield** Colorado, USA
12B3 **Springfield** Illinois, USA
14D1 **Springfield** Massachusetts, USA
11C3 **Springfield** Minnesota, USA
17D2 **Springfield** Missouri, USA
12C3 **Springfield** Ohio, USA
18B2 **Springfield** Oregon, USA
15B1 **Springfield** Tennessee, USA
13E2 **Springfield** Vermont, USA
74D3 **Springfontein** S Africa
5J4 **Springhill** Can
19C3 **Spring Mts** USA
74D2 **Springs** S Africa
14A1 **Springville** New York, USA
19D2 **Springville** Utah, USA
14B1 **Springwater** USA
18D2 **Spruce Mt** USA
35F5 **Spurn Head** *C* Eng
33D3 **Spurn Head** *Pt* Eng
18B1 **Spuzzum** Can
3D4 **Squamish** Can
49R3 **Sredhekolymsk** Russian Fed
49S4 **Sredinnyy Khrebet** *Mts* Russian Fed
44F5 **Sredne-Russkaya Vozvyshennost'** *Upland* Russian Fed
49M3 **Sredne Sibirskoye Ploskogorye** *Tableland* Russian Fed
44K4 **Sredniy Ural** *Mts* Russian Fed
55D3 **Srepok** *R* Camb
50E1 **Sretensk** Russian Fed
55C3 **Sre Umbell** Camb
62C1 **Srīkākulam** India
59G5 **Sri Lanka** Republic, S Asia
60C2 **Srīnagar** India
62A1 **Srīvardhan** India
42D2 **Sroda Wielkopolski** Pol
34C2 **Stack Skerry** *I* Scot
42B2 **Stade** Germany
34B3 **Staffa** *I* Scot
35D5 **Stafford** County, Eng
35D5 **Stafford** Eng
14D2 **Stafford Springs** USA
Stalingrad = Volgograd
3D2 **Stalin,Mt** Can
74B3 **Stallberg** *Mt* S Africa
7J1 **Stallworthy,C** Can
43E2 **Stalowa Wola** Pol
14D2 **Stamford** Connecticut, USA
14C1 **Stamford** New York, USA
16C3 **Stamford** Texas, USA
74B1 **Stampriet** Namibia
74D2 **Standerton** S Africa
12C2 **Standish** USA
18D1 **Stanford** USA
74E2 **Stanger** S Africa
20B2 **Stanislaus** *R* USA
41E2 **Stanke Dimitrov** Bulg
75E3 **Stanley** Aust
25E8 **Stanley** Falkland Is
18D2 **Stanley** Idaho, USA
11B2 **Stanley** N Dakota, USA
62B2 **Stanley Res** India
Stanleyville = Kisangani
21D3 **Stann Creek** Belize
50F1 **Stanovoy Khrebet** *Mts* Russian Fed
37C1 **Stans** Switz
75D1 **Stanthorpe** Aust
34B3 **Stanton Banks** *Sand-bank* Scot
16B1 **Stapleton** USA
43E2 **Starachowice** Pol
41E2 **Stara Planiná** *Mts* Bulg
44E4 **Staraya Russa** Russian Fed
41F2 **Stara Zagora** Bulg
42D2 **Stargard Szczecinski** Pol
17E3 **Starkville** USA
42C3 **Starnberg** Germany
43D2 **Starogard Gdanski** Pol
43F3 **Starokonstantinov** Ukraine
35D6 **Start Pt** Eng
45F5 **Staryy Oskol** Russian Fed
14B2 **State College** USA
14C2 **Staten I** USA
15C2 **Statesboro** USA
15C1 **Statesville** USA
13D3 **Staunton** USA
32F7 **Stavanger** Nor
36C1 **Stavelot** Belg
45G6 **Stavropol'** Russian Fed
75B3 **Stawell** Aust
42D2 **Stawno** Pol
18B2 **Stayton** USA
16A1 **Steamboat Springs** USA
10F3 **Stebbins** USA
10K3 **Steele,Mt** Can
14B2 **Steelton** USA
3E2 **Steen** *R* Can
3E2 **Steen River** Can
18C2 **Steens Mt** USA
7N2 **Steenstrups Gletscher** *Gl* Greenland
6H2 **Stefansson I** Can
74E2 **Stegi** Swaziland
37D1 **Steinach** Austria
4B4 **Steinbach** Can
44A3 **Steinkjer** Nor
74B2 **Steinkopf** S Africa
3D3 **Stein Mt** Can
74C2 **Stella** S Africa
5J4 **Stellarton** Can
74B3 **Stellenbosch** S Africa
22C2 **Stemaco** Mexico
36C2 **Stenay** France
42C2 **Stendal** Germany
45H8 **Stepanakert** Azerbaijan
11C2 **Stephen** USA
78B2 **Stephens,C** NZ
75B2 **Stephens Creek** Aust
12B1 **Stephenson** USA
10M4 **Stephens Pass** USA
7N5 **Stephenville** Can
16C3 **Stephenville** USA
10F4 **Stepovak B** USA
74D3 **Sterkstroom** S Africa
16B1 **Sterling** Colorado, USA
12B2 **Sterling** Illinois, USA
16C2 **Sterling** Kansas, USA
11B2 **Sterling** N Dakota, USA
16B3 **Sterling City** USA
12C2 **Sterling Heights** USA
44K5 **Sterlitamak** Russian Fed
3F3 **Stettler** Can
12C2 **Steubenville** USA
4B3 **Stevenson L** Can
12B2 **Stevens Point** USA
6D3 **Stevens Village** USA
3B2 **Stewart** Can
19C3 **Stewart** USA
10L3 **Stewart** *R* Can
10L3 **Stewart Crossing** Can
78A3 **Stewart I** NZ
77F1 **Stewart Is** Solomon Is
6E3 **Stewart River** Can
14B3 **Stewartstown** USA
11D3 **Stewartville** USA
74D2 **Steyn** S Africa
74D3 **Steynsburg** S Africa
42C3 **Steyr** Austria
74C3 **Steytlerville** S Africa
37D3 **Stia** Italy
10L4 **Stika** USA
3B2 **Stikine** *R* Can
10M4 **Stikine Ranges** *Mts* Can
11D2 **Stillwater** Minnesota, USA
17C2 **Stillwater** Oklahoma, USA
19C3 **Stillwater Range** *Mts* USA
4E4 **Stimson** Can
16B2 **Stinett** USA
75A2 **Stirling** Aust
34D3 **Stirling** Scot
36E3 **Stockach** Germany
14D1 **Stockbridge** USA
42D3 **Stockerau** Austria
32H7 **Stockholm** Sweden
35D5 **Stockport** Eng
20B2 **Stockton** California, USA
35E4 **Stockton** Eng
16C2 **Stockton** Kansas, USA
17D2 **Stockton L** USA
35D5 **Stoke-on-Trent** Eng
4E4 **Stokes Bay** Can
32A2 **Stokkseyri** Iceland
32G5 **Stokmarknes** Nor
49P2 **Stolbovoy, Ostrov** *I* Russian Fed
32K8 **Stolbtsy** Belarus
43F2 **Stolin** Belarus
14C3 **Stone Harbor** USA
34D3 **Stonehaven** Scot
17C3 **Stonewall** USA
10H3 **Stony** *R* USA
5K3 **Stony I** Can
3J2 **Stony L** Can
4E3 **Stooping** *R* Can
32H5 **Storavan** *L* Sweden
32G6 **Støren** Nor
75E3 **Storm B** Aust
11C3 **Storm Lake** USA
34B2 **Stornoway** Scot
43F3 **Storozhinets** Ukraine
14D2 **Storrs** USA
32G6 **Storsjön** *L* Sweden
32H5 **Storuman** Sweden
11A3 **Story** USA
3H4 **Stoughton** Can
14E1 **Stoughton** USA
36A1 **Stour** *R* Eng
35F5 **Stowmarket** Eng
53C1 **Stoyba** Russian Fed
34B4 **Strabane** N Ire
75E3 **Strahan** Aust
42C2 **Stralsund** Germany
74B3 **Strand** S Africa
32F6 **Stranda** Nor
32H7 **Strängnäs** Sweden
34C4 **Stranraer** Scot
38D2 **Strasbourg** France
13D3 **Strasburg** USA
20C2 **Stratford** California, USA
4E5 **Stratford** Can
14D2 **Stratford** Connecticut, USA
78B1 **Stratford** NZ
16B2 **Stratford** Texas, USA
35E5 **Stratford-on-Avon** Eng
75A3 **Strathalbyn** Aust
34C4 **Strathclyde** Region, Scot
3F3 **Strathmore** Can
13E1 **Stratton** USA
12B2 **Streator** USA
37C2 **Stresa** Italy
40D3 **Stretto de Messina** *Str* Italy/Sicily
40D3 **Stroboli** *I* Italy
28C4 **Stroeder** Arg
34D2 **Stromness** Scot
32D3 **Strømø** Faroes
17C1 **Stromsburg** USA
32H6 **Stromsund** Sweden
32G6 **Ströms Vattudal** *L* Sweden
34D2 **Stronsay** *I* Scot
35D6 **Stroud** Eng
14C2 **Stroudsburg** USA
41E2 **Struma** *R* Bulg
35C5 **Strumble Head** *Pt* Wales
41E2 **Strumica** Macedonia
43E3 **Stryy** Ukraine
43E3 **Stryy** *R* Ukraine
75B1 **Strzelecki Creek** *R* Aust
15E4 **Stuart** Florida, USA
11C3 **Stuart** Nebraska, USA
3D3 **Stuart** *R* Can
10F3 **Stuart I** USA
3D3 **Stuart L** Can
37D1 **Stubaier Alpen** *Mts* Austria
32H8 **Stubice** Pol
55D3 **Stung Sen** Camb
55D3 **Stung Treng** Camb
4C2 **Stupart** *R* Can
40B2 **Stura** *R* Italy
79G7 **Sturge I** Ant
12B2 **Sturgeon Bay** USA
4F4 **Sturgeon Falls** Can
4C4 **Sturgeon L** Can
12B3 **Sturgis** Kentucky, USA
12B2 **Sturgis** Michigan, USA
11B3 **Sturgis** S Dakota, USA
76B2 **Sturt Creek** *R* Aust
75B1 **Sturt Desert** Aust
74D3 **Stutterheim** S Africa
17D3 **Stuttgart** USA
42B3 **Stuttgart** Germany
32A1 **Stykkishólmur** Iceland
43F2 **Styr'** *R* Ukraine
49M4 **Styudyanka** Russian Fed
29D2 **Suaçuí Grande** *R* Brazil
66C3 **Suakin** Sudan
54A3 **Suan** N Korea
52E5 **Su-ao** Taiwan
28C2 **Suardi** Arg
56C2 **Subi** *I* Indon
41D1 **Subotica** Serbia, Yugos
45D6 **Suceava** Rom
22C2 **Suchixtepec** Mexico
26E7 **Sucre** Bol
29B2 **Sucuriú** R, Brazil
72C2 **Sudan** Republic, Africa
4E4 **Sudbury** Can
35F5 **Sudbury** Eng
72C3 **Sudd** *Swamp* Sudan
27G2 **Suddie** Guyana
65B4 **Sudr** Egypt
72C3 **Sue** *R* Sudan
10M4 **Suemez I** USA
64B4 **Suez** Egypt
64B3 **Suez Canal** Egypt
64B4 **Suez,G of** Egypt
14C2 **Suffern** USA
35F5 **Suffolk** County, Eng
13D3 **Suffolk** USA
13E2 **Sugarloaf Mt** USA
75D2 **Sugarloaf Pt** Aust
3H3 **Suggi L** Can
49R3 **Sugoy** *R* Russian Fed
67G2 **Suhār** Oman
50D1 **Sühbaatar** Mongolia
60B3 **Sui** Pak
53C2 **Suibin** China
52C2 **Suide** China
53C3 **Suifenhe** China
53B2 **Suihua** China
53B2 **Suileng** China
52B3 **Suining** China
36C2 **Suippes** France
33B3 **Suir** *R* Irish Rep
52C3 **Sui Xian** China
52E1 **Suizhong** China
60C3 **Sujāngarh** India
56C4 **Sukabumi** Indon
56D3 **Sukadana** Borneo, Indon
56C4 **Sukadana** Sumatra, Indon
53E4 **Sukagawa** Japan
56D3 **Sukaraya** Indon
44F5 **Sukhinichi** Russian Fed
44G4 **Sukhona** *R* Russian Fed
45G7 **Sukhumi** Georgia
7N3 **Sukkertoppen** Greenland
7N3 **Sukkertoppen Isflade** *Gl* Greenland
32L6 **Sukkozero** Russian Fed
60B3 **Sukkur** Pak
62C1 **Sukma** India
53D2 **Sukpay** *R* Russian Fed
73B6 **Sukses** Namibia
54B4 **Sukumo** Japan
3D2 **Sukunka** *R* Can
45F5 **Sula** *R* Russian Fed
60B3 **Sulaiman Range** *Mts* Pak
34B2 **Sula Sgeir** *I* Scot
57B3 **Sulawesi** *I* Indon
57B3 **Sulawesi Sulatan** Prov, Indon
57B3 **Sulawesi Tengah** Prov, Indon
57B3 **Sulawesi Tenggara** Prov, Indon
57B3 **Sulawesi Utara** Prov, Indon
71H4 **Suleja** Nig
34C2 **Sule Skerry** *I* Scot
41F1 **Sulina** Rom
32H5 **Sulitjelma** Nor
26B4 **Sullana** Peru
17D2 **Sullivan** USA
3C3 **Sullivan Bay** Can
3F3 **Sullivan L** Can
36B3 **Sully-sur-Loire** France
40C2 **Sulmona** Italy
17D3 **Sulphur** Louisiana, USA
17C3 **Sulphur** Oklahoma, USA
17C3 **Sulphur Springs** USA
4E4 **Sultan** Can
45E8 **Sultan Dağlari** *Mts* Turk
61B2 **Sultānpur** India
57F9 **Sulu Arch** Phil
51E6 **Sulu S** Philip
36E2 **Sulz** Germany
25D3 **Sumampa** Arg
56A2 **Sumatera** *I* Indon
57B4 **Sumba** *I* Indon
56E4 **Sumbawa** *I* Indon
56E4 **Sumbawa Besar** Indon
73D4 **Sumbawanga** Tanz
34E2 **Sumburgh Head** *Pt* Scot
56D4 **Sumenep** Indon
45H7 **Sumgait** Azerbaijan
73B5 **Sumbe** Angola
50H3 **Sumisu** *I* Japan
3E4 **Summerland** Can
5J4 **Summerside** Can
3B2 **Summer Str** USA
6F4 **Summit Lake** Can
19C3 **Summits Mt** USA
78B2 **Sumner,L** NZ
54B4 **Sumoto** Japan
15C2 **Sumter** USA
45E5 **Sumy** Ukraine
18D1 **Sun** *R* USA
54D2 **Sunagawa** Japan
54A3 **Sunan** N Korea
14B2 **Sunbury** USA
28C2 **Sunchales** Arg
28C1 **Suncho Corral** Arg
53B4 **Sunch'ŏn** N Korea
53B5 **Sunch'ŏn** S Korea
11B3 **Sundance** USA
61B3 **Sundargarh** India
61C3 **Sunderbans** *Swamp* India
34E4 **Sunderland** Eng
3F3 **Sundre** Can
13D1 **Sundridge** Can
32H6 **Sundsvaall** Sweden
56E3 **Sungaianyar** Indon
56B3 **Sungaisalak** Indon
56F6 **Sungai Siput** Malay
56F6 **Sungei Petani** Malay
57A4 **Sungguminasa** Indon
18C1 **Sunnyside** USA
19B3 **Sunnyvale** USA
12B2 **Sun Prairie** USA
49N3 **Suntar** Russian Fed
63E3 **Suntsar** Pak
18D2 **Sun Valley** USA
53B2 **Sunwu** China
71F4 **Sunyani** Ghana
44E3 **Suojarvi** Russian Fed
54B4 **Suō-nada** *B* Japan
32K6 **Suonejoki** Fin
61C2 **Supaul** India
19D4 **Superior** Arizona, USA
17C1 **Superior** Nebraska, USA
12A1 **Superior** Wisconsin, USA
12B1 **Superior,L** USA/Can
55C3 **Suphan Buri** Thai
64D2 **Süphan Daǧ** Turk
51G7 **Supiori** *I* Indon
57C2 **Supu** Indon
66D3 **Sūq 'Abs** Yemen
64E3 **Suq ash Suyukh** Iraq
65D1 **Suqaylibīyah** Syria
52D3 **Suqian** China
Suqutra = Socotra
67G2 **Sūr** Oman
44H5 **Sura** *R* Russian Fed
56D4 **Surabaya** Indon
54C4 **Suraga-wan** *B* Japan
56D4 **Surakarta** Indon
65D1 **Sūrān** Syria
75C1 **Surat** Aust
60C4 **Sūrat** India
60C3 **Sūratgarh** India
55B4 **Surat Thani** Thai
60C4 **Surendranagar** India
14C3 **Surf City** USA
48J3 **Surgut** Russian Fed
62B1 **Suriāpet** India
38D2 **Sürich** Switz
57G9 **Surigao** Phil
55C3 **Surin** Thai
27G3 **Surinam** Republic, S America
20B2 **Sur,Pt** USA
35E6 **Surrey** County, Eng
37C1 **Sursee** Switz
69A1 **Surt** Libya
32A2 **Surtsey** *I* Iceland
56B3 **Surulangan** Indon
37B2 **Susa** Italy
54B4 **Susa** Japan
54B4 **Susaki** Japan
19B2 **Susanville** USA
37D1 **Süsch** Switz
10J3 **Susitna** *R* USA
14C2 **Susquehanna** USA
14B3 **Susquehanna** *R* USA
14C2 **Sussex** USA
35E6 **Sussex West** Eng
3C2 **Sustut Peak** *Mt* Can
74C3 **Sutherland** S Africa
16B1 **Sutherland** USA
60C2 **Sutlej** *R* Pak
19B3 **Sutter Creek** USA
12C3 **Sutton** USA
4E3 **Sutton** *R* Can
54D2 **Suttsu** Japan
10G4 **Sutwik I** USA
77G2 **Suva** Fiji
53D4 **Suwa** Japan
43E2 **Suwałki** Pol
15C3 **Suwannee** *R* USA
65C2 **Suweilih** Jordan
53B4 **Suwŏn** S Korea
52D3 **Su Xian** China
54C3 **Suzaka** Japan
52E3 **Suzhou** China
53D4 **Suzu** Japan
54C4 **Suzuka** Japan
54C3 **Suzu-misaki** *C* Japan
48C2 **Svalbard** *Is* Barents S
43E3 **Svalyava** Ukraine
7N2 **Svartenhuk Halvø** *Region* Greenland
32G5 **Svartisen** *Mt* Nor
55D3 **Svay Rieng** Camb
32G6 **Sveg** Sweden
32G7 **Svendborg** Den
7J1 **Sverdrup Chan** Can
6H2 **Sverdrup Is** Can
53D2 **Svetlaya** Russian Fed
43E2 **Svetlogorsk** Russian Fed
32K6 **Svetogorsk** Russian Fed
41E2 **Svetozarevo** Serbia, Yugos
41F2 **Svilengrad** Bulg
43F2 **Svir'** Belrussia
44E3 **Svir'** *R* Russian Fed
42D3 **Śvitavy** Czech Republic
53B1 **Svobodnyy** Russian Fed
32G5 **Svolvaer** Nor
77E3 **Swain Reefs** Aust
77H2 **Swains** *I* American Samoa
15C2 **Swainsboro** USA
74B1 **Swakop** *R* Namibia
74A1 **Swakopmund** Namibia
35E4 **Swale** *R* Eng

Warmbad
Wind Cave Nat Pk

73C6 **Warmbad** S Africa
14C2 **Warminster** USA
19C3 **Warm Springs** USA
42C2 **Warnemünde** Germany
18B2 **Warner Mts** USA
15C2 **Warner Robins** USA
75B3 **Warracknabeal** Aust
75A1 **Warrandirinna,L** Aust
76D3 **Warrego** *R* Aust
17D3 **Warren** Arkansas, USA
75C2 **Warren** Aust
11C2 **Warren** Minnesota, USA
12C2 **Warren** Ohio, USA
4E5 **Warren** Michigan, USA
13D2 **Warren** Pennsylvania, USA
14E2 **Warren** Rhode Island, USA
35B4 **Warrenpoint** N Ire
17D2 **Warrensburg** USA
74C2 **Warrenton** S Africa
13D3 **Warrenton** USA
71H4 **Warri** Nig
75A1 **Warrina** Aust
35D5 **Warrington** Eng
15B2 **Warrington** USA
75B3 **Warrnambool** Aust
11C2 **Warroad** USA
Warsaw = Warszawa
14A1 **Warsaw** USA
72E3 **Warshiikh** Somalia
43E2 **Warszawa** Pol
43D2 **Warta** *R* Pol
75D1 **Warwick** Aust
35E5 **Warwick** County, Eng
35E5 **Warwick** Eng
14C2 **Warwick** New York, USA
14E2 **Warwick** Rhode Island, USA
19D3 **Wasatch Range** *Mts* USA
74E2 **Wasbank** S Africa
20C3 **Wasco** USA
11D3 **Waseca** USA
3G2 **Wasekamio L** Can
63E3 **Washap** Pak
12A1 **Washburn** USA
6H2 **Washburn L** Can
18D2 **Washburn,Mt** USA
60D4 **Wāshīm** India
9F3 **Washington** District of Columbia, USA
15C2 **Washington** Georgia, USA
12B3 **Washington** Indiana, USA
11D3 **Washington** Iowa, USA
17D2 **Washington** Missouri, USA
15D1 **Washington** N Carolina, USA
14C2 **Washington** New Jersey, USA
12C2 **Washington** Pennsylvania, USA
8A2 **Washington** State, USA
19D3 **Washington** Utah, USA
12C3 **Washington Court House** USA
7M1 **Washington Land** *Region* Can
13E2 **Washington,Mt** USA
16C2 **Washita** *R* USA
35F5 **Wash,The** Eng
60A3 **Washuk** Pak
10J3 **Wasilla** USA
7L4 **Waskaganish** Can
23A4 **Waspán** Nic
20C1 **Wassuk Range** *Mts* USA
36C2 **Wassy** France
4F4 **Waswanipi L** *L* Can
57B3 **Watampone** Indon
57A3 **Watansoppeng** Indon
74D3 **Waterberge** *Mts* S Africa
14D2 **Waterbury** USA
3G2 **Waterbury L** Can
35B5 **Waterford** County, Irish Rep
33B3 **Waterford** Irish Rep
35B5 **Waterford Harbour** Irish Rep
36C1 **Waterloo** Belg
4E5 **Waterloo** Can
11D3 **Waterloo** USA
12B1 **Watersmeet** USA
18D1 **Waterton-Glacier International Peace Park** USA
13D2 **Watertown** New York, USA
11C3 **Watertown** S Dakota, USA
12B2 **Watertown** Wisconsin, USA
74E2 **Waterval-Boven** S Africa
13F2 **Waterville** Maine, USA
14C1 **Waterville** New York, USA
14D1 **Watervliet** USA
6G4 **Waterways** Can
35E6 **Watford** Eng
11B2 **Watford City** USA
14B1 **Watkins Glen** USA
16C2 **Watonga** USA
8C1 **Watrous** Can
16B2 **Watrous** USA
72C3 **Watsa** Zaïre
10N3 **Watson Lake** Can
20B2 **Watsonville** USA
3E2 **Watt,Mt** Can
57B3 **Watukancoa** Indon
51H7 **Wau** PNG
72C3 **Wau** Sudan
75D2 **Wauchope** Aust
15E4 **Wauchula** USA
12B2 **Waukegan** USA
12B2 **Waukesha** USA
12B2 **Waupaca** USA
12B2 **Waupun** USA
17C3 **Waurika** USA
12B2 **Wausau** USA
12B2 **Wauwatosa** USA
76C2 **Wave Hill** Aust
35F5 **Waverey** *R* Eng
11D3 **Waverly** Iowa, USA
14B1 **Waverly** New York, USA
12C3 **Waverly** Ohio, USA
36C1 **Wavre** Belg
7K5 **Wawa** Can
71G4 **Wawa** Nig
69A2 **Wāw Al Kabīr** Libya
69A2 **Wāw an Nāmūs** *Well* Libya
20C2 **Wawona** USA
17C3 **Waxahachie** USA
57C2 **Wayabula** Indon
15C2 **Waycross** USA
11C3 **Wayne** USA
15C2 **Waynesboro** Georgia, USA
17E3 **Waynesboro** Mississippi, USA
14B3 **Waynesboro** Pennsylvania, USA
13D3 **Waynesboro** Virginia, USA
17D2 **Waynesville** Missouri, USA
15C1 **Waynesville** N Carolina, USA
60B2 **Wazi Khwa** Afghan
35F6 **Weald,The** *Upland* Eng
34D4 **Wear** *R* Eng
16C2 **Weatherford** Oklahoma, USA
17C3 **Weatherford** Texas, USA
18B2 **Weaverville** USA
12C1 **Webbwood** Can
14B1 **Webster** New York, USA
11C2 **Webster** S Dakota, USA
14E1 **Webster** USA
11D3 **Webster City** USA
12A3 **Webster Groves** USA
57C2 **Weda** Indon
25D8 **Weddell I** Falkland Is
79G2 **Weddell S** Ant
3D3 **Wedge Mt** Can
5H5 **Wedgeport** Can
18B2 **Weed** USA
14A2 **Weedville** USA
74E2 **Weenen** S Africa
75C2 **Wee Waa** Aust
52D1 **Weichang** China
42C3 **Weiden** Germany
52D2 **Weifang** China
52E2 **Weihai** China
52C3 **Wei He** *R* Henan, China
52C2 **Wei He** *R* Shaanxi, China
75C1 **Weilmoringle** Aust
36E2 **Weinheim** Germany
52A4 **Weining** China
76D2 **Weipa** Aust
12C2 **Weirton** USA
18C2 **Weiser** USA
52D3 **Weishan Hu** *L* China
42C2 **Weissenfels** Germany
15B2 **Weiss L** USA
3G2 **Weitzel L** Can
4B3 **Wekusko** Can
12C3 **Welch** USA
72E2 **Weldiya** Eth
20C3 **Weldon** USA
74D2 **Welkom** S Africa
13D2 **Welland** Can
35E5 **Welland** *R* Eng
76C2 **Wellesley Is** Aust
10L3 **Wellesley L** Can
14E2 **Wellfleet** USA
35E5 **Wellingborough** Eng
75C2 **Wellington** Aust
16B1 **Wellington** Colorado, USA
17C2 **Wellington** Kansas, USA
20C1 **Wellington** Nevada, USA
78B2 **Wellington** NZ
74B3 **Wellington** S Africa
16B3 **Wellington** Texas, USA
7J2 **Wellington Chan** Can
3D3 **Wells** Can
35D6 **Wells** Eng
18D2 **Wells** Nevada, USA
14C1 **Wells** New York, USA
14B2 **Wellsboro** USA
78B1 **Wellsford** NZ
76B3 **Wells,L** Aust
4A2 **Wells L** Can
14B1 **Wellsville** USA
42C3 **Wels** Austria
35D5 **Welshpool** Wales
3E2 **Wembley** Can
7L4 **Wemindji** Can
18B1 **Wenatchee** USA
18C1 **Wenatchee** *R* USA
71F4 **Wenchi** Ghana
52E2 **Wenden** China
18D2 **Wendover** USA
52E4 **Wenling** China
52A5 **Wenshan** China
76D4 **Wenthaggi** Aust
75B2 **Wentworth** Aust
3F2 **Wentzel L** Can
52A3 **Wen Xian** China
52E4 **Wenzhou** China
52C4 **Wenzhu** China
74D2 **Wepener** S Africa
74C2 **Werda** Botswana
10L2 **Wernecke Mts** Can
42C2 **Werra** *R* Germany
75D2 **Werris Creek** Aust
36D1 **Wesel** Germany
42B2 **Weser** *R* Germany
16B2 **Weskan** USA
17F4 **Weslaco** USA
7N5 **Wesleyville** Can
76C2 **Wessel Is** Aust
36E1 **Wesser** *R* Germany
36E1 **Wesserbergland** Region, Germany
11C3 **Wessington Springs** USA
12B2 **West Allis** USA
xxviiiF5 **West Australian Basin** Indian O
xxviiiF6 **West Australian Ridge** Indian O
17E3 **West B** USA
61C3 **West Bengal** State, India
14C1 **West Branch Delaware** *R* USA
14A2 **West Branch Susquehanna** *R* USA
35E5 **West Bromwich** Eng
13E2 **Westbrook** USA
12A2 **Westby** USA
14C3 **West Chester** USA
20D3 **Westend** USA
36D1 **Westerburg** Germany
42B2 **Westerland** Germany
14E2 **Westerly** USA
76B3 **Western Australia** State, Aust
74B3 **Western Cape** Province, S Africa
62A1 **Western Ghats** *Mts* India
34B3 **Western Isles** Scot
70A2 **Western Sahara** Region, Mor
77H2 **Western Samoa** *Is* Pacific O
36B1 **Westerschelde** *Estuary* Neth
36D1 **Westerwald** Region, Germany
38D1 **Westfalen** Region, Germany
25D8 **West Falkland** *I* Falkland Is
14D1 **Westfield** Massachusetts, USA
13D2 **Westfield** New York, USA
14B2 **Westfield** Pennsylvania, USA
12B3 **West Frankfort** USA
75C1 **Westgate** Aust
35D6 **West Glamorgan** County, Wales
13F1 **West Grand L** USA
xxxE4 **West Indies** *Is* Caribbean S
12C3 **West Liberty** USA
3F3 **Westlock** Can
12C2 **West Lorne** Can
35B5 **Westmeath** County, Irish Rep
17D2 **West Memphis** USA
35E5 **West Midlands** County, Eng
35E6 **Westminster** Eng
14B3 **Westminster** Maryland, USA
15C2 **Westminster** S Carolina, USA
74D1 **West Nicholson** Zim
56E1 **Weston** Malay
12C3 **Weston** USA
35D6 **Weston-super-Mare** Eng
15E4 **West Palm Beach** USA
17D2 **West Plains** USA
20B1 **West Point** California, USA
17E3 **West Point** Mississippi, USA
11C3 **West Point** Nebraska, USA
14D2 **West Point** New York, USA
10K3 **West Point** *Mt* USA
78B2 **Westport** NZ
4A3 **Westray** Can
33C2 **Westray** *I* Scot
3D3 **West Road** *R* Can
35F5 **West Side** *Oilfield* N Sea
9E3 **West Virginia** State, USA
20C1 **West Walker** USA
75C2 **West Wyalong** Aust
18D2 **West Yellowstone** USA
35E5 **West Yorkshire** County, Eng
57C4 **Wetar** *I* Indon
3F3 **Wetaskiwin** Can
72D4 **Wete** Tanz
36E1 **Wetter** *R* Germany
36E1 **Wetzlar** Germany
Wevok = Cape Lisburne
76D1 **Wewak** PNG
17C2 **Wewoka** USA
35B5 **Wexford** County, Irish Rep
35B5 **Wexford** Irish Rep
6H5 **Weyburn** Can
35D6 **Weymouth** Eng
14E1 **Weymouth** USA
78C1 **Whakatane** NZ
78C1 **Whakatane** *R* NZ
34E1 **Whalsay** *I* Scot
78B1 **Whangarei** NZ
35E5 **Wharfe** *R* Eng
17C4 **Wharton** USA
11A3 **Wheatland** USA
14B3 **Wheaton** Maryland, USA
11C2 **Wheaton** Minnesota, USA
3G2 **Wheeler** *R* Can
19D3 **Wheeler Peak** *Mt* Nevada, USA
16A2 **Wheeler Peak** *Mt* New Mexico, USA
20C3 **Wheeler Ridge** USA
5H2 **Wheeler** *R* Can
12C2 **Wheeling** USA
3D3 **Whistler** Can
35E4 **Whitby** Eng
4F5 **Whitby** Can
17D2 **White** *R* Arkansas, USA
10K3 **White** *R* Can
16A1 **White** *R* Colorado, USA
12B3 **White** *R* Indiana, USA
11B3 **White** *R* S Dakota, USA
7N4 **White B** Can
11B2 **White Butte** *Mt* USA
75B2 **White Cliffs** Aust
33C2 **White Coomb** *Mt* Scot
3E3 **Whitecourt** Can
18D1 **Whitefish** USA
4D4 **Whitefish B** Can/USA
12B1 **Whitefish Pt** USA
7M4 **Whitegull L** Can
13E2 **Whitehall** New York, USA
14C2 **Whitehall** Pennsylvania, USA
12A2 **Whitehall** Wisconsin, USA
35D4 **Whitehaven** Eng
10L3 **Whitehorse** Can
78C1 **White I** NZ
17D4 **White L** USA
75E3 **Whitemark** Aust
19C3 **White Mountain Peak** *Mt* USA
20C2 **White Mountain Peak** *Mt* USA
20C2 **White Mountain Peak** *Mt* USA
10J2 **White Mts** Alaska, USA
20C2 **White Mts** California, USA
13E2 **White Mts** New Hampshire, USA
72D2 **White Nile** *R* Sudan
4C4 **White Otter L** Can
14D2 **White Plains** USA
7K5 **White River** Can
11B3 **White River** USA
13E2 **White River Junction** USA
White S = Beloye More
3C3 **Whitesail L** Can
18B1 **White Salmon** USA
3H3 **Whitesand** *R* Can
4B3 **Whiteshell Prov Park** Can
18D1 **White Sulphur Springs** USA
15D2 **Whiteville** USA
71F4 **White Volta** *R* Ghana
12B2 **Whitewater** USA
3H3 **Whitewood** Can
34C4 **Whithorn** Scot
15C2 **Whitmire** USA
4F4 **Whitney** Can
20C2 **Whitney,Mt** USA
10J3 **Whittier** Alaska, USA
20C4 **Whittier** California, USA
6H3 **Wholdaia L** Can
75A2 **Whyalla** Aust
12C2 **Wiarton** Can
71F4 **Wiawso** Ghana
11B2 **Wibaux** USA
17C2 **Wichita** USA
16C3 **Wichita** *R* USA
16C3 **Wichita Falls** USA
16C3 **Wichita Mts** USA
34D2 **Wick** Scot
19D4 **Wickenburg** USA
35B5 **Wicklow** County, Irish Rep
35B5 **Wicklow** Irish Rep
35B5 **Wicklow** *Mts* Irish Rep
75C1 **Widgeegoara** *R* Aust
36D1 **Wied** *R* Germany
43D2 **Wielun** Pol
42D3 **Wien** Austria
42D3 **Wiener Neustadt** Austria
43E2 **Wieprz** *R* Pol
36E1 **Wiesbaden** Germany
36D3 **Wiese** *R* Germany
35D5 **Wigan** Eng
17E3 **Wiggins** USA
34C4 **Wigtown** Scot
34C4 **Wigtown B** Scot
37C1 **Wil** Switz
18C1 **Wilbur** USA
75B2 **Wilcannia** Aust
19C3 **Wildcat Peak** *Mt* USA
37B1 **Wildhorn** *Mt* Switz
3F4 **Wild Horse** Can
37D1 **Wildspitze** *Mt* Austria
15C3 **Wildwood** Florida, USA
14C3 **Wildwood** New Jersey, USA
16B2 **Wiley** USA
74D2 **Wilge** *R* S Africa
76D1 **Wilhelm,Mt** PNG
42B2 **Wilhelmshaven** Germany
14C2 **Wilkes-Barre** USA
79F8 **Wilkes Land** Ant
3G3 **Wilkie** Can
18B2 **Willamette** *R* USA
75B2 **Willandra** *R* Aust
18B1 **Willapa B** USA
19E4 **Willcox** USA
23D4 **Willemstad** Curaçao
3G2 **William** *R* Can
75A1 **William Creek** Aust
75B3 **William,Mt** Aust
19D3 **Williams** Arizona, USA
19B3 **Williams** California, USA
13D3 **Williamsburg** USA
3D3 **Williams Lake** Can
12C3 **Williamson** USA
14B2 **Williamsport** USA
15D1 **Williamston** USA
14D1 **Williamstown** Massachusetts, USA
12C3 **Williamstown** W Virginia, USA
14D2 **Willimantic** USA
14C2 **Willingboro** USA
3E3 **Willingdon,Mt** Can
76E2 **Willis Group** *Is* Aust
15C3 **Williston** Florida, USA
11B2 **Williston** N Dakota, USA
74C3 **Williston** S Africa
3D2 **Williston L** Can
11C2 **Willmar** USA
75A3 **Willoughby,C** Aust
3D3 **Willow** *R* Can
11A2 **Willow Bunch** Can
74C3 **Willowmore** S Africa
18B2 **Willow Ranch** USA
19B3 **Willows** USA
17D2 **Willow Springs** USA
75A2 **Wilmington** Aust
14C3 **Wilmington** Delaware, USA
15D2 **Wilmington** N Carolina, USA
14D1 **Wilmington** Vermont, USA
16C2 **Wilson** Kansas, USA
15D1 **Wilson** N Carolina, USA
14A1 **Wilson** New York, USA
9F3 **Wilson** USA
16C2 **Wilson** *L* USA
75B1 **Wilson** *R* Aust
7K3 **Wilson,C** Can
20C3 **Wilson,Mt** California, USA
16A2 **Wilson,Mt** Colorado, USA
18B1 **Wilson,Mt** Oregon, USA
75C3 **Wilsons Promontory** *Pen* Aust
35E6 **Wiltshire** County, Eng
36C2 **Wiltz** Lux
76B3 **Wiluna** Aust
12B2 **Winamac** USA
74D2 **Winburg** S Africa
14D1 **Winchendon** USA
13D1 **Winchester** Can
35E6 **Winchester** Eng
12C3 **Winchester** Kentucky, USA
14D1 **Winchester** New Hampshire, USA
13D3 **Winchester** Virginia, USA
18E2 **Wind** *R* USA
14A2 **Windber** USA
11B3 **Wind Cave Nat Pk** USA

Yirshi Zyyi

49N5 **Yirshi** China
52B5 **Yishan** China
52D2 **Yishui** China
41E3 **Yíthion** Greece
53A1 **Yitulihe** China
32J6 **Yivieska** Fin
52C4 **Yiyang** China
44D2 **Yli-Kitka** *L* Fin
32J5 **Ylilornio** Sweden
44C3 **Ylivieska** Fin
17C4 **Yoakum** USA
71J3 **Yobe** *State* Nig
22C2 **Yogope** Mexico
56D4 **Yogyakarta** Indon
3E3 **Yoho Nat Pk** Can
72B3 **Yokadouma** Cam
54C4 **Yokkaichi** Japan
71J4 **Yoko** Cam
54D3 **Yokobori** Japan
54C3 **Yokohama** Japan
54C3 **Yokosuka** Japan
54D3 **Yokote** Japan
71J4 **Yola** Nig
53C4 **Yonago** Japan
54A3 **Yŏnan** N Korea
53E4 **Yonezawa** Japan
54A4 **Yongam** S Korea
52D4 **Yong'an** China
52A2 **Yongchang** China
53B4 **Yŏngch'on** S Korea
52B4 **Yongchuan** China
54A3 **Yŏngchŭng-man** *I* N Korea
52A2 **Yongdeng** China
52D5 **Yongding** China
52D2 **Yongding He** *R* China
53B4 **Yŏngdŏk** S Korea
54A3 **Yŏnggwang** S Korea
53B4 **Yŏnghŭng** N Korea
54A3 **Yŏngil-man** *B* S Korea
53B3 **Yongji** China
53B4 **Yongju** S Korea
52B2 **Yongning** China
56G7 **Yong Peng** Malay
54A3 **Yŏngsanp'o** S Korea
54A3 **Yŏngyang** S Korea
14D2 **Yonkers** USA
36B3 **Yonne** Department, France
38C2 **Yonne** *R* France
35E5 **York** Eng
17C1 **York** Nebraska, USA
14B3 **York** Pennsylvania, USA
76D2 **York,C** Aust
75A2 **Yorke Pen** Aust
75A3 **Yorketown** Aust
7J4 **York Factory** Can
51F8 **York Sd** Aust
35D4 **Yorkshire Dales Nat Pk** Eng
33C3 **Yorkshire Moors** *Moorland* Eng
35E4 **Yorkshire Wolds** *Upland* Eng
3H3 **Yorkton** Can
13D3 **Yorktown** USA
14E1 **York Village** USA
71G4 **Yorubaland Plat** Nig
20B2 **Yosemite L** USA
20C1 **Yosemite Nat Pk** USA
54B4 **Yoshii** *R* Japan
54B4 **Yoshino** *R* Japan
44H4 **Yoshkar Ola** Russian Fed
53B5 **Yŏsu** S Korea
65C4 **Yotvata** Israel
33B3 **Youghal** Irish Rep
52B5 **You Jiang** *R* China
75C2 **Young** Aust
28D2 **Young** Urug
78A2 **Young Range** *Mts* NZ
3F3 **Youngstown** Can
14A1 **Youngstown** New York, USA
12C2 **Youngstown** Ohio, USA
20A1 **Yountville** USA
71A2 **Youssoufia** Mor
52B4 **Youyang** China
53A2 **Youyi** China
64B2 **Yozgat** Turk
29A3 **Ypané** *R* Par
18B2 **Yreka** USA
32G7 **Ystad** Sweden
35D5 **Ystwyth** *R* Wales
34D3 **Ythan** *R* Scot
52C4 **Yuan Jiang** *R* Hunan, China
52A5 **Yuan Jiang** *R* Yunnan, China
52A4 **Yuanmu** China
52C2 **Yuanping** China
19B3 **Yuba City** USA
53E3 **Yūbari** Japan
70A2 **Yubi,C** Mor
21D3 **Yucatan** *Pen* Mexico
21D2 **Yucatan Chan** Mexico/Cuba
19D4 **Yucca** USA
52C2 **Yuci** China
53A1 **Yudi Shan** *Mt* China
49P4 **Yudoma** *R* Russian Fed
52D4 **Yudu** China
52A4 **Yuexi** China
52C4 **Yueyang** China
44L2 **Yugorskiy Poluostrov** *Pen* Russian Fed
41D2 **Yugoslavia** Federal Republic, Europe
52B5 **Yu Jiang** *R* China
10G3 **Yukon** *R* USA/Can
6E3 **Yukon Territory** Can
55E1 **Yulin** Guangdong, China
52C5 **Yulin** Guangxi, China
52B2 **Yulin** Shaanxi, China
19D4 **Yuma** USA
50C3 **Yumen** China
52D2 **Yunan** China
10D5 **Yunaska** *I* USA
28A3 **Yungay** Chile
52C5 **Yunkai Dashan** *Hills* China
75A2 **Yunta** Aust
52C3 **Yunxi** China
52C3 **Yun Xian** China
52B3 **Yunyang** China
26C5 **Yurimaguas** Peru
52E5 **Yu Shan** *Mt* Taiwan
44E3 **Yushkozero** Russian Fed
53B3 **Yushu** Jilin, China
59H2 **Yushu** Tibet, China
29A4 **Yuty** Par
52A5 **Yuxi** China
54D3 **Yuzawa** Japan
53F3 **Yuzhno-Kuril'sk** Russian Fed
53E2 **Yuzhno-Sakhalinsk** Russian Fed
43F3 **Yuzhnyy Bug** *R* Ukraine
44K5 **Yuzh Ural** *Mts* Russian Fed
36A2 **Yvelines** Department, France
37B1 **Yverdon** Switz
36A2 **Yvetot** France

Z

42A2 **Zaandam** Neth
45G8 **Zab al Asfal** *R* Iraq
64D2 **Zāb al Babir** *R* Iraq
64D2 **Zāb asŞaghīr** *R* Iraq
50E2 **Zabaykal'sk** Russian Fed
66D4 **Zabīd** Yemen
63E2 **Zābol** Iran
42D3 **Zabreh** Czech Republic
43D2 **Zabrze** Pol
22B2 **Zacapu** Mexico
22B1 **Zacatecas** Mexico
22B1 **Zacatecas** State, Mexico
22C2 **Zacatepec** Morelos, Mexico
22C2 **Zacatepec** Oaxaca, Mexico
22C2 **Zacatlan** Mexico
22B2 **Zacoalco** Mexico
22C1 **Zacualtipan** Mexico
40D2 **Zadar** Croatia
55B3 **Zadetkyi** *I* Myanmar
39A2 **Zafra** Spain
69C1 **Zagazig** Egypt
70B1 **Zagora** Mor
40D1 **Zagreb** Croatia
Zagros Mts = Kūhhā-ye Zagros
63E3 **Zāhedān** Iran
65C2 **Zahle** Leb
39C2 **Zahrez Chergui** *Marshland* Alg
44J4 **Zainsk** Russian Fed
72C4 **Zaïre** Republic, Africa
72B4 **Zaïre** *R* Zaïre/Congo
41E2 **Zajecăr** Serbia, Yugos
50D1 **Zakamensk** Russian Fed
45H7 **Zakataly** Azerbaijan
63E1 **Zakhmet** Turkmenistan
64D2 **Zakho** Iraq
41E3 **Zákinthos** *I* Greece
43D3 **Zakopane** Pol
42D3 **Zalaegerszeg** Hung
41E1 **Zalău** Rom
42C2 **Zalew Szczeciński** *Lg* Pol
66D2 **Zalim** S Arabia
72C2 **Zalingei** Sudan
49P4 **Zaliv Akademii** *B* Russian Fed
53E2 **Zaliv Aniva** *B* Russian Fed
49M2 **Zaliv Faddeya** *B* Russian Fed
45J7 **Zaliv Kara-Bogaz-Gol** *B* Turkmenistan
10C2 **Zaliv Kresta** *B* Russian Fed
53C3 **Zaliv Petra Velikogo** *B* Russian Fed
49R3 **Zaliv Shelikhova** *B* Russian Fed
53E2 **Zaliv Turpeniya** *B* Russian Fed
69A2 **Zaltan** Libya
67E3 **Zamakh** Yemen
68H9 **Zambesi** *R* Mozam
73C5 **Zambezi** Zambia
73C5 **Zambezi** *R* Zambia
73C5 **Zambia** Republic, Africa
57F9 **Zamboanga** Phil
57F9 **Zamboanga Pen** Phil
43E2 **Zambrów** Pol
71H3 **Zamfara** *R* Nig
26C4 **Zamora** Ecuador
22B2 **Zamora** Mexico
39A1 **Zamora** Spain
20B1 **Zamora** USA
43E2 **Zamość** Pol
52A3 **Zamtang** China
72B4 **Zanaga** Congo
22D2 **Zanatepec** Mexico
39B2 **Záncara** *R* Spain
60D2 **Zanda** China
12C3 **Zanesville** USA
60D2 **Zangla** India
63B1 **Zanjān** Iran
28B2 **Zanjitas** Arg
28B2 **Zanjon** *R* Arg
72D4 **Zanzibar** Tanz
72D4 **Zanzibar** *I* Tanz
70C2 **Zaouatallaz** Alg
52D3 **Zaozhuang** China
64D2 **Zap** *R* Turk
32K7 **Zapadnaja Dvina** *R* Russian Fed
43G1 **Zapadnaya Dvina** Russian Fed
53E1 **Zapadno-Sakhalinskiy** *Mts* Russian Fed
44L3 **Zapadno-Sibirskaya Nizmennost'** Lowland, Russian Fed
49L4 **Zapadnyy Sayan** *Mts* Russian Fed
28A3 **Zapala** Arg
17F4 **Zapata** USA
44E2 **Zapolyarnyy** Russian Fed
45F6 **Zaporozh'ye** Ukraine
64C2 **Zara** Turk
22B1 **Zaragoza** Mexico
39B1 **Zaragoza** Spain
63C1 **Zarand** Iran
63D2 **Zarand** Iran
63E2 **Zaranj** Afghan
26E2 **Zarara** Ven
43F1 **Zarasai** Lithuania
28D2 **Zárate** Arg
63B2 **Zard Kuh** *Mt* Iran
10M4 **Zarembo I** USA
60B2 **Zarghun Shahr** Afghan
60B2 **Zargun** *Mt* Pak
71H3 **Zaria** Nig
64C3 **Zarqa** Jordan
65C2 **Zarqa** *R* Jordan
26C4 **Zaruma** Ecuador
42D2 **Zary** Pol
71E2 **Zarzis** Tunisia
60D2 **Zāskār** *Mts* India
60D2 **Zāskār** *R* India
74D3 **Zastron** S Africa
65D2 **Zatara** *R* Jordan
Zatoka Gdańska = Gdańsk,G of
53E2 **Zavety Il'icha** Russian Fed
53B1 **Zavitinsk** Russian Fed
61E2 **Zavū** China
43D2 **Zawiercie** Pol
49M4 **Zayarsk** Russian Fed
48K5 **Zaysan** Kazakhstan
48K5 **Zaysan, Ozero** *L* Kazakhstan
50C4 **Zayü** *Mt* China
43D2 **Zduńska Wola** Pol
36B1 **Zeebrugge** Belg
65C3 **Zeelim** Israel
74D2 **Zeerust** S Africa
65C2 **Zefat** Israel
70C3 **Zegueren** *Watercourse* Mali
72E2 **Zeila** Somalia
42C2 **Zeitz** Germany
52A2 **Zekog** China
44E2 **Zelenoborskiy** Russian Fed
44H4 **Zelenodol'sk** Russian Fed
32K6 **Zelenogorsk** Russian Fed
37D1 **Zell** Austria
37B1 **Zell** Germany
37E1 **Zell am See** Austria
72C3 **Zemio** CAR
48F1 **Zemlya Aleksandry** *I* Russian Fed
48F2 **Zemlya Frantsa Josifa** *Is* Russian Fed
48F1 **Zemlya Georga** *I* Russian Fed
48H1 **Zemlya Vil'cheka** *I* Russian Fed
41D2 **Zenica** Bosnia-Herzegovina
65C3 **Zenifim** *R* Israel
52B4 **Zenning** China
71C2 **Zergoun** *R* Alg
37B1 **Zermatt** Switz
45G7 **Zestafoni** Georgia
65B1 **Zevgari,C** Cyprus
49O4 **Zeya** Russian Fed
53B1 **Zeya** *R* Russian Fed
49O4 **Zeya Res** Russian Fed
39A1 **Zézere** *R* Port
65C1 **Zghorta** Leb
43D2 **Zgierz** Pol
53B3 **Zhangguangcai Ling** *Mts* China
52D1 **Zhangjiakou** China
52D4 **Zhangping** China
52D2 **Zhangwei He** *R* China
52E1 **Zhangwu** China
52A2 **Zhangye** China
52D5 **Zhangzhou** China
52C5 **Zhanjiang** China
52A4 **Zhanyi** China
53B2 **Zhaodong** China
52C5 **Zhaoqing** China
52A4 **Zhaotong** China
52D2 **Zhaoyang Hu** *L* China
53A2 **Zhaoyuan** China
45K6 **Zharkamys** Kazakhstan
43G1 **Zharkovskiy** Russian Fed
43G3 **Zhashkov** Ukraine
49O3 **Zhatay** Russian Fed
52D4 **Zhejiang** Province, China
44J3 **Zheleznodorozhnyy** Russian Fed
46G4 **Zhengou** China
52C3 **Zhengzhou** China
52D3 **Zhenjiang** China
53A2 **Zhenlai** China
52A4 **Zhenxiong** China
52B4 **Zhenyuan** China
45G5 **Zherdevka** Russian Fed
52C3 **Zhicheng** China
50D1 **Zhigalovo** Russian Fed
49O3 **Zhigansk** Russian Fed
52B4 **Zhijin** China
43F2 **Zhitkovichi** Belarus
43F2 **Zhitomir** Ukraine
43F2 **Zhlobin** Belarus
43F3 **Zhmerinka** Ukraine
60B2 **Zhob** Pak
43F2 **Zhodino** Belarus
61B2 **Zhongba** China
52B2 **Zhongning** China
52C5 **Zhongshan** China
79G10 **Zhongshan** *Base* Ant
52B2 **Zhongwei** China
50C4 **Zhougdian** China
52E3 **Zhoushan Quandao** *Arch* China
43G3 **Zhovten'** Ukraine
52E2 **Zhuanghe** China
52A3 **Zhugqu** China
52C3 **Zhushan** China
52C4 **Zhuzhou** China
52D2 **Zibo** China
76C3 **Ziel,Mt** Aust
42D2 **Zielona Góra** Pol
65A3 **Zifta** Egypt
55A1 **Zigaing** Myanmar
52A4 **Zigong** China
70A3 **Ziguinchor** Sen
22B2 **Zihuatanejo** Mexico
65C2 **Zikhron Ya'aqov** Israel
43D3 **Žilina** Slovakia
69A2 **Zillah** Libya
37D1 **Ziller** *R* Austria
37D1 **Zillertaler Alpen** *Mts* Austria
43F1 **Zilupe** Latvia
49M4 **Zima** Russian Fed
22C1 **Zimapan** Mexico
22C2 **Zimatlan** Mexico
74D1 **Zimbabwe** Republic, Africa
65C3 **Zin** *R* Israel
22C2 **Zinacatepec** Mexico
22B2 **Zinapécuaro** Mexico
70C3 **Zinder** Niger
71F3 **Ziniaré** Burkina
20D3 **Zion Nat Pk** USA
52C4 **Zi Shui** China
22B2 **Zitácuaro** Mexico
42C2 **Zittau** Germany
52D2 **Ziya He** *R* China
52A3 **Ziyang** China
44K4 **Zlatoust** Russian Fed
48K4 **Zmeinogorsk** Russian Fed
43D2 **Znin** Pol
42D3 **Znoimo** Czech Republic
74D1 **Zoekmekuar** S Africa
37B1 **Zofinger** Switz
52A3 **Zoigê** China
43E3 **Zolochev** Ukraine
43G3 **Zolotonosha** Ukraine
73D5 **Zomba** Malawi
72B3 **Zongo** Zaïre
64B1 **Zonguldak** Turk
70B4 **Zorzor** Lib
70A2 **Zouerate** Maur
41E1 **Zrenjanin** Serbia, Yugos
37C1 **Zug** Switz
45G7 **Zugdidi** Georgia
37D1 **Zugspitze** *Mt* Germany
39A2 **Zújar** *R* Spain
73D5 **Zumbo** Mozam
11D3 **Zumbrota** USA
22C2 **Zumpango** Mexico
71H4 **Zungeru** Nig
16A2 **Zuni** USA
16A2 **Zuni Mts** USA
52B4 **Zunyi** China
55D1 **Zuo** *R* China
52B5 **Zuo Jiang** *R* China
37C1 **Zürich** Switz
37C1 **Zürichsee** *L* Switz
71H3 **Zuru** Nig
69A1 **Zuwārah** Libya
69A2 **Zuwaylah** Libya
44J4 **Zuyevka** Russian Fed
43G3 **Zvenigorodka** Ukraine
73C6 **Zvishavane** Zim
43D3 **Zvolen** Slovakia
41D2 **Zvornik** Bosnia-Herzegovina
53D1 **Zvoron, Ozero** *L* Russian Fed
36D2 **Zweibrücken** Germany
37B1 **Zweisimmen** Switz
42C2 **Zwickau** Germany
42B2 **Zwolle** Neth
43E2 **Zyrardów** Pol
49R3 **Zyryanka** Russian Fed
48K5 **Zyryanovsk** Kazakhstan
43D3 **Żywiec** Pol
65B1 **Zyyi** Cyprus

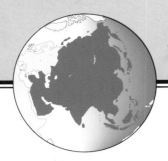

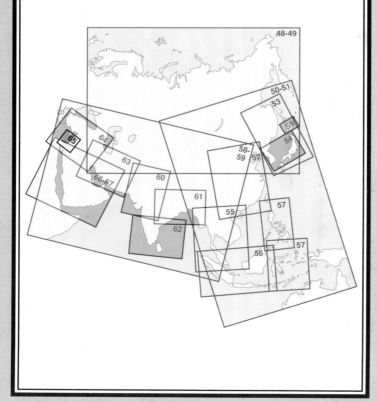

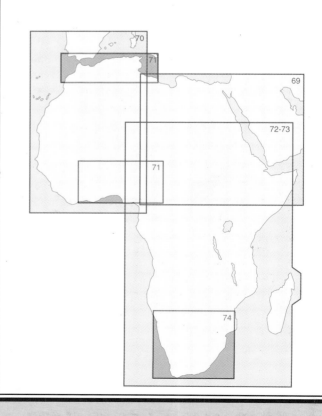